COVER PHOTO:
Edith Lake - Tourism Kamloops/Kelly Funk

Official Partners:

THE TEAM

DIRECTORS
Russell Mussio
Wesley Mussio

VICE PRESIDENT
Chris Taylor

EDITOR IN CHIEF
Russell Mussio

GIS & CARTOGRAPHY

MANAGER
Andrew Allen

GIS SPECIALISTS
Farah Aghdam
David Mancini

CARTOGRAPHERS
Aaron Dixon
Oliver Herz
Dale Tober

MARKETING & CREATIVE SERVICES

MANAGERS
Nazli Faghihi
Farnaz Faghihi

GRAPHIC & LAYOUT DESIGN
Elisa Codazzi
Nicky Forshaw

SOCIAL MEDIA
Carly Watson

CONTENT WRITERS
Sean Anderson
Leslie Bryant MacLean
Trent Ernst
Brian Harris
Jay Hoare
Colin Hughes
Mike Manyk
Jason Marleau
Russell Mussio
Stepan Soroka

SALES
Basilio Bagnato
Chris Taylor

ADMINISTRATION
Shaun Filipenko
Jo-ana Maki

TECH SUPPORT
Sal Kahila
Matthew Steblyna

ACKNOWLEDGEMENTS

This book could not have been compiled without the dedicated and talented people at Mussio Ventures Ltd. Thanks to Sean Anderson, Leslie Bryant MacLean, Lorne Collicutt, Jay Hoare, Colin Hughes and Stepan Soroka who continued with the work of Trent Ernst, Brian Harris, Mike Manyk, Jason Marleau and others of sifting through the incredible amount of recreational opportunities in southern BC. Combined with the talented efforts of Farah Aghdam, Andrew Allen, Basilio Bagnato, Elisa Codazzi, Aaron Dixon, Farnaz Faghihi, Nazli Faghihi, Shaun Filipenko, Nicky Forshaw, Oliver Herz, Sal Kahila, Jo-ana Maki, David Mancini, Matthew Steblyna, Chris Taylor, Dale Tober and Carly Watson we were able to produce the most comprehensive guidebook for this recreational hotbed of British Columbia.

For each edition we consult a variety of people and resources to help ensure our information is as up to date as possible. These sources range from the very helpful Recreation Sites and Trails personnel, including John Crooks and Noelle Kekula to BC Parks and Protected Areas supervisors such as Ed Atkinson and Kevin Wilson. We would also like to thank Craig Morrison of the Mountain Resorts Branch and Connie Falk from Employment Services in Barrière. And, as always, we turn to many other resources such as the Shuswap Trails Alliance, Trail Peak and Club Tread along with various other backcountry trail information sources to dig up more information on the many hidden treasures in the area.

Another incredible resource for our updates is our readers, many of who have taken advantage of our GPS Track Submission Program. We have many notable contributors that include Fred Swirp from the Vernon Outdoors Club, Russell Grosser, Steve McAbee, Brian Stainsby and Stan Wieczorek for their impressive trail track collections, Ryan Klassen (mountain biker extraordinaire) and Arnold Grimm and Meredith Twaites for their road edits. This is by no means a complete list; so please continue to send your tracks and updates our way!

These maps are a synthesis of a variety of sources, mostly from the Federal, Provincial and Municipal Government. We would like to express our gratitude to the helpful map providers at the Department of Natural Resources Canada. The maps also contain information licensed under the Open Government License – British Columbia, as well as information licensed under the Open Government Licence - Kamloops. We would also like to thank the cities of Penticton, Vernon and Kelowna.

Finally we would like to thank Allison, Devon, Jasper, Madison, Nancy and Penny Mussio for their continued support of the Backroad Mapbook Series. As our family grows, it is becoming more and more challenging to break away from it all to explore our beautiful country.

Sincerely,

Russell and Wesley Mussio

Library and Archives Canada Cataloguing in Publication
Mussio, Russell, 1969
Backroad Mapbook, Thompson Okanagan BC
[cartographic material] / Russell Mussio. -- 4th ed.

ISBN 978-1-926806-52-5

1. Recreation areas--British Columbia--Okanagan Valley (Region)--Maps. 2. Recreation areas--British Columbia--Thompson-Nicola--Maps. 3. Outdoor recreation--British Columbia--Okanagan Valley (Region)--Guidebooks. 4. Outdoor recreation--British Columbia--Thompson-Nicola--Guidebooks. 5. Okanagan Valley (B.C. : Region)--Maps. 6. Thompson-Nicola (B.C.)--Maps. 7. Okanagan Valley (B.C. : Region)--Guidebooks. 8. Thompson-Nicola (B.C.)--Guidebooks. I. Mussio Ventures Ltd. II. Title. III. Title: Thompson Okanagan BC, backroad mapbook.

G1172.T56E63M87 2013   796.509711'72   C2013-901590-6

DISCLAIMER

Backroad Mapbooks does not warrant that the backroads, paddling routes and trails indicated in this Mapbook are passable nor does it claim that the Mapbook is completely accurate. Therefore, please be careful when using this or any source to plan and carry out your outdoor recreation activity.

Please note that traveling on logging roads, river routes and trails is inherently dangerous, and without limiting the generality of the foregoing, you may encounter poor road conditions, unexpected traffic, poor visibility, and low or no road/trail maintenance. Please use extreme caution when traveling logging roads and trails.

Please refer to the Fishing and Hunting Regulations for closures and restrictions. It is your responsibility to know when and where closures and restrictions apply.

HELP US HELP YOU

A comprehensive resource such as Backroad Mapbooks for Thompson Okanagan BC could not be put together without a great deal of help and support. Despite our best efforts to ensure that everything is accurate, errors do occur. If you see any errors or omissions, please continue to let us know.

* ALL UPDATES WILL BE POSTED ON OUR WEBSITE

CONTACT US

☎ 604-521-6277
toll free 1-877-520-5670

✉ updates@backroadmapbooks.com

🖷 604-521-6260

📍 Unit 106- 1500 Hartley Ave
Coquitlam, BC, V3K 7A1

🌐 backroadmapbooks.com

INTRODUCTION

Lac Du Bois
©Tourism Kamloops/Kelly Funk

WELCOME

Welcome to the 4th edition of the Thompson Okanagan Backroad Mapbook.

In reality, this is the seventh edition of the former Kamloops/Okanagan Mapbook that we have expanded north to include the North Thompson, or the area from Clearwater to McBride. We now cover the heart of the interior of British Columbia and include the areas around Kamloops, Kelowna, Merritt, Penticton, Princeton and Vernon, to name a few.

▶ **THE AREA:** There are few places in this country that say "summer" like the Interior of British Columbia. Summers are hot and dry with golden beaches, delightfully warm lakes and crystal-clear rivers that hold the collective memories of folks from across the country, many of whom make an annual pilgrimage to explore and enjoy Okanagan Lake, Shuswap Lake, and elsewhere.

But there is more to this land than just big lakes and big beaches. It is home to the most famous section of one of Canada's best-known multi-use trails, the Kettle Valley Railway. Trout anglers from around the world visit this area in hopes of landing a trophy rainbow on the fly. And there are many places to camp at and even more places to explore. In the winter, this area also boasts some of the best skiing conditions in the country. In your hands you hold your guide to all of it. From Osoyoos in the south to Mount Robson in the north, from Manning Park to Christina Lake, this book will guide you to the best the Thompson and Okanagan areas have to offer.

▶ **THE BACKROADS:** The Southern Interior is a backroader's paradise. If you prefer highways or paved roads, there are few better roads to explore than the Crowsnest Highway from Hope west to Alberta. Of course, other quiet routes like Highway 6 from Vernon towards Nakusp are also worth touring. Those looking for more of a backroad feel can explore some great road systems that will take you through the heart of this area. The Christian Valley/Kettle River Forest Service Road and the North Fork/Burrell Creek Forest Service Road are two such roads in the south. The Mabel Lake and Adams West Forest Service Roads also lead past countless recreational gems. Adventurous travelers tell us they love our books because we are one of the few sources that show the rarely driven roads that lead to those truly special wilderness areas. We also list trails and camping areas few have ever heard of. This is what British Columbia is all about.

▶ **THE BOOK:** This book is full of many changes and improvements. We have updated the roads, added countless new trails and paddling routes (including motorized riding areas) and expanded on the activity and Adventure sections of the mapbook. Another new feature is the Community Profiles that highlight many of the areas covered in the mapbook. These are just a few of the many improvements and tweaks to one of our best-selling mapbooks.

The Backroad Mapbook is much more than a set of maps; it is an explorer's guide. Whether from the comfort of your armchair or from the cab of your four-wheel drive vehicle, let our writing and maps take you to places most only dream of!

BACKROAD HISTORY

The Backroad Mapbook idea came into existence when Wesley and Russell Mussio were out exploring. They had several books and a few maps to try to find their way through the maze of logging roads around southern BC. The brothers were getting very frustrated trying to find their way and eventually gave up. Not to be outdone, the two ambitious brothers started brainstorming. Eventually the Backroad Mapbook idea was born.

They published their first book in January 1994 and it quickly sold out. Rather than simply reprinting it, they listened to the feedback of customers and made several alterations that helped improve the book. This formula of continuing to make the product better continues today and has helped establish the Backroad Mapbook series as the top selling outdoor recreation guidebook series in the country. From the tiny beginnings in that Vancouver apartment with maps strewn all over the walls, to one of the most sought-after outdoor products in the country, the Backroad Mapbook series has truly come a long way.

RESOURCE ROADS ARE PLANNED AND CONSTRUCTED TO DEVELOP AND PROTECT BC'S NATURAL RESOURCES; WHILE PRIMARILY USED BY FORESTRY, AGRICULTURE, MINING, AND OIL AND GAS THEY ALSO PROVIDE ACCESS TO RECREATIONAL OPPORTUNITIES.

WHAT TO EXPECT

Resource roads are gravel or dirt and they may be single lane with sharp turns, soft shoulders, narrow bridges, poor alignment and grades steeper than on highways. Not all hazards will be marked and there might not be protective barriers at dangerous or steep sections; roadside brush may limit visibility.

APPLY THE SAME RULES OF THE ROAD AS USED ON HIGHWAYS

Drive on the right hand side. Wear your seatbelt. Don't drink and drive. Take your license and insurance. Obey the speed limit – unless posted otherwise, it's up to 80 km/hr. but many roads are designed and built for 60 km/hr. or less.

DRIVE ACCORDING TO ROAD CONDITIONS

Travel a speed that allows you to stop within half of your line of sight (other vehicles need room to stop too). If dusty or slippery, slow down so you can react to oncoming traffic, potholes, wildlife, changing road conditions and unexpected hazards; large industrial vehicles can't manoeuver as quickly as passenger vehicles.

FOCUS ON YOUR DRIVING; EXERCISE CAUTION, PATIENCE AND COURTESY

Keep your headlights and taillights on. Industrial drivers are familiar with the road; let them go ahead and give them room to do their job. It might be advantageous for you to follow industrial vehicles, watch for brake lights and make sure you find a turn out when they do (to clear oncoming traffic).

OBSERVE AND OBEY THE SIGNS

Signs communicate information about the road, traffic you can expect, active worksites or hazardous conditions; take time to read and understand signs at the start of the road and along the way.

STOP IN THE RIGHT SPOT

If you must stop along the road find a pull out or straight section that provides good visibility from both directions and is wide enough for traffic to pass. Pull over onto the shoulder; avoid stopping in a curve or on the crest of a hill.

BE PREPARED

Plan your trip before you go! Beware of road conditions and traffic; share trip information with a reliable contact, bring a map and GPS. Carry extra clothing, footwear, food, water and fuel. Have an emergency first aid kit. Make sure your vehicle is ready for the trip – good tires, a spare, chains in winter, tools including a shovel and a fire extinguisher.

BC Forest
Safety Council
1-877-741-1060
VINBC.CA

KEEP AN EYE OUT FOR THE VIN PROGRAM

BC **Forest Safety**
Unsafe is Unacceptable

REPORT A CONCERN OR COMPLIMENT ABOUT A VEHICLE AT 1 877 741 1060 OR VINBC.CA

VISITOR CENTRES

Watch for the Visitor Centre signs located thoughout the Thompson Okanagan Region.
Visitor Centres can help with:

- Hotel and activity/attraction bookings
- Maps and directions
- Travel advice and free guides
- In-depth knowledge of the community and region
- National and BC parks information
- Many other travel-related services

THOMPSON OKANAGAN BRITISH COLUMBIA

Visitor Centre

Armstrong
Visitor Centre
(Year Round)   See Map 24/D5

Situated in the Okanagan Valley, we offer visitors a warm welcome and a hometown atmosphere that will leave visitors with great memories of their visit.

3550 Bridge St
Armstrong, BC V0E 1B0
250-546-8155
manager@aschamber.com
/ASChamberofCommerce
@AstrongChamber

www.aschamber.com

Barriere
Tourist/Visitor Info Booth
(Year Round)   See Map 28/E1

Get back to your rural roots at the North Thompson Fall Fair. Hike, Bike, Horseback ride, Golf, Ski, Canoe and Kayak, Fish, Swim, Camp; come and see all the adventures we have to offer.

Suite 3, 4353 Conner Rd
Barriere, BC V0E 1E0
250-672-9221
bcoc@telus.net
/barrierechamber

www.norththompson.ca

Cache Creek
Tourist/Visitor Info Booth
(Seasonal: May to September)   See Map 26/D7

Cache Creek is abound with outdoor recreational activities for every interest. Hunting, fishing, hiking, and biking activities are right on your doorstep as are winter sports such as snowmobiling, cross country skiing and ice fishing.

1270 Stage Rd
Cache Creek, BC V0K 1H0
250-457-7661
cachecreekinfo@telus.net
/cache.creekactivities

www.cachecreekvillage.com

Chase
Visitor Centre
(Year Round)   See Map 29/D7

The friendly village of Chase on the beautiful Little Shuswap lake offers public sandy beach, wharf & boat launch. Come see the waterfalls. Go for a hike and Big Horn Sheep may await you in our awe-inspiring wilderness. And for the kids, we have a wading pool & playgrounds.

400 Shuswap Ave
Chase, BC, V0E 1M0
250-679-8432
admin@chasechamber.com
/ChaseChamber1

www.chasechamber.ca

Christina Lake
Visitor Centre
(Year Round)   See Map 6/E5

Christina Lake is British Columbia's recreation paradise. The scenery is spectacular, the climate wonderful. Whether you are planning a vacation, wedding, reunion, or looking for a quieter lifestyle, Christina Lake has a lot to offer any time of year.

1675 Hwy 3
Christina Lake, BC V0H 1E2
250-447-6161
tourism@christinalake.ca
/ChristinaLakeVisitorInformation Centre

www.christinalake.com

Clearwater
Visitor Centre
(Seasonal: May to Mid-October)   See Map 33/F1

Located at the entrance to Wells Gray Provincial Park, the Clearwater Visitor Centre offers a park-like setting with all amenities for the travelling public. Friendly service & free maps. COME VISIT JERRY THE MOOSE!

416 Eden Rd
Clearwater, BC V0E 1N1
250-674-3334
wellsgray@gmail.com
/wellsgraypark

www.wellsgraypark.info

Enderby
Visitor Centre
(Year Round)   See Map 24/E3

Where the Shuswap meets the Okanagan! Paddle or float down the Shuswap River. Take a stroll down our scenic Riverwalk. Hike the Enderby Cliffs. Enjoy fishing at many nearby lakes.

700 Railway St
Enderby, BC V0E 1V0
250-838-6727
info@enderbychamber.com
/EnderbyChamber
@EnderbyChamber

www.exploringenderby.com

VISITOR CENTRES

Greenwood
Visitor Centre
(Seasonal)
See Map 5/F5

Visit Historic Greenwood, Canada's smallest city. Step back in time, visit the museum & heritage buildings. Self-guided walking tour & Smelter ruins brochures. Gift shop, Internet.

214 South Copper Ave
Greenwood, BC V0H 1J0
250-445-6355
museum@shaw.ca
/GreenwoodMuseumBC

www.greenwoodmuseum.com

Kamloops
Visitor Centre
(Year Round)
See Map 22/C2

Welcome to BC's Friendliest City and Canada's Tournament Capital! Blending energizing outdoor recreational opportunities with a culture of warm, welcoming people, Kamloops is an amazing place for any visitor to let loose and just play.
#explorekamloops

1290 West Trans Canada Hwy
Kamloops, BC V2C 6R3
1-800-662-1994
250-374-3377
inquiry@tourismkamloops.com
/tourismkamloops
@TourismKamloops

www.tourismkamloops.com

Kelowna
Visitor Centre
(Year Round)
See Map 17/A7

The scenic urban centre and international gateway to BC's spectacular Okanagan Valley offers an adventure around every corner. Wine, dine, tour, hike, bike, boat, swim, camp, ski, golf, spa, shop, gallery hop... the list of options is endless.

544 Harvey Ave (Hwy 97)
Kelowna, BC V1Y 6C9
1-800-663-4345
250-861-1515
info@tourismkelowna.com
/TourismKelowna
@Tourism_Kelowna

www.tourismkelowna.com

Keremeos
Visitor Centre
(Year Round)
See Map 3/D4

"The Western Gateway to Wine Country"
Come and visit the picturesque Lower Similkameen Valley. With attractions such as the Red Bridge and the Keremeos Columns there is a lot to see and do here in the valley. Come Join us!

417 - 7th Ave
Keremeos, BC V0X 1N0
250-499-5225
siminfo@nethop.net

www.similkameencountry.org

Logan Lake
Visitor Centre
(Seasonal: May to Mid-October)
See Map 21/D5

"Discover our Nature" With Magnificent mountains, lakes & forests, this region is perfect for the outdoor enthusiast.
Come see us in BC's most unique Visitor Centre.

31 Chartrand Ave
Logan Lake, BC V0K 1W0
1-800-331-6495
250-523-6322
tourism@loganlake.ca
/DistrictofLoganLake

www.loganlake.ca

Lumby
Visitor Centre
(Seasonal: May to September)
See Map 17/G1

Pristine lakes, trails, mountain rivers, and snow-capped peaks are only part of our natural lure. Wildlife viewing and awe-inspiring outdoors bekons you year round.

1882 Vernon St
Lumby, BC V0E 2G0
250-547-2300
lumbychamber@shaw.ca

www.monasheetourism.com

Merritt
Visitor Centre
(Year Round)
See Map 14/E4

Courteous, knowledgeable staff provide professional visitor counselling and itinerary planning, accommodation reservations plus attraction and transportation ticketing, and helpful travel information including transportation and community information on all areas of British Columbia.

Junction Of Hwys 5 & 97C (exit 286)
Merritt, BC V1K 1B8
250-315-1342
BCVCMerritt@destinationbc.ca
/HelloBC
@HelloBC #exploreBC

www.hellobc.com

Mt. Robson
Visitor Centre
(Seasonal: Mid-May to Mid-October)
See Map 51/A6

Visitor Centre located in Mount Robson Provincial Park and Protected Area. Our beautiful building set against the backdrop of Mount Robson includes a store, Visitor information Centre, Museum, and the Berg Lake Trail overnight booking services.

Hwy 16, Mt. Robson Prov. Park
Mount Robson, BC V0E 2Z0
250-566-4038
mountrobson@shaw.ca
Mount Robson Visitor
  Information Centre

www.env.gov.bc.ca/bcparks

Oliver
Visitor Centre
(Year Round)
See Map 4/A4

Located in the historic CPR building along Oliver's 18.8 km Hike & Bike Trail (KVR Trail) at the south end of Lions Park. Ask about Sample Cycling! Biking the Wine Capital Of Canada is an ideal way to tour the valley's southern wineries.

6431 Station St
Oliver, BC V0H 1T0
1-844-896-3300
778-439-2363
info@winecapitalofcanada.com
/WineCapitalofCanada
@WineCapital

www.winecapitalofcanada.com

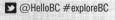

Osoyoos
Visitor Centre
(Year Round) — See Map 4/B6

Courteous, knowledgeable staff provide professional visitor counselling and itinerary planning, accommodation reservations plus attraction and transportation ticketing, and helpful travel information including transportation and community information on all areas of British Columbia.

9912 Hwy 3 (Junction Hwy 3 & 97)
Osoyoos, BC V0H 1V0
250-495-5410
BCVCOsoyoos@destinationbc.ca
f /HelloBC
🐦 @HelloBC #exploreBC

www.hellobc.com

Peachland
Visitor Centre
(Year Round) — See Map 9/E2

Peachland, the get-a-way you have been longing for! Enjoy unique specialty shops, restaurants, wineries, dock your boat in the day wharf, suntan on our beaches, visit Swim Bay, golf, enjoy hiking trails, back country adventure & much more!

5684 Beach Ave
Peachland, BC V0H 1X6
250-767-2455
visitpeachland@gmail.com
f /PeachlandBC
🐦 @PeachlandBC

www.destinationpeachland.com

Princeton
Visitor Centre
(Year Round) — See Map 6/B6

Enjoy 300 hours of winter sunshine. Hike or bike our historic trails, the scenic Trans Canada Trail, or just relax fishing one of our 49 lakes. Explore 100s of miles of backcountry road or our renovated museum. We have something for everyone!

169 Bridge St
Princeton, BC V0X 1W0
250-295-0235
visitorinfo@princeton.ca

www.princeton.ca

Salmon Arm
Visitor Centre
(Year Round) — See Map 24/C1

Located on beautiful Shuswap Lake, surrounded by lush hills and mountains, Salmon Arm offers outstanding adventures in hiking, biking, trail riding, fishing, camping and water activities.

#101- 20 Hudson Ave NE
Salmon Arm, BC V1E 4P2
1-877-725-6667
250-832-2230
info@visitsalmonarm.com
f /salmonarmchamber
🐦 @SArmChamber

www.sachamber.bc.ca

Sicamous
Visitor Centre
(Year Round) — See Map 30/G6

The Houseboat Capital of Canada & The Eastern Gateway to the Shuswap. "Spring, Summer, Winter, Fall" For All Your Four Season Recreational Needs Just Call.

#3 446 Main St
Sicamous, BC V0E 2V0
1-866-250-4055
250-836-3313
vc@sicamouschamber.bc.ca
f /sicamous.visitorcentre

www.sicamouschamber.bc.ca

Summerland
Visitor Centre
(Year Round) — See Map 9/F4

Minutes from back road adventures: hiking, biking, fishing, hunting, ATV Fun, Trans Canada Trail, Kettle Valley Stream Train, 20 wineries & cideries, B&B's, galleriesm shops, restaurants, beaches, golfing, horseback riding and more! Free Wifi at centre.

15600 Hwy 97,
Summerland, BC V0H 1Z0
250-494-2686
visitors@summerlandchamber.com
f /VisitSummerLand
🐦 @TourSummerland

www.tourismsummerland.com

Valemount
Visitor Centre
(Seasonal: May to September) — See Map 47/A3

Make the Valemount Visitor Centre your first stop for great local and provincial information. We offer a range of services including free WiFi, adventure activity and accomodations bookings, local arts and crafts, clothing and souvenirs, nature displays, fishing licences and attraction tickets.

785 Cranberry Lake Rd
Valemount, BC V0E 2Z0
250-566-9893
visitorcentre@valemount.ca
f /ValemountVisitorCentre
🐦 @VisitValemount

www.visitvalemount.ca

Vernon
Visitor Centre
(Year Round) — See Map 17/C1

Surrounded by 3 lakes, 5 Provincial Parks and the Monashee Mountains, Vernon offers small city charm with urban amenities and abundance of outdoor activities to experience. Golfing, biking, hiking, skiing and local orchards are at your doorstep to explore. Ask us – we are your local experts. Activate your vacation in Vernon.

3004 39th Ave
Vernon, BC V1T 3C3
1-800-665-0795
250-542-1415
info@tourismvernon.com
f /Tourism.Vernon
🐦 @TourismVernon

www.tourismvernon.com

West Kelowna
Visitor Centre
(Year Round) — See Map 9/F1

Nestled in the sunny Okanagan Valley, visit our award winning wineries, executive golf courses, and family attractions. Winter ski & Telemark. Four-season playground.

2376 Dobbin Rd
West Kelowna, BC V4T 2H9
250-768-0110
wkvisitorcentre@gmail.com
f /VisitWestside
🐦 @VisitWestside

www.visitwestside.com

NAVIGATING

Each of our Backroad Mapbooks is filled with amazing experiences that show you how to enjoy the outdoors and create unforgettable memories. Visit backroadmapbooks.com for our other great products, tips & tutorials, features and updates to further enhance your outdoor experiences.

INTRODUCTION

After a brief introduction to the region, you can find valuable planning tools such as information on Travel/Tourism and Visitor Centres, and the ever-so-important Map Legend.

ADVENTURES

Exclusive to Backroad Mapbooks, this section is filled with adventure write-ups, put together by our team of outdoor researchers and with the help of local residents & communities. From backroad attractions to fishing hotspots and winter adventures, you have access to the most comprehensive backcountry planning tool available on the market.

COMMUNITY PROFILES

This section features detailed overviews and photos provided by community locals, providing insight into major towns and cities within the region and what each community has to offer, as you trek into the backcountry.

TOPO MAPS

Containing the core foundation of our Mapbooks, this section begins with a regional map key and leads into our nationally-acclaimed topographic maps, with hundreds of thousands of kilometers of backroads, backcountry trails and points of interest.

SERVICE DIRECTORY

Another essential trip planning resource, the Service directory allows you to find details on some of the best Accommodations, Sales /Services and Tours/Guides in the area.

MAP & ADVENTURES INDEXES

A full map and adventures index of the guide's contents is included with page numbers and map coordinates for easy reference.

TRIP PLANNING

Everything you need to know before heading into the outdoors, including important contact information for general services, parks, wildlife, club & association contacts, distance chart, alongside a list of advertisers featured in the mapbook. We also have included handy pages for making general notes or reservations.

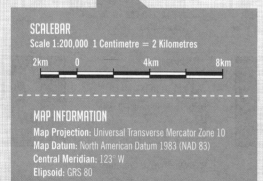

SCALEBAR
Scale 1:200,000 1 Centimetre = 2 Kilometres

2km   0   4km   8km

MAP INFORMATION
Map Projection: Universal Transverse Mercator Zone 10
Map Datum: North American Datum 1983 (NAD 83)
Central Meridian: 123° W
Elipsoid: GRS 80

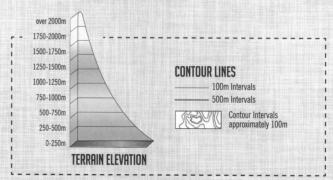

over 2000m
1750-2000m
1500-1750m
1250-1500m
1000-1250m
750-1000m
500-750m
250-500m
0-250m

TERRAIN ELEVATION

CONTOUR LINES
——————— 100m Intervals
——————— 500m Intervals

Contour Intervals approximately 100m

MAP LEGEND

AREA INDICATORS

National / Provincial Parks

Community Forests / Interpretive Forests / Recreation Sites / Regional Parks

Conservancy / Ecological Reserve / Protected Area / Wildlife Area

Canadian Forces Base / Mining / Restricted Area / Motorized Closures

City

First Nations

Glacier

Water

Swamps

WMU (Wildlife Management Units)

TFL (Tree Farm Licence Area)

Municiple / Regional District

LINE CLASSIFICATIONS

Freeways

Highways

Secondary Highways

Arterial Paved Roads

Rural Paved Roads

Local Paved Roads

Railways

Unpaved Secondary Highways

Forest Service & Main Industry Roads

Active Industry Roads (2wd)

Other Industry Roads (2wd / 4wd)

Unclassified & 4wd Roads

Deactivated Roads

Ferry Routes

Trans Canada Trail

Long Distance Trails

Snowmobile Trails

Motorized Trails ATV/OHV & Snowmobile

Developed Trails

Routes (Undeveloped Trails)

Portage Routes

Lake Paddling Routes

River Paddling Routes

Transmission Lines

Pipelines

Cut / Seismic Lines

MAP SYMBOLS

ON THE TRAIL

- ATV / OHV / Motorbiking
- BC Recreation Site (Camping)
- BC Recreation Site (Camping-RV)
- Cabin / Chalet / Hut / Shelter
- Campsite (back country / water access only)
- Campsite / Limited Facilities
- Caving / Spelunking
- Cross Country Skiing / Back Country Ski Touring
- Cycling / Mountain Biking
- Hiking
- Horseback Riding
- Interpretive Trail
- Picnic Site
- Ranger Station / Patrol Cabin
- Rock Climbing
- RV Campsite / Trailer Park
- Ski Area
- Snowmobiling
- Snowshoeing
- Trailhead
- Viewpoint / Forestry Lookout (abandoned)
- Wildlife Viewing

ON THE WATER

- Anchorage
- Beach
- Beacon
- Boat Launch
- Canoe Access Put-in / Take-out
- Dam
- Diving
- Ferry
- Float Plane Landing
- Fish Hatchery
- Fish Spawning / Ladder
- Hotspring
- Marsh
- Paddling (canoe-kayak)
- Portage
- P2100m Portage Distance
- Waterfall

ON THE ROAD

- Airport
- Airstrip
- Gate
- Highway: Trans Canada
- Highway Interchange
- Information Centre
- Parking
- Visitor Centre

OTHER

- Arrow / Location Pointer
- BRMB Geocache
- City, Town, Village Indicator
- Customs
- Golf Course
- Hang-gliding
- Microwave Tower
- Mine Site
- Point of Interest
- Resort
- Resort (BCFROA)
- Wilderness Area / Wildlife Area / Wildlife Reserve
- Winery

Visit **backroadmapbook.com** to see tutorials on how to use different elements of our legend

IX

TOPOGRAPHIC MAPS

MAP KEY

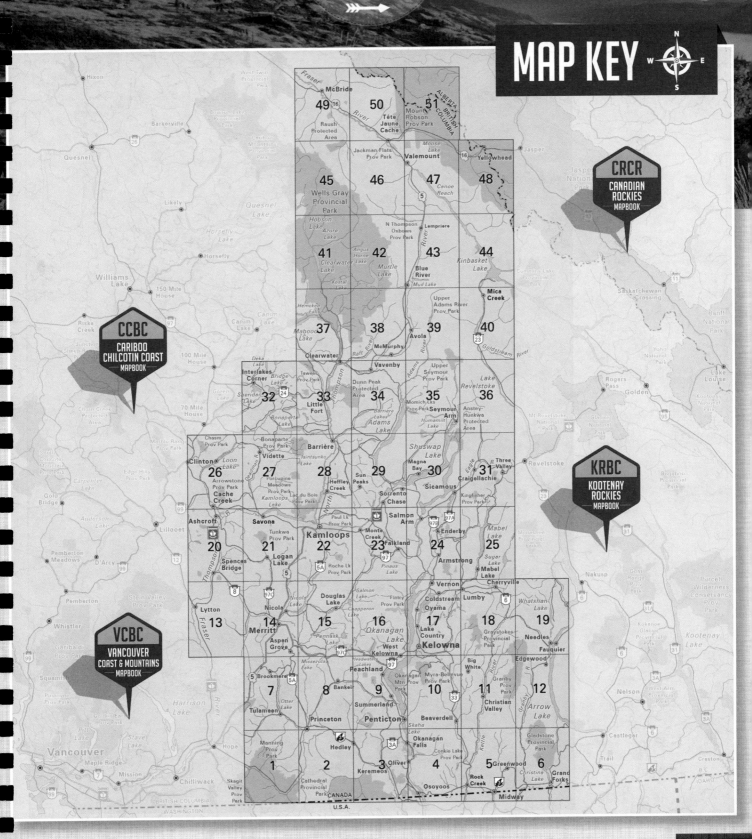

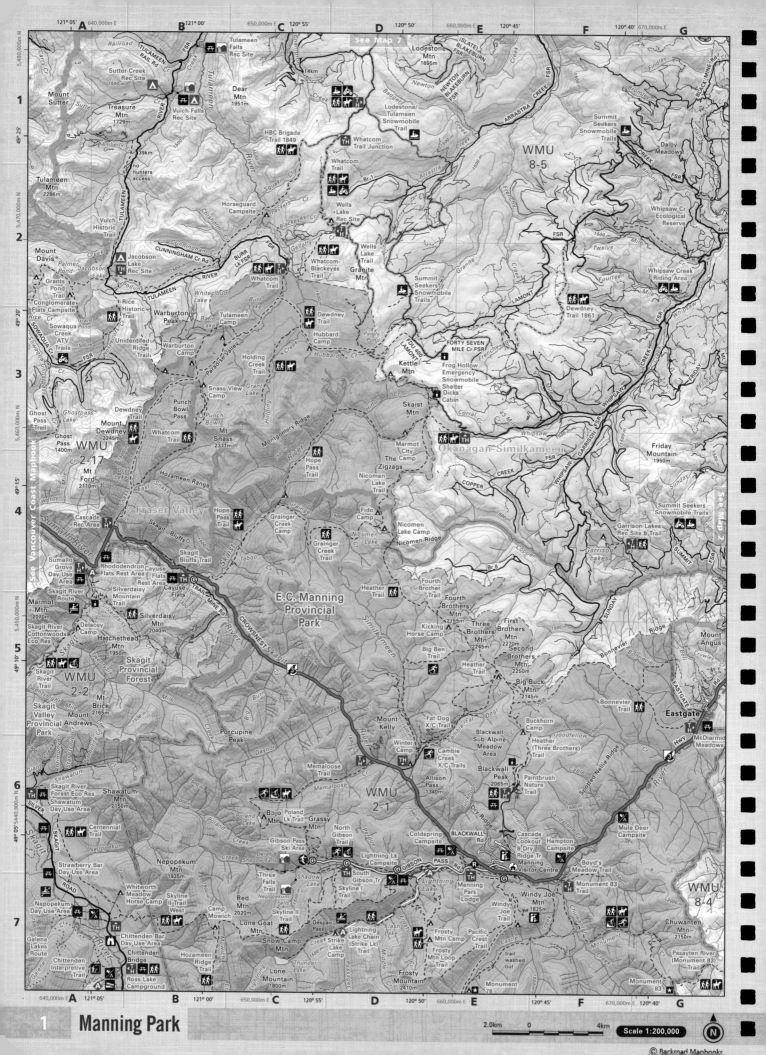

Manning Park

1

Scale 1:200,000

2.0km   0   4km

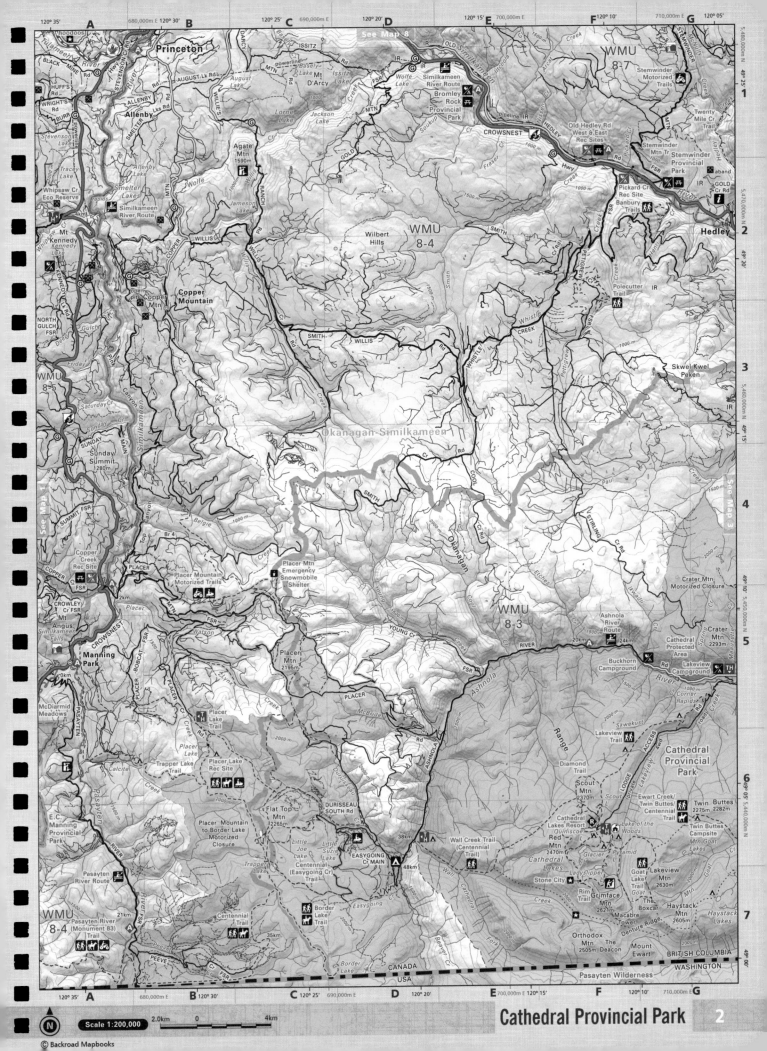

Cathedral Provincial Park

2

Scale 1:200,000   2.0km   0   4km

© Backroad Mapbooks

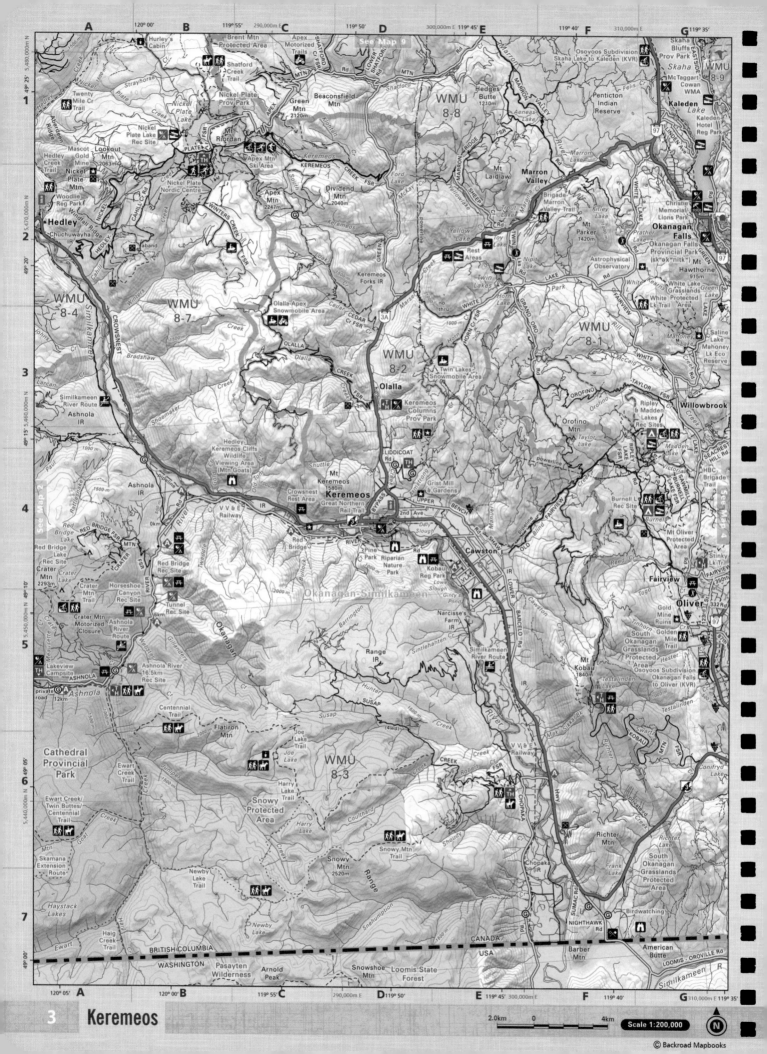

Scale 1:200,000

© Backroad Mapbooks

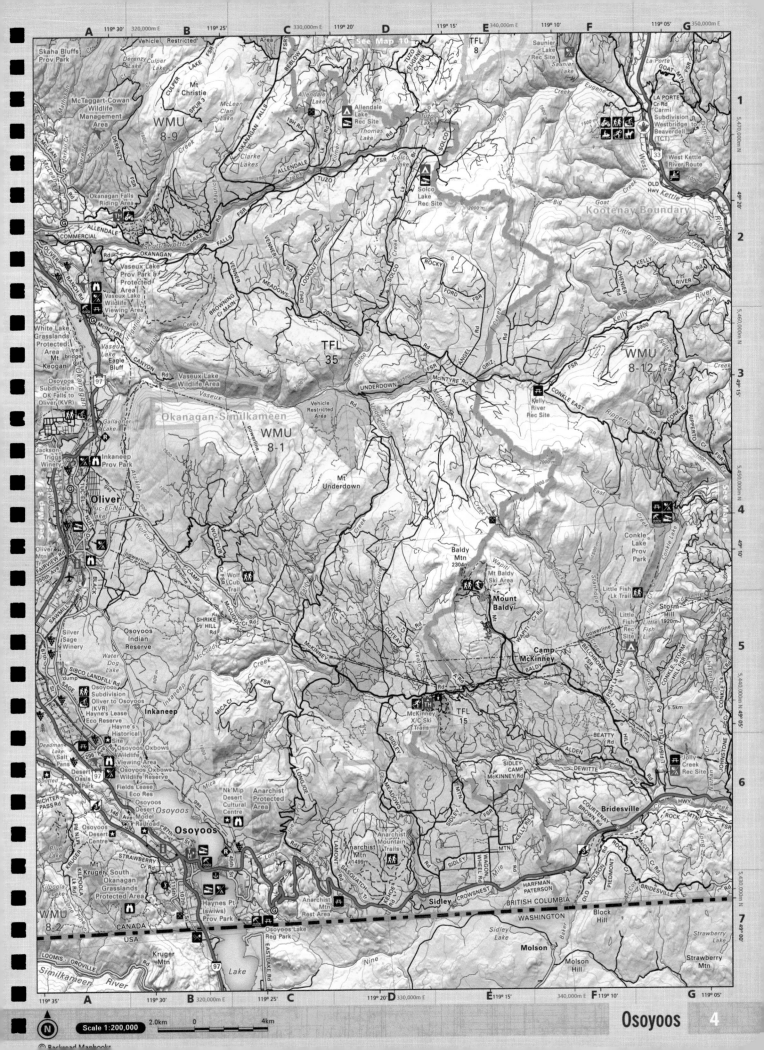

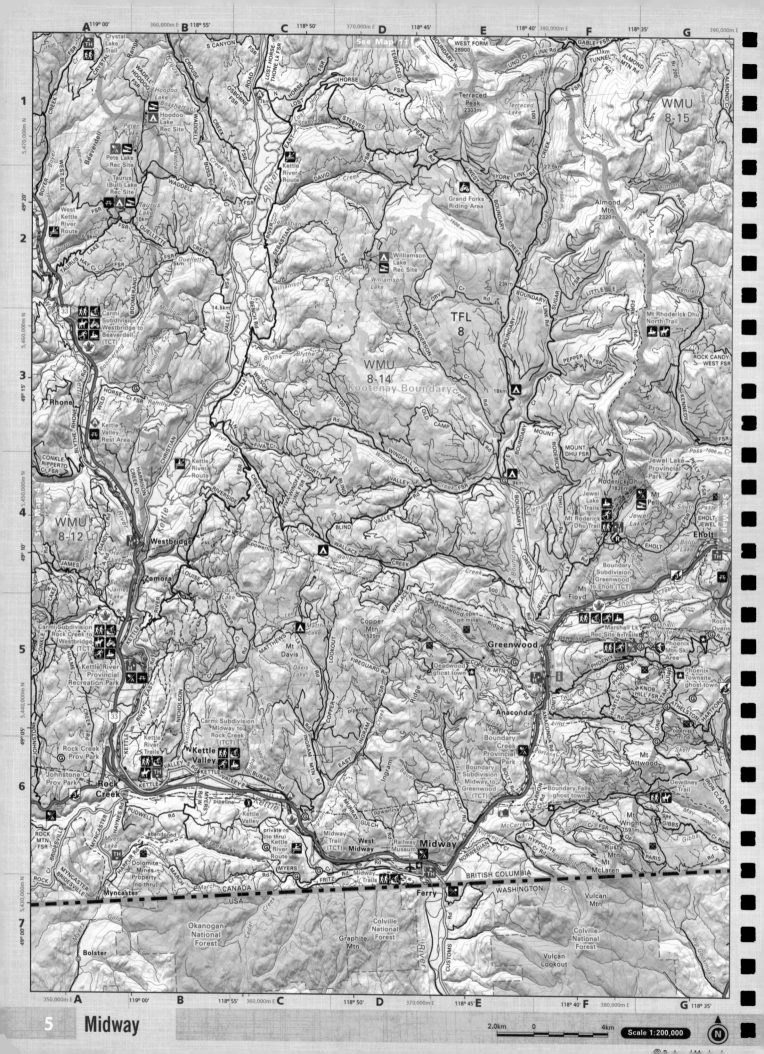

Scale 1:200,000

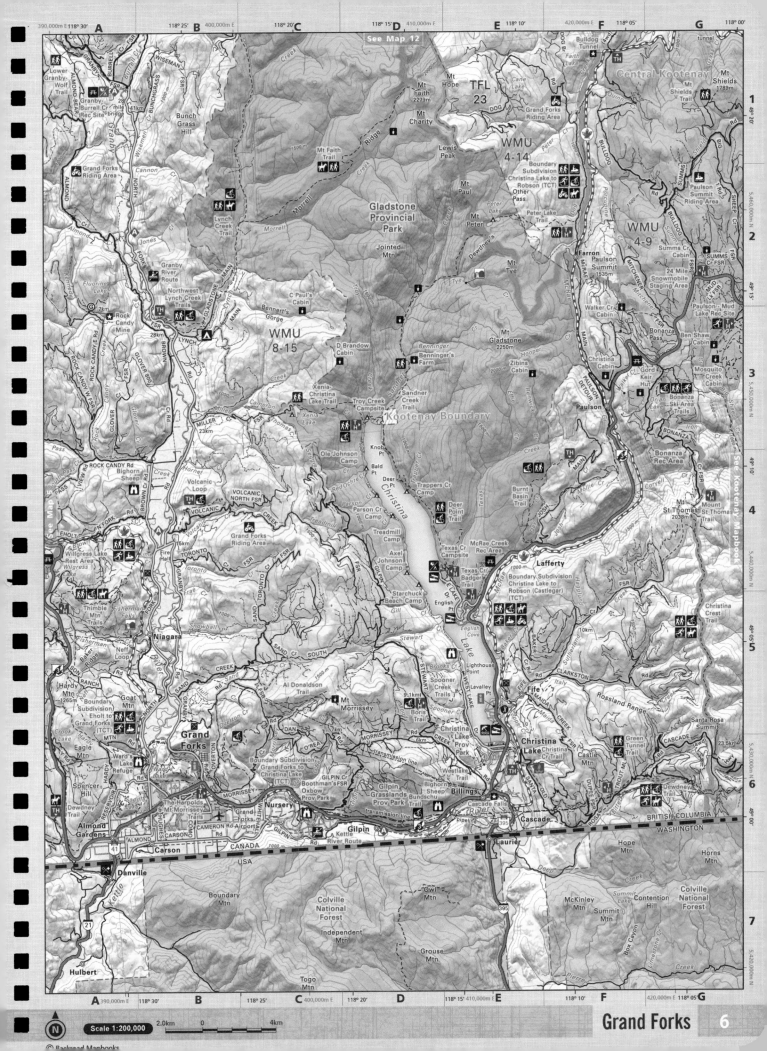

Scale 1:200,000   2.0km   0   4km

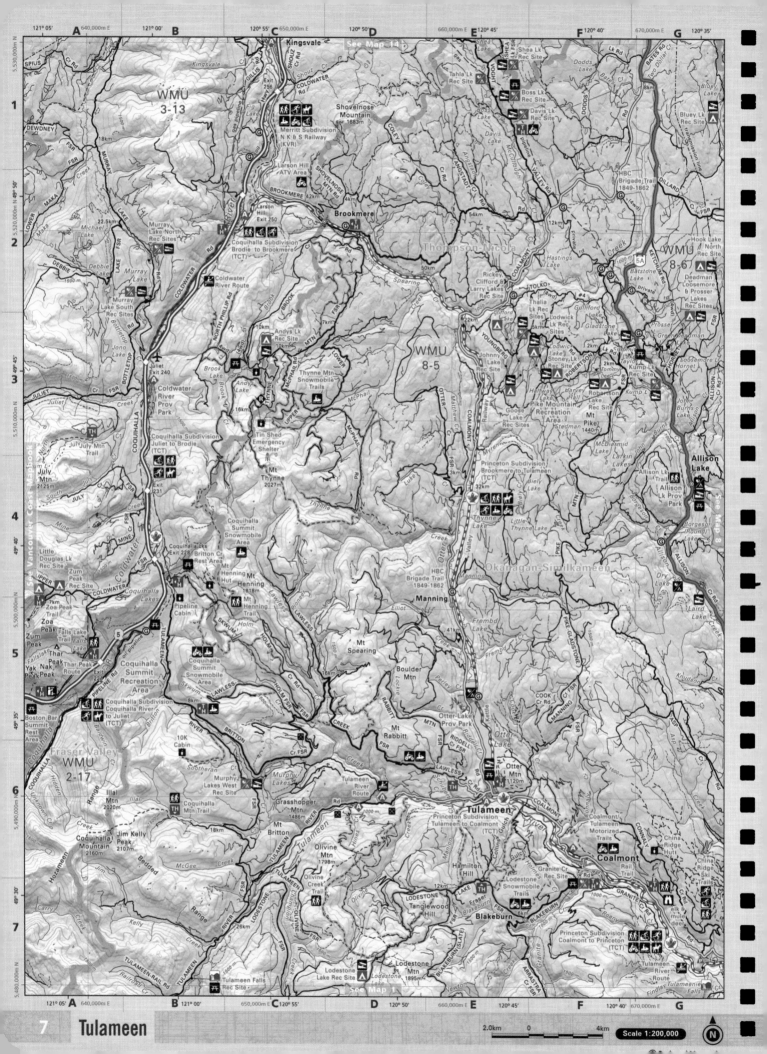

Scale 1:200,000

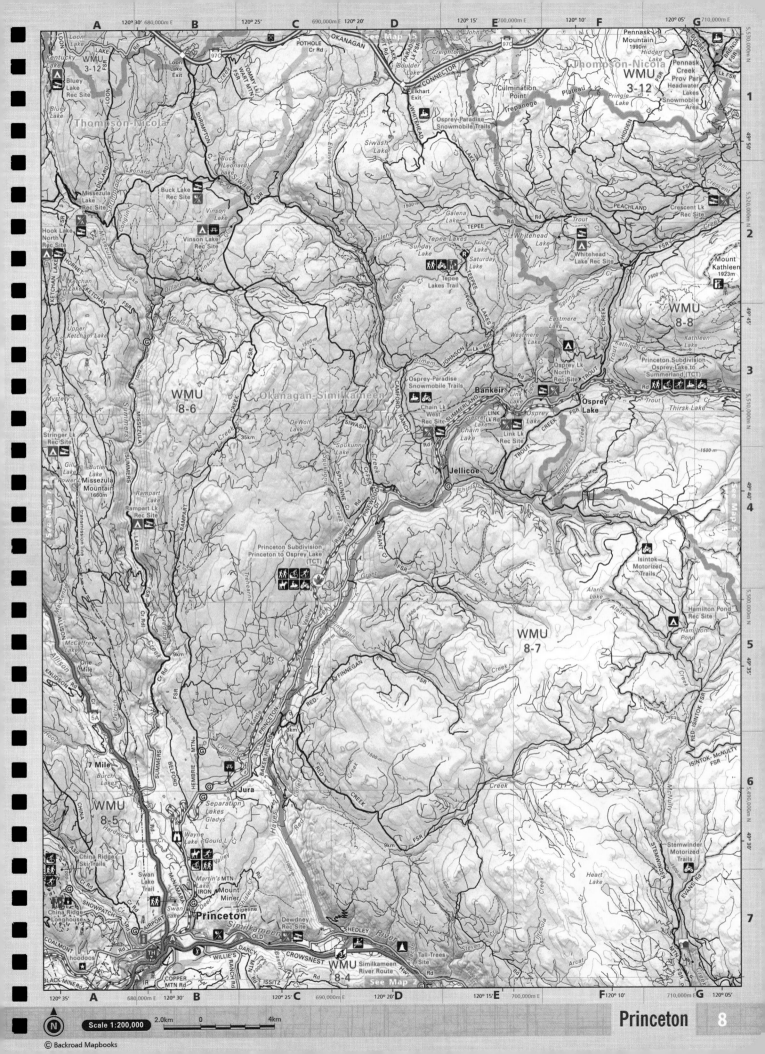

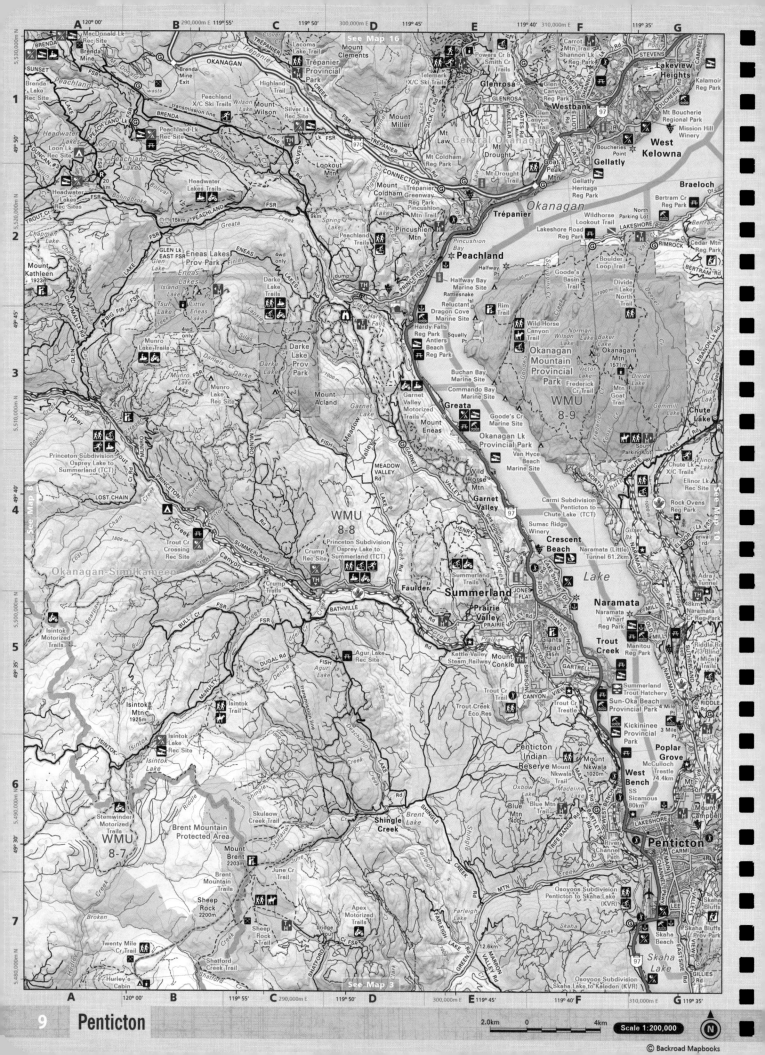

Scale 1:200,000

2.0km   0   4km

© Backroad Mapbooks

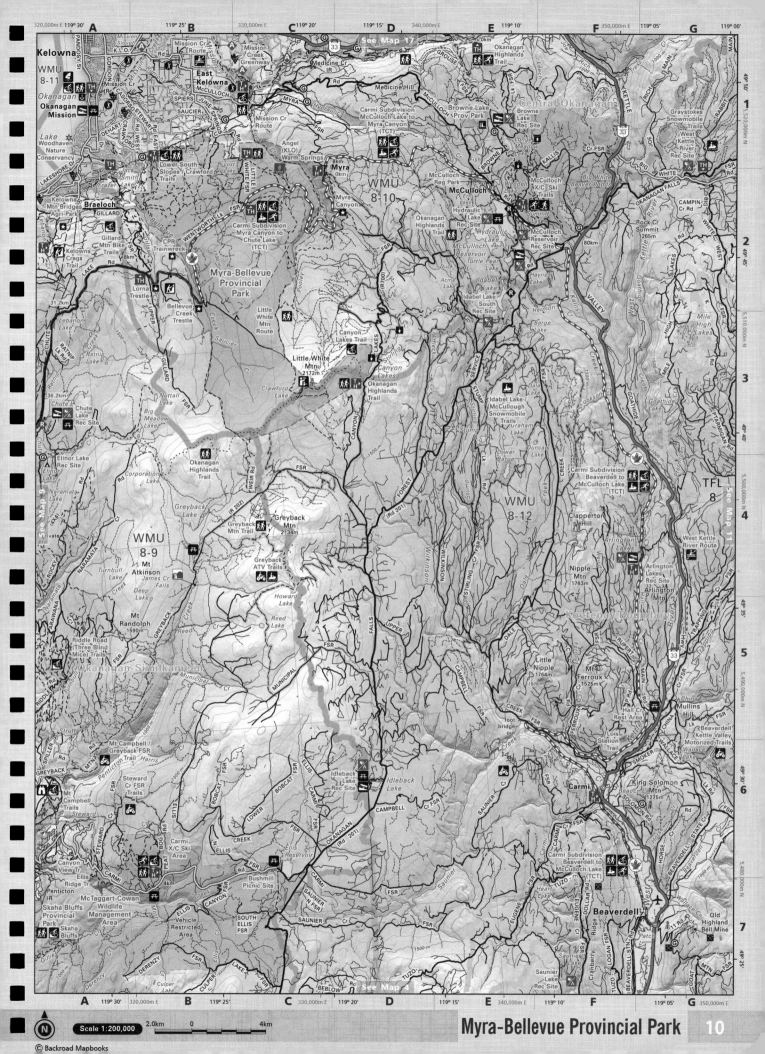

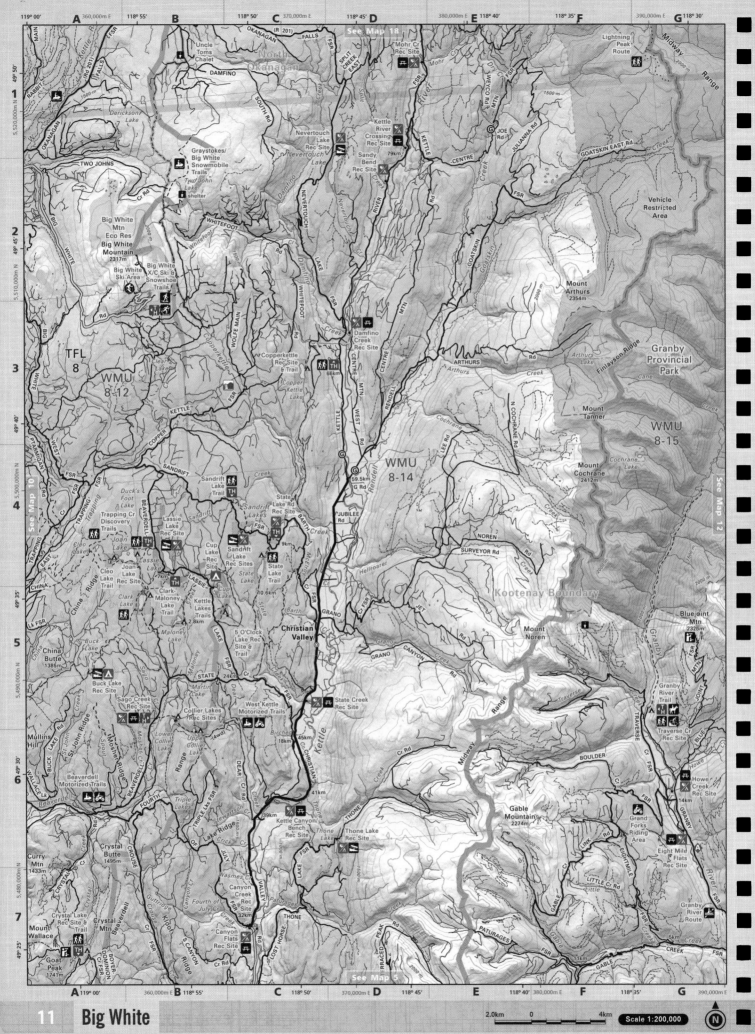

Scale 1:200,000

© Backroad Mapbooks

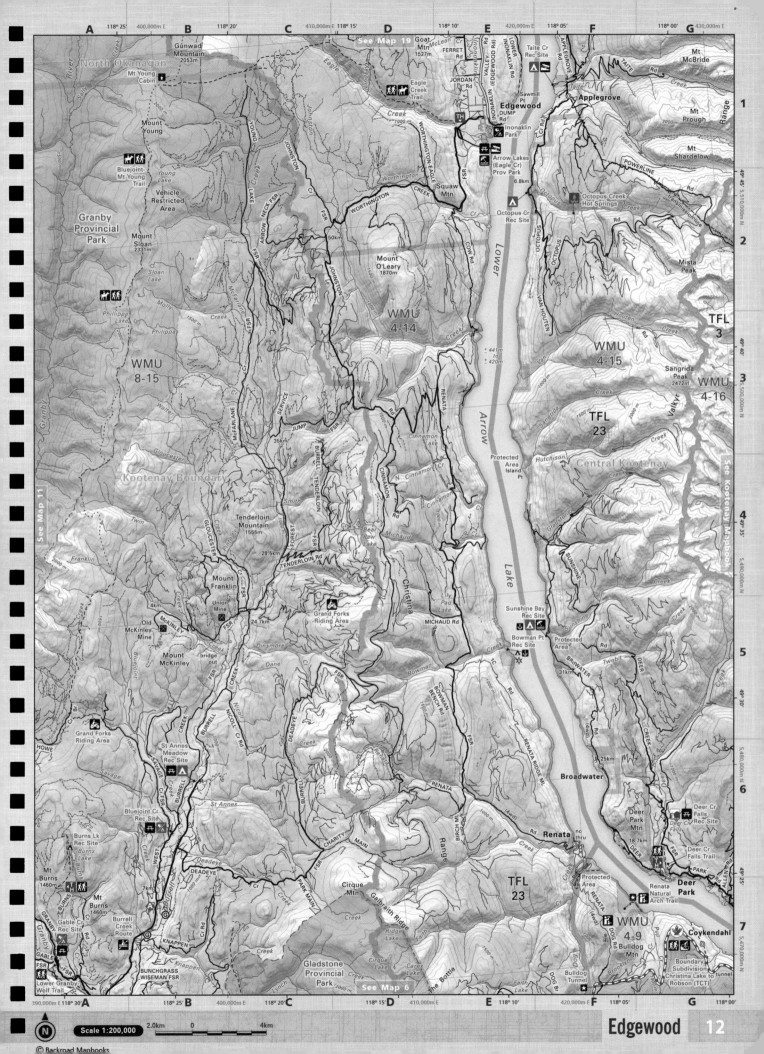

Scale 1:200,000

© Backroad Mapbooks

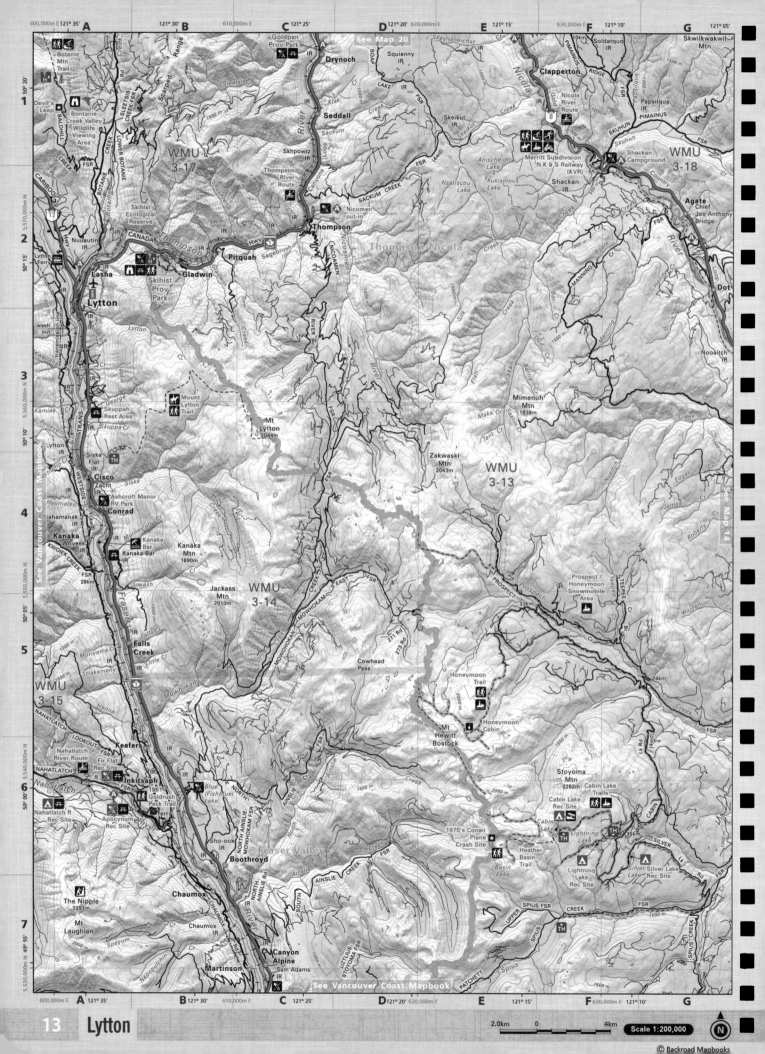

Scale 1:200,000

2.0km   0   4km

© Backroad Mapbooks

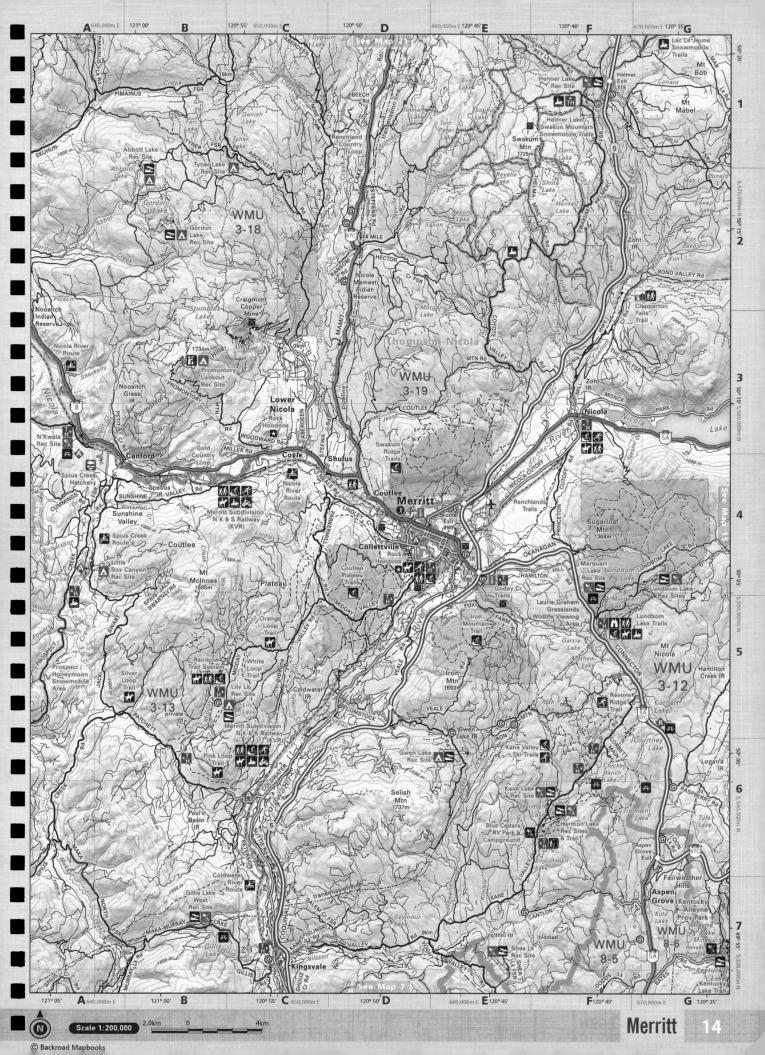

Scale 1:200,000

© Backroad Mapbooks

Scale 1:200,000

© Backroad Mapbooks

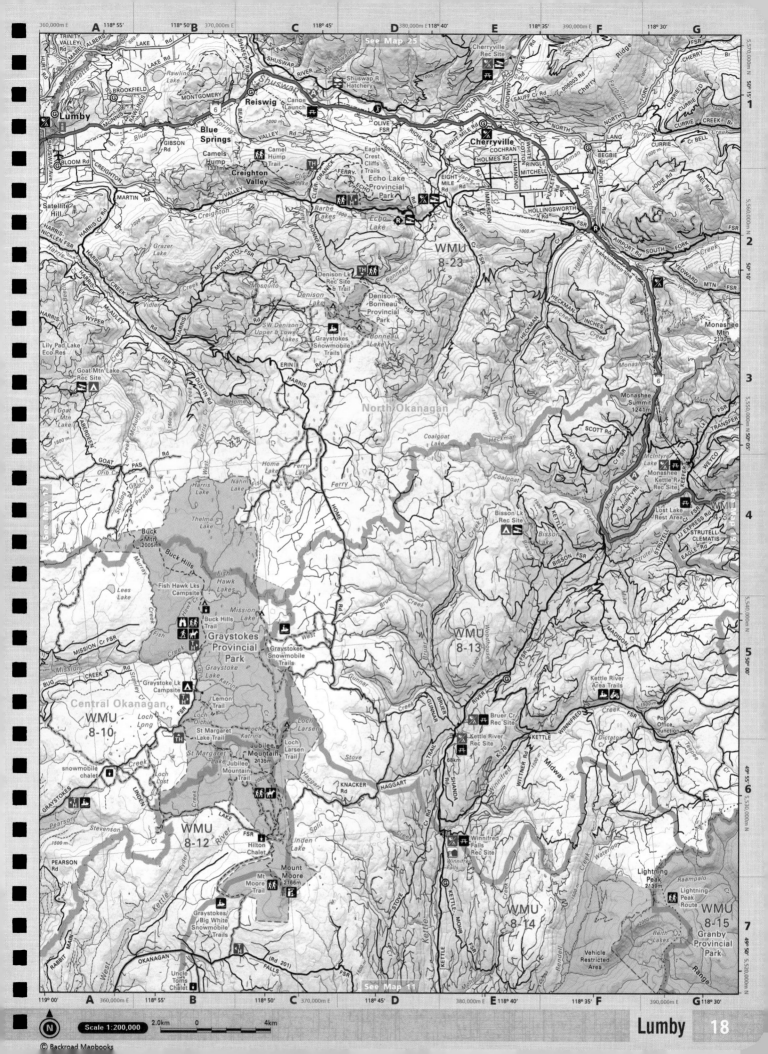

Scale 1:200,000

© Backroad Mapbooks

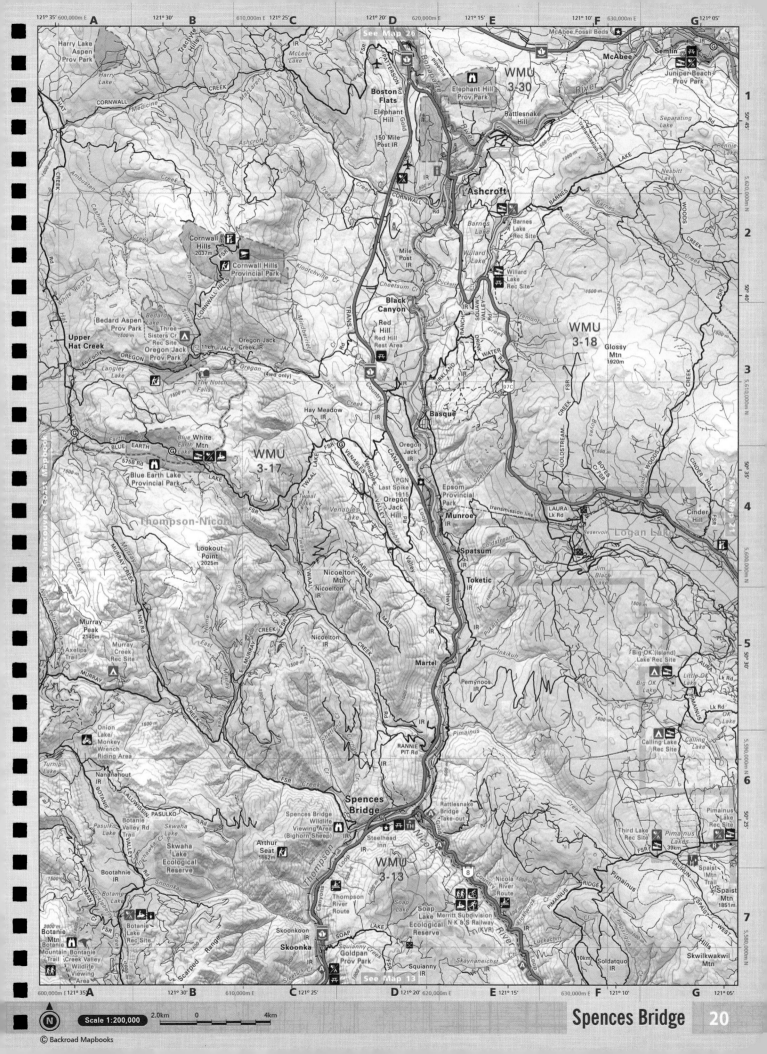

Scale 1:200,000

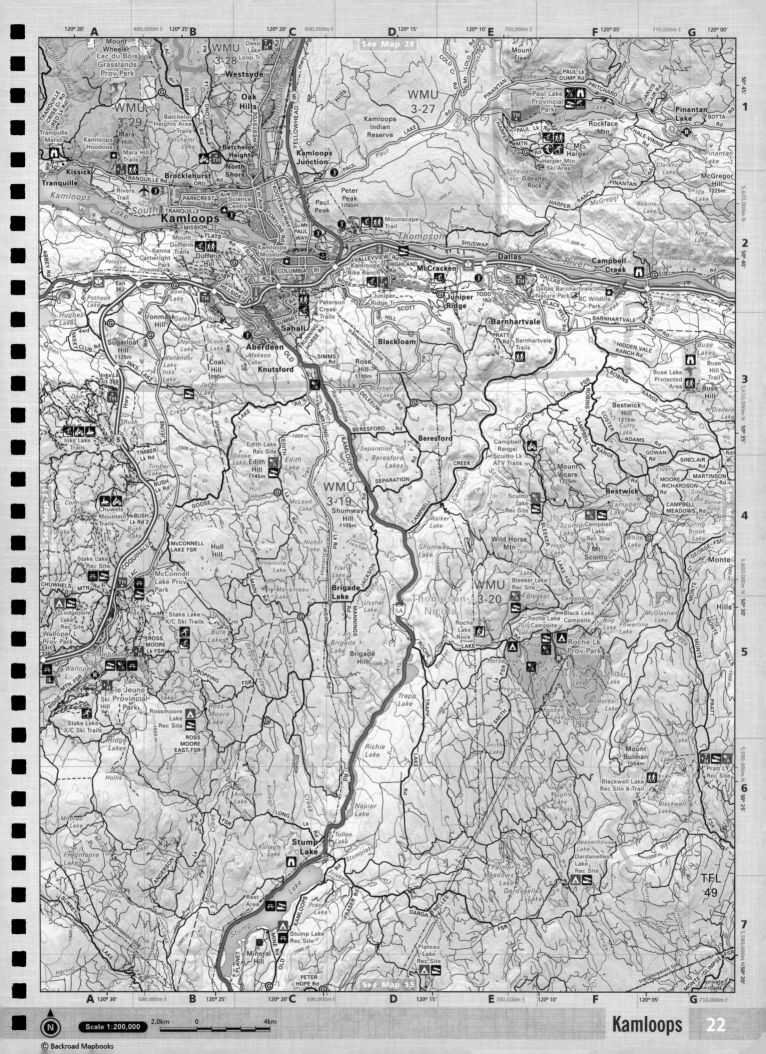

Scale 1:200,000

2.0km   0   4km

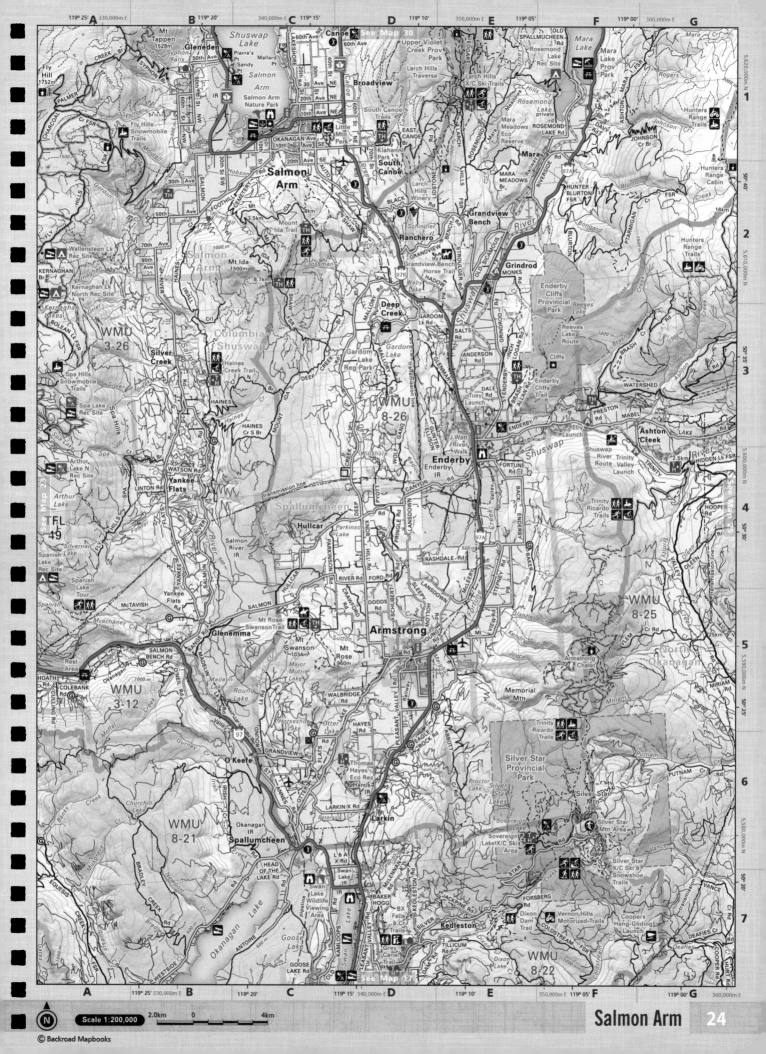

Scale 1:200,000

© Backroad Mapbooks

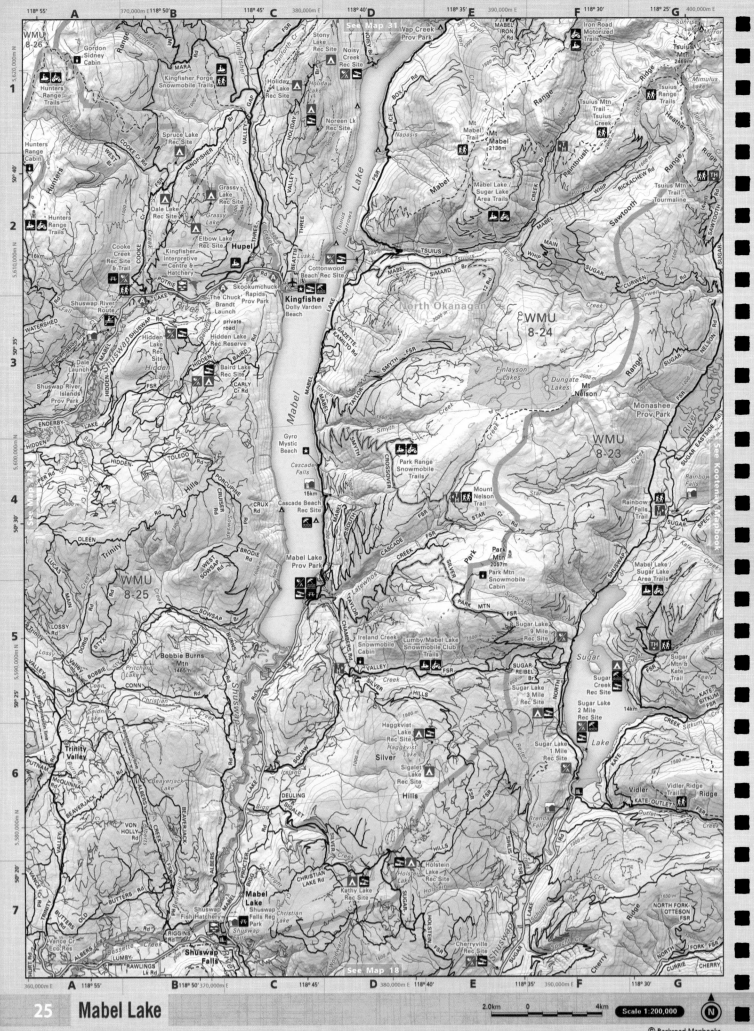

Scale 1:200,000

© Backroad Mapbooks

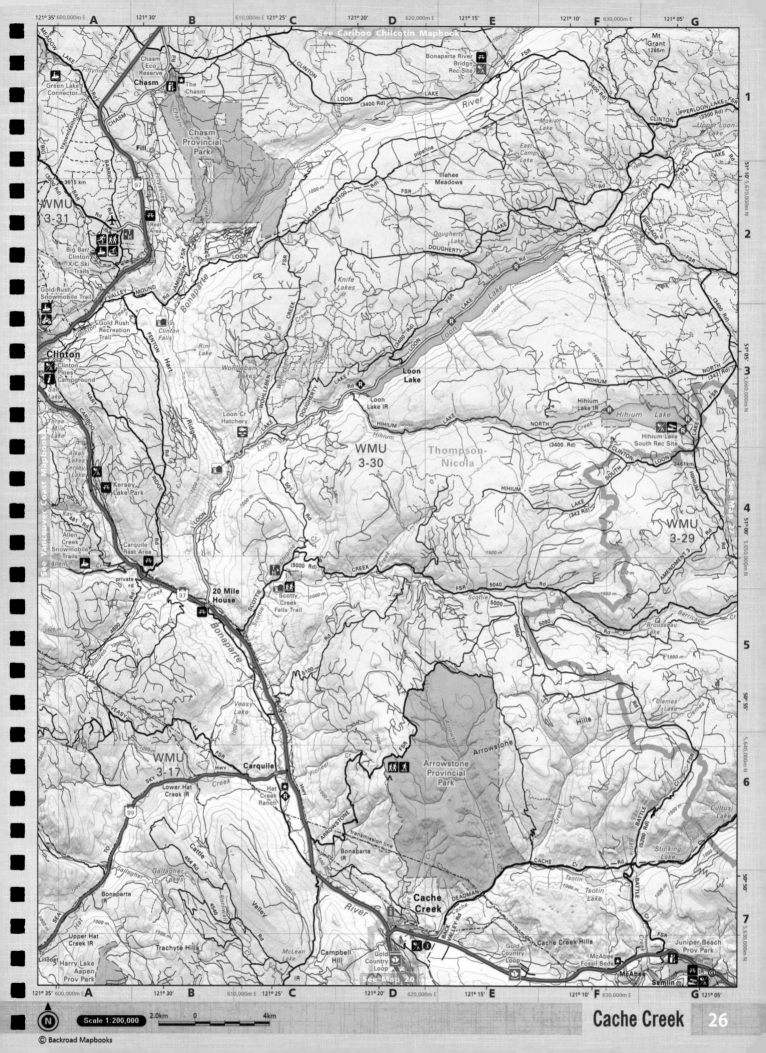

Scale 1:200,000   2.0km   0   4km

© Backroad Mapbooks

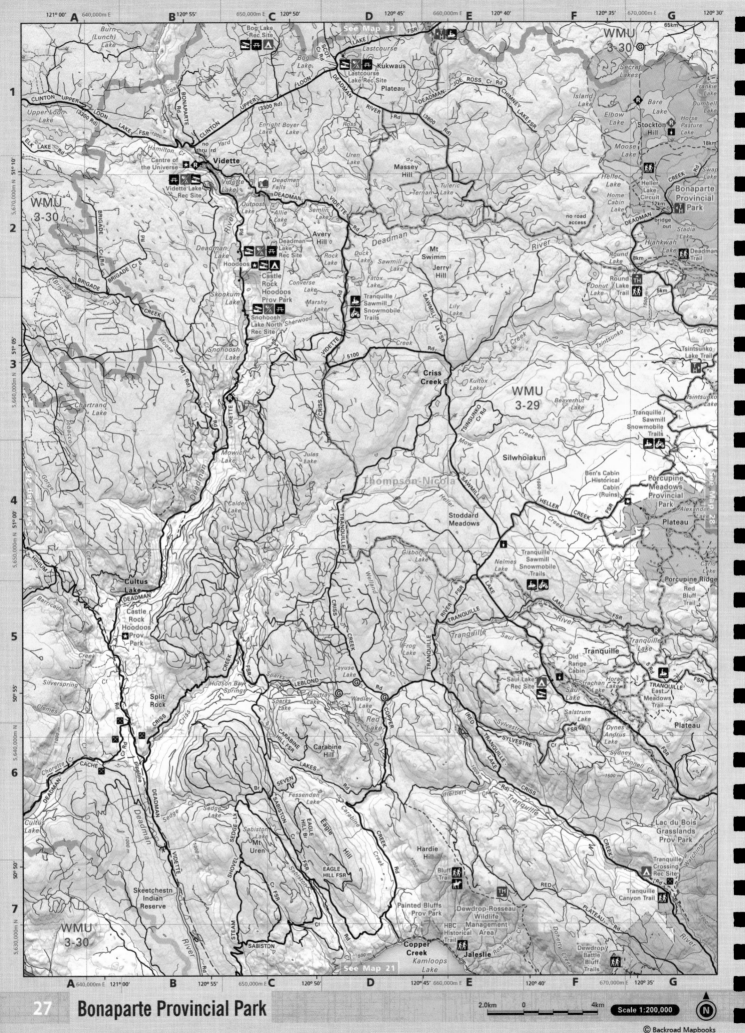

Scale 1:200,000

© Backroad Mapbooks

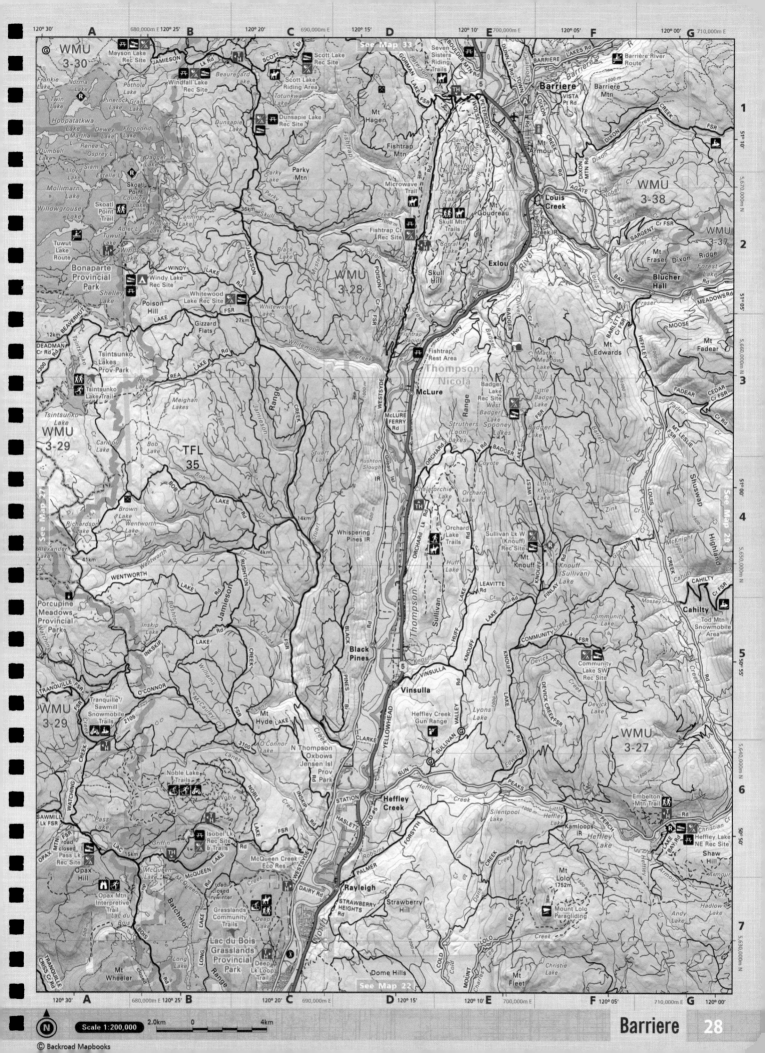

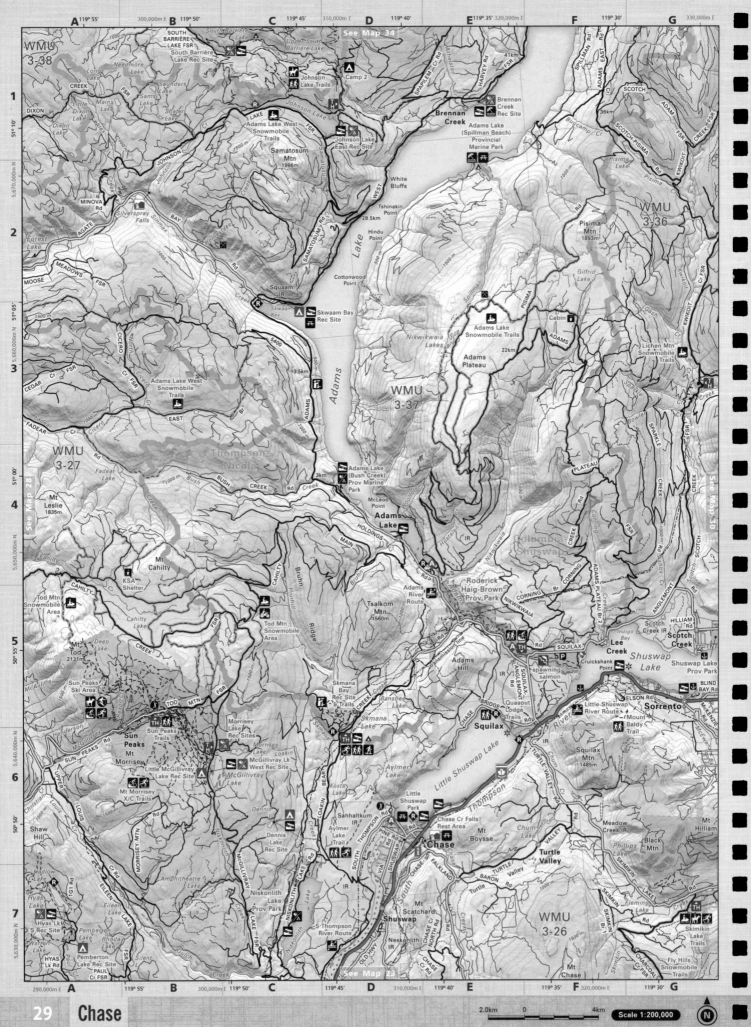

2.0km 0 4km | Scale 1:200,000 | N

© Backroad Mapbooks

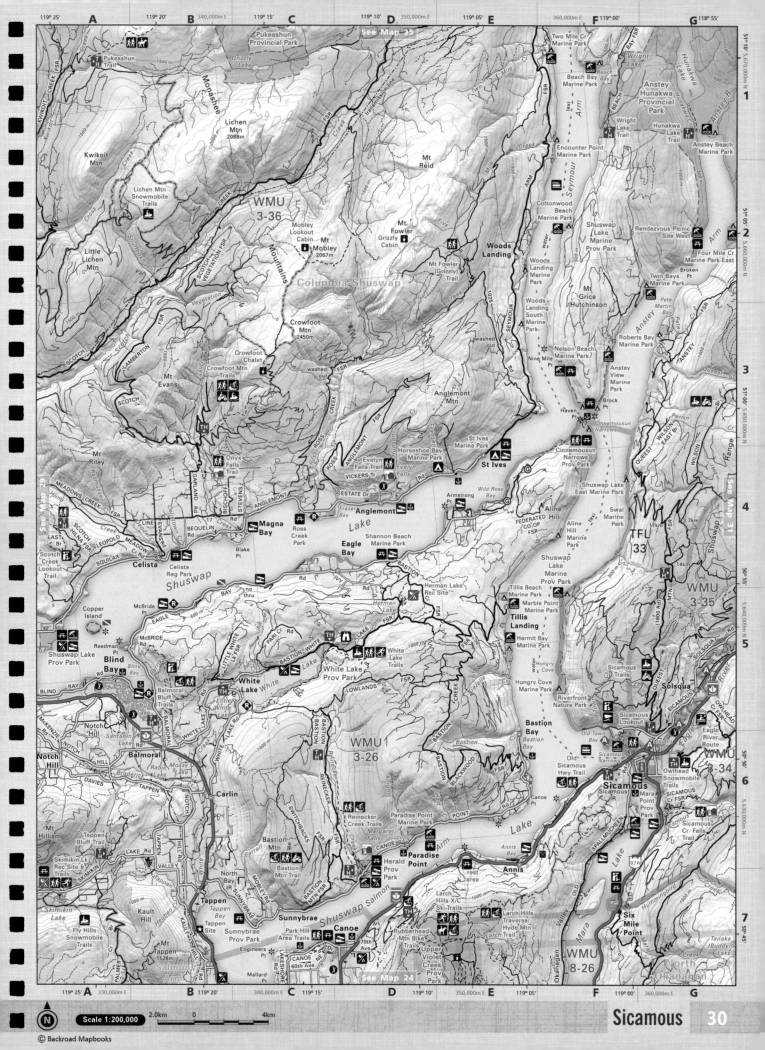

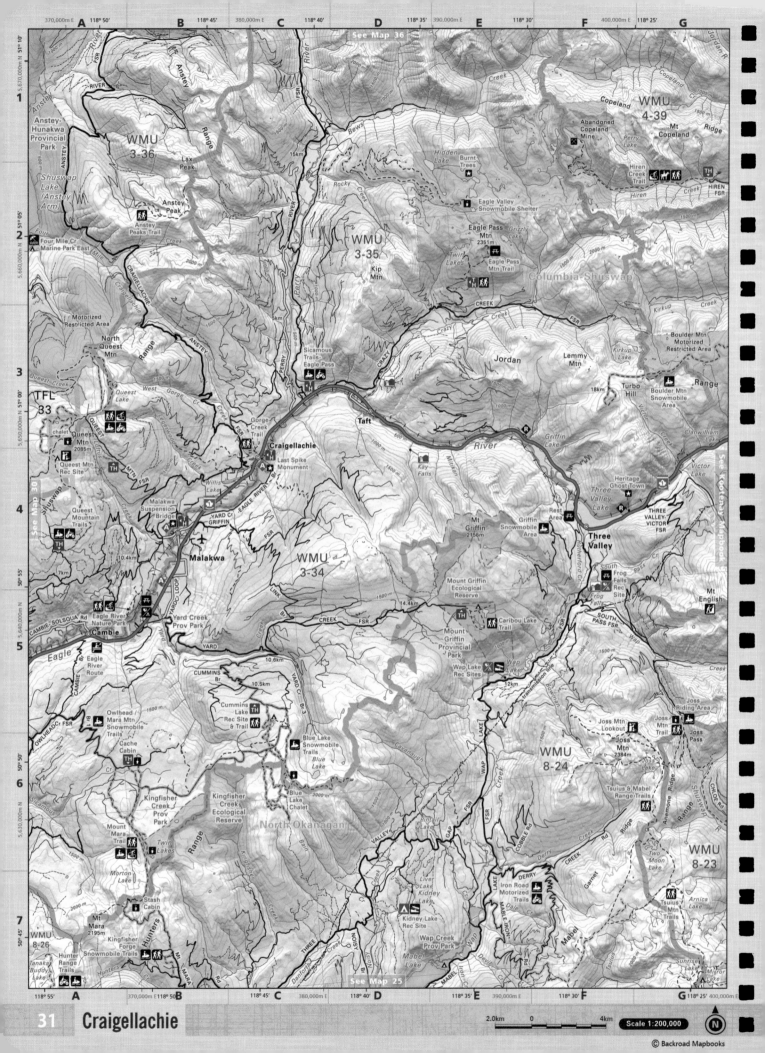

Scale 1:200,000

2.0km   0   4km

© Backroad Mapbooks

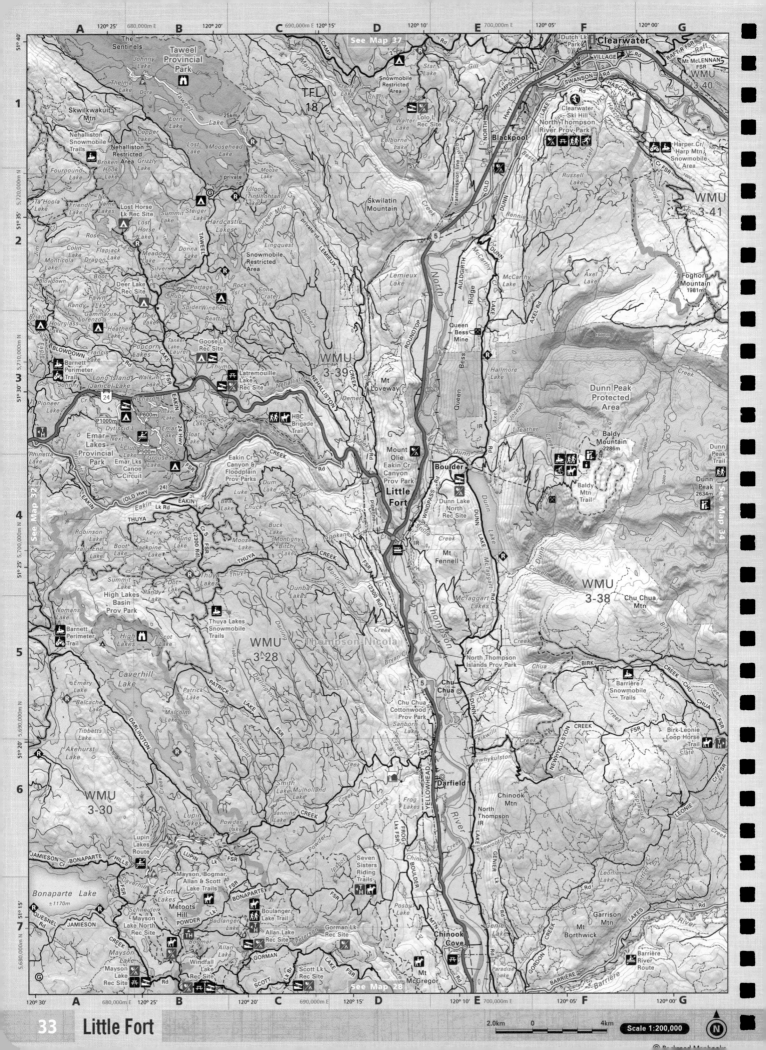

Scale 1:200,000

2.0km   0   4km

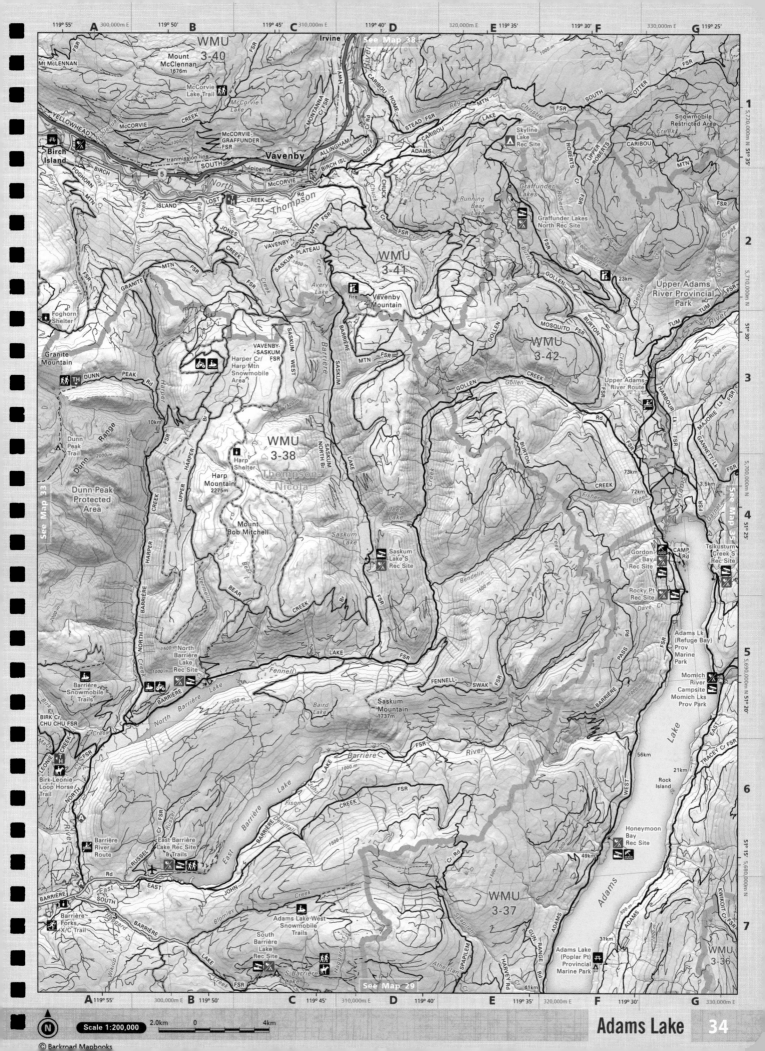

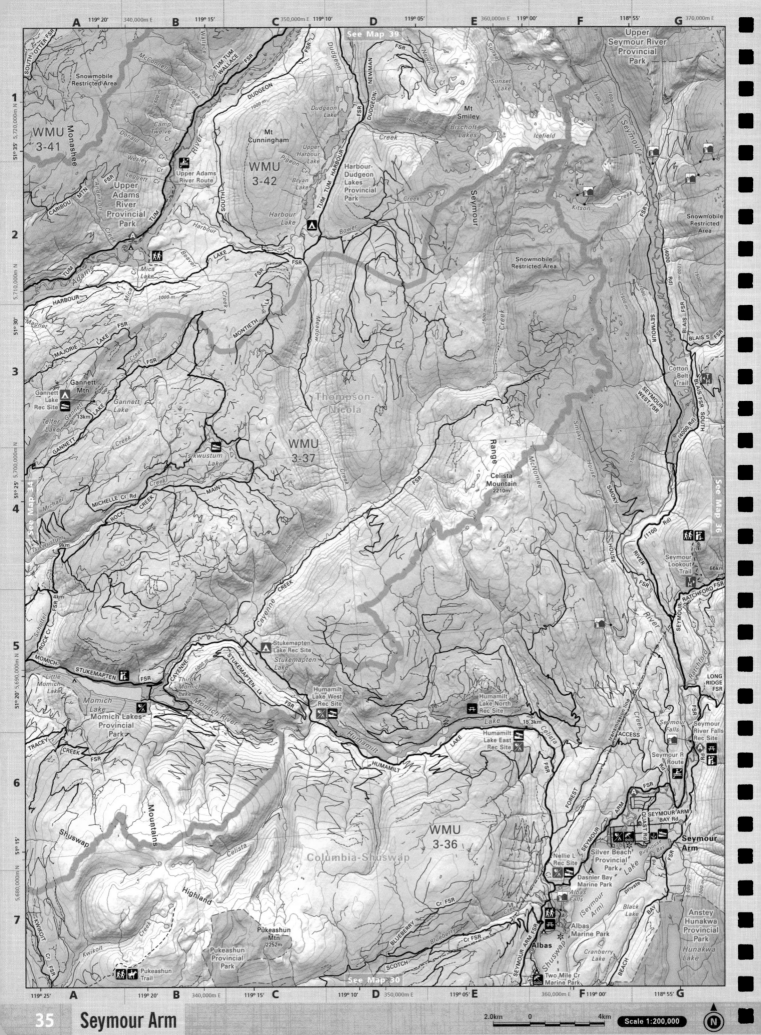

Scale 1:200,000

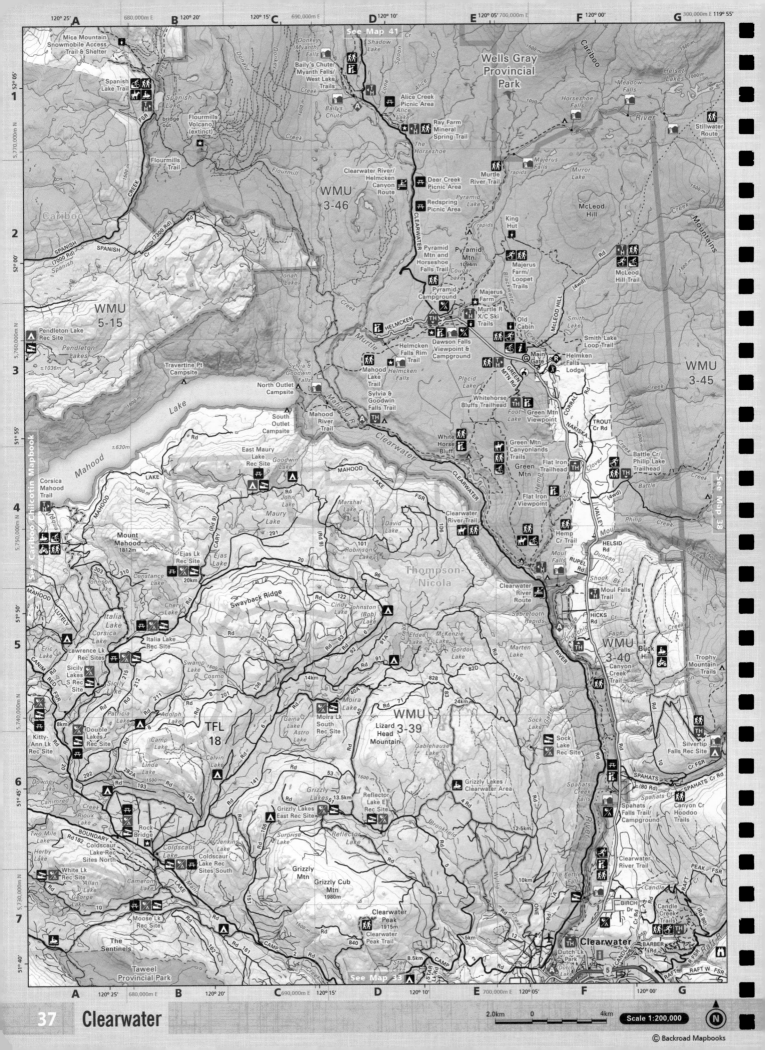

Scale 1:200,000

2.0km   0   4km

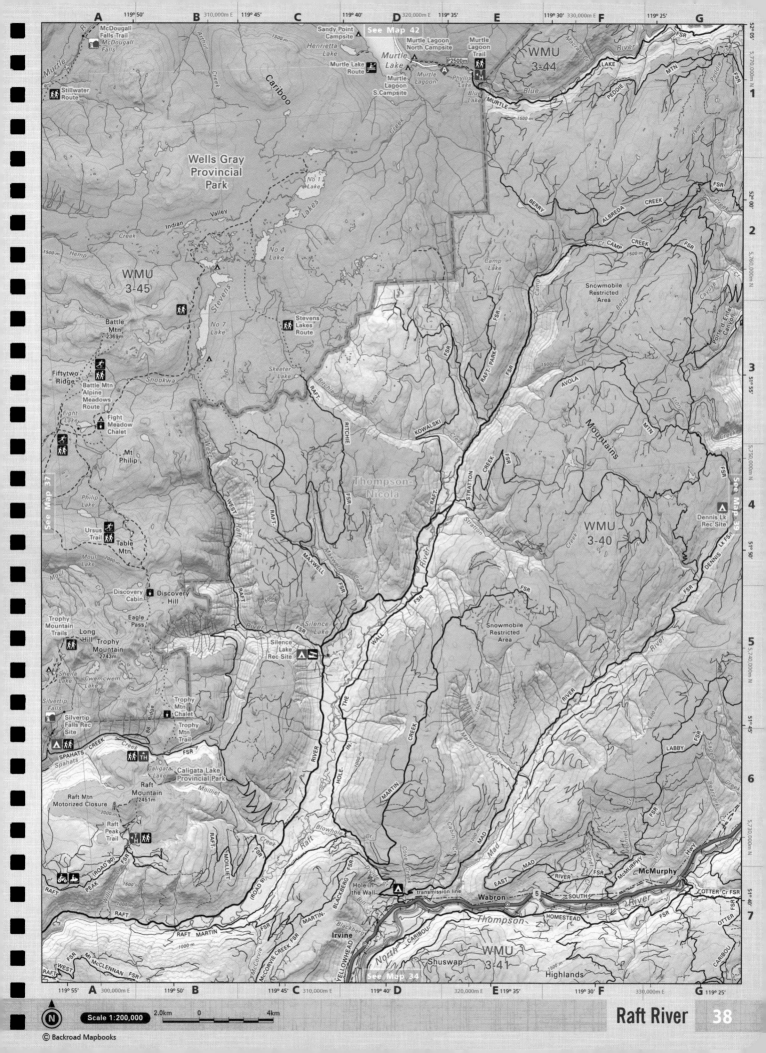

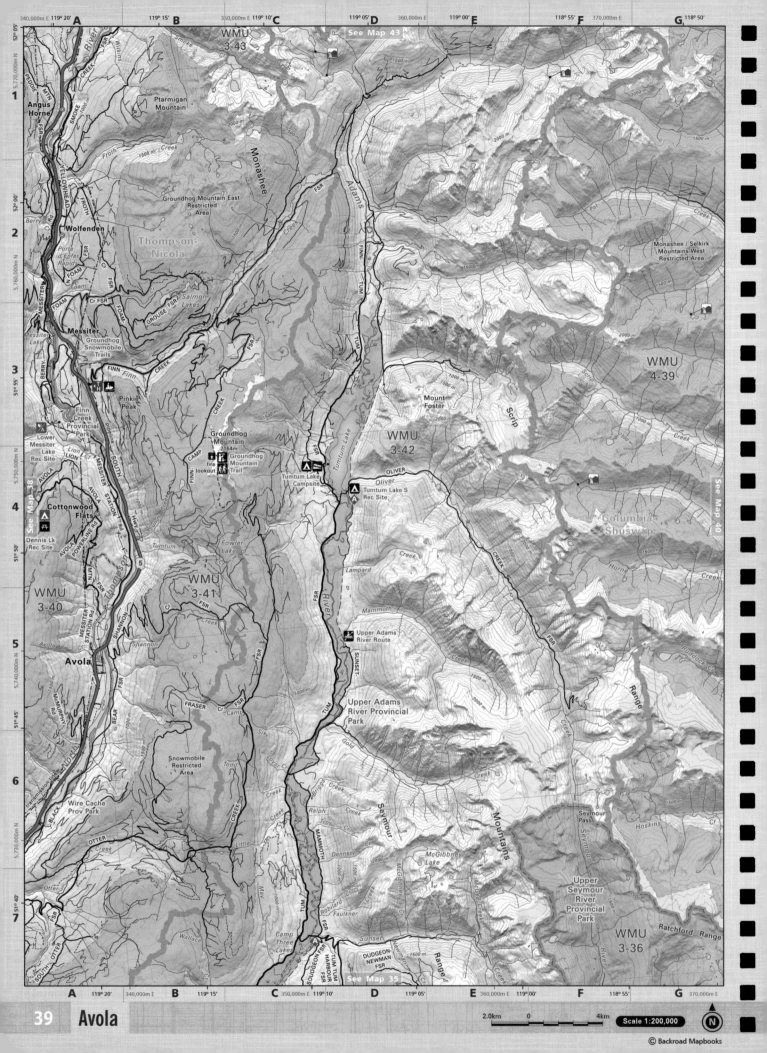

Scale 1:200,000

© Backroad Mapbooks

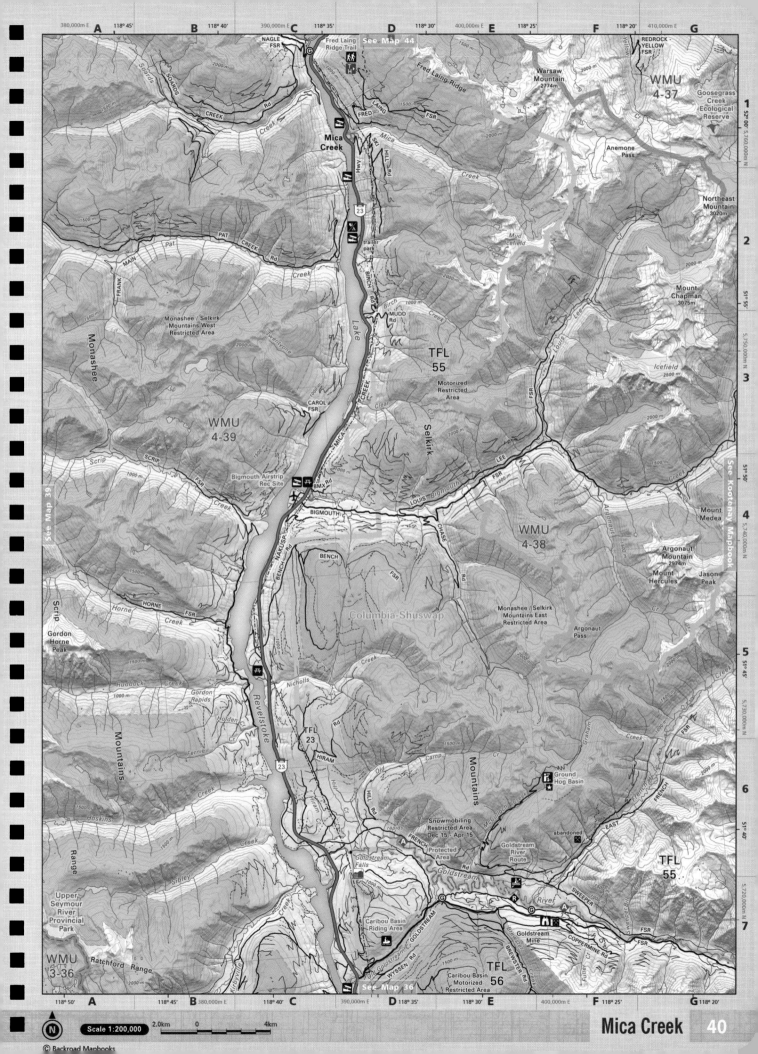

WMU
5-15

WMU
3-46

WMU
3-45

WMU
5-15

Thompson-Nicola

Wells Gray
Provincial
Park

See Cariboo Chilcotin Mapbook

See Map 42

See Map 37

Hamany

Hall Creek

Baking Creek

Powder Creek

Lickskillet Creek

Hobson Lake

De Weiss Lake

±858m

Mount Hugh Neave

Cariboo Creek

2000 m

1500 m

Garnet Peak 2900m

Buchanan Peak 2469m

Azure River

Azure Creek

Tryfan Mountain

Batoche Peak

Mount Huntley 2429m

Huntley Col

Huntley Column Route

Four and a Half Mile Campsite

Garnet Falls

Garnet Cr

Goat Creek

Embry Cr

bridge out

Sundt Falls

Indian Pt Campsite

P500m

Osprey Campsite

Azure

±681m

Rainbow Falls Campsite

Clearwater/ Azure Lakes Route

Rainbow Falls

Airgus Creek

Horne Creek

Lake

Clearwater Lake

Barella Cr Campsite

Hobson Lake Trail

Barella Creek

Clearwater

Zodiac Mtn

Azure Mtn 2495m

Mountains

Molen

Archer Cr Campsite

Clearwater/ Azure Lakes Route

±679m

Huckleberry Campsite

Zodiac Peak Route

Ivor Creek

Extinct Volcano

File Creek

McDougall Lake

Archer Creek

Ivor Creek Campsite

Huckleberry Beach

Mount Ray 2046m

Goat Peaks 2450m

Bar View Campsite

Falls (Ray) Lake

Divers Bluff Campsite

Cranberry Lake

Snowmobile Restricted Area

Chain Lake

Cariboo Beach Campsite

Chain Meadow/ Easter Bluffs Loop

Kostal Lake

Kostal Volcano (extinct)

McKusky Creek

Daniel Creek

A

CLEARWATER

Lava Flow

Sticta & Osprey (Clegeral) Falls

Majerus Lake

Pillpill Mountain

Mica Mountain 2122m

Cariboo

CW Shook/ Dragon's Tongue Trail

Clearwater Lake & Falls Creek Campgrounds

Falls Creek

Spoon Creek

Mica Mountain Snowmobile Access Trail & Shelter

Beaver Creek

VALLEY

Zellers Lake

Chain Meadows

Shadow Lake

Kilpill Mountain

Clearwater River

Rd

2.0km   0   4km

Scale 1:200,000

N

© Backroad Mapbooks

Scale 1:200,000   2.0km   0   4km

© Backroad Mapbooks

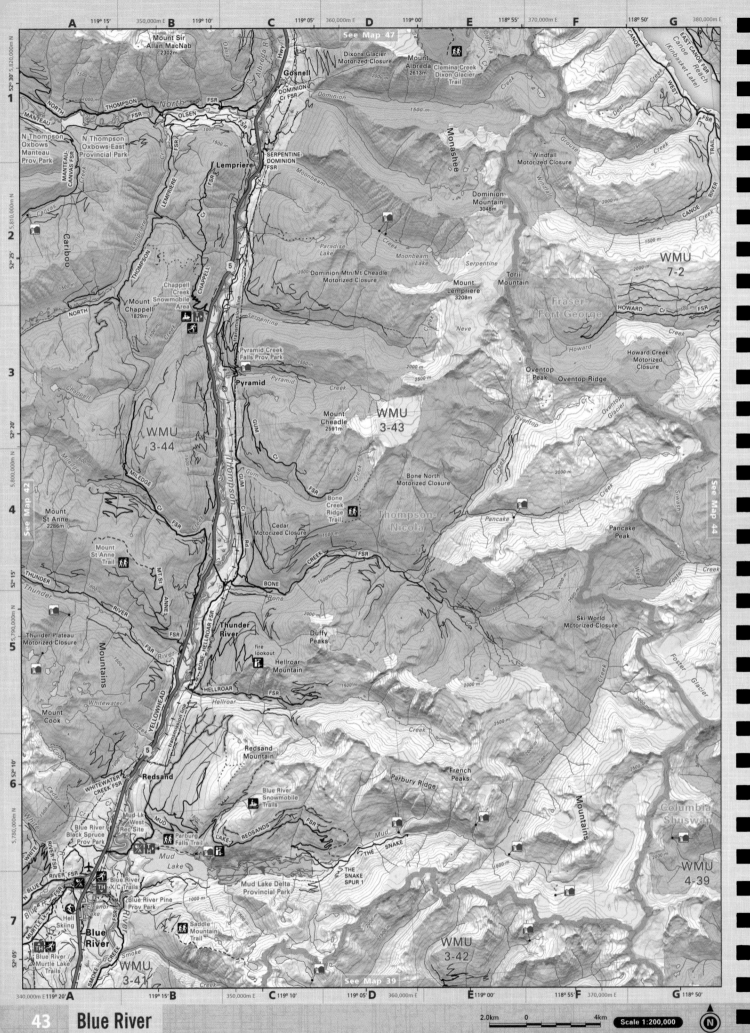

Scale 1:200,000

2.0km 0 4km

WMU 7-2

LITTLE FROG FSR

Mount Blackman

Rocky

Mallard Peak

Jasper National Park

Canoe Pass 2050m

BC / AB

Athabasca Pass Trail

Mount Brown

Mount Brown Icefield

Hugh Allan Ridge

ALLAN

SILVERTIP FSR

SOUTH FORK

Bryan Peak

Anderson Mtn

Amie Peak

Edward Peak

East Iroquois Creek

Fraser-Fort George

Selwyn

Canoe Mountain

Windfall Bay

Howard Bay

CANOE FSR

HOWARD CREEK

Howard Creek

Buster Creek

BUSTER/HOWARD FSR

Monashee

Foster Creek Motorized Closure

See Map 43

Foster Arm Protected Area

Trench

Baker Cr

BAKER

FSR

Lemmy Mountain

WMU 4-40

Dunkirk Mountain

Dawson Creek

Hallam Glacier

Hallam Peak

Mountains

Foster Arm

Foster Creek

Kelly Cr

Reach

Harvey Bay

Harvey Creek

Mount Dainard

DAINARD FSR

Dainard Cr

Range

Mountains

Mount Molson 2498m

Columbia-Shuswap

Molson Creek

Molson Bay

Wood Arm

Encampment North Motorized Closure

Franchere Creek

Kinbasket Lake (McNaughton Lake)

Garnet Islands

WOOD RIVER FSR

GOATBUSTER CREEK Rd

Cummins Lookout

Mount Cummins 2586m

WMU 4-39

Mount Nagle 2271m

Little Chief Lake

Little Chief Ridge

Dutchman's Ridge

DUTCHMAN

Encampment

Creek Rd

Sprague Bay Rec Site

Sprague Bay

ROCK

Bodleigh

WOOD ARM FSR

REDROCK SPRAGUE FSR

Redrock Harbour

Rd

YELLOW

Columbia

CREEK

Yellow Bay

Monashee / Selkirk Mountain West Restricted Area

Nagle Creek

RED

Potlatch Cr Rec Site

Mica Dam

WMU 4-38

23

Private

Gorge

Fred Laing Ridge

Fred Laing Cr

Selkirk Mountains

Yellow Creek

REDROCK YELLOW FSR

YELLOW FSR

WMU 4-37

Goosegrass Creek Ecological Reserve

Soards

TFL 55

NAGLE Creek

FSR

Fred Laing Ridge Trail

See Map 40

Wells Gray Provincial Park

Scale 1:200,000

© Backroad Mapbooks

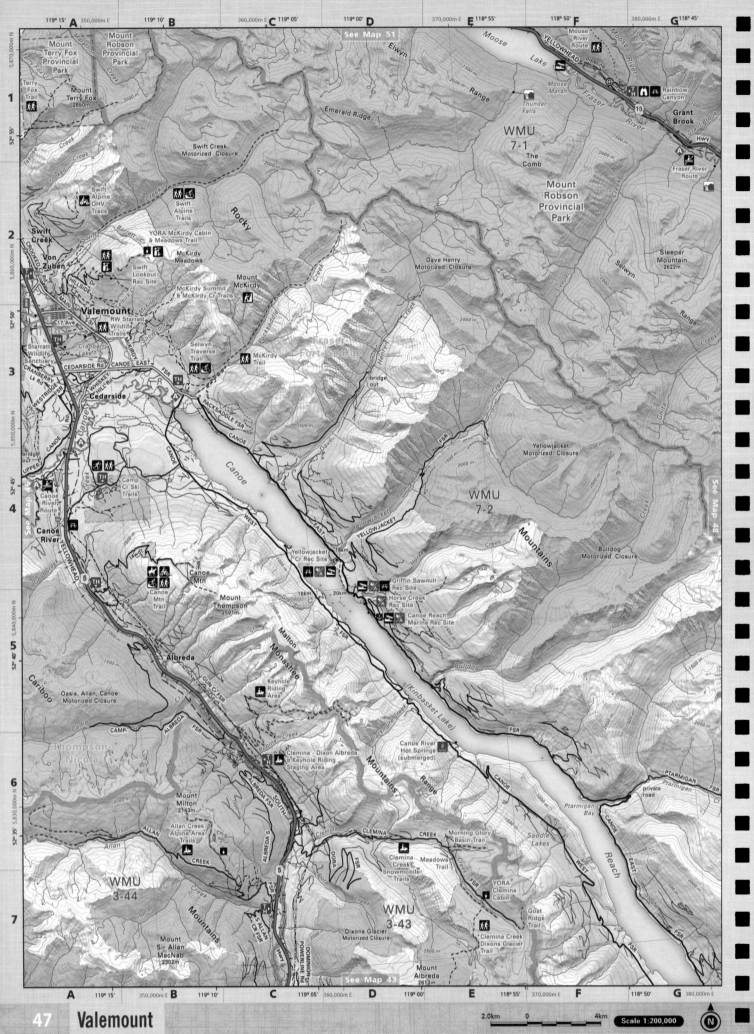

Scale 1:200,000

2.0km 0 4km

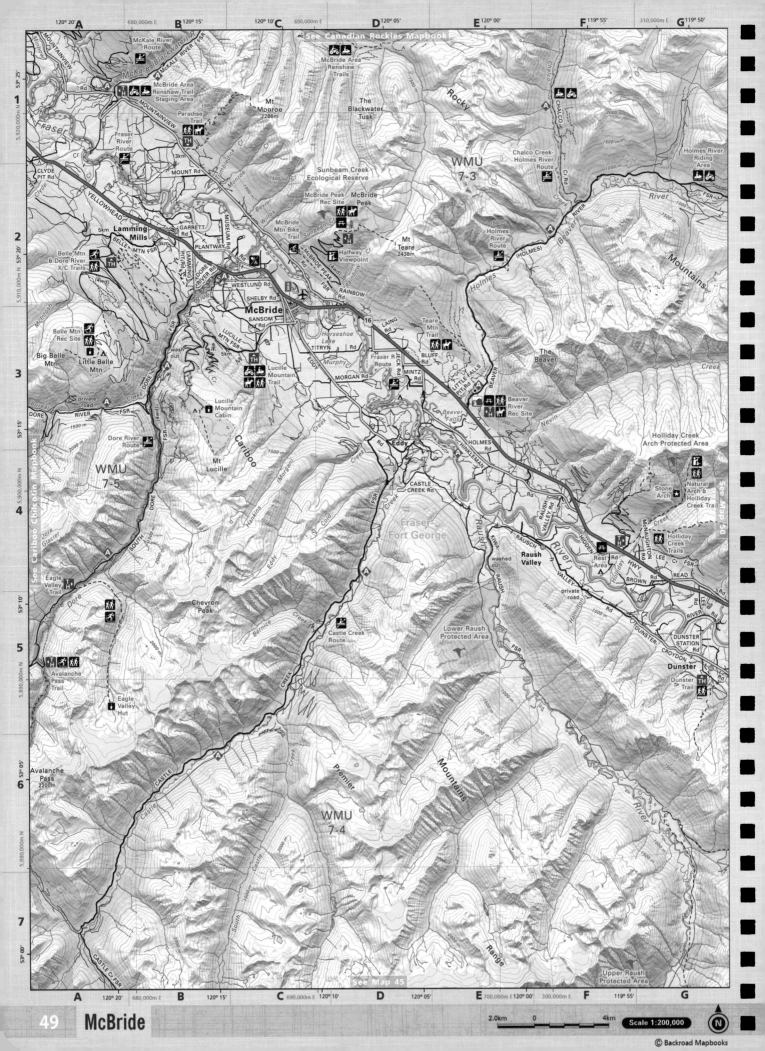

Scale 1:200,000

© Backroad Mapbooks

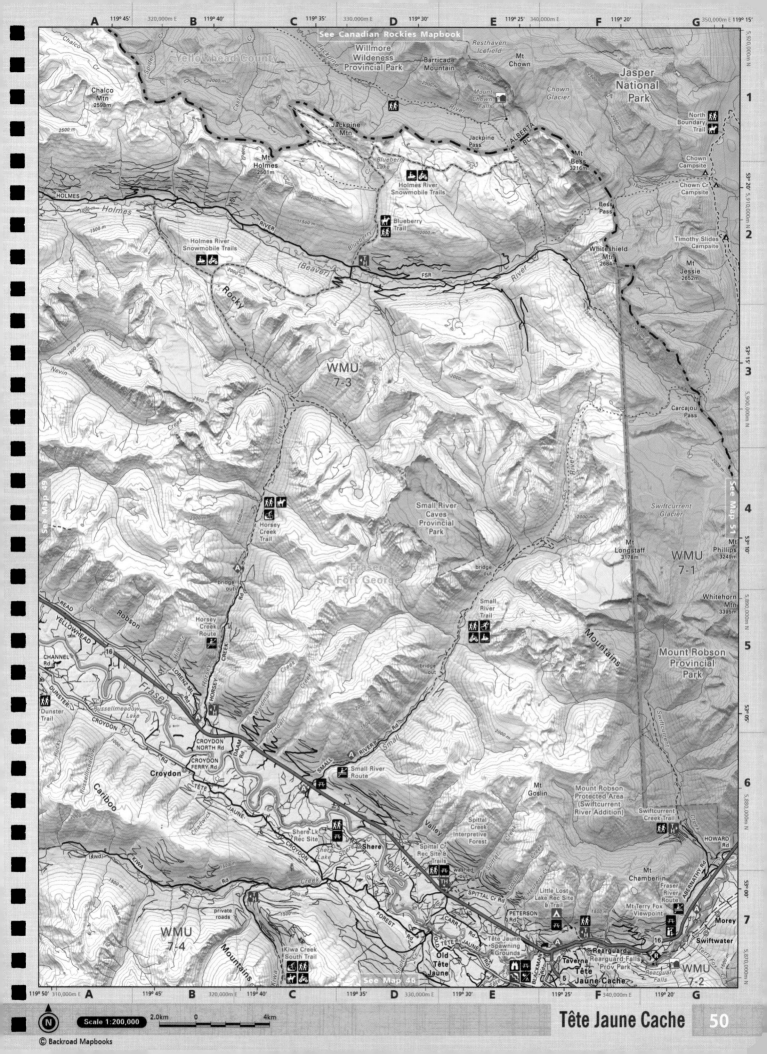

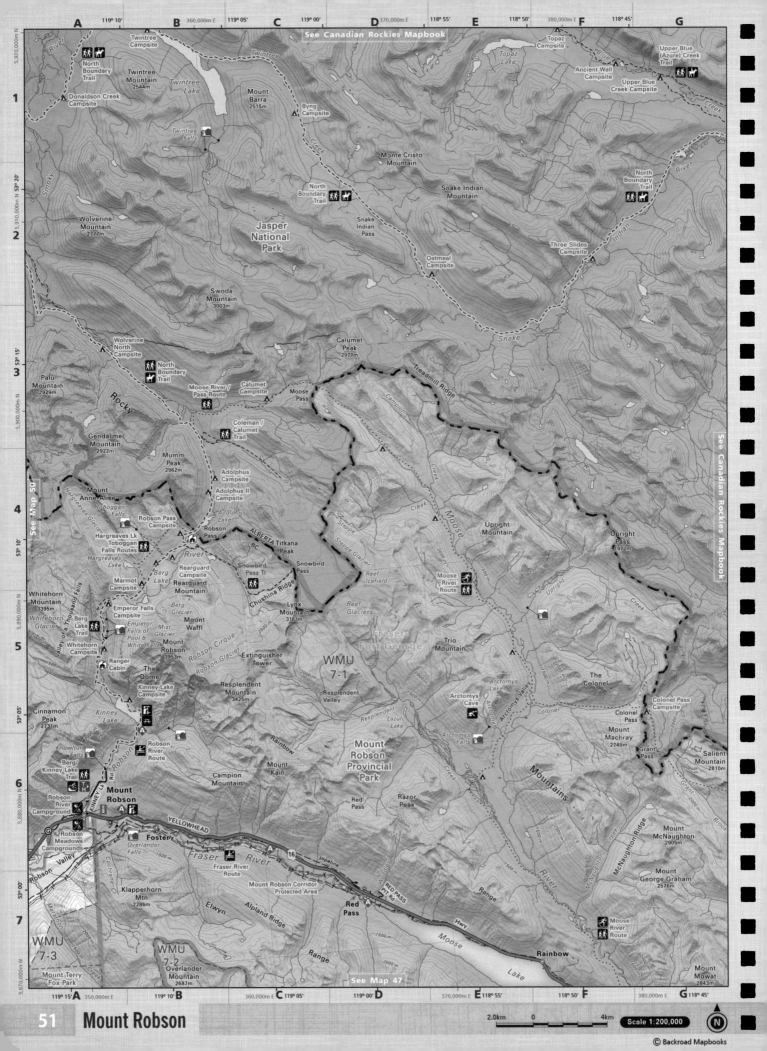

Scale 1:200,000

2.0km   0   4km

© Backroad Mapbooks

DISTANCE CHART

BRITISH COLUMBIA / ALBERTA

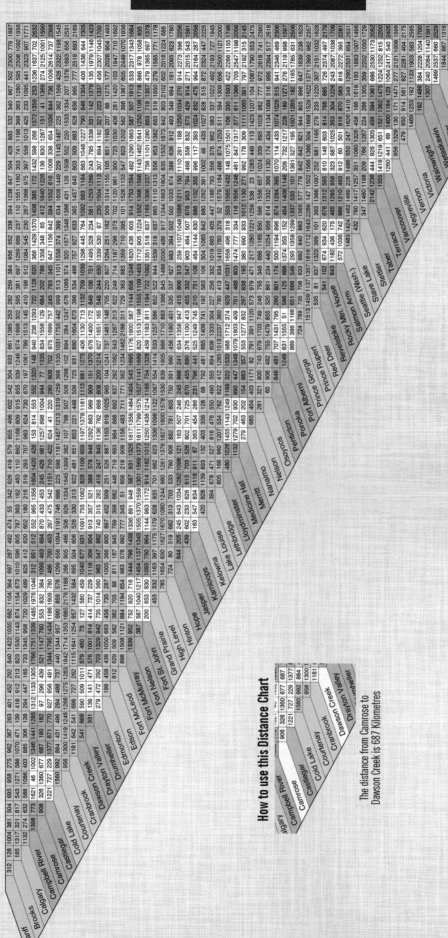

How to use this Distance Chart

The distance from Camrose to Dawson Creek is 687 Kilometres

1 Mile = 1.6 Kilometres

1 Kilometre = 0.621 Mile

Speed Conversion Chart

Km / hr														
0	10	20	30	40	50	60	70	80	90	100	110	120	130	140

MPH									
0	10	20	30	40	50	60	70	80	90

Reservations:

SD
SERVICE DIRECTORY

Find what you are looking for, from our trusted Service Directory Members.

▶**Accommodations** ▶ **Tours & Guides** ▶ **Sales & Services**

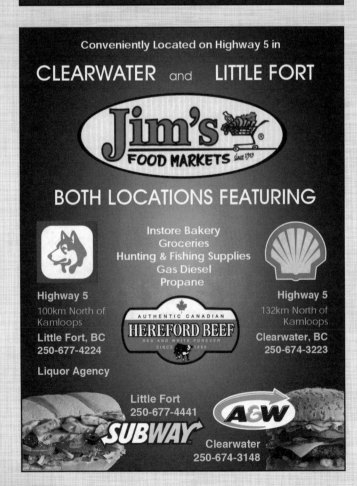
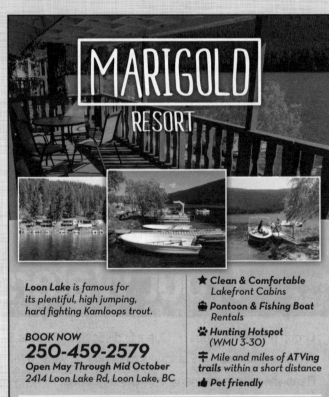
FISHING BC

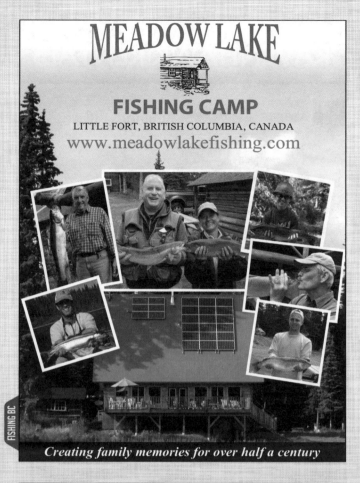

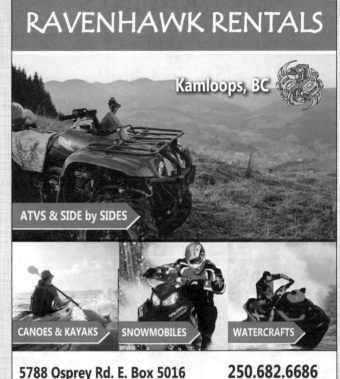
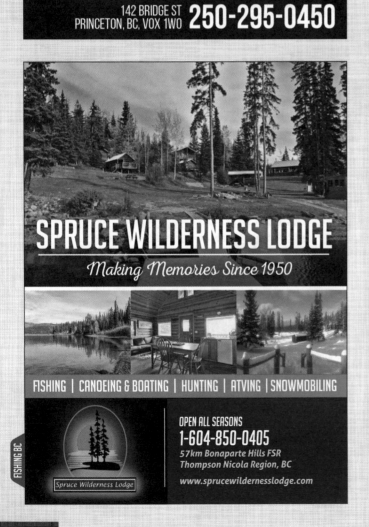

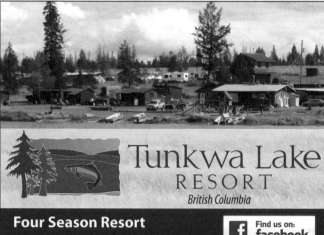

58

FISHING BC

We've Got Your Back in the Back Country!

HORSE COUNCIL
BRITISH COLUMBIA

HCBC supports recreational and trail riders in BC by providing excellent third party liability and accidental death and dismemberment coverage from Capri Insurance with our yearly membership.

Preservation, access to trails, and safety is of great importance to all those who enjoy the pleasure of a ride through the countryside. Horse Council BC provides safety manuals, educational resources, funding, and guidance and support to members interested in building, maintaining, and using the trail systems in BC.

For more information please visit the Horse Council BC website at: www.hcbc.ca or contact us directly at recreation@hcbc.ca

Follow Us Online!

Trip Planning Notes:

ADVENTURES

FISHING

HUNTING

PADDLING

BACKROAD

PARK

RECSITE

WINTER

TRAIL

ATV [OHV]

SNOWMOBILE

WILDLIFE

Awaken the adventurer within as you explore the thousands of backcountry adventures we have put together for you in the following section. With no shortage of year-round recreational opportunities in the Thompson Okanagan region of BC, our adventure section can guide you through alpine skiing and ocean kayaking in the same day. Or, choose to spend the day hiking through old growth forests, going on a hunting expedition, driving along scenic backcountry roads or fishing one of the hundreds of lakes and rivers. Hardcore adventurers will enjoy trekking to some of Canada's highest waterfalls, biking down single-track trails through the rainforest or experiencing the thrill of snowmobiling among massive snow-capped mountain peaks. No matter what your ideal adventure may be, from hunting to fishing, wildlife viewing to camping, ATVing to horseback riding, the following 11 adventure sections will have you outdoors and exploring in no time. Make sure to read through the adventure Summary at the beginning of each section, for a quick overview summary of that activity as it pertains to the region. Each Adventure section is made up of countless listings and descriptions of different activities offering endless possibilities when it comes to planning your next adventure. Make sure to check out the symbols beside each listing, showcasing the numerous nearby activities. Once you find the perfect adventure listing, use the map reference to locate and explore your next excursion on our maps. We hope you enjoy exploring these adventures, as much as we enjoyed bringing them to you!

Helmcken Falls
Wells Gray Park / Clearwater

BACKROAD
ADVENTURES

The Southern Interior is blessed with a good combination of highways and logging roads. In fact, outside of a few notable exceptions, there are few areas in this region that are not accessible by some sort of motorized vehicle. This makes getting to that backcountry lake or hidden trailhead all that much easier.

Cars or RVs can travel many of the secondary roads, most of which are paved or surfaced with hard packed gravel. The paved roads are shown on the maps with coloured lines, while the thicker black lines mark the better gravel or main roads. Branching from the main roads are side roads and trails of all shapes and sizes. These routes, marked by thinner black lines and dashed lines on our maps, should be left to the off-road enthusiasts and trail users.

Road conditions can change very quickly. The weather, the status of road systems and the degree of maintenance can all affect the road systems. Weekdays from 6am–6pm or at times of extreme fire hazard, logging and rural roads may be closed to the public. Other roads may be gated to protect equipment in the area or private property. Roads are deactivated, and bridges and culverts are sometimes removed, making the roads virtually impassable. Be sure to pay attention to road and private property signs and always watch for logging trucks. It is also a good idea to contact the nearest Forest District Office for information on specific road conditions. Having a CB radio tuned to the channel listed on signs and used by logging trucks will often give you a heads up of what's ahead.

People without access to a four-wheel drive or an ATV may find it more difficult to access the backcountry. However, backroaders with a lot of patience can get off of the main roads if they allow a bit of extra time to get to their destination. Wilderness Use Roads (roads that are no longer graded or brushed) are usually passable by one means or another. For those looking to get away from it all, it is these wilderness or backcountry roads that can lead to really interesting destinations.

While many choose to enjoy travel in this area off the beaten path, those who do decide to stay on pavement will still find lots of great and interesting places to visit in the region. Museums, lots of great wineries, hiking, mountain biking and natural geological features such as hoodoos (naturally created stone towers) offer plenty of destinations to visit. In season, enjoy succulent, chin dripping fruit and fresh veggies at fruit stands throughout the Okanagan and Similkameen Valleys.

GOLD COUNTRY
GEOTOURISM ADVENTURES
— MODERN DAY TREASURE HUNT —

Field Guide providers
can be found at www.goldtrail.com
Available in English and French

Gold
Country
GEOTOURISM
P R O G R A M
www.goldtrail.com

Adams River (Map 29/F5)

The Adams River supports British Columbia's largest run of Sockeye Salmon, which happens every October and peaks every four years (next peak year is 2018). Even during the other years, it still is impressive. This is partly due to the relentless efforts to rehabilitate the spawning area in Roderick Haig-Brown Provincial Park. The park has recently added a paved wheelchair accessible walkway to the viewing platform.

Angel [KLO] Warm Springs (Map 10/C2)

These warm springs can be reached via a one hour hike into Myra-Bellevue Provincial Park. The main springs average about 23°C (73°F), but if you head up the tufa deposits you can find some warmer seeps closer to 32°C (90°F).

BC Orchard Industry Museum (Map 17/A7)

Opened in 1989 in Kelowna, the museum tells the story of the Okanagan Valley's transformation from wide open cattle range to manicured orchards. Exhibits include packing, processing, home preserves, orchards and marketing. It is found at 1304 Ellis Street near Prospera Place and is open Tuesday to Saturday.

BC Wildlife Park (Map 22/F2)

Found just east of Kamloops on Dallas Drive, the BC Wildlife Park focuses on the indigenous wildlife found in the province. The park covers 50 hectares and features over 65 species of wildlife, from cougars to moose to snakes, bears, wolves and mountain goats. The park has a special bird of prey area, with the largest breeding facility for burrowing owls in North America. The park offers visitors a chance to interact with and learn about wildlife rarely seen. Visit the park website at *bcwildlife.org* for full details.

BC Wine Museum & VQA Wine Shop (Map 17/A7)

Located in the same building as the BC Orchard Industry Museum in Kelowna, this museum, opened 15 years ago, brings the history of the Okanagan Wine Region to visitors. It also carries over 600 wines from over 90 wineries; a great one stop shop to explore all the wines the area has to offer. The museum and wine shop are open daily.

Canoe River Hot Springs (Map 47/B4)

These hot springs are located approximately 32 km southeast of Valemount on the west end of Kinbasket Lake. The hot springs, with a temperature of around 67°C, are submerged most of the year.

Take care of the areas we love by packing out everything you pack in, and leaving behind only footprints.

Castle Rock Hoodoos (Map 27/B5)

The Castle Rock Hoodoos are an impressive set of Hoodoos located along the Deadman River. In fact, the Deadman Valley itself is also worth a drive. Because the eco-system is very fragile, visitors are asked to view the formations as opposed to walking, hiking or climbing in the area.

Douglas Lake Ranch (Map 15/E3)

The Douglas Lake Ranch is Canada's largest working cattle ranch. Its history dates back to the mid-1880s and the name honours John Douglas Sr., who first homesteaded 320 acres along the shore of the lake. Visitors are welcome to try their hand at horseback riding, fly-fishing and more. Accommodations include cabins, yurts and a full amenity lodge. Visit *douglaslake.com* for more information or to make a reservation.

Grist Mill & Gardens – Keremeos (Map 3/C4)

The Keremeos Grist Mill opened in August 1877. It was significant to local residents as this meant they were no longer forced to travel 170 miles to get flour. The mill still produces flour despite being converted to an informative historical site with a campground and ongoing special events throughout the year. Visit *oldgristmill.ca* for more information.

Hat Creek Ranch (Map 26/C6)

Rich in history, Hat Creek Ranch is home to an 1860 roadhouse, a heritage apple orchard, gardens, First Nations interpretive centres and more. The roadhouse catered to miners heading to the interior during the gold rush and operated until 1916. There are a number of interpretive activities, including stagecoach rides along the historic "wagon road." Camping is available as well in various forms including tent and RV, miners' tents, covered wagons, teepees, cabins

and more. The tourist attraction is found off Highway 99 near its junction with Highway 97. Visit the ranch website at *hatcreekranch.ca* for full details.

Helmken & Dawson Falls (Map 37/D3)

According to the official books, Helmken is Canada's fourth largest waterfall, falling 141 metres (463 ft). While the viewing platform hangs over the lip of the canyon, if you prefer a close-up view, take a one hour hike along the Rim Trail for even more spectacular viewing. During the winter, the waterfall freezes and offers a different but equally impressive view. Nearby Dawson Falls are much easier to see since they rest next to the main road. They are 90 metres (295 ft) wide and 20 metres high.

Highland Valley Copper Mine Tour (Map 21/A5)

The Highland Valley Copper Mine, located west of Logan Lake, is one of the world's largest copper mines. Every year in summer, the mine hosts tours. The two hour tours include views over the pit, a tour of the mill and even a drive through the reclaimed land. The tours are free, but no open-toed footwear or dresses are permitted. Be sure to call 1-855-523-3429 to find out when the tours are being offered.

Gyro Mystic Beach (Map 25/D4)

Discover the Fantasy Forest next to Mabel Lake. The trail starts at the Shoe Tree just past Cascade Falls off the Mable Lake Forest Service Road and leads past countless fairy tale characters, creative wood art, teepees and more. There is a geocache to find as well. A must see if you are in the area!

Kamloops Hoodoos (Map 22/A2)

The Okanagan is home to many hoodoos, some are visible from the roadside, and some you have to hike to. One of the more impressive sets of hoodoos is located just outside of Kamloops. Travel 3.5 kilometres west along the road leading to the Kamloops airport and look for a pullout. From here, you can pick your way northwest into the sandstone hills. A trail heads up to the right into a canyon, where you will find a dramatic series of hoodoos. A return trip is about 10 km (6 miles) long.

Kamloops Heritage Railway (Map 22/B2)

On a dark, stormy Halloween night in 1915, a train carrying 44 passengers and crew left Kamloops Junction destined for the town of Blue River. The train disappeared in a thick fog while passing through Wolfenden and never reappeared. A restored 2141 steam locomotive now makes special Halloween trips. The Spirit of Kamloops railtour also operates throughout July and August and during Christmas out of 510 Lorne Street. Visit *kamrail.com* for more information on the different excursions offered.

Kamloops Museum (Map 22/C2)

Explore the history of the Kamloops area, from First Nations to fur trade to gold rush and beyond. Found at 207 Seymour Street in downtown Kamloops, admission is by donation. Details regarding current exhibits, hours of operation and more can be found at *kamloops.ca/museum/index.shtml*.

Kelowna Mountain Bridges Agri-Park (Map 10/A2)

In 2003, the Okanagan Mountain Park fire destroyed the entire south slopes area of the park. Today, a unique outdoor adventure area has created four bridges to cross as you explore the area. These include the 122 metre (400 ft) Earth Bridge travelling from cliff to cliff, the Sun Bridge which travels 30 metres (100 ft) over an ice wine vineyard, the 244 metre (800 ft) Water Bridge over a 30 metre (100 ft) waterfall and the Vine Bridge, which visits a Koi Fish Pond. The welcome centre features local artisan crafts as well as food and more. Visit *kelownamountainbridges.com* for more information.

Kettle River Museum (Map 5/D7)

Plan to set some time aside to visit the Midway CPR Station/Museum at Mile "0." In addition to the original station house, there is a restored CPR caboose and many other outdoor artifacts. For added adventure, this can be the start or end of an extended hike or bike along the famed Kettle Valley Railway cum Trans Canada Trail.

Kettle Valley Steam Railway (Map 9/E5)

After the Kettle Valley Railway was retired in the 1970s, most of the track was ripped out and replaced by a multi-use trail system that has recently been added to the Trans Canada Trail system. The only section still intact is the 16 km (10 mi) portion of the track near Summerland that has been rebuilt. During the summer, a restored steam train runs tours from the Trout Creek Bridge (73 metres/240 ft above the canyon floor) through orchards and fields common to the Okanagan. Rates and schedules and additional railroad historic details can be found at *kettlevalleyrail.org*.

Last Spike Monument (Map 31/C4)

Craigellachie, found 37 km west of Revelstoke, is home to one of the most monumental achievements in Canadian history. On a cold November day in 1885, the last spike of the Canadian Pacific Railway was ceremoniously driven home by Sir Donald Alexander Smith, marking a railway stretching from the Pacific to the Atlantic Ocean. Today, the Revelstoke Railway Museum, open from May to October, along with a plaque and cairn at the highway rest stop are found here. Visit *railwaymuseum.com* for more information.

Malakwa Suspension Bridge (Map 31/C4)

This unique swinging bridge spans the Eagle River and was originally built in 1915 to link farmers with local communities. Now a popular tourist attraction, the bridge is accessed from Malakwa Suspension Bridge Road and leads to a 4 km walking loop along scenic country roads, eventually crossing another smaller suspension bridge and leading back to the parking area.

Mascot Gold Mine (Map 3/A2)

Perched on the side of Nickleplate Mountain, high above the small town of Hedley, this particularly audacious bit of history was built in 1897. Although it was closed in 1949, it was re-opened in 2004 as a tourist attraction. After a long, winding bus ride up to the mine site, visitors walk down a long staircase (583 steps) to the 80-year-old mine buildings. Allow about three hours for the tour, which features impressive view over the valley.

McAbee Fossil Beds (Map 26/F7)

Once a shallow lake, there are many unique fossils found here. The area is accessible from May to October and guided tours are available. Note that you can no longer hunt for fossils or do any rock hunting because the area is now a designated heritage site.

Moul Falls (Map 37/F5)

Moul Falls are accessed by a rough moss and root covered trail which takes approximately an hour to hike from the Clearwater Valley Road. There is a viewing platform at the top, but if you continue down to the base of the chute, you can slide in between the falls and the canyon for a unique viewing experience.

Mount Robson (Map 51/B5)

While it is not the highest peak in Canada (that would be Mount Logan), or even in BC (that honour goes to Mount Waddington), it is the highest point in the Canadian Rockies at an elevation of 3,954 metres (12,972 ft). The Yellowhead Highway Passes within about 10 km from the base of the mountain and there are terrific views of the mountain from the visitor's centre down the Robson Valley. To really experience the mountain, though, we recommend hiking to Kinney Lake, at the base of Robson. More adventurous backpackers can make the two-day trek to Berg Lake.

Myra Canyon Trestles (Map 10/C2)

Resting high above Kelowna, this section of the famous Kettle Valley Railway was quite an engineering feat. Today, the trestles are a popular destination for locals and area visitors. Recently rebuilt after the infamous Okanagan Mountain Fire in 2003, there are 18 trestles and a few tunnels around the scenic canyon. If only doing a short excursion, the easiest access is from the Myra Forest Service Road (the northeastern access point). It is a 12.5 km (7.8 mi) one-way route between the Myra and Little White Forest Service Roads. Access points are also available at either the Myra Station or Ruth Station. From the Myra Station, it is 1 km to the first trestle, 2 km to cross six trestles to reach the first of two tunnels and 6 km to the largest trestle making it a 12 km return trip.

Nk'Mip Desert Cultural Centre (Map 4/B6)

Discover both the history of Canada's only desert and the living culture of Okanagan First Nations around present day Osoyoos. At the heart of this 22 hectare site is the Interpretive Cultural Centre. From here enjoy cultural exhibits, walking trails, outdoor sculptures and hands-on interactive displays. Explore a reconstructed Aboriginal village and animal exhibits. Visit *nkmipdesert.com* for more information.

Okanagan Vineyard Tours (Maps 3, 4, 9, 10, 16, 17, 24)

There are over sixty vineyards and counting in the Okanagan Valley, from Larch Hills Winery near Armstrong, all the way south to Osoyoos' Golden Beaver. Along the way, you can taste-test your way through some of the world's greatest wineries, including Jackson-Triggs near Oliver, Sumac Ridge near Penticton and Mission Hill near Kelowna, just to name a few. Many wineries also feature award winning restaurants. Quail's Gate in West Kelowna and Grey Monk in Lake Country are examples of fine fair with breathtaking views over Okanagan Lake.

Osoyoos Desert Model Railroad (Map 4/A6)

Filling an entire 1,220 m2 (4,000 ft2) warehouse, allow at least two hours to view the multiple interconnected themed layouts, including several European railways. A good time to visit is when the building is changed from day to night and thousands of small lights recreate evening scenes, including a forest fire. Recently featured on the Amazing Race Canada, the railway is found west of town next to Highway 3 at 1161, 115th Street. Visit *osoyoosrailroad.com* for more information.

Osoyoos Pocket Desert (Map 4/A6)

When people talk about BC having such a diverse landscape – from desert to ocean to glaciated peak is how it usually goes – this is the desert they are referring to. It is, in fact, Canada's only desert. This region is home to one of the most fragile and endangered ecosystems in North America. It is home to an exceptional array of desert plants and animals, some found nowhere else in Canada and many on the brink of extinction. The Nk'Mip Desert Cultural Centre helps explain all the amazing features; visit *desert.org*.

If you plan to travel through remote areas it is imperative that you leave a detailed itinerary with friends or family.

Rock Candy Mine (Map 6/A3)

The Rock Candy Mine was named by its' first miners for the colourful crystals of fluorite and barite found there. Discovered in 1911, it operated until 1929. The mine now offers family-friendly nature tours where you can collect quartz crystal, enjoy the mountain scenery and explore the Rock Candy ghost town with its' historical artefacts. Book your visit through the Grand Forks Visitor Centre or visit *rockcandymine.com*.

R.W Staratt Wildlife Sanctuary (Map 47/A3)

Found near Valemount, the R.W Staratt Wildlife Sanctuary is home to over 140 different song birds and waterfowl. The sanctuary also offers over 7 km (4.3 mi) of trails to explore as well as quiet marshes to canoe in.

Savona Caves (Map 21/D3)

Home to First Nations legends and cultural rituals, these caves on Savona Mountain also feature fascinating rock formations full of green opals and agates. The hike from the Tunkwa Lake Road to the base of the cliffs is around 2 km one-way and usually takes 2 hours to complete, with the final part of the trail a steep scramble. It is a great place for rock hounders to visit.

Spahats Creek Falls (Map 37/F6)

Spahats Creek Falls is the most dramatic of all the waterfalls in Wells Gray Provincial Park. Found near the entrance of the park, the falls are only a five minute walk from the Clearwater Valley Road. Volcanic rock deposits here have created a layer-cake-like canyon where the falls drop some 80 metres (260 ft) through a keyhole in the rock surface to the Clearwater River.

Spotted Lake (Map 4/A6)

This culturally and ecologically sensitive area is a medicine lake for the Okanagan (Sylix) peoples. Although closed to the public, you can view it from a highway pull-off north of Osoyoos. How it was formed is still a mystery, but the salt and water seems to change regularly, creating new spots in the water.

SS Sicamous (Map 9/G6)

The largest surviving steel-hulled sternwheeler in Canada, the SS Sicamous was built in 1914, and sailed Okanagan Lake until 1936, when she was retired. Now, she is the heart of the Okanagan Inland Marine Park in Penticton. There is a small fee to tour the historic vessel.

Vidette Lake (Map 27/B2)

Vidette Lake is a nice, unassuming lake found well off the beaten path. The lake sits along the gold rush era route from Kamloops to the Cariboo Goldfields. From 1933 to 1939, the Vidette Lake Mine operated on the east side of the lake producing 28,869 ounces of gold, 46,573 ounces of silver and 48 tons of copper. However, the lake's claim to fame is that it is the Centre of the Universe. Seriously! In 1980, Tibetan Buddhist monks visiting the area declared a location overlooking the lake to be the Centre of the Universe. The site is on the property of the Vidette Lake Gold Mine Lodge and access is by permission only.

FISHING ADVENTURES

Some of the best fishing in the province is found in the Thompson Okanagan region. This region offers an amazing selection of lakes and streams and is home to the world famous Kamloops rainbow trout. The abundance of nutrient rich alkaline waters in the region means that fish are faster growing and achieve larger sizes than other lakes in the province.

Big fish, combined with a wide variety of waterbodies – from huge valley-bottom lakes, like Okanagan and Shuswap Lakes, to mountainside streams – provide anglers with a wide variety of opportunities.

This book covers two fishery regions. The Thompson/Nicola Region, or Region 3, is found to the west and stretches from Hope all the way past Kamloops and Clearwater along the Thompson River system. To the east, the big valley lakes from Osoyoos north to Revelstoke define the Okanagan Region, or Region 8.

There are nearly 500 lakes described here and there are still plenty of lakes not mentioned. Fly-fishing is extremely popular, as this is arguably the best way to land a famous Kamloops trout on the smaller lakes, while trollers will find many big lakes to sample in the valley bottoms. Although the area sees a lot of fishing pressure, fisheries does a great job of managing both quality lakes (those that hold trophy sized trout) and stocked lakes (those that are generally easier to fish). We have marked the lakes that have been stocked in the last few years with the ⬛ symbol.

With so many great fishing lakes in this area, stream fishing is often ignored. This is too bad, as the Thompson Okanagan Region has many rivers and streams with very good fishing for small wild rainbow, brook trout or Dolly Varden. A few streams, most notably the Thompson River, also offer runs of Pacific Salmon and the ever popular steelhead.

Anglers looking for more detailed lake information, including depth charts and fishing tips, are advised to pick up a copy of either (or both) of the Fishing Mapbooks that cover this region. The Southwest BC Fishing Mapbook and the Southeast BC Fishing Mapbook cover many of the best lakes and streams in this region and are perfect angling companions.

Please note there are regulations imposed for many of the lakes and almost all of the streams in order to preserve the quality of fisheries. Some of the regulations include bait bans, artificial fly only lakes, boating restrictions, catch and release and closures. Check the Freshwater Fishing Regulations before fishing!

DID YOU KNOW?

OUR FISHING MAPBOOKS INCLUDE EVERYTHING YOU NEED TO REEL IN THAT CATCH OF THE DAY!

〰 LAKES & RIVERS

Each fishing lake and river receives a full-page description with bathymetric (depth) lake charts, river maps, descriptions, species, stocking info directions and access points.

💡 TIPS & TECHNIQUES

From trolling to ice fishing, to fly fishing and jigging, we provide you with some of the best fishing tips and techniques, including information on baits, lures and equipment.

 backroadmapbooks.com/fishing-maps

Stocking Charts

Many lakes in the Thompson Okanagan region are stocked in order to provide enhanced fishing opportunities to anglers. Stocking takes place in the spring and fall and many lakes are stocked each year. Stocked populations of Rainbow Trout, Brook Trout and Kokanee can be found throughout the region.

Rainbow Trout Stocking	MAP	BROOK TROUT	BURBOT	KOKANEE	LAKE TROUT	RAINBOW TROUT	OTHER
Abbott Lake	14/B2					•	
Agur Lake	9/D5	•				•	
Aileen Lake	17/F4					•	
Alkali Lakes	26/A3	•				•	
Allendale Lake	4/D1					•	
Allen Meadows Lake	21/C4					•	
Alleyne Lake	14/G7-15/A7			•		•	
Allison Lake	7/G4			•		•	
Amphitheatre Lake	29/B7					•	
Andy Lake	28/G7					•	
Armour Lake	29/A7					•	
Arthur Lake	24/A4					•	
Badger and Spooney Lakes	28/E3					•	
Baird Lake	25/C3					•	
Baker Lake	9/F3					•	
Bardolph Lake	17/F1					•	
Bare Lake	27/G1					•	
Barnes Lake	20/E2					•	
Barton Lake	16/C4					•	
Beacon Lake	10/G6					•	
Beaton Lake	21/F2					•	
Beaver (Swalwell) Lake	17/D4					•	
Bear Paw (Russel) Lake	12/D4					•	
Beautiful Lake	16/A1					•	
Biely Lake	7/E4	•				•	
Big Ok Lake	20/G5					•	
Big White Beaver Ponds	10/F2					•	
Billy Lake	21/C6					•	
Birch Lake	32/G4			•		•	
Bisson Lake	18/E4					•	
Black Lake	22/F5	•				•	
Blackwell Lake	22/G6					•	
Bleeker Lake	22/E5					•	
Blue Lakes	15/E2					•	
Bluey Lake	8/A1					•	
Bob's Lake	15/D7					•	
Bog Lake	27/C1					•	
Bonneau Lake	18/D3					•	
Boot Lake	15/C7					•	
Borgeson (Round) Lake	7/G4					•	
Bose Lake	21/B5					•	
Boss Lake	7/E1					•	
Boulder Lake	8/D1					•	
Brenda Lake	16/A7					•	

Lake Fishing

Abbott Lake (Map 14/B2)
Abbott Lake is a 15 hectare (37 ac) lake with reasonable fishing for stocked rainbow trout up to 1 kg (2 lbs) throughout the ice-free season. The high elevation lake is found on a four-wheel drive spur road east of Highway 8 and offers a small recreation site with a cartop boat launch. Check the regulations for special restrictions and retention limits before heading out.

Aberdeen Lake (Map 17/F3)
Aberdeen Lake offers decent fishing for wild rainbow trout up to 1 kg (2 lbs). Drawdown affects the summer fishery in this tea-coloured waterbody. Trolling is the preferred method here.

Adams Lake (Map 29/D4–34/G4)
Adams Lake is one of the big lakes in this region, measuring 65 km long and averaging 3 km wide. The lake has a steep, rocky shoreline and is prone to unpredictable winds. In the late spring (May and June) fishing is at its best, as the fish are actively feeding near the surface on salmon fry. To take advantage of the feed, it is best to troll a Silver Bucktail or Silver Spoon quickly on the surface. Often times, the salmon fry hold up in small bays and fly-fishing or spincasting in these areas is very effective. By the summertime, the rainbow creep to the depths as the water warms and it is best to troll with a downrigger at 10-25 metres (30-90 ft) using a plug, Apex or Flatfish. The lake contains rainbow trout that average 3 kg (6 lbs) as well as some larger lake trout and Dolly Varden (up to 10 kg/22 lbs). Kokanee fishing can be effective in August through October. Check the regulations for special restrictions.

Akehurst Lake (Map 33/A6)
A 220 hectare (543 ac) lake located north of Bonaparte Lake off the Darlington Creek Forest Service Road, this high elevation lake has rainbow that reach 2 kg (4.5 lbs). The best time to fish is in the spring or fall by fly-fishing (chironomids, damsel flies or leeches) or trolling. There is a resort on the lake.

Alex Lake (Map 17/D4)
Alex Lake has good fishing for wild rainbow trout due to its rough access (four-wheel drive or hiking). The 8 hectare (20 ac), high elevation lake does not have any developed facilities. The lake is found off the Dee Lake Road and is best fished in the summer and fall.

Alice Lake (Map 37/D1)
Found in Wells Gray Provincial Park off the east side of the Clearwater Valley Road, Alice Lake offers some of the best small lake fishing in the park...assuming that fish survive the winter in the shallow lake. The lake is accessed by a short trail. Most people carry a canoe or small cartopper to the lake.

Allan Lake (Map 33/B7)
West of Barrière, off Jamieson Creek Forest Service Road, this 149 hectare (368 ac) lake sees heavy fishing pressure throughout the ice-free season for rainbow trout and whitefish. At the east end of the lake there is a recreation site with a cartop boat launch and camping facilities.

Allendale Lake (Map 4/D1)
This remote lake is located off the Okanagan Falls Forest Service Road, 7 km north of the junction with Ripperto Forest Service Road, high in the hills above Penticton. Stocked with rainbow trout, the lake has a recreation site with a campground and cartop boat launch.

Alleyne Lake (Map 14/G7–15/A7)
Part of the Kentucky-Alleyne Provincial Park, this lake is a popular destination in the open water season with picnicking, boat launch facilities and camping. The 55 hectare (135 ac) lake offers stocked rainbow up to 2 kg (4.5 lbs) as well as stocked kokanee. The lake is often trolled but you can achieve success by fly-fishing (shrimp and chironomids) the many marshy areas that ring the lake. Check the regulations for boating restrictions.

Allison Lake (Map 7/G4)
Allison Lake covers 71 hectares (175 ac) and is one of the most popular lakes in the area, due in no small part to the fact that the lake stretches alongside Highway 5A. It features camping and a boat launch at a provincial park on the south end of the lake. Despite its easy access, the lake offers a fairly good summer and winter fishery for stocked rainbow trout that can reach 1 kg (2 lbs) and small kokanee.

Amphitheatre Lake (Map 29/B7)

Found south of the Sun Peaks Ski Area along the Eileen Lake Forest Service Road, this 11.8 hectare lake holds stocked rainbow trout. Those wanting to make a weekend of it will find several recreation sites within the area. Check the regulations for special restrictions and retention limits before heading out.

Anderson Lake (Map 42/B6)

Found in Wells Gray Provincial Park, Anderson is a remote lake that can only be reached by a long trail from the shore of Murtle Lake. The trip is worth it, since Anderson Lake provides good fishing much of the time for some decent sized rainbow trout.

Andy's Lake (Map 7/C3)

This high elevation lake holds good numbers of small rainbow that can be caught using a bobber and bait, by fly-fishing or by spincasting from a float tube or shore. Casting towards the many weed beds is your best bet. The 12 hectare (30 ac) lake receives very little fishing pressure.

Antler Lake (Map 21/C7)

Located on a four-wheel drive spur road north of Chataway Lake, this lake is reasonably good for rainbow trout up to 1.5 kg (3 lbs) best caught on a fly. The lake is at a fairly high elevation, but still warms up in the summer. The sedge hatch begins in late June and is usually the best time to fly-fish. There is a campsite on the lake as an opportunity to launch small boats. Check the regulations for special restrictions and retention limits before heading out.

Arlington Lakes (Map 10/F4)

A trio of lakes located on a two-wheel drive road just west of Highway 33 and next to the Kettle Valley Railway. All three lakes hold fair numbers of small rainbow trout, caught primarily by fly-fishing or trolling. There is a recreation site at the southern lake, complete with cartop boat launch and camping facilities. The lakes are high enough that fishing remains consistent throughout the summer.

Arrow Lakes (Map 12/G7–19/G3)

Before the construction of the Hugh Keenleyside Dam, there were actually two separate lakes here. While the dam has created one large lake, the fish still behave as if there are two. The kokanee prefer Lower Arrow, while the trout, which can get up to (and over) 8 kg (20 lbs), seem to favour the Upper. There are also plenty of dollies, whitefish and burbot. The best fishing on the upper lake is generally between Nakusp and Shelter Bay using a plug that looks like a minnow or even a silver or bronze coloured wobbler on a fast troll. Fishing on the lower lake is usually better north of Deer Park until early September. The lakes are subject to significant drawdown in the summer months, have lots of debris and can get quite windy.

Arthur Lake (Map 24/A4)

Found off the Bolean Lake Road (good two-wheel drive access), Arthur Lake has a recreation site complete with a cartop boat launch. The 75 hectare (185 ac) lake offers good fishing for stocked rainbow through the summer. The best time to fish the lake is in early June on a fly.

Azure Lake (Map 41/C4–F3)

Found in Wells Gray Provincial Park, Azure Lake is accessed by plane or via canoe from Clearwater Lake. The fishing on the big lake can be quite good for rainbow trout and bull trout that can reach 3 kg (6.5 lbs) in size. Trolling works best. Check the regulations for special restrictions.

Badger and Spooney Lakes (Map 28/E3)

Badger and Spooney Lakes are separated by a narrow channel that offers fishing for rainbow. For fly anglers, the sedge hatch in mid-June and the spring mayfly hatch are goods times to find fish. Later in the spring and into the fall, try a caddisfly or dragonfly pattern. Also, try casting towards one of the many shoals that line the dark lakes. Also in the area are Little Badger and Little Spooney Lakes. Badger is stocked occasionally with rainbow.

Baird Lake (Map 25/C3)

Baird Lake is easily accessed on the Hidden Lake Road just east of Hidden Lake. This small lake has a recreation site with a boat launch as well as camping facilities. The primary method of fishing for the many small stocked rainbow that inhabit the lake is fly-fishing. There is an electric motor only restriction on the lake.

Baker Lake (Map 9/F3)

Baker Lake is located within Okanagan Mountain Provincial Park and requires a good hiking to access it. Those that do make it in will find rainbow that are stocked regularly. Wilderness camping is allowed at the lake.

Rainbow Trout Stocking	MAP	BROOK TROUT	BURBOT	KOKANEE	LAKE TROUT	RAINBOW TROUT	OTHER
Bridge Lake	32/D3		•	•	•	•	•
Browne (Island) Lake	10/E1					•	
Brunette Lake	17/E4					•	
Bryden and Pement Lake	23/F1					•	
Buck Lake	11/A5					•	
Buck (Leonard) Lake	8/B2	•					
Bulman Lake	22/F5					•	
Burn (Lunch) Lake	27/B1					•	
Burnell (Sawmill) Lake	3/G4					•	
Burns Lake	12/A7					•	
Butterball Lake	22/F5					•	
Butler Lake	8/A4					•	
Calling Lake	20/G6					•	
Chain Lake	8/E3					•	
Clark Lakes	4/C1					•	
Clear Lake	11/B3					•	
Clifford (Cliff) Lake	7/E3					•	
Club Lake	33/B4					•	
Coalgoat Lake	18/D4					•	
Collier Lakes	11/B6					•	
Community Lake	28/F5					•	
Conkle (Fish) Lake	4/G4					•	
Corbett Lake	14/G5					•	
Courtney Lake	14/G6					•	•
Crystal Lake	32/D4					•	
Cup Lake	11/B5					•	
Dagger Lake	28/B1					•	
Dairy Lake	21/E3					•	
Dardanelles Lake	22/F7					•	
Darke (Fish) Lake	9/C3	•				•	
Davis Lake	7/E1					•	
Deadman Lake	7/G3					•	•
Deadman Lake	27/C2					•	
Dee Lake	17/E3					•	
Deep Lake	28/C7	•				•	
Deka Lake	32/C1			•	•	•	
Denison Lakes	18/C3					•	
Dennis Lake	29/C6					•	
Derenzy Lake	4/B1					•	
DeWolf Lake	8/C4					•	
Divide Lake	9/G3					•	
Dobbin Lake	16/C6	•				•	
Dominic Lake	21/F4					•	
Donut Lake	27/F2					•	
Doreen Lake	17/E3					•	
Dot Lake	21/C7					•	
Dry Lake	7/G4					•	
Drum Lake	23/B7					•	
Duffy Lake	21/E3					•	
Dutch Lake	33/F1			•	•	•	
Dytiscid Lake	33/B3					•	
Eastmere & Westmere Lakes	8/F3					•	
Echo (Lumby) Lake	18/D2			•	•	•	
Echo Lake	17/D4					•	
Edith Lake	22/C4	•				•	

Rainbow Trout Stocking	MAP	BROOK TROUT	BURBOT	KOKANEE	LAKE TROUT	RAINBOW TROUT	OTHER
Eileen Lake	16/C5					•	
Elbow Lake	25/B2					•	
Englishmen Lake	14/F6					•	
Ernest Lake	22/F5					•	
Face Lake	21/F4					•	
Fatox Lake	27/D2					•	
Faulkner Lake	32/F3					•	
Fawn Lake	32/A3					•	
Five O'Clock Lake	11/C5					•	
Float Lake	33/B4					•	
Flourine Lake	6/A2					•	
Flyfish Lakes	17/E4					•	
Foot Lake	37/E3					•	
Forest Lake	29/A2					•	
Fred Lake	22/B5	•				•	
French Lake	32/D2					•	
Frisken Lake	22/F5					•	
Frogmoore Lakes	21/G6					•	
Gammarus Lake	33/A3					•	
Gardom Lake	24/D3					•	
Garnet Lake	9/D3	•				•	
Garrison Lakes	1/F4					•	
Gellately Lake	16/D7					•	
Gill Lake	8/A4					•	
Gillis Lake	14/B7					•	
Gladstone Lake	7/G3					•	
Glen Lake	9/B2	•				•	
Glimpse Lake	15/D2					•	
Goose Lake	7/E3					•	
Gordon Lake	14/B2					•	
Gorman Lake	33/D7					•	
Grassy Lake	25/B2					•	
Greyback Lake	10/B4					•	
Grizzly Lake	17/F4					•	
Gump Lake	21/C6					•	
Gwen Lake	14/E6					•	
Gypsum Lake	21/C7					•	
Haggkvist Lake	25/D6					•	
Hall Road Pond	17/B7					•	
Hamilton Lake	14/F4	•				•	
Hammer Lake	32/E7					•	
Harmon Lake	14/F6					•	
Harper Lake	23/D1					•	
Hathaway Lake	32/C1			•	•	•	
Hatheume Lake	15/G6					•	
Haynes Lake	10/E2					•	
Headwater Lakes	9/A2	•				•	
Heather Lake	33/A3					•	
Heffley Lakes	28/F6					•	
Herman Lake	30/D5					•	
Hidden Lake	25/B3					•	
High Lake	17/D3					•	
Hihium Lake	26/G3					•	
Holiday Lake	25/C1					•	
Holstein Lake	25/D7					•	

Bardolph Lake (Map 17/F1)

While this 10 hectare (25 ac) lake is not a high elevation lake, it is deep enough to remain cool during the summer. A small stream runs into the lake near the recreation site at the lake's north end. This is one of the best places to fish for small rainbow that can be caught throughout the open water season and again during winter. The four-wheel drive access lake is stocked with rainbow.

Bare Lake (Map 27/G1)

Bare Lake is a large (230 hectare/570 ac), remote lake reached by a 6 km hike along the Heller Lake Trail. The lake offers good fishing throughout the ice free season for stocked rainbow up to 1.5 kg (3 lbs) in size primarily by fly-fishing or spincasting. Fly anglers should try using chironomids, mayflies, sedges and leeches around the many shoals of the high elevation lake. There is a resort on the lake. Check the regulations for special restrictions and retention limits before heading out.

Barge Lake (Map 10/E3)

This small 5 hectare (12 ac) lake has brook trout and rainbow trout that both grow up to 1 kg (2 lbs). The lake offers good fishing throughout the spring and fall primarily due to its hike-in access. The trail/old road is found near the south end of Idabel Lake off the Okanagan Falls Forest Service Road.

Barnes Lake (Map 20/E2)

Barnes Lake is easily accessed off Highway 97C on the Barnes Lake Road. The lake has a recreation site complete with cartop boat launch. The lake provides reasonably good fishing for stocked rainbow trout up to 1 kg (2 lbs) by trolling or fly-fishing. It is possible to cast a line from shore, especially in the summer when the lake suffers from drawdown and the shoreline expands.

Barton Lake (Map 16/C4)

Small rainbow trout are found in this 45 hectare (110 ac) lake. The lake is stocked regularly and is best fished during the spring and fall. Access to this lake is by a long hike/four-wheel drive road, ensuring little fishing pressure.

Beaver Lake [Swalwell Lake] (Map 17/D4)

Despite its popularity, this stocked lake still produces extremely well for rainbow trout up to 2 kg (4.5 lbs) by trolling or fly-fishing throughout the early summer or fall. Ice fishing is also common. There is camping and a resort on the lake.

Becker Lake (Map 17/E1)

Becker Lake is a small fishing lake east of Vernon. The lake is not quite high enough to keep cool in the summer, making spring, fall and winter (after the ice forms) the best times to fish. The lake is stocked annually with brook trout that grow up to 1 kg (2 lbs). Access to the lake is along the two-wheel drive Becker Road and there is a recreation site with cartop boat launch and campground. A float tube would be a real advantage, though there are plenty of places to fish from shore.

Berg and Kinney Lakes (Map 51/B5)

These two lakes are among the prettiest lakes in the province, which is good, because you're going to be staring at them for a long time if you try fishing here. While the lakes do contain rainbow trout, the water's high glacial till content makes finding them difficult.

Biely Lake (Map 7/E4)

Biely Lake is found in the Pike Mountain area between Coalmont Road and Highway 5A west of Allison Lake. Anglers making their way into here will find rainbow that are stocked annually as well as eastern brook trout.

Big Meadow Lake (Map 10/A3)

Big Meadow is an 18 hectare (45 ac) lake that once held rainbow trout. Summer drawdown has all but wiped out the fishery. The high elevation lake is accessed by a deactivated road system that also discourages many would be visitors.

Big Ok Lake [Island Lake] (Map 20/G5)

Big Ok is a heavily regulated catch-and-release, fly-fishing only lake. As a result, some big trout (up to 5 kg/10 lbs) are caught annually. Chironomid, caddisfly and mayflies are the preferred patterns, but do not rule out leeches. Casting from a float tube towards the weeds and sunken island can be very effective on the stocked lake. Nearby Ok Lake is also stocked annually with rainbow. Double check the regulations before heading out for retention limits and other restrictions.

Billy Lake (Map 21/C6)

Billy Lake is located on a four-wheel drive road north of Chataway Lake. It is possible to catch a rainbow in the 2-3 kg (4.5-6 lb) category but most of the stocked fish are significantly smaller. The nutrient-rich lake usually produces well throughout the summer months for small rainbow on a fly or by spincasting. For the fly anglers, try a shrimp, dragonfly or leech pattern for best results.

Birch Lake (Map 32/G4)

Southeast of Lac des Roches and Highway 24, Birch Lake is best fished by fly-fishing or trolling throughout the ice free season for stocked rainbow that reach 2 kg (4.5 lbs) in size. There is also a fishery for burbot. Effective fly patterns include chironomids, mayflies, damselflies, sedges and leeches. The lake has cartop boat launch facilities as well as a resort. Check the regulations for special boating restrictions.

Bisson Lake (Map 18/E4)

Rainbow trout up to 2 kg (4.5 lbs) are found in this 15 hectare (37 ac) lake. The lake is stocked annually with rainbow and trolling or fly-fishing during the early summer or in the fall can be productive. A four-wheel drive spur road off the Kettle River Forest Service Road accesses the lake.

Black Lake (Map 22/F5)

Set in Roche Lake Provincial Park, Black Lake has a misleading name since the lake has crystal clear water. The lake has rainbow trout up to 2 kg (4.5 lbs), which are stocked annually, as well as stocked brook trout. The lake is found east of Roche Lake on a rough road.

Blackwell Lake (Map 22/G6)

Blackwell Lake is reached by a 3 km hike from the Pratt Lake Recreation Site. Set below Mount Bulman, the scenic lake has a rustic recreation site and offers good fly-fishing or spincasting for stocked rainbow that can grow up to 1 kg (2 lbs). The waters are quite nutrient-rich allowing for good fly-fishing throughout the open water season.

Bleeker Lake (Map 22/E5)

Bleeker Lake is a shallow lake located north of Roche Lake along a four-wheel drive road. The murky, nutrient-rich waters allow rainbow to grow up to 3 kg (6 lbs). The stocked lake is best fly-fished using a shrimp, leech or dragonfly pattern in the early spring or late fall. The lake is used for irrigation so drawdown and the warm days really affect fishing in the summer. The lake is also aerated to help with winterkill, but this does make ice dangerously thin in the winter.

Blue Earth Lake (Map 20/B4)

Located south of Upper Hat Creek on the Earth Lake Road (two-wheel drive access), this lake is not overly popular despite its scenic surroundings, crystal clear water and prominent shoals. It offers a good fishery for rainbow trout up to 1 kg (2 lbs) by fly-fishing (shrimp, dragonfly and damselfly patterns) or trolling a lake troll. A recreation site at the lake provides boat launching facilities and a small campsite.

Blue Lakes (Map 15/E2)

Known for its good-sized rainbow (up to 2 kg/4.5 lbs), Blue Lake is also notoriously difficult to fish. Your best bet is to cast a sinking line towards one of the shoals or into the deep section of the lake (towards the middle). The 12 hectare (30 ac) lake is stocked annually with rainbow and is an artificial fly (and other restrictions) only lake with no ice fishing allowed. Rustic camping and a cartop boat launch are available at the lake. Nearby Little Blue Lake grows some pretty big fish, with rainbow that can reach 1.5 kg (3 lbs). The difficult four-wheel drive access discourages some fishers.

Bluey Lake (Map 8/A1)

Road access into Bluey was recently fixed up and this, combined with an intensive stocking program, makes this a popular fishery. Rainbow have been reported up to 2 kg (4.5 lbs) in the past. It is possible to launch small cartoppers here, while camping is found at nearby Kentucky Lake. The nearby pothole lake is also stocked.

Bob's Lake (Map 15/D7)

The 10 hectare (25 ac) lake has a recreation site with a cartop boat launch and a camping area. The lake provides good fishing for small stocked rainbow that can reach 1 kg (2 lbs) in size. There is a special retention limit here.

Bog Lake (Map 22/F5)

Bog Lake is noted for its large, stocked brook trout that come readily to a lure and bait in the fall or bait and hook during ice fishing season. The small lake is found in Roche Lake Provincial Park, which contains a few campgrounds.

Bogmar Lake (Map 33/B7)

Bogmar Lake is located to the east of Mayson Lake off the Jamieson Creek Forest Service Road. A short hike is required to reach the 15 hectare (37 ac), high elevation lake. The lake contains a variety of fish including bull and rainbow trout, sucker and carp.

Rainbow Trout Stocking

Lake	MAP	BROOK TROUT	BURBOT	KOKANEE	LAKE TROUT	RAINBOW TROUT	OTHER
Hoodoo Lake	5/B1					•	
Hook Lake	8/A2	•				•	
Horseshoe Lake	22/F5	•				•	
Hosli Lake	22/F4					•	
Hudson Bay Lake	16/E3	•				•	
Hyas & Area Lakes	29/A7					•	
Hydraulic Lake (McCulloch Res)	10/E2					•	
Ida Lake	22/G2					•	
Idleback Lake	10/D6					•	
Isintok Lake	9/B6					•	
Island Lake	15/D7					•	
Island Lake	27/F1					•	
Isobel Lake	28/B6					•	
Jacko Lake	22/B3					•	
Jackpine Lake	16/D7					•	
Jackson Lake	15/G5					•	
Jewel Lake	5/F4			•		•	
Jimmy Lake	23/C7					•	
John Burns Lake	7/G3	•				•	
John Frank Lake	22/F5					•	
Johnny Lake	7/E3					•	
Johnson Lake	29/C1					•	
Joyce (Green) Lake	23/F3					•	
Kane Lakes	14/F6	•				•	
Kathy Lake	25/D7					•	
Kentucky Lake	15/A7					•	
Kersey (Five Mile) Lake	26/A4					•	
Kidd Lake	14/G7					•	
Kidney & Liver Lakes	31/D7					•	
Kilpoola Lake	4/A7			•		•	
Knight (Echo) Lake	21/B6					•	
Kump Lake	7/G3					•	
Lac Des Roches	32/F3-G4				•	•	
Lac Le Jeune	22/A5					•	
Laird McKenzie) Lake	7/G5			•		•	
Lambly (Bear) Lake	16/E6					•	
Larkin Lakes	7/F4					•	
Larry (Cliff) Lake	7/E3					•	
Lassie Lake	11/B4					•	
LeRoy Lakes	21/C6					•	
Lily Lake	14/C5					•	
Link Lake	8/E3					•	
Little Lac Des Roches	32/E3					•	
Loch Drinkie	16/E3					•	
Loch Larsen	18/C6					•	
Lodestone Lake	7/D7					•	
Lodgepole Lake	22/A5					•	
Lodwick (Ludwick) Lake	7/F3					•	
Logan Lake	21/D5					•	
Lolo Lake	33/D1					•	
Loon Lake	9/A1	•				•	
Loon Lake	17/E4					•	
Loosemore Lake	7/G3					•	
Lost Lake	17/E4					•	
Luke (Little Dum) Lake	33/C4					•	

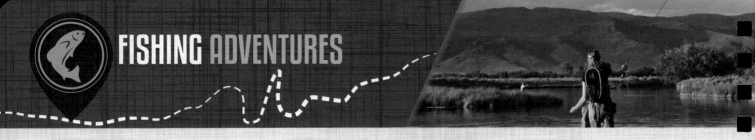

Rainbow Trout Stocking

	MAP	BROOK TROUT	BURBOT	KOKANEE	LAKE TROUT	RAINBOW TROUT	OTHER
Lundbom Lake	14/G4					•	
Lynn Lake	33/B3	•				•	
MacDonald Lake	16/A7					•	
Machete Lake	32/F5			•		•	
Madden Lake	3/G4	•				•	
Marquart Lake	14/F5	•				•	
Marshall (Providence) Lake	5/G5					•	
Martin's Lake	8/B7					•	
McCaffery Lake	8/A5	•				•	
McCall Lakes	9/D2	•				•	
McConnell Lake	22/B4					•	
McCormick and Twin Lakes	43/A7					•	
McLean Clan Lake	4/B1					•	
Mildred Lake	22/A6					•	
Miller Lake	23/E3					•	
Minnow Lake	10/E2					•	
Missezula Lake	8/A2	•		•		•	
Monte Lake	23/C5			•		•	
Moore Lake	5/A2					•	
Moore (Bullman) Lake	17/D5					•	
Moose Lake	37/B7					•	
Morgan Lake	21/E1					•	
Munro Lake	9/B3					•	
Murphy Lakes	7/C6	•				•	
Murray Lake	7/B2					•	
Naramata Lake	10/A4					•	
Nellies Lake	35/F7					•	
Nevertouch Lake	11/D2					•	
Nickel Plate Lake	3/B1					•	
Niskonlith Lake	29/C7			•		•	
Noble Lake	28/B6					•	
Norman Lake	9/F3					•	
Norman Lake	21/E3					•	
Nomans Lake	33/A5					•	
Nugget Lake	23/C7					•	
Orian Lake	6/F3					•	
Osprey Lake	8/F3					•	
Otter Lake	7/E5	•		•	•	•	
Oyama Lake	17/D3					•	
Pass Lake	28/A6					•	
Paul Lake	22/F1			•		•	
Peachland Lake	9/B1					•	
Pear Lake	10/E2					•	
Peter Hope Lake	15/D1					•	
Peter (Pete`s) Lake	5/A2					•	
Phillips Lake	29/F7	•				•	
Phinetta Lake	32/G4					•	
Pillar Lake	23/E3					•	
Pinantan Lake	22/G1					•	
Pinaus & Area Lakes	23/F6					•	
Pinnacle Lake	15/G6					•	
Pintail Lake	31/D6					•	
Placid Lake	37/E3					•	
Plateau Lake	15/D1					•	
Polson Park Pond	17/C1					•	

Bolean Lake (Map 23/G4)

With a resort, campground, cabins and rentals, this 78 hectare (193 ac) lake certainly sees its share of anglers. As a result, the rainbow rarely grow over 1 kg (2 lbs) in size and can be a bit more challenging to hook. The tea coloured lake is best worked near the deeper northwest end. Attractor type fly patterns or lures with bait can be effective.

Bonaparte Lake (Map 32/E7–33/A7)

Bonaparte Lake is the largest lake on the Bonaparte Plateau north of Kamloops at 33,674 hectares (83,210 ac). The lake is high and deep enough to stay cool through summer, meaning that fishing is good throughout the open water season. Bonaparte is also a good ice fishing lake. Fishing can be slow, but the big rainbow (over 5 kg/10 lbs) makes the wait well worth it. Trolling is the mainstay of the lake with plugs and Crocodile lures working the best when your gear is trolled deep. There is also a good number of small kokanee that can be taken by trolling. There are a number of resorts on the lake, as well as a recreation site with a cartop boat launch and camping.

Boot Lake (Map 15/C7)

Boot Lake is a high elevation lake, which offers a good fishery for stocked rainbow trout up to 1 kg (2 lbs) throughout the summer months. The access into the 30 hectare (74 ac) lake is a little rough but there is a rustic campsite and a cartop boat launch.

Borgeson Lake [Round Lake] (Map 7/G4)

Like the other lakes in the area found beside Highway 5A, the 15 hectare (37 ac) Borgeson Lake receives heavy use. Despite being stocked with both spring catchable and yearling trout, the fishing is reported to be slower than Allison Lake to the north or Dry Lake to the south. Trolling is the most popular method of fishing although fly anglers and bait anglers can meet with success. The lake has a launching area for small boats.

Bose Lake (Map 21/B5)

Bose Lake is located north of Highway 97C on a four-wheel drive road (Bose Lake Road). The high elevation lake offers good fishing for rainbow trout up to 1 kg (2 lbs) in size on a fly. The lake has a small recreation site with camping and a cartop boat launch. Rainbow are stocked annually at the 30 hectare (74 ac) lake. Check the regulations for the no fishing zone.

Boss Lake (Map 7/E1)

Boss Lake offers a good retreat for anglers who want to enjoy the sunny open rangeland that the Voght Valley has to offer. There is a popular campsite at the lake with a cartop boat launch. The 20 hectare (50 ac) lake is often trolled for stocked rainbow that reach 1 kg (2 lbs) in size, but fly-fishing is certainly possible.

Botanie Lake (Map 20/A7)

This lake has decent fishing for rainbow, which are best caught by trolling or fly-fishing. Although there is a smaller recreation site on the west end of the lake, be sure to respect the private Indian Reserve lands in the area.

Boulder Lake (Map 8/D1)

Boulder Lake is a hike-in lake north of the Okanagan Connector (Hwy 97C) offering reasonably good fishing for small rainbow on a fly, using bait or by spincasting. The lake is 20 hectares (50 ac) in size and offers fishing throughout the summer months because of its high elevation.

Bouleau Lakes (Map 16/E1)

Good fishing for small wild rainbow trout is offered at Bouleau Lake. Because of its proximity to Vernon and campsite with launch, the lake sees heavy pressure, although the fishing is usually fairly consistent. To the west is Little Bouleau Lake, a 15 hectare (37 ac) lake that is best reached by a four-wheel drive vehicle.

Brenda Lake (Map 15/G7–16/A7)

Brenda Lake offers fair fishing for stocked rainbow trout growing up to 2 kg (4.5 lbs). The lake covers 9 hectares (22 ac) and is high enough to remain cool in the summer. Or at least it would be if it wasn't so shallow. The ice is not usually off the lake until May, and by July, the heat and drawdown make fishing here difficult. But in June the fishing can be terrific as the lake holds plenty of shrimp and the fish grow fast. Camping facilities are available at a recreation site.

Bridge Lake (Map 32/D3)

Bridge Lake is a very popular fishing retreat found on Highway 24. The 1,370 hectare (3,385 ac) lake holds arctic char that are best caught shortly after ice-off in early to mid-May when they congregate in the shallows. In addition, the lake is stocked with rainbow and kokanee and also holds lake trout, burbot and a number of coarse fish. Kokanee are best fished in June before the fish retreat to the depths of the lake in late summer. Rainbow trout can grow to 3 kg (6.5 lbs), with the best

fishing in the early spring or just before ice-over in the fall. The lake trout grow up to 9 kg (20 lbs) and are best caught on a deep troll using a large spoon such as an Apex. It is catch-and-release only for lake trout. There are numerous resorts and access areas scattered around the lake.

Brook Lake (Map 7/C3)
Brook Lake is accessed off the Brook Creek Road but will require a short hike given the deteriorating road conditions. The 15 hectare (37 ac) lake, like neighbouring Andy's Lake, offers a secluded experience where you are likely to catch a number of small rainbow using bait, flies or a lure. Electric motors only.

Browne Lake [Island Lake] (Map 10/E1)
Browne Lake is one of the better fishing lakes in the McCulloch area and is blessed with a recreation campsite and boat launch. The 25 hectare (62 ac) lake contains good numbers of rainbow trout that grow up to 2 kg (4.5 lbs) in size. The lake is best fished is in the spring and fall. It is a fly-fishing only lake; check for other restrictions.

Brunette Lake (Map 17/E4)
This high elevation lake supports a good population of large rainbow trout. The reason for the large fish is the hike-in access and the limited stocking program. The 10 hectare (25 ac) lake is best fished during the summer and fall

Bryden and Pement Lake (Map 23/F1)
Bryden and Pement Lakes are accessed by a trail off the Charcoal Creek Forest Service Road. The lakes total 16 hectares (40 ac) and are best fished for the small rainbow. Fishing remains fairly good from June to September as the number of fish in both lakes is very good. Pement is stocked every other year.

Buck Lake (Map 11/A5)
Buck Lake is best accessed from the west off the Trapping Creek and then China Lake Forest Service Roads. Because there isn't heavy fishing pressure, the 25 hectare (62 ac) lake produces very well for stocked rainbow up to 2 kg (4.5 lbs). The lake is high enough to remain cool over summer (meaning the fishing stays hot) and sports a recreation site, complete with cartop boat launch. The lake is best fished with a fly rod from a float tube or by trolling.

Buck Lake [Leonard Lake] (Map 8/B2)
This small lake is found east of Missezula Lake along the Shrimpton Creek Forest Service Road. Offering angling for stocked rainbow and natural populations of brook trout, there is a small recreation site with a few campsites and a boat launch here. Check the regulations for special retention limits and other restrictions.

Bulman Lake (Map 22/F5)
Bulman Lake, in Roche Lake Provincial Park, produces large insect populations, which in turn feed the stocked rainbow. The lake is very moody with fly-fishing during the sedge hatch in late June or the water boatman hatch in the fall being your best bet. Check the regulations for special restrictions and retention limits before heading out.

Burnell Lake [Sawmill Lake] (Map 3/G4)
Locally known as Burnell Lake, this lake is a popular catch-and-release fishery east of the Fairview White Lake Road. The restrictions, along with a new aerator to help combat winterkill, have helped turn this lake into a quality fishery with stocked rainbow trout that can grow up to 2.5 kg (5 lbs) or 70 cm (28 in) in size. The lake is best fished in the spring and fall since it can suffer from drawdown and warm quickly in the summer. Try using chironomids/other flies around shoals or near underwater islands. Check the regulations for special retention limits and other restrictions.

Butler Lake (Map 8/A4)
Found north of Missezula Mountain, Butler Lake is one of a few nice small fishing lakes in the area. Fishing here is for stocked rainbow, while camping can be found at the nearby Stringer Lake Recreation Site. Check the regulations for special retention limits and other restrictions.

Butterball Lake (Map 22/F5)
Found east of the southern boundary of Roche Lake Provincial Park, this small lake is stocked with rainbow trout on an annual basis. Camping can be found back at Rocke Lake Provincial Park.

Calling Lake (Map 20/G6)
Calling Lake is a 30 hectare (74 ac), high elevation lake, which suffers from both winterkill and summer drawdown. Still, the lake produces well for rainbow trout up to 1 kg (2 lbs) in size throughout the spring and fall by trolling (lake troll or leech pattern) or by fly-fishing (shrimp pattern). The lake is comprised of dark, nutrient rich waters and is stocked annually. Check the regulations for special quotas on rainbow.

Rainbow Trout Stocking	MAP	BROOK TROUT	BURBOT	KOKANEE	LAKE TROUT	RAINBOW TROUT	OTHER
Postill Lake	17/E5	•				•	
Powerline Lake	22/F5	•				•	
Pratt Lake	22/G6					•	
Prosser Lake	7/G3					•	
Rampart Lake	8/B4					•	
Red Lake	27/D6	•				•	
Renees Pothole	14/G7					•	
Rexford Lake	28/E2					•	
Richard Lake	33/B3					•	
Rickey (Rick) Lake	7/E3					•	
Ripley Lake	3/G3					•	
Robertson Lake	7/F3					•	
Roche Lake	22/F5					•	
Rod Lake	17/E4					•	
Rose Lake	22/F5	•				•	
Rose Valley Lake	16/G7					•	
Ross Moore Lake	22/B5					•	
Ruth Lake	17/E4					•	
Salmon Lake	16/A1					•	
Sandrift Lakes	11/C4					•	
Scott Lakes	33/B7					•	
Secret Lake	3/B1					•	
Secret Lake	8/E3	•				•	
Sedge (Bonanza) Lake	33/B3					•	
Seidner Lake	25/A5					•	
Shannon Lake	9/F1					•	
Sharpe Lake	32/C6					•	
Shea Lake	7/E1					•	
Sheridan Lake	32/B3					•	
Sigalet Lake	25/E6				•		
Silence Lake	38/C5					•	
Silent Lake	29/B7					•	
Silver Lake	9/C1					•	
Six Mile (Pat) Lake	21/E1					•	
Skmana and Little Skmana	29/D6					•	
Skimikin Lake	30/A7					•	
Smith Lake	37/F3	•				•	
Snake Lake	28/E2					•	
Spanish Lake	24/A5					•	
Spectacle Lake	32/C6					•	
Spring Lake	9/D2					•	
Spukunne Lake	8/C4					•	
Square Lake	23/F6					•	
Stake Lake	22/A5					•	
Stony (Stoney) Lake	7/F3					•	
Streak Lake	17/D3					•	
Stringer Lake	8/A4					•	
Stump Lake	22/C7			•	•	•	
Sulphorous Lake	32/C1	•				•	
Summit Lake	7/G3					•	
Summit Lake	33/B4					•	
Surrey Lake	21/G7					•	
Swan Lake	24/D7					•	
Tahla Lake	7/E1					•	
Taurus (Bull) Lake	5/B2					•	

FISHING ADVENTURES

Rainbow Trout Stocking

	MAP	BROOK TROUT	BURBOT	KOKANEE	LAKE TROUT	RAINBOW TROUT	OTHER
Taylor (Gulliford) Lake	3/F4	•				•	
Taylor Lake	7/G3					•	
Teepee Lakes	8/D2					•	
Terraced Lake	5/E1					•	
Thalia Lake	7/E3					•	
Thomas Lake	4/D1					•	
Thone Lake	11/D7					•	
Tom Campbell Lake	22/F5					•	
Tsotin Lake	26/F7	•				•	
Tulip Lake	22/F5	•				•	
Tunkwa Lake	21/C3					•	
Tupper Lake	21/C6					•	
Tuzo Lake	4/D1					•	
Twin Lakes	3/E2	•		•		•	•
Two Mile	37/A6					•	
Tyner Lake	14/B2					•	
Victor Lake	31/G4			•	•	•	•
Vinson Lake	8/B2					•	
Walker Lake	15/F7					•	
Ware Lake	21/C4					•	
Warren Lake	29/A7					•	
Wasley Lake	15/E5					•	
West Badger Lake	28/E3					•	
West Lake	37/D1					•	
White Lake	30/C5					•	
Whitehead Lake	8/F2					•	
Wilgress Lake	6/A4	•				•	
Williamson Lake	5/D2					•	
Windy Lake	28/A2					•	
Wineholt Lake	33/B2					•	
Wollaston Lakes	17/E4					•	
Woods Lake	23/D6					•	
Wyse Lakes	21/E4					•	
Xenia Lake	6/C3					•	
Yellow Lake	3/E2				•	•	

Cameron Lake (Map 16/C6)
This high elevation lake has many small rainbow trout easily caught by trolling or fly-fishing in the spring or fall. The lake is located along a good mainline logging road (Bear Creek Main) and sports a recreation site.

Cameron Lake (Map 37/B7)
Found just off the Camp 2 Road, this small lake offers good fishing for stocked brook trout up to 1 kg (2 lbs). There are also unconfirmed reports of rainbow in the lake. Fly-fishing is most effective, although trolling a small spoon or fly can also produce results. A rustic camping and launch are available at the lake.

Campbell Lake (Map 22/F4)
Campbell Lake covers 110 hectares (272 ac) and is considered a great fly-fishing lake for the skilled angler, especially in the late spring during the caddisfly hatch. This lake suffers from an algae bloom in the summer due to its shallow, dark and nutrient-rich waters. Winds also play havoc to boaters. The rainbow trout can reach 5 kg (10 lbs) in size but average 1.5 kg (3 lbs).

Canyon Lakes (Map 10/D3)
Rainbow trout can be caught by fly-fishing or trolling during the summer and fall at the southern lake, which is 18 hectares (45 ac) in size. The lakes are accessed by a four-wheel drive forestry road south of Kelowna.

Caribou Lakes [North and South] (Map 19/F1)
These lakes, totalling 22.5 hectares in size, offer good small rainbow fishing caught primarily on the fly. There is a recreation site with a cartop boat launch for electric motor only boats.

Cathedral Park Lakes (Map 2/F7)
Cathedral Park offers a truly rugged mountain experience. Within the park are a number of small alpine lakes, four of which were stocked back in the 1930s with rainbow and/or cutthroat and now have a self-supporting population. The turquoise-coloured lakes and the spectacular scenery will add to the enjoyable fishing experience. Given the high elevation, fishing is best in late July through October. Most of the fishing happens in the core lakes – Quiniscoe, Pyramid, Ladyslipper and Lake of the Woods – but there are also fish in Haystack Lakes. Of all the lakes, Ladyslipper offers the best fishing.

Caverhill Lake (Map 33/B6)
Caverhill Lake has rainbow up to 1 kg (2 lbs) best caught by trolling, fly-fishing (chironomids, mayflies, sedges or leeches) or spincasting small lures throughout the ice-free season. Despite its size, the 542 hectare (1,340 ac) lake has many bays and islands that are ideal for casting a line. A boat access resort on the lake provides the ideal getaway including hiking trails and rentals.

Chain Lake (Map 8/E3)
This 42 hectare (104 ac) lake has very good fishing for small stocked rainbow that can reach 3 kg (6 lbs) in size. Trolling is the most popular method of fishing although fly-fishing and spincasting can also be productive. The lake, which offers a campsite and boat launch, is heavily stocked, but is also heavily fished. Check the regulations for special retention limits and other restrictions.

Chapman Lake (Map 9/A2)
This small 8 hectare (20 ac) lake has small rainbow trout best fished in the spring or fall using a fly or by spincasting. Access is by a long trail (along an old road), which should ensure that you would be the only one at the lake when you get there. No ice fishing is allowed.

Chapperon Lake (Map 15/G2)
Found in the heart of the Douglas Lake Ranch, this is a private lake that offers good fly-fishing for rainbow up to 2 kg (4.5 lbs). The 393 hectare (970 ac) lake is quite shallow and is subject to winterkill.

Chataway Lake (Map 21/C7)
Chataway Lake is a popular high elevation lake that serves as the hub of several small mountain lakes (including Antler, Billy, Dot, Gump, Gypsum, Knight and Roscoe Lakes). Despite the heavy fishing pressure, it consistently produces small rainbow with some reaching 2 kg (4.5 lbs). The 15 hectare (37 ac) lake is best trolled, although fly-fishing is popular. The most productive fly patterns are attractor type patterns like a woolly bugger or a Doc Spratley. There is a nice fishing resort as well as camping facilities and a boat launch at the lake, but note that it is electric motors only here.

Chicken Ranch Lake (Map 14/F6)
This tiny 5 hectare (12 ac) lake is found northeast of the Kane Lakes. The stocked lake is heavily managed to ensure a good fishery for small brook trout. For best success, it is recommended that you cast your lure or fly towards many of the weed beds that line the shores. There is opportunity to launch a small boat at the lake.

Christie Lake (Map 28/E7)
This 3 hectare (7.4 ac) lake is unique because its best fishing is during the winter, when the brook trout come readily to a hook and bait. However, the lake is subject to winterkill. To counteract this, it is stocked annually.

Christina Lake (Map 6/D3–E6)
On Highway 3, east of Grand Forks, this large (2,509 hectare/6,200 ac) recreation lake is very popular for water sports given its warm waters. Trolling for large rainbow up to 9 kg (20 lbs), small kokanee and whitefish can be productive, particularly in the spring or fall, while smallmouth and largemouth bass are your better bet during the summer. Spincasting or fly-fishing for smallmouth bass and rainbow in the shallow bays and at the creek mouths, especially at the north end of the lake, is excellent. The southern end of the lake is well developed and has several resorts and campgrounds to accommodate visitors. Check the regulations for special restrictions.

Churchill Lake (Map 24/B6)
This small lake is found in the hills northwest of Okanagan Lake. Anglers making their way into this lake will find stocked eastern brook trout. The best access is from the Irish Creek Road leading off of Highway 97 north of Spallumcheen.

Chute Lake (Map 9/G3–10/A3)

There is a 10 hp maximum engine restriction on this well-known lake between Penticton and Kelowna. Fishing is best in the spring and fall. The 40 hectare (99 ac) lake has good fishing for small wild rainbow trout despite consistent use from visitors to the recreation site and the popular resort. There is an engine power restriction here.

Clanwilliam Lake (Map 31/G4)

Clanwilliam Lake is a 7.3 hectare (18 ac) widening of the Eagle River. The lake contains rainbow and cutthroat trout. This is a low elevation lake that opens up sooner than others in the area, but it is subject to the summer doldrums. You will also find lake trout and Dolly Varden, but these species are catch and release only.

Clark Lake (Map 11/B5)

Clark Lake is a small hike-in lake to the south of Joan Lake. It offers very good fishing for its small rainbow trout primarily by fly-fishing or using a float with bait. The 2.2 km trail in starts from the 7 km mark of the Lassie Lake Forest Service Road.

Clearwater Lake (Map 41/D7–B4)

Clearwater Lake is the primary water access route to the interior of Wells Gray Provincial Park. The large lake offers fishing for rainbow trout, lake trout and bull trout. Trolling is the preferred method since the trout are hard to come by. Patient anglers may be rewarded with rainbow and bull trout up to 3 kg (6.5 lbs) and lake trout that can top 6 kg (13 lbs) in size. Check the regulations for special restrictions.

Coalgoat Lake (Map 18/D4)

This small kidney shaped is located in a remote area east of Graystokes Provincial Park. You will have to navigate the backroads southeast of the Harris Creek Road and make a short hike-into the lake to reach it. Those that do make it here will find good fishing for rainbow that are stocked on a regular basis.

Coldscour Lake (Map 37/B7)

West of Clearwater, this long, narrow lake can be found via the Camp 2 Road. The lake offers productive fishing for rainbow trout up to 1.5 kg (3.5 lbs). Fly-fishing or trolling during the spring or fall periods will increase your chances. A recreation site complete with a boat launch is also found at the lake.

Collier Lakes (Map 11/B6)

Lower Collier Lake is a small 12 hectare (30 ac) lake that can be accessed by a steep 1 km trail from Sago Creek Recreation Site at 18 km on the Beaverdell/State Creek Forest Service Road. Upper Collier Lake is 2 km further east along an easy grade trail. These lakes can also be accessed from the east by using the Dear Creek Road (four-wheel drive recommended), which is found at the 38 km mark on the Christian Valley/Kettle River Main Road. Both lakes are stocked annually with rainbow trout.

Community Lake (Map 28/F5)

Community Lake is located on a good road off the Knouff Lake Road. The high elevation allows fishing to remain good throughout the summer months, although drawdown in some years may limit summer fishing. The sedge hatch in mid-June and the spring chironomid hatch are the best times to fly-fish. The 40 hectare (99 ac) lake is stocked nearly every year with rainbow and has a recreation site with a cartop boat launch and camping facilities. Check the regulations for special restrictions and retention limits before heading out.

Conkle Lake [Fish Lake] (Map 4/G4)

This 124 hectare (305 ac) lake is accessed by rough two-wheel drive road from Highway 3 or from Highway 33.The lake is home to a beautiful provincial park that offers a boat launch, camping and hiking trails. The lake has pretty good fishing for stocked rainbow trout that reach 2 kg (4.5 lbs) in size, with trolling being the popular fishing method. There is an engine power restriction on the lake.

Copperkettle Lake (Map 11/C3)

It is a 3 km hike from the Christian Valley Road to Copperkettle Lake. In the spring and fall the lake provides good fly-fishing (no bait or spinners allowed) for rainbow up to 1 kg (2 lbs). A rustic campground adds to the remote wilderness setting.

Coquihalla Lakes (Map 7/B5)

The 10 hectare (25 ac) Coquihalla Lakes receives very little fishing pressure, despite the fact that it lies alongside a major highway and has a quaint resort. Even more surprising, the lake offers good fishing for rainbow trout up to 1 kg (2 lbs) by trolling. The fishing season begins in early summer and lasts to the fall. The resort offers cabins and camping.

Corbett Lake (Map 14/G5)

This private, fly-fishing only lake is located right next to the Okanagan Connector (Hwy 97C). The, clear, shallow, 29 hectare (72 ac) lake is stocked annually with rainbow to ensure reasonable success for paying guests.

Corsica Lake (Map 37/A5)

Off the Branch 231 forestry road, Corsica Lake offers good fishing for rainbow trout that can reach up to 2 kg (4.5 lbs). Trolling, fly-fishing and spincasting all produce results. A high clearance vehicle is required to access the lake.

Courtney Lake (Map 14/G6)

Located alongside Highway 97C, the 74 hectare (183 ac) Courtney Lake contains redside shiners (much to the dismay of most anglers) and stocked rainbow. Despite its close proximity to the highway, the good-sized trout (up to 1.5 kg /3 lbs) and large shoals, Courtney is often overlooked as a fly-fishing destination. Check the regulations for restrictions.

Crater Lake (Map 15/A7)

Near the Kentucky-Alleyne Park, this lake offers surprisingly good fishing for smaller rainbow. Trolling is the mainstay of the 20 hectare (50 ac) lake.

Crooked Lake (Map 17/D4)

Crooked Lake is one of the many recreational lakes found in the Dee Lakes area east of Lake Country. Anglers here can expect to find rainbow trout. The lake is dammed, so the water level tends to fluctuate in the summer. No ice fishing is allowed.

Crystal Lake (Map 32/D4)

Located on the North Bonaparte Lake Road (two-wheel drive) southwest of Bridge Lake and Highway 24, Crystal Lake offers reasonably good fishing for stocked rainbow trout. The fish average less than 1 kg (2 lbs), although a 6.3 kg (14 lb) rainbow is on record. In addition to a guest ranch, there is a recreation site on the north shore of the lake where you can launch a cartopper. Trolling and fly-fishing both work well here, as does ice fishing in the winter with bait.

Crescent Lake (Map 8/G2)

This 30 hectare (74 ac) lake has rainbow trout up to 2 kg (4.5 lbs) that average much smaller. There is recreation site with camping and a cartop boat launch on the lake, which is high enough in elevation to maintain a summer fishery.

Cultus Lake (Map 26/G6–27/A6)

This 48 hectare (119 ac) lake is easily accessed of the Deadman-Cache Creek Road and offers fair fishing for small rainbow. This shallow lake does suffer from the summer doldrums.

Cup Lake (Map 11/B5)

Cup Lake is a small, 9 hectare (22 ac), scenic lake that is easily accessed via the Lassie Lake Road. Most of the stocked rainbow remain small, although some reach 1 kg (2 lbs) in size. Trolling or fly-fishing from a float tube is very effective. A recreation site is located at the north end of the lake where you will find a cartop boat launch for electric motors only and a wharf for casting.

Be careful when wading into the water in spring — you might unknowingly walk through a spawning bed and destroy a lot of eggs. Trout usually turn over small rocks when laying eggs, exposing algae-free undersides — look for shiny or lighter coloured rocks that may indicate a spawning bed.

Curtis Lake (Map 17/G3)

Curtis Lake has an abundance of small rainbow trout that offer fast fishing during the spring or fall with bobber and bait or by fly-fishing. A four-wheel drive road off the Hadoo Main accesses the lake.

Dairy Lake (Map 21/E3)

This 25 hectare (62 ac) lake is located along a two-wheel drive road to the east of Greenstone Mountain. The lake is subject to winterkill and drawdown in the summer, but an aggressive rainbow trout stocking program helps maintain the fishery. The lake is best fished by trolling, although fly-fishing can be effective at times. There is a cartop boat launch at the recreation site on the northeast shore.

Damer Lake [Round Lake] (Map 17/D3)

This 7 hectare (17 ac) lake is accessed by a four-wheel drive road off Oyama Lake Road. The lake has camping and a rough boat launch at the lakeshore recreation site. Since the lake is subject to summer drawdown, the rainbow trout are best caught throughout the spring and fall using a fly or by trolling.

Dardanelles Lake (Map 22/F7) 🎣

Dardanelles Lake has very good fly-fishing for stocked rainbow up to 1.5 kg (3 lbs). In the spring, there is a good caddisfly and chironomid hatch to imitate, while a strong sedge hatch occurs in mid-June. In the fall, water boatmen patterns can be effective. At other times of the year, slowly trolling a leech pattern will produce. There is a special retention limit here.

Darke Lake [Fish Lake] (Map 9/C3) 🎣

Brook and rainbow trout are stocked regularly in this 40 hectare (99 ac) lake. The fish, which can reach 2 kg (4.5 lbs) in size, are best caught in the spring or fall as the lake is subject to severe drawdown in summer. Located in Darke Lake Park, the lake is accessed by two-wheel drive road and has camping and boat launching facilities. Brook trout provide a good ice fishing experience in winter

Davis Lake (Map 7/E1) 🎣

This 23 hectare (57 ac) lake holds stocked rainbow up to 2 kg (4.5 lbs) that are best caught by trolling, although fly-fishing or bait and bobber can be effective. The lake is very popular and has a large campsite and cartop boat launch.

Deadman Lake (Map 7/G3) 🎣

A small 6 hectare (15 ac) lake that is accessed by a four-wheel drive road, Deadman Lake has stocked rainbow as well as smallmouth and largemouth bass. There is a recreation site with a campground at the lake.

Deadman Lake (Map 27/C2) 🎣

Deadman Lake is located off the sometimes rough Deadman Vidette Road. The 49 hectare (121 ac) lake has reasonably good fishing for stocked rainbow and kokanee that reach 1 kg (2 lbs) in size and are best caught by fly-fishing or trolling. The lake has a recreation site on the eastern shore.

Dee Lake (Map 17/E3) 🎣

Dee Lake is accessed off the good two-wheel drive Dee Lake Road and it offers good fishing for rainbow caught by either fly-fishing or trolling. Stocked and known to produce some large rainbow (up to 2 kg/4.5 lbs), there is a boat launch and rustic resort on Dee Lake. Check the regulations for special restrictions.

Deep Lake (Map 17/D2)

Deep Lake is a tiny 5 hectare (12 ac) lake with hike-in access from Kalamalka Lake Park. The lake contains rainbow trout, which do not see many hooks so usually take readily to flies; especially during the spring hatches.

Deep Lake (Map 28/C7) 🎣

This 3.6 hectare (8.9 ac) hike-in lake is located off the Grasslands Community Trail in Lac du Bois Grasslands Provincial Park. Anglers will find eastern brook and rainbow trout; both are stocked on a regular basis to help maintain the fishery. Living up to its name, the lake has a maximum depth of nearly 13 meters (43 ft), making shore fishing relatively easy. Check the regulations for special retention limits.

Deer Lake (Map 17/E3)

Part of the popular Dee Lake Chain, Deer Lake is most often accessed by canoe or small boat from Island Lake to the north. It is yet another option in the area for anglers going after rainbow trout. No ice fishing is allowed.

Deer Lake (Map 33/B3)

You can find Deer Lake off Taweel Lake Forest Service Road. The lake provides fishing opportunities for rainbow trout that can reach up to 1 kg (2 lbs). Fly anglers should try a leech imitation, like a woolly bugger, for added success. There is a rustic campsite and boat launch at the lake.

Deka Lake (Map 32/C1) 🎣

This good sized lake (1,153 hectares/2,849 ac) is found west of Little Fort, north of Highway 24. Anglers here will find lake trout, rainbow and kokanee. Both rainbow and kokanee are stocked heavily each year. You will want a decent boat to get out and explore the lake, but take caution when going between the two main sections of the lake, as the area in between is very shallow – watch for markers. The Deka Lake Volunteer Fire Department hosts an annual fishing derby on the BC Day Long Weekend – inquire locally for specifics on the event.

Dennis Lake (Map 29/C6) 🎣

This 6 hectare (15 ac) lake is subject to winterkill but can be fairly productive in good years for stocked rainbow that can reach 1 kg (2 lbs). There is a small recreation site and a cartop boat launch on the lake, which may require a four-wheel drive vehicle to reach.

Desmond Lake (Map 21/F6)

Desmond Lake is located on the rough Surrey Lake Forest Service Road just south of the Meadow Creek Road west of Highway 5.The 25 hectare (62 ac) lake has spotty fishing for rainbow trout up to 1 kg (2 lbs), with three distinct holes to work.

Divide Lake (Map 9/G3) 🎣

One of two small trail-access lakes (this one covers just 4 hectares/9.9 ac) in Okanagan Mountain Park worth fishing, Divide Lake has lots of small stocked rainbow. To catch some, try using a fly or spincasting anytime during the early summer or fall.

Dixon Lake (Map 24/E7)

This small 13 hectare (32 ac) lake is located on the Dixon Creek Road and provides good fishing for small rainbow by fly-fishing or spincasting. Most attractor type flies or small lures work on the easily caught rainbow.

Dobbin Lake (Map 16/C6) 🎣

One of the Horseshoe Lakes, Dobbin is a 10 hectare (25 ac) lake that was stocked in the past with brook trout. The high elevation lake also offers stocked rainbow trout. The lake is accessed by a two-wheel drive road and has a cartop boat launch. Electric motors only.

Dominic Lake (Map 21/F4) 🎣

The 35 hectare (86 ac) Dominic Lake is located north of Face Lake on the Paska Lake Road (four-wheel drive recommended). The lake offers good fishing for stocked rainbow up to 1 kg (2 lbs) best caught by fly-fishing (attractor patterns) or trolling a lake troll. There is an undeveloped campsite on the east end of the lake as well as a resort with camping facilities.

Doreen Lake (Map 17/E3) 🎣

Doreen Lake is located off the Dee Lake Road (two-wheel drive) and has a large recreation site with camping and a cartop boat launch. The 40 hectare (99 ac) lake is a fly-fishing only lake and holds good numbers of rainbow in the 2 kg (4.5 lbs) range. Although there are many stocked fish to entice the angler, the rainbow tend to be extremely moody. No ice fishing is allowed.

Double Lakes (Map 37/A5)

Double Lakes is really one lake that gives the illusion of two lakes if viewed from above. The lake is accessible off Road 20 west of Clearwater. Fishing is fair for rainbow trout up to 1 kg (2 lbs). There is a recreation site equipped with a boat launch available at the lake.

Douglas Lake (Map 15/E3)

Douglas Lake is located along the paved Douglas Lake Road. The lake is noted more for cattle ranching than for fishing, but it is possible to catch rainbow up to 1 kg (2 lbs), small kokanee and burbot (through the ice – catch and release only). The Douglas Lake Cattle Company offers a campground with a boat launch that can be used for a fee.

Dry Lake (Map 7/G4) 🎣

Rainbow are stocked annually at the 35 hectare (86 ac) lake and some of them grow to be 2 kg (4.5 lbs) in size, although most are quite small given the heavy fishing pressure. There are also some brook trout available at the lake. Trolling is the mainstay of the lake. There is an engine power restriction here.

Duffy Lake (Map 21/E3) 🎣

This 23 hectare (57 ac) lake is located on a two-wheel drive road south of Cherry Creek. The lake is stocked annually with rainbow that can reach 2 kg (4.5 lbs) in size, although the average catch is quite small. Both trolling and fly-fishing can be quite effective throughout the spring and fall. For the fly angler, try a shrimp, dragonfly or mayfly pattern, depending on the hatch. The lake has a small recreation site with camping and boat launch facilities.

Dum Lake (Map 33/C4)

You can find Dum Lake off a rough four-wheel drive road, south of Little Fort. The lake offers good fishing for small rainbow trout that can reach 1 kg (2 lbs) on occasion. Fly-fishing can be very good in the spring or fall with a caddisfly or dragon fly pattern. Check the regulations for special restrictions and retention limits before heading out.

Dunn Lake (Map 33/E4)

This long, deep lake can be found via the Dunn Lake Road just east of Little Fort. The scenic lake offers fishing opportunities for rainbow trout, lake trout, bull trout and the odd kokanee. Due to the depth of this lake, the water remains fairly cool. Trolling is the most effective fishing method, especially in the heat of the summer. There is a resort on the southern shore of the lake and a recreation site with a cartop boat launch along the northern shore.

FISHING ADVENTURES

Dunsapie Lake (Map 28/C1)
This 10 hectare (25 ac) lake is located along the Jamieson Creek Road. It has a nice recreation site with camping and a cartop boat launch. The lake is primarily trolled for the fair number of rainbow up to 1 kg (2 lbs). The high elevation lake has reasonably good fishing throughout the summer months. Fly fishers will find that spring and fall are the better times to fish.

Dutch Lake (Map 33/F1)
Dutch Lake lies within the town of Clearwater and offers generally fair fishing for small stocked rainbow. Brookies were stocked here in the past and still offer a fishery for this elusive trout. Recently, kokanee have also been stocked here on an annual basis. Home to a nice park, the lake receives significant angling pressure throughout the year. Regardless, it is still possible to have a good day with a canoe or float tube on this lake. Check the regulations for engine power restrictions.

Eagan Lake (Map 32/D5)
Northwest of Bonaparte Lake along the Egan-Bonaparte Forest Service Road (3300 Rd), this 410 hectare (1,013 ac) lake offers fairly good fishing for rainbow that can reach 1 kg (2 lbs) in size. There are also some small kokanee that inhabit the lake. The lake has a resort on the north end of the lake. Check the regulations for special restrictions.

East Barrière Lake (Map 34/C6)
A long narrow lake found on the East Barrière Forest Service Road (two-wheel drive access), this 1,036 hectare (2,560 ac) lake is usually trolled. Try working flies or a lake troll near the many shoals for the Dolly Varden, rainbow trout, lake trout and kokanee that inhabit the lake. The lake sports an airstrip, a recreation site with camping and a boat launch as well as a resort on the west end of the lake.

Eastmere & Westmere Lakes (Map 8/F3)
These small, remote mountain lakes can be reached by a 4 km trail/old road from Osprey Lake. As a result, the lakes are a great place to go for a secluded fishing experience with a good possibility of catching small stocked rainbow. Check the regulations for special retention limits and other restrictions.

Echo Lake [Lumby Lake] (Map 18/D2)
Home to a nice resort and an undeveloped provincial park, the 75 hectare (185 ac) lake has good numbers of stocked rainbow trout that grow up to 4 kg (9 lbs). There are also a few kokanee and some lake trout that grow up to 5 kg (11 lbs). Trolling is the preferred method of fishing, but the lake can be fly-fished with some success, particularly at the shoals at the western end of the lake. The lake has a large shrimp population, which allows the fish to grow to large sizes. The picturesque lake does receive heavy fishing pressure.

Edith Lake (Map 22/C4)
Edith Lake is easily accessed off a two-wheel drive road from Knutsford. The lake covers 27 hectares (67 ac) and has a surprisingly good fishery for brook trout in the early spring and late fall, as well as during ice fishing season. The fish are best caught by a small lure with bait during the open water season or bait and hook during ice fishing season. The lake is rumoured to have a few big rainbow that are very hard to catch. Both brook trout and rainbow are stocked annually at the lake to counteract winterkill. There is a special rainbow trout retention limit here.

Edna Lake (Map 14/E6)
Edna Lake covers 11 hectares (27 ac) and is located on a two-wheel drive access road. It is considered a reasonably good lake for fishing small stocked brook trout. However, brookies up to 2 kg (4 lbs) can be pulled through the ice. It is possible to launch small boats at the lake.

Eileen Lake (Map 16/C5)
Eileen Lake is found on a two-wheel drive access road south of Sun Peaks and provides a reasonably good fishery for small stocked rainbow. The 10 hectare (25 ac) lake warms in the summer so it is best to fish in the spring or fall. It is possible to launch small boats at the lake.

Ejas Lake (Map 37/B4)
Ejas Lake offers good fishing for rainbow trout up to 2 kg (4.5 lbs). Trolling or fly-fishing are your best bets for success, especially during the spring or fall periods. A recreation site with a boat launch is also found at the lake.

Elbow Lake (Map 25/B2)
You will have to hike-in to Elbow Lake, along the Heller Lake Trail, but you will not have to carry a tent if you're planning on staying (unless you want to), as there is a resort on the west end of the lake. Elbow offers great fishing for stocked rainbow trout up to 1 kg (2 lbs) by fly-fishing or spincasting. Fishing remains fairly active throughout the ice-free season. Fly anglers can try chironomids, mayflies, damselflies or leeches around the shoals. Check the regulations for special restrictions and retention limits before heading out.

Elinor Lake (Map 9/G4)
Many small rainbow trout can be caught in this 8 hectare (20 ac) lake, which is best accessed from Chute Lake to the north. The best time for fishing is during the early summer or fall since the lake is subject to drawdown. The lake is popular with fly anglers, though spincasting is productive as well.

Emar Lake (Map 33/B3)
Accessed by trail from Grouse Lake south of Highway 24, Emar Lake is inhabited by rainbow trout that can reach up to 2 kg (4.5 lbs). There are some superb shoals found around the lake that produce well for fly anglers. There is a bait ban in effect on the lake.

Making sure your hooks are high quality and sized properly can make a world of difference. Spending a little extra time to replace worn out hooks with top-quality hooks will increase your chances for landing that big one.

Eneas Lakes (Map 9/B2)
The Eneas Lakes are comprised of a trio of lakes: Island Lake, Eneas Lake and Tsuh Lake that total 18 hectare (45 ac) in size. All three are found in Eneas Lakes Provincial Park and have fair numbers of rainbow trout that are caught using a fly or by spincasting anytime during the open water season. Eneas Lake has a cartop boat launch and is accessed by the Eneas Lake Road (two-wheel drive). Island Lake requires a short hike, while Tsuh Lake is along a four-wheel drive road (you can hike the road to the lake) and also has a place to launch small boats.

English Lake (Map 32/E2)
Finding English Lake is a difficult task due to the tricky nature of the logging roads in the area. The last reports are that the roads have been deactivated, so the drive will involve travelling through numerous cross-ditches. This high elevation lake does not become fishable until mid to late May, but the fishing for rainbow remains active throughout the ice-free season.

Englishmen Lake (Map 14/F6)
Covering 13 hectares (32 ac), this lake is being intensively managed so that there is now some reasonably good fly-fishing for stocked rainbow trout up to 1 kg (2 lbs) in size. For best results, try casting towards the many weed beds. Check the regulations for special restrictions.

Ern Lake (Map 10/E2)
Ern Lake is stocked regularly with brook trout which average 20-30 cm (8-12 in) in size. Try bait fishing or spincasting in the spring or fall for best results. The lake is found just northeast of Hydraulic Lake.

Ernest Lake (Map 22/F5)
Ernest Lake is a small 28 hectare (69 ac) lake in Roche Lake Provincial Park that can be quite moody despite the fact the rainbow trout are stocked. It is a fly-fishing only lake with an electric motor only restriction, no ice fishing and other restrictions. There is a rustic campground and boat launch for those with a four-wheel drive vehicle.

Esperon Lake (Map 16/D4)
The 20 hectare (50 ac) Esperon Lake has rainbow that tend to be small and rather scarce. There is a place to launch small boats and a snowmobile cabin on the lake. The high elevation lake is not ice-free until June.

Face Lake (Map 21/F4)
Face Lake is located north of Highway 97C on Paska Lake Road (four-wheel drive). A nice recreation site lies on the north end of the lake offering a boat launch as well as camping facilities. The 60 hectare (150 ac) lake is best trolled for stocked rainbow. Check the regulations for special retention limits.

Falls Lake (Map 7/A5)
Located west of the Coquihalla Toll Booth, Falls Lake is accessed by a gentle 2 km trail from Exit 221 on Highway 5. Not many anglers venture into this scenic mountain lake, which provides fast action for small rainbow on a fly or by spincasting.

Faulkner Lake (Map 32/F3)

A four-wheel drive vehicle is recommended to access the lakes northeast of Bridge Lake. Fishing for the stocked rainbow trout remains good throughout most of the ice-free season, except in heat of summer. Although not abundant, the odd 2.5 kg (5.5 lb) trout is lured from the depths. There is a small lakeshore camping area on the northern shore where a small boat can be launched.

Fawn Lake (Map 32/A3)

Fawn Lake is situated north of Highway 24, about 27 km west of Bridge Lake. The popular fishing hole is home to a resort and regularly yields rainbow trout in the 2-3 kg (4.5-6.5 lb) size range on the fly. There are also rumours of some fish exceeding 5 kg (10 lbs). The 32 hectare (79 ac) lake is stocked and there is public access with a boat launch for electric motors only. The best action seems to occur along the middle section of the southeastern shoreline where the lake drops off quickly. Note the retention limit.

Fish Hawk Lake (Map 18/B5)

This 40 hectare (99 ac) lake has rainbow trout up to 1 kg (2 lbs) in size caught in the summer and early fall with bait, by spincasting or by fly-fishing. The high elevation lake has a recreation site with camping and a cartop boat launch. The lake is accessed by the Graystokes Road, which is best travelled by a four-wheel drive or mountain bike.

Five O'Clock Lake (Map 11/C5)

This 8 hectare (20 ac) lake is home to stocked rainbow that can reach up to 1 kg (2 lbs). Because the lake is located off the Lassie Lake Forest Service Road via a 1 km trail, it doesn't see as much pressure as many of the roadside lakes in the area. There is a small walk-in recreation site on the lakeshore. It is best to bring along a float tube as it is difficult to fish from shore. Check the regulations for special retention limits and other restrictions.

Flapjack Lake (Map 33/A2)

This small lake can be found via a short trail from a rough access road northwest of Little Fort. The lake offers good fishing for small rainbow trout, which are best caught on the fly. Electric motors only.

Flourine Lake (Map 6/A2)

This small lake is found north of Grand Forks near the private Rock Candy Mine area; please respect the landowner by not trespassing. Anglers that make their way into this remote lake will find rainbow trout that are stocked on a regular basis.

Flyfish Lakes (Map 17/E4)

These two lakes are fly-fishing only. The stocked lakes offer good fishing for rainbow that can grow up to 1.5 kg (3 lbs) but are generally much smaller. There is a short hike to access the smaller lake (Flyfish 1), whereas the larger lake (Flyfish 2) can be accessed by a four-wheel drive road off the mainline. There is camping at both lakes. Check the regulations for special retention limits and other restrictions.

Foot Lake (Map 37/E3)

This small 3.7 hectare lake is located within Wells Gray Provincial Park and offers a wilderness fishing adventure without having to travel too far into the wilderness. Located just a short hike from Green Mountain Road, Foot Lake offers stocked rainbow trout.

Fred Lake (Map 22/B5)

Fred Lake has stocked rainbow as well as rumours of brook trout which can both reach 2 kg (4.5 lbs). The 10 hectare (25 ac) lake is found on a four-wheel drive road east of Lac Le Jeune and has a cartop boat launch but no developed camping. The lake is best fished using bait or by spincasting or fly-fishing with attractor type patterns. The lake is subject to winterkill. Check the regulations for special restrictions and retention limits before heading out.

French Lake (Map 32/D2)

French lake is situated north of Bridge Lake off the Windy Mountain Forest Service Road (1900 Road). If you have a four-wheel drive vehicle, it is possible to bring a small boat down to the recreation site on the lake. Fishing for rainbow is best from late May into June. Barbless hooks, no ice fishing, bait ban and powerboat restrictions are in effect for this lake. The Freshwater Fisheries Society of BC keeps the lake well stocked with 3,000 yearling rainbow each year.

Friendly Lake (Map 33/A2)

Friendly Lake is inhabited by good numbers of rainbow trout, some of which reach 2 kg (4.5 lbs) in size. The lake is quite deep; therefore, it is not subject to winterkill, which is common to several lakes in this region. The lake can be reached off Wavey Lake Forest Service Road, north of Highway 24.

Frisken Lake (Map 22/F5)

Frisken Lake is very productive, with stocked rainbow growing up to 2 kg (4.5 lbs)...if winterkill does not occur. The lake offers good fly-fishing during the chironomid hatch in mid-May and the sedge hatch in late June. There is a cartop boat launch and camping at the 30 hectare (74 ac) lake, which is accessed by four-wheel drive road in Roche Lake Provincial Park. Check the regulations for special retention limits.

Frogmoore Lakes (Map 21/G6)

A pair of lakes covering 80 hectares (200 ac) in total, the Frogmoores have stocked rainbow trout that grow up to 2 kg in size on occasion. The lakes tend to get too warm to fish in summer, making them a better spring or fall destination.

Galena Lake (Map 8/E2)

Galena Lake is located on a four-wheel drive spur road off the Whitehead Lake Road and does not get as much fishing pressure as many of the lakes in the area. The lake covers an area of 20 hectares (50 ac) and offers fairly good fishing for rainbow by trolling or fly-fishing.

Gannett Lake (Map 35/A3)

Found near the 13 km mark of the Gannett Lake Forest Service Road, the side road to this lake may require a four-wheel drive vehicle. The rainbow are generally small but there are expansive shallows and weed beds to provide good cover. Fly anglers should work these areas, while trollers should work the deeper parts of the 78 hectare (193 ac) lake. There is a recreation site on the northern shore that offers a cartop boat launch.

Gardom Lake (Map 24/D3)

Just off Highway 97B between Enderby and Salmon Arm, Gardom Lake is a popular destination with a nice park and boat launch. The lake was recently rehabilitated and reports of stocked rainbow trout over 1 kg (2.5 lbs) are being caught. The lake is known for its crystal clear water. Check the regulations for special retention limits and the electric motor restriction.

Garcia Lake (Map 14/F5)

This small lake is easily accessed from the Coquihalla Connector not far from the town of Merritt. Anglers here can expect to find naturally reproducing rainbow trout.

Garnet Lake (Map 9/D3)

Garnet Lake has good fishing for both rainbow trout and brook trout that are stocked annually. The fishing success holds throughout the summer for the rainbow, and there are ice-fishing possibilities for brook trout in the winter. The Garnet Valley Road has restricted access and you will have to scramble down the steep bank near the south end of the lake. People still haul in small boats (electric motors only).

Garrison Lakes (Map 1/F4)

A rustic trail leads off the Sunday Summit Forest Service Road to two scenic sub-alpine lakes. The lakes have 45 hectares (110 ac) of open water between the both of them and produce stocked rainbow trout up to 2 kg (4.5 lbs) by fly-fishing. Given the elevation, fishing is best left to the early summer through fall. Check the regulations for special retention limits and other restrictions.

Gill Lake (Map 8/A4)

This small lake is found east of Allison Lake amongst several other small fishing lakes. Access into here is best from the north from the Ketchan Lake Forest Service Road. Anglers will find stocked rainbow trout and camping at Stringer Lake Recreation Site.

Gillis Lake (Map 14/B7)

This popular 15 hectare (37 ac) lake is easily accessed off the Coquihalla Highway and is home to a popular recreation site with cartop boat launch. Fishing for rainbow trout up to 1.5 kg (3 lbs) in size remains steady, due in part to the stocking program. The best time for fishing is during the spring and fall using a fly or by trolling.

Gladstone Lake (Map 7/G3)

Another in a series of small rainbow lakes (this one covers 9 hectares/22 ac) next to Highway 5A, Gladstone produces well in both the open water and ice fishing seasons. The lake has a cartop boat launch as well as picnic facilities. It is stocked annually with rainbow.

Glen Lake (Map 9/B2)

Glen Lake is a small 11 hectare (27 ac) lake, with fair fishing for rainbow and brook trout that can grow up to 1.5 kg (3 lbs) in size. Both species are stocked regularly. The lake is fairly nondescript but offers some great fishing.

Glimpse Lake (Map 15/D2)
Glimpse Lake provides good fishing for rainbow trout up to 1 kg (2 lbs). Your best bet is to fly-fish or troll any time during the open water season for the stocked rainbow. For fly anglers, a sedge pattern in the early summer or a damselfly nymph pattern in the spring meet with success. The lake has a cartop boat launch, camping facilities and a resort. The lake has an electric motor only restriction.

Goat Mountain Lake (Map 18/A3)
This lake is found along a two-wheel drive forestry road and offers good fishing for small rainbow trout. Fly-fishing is the preferred method of fishing with the spring and fall being the best time to fish. There are camping facilities and a boat launch at a small lakeshore recreation site.

Goodwin Lake (Map 37/C4)
This small lake is found off the rough Road 9 south of Mahood Lake. Goodwin offers fishing opportunities for rainbow trout up to 1 kg (2 lbs) that are best taken on the fly. The lake is home to a small recreation site complete with a cartop boat access.

Goose Lake (Map 7/E3)
Goose Lake receives heavy use, but the fishing still remains fairly good for small rainbow taken by trolling or fly-fishing, likely due to the extensive stocking program in effect. There are campsites at both ends of the 30 hectare (74 ac) lake but the southern location is much better for accessing the lake. Some rainbow can reach 1.5 kg (3 lbs) in size. This lake has an electric motors only restriction.

Goose Lake (Map 24/C7)
Easily accessed from Vernon, this lake is not a popular fishery but is best known for its carp fishing when the water levels are down.

Gordon Lake (Map 14/B2)
Gordon Lake provides good fishing for stocked rainbow trout up to 1.5 kg (3 lbs). The preferred methods of fishing are fly-fishing and trolling, particularly during the spring or fall. Access to this shallow, high elevation lake is by four-wheel drive road off the Tyner Forest Service Road. There is a campsite with a cartop boat launch here.

Gorman Lake (Map 33/D7)
West of Barrière, Gorman Lake covers an area of 20 hectares (50 ac) and is high enough and deep enough to remain cool throughout the summer months. Despite the easy access and recreation site complete with cartop boat launch and camping facilities, the lake offers fairly good fishing for stocked rainbow trout.

Grassy Lake (Map 25/B2)
Grassy Lake is found west of Mabel Lake along a rough four-wheel drive spur road off the Cooke Grassy Forest Service Road. The lake is best fished for the stocked rainbow from a boat, but due to the marshy shoreline a small cartop aluminium boat or canoe is your best bet. There is a recreation site at the lake that offers camping.

Graystoke Lake (Map 18/B5)
This area northeast of Kelowna is a high elevation plateau known as the Graystokes. The 46 hectare (114 ac) lake is accessed by the Graystokes Forest Service Road, which is best travelled by a four-wheel drive. There is a recreation site and fishing for rainbow in the summer and early fall.

Green Lake (Map 3/G3)
Rainbow trout up to 2 kg (4.5 lbs) in size are found in this 18 hectare (45 ac) lake. Fishing is hit-and-miss, with spring and fall being the best time to fish by trolling, spincasting or fly-fishing. Access to the lake is by a good two-wheel drive road (Green Lake Road) south of Okanagan Falls.

Greyback Lake (Map 10/B4)
Access to Greyback Lake is by a good two-wheel drive road (Greyback Road) east of Okanagan Lake. There is a picnic area as well as a boat launch on the lake, which is stocked annually. Fishing for the many small rainbow trout is best by trolling in the early summer or fall.

Griffin Lake (Map 31/F4)
Griffin Lake is located next to Highway 1 northwest of Three Valley Gap. The 35 hectare (86 ac) lake has a small population of rainbow trout, lake trout and dollies, which reach 2 kg (4.5 lbs) on occasion. Your best chance for success is to troll a willow leaf, plug or Flatfish. Check the regulations for special retention limits.

Grizzly Lake (Map 17/F4)
Grizzly Lake used to offer fishing for large rainbow trout but the quality of fishing has declined over the years since the dam went in (1978). The lake still offers fish up to 45 cm (18 in) since it is stocked regularly. The reservoir covers 138 hectares (340 ac) and is best fished in the spring or fall by trolling. The lake has two places to launch boats and rustic camping opportunities.

Grizzly Lakes (Map 37/C6)
Grizzly Lake offers fishing opportunities for rainbow that grow to a healthy 3 kg (6.5 lbs) in size. A good area to focus your fishing efforts is near the inflow or outflow creeks found on the lake. There is a recreation site available with a boat launch. Check the regulations for special restrictions.

Grouse Lake (Map 33/B4)
Grouse Lake can be reached via portage or by a trail in Emar Lakes Provincial Park. The lake provides good fly-fishing for rainbow trout up to 2 kg (4.5 lbs), especially during spring chironomid hatches.

Gulliford Lake (Map 7/F2)
This 6 hectare (15 ac) lake is located west of Highway 5A. The lake can be productive during the spring or fall for small rainbow, which can reach 1 kg (2 lbs) in size. Bobber and bait, fly-fishing or spincasting are the preferred methods of catching the rainbow. There is a cartop boat launch at the lake.

Gump Lake (Map 21/C6)
The 20 hectare (50 ac) Gump Lake contains stocked rainbow that can reach 2 kg (4.5 lbs) in size, but do not expect to catch too many of these cagey fish. Fly-fishing is the preferred method of fishing with the spring chironomid and mayfly hatches or the mid-June sedge hatch being the best times to fish. The shallow, clear lake is accessed along the rough Highmont Road and there is a small recreation site with camping. Check the regulations for special restrictions and retention limits before heading out.

Gwen Lake (Map 14/E6)
Gwen Lake is accessed off the Comstock Road (four-wheel drive recommended) and holds stocked rainbow up to 2 kg (4.5 lbs). The fishing remains reasonably productive throughout the open water season. Visitors will find a campsite next to the 20 hectare (50 ac) lake.

Gypsum Lake (Map 21/C7)
The 12 hectare (30 ac) Gypsum Lake provides a fishery for stocked rainbow trout. The best time for fishing is during the spring and fall at which time spincasting and fly-fishing can be productive. A cartop boat launch (electric motors only) and camping facilities are available at the high elevation lake. Access to the lake is via a four-wheel drive road.

Haddo Lake (Map 17/F4)
This man-made lake has rainbow trout up to 2 kg (4.5 lbs), best caught by trolling or fly-fishing in the spring and fall. Access is fairly rough and the rustic camping area is not as popular as others in the area. The lake is used for domestic watershed purposes, so summer drawdown is a problem. Try fishing around the lake's three small islands, especially the middle island.

Hallmore Lake (Map 33/E3)
Hallmore Lake can found off the Dunn Lake Road south of Clearwater. The lake offers fair fishing for rainbow that can reach 1 kg (2 lbs) in size. Fly-fishing or trolling can prove successful. There is an informal camping area at the lake.

Hamilton Lake (Map 14/F4)
Hamilton Lake is a 22 hectare (54 ac) lake that suffers from winterkill. Brook trout can migrate into the lake and the best time to fish is in the fall just before spawning season. At this time, the fish are taken easily on large fly patterns and lures (Deadly Dicks) with a worm. In the past couple of years rainbow have been stocked into the lake to help establish that fishery. Check the regulations for special angling restrictions.

Hammer Lake (Map 32/E7)
Hammer Lake has a good sedge fly hatch, which means that fly-fishing is best in late June and into July. Be forewarned that the lake can be quite moody, especially in the summer when the shallow waters get quite warm. The lake contains stocked rainbow in the 1-2 kg (2-4.5 lb) range, although there is the odd fish that reaches 3 kg (6 lbs). The lake covers 68 hectares (168 ac) and has a recreation site found along the Egan-Bonaparte Forest Service Road (3700 Rd). Electric motors only.

Harbour Lake (Map 35/C2)
Harbour Lake can be reached via the Harbour Lake Forest Service Road northeast of Adams Lake. Harbour Lake produces well for small rainbow trout that can reach up to 1 kg (2 lbs) in size. There is a small rustic campsite and cartop boat launch next to the lake.

Hardcastle Lakes (Map 33/B2)
These two secluded lakes can be accessed off the Taweel Lake Forest Service Road. The lakes offer fishing opportunities for rainbow that reach 2 kg (4.5 lbs) in size on occasion. The Lower Hardcastle Lake is quite shallow and experiences winterkill from time to time.

Harmon Lake (Map 14/F6)

Probably the most popular lake in the Kane Valley, there are several recreation sites that surround the 21 hectare (52 ac) lake. Despite the heavy fishing pressure, fishing remains consistent year round for the stocked rainbow trout that reach 2 kg (4 lbs) on occasion. The lake is usually fly-fished at the south end of the lake in the shallows and trolled along the west side of the lake with a lake troll or leech. Nearby Little Harmon Lake is also stocked with rainbow.

Harper Lake (Map 23/D1)

On a secondary road off the Chase-Falkland Road, this 28 hectare (69 ac) lake offers fair fishing for stocked rainbow, which can reach 2 kg (4.5 lbs). The preferred method of fishing is by fly as there is a bait ban, ice fishing ban and other restrictions at the lake. Fly anglers should have a little patience and a good selection of leeches, shrimp, and, during the summer, dragonfly patterns.

Harvey Hall Lake (Map 7/F3)

The 8 hectare (20 ac) Harvey Hall Lake produces fairly well for brook trout and rainbow up to 1 kg (2 lbs) in size. Fishing is only really possible from either a float tube or small boat.

Hastings Lake (Map 7/F2)

This 30 hectare (74 ac) lake offers reasonable fishing for rainbow, with the best option being a bobber or spinner with bait (worms). There is an undeveloped campground on the lake, which is fished throughout the summer months with reasonable success.

Hathaway Lake (Map 32/C1)

One of many great fishing lakes in the area, Hathaway Lake, at 152 hectares (375 ac), is a good medium sized lake for rainbow and lake trout and kokanee. Both rainbow and kokanee are stocked heavily in this lake. Being a large, deep lake, fishing here can remain decent throughout the entire ice free season (late May to October). Access is off Mahood Lake Forest Service Road; there is a resort on the south end of the lake and a picnic site and boat launch on the western shore.

Hatheume Lake (Map 15/G6)

The 134 hectare (330 ac) Hatheume Lake is a catch-and-release fishery for stocked rainbow that can reach 1.5 kg (3 lbs) in size. It is ideal for fly-fishing with a good spring chironomid hatch and late June sedge hatch. The high elevation lake has a resort as well as a recreation site with camping facilities. Double check the regulations for retention limits and other restrictions before heading out.

Headwater Lakes (Map 9/A2)

This series of four lakes receive heavy fishing pressure throughout the open water season. However, you can still expect decent fishing for small stocked rainbow trout in lakes 2 through 4 and stocked brook trout in the first lake. The fish are best caught by trolling, although fly-fishing the many peat shoals or weed beds that line the lakes can produce well, too. A nice resort and recreation site are available for visitors. The first lake has some unique floating islands which provide cover for the fish. Check the regulations for special restrictions.

Heffley Lakes (Map 28/F6)

On the paved Sun Peaks Road, Heffley Lake covers 203 hectares (500 ac), while the nearby Little Heffley Lake only covers 7. Heffley Lake has two resorts as well as a large recreation site and numerous private homes. Due to their good access, the stocked lakes receive heavy fishing pressure but they do offer some reasonable fishing for rainbow trout up to 1.5 kg (3 lbs) throughout the ice-free season. Most troll the bigger lake but fly anglers can try the shoals at the west end of the smaller lake during the spring damselfly or mayfly hatch. Check the regulations for special boating restrictions.

Heller Lake (Map 27/F2)

Heller Lake is another hike-in lake, accessed along the Heller Lake Trail, which starts at the south end of the Bonaparte Provincial Park. The lake is high enough to provide very good fishing for rainbow trout up to 1.5 kg (3.5 lbs) in size throughout the ice-free season.

Helmer Lake (Map 14/F1)

This 15 hectare (37 ac) lake offers some good fishing for small rainbow trout during the spring and fall. During summer, irrigation drawdown can be a problem. The lake is accessed off a two-wheel drive road (Helmer Road) from the Coquihalla Highway and is home to a small recreation site.

Hereron Lake (Map 17/E5)

This small 10 hectare (25 ac) hike-in lake is found east of Postill Lake area. The 4 km hike deters most other anglers, meaning you could have this lake all to yourself. This lake has good fishing for small rainbow trout.

Herman Lake (Map 30/D5)

Although this lake is only 4 hectares (9.9 ac) in size, it is worth mentioning because it offers very good fishing for small stocked rainbow trout. The lake is located on a rough two-wheel drive road and has a recreation site, complete with a boat launch and campground.

Hiahkwah Lake (Map 27/G2)

This lake can be reached by a four-wheel drive road or trail and has a good population of rainbow that can grow up to 1 kg (2 lbs). Fly-fishing around the shoals with sedge flies at dusk in June and July is quite effective. Chironomids, mayflies and leeches also work. The lake is at 1,325 metres (4,350 ft) in elevation.

Hidden Lake (Map 8/G1, 15/G7)

This 10 hectare (25 ac) lake is reached by way of a rough two-wheel drive road and then a hike. This reduces the fishing pressure and results in good fishing for small rainbow trout. The lake is best fished during the early summer and fall by spincasting or fly-fishing.

Hidden Lake (Map 25/B3)

Hidden Lake offers good trolling for stocked rainbow that can reach 3 kg (6 lbs). The 130 hectare (320 ac) lake is best fished in the spring and fall. There are also possibilities to fly-fish the outlet stream at the north end of the lake as well as the creek estuaries at the south end of the lake.

Hihium Lake (Map 26/G3)

This 350 hectare (865 ac) lake is located by two-wheel drive road from Loon Lake or from the east on the 3400 Road. The lake is an excellent fly-fishing lake, given its abundant weed beds and rocky shoals, which provide natural cover for the stocked rainbow that reach 2 kg (4.5 lbs). The high elevation, windy lake has two recreation sites and a boat access fish camp on its shores. Double check the regulations for boating and angling restrictions before heading out.

Hobson Lake (Map 41/B3–45/D6)

Hobson Lake is another big, remote lake found within Wells Gray Provincial Park. Access is limited as the trail leading from the north end of Clearwater Lake has been closed due to the lack of a bridge over Lickskillet Creek. As a result, anglers are few and far between. If you can bring a floatation device, you will increase your chances of success for the big rainbow and bull trout dramatically.

Holmes Lake (Map 19/C3)

This 36 hectare (89 ac) lake is a 20-minute hike from the Keefer Lake Resort. You can rent a boat from the resort, or bring a tube. There is a walk-in campsite at the lake (often used by ATVers). The small, intimate lake used to produce some huge fish, but these days it produces rainbow and brook trout less than 30 cm (12 in). Fly-fishing, spincasting and trolling all seem to be effective.

Fishing requires a lot of patience. Bring along snacks, drinks, a radio (not too loud), and your best friends to make the wait for that prize catch a pleasure, not a chore.

Holstein Lake (Map 25/D7)

A small, secluded, 11 hectare (27 ac) lake that has a fair population of small stocked rainbow. The marshy shoreline restricts shore fishing and makes access difficult in the spring. The fishing is slow in the summer, making fall the best time to fish here.

Hoodoo Lake (Map 5/B1)

Hoodoo Lake is located at the 14 km mark on the Waddell Creek Forest Service Road (two-wheel drive) and offers fairly good fishing for small stocked rainbow by trolling or fly-fishing. A small recreation site offers a cartop boat launch and camping facilities.

Hook Lake (Map 8/A2)

Found on a two-wheel drive road off the Ketchan Lake Forest Service Road, this lake offers fair fishing for some large rainbow (up to 2 kg/4.5 lbs) and the occasional brook trout. The lake has a recreation site complete with a cartop boat launch and is stocked regularly with rainbow.

Hoopatatkwa Lake (Map 28/A1)

Located near the north end of Bonaparte Provincial Park, this lake is accessible only by trail or float plane. The high elevation lake has good fishing for rainbow trout up to 2 kg (4.5 lbs). There is a resort at the lake.

Horseshoe Lake (Map 22/F5) 🐟

Horseshoe Lake has both brook trout and rainbow trout that can grow up to 3 kg (6 lbs) in size. Although both species are stocked, an aerator has been installed to prevent winterkill. Fly-fishing using a shrimp, dragonfly or damselfly pattern can be productive at times. Check the regulations for special retention limits.

Hosli Lake (Map 22/F4) 🐟

Hosli Lake is stocked annually with rainbow trout that can reach 2 kg (4.5 lbs) in size. There are a bait and ice-fishing ban and other restrictions in effect so your best options are to fly-fish or spincast in the spring or fall. Casting around the sunken island or near the drop-offs during the June sedge hatch can be great. It is possible to launch cartop boats or even camp at lakeside.

Howard Lake (Map 10/C5)

This small 7 hectare (17 ac) lake is another hike-in lake, which offers decent fishing for small rainbow trout in the summer and fall. The high elevation lake is reached by trail off the Greyback Road.

Hudson Bay Lake (Map 16/E3) 🐟

Although fishing can be slow, rainbow trout and brook trout up to 2 kg (4.5 lbs) are found in this small 5 hectare (12 ac) lake. The lake is accessed by a two-wheel drive spur road south of Whiteman Creek Forest Service Road. The rainbow population is supplemented with a healthy annual stocking program and a retention limit of only two fish.

Humamilt Lake (Map 35/E6)

Humamilt Lake is a long, narrow lake – actually a chain of three small lakes – totalling 465 hectares (1,150 ac). The lakes hold some small rainbow trout, but mostly a lot of coarse fish and suckers.

Hunakwa Lake (Map 30/G1–35/G7)

This remote lake can only be accessed by boat and then on foot from the north end of Anstey Arm of Shuswap Lake. Needless to say, there are few visitors to this 497 hectare (1,230 ac) lake. Trolling, fly-fishing and spincasting can all produce.

Hyas & Area Lakes (Map 29/A7) 🐟

North of Paul Lake, a series of small mountain lakes offer good fishing due in part to the four-wheel drive access. Hyas Lake has fair fishing for rainbow up to 2 kg (4.5 lbs). The deep, clear lake is best trolled and is home to a resort and recreation site. A short hike to the northwest leads to Hadlow Lake, which holds stocked rainbow up to 1 kg (2 lbs). Nearby Pemberton Lake has rainbow that can reach 1.5 kg (3 lbs).

Hydraulic Lake [McCulloch Reservoir] (Map 10/E2) 🐟

This 260 hectare (645 ac) man-made lake has stocked rainbow trout that reach 2 kg (4.5 lbs) in size. The lake is home to the McCulloch Lake Resort, a popular destination with anglers as well as travellers on the Kettle Valley Railway. The lake also has a recreation site with a campground and boat launch and is best fished in the spring or fall by trolling. Check the regulations for engine power restrictions.

Idabel Lake [Cariboo Lake] (Map 10/E2) 🐟

Idabel has a healthy population of freshwater shrimp, which means good fishing for large rainbow and stocked brook trout particularly in the spring and fall by fly-fishing or trolling. The lake covers an area of 46 hectares (114 ac) and has a scenic resort and private cabins as well as a boat launch. The lake is close to Kelowna and quite popular.

Ideal Lake [Belgo Lake] (Map 17/F5)

This is indeed an ideal family lake that offers good fishing for small rainbow. The 145 hectare (360 ac) lake is best fished in the spring or fall by trolling or fly-fishing since summer drawdown is a problem. For fly anglers, there is a prominent June damselfly hatch as well as a good spring caddisfly hatch. Try casting near the small island or the shallow bay. Accessed by a two-wheel drive road, there is a lakeside recreation site offering camping and a boat launch.

Idleback Lake (Map 10/D6) 🐟

Next to the Okanagan Falls Forest Service Road (good two-wheel drive access), Idleback Lake covers 14 hectares (35 ac) and has stocked rainbow that can reach 3 kg (6 lbs). This high elevation lake offers a fly-fishing-only experience and is considered one of the finest lakes in the region. There are also restrictions on ice fishing (not allowed) and boat motors (electric only). The lake is best fished in the early summer or fall when the hatches are at their peak. A cartop boat launch is found at the recreation site on the lake's north shore. Check the regulations for special restrictions.

Isintok Lake (Map 9/B6) 🐟

Camping and a cartop boat launch at the lakeshore recreation site help you enjoy this 40 hectare (99 ac) lake. The decent fishing for stocked rainbow trout that grow up to 1.5 kg (3 lbs) in size also attracts visitors.

Brook Trout Stocking	MAP	BROOK TROUT	BURBOT	KOKANEE	LAKE TROUT	RAINBOW TROUT	OTHER
Alkali Lakes	26/A3	•				•	
Becker Lake	17/E1	•					
Black Lake	22/F5	•				•	
Bog Lake	22/F5	•				•	
Cameron Lake	37/B7	•					
Chicken Ranch Lake	14/F6	•					
Christie Lake	28/E7	•				•	
Churchill Lake	24/B6	•					
Darke (Fish) Lake	9/C3	•				•	
Deep Lake	28/C7	•				•	
Duo Via Lake	16/E4	•					
Edith Lake	22/C4	•				•	
Edna Lake	14/E6	•					
Ern Lake	10/E2	•					
Fish Lake	10/E1	•				•	
Garnet Lake	9/D3	•				•	
Glen Lake	9/B2	•				•	
Headwater Lakes	9/A2	•				•	
Horseshoe Lake	22/F5	•				•	
Idabel Lake	10/E2	•				•	
Jewel Lake	5/F4	•				•	
Kane Lakes	14/F6	•				•	
Kersey (Five Mile) Lake	26/A4	•				•	
Lemieux Lake	33/D2	•					
Loon Lake	9/A1	•				•	
Marquart Lake	14/F5	•				•	
McGlashan Lake	22/G5	•					
McIntyre Lake	18/F4	•					
Missezula Lake	8/A2	•		•		•	
Phillips Lake	29/F7	•					
Powerline Lake	22/F5	•				•	
Red Lake	27/D6	•				•	
Rose Lake	22/F5	•				•	
Second Lakes	14/F6	•					
Seidner Lake	25/A5	•					
Taylor (Gulliford) Lake	3/F4	•				•	
Tsotin Lake	26/F7	•					
Tulip Lake	22/F5	•				•	
Turtle Lake	10/E2	•					
Twin Lakes	3/E2	•		•		•	•

Islaht Lake (Map 16/D6)

One of the Horseshoe Lakes, north of the Bear Creek Main, Islaht Lake is a high elevation lake that offers reasonable fishing for rainbow trout up to 1 kg (2 lbs) in size. The lake also holds brook trout and can be fished with success anytime during the open water season by spincasting or by fly-fishing. Nearby West Lake is too shallow to hold fish but Dobbin Lake offers good brook trout fishing. Electric motors only.

Island Lake (Map 9/B3)

Island Lake offers small rainbow that can be caught fairly regularly throughout the ice-free season. There is a recreation site next to the 34 hectare (84 ac) lake.

Island Lake (Map 15/D7) 🐟

This 42 hectare (104 ac) lake is located just north of Highway 97C along the Paradise Lake Road. Anglers heading this way will find stocked rainbow and a nice recreation site that offers camping. There are several other angling options nearby, but you might want to consider trying this lake first as it is considered a trophy lake.

Island Lake (Map 17/E4)
Located east of Lake Country, this is one of a chain of recreational lakes centred around Dee Lake. Anglers will find rainbow trout along with a nice campsite and boat launch. Check the regulations for special restrictions.

Island Lake (Map 27/F1)
Island Lake, located just west of Bonaparte Provincial Park, is one of many angling options in the area. Anglers trying their luck here should expect to find stocked rainbow trout in this 49 hectare (121 ac) lake. Check the regulations for special restrictions and retention limits before heading out.

Isobel Lake (Map 28/B6)
Isobel Lake is a small 14 hectare (35 ac) lake with a good population of stocked rainbow trout that are best caught in the fall or through the ice. If fishing is slow, there are several trails in the area to explore. Check the regulations before fishing here.

Issitz Lake (Map 2/D1)
Located just west of Wolfe Lake, the 16 hectare (40 ac) Issitz Lake offers small rainbow. Fishing can be quite good in the early spring by trolling.

Italia Lake (Map 37/B5)
Italia Lake offers good spring or fall fishing for small rainbow trout. By summer the water warms and the fishing slows down. A fishing camp and a recreation site are found at the lake, which is accessible via the well-maintained Road 20.

Jacko Lake (Map 22/B3)
Promoted as one of the better lakes around Kamloops, Jacko Lake has stocked rainbow that can reach 2 kg (4.5 lbs) in size. Along with chironomids, shrimp and leeches make up the majority of the trout's diet. The 40 hectare (99 ac) lake is one of the first in the area to open up (in early April), but no ice fishing is allowed. Shore fishing is possible but a float tube or small boat is an asset.

Jackpine Lake (Map 16/D7)
Jackpine Lake is a popular recreation lake with good two-wheel drive access, a resort, camping and boat launch facilities. The lake has reasonable fishing for stocked rainbow trout that are best caught in the spring or fall. The lake can be extremely popular with anglers out of Kelowna. Check the regulations for special boating regulations.

Jackson Lake (Map 15/G5)
Jackson is reached by a short trail from the north end of Pennask Lake or from a slightly longer trail from the Mellin Forest Service Road to the north. The lake offers good fishing for stocked rainbow trout up to 2 kg (4.5 lbs) throughout the ice-free season. Try casting a lure with bait or fly (caddisfly, leech or dragonfly pattern). Check the regulations for special restrictions and retention limits before heading out.

James Lake [Trapper Lake] (Map 17/D6)
This 55 hectare (135 ac) lake has good fishing for small rainbow trout that can be caught any time during the open water season by trolling or fly-fishing. The lake is also a good ice fishing destination. Access to this lake is via a two-wheel drive road.

Jamieson Lake (Map 2/C2)
Jamieson Lake is reached by a short hike off of the often gated Darcy Mine Road. Because of the limited access, the 20 hectare (50 ac) lake has fairly good fishing for small rainbow.

Janning Lake (Map 33/C6)
This 10 hectare (25 ac) lake provides fishing for rainbow trout up to 1 kg (2 lbs), primarily by trolling or fly-fishing.

Jewel Lake (Map 5/F4)
In the past, Jewel Lake was famous for its unbelievably large trout. The largest, rumour has it, was 25 kg (56 lbs). But when minnows were introduced the dynamics of the lake changed. The rainbow have started to rebound. You can find rainbow up to 3 kg (6 lbs) and smaller brookies. Both species are stocked annually. The 72 hectare (178 ac) lake has a provincial park at the north end of the lake and a boat launch at the south. Trolling works well here, as does fly-fishing. Check the regulations for boating restrictions.

Jimmy Lake (Map 23/C7)
Jimmy Lake is located on a two-wheel drive road south of Ingram Creek Forest Service Road and has a recreation site with a cartop boat launch. The lake is highly regulated; including the requirement to release any fish under 50 cm (21 in). As a result, the lake is now producing rainbow up to 3 kg (6 lbs). The stocked trout are pretty tough to catch but are best fished by fly-fishing. There is a good spring chironomid hatch, followed by a prolific sedge hatch beginning in late June. Check the regulations for special restrictions.

Joan Lake (Map 11/A4)
This 50 hectare (125 ac), high elevation lake is accessed by an easy 1.5 km walk from the 6.5 km mark on the Lassie Lake Forest Service Road. The lake offers very good fishing for small rainbow in the spring and fall from a float-tube. There is a recreation site on the lake.

Joe Lake (Map 3/C6)
Your shortest point of access to this small sub-alpine lake is from the end of Susap Creek Forest Service Road. It still means hiking a couple kilometres. The lake has good fishing for small rainbow and cutthroat, which can be caught on just about anything.

John Frank Lake (Map 22/F5)
John Frank Lake is located in the heart of Roche Lake Provincial Park on a four-wheel drive road leading past the resort area. The lake is best fly-fished by casting a leech or dragonfly pattern near the lily pads that line the shallow lake. The 20 hectare (50 ac) lake has dark, nutrient-rich waters, which have been dammed for a Ducks Unlimited irrigation project. The stocked rainbow grow rapidly, but only reach 2 kg (4.5 lbs) in size because of winterkill problems. Cartop boat launching facilities are available at the lake, which has a bait and ice-fishing ban in effect.

Johnny Lake (Map 7/E3)
Access into this 10 hectare (25 ac) lake can be a little rough, but the recreation site and cartop boat launch still remains busy. The lake is very productive for small stocked rainbow that come readily to a fly, bait or a lure. Electric motors only.

Johnson Lake (Map 29/C1)
Johnson Lake covers an area of 362 hectares (895 ac) and is easily accessed off the Johnson Lake Road. The lake is best trolled for stocked rainbow that can reach 2 kg (4.5 lbs). There is a resort on the lake offering cabins and campsites as well as a recreation site.

Joyce Lake [Green Lake] (Map 23/F3)
This small 8 hectare (20 ac) lake is located beside the Chase-Falkland Road (good two-wheel drive access) and offers reasonable fishing for rainbow trout that can reach 1 kg (2 lbs) in size. The low elevation lake is stocked regularly and has a recreation site on the north end of the lake.

Kalamalka Lake (Map 17/B4–C2)
In the heart of the Okanagan Valley, this big, beautiful lake (called one of the ten most beautiful in the world by none other than National Geographic) is known more for water sports than fishing. There are lots of fish, but they are hard to find in the big lake. There are a few lake trout and rainbow trout, both growing up to 8 kg (18 lbs), as well as a few small kokanee and even some carp. Check the regulations for special restrictions.

Kamloops Lake (Map 21/C1–22/B2)
This very large (5,585 hectare/13,800 ac), deep lake extends along Highway 1 eastward from Kamloops. As with most big lakes, anglers will need to be patient and work the creek mouths or rocky cliffs. Rainbow, small kokanee and Dolly Varden all reside in the lake and are best caught by trolling. Rumour has it that the bigger fish are caught in the winter.

Kane Lakes (Map 14/F6)
This pair of small lakes is ideal for fly-fishing with nice shoals and dark, nutrient rich waters. However, fishing is quite spotty for the stocked rainbow and brook trout that reach 2 kg (4.5 lbs). There is a popular campsite on the Lower Kane Lake as well as several places to launch small boats or float-tubes. Check regulations before heading out.

Kathy Lake (Map 25/D7)
This tiny lake has good fishing for small rainbow trout and brook trout. It is best fished by casting a lure, bait or fly in the early summer or fall. The high elevation lake is stocked annually with rainbow and offers camping and a cartop boat launch at the recreation site on the east side.

Keefer Lake (Map 19/B3)
Home to the popular Keefer Lake Resort, this 69 hectare (110 ac) lake is also home to good fishing for rainbow that can get up to 1 kg (2 lbs). There is a boat launch at the resort, as well as boat rentals. The lake has suffered from overfishing, but populations are improving.

Kentucky Lake (Map 15/A7)
Part of the Kentucky-Alleyne Recreation Area, this is a popular destination in the open water season. There is camping on the lake as well as a trail around the lake providing good shore access. The 36 hectare (89 ac) lake holds stocked rainbow up to 2 kg (4.5 lbs). Just north of Kentucky Lake are some ponds that are stocked on an annual basis. Check the regulations for special restrictions.

Kernaghan Lake (Map 23/G3)

On a four-wheel drive road south of Wallensteen Lake, Kerneghan Lake has good numbers of small rainbow easily taken by trolling a Willow Leaf and worm, small lure or Flatfish. There is a recreation site at the 7 hectare (17 ac) lake. Expect to carry your boat to the lake.

Ketcham Lake (Map 8/A3)

Best accessed from the north, Ketcham Lake is a moody lake that is best fished earlier in the year. The shallow lake holds rainbow trout.

Kidd Lake (Map 14/G7)

Found next to Highway 5A south of Aspen Grove, this 19 hectare (47 ac) lake has lots of shallows and bulrushes. The lake has been managed as a catch-and-release fishery and now produces some of BC's biggest trout even though the rainbow are stocked annually. You should expect to find the larger fish at the north end, but more fish in the southern end. Check the regulations for special retention limits and other restrictions.

Kidney & Liver Lakes (Map 31/D7)

Located on a rough two-wheel drive spur road off the Three Valley-Mabel Forest Service Road, Kidney Lake offers fairly good fishing for stocked rainbow that can reach 2 kg (4.5 lbs). The best way to fish the lake is to use a float tube and fly-fish the many shallows. A campsite and cartop boat launch are available at the lake. Just to the north of Kidney is the tiny 3 hectare (7.4 ac) Liver Lake. The lake has many small stocked rainbow primarily caught by fly-fishing.

Kilpoola Lake (Map 4/A7)

This lake is accessed by a gated road off Highway 3 west of Osoyoos. It has fair fishing for rainbow and brook trout that can grow up to 1 kg (2 lbs). The lake is stocked regularly with catchable rainbow and is prone to winterkill. There is an undeveloped boat launch at the lake.

Kinbasket Lake [McNaughton Lake] (Map 44/G7–47/B3)

This glacier fed lake is actually a large man-made reservoir of the Columbia River drainage that was created by the Mica Dam in 1973. Access to the many arms of the lake can be found off of a number of good forestry roads. Boat launches and campsites are well spaced along the lake. The lake has good numbers of bull trout, in addition to burbot, rainbow, kokanee and whitefish. Try casting a Kamlooper, Red Devil or Krocodile for bull trout. Watch for the closure in Bush Arm near the bridge on the Bush-Sullivan Road. The low elevation lake covers 43,200 hectares (106,710 ac) and gets very deep (over 100 metres/325 ft).

King Edward Lake (Map 17/D3)

Summer drawdown can transform this 30 hectare (74 ac) lake from a jewel in the rough to an unsightly mud pit. If you time it right, fishing for rainbow trout up to 1.5 kg (3 lbs) can be good. Trolling or fly-fishing in the spring or fall should meet with success.

Knight Lake [Echo Lake] (Map 21/B6)

Knight Lake is a small 6 hectare (15 ac) lake accessed by a short trail leading west from Roscoe Lake. The lake receives little fishing pressure but offers some very good fishing for smaller, stocked rainbow if you can get beyond the muddy shoreline and lily pads. The weed beds to the south end of the lake are the best place to cast your line. Chataway Lake Resort has boats at this hike-in lake.

Knouff Lake [Sullivan Lake] (Map 28/F4)

Knouff Lake offers good fishing for rainbow trout throughout the ice-free season by fly-fishing or trolling. The rainbow are generally small although some grow to 1.5 kg (3 lbs) in size. For fly anglers, try casting a fly near one of the many shoals or sunken islands that are easily seen through the clear water. There is a recreation site at the north end as well as a resort. Check the regulations for special retention limits before heading out.

Kostal Lake (Map 41/F6)

Reached via a long, rugged hike through the backcountry of Wells Gray Provincial Park, the rough access ensures very few visitors and as a result fishing is known to be good for some nice sized rainbow trout. The scenic lake sits next to an extinct volcano.

Kump Lake [Lost Lake] (Map 7/G3)

Also known as Lost Lake, this lake offers a popular recreation site to access the lake. This 17 hectare (42 ac) lake is managed as a trophy lake for rainbow, which can be taken by fly-fishing only. The fishing is spotty and does suffer from the summer doldrums, but the stocked rainbow grow up to 2.5 kg (5 lbs). Check the regulations for special retention limits and other restrictions.

Lac Des Roches (Map 32/F3–G4)

Lac Des Roche is a popular resort fishery located next to Highway 24. The 657 hectare (1,623 ac) lake is separated into two distinct bays by a narrow channel. There are a few burbot and the stocked rainbow trout average 1-1.5 kg (2-3 lbs) with some growing to the 3.5 kg (8 lb) category. For fly anglers, the lake offers a good spring chironomid hatch as well as one of the best mayfly hatches in the Cariboo that begins in late May and extends into the early part of June. Try focusing around the deeper water and along the steep drop-offs. There are boat launches and a few resorts scattered around the lake.

Lac Le Jeune (Map 22/A5)

Lac Le Jeune is a popular 149 hectare (368 ac) lake that offers reasonably good fishing throughout the ice-free season. Stocked rainbow up to 2 kg (4.5 lbs) can be caught on a fly or by trolling. For fly anglers, the many bays and shoals make ideal casting areas. Try hitting the lake during the caddisfly hatch beginning in late June or during the mayfly and damsel fly hatches. There is a provincial park that offers camping, picnicking and a boat launch as well as a full service resort on the lake. Check the regulations for special boating restrictions.

Lacoma Lake (Map 16/C7)

Lacoma is a small 5 hectare (12 ac) hike-in lake with good fly-fishing and spin-casting in the spring and fall. It is home to good numbers of rainbow trout up to 1 kg (2 lbs).

Laird Lake [McKenzie Lake] (Map 7/G5)

Laird Lake receives heavy fishing pressure given its proximity to Highway 5A but still offers good numbers of small rainbow and brook trout caught by trolling, fly-fishing or spincasting. The 27 hectare (67 ac) lake is best fished in the spring or fall. A cartop boat launch is available at the lake, which is stocked regularly with rainbow.

Lake Revelstoke (Map 36/G5–40/D1)

This large, narrow reservoir (stretching 130 km/79 mi north from the Revelstoke Dam to the Mica Dam) was created when the Revelstoke Dam was completed in 1985. The lake offers fair to good fishing for rainbow up to 4 kg (10 lbs), lingcod, bull trout up to 8 kg (20 lbs) and whitefish and kokanee up to 1 kg (2 lbs). The preferred method of fishing is trolling but if you try fishing at a creek mouth or along the rocky shoreline with a float and bait you may get good results. A fast troll at 12-30 metres (40-100 ft) with any plug that looks like a minnow usually meets with success, particularly in the early spring or late fall. The lake produced a 12.7 kg (32 lb) bull trout a number of years back and there is always a chance you may land a monster. There are a number of access points and camping spots along Highway 23. Watch for closures around the Mica Dam and be aware of wind and debris on the lake.

Although you may be compelled to fish where you have recently had the most success, fish move around according to the season. Choose your spot according to the current conditions, regardless of your past catches.

Lambly Lake [Bear Lake] (Map 16/E6)

Despite easy access (and the resulting heavy pressure) to this 75 hectare (185 ac) lake it still produces well for nice-sized rainbow trout throughout the spring or fall by trolling (electric motors only) or fly-fishing. Perch are now quite abundant and can easily be caught by trolling a Wedding Ring with a worm. The trout are stocked to try to counteract the perch infestation.

Lassie Lake (Map 11/B4)

This Christian Valley lake is a popular place for area anglers interested in good fishing and a scenic place to visit. The lake is well stocked with rainbow that can grow up to 1 kg (2 lbs) or more. The lake is easily accessed by the Lassie Lake Road and, not surprisingly, has a recreation site on its southern shore. There is a boat launch and hiking trails in the area. The high elevation lake is deep enough to be trolled, but fly-fishing around the inflow of an unnamed creek on its northern shores, or the outflow of Sandrift Creek on its east, are also good bets.

Latremouille Lake (Map 33/B3)

This 96 hectare (237 ac) lake is located just off Highway 24. There is consistent fishing for rainbow trout up to 1.5 kg (3 lbs) that are reported to come readily to chironomid and leech fly patterns. A recreation site providing camping and a cartop boat launch is found along the east end of the lake.

Laurel Lake (Map 33/B3)

Laurel Lake can be reached by a short trail from the Taweel Lake Forest Service Road west of Little Fort. It is a productive fly-fishing lake inhabited by numerous small rainbow trout, although the odd rainbow can reach up to 2 kg (4.5 lbs). Try working chironomids off the shoal areas in the spring. There are a few hike-in lakes beyond Laurel Lake that see few people and as a result have excellent fishing.

Leighton Lake (Map 21/C3)

Found within the borders of Tunkwa Provincial Park, Leighton Lake usually provides good fly-fishing and trolling for rainbow trout up to around 2-3 kg (4.5-6 lbs). Unfortunately, the lake suffers from drawdown, winterkill and heavy fishing pressure. Shore fishing is possible and fly anglers should try the damselfly hatch in June. The 55 hectare (135 ac) lake has a campsite with a boat launch. Check the regulations for special restrictions.

LeRoy Lakes (Map 21/C6)

These two side by side lakes found southwest of Logan Lake offers anglers another option in the area for going after stocked rainbow trout. Camping is possible at the user maintained recreation site.

Lesser Fish Lake (Map 32/D3)

Lesser Lake lies just west of Bridge Lake off the Bridge Lake North Road. Lesser Lake produces well for rainbow trout that average 35-40 cm (14-16 in) and can reach up to 2 kg (4.5 lbs). Fishing remains steady throughout the ice-free season.

Lightning Lake Chain (Map 1/D7)

Found within Manning Provincial Park, this high elevation chain of lakes provides good fishing throughout the summer and early fall. There is a popular campsite and launch on Lightning Lake, where anglers can find many small cutthroat and rainbow caught by fly-fishing or spincasting. A good trail system leads past Flash, Strike and then Thunder Lake. These smaller lakes offer generally small rainbow.

Linden Lake (Map 18/C7)

The rough access (four-wheel drive only) prevents some anglers from enjoying this scenic 12 hectare (30 ac) lake set below Mount Moore. Spring or fall are the best times to fly-fish or spincast for the rainbow trout that grow up to 1 kg (2 lbs).

Link Lake (Map 8/E3)

This 15 hectare (37 ac) lake has a nice campsite and a cartop boat launch. Despite easy access, the lake still provides a reasonable fishery for rainbow that can reach 2 kg (4.5 lbs) in size. The lake is plagued by winterkill. An annual stocking program helps maintain the fishery. The lake is quite shallow around the shore and a tube or small boat is needed to get out to the drop-off. Electric motors only.

Little Shuswap Lake (Map 29/E6)

Little Shuswap Park offers a boat launch, beach and picnic site. There is private camping along the lake as well. Like Shuswap Lake, this lake offers reasonable fishing for rainbow up to 5 kg (10 lbs) primarily by trolling Bucktails, Apex or a plug near the surface in May to June and October to November. Fishing slows during the summer months and requires a downrigger to fish in the 10-25 metre (30-90 ft) range.

Loch Drinkie (Map 16/E3)

This 17 hectare (42 ac) lake's claim to fame (other than the amusing name) is that it is home to some surprisingly large rainbow trout. The lake is stocked regularly and receives light fishing pressure, no doubt due to the hike-in (about 2 km; if you can make it to the end of the rough logging road). Fishing remains fairly good throughout the ice-free season. Check the regulations for special retention limits and other restrictions.

Lodestone Lake (Map 7/D7)

Lodestone is a lovely little lake located at the end of the Lodestone Forest Service Road (or by foot or horse along the Hope Brigade Trail). The high elevation lake offers fast fishing for small stocked rainbow beginning in early July through to October. A small campsite and cartop boat launch is available.

Lodgepole Lake (Map 22/A5)

Lodgepole Lake offers fair fishing for stocked rainbow. Fly-fishing is the mainstay of the lake with dragonfly or shrimp patterns being the most consistent flies. The lake has a recreation site with a cartop boat launch and wharf. There is an electric motor only restriction on the lake.

Lodwick Lake [Ludwick Lake] (Map 7/F3)

Found in an area riddled with fine fishing lakes, Lodwick is also blessed with a campsite at each end of this long, narrow 19 hectare (47 ac) lake. Accessed off

Youngsberg Road, most two-wheel drive vehicles should be able to navigate their way into the lake. The rainbow here are supplemented with stocking each year, allowing for decent rainbow fishing, especially around the islands and prominent shoals.

Logan Lake (Map 21/D5)

Despite the proximity to town, Logan Lake offers good fishing for large rainbow trout. The stocked trout have been known to reach 7 kg (15 lbs), due in part to the redside shiners that infest the lake. The fishing remains fairly good throughout the spring and fall as well as during ice fishing season (be aware of the aerators installed to prevent winterkill). There is a campground, wharf and boat launch on the 12 hectare (30 ac) lake. Check the regulations for special restrictions.

Lolo Lake (Map 33/D1)

Accessible via Road 31 from the Camp 2 Road west of Clearwater. The lake offers fair to good fishing for stocked rainbow trout in the spring and fall. There is a recreation site at the lake that is home to a rough cartop boat launch. Electric motors only.

Long Island Lake [Janice Lake] (Map 33/A3)

Providing the main access to the Emar Lakes, this 146 hectare (360 ac) lake is accessed off Highway 24, west of Little Fort. There is a fishing camp as well as a rustic camping area with rough boat launch. The lake is a good fishing lake for rainbow up to 1.5 kg (3.5 lbs) with plenty of shoals and shallows ideal for fly-fishing. A few of the more productive flies include caddisfly, mayfly, leech and scud imitations. To maintain the fishery, there is an ice fishing ban, bait ban and single hook regulations in effect.

Long Lake (Map 28/B7)

Long Lake is an 80 hectare (200 ac) lake inside Lac Du Bois Grasslands Provincial Park. The lake offers fairly good fishing for rainbow trout that can reach 2 kg (4.5 lbs) in size. An ice-fishing ban is in effect.

Loon Lake (Map 9/A1)

This Loon Lake is found just north of the Headwater Lakes off the west side of the Sunset Lake Forest Service Road. Anglers will have the option of either going after brook trout or rainbow trout here. Both species are stocked to help the fishery.

Loon Lake (Map 15/A7)

Loon Lake is found just east of the Kentucky-Alleyne Provincial Park on the south side of Loon Lake Road. The small lake offers anglers another option for going after rainbow trout in the area.

Loon Lake (Map 17/E4)

Loon Lake receives steady fishing pressure due to its easy access and general popularity. The 10 hectare (25 ac) lake holds fair numbers of rainbow trout up to 2 kg (4.5 lbs) that are caught primarily by fly-fishing or trolling. The lake is stocked regularly and is best fished during the early summer and fall. Camping facilities are available at a small treed recreation site. Check the regulations for special retention limits and other restrictions.

Loon Lake (Map 26/D3–F2)

Easily accessed on the Loon Lake Road southeast of Clinton, this 970 hectare (2,395 ac) lake is consistently ranked as one of the top 10 naturally stocked lakes in North America. Although, the rainbow trout here are generally smaller, averaging 0.5 kg (1-1.5 lbs), what they lack in size they make up in quantity and fight as they are acrobatic Kamloops strain of trout. Fishing remains active throughout the season and there are resorts, camping and boat launch available. Check the regulations before heading out.

Loosemore Lake (Map 7/G3)

This small 5 hectare (12 ac) lake is found east of Highway 5A and provides fair fishing for small stocked rainbow trout. The lake has a campsite and a cartop boat launch and can be fished effectively by using similar gear as Deadman Lake to the north.

Lorenzo Lake (Map 33/A3)

Accessible via a rough spur road from the Blowdown Forest Service Road, Lorenzo Lake offers fair fishing for rainbow trout that can reach up to 3 kg (6.5 lbs). Fly-fishing or spincasting along the deep holes found in the northern portion of the lake is your best bet for results. Rustic camping and a cartop boat launch are available at the lake. Check the regulations for special retention limits before heading out.

Lorne Lake (Map 2/C1)

This 40 hectare (99 ac) hike-in lake has reasonably good fishing for rainbow that average 20-25 cm (8-10 in). The rainbow are caught by spincasting, by fly-fishing or with bait.

Lost Horse Lake (Map 33/B2)

You can find this lake via a branch road off the Taweel Lake Forest Service Road north of Highway 24. Fishing is good at times for average sized rainbow trout. There are ample shoal areas around the lake ideal for insect activity and perfect for fly anglers and spincasters to work their magic. A recreation site if found on the north end of the lake.

Lundbom Lake (Map 14/G4)

Boasting trout up to (and over) 5 kg (12 lbs), this popular 47 hectare (116 ac) lake is stocked annually with rainbow and offers a large recreation site. Trolling is the primary fishing method although fly anglers do well in late June by matching the sedge hatch or by using a scud or leech pattern in the fall. There are special retention and other restrictions here.

Lupin Lakes (Map 33/B6)

Better known for their canoeing than their fishing, this series of mountain lakes strung out along Caverhill Creek offers rainbow up to 1 kg (2 lbs) by spincasting or fly-fishing. Fishing remains fairly active throughout the ice-free season.

Lynn Lake (Map 33/B3)

Lynn Lake can be found by an access road that branches south off Highway 24. The clear, shallow lake contains stocked rainbow and naturally reproducing brook trout. Try fly-fishing near the small creek mouths or trolling the lake. The lake is closed to ice fishing.

Mab Lake (Map 14/G2)

Good fishing for rainbow trout is offered in the spring and fall. The access to this 25 hectare (62 ac) lake is via two-wheel drive road north of Nicola Lake.

Mabel Lake (Map 25/C5–E1)

This large lake is found east of Enderby and is primarily a trolling lake for the large rainbow, which reach 4 kg (9 lbs). You will also find small kokanee, large lake trout (up to 7 kg/15 lbs) and large Dolly Varden (up to 4 kg/9 lbs). Unique to this lake is the fact big Chinook salmon (over 7 kg/15 lbs) can be found holding near the river mouth and can be caught with trolling salmon gear. The lake has full facilities including several recreation sites with boat launches and a nice resort. A provincial park is located at the south end of the lake. Check the regulations for special restrictions.

MacDonald Lake (Map 16/A7)

MacDonald Lake has a good population of small rainbow trout, which are stocked regularly. The high elevation lake can be fished with success any time during the ice-free season with bait, a fly or spinner. The 5 hectare (12 ac) lake is found next to Brenda Lake and a lakeshore recreation site.

Machete Lake (Map 32/F5)

Machete Lake is a 440 hectare (1,087 ac) lake, 18 km south of Highway 24 on Machete Lake Road. It is a popular recreation lake, complete with camping, resorts, picnicking and boat launching facilities. It has fair fishing for stocked rainbow trout and kokanee up to 1 kg (2 lbs). The preferred methods of fishing are by trolling (lures or leech patterns) and ice fishing. Check the regulations before heading out.

Madden Lake (Map 3/G4)

Madden Lake has a fair population of stocked rainbow trout up to 2 kg (4.5 lbs) and a few brook trout. The 11 hectare (27 ac) lake is best fished in the spring or fall by trolling or fly-fishing. The lake has camping and cartop boat launch facilities at a recreation site. Access to this lake is by two-wheel drive road (Fairview Road) northwest of Oliver.

Mahood Lake (Map 37/A4–C3)

This big, 3,311 hectare (8,181 ac) lake forms the southwest boundary of Wells Gray Park. The lake offers fishing for rainbow trout up to 4.5 kg (10 lbs) and lake trout up to 9 kg (20 lbs) along with the odd kokanee. Fishing can be steady right from May to October. Ice fishing is also possible. Trolling is the most productive angling method used; for fly anglers and spincasters, try near one of the creek or river mouths. There is a campground with a boat launch at the western end as well as a number of boat access lakeshore campsites on the lake. Check the regulations for special restrictions.

Maloney Lake (Map 11/B5)

Maloney Lake is a hike-in lake in the ever-popular Christian Valley. This beautiful lake requires a 3.5 km hike from Cup Lake that can be extended to loop past Clark Lake to the road southwest of Lassie Lake. Maloney Lake has a recreation site and reasonably good fishing for rainbow averaging 20-25 cm (8-10 in). The lake is best fished from a float tube using flies, although spincasting also works.

Mamit Lake (Map 21/D7)

Accessed by paved road (Highway 97C) between Logan Lake and Merritt, Mamit has a cartop boat launch and fair fishing during the open water season for rainbow trout reaching 1.5 kg (3 lbs). Your best bet is to try trolling the lake, although fly-fishing during the spring mayfly hatch or with an attractor type pattern through the spring or fall can be effective. This a popular ice fishing hole with both rainbow and burbot (they must be released) providing decent results.

Mara Lake (Map 24/F1–30/G6)

Mara Lake is more of a recreational lake than a fishing lake, although it does offer rainbow, lake trout and Dolly Varden that can reach 2 kg (4.5 lbs). Kokanee fishing can be fairly good from July to October. The lake offers full facilities including a resort and a provincial park. It is easily accessed by Highway 97A south of Sicamous.

Marquart Lake (Map 14/F5)

This 23 hectare (57 ac) lake has big rainbow and brook trout (rumoured to reach 3.5 kg/8 lbs) that can be caught any time of the year, including winter. The lake offers a recreation site and is stocked annually with both species.

Marshall Lake [Providence Lake] (Map 5/G5)

Also known as Providence Lake, Marshall Lake is a small 3 hectare (7.4 ac) man-made lake created by Granby Mines. The easily accessed lake sits near the Phoenix Mountain Ski Area east of Greenwood and offers a recreation site with a cartop boat launch and a series of good trails to explore. The lake also has a reasonably good population of small stocked rainbow. Note that the dam is being deactivated and the lake will be lowered to original pond levels. This may affect the fishing and camping opportunities. Check the regulations for boating restrictions.

Matthews Lake (Map 5/C5)

Matthews Lake is a small 5 hectare (12 ac) mountain lake, set beneath Mount Davis. The lake offers fairly good fishing for small rainbow, primarily by fly-fishing, bait fishing or spincasting. There is a quiet recreation site on the lakeshore that can be accessed by a two-wheel drive forestry road.

Maury Lake (Map 37/C4)

Maury Lake offers good fishing for rainbow trout that can reach 1 kg (2 lbs). Fly-fishing and trolling can both be productive. There is a recreation site and boat launch available at the lake.

McCaffery Lake (Map 8/A5)

This small lake offers a surprisingly good fishery for small rainbow and given its easy access, it is a good choice for a family outing. The lake also produces well during ice fishing season for the brook trout that inhabit the lake. An undeveloped boat launch and picnic area is available at the lake, which is stocked annually with rainbow.

McCall Lakes (Map 9/D2)

Located in the hills west of Peachland, the McCall Lakes offer a nice fishery not too far from town. Offering eastern brook trout and stocked rainbow trout, it is possible to launch small cartop boats or a canoe at the bigger of the two lakes.

McConnell Lake (Map 22/B4)

Next to Lac Le Jeune Road, this high elevation lake has fairly good fishing for rainbow trout throughout the ice-free season. It is stocked annually and is best trolled (leech pattern or lake troll) or fly-fished (Doc Spratley, Woolly Bugger or dragonfly pattern).

McCormick and Twin Lakes (Map 43/A7)

McCormick is a tiny 2.9 hectare (7.2 ac) lake found just west of Blue River along the North Blue Forest Service Road. The lake offers a nice little fishery for stocked rainbow trout. Nearby Twin Lake also offers stocked rainbow.

McDougall Lake (Map 41/G5)

McDougall Lake is a secluded lake found within the heart of Wells Gray Provincial Park. It is an arduous journey to reach this lake, involving a long paddle with some difficult portages followed by a long hike. Once you reach the lake, you will be rewarded with pristine scenery and good fishing for some nice sized rainbow trout.

McGillvray Lake (Map 29/C6)

The dark, nutrient rich water means fishing can be great for rainbow reaching over 1.5 kg (3 lbs) in size. Fly anglers can try caddisflies (in early spring), chironomids, May and damsel nymphs and leeches around the shoals. A slow troll with a Deadly Dick or Flatfish can also be effective. The lake sees a lot of traffic as it is has good road access and a recreation site. A bait ban and gear restrictions are in effect on the lake.

McGlashan Lake (Map 22/G5)

This small lake contains stocked brook trout that grow up to 2 kg (4.5 lbs). The best time to fish is in the fall and during ice fishing season. Spincasting and trolling are the most productive methods of fishing although fly anglers will find success when casting towards one of the many weed beds that line the lake.

McLean Clan Lake (Map 4/B1)

This small lake located on the southeastern slope of Mount Christine, east of Okanagan Falls, is stocked on a regular basis with rainbow trout. Access requires bushwhacking in from a side road off the Okanagan Falls Forest Service Road; this discourages many anglers.

McTaggart Lakes (Map 33/E5)

On the Dunn Lake Road, these two small lakes (about 18 hectares/45 ac in size each) offer some reasonably good fishing for rainbow trout that can reach 1 kg (2 lbs). The lakes are best fished in the spring and fall.

Meadow Lake (Map 17/E6)

Meadow Lake requires a short hike from Victor Main or a longer hike from Postill Lake to the north. Anglers can expect good numbers of rainbow up to 1.8 kg (4 lbs) frequently taken by fly-fishing or spincasting. Check the regulations for special retention limits and other restrictions.

Meadow Lake (Map 33/B2)

Meadow Lake is one of the many pothole lakes found northwest of Little Fort, off Taweel Lake Forest Service Road. Fishing in the lake is generally fair for small rainbow that can reach 1.5 kg (3 lbs) on occasion. The shallow lake heats up considerably during the summer, reducing angling success at that time. There is a private fishing camp located on the lake.

Minnie and Stoney Lakes (Map 15/B5)

Although public lakes, access into Minnie and nearby Stoney Lake lies in the Douglas Lake Ranch east of Merritt. The ranch has gated and marked the access private, but officially the lakes and Stoney Lake Road, which runs along the north shore of the lake, are public. Both lakes offer good trout fishing if you can get to them legally.

Missezula Lake (Map 8/A2)

Missezula is a large, popular lake found in the hills north of Princeton. The lake has stocked rainbow and is occasionally stocked with brook trout up to 2 kg (4.5 lbs). There are also a few kokanee. There is a recreation site at the north end of the lake, which is considered a good trolling lake. Fly-fishing and spincasting can also work around one of the many inlet streams.

Mission Lake (Map 18/C5)

Mission Lake is a high elevation lake, accessed by a long trail. It is 6 km from Fish Hawk Lake, which in turn requires a four-wheel drive vehicle to access, so the fishing is fairly good for rainbow trout up to 1.5 kg (3 lbs) in size.

Moira Lake (Map 37/D5)

Easily accessed off a main haul logging road, Moira Lake offers quite good fishing throughout the ice-free season for rainbow trout up to 1 kg (2 lbs). Fly anglers can do exceptionally well at the lake, although if you troll a small spoon or spinner you should find some success. For overnight campers, there is a recreation site with an established boat launch available.

Momich Lakes (Map 35/A5)

A series of scenic valley lakes have been protected by the creation of the Momich Lakes Park. In addition to camping and boat launches, the park makes a fine canoeing or fishing destination. The big lake is best trolled for rainbow trout and Dolly Vardens, which grow up to 2 kg (4.5 lbs). The fish are somewhat difficult to catch, especially in the summer. Little Momich Lake can be reached by canoe from the main lake, while the Third Momich Lake is best reached by road.

Monte Lake (Map 23/C5)

Monte Lake is located next to a quiet stretch of Highway 97. Trolling for the stocked rainbow trout up to 2 kg (4.5 lbs) is your best bet, but you will also find stocked kokanee here. Facilities include a decent boat launch at the north end, private campgrounds and an undeveloped provincial park with a nice beach.

Monticola Lake (Map 32/G2–33/A2)

Accessible via trail from a rough road off the Blowdown Forest Service Road, this 74 hectare (182 ac) lake offers some good fishing for rainbow trout that can reach 1.5 kg (3.5 lbs) in size. Trolling is a popular angling method on the lake. Rustic camping is available at the lake.

Moore Lake [Bullman Lake] (Map 17/D5)

Moore Lake is found north of Postill Lake. The stocked lake produces well for small rainbow trout during the early summer and into the fall despite the drawdown and winterkill problems. The lake has a lakeside recreation site.

Moose Lake (Map 27/G1)

This high elevation hike-in lake is reached by the Heller Lake Trail in Bonaparte Provincial Park. The lake offers fishing for rainbow trout.

Moose Lake (Map 32/B6)

Moose Lake is found off the south side of the Eagan-Bonaparte Forest Service Road (3700 Rd) to the west of the bigger Bonaparte Lake. The lake is home to a recreation site with boat launch and holds rainbow trout.

Moose Lake (Map 33/C2)

Moose Lake is a small, shallow lake and has rainbow trout. Success on the lake is best during the spring before the water warms. You can find Moose Lake off private Taweel Lake Road at the south end of the park.

Moose Lake (Map 37/B7)

Moose Lake, west of Clearwater off Road 10, is stocked on a regular basis with rainbow trout making for a nice fishery. A recreation site with boat launch is located at the 8 hectare (20 ac) lake for those wanting more than just a day trip.

Moose Lake (Map 47/F1–51/D7)

This big lake lies just off the south side of Highway 16 in Mount Robson Park. The lake offers fishing opportunities for rainbow trout, lake trout, kokanee, bull trout, whitefish and burbot. Trolling is the main angling method used on the lake. There is a boat launch at the eastern end of the lake.

Morgan Lake (Map 21/E1)

Morgan Lake was created just a few years ago as part of a watershed improvement program and has already become a local favourite. The low-elevation lake is one of the first to be ice-free in spring and is stocked with sterile rainbow, which grow big and fast. The lake is managed as a trophy catch and release (plus other restrictions) lake and fish have been caught in excess of 4.5 kg (10 lbs) here.

Morrissey Lake (Map 29/C6)

Morrissey Lake is just down the road from McGillvray Lake but is much smaller. Morrissey also has dark, nutrient rich waters and produces rainbow up to (and over) 1.5 kg (3 lbs). These fish can be caught by a slow troll or fly-fishing. There is a small recreation site as well as a bait ban and gear restrictions on the lake.

Mowich Lake (Map 27/B4)

The 29 hectare (72 ac) Mowich Lake has fair fishing for small rainbow and kokanee best caught by fly-fishing or spincasting throughout the spring and fall. There is a resort on the north end of the lake.

Mulholland Lake (Map 33/C6)

This lake is accessed by a short hike and has rainbow up to 1 kg (2 lbs). The preferred methods of fishing are bait and bobber, fly-fishing and spincasting throughout the spring or fall.

Murphy Lakes (Map 7/C6)

A short hike off the Lawson-Britton Creek Forest Service Road leads to these popular mountain lakes, which offer rustic campsites. Both lakes have rainbow and brook trout, although rumours are the eastern lake has the bigger fish. The lakes are stocked regularly with rainbow and receive heavy fishing pressure.

Murray Lake (Map 7/B2)

Murray Lake is accessed off the Coquihalla Highway (Hwy 5). There are two recreation sites and a boat launch here. Trolling and fly-fishing with dragonflies, leeches or shrimp patterns are your best bet for the stocked rainbow.

Murtle Lake (Map 38/D1–42/D5)

Murtle Lake is a big lake that provides access to the eastern region of Wells Gray Provincial Park. It can be reached by a 2.5 km portage from the Blue River Forest Service Road. Murtle Lake is a beautifully scenic interior lake that offers good fishing for rainbow trout that are best caught by trolling. Fly-fishing or spincasting near any one of the many streams that enter the lake is also a good bet for success. Check the regulations for special restrictions.

Naramata Lake (Map 10/A4)

Located in the hills above Naramata along the deactivated Elinor Lake Forest Service Road, this small lake is stocked annually with rainbow trout. Most anglers access this lake from the north.

Needa Lake (Map 32/D2)

Windy Mountain Forest Service Road (1900 Rd) provides good access to Needa Lake. The 188 hectare (464 ac) lake offers good fishing for average sized rainbow, mainly by trolling. A popular recreation site with a steep cartop boat launch provides a good base from which to explore the lake.

Nellies Lake (Map 35/F7)

This pretty, but small, lake is found southwest of the community of Seymour Arm. Anglers heading here will find rainbow trout that get stocked on occasion. Since the lake is a long way from a major community, it is well serviced by a small recreation site with four camping spots.

Nevertouch Lake (Map 11/D2)

On a two-wheel drive secondary road off the Kettle River Main, Nevertouch Lake has good fly-fishing for rainbow that can reach 1 kg (2 lbs). Although most of the fish are quite small, fishing remains reasonably good throughout the summer. The lake has a recreation site and is stocked annually.

Next Lake (Map 33/A3)

Next Lake is often confused with the larger Club Lake to the east since they are actually connected by a small shallow channel. The rainbow in Next Lake are smaller, but it is a better fly-fishing lake.

Nickel Plate Lake (Map 3/B1)

This 80 hectare (200 ac) lake is located below Apex Mountain and is home to a campsite and a well-developed trail system. Fishing is fairly good for small stocked rainbow throughout the summer months. Adventurous anglers may be interested in the small lake, which is about a 15-minute walk to the north. This lake holds small rainbow that readily take most offerings.

Nicklen Lake (Map 17/G3)

Nicklen Lake has wild rainbow up to 2 kg (4.5 lbs). In summer the lake suffers from drawdown. The lake is found along a good two-wheel drive road and offers camping and a cartop boat launch at the recreation site.

Nicola Lake (Map 14/F3–15/B2)

This large 6,215 hectare (15,350 ac) lake offers fair fishing for small kokanee and rainbow trout. There are rumours of trout reaching 9 kg (20 lbs). Trolling a small spin-n-glo or a Willow Leaf with bait (maggots or worm) in June to mid-July is most effective for the kokanee. In the winter, burbot fishing can be very effective, but they are catch and release. The popular recreational lake is home to a provincial park and is easily accessed by paved road.

Nicomen Lake (Map 1/D4)

As the crow flies, Nicomen Lake is 10 km from the nearest road, but the hike-in is nearly double that, along the Hope Pass Trail/Grainger Creek Trail. Given the tough access, you can usually expect some good fishing for small rainbow. A small, scenic tenting site is located at the lake.

Niskonlith Lake (Map 29/C7)

East of the South Thompson River, this lake offers fair fishing for small rainbow and kokanee. Rainbow trout are stocked on occasion. For fly anglers, good hatches are offered in the spring and summer with the best place to fish being around the island. There are boat launching and camping facilities on the west side of the 370 hectare (915 ac) lake, which is easily accessed off the Niskonlith Lake Road. Check the regulations for boating restrictions.

Noble Lake (Map 28/B6)

Noble Lake is located on a four-wheel drive access road off the Dairy Creek Road north of Isobel. It is a small, 8 hectare (20 ac) lake with fairly good fishing for stocked rainbow that can reach 1 kg (2 lbs) in size. For fly anglers, try a dragonfly pattern, Woolly Bugger or Doc Spratley.

Noreen Lake (Map 25/C1)

This 5 hectare (12 ac) lake is located on a four-wheel drive road north of the Kingfisher resort area of Mabel Lake. The lake has a recreation site with a campground and cartop boat launch and is best fished in the spring or fall. Fly-fishing and spincasting often produce small rainbow.

North Barrière Lake (Map 34/B5)

North Barrière Lake produces large dollies, rainbow and lake trout (up to 4 kg/9 lbs) as well as some smaller kokanee, whitefish and lingcod. The preferred method of fishing is trolling with the spring and fall being the best times. There is a recreation site on the north side of the lake.

Nugget Lake (Map 23/C7)

Nugget Lake is managed as a quality fishery ideal for the fly angler. It covers 8 hectares (20 ac) and is located by four-wheel drive road south of Jimmy Lake. The stocked rainbow can grow to over 1.5 kg (3 lbs). Check the regulations before heading out.

Okanagan Lake (Maps 9, 10, 16, 17, 24)

This huge recreational lake is known more for its beaches and water sports than its fishing. It does hold quite a few rainbow and the kokanee have started to rebound in recent years. Whitefish can be fun to catch south of Bear Creek Park, as are carp. Anglers looking for trout that on occasion reach over 5 kg (11 lbs) will find better luck in October to March using a plug, spoon or Bucktail. The best areas are near Fintry, Okanagan Mountain Park, Okanagan Centre or Rattlesnake Island. During the summer, smaller trout and kokanee can be caught on lake trolls. There is no shortage of places to access the lake as several resorts, campsites and provincial parks line the lake. Be sure to check the regulations for current limits.

Orian Lake (Map 6/F3)

This higher elevation, 2.1 hectare (5.2 ac) lake is found along the western side of the Bonanza Forest Service Road. Anglers here will find fishing for rainbow that are stocked on a regular basis.

Osoyoos Lake (Map 4/A6–B7)

This is Canada's warmest lake with average summer temperatures at around 24°C. In the spring, trolling can often be successful for large rainbow trout (up to 5 kg/11 lbs), while a few kokanee can also be found. Later in the year, there is an opportunity to spincast for largemouth or smallmouth bass, black crappie, perch or carp. Some large bass are caught here. Check the regulations for special retention limits and other restrictions.

Osprey Lake (Map 8/F3)

Osprey Lake is the heart of the three lakes area and is home to nice campsite. The lake offers a reasonably good fishery with stocked rainbow that can grow up to 2 kg (4.5 lbs) in size. The lake is best trolled, although fishing from shore can be productive. Check the regulations for engine power restrictions.

Otter Lake (Map 24/C6)

Found north of Vernon, this lake is easily accessed off the Otter Lake Road. Fishing for rainbow and Dolly Varden is slow.

Otter Lake (Map 7/E5)

This lake is a popular recreation lake with private cabins, camping, a boat launch and a beach at the Otter Lake Provincial Park. A good two-wheel drive road skirts the west side of the lake, while the Kettle Valley Railway runs along the east side. The lake was stocked in the past with brook trout, but currently rainbow and kokanee are stocked to bolster the fishery. There are also some lake trout and whitefish available. The best method of fishing is trolling during the early spring or late fall as the lake warms due to the low elevation.

Oyama Lake (Map 17/D3)

Oyama Lake has surprisingly large rainbow trout that can reach 3 kg (6 lbs) is size despite the relatively heavy fishing pressure and the fact the fish are stocked. The lake is accessed by a four-wheel drive road and is best fished in the spring or fall with fly-fishing around the many islands being the preferred method. The spring caddisfly hatch is the best time.

Paradise Lake (Map 15/D7)

Paradise Lake is the largest in a cluster of lakes north of the Okanagan Connector (Hwy 97C). It offers many small rainbow trout easily caught by fly-fishing or trolling during the open water season. In fact, the limit of eight fish attests to how good the fishing can be. The high elevation lake has dark, nutrient rich water making an attractor type lure or fly your best bet. There is a small campsite, cartop boat launch and a resort on the lake.

Paska Lake (Map 21/F5)

Paska Lake has rainbow up to 1 kg (2 lbs) that are caught throughout the spring and fall by trolling a Flatfish or leech pattern or by casting a damselfly or attractor fly. The lake has a cartop boat launch and camping facilities at a small recreation site on its northwest shore. Check the regulations for boating restrictions.

Pass Lake (Map 28/A6)

Pass Lake is managed as a quality fishery and there are many restrictions that help grow the stocked rainbow trout to over 4 kg (8 lbs). Of course, the bigger fish are notoriously hard to catch. Try matching the early spring chironomid or mayfly hatches and casting near the northeastern shoals. Later in the spring or into the fall, leech, dragonfly, sedge or caddisfly patterns work. A recreation site offers a nice place to camp and launch a small boat. Check the regulations before fishing here.

Kokanee Stocking

	MAP	BROOK TROUT	BURBOT	KOKANEE	LAKE TROUT	RAINBOW TROUT	OTHER
Bridge Lake	32/D3		•	•	•	•	•
Deadman Lake	27/C2			•		•	
Deka Lake	32/C1			•	•	•	
Dutch Lake	33/F1	•		•		•	
Machete Lake	32/F5			•		•	
Monte Lake	23/C5			•		•	
Otter Lake	7/E5	•		•	•	•	•
Paul Lake	22/F1			•		•	
Stump Lake	22/C7			•		•	
Sulphorous Lake	32/C1	•	•	•	•	•	
Twin Lakes	3/E2			•		•	•
Yellow Lake	3/E2			•		•	

Pasulko Lake (Map 20/A6)
This lake holds rainbow that are fairly easy to catch during the spring and fall. The lake has a cartop boat launch and is easily accessed.

Patrick Lake (Map 33/B5)
Patrick Lake provides good fishing throughout the summer months for rainbow up to 1 kg (2 lbs) by spincasting or fly-fishing. The lake covers an area of 15 hectares (37 ac) and is accessed off the Patrick Creek Forest Service Road.

Paul Lake (Map 22/F1)
This large lake offers a provincial park with camping and picnicking facilities as well as a boat launch. The lake is stocked annually with rainbow that can reach 2.5 kg (5 lbs) and are best caught by trolling near the shoals in the spring or fall. It is a renowned mayfly lake but chironomids, caddisflies and even minnow patterns (in August) can produce at other times in the year. Ice fishing is possible. Recently kokanee have been stocked into the lake.

Peachland Lake (Map 9/B1)
This popular lake experiences heavy fishing pressure, resulting in slow fishing for generally small rainbow trout. A stocking program is in effect to help increase the population of rainbow and counteract the coarse fish problem. The 110 hectare (272 ac) lake is found along a good two-wheel drive road (Peachland Forest Service Road). Your best bet is to troll the lake in the spring or fall, as drawdown is a problem in the summer. A large open recreation site lines the lake.

Pefferle Lake (Map 15/F5)
Pefferle Lake contains rainbow trout that can reach 1.5 kg (3 lbs). Access is from the northwest shore of Pennask Lake via boat or along a four-wheel drive spur road off the Pennask Lake Forest Service Road. Fishing is usually good in the spring and fall due to the limited access.

Pendleton Lakes (Map 37/A3)
Pendleton Lakes lie north of the much bigger Mahood Lake and can be reached via the rough Pendleton Lake Forest Service Road (7100 Road); a four-wheel drive vehicle is recommended. The main lake is inhabited by generally small rainbow trout, although they can reach up to 1.5 kg (3.5 lbs) on occasion. A good place to try is off one of the small islands found on the lake. There is a recreation site and a steep boat launch here.

Pennask Lake (Map 15/F6)
The largest lake in the immediate area, Pennask Lake produces brood stock to help stock many of the lakes in the province with feisty rainbow trout. Fishing here is limited to fly-fishing only but there are a lot of small rainbow in the lake. The most consistent fly patterns seem to be shrimp or mayflies although many others work. The high elevation lake is accessed by rough roads and has a members only resort as well as rustic camping and boat launch facilities. Several smaller lakes in the area also offer good fishing. Check the regulations for special restrictions.

Peter Hope Lake (Map 15/D1)
Peter Hope Lake has succumbed to development which may affect the once renowned fishery. Regardless, the lake has numerous shoals and sunken islands that hold large rainbow (rumours of 5 kg/10 lb fish circulate). However, you should be prepared for many long hours before you will be able to hook one of these beauties. In addition to the private cabins, there is a popular recreation site on the lake. Watch for bait and ice fishing bans.

Peter [Pete's] and Moore Lakes (Map 5/A2)
These small lakes (Peter at 7 hectares and Moore at 6) offer reasonably good fishing for small stocked rainbow in spring and fall. The lake offers a treed recreation site with boat launch. Check the regulations for special restrictions and retention limits before heading out.

Phillips Lake (Map 29/F7)
Phillips Lake is shallow and warms quickly in the summer. The lake was closed for a time due to an infestation of perch, but has recovered and now is being stocked with both eastern brook trout and rainbow.

Phinetta Lake (Map 32/G4)
Accessed via Eakin Creek Road off Highway 24, this 23 hectare (56 ac) lake has many shoals ideal for insect growth. It is a productive fly-fishing lake for stocked rainbow trout that is home to a small recreation site with a boat launch.

Pillar Lake (Map 23/E3)
Named for the dramatic basalt Pillars to the east of the lake, Pillar Lake offers good fly-fishing, bait fishing and trolling in May and June for rainbow that can reach 1 kg (2 lbs) in size. Fly anglers should try casting a damselfly or dragonfly pattern during the spring hatches towards the shoals that are found at the north end of the lake. The lake has a private resort as well as a recreation site with a boat launch and camping. The access to the lake is via the Chase-Falkland Road (good two-wheel drive access). There are special boating regulations here.

Pimainus Lakes (Map 20/G6)
Rainbow trout up to 1 kg (2 lbs) in size are found in this 40 hectare (99 ac) lake. Most fishermen fly-fish or troll in the spring or fall. The access to the lake is via four-wheel drive road off the Pimainus Lake Road. When you reach the lake, you will find a cartop boat launch, campground and a resort.

Pinantan Lake (Map 22/G1)
This 68 hectare (168 ac) lake on the Paul Lake Road is surrounded by private homes and has a resort with camping. Regardless, the lake is still fairly good for fishing for rainbow that can reach 2 kg (4.5 lbs). Trolling is the mainstay of the deep lake, which is stocked annually to maintain the fishery. Fly-fishing is generally spotty, although it can produce around the shoals in the spring and fall with attractor patterns being the best bet. Electric motors only.

Pinaus & Area Lakes (Map 23/F6)
Accessed by the Pinaus Lake Road, there are several lakes that can be accessed in the area. The most popular is Pinaus Lake due, in no small part, to the camping facilities and a resort. The stocked lake offers fair fishing for rainbow trout on a troll or by fly-fishing. Trout in the 2-3 kg (6 lb) range are possible, although the windy lake is infested with perch and it is best to avoid the weedy areas if fishing for trout. Nearby Lady King Lake is also infested with perch, but is also stocked with rainbow. The lake still produces the odd large trout, but is being rehabilitated to re-establish this fishery. There is an ice fishing ban on the lake. Little Pinaus Lake is a 20 hectare (50 ac) lake east of Pinaus Lake proper that is a popular fishery with the kids since the trout are small and the perch are easy to catch. Shore fishing is possible here.

Placer Lake (Map 2/B6)
This small sub-alpine lake is located in the Placer Mountain Motorized Regulated Area and can be accessed by trail. The remote access results in very good fly-fishing for small wild rainbow.

Placid Lake (Map 37/E3)
This little lake can be reached by the Placid Lake Trail, which is found off the Clearwater Valley Road. The scenic lake provides fair to good fishing opportunities for small rainbow. Fly-fishing is popular, although spincasters can have good days on this lake. The better time to try this lake is in the early summer period. Check the regulations for special restrictions and retention limits before heading out.

Plateau Lake (Map 15/D1)
Plateau Lake is found via a four-wheel drive road east of Stump Lake and is home to a recreation site with cartop boat launch. You will find good fishing for rainbow up to 2 kg (4.5 lbs) by fly-fishing, spincasting or trolling a lake troll or leech patterns. For fly anglers, the sedge hatch in early July is the best time to cast your line. An annual stocking program is in effect to offset the winterkill problem. Check the regulations for restrictions.

Postill Lake (Map 17/E5)
Postill Lake forms the hub of a popular fishing destination northeast of Kelowna. Overnight visitors will find good access to the recreation site and the resort. The mixed population of brook trout and stocked rainbow are best caught in the spring or fall by trolling or spincasting. Also in the area are several hike-in lakes to explore.

Pothole Lake (Map 15/A6)

Despite its close proximity to the Coquihalla Connector (Hwy 97C), this small 4.3 hectare (10.6 ac) lake is rather difficult to access. The lake also supports good insect growth and as a result the fishing is good for rainbow up to 1.5 kg (3 lbs).

Pratt Lake (Map 22/G6)

The 30 hectare (74 ac) Pratt Lake is used extensively for irrigation purposes and drawdown can be extreme in hot, dry summers. It holds a fair number of rainbow that reach 1 kg (2 lbs). Casting a fly (leech or caddisfly pattern) or trolling (leech or Willow Leaf) can be effective. The lake has a cartop boat launch and has camping facilities.

Pressy Lake (Map 32/A5)

Located along the North Bonaparte Road, Pressy Lake is a long, thin 57 hectare (140 ac) lake with a recreation site providing camping and a boat launch. The 57 hectare (140 ac) lake offers a good fishery for rainbow trout up to 1 kg (2 lbs) in size throughout the spring and fall. Check the regulations for engine restrictions.

Procter Lake (Map 24/E6)

Procter Lake is found on a four-wheel drive road south of Armstrong and offers decent fishing for rainbow trout that can grow up to 1 kg (2 lbs). Try in the early summer or fall with a fly or small spinner.

Rampart Lake (Map 8/B4)

Rampart Lake is an isolated lake found off of Hombrie Mountain Road to the south. The lake has a recreation site and is stocked regularly with scrappy rainbow that can grow up to 2 kg (4.5 lbs). It is a fly-fishing only lake, with a good chironomid hatch in the spring. Check the regulations for special restrictions.

Ratnip Lake (Map 10/A3)

Ratnip Lake is found via a short hike off Chute Lake Road. There are lots of small rainbow trout at the 20 hectare (50 ac) lake and it shouldn't be too hard to hook one or two. The best time for fishing is during the spring and fall since the lake warms in the summer.

Raymer Lake (Map 16/C6)

Accessed by a four-wheel drive road off the Bear Creek Main, this lake has rainbow trout up to 1 kg (2 lbs). The high elevation lake is best fished in the early summer or fall by bait fishing, spincasting or fly-fishing.

Red Lake (Map 27/D6)

Red Lake is set below Carbine Hill on the Copper Creek Road north of Kamloops Lake. It has a fairly good population of stocked brook trout, which are best fished during the fall or during ice fishing season. Rainbow are also stocked annually. The lake has undergone recent amenity improvements, including a new boat launch and outhouses. This is a popular ice fishing destination, despite difficult access during the winter. There is an engine horsepower restriction here.

Reeves Lake (Map 24/F3)

Found in the Enderby Cliffs Protected Area, this is a small walk-in trout lake. The terrain around the lake is quite wet and marshy, although there are a couple dry spots to set up a tent or fish from.

Reflector Lake (Map 37/D6)

Reflector Lake can be found off Road 5 west of Clearwater. The lake holds a fair number of rainbow trout that can reach up to 2 kg (4.5 lbs) in size. Look for the shoal areas or creek mouths to focus your efforts. There is a recreation site at the lake complete with a cartop boat launch.

Renees Pothole (Map 14/G7)

Found on the southern side of Bates Road on the way to Kentucky-Alleyne Provincial Park, this tiny lake is stocked annually with rainbow. Camping can be found at the park down the road.

Reservoir Lake (Map 15/E7)

This lake offers good fishing throughout the open water season for rainbow trout up to 1 kg (2 lbs). Access leading to the recreation site with a cartop boat launch is by a four-wheel drive road. Leading from the recreation site are trails to nearby Skunk and Walker Lakes.

Rey Lake (Map 21/E7)

Good fishing for rainbow trout is offered at this 25 hectare (62 ac) lake. Access to the lake is via a two-wheel drive road east of Mamit Lake. Try trolling or fly-fishing for best success.

Rexford Lake (Map 28/E2)

Rexford Lake is located southwest of Barriere in the cluster of small lakes to the east of Westsyde Road. Although it is relatively close to a main road, a four-wheel drive vehicle may be preferred to reach this 3.8 hectare lake. It is possible to launch small cartoppers to get at the stocked rainbow trout.

Rickey Lake [Rick Lake], Larry and Clifford Lake [Cliff Lake] (Map 7/E3)

Youngberg Road runs east from the Coalmont Road and provides decent access to this trio of small lakes. There are nice campsites at Rickey and Clifford Lakes (sometimes called just Rick and Cliff Lake). Fishing is for generally small stocked rainbow that suffer from winter kill. The marshy area surrounding the lake helps produce plenty of insects for the fish and mosquitoes for the campers. Check the regulations for restrictions.

Ridge Lakes (Map 22/A6)

These two small lakes (they cover a total of 18 hectares/45 ac) are located on a four-wheel drive road south of Lac Le Jeune. The high elevation lakes offer good rainbow fishing beginning in the early summer and running into the fall. Since the water in the lakes is dark due to the organic content, leech and other attractor patterns work well for fly anglers. There are undeveloped camping and cartop boat launch facilities at both lakes.

Rioux Lake (Map 37/A6)

Rioux Lake is home to a fishing camp and offers good fishing for rainbow trout that can be found up to 2 kg (4.5 lbs). Trolling and fly-fishing are both effective angling methods for this lake.

Ripley Lake [Bear Lake] (Map 3/G3)

Ripley Lake is located north of Madden Lake on a spur road. The 6 hectare (15 ac) lake offers fairly good fishing for rainbow. It is stocked annually with rainbow and is subject to drawdown. A small recreation site offers camping and a cartop boat launch.

Robertson Lake (Map 7/F3)

This 9 hectare (22 ac) lake is located by four-wheel drive road to the west of Highway 5A. The lake is best fished during ice fishing season, although there is a decent fly-fishing or trolling fishery for stocked rainbow during the spring and fall. Electric motors only.

Roche Lake (Map 22/F5)

Roche Lake is a very popular lake, complete with a resort, campground and good rainbow fishing. Due to the clear waters, most anglers troll the 134 hectare (330 ac) lake for the stocked rainbow that can reach 3 kg (6 lbs). Die-hard fly anglers can do well by casting a line near the drop-offs or near one of the many shoals that line the lake. A good chironomid hatch occurs in the spring, while a smaller sedge hatch begins in early June. Check the regulations for special restrictions.

Rock Island Lake (Map 33/B2)

Rock Island Lake is a good fly-fishing lake that holds rainbow trout in the 1 kg (2 lb) size range. Try fishing the numerous shoals and along the deep pockets that are found around the lake. There is a rustic campsite at the southern end of the lake and a resort along the north shore. No ice fishing is allowed.

Roscoe Lake (Map 21/B7)

Roscoe Lake is a small 25 hectare (62 ac) lake located on a tough to find two-wheel drive road northwest of Chataway Lake. The lake is good for small rainbow in the spring and fall taken by fly-fishing or trolling, but do not expect any big fish. The lake can be easily fished from shore, as there is a trail around the entire lake that also leads to nearby Knight Lake. A cartop boat launch and campground are available at the south end of the lake.

Rosemond Lake (Map 24/F1)

Situated at the south end of Mara Lake, this small lake is also known by locals as Mud Lake. To access the forestry recreation site you will need to take the longer route that switchbacks east from the Rosemond Branch Forestry Road. Or you can take a canoe or rowboat under the railway trestle from Mara Lake; motorboats are not allowed. Fishing here is similar to Mara Lake, with rainbow, lake trout and Dolly Varden roaming the lakes.

Rose Valley Lake (Map 16/G7)

Found just north of West Kelowna, this 42 hectare (104 ac) lake is an important watershed in the area. In addition to a series of trails around the lake, anglers will find a nice local fishery for stocked rainbow. Those that want to carry in boats should note the electric motor only restriction.

FISHING ADVENTURES

Ross Moore Lake (Map 22/B5) 🛶

This lake has stocked rainbow trout up to 2 kg (4.5 lbs), which are caught either by trolling or fly-fishing. For best results, hit the chironomid hatch in the spring or try a leech or dragonfly pattern until early summer or again in the fall. There is a cartop boat launch as well as camping facilities at the lakeshore recreation site. A four-wheel drive vehicle is recommended to access the lake. Check the regulations for special restrictions and retention limits before heading out.

Ruth Lake (Map 17/E4) 🛶

Ruth Lake has good fishing for rainbow trout up to 2 kg (4.5 lbs), best caught in the spring or fall. The 10 hectare (25 ac) lake is stocked annually and has camping at a rustic, user-maintained recreation site. Access to this lake is by hiking from the Flyfish #2 Lake.

Sabiston Lake (Map 27/C6)

Sabiston Lake is located along the two-wheel drive Sabiston Creek Road and provides a fair fishery for brook trout during the fall or during ice fishing season. Unfortunately, the lake is subject to winterkill.

Salmon Lake (Map 16/A1) 🛶

You would think that Salmon Lake, found along the Douglas Lake Road would have salmon, wouldn't you? Instead, the lake is a popular fly-fishing destination for stocked rainbow trout. Most fly anglers cast towards the weed beds that line the west side of the lake using a damselfly (green), shrimp or chironomid pattern. Trolling a leech pattern is also fruitful. The lake is quite shallow and awfully silty so it warms significantly in the summer. Check the regulations for special restrictions, including no ice fishing.

Sandrift Lakes (Map 11/C4) 🛶

Sandrift Lakes are a trio of small, shallow lakes located along the Sandrift Forest Service Road (two-wheel drive access). They all offer good fishing for small stocked rainbow with the preferred method of fishing being fly-fishing. There are small recreation sites on Sandrift 2 & 3.

Saskum Lake (Map 34/D4)

Saskum Lake is home to nice sized rainbow trout, dollies and kokanee. The lake has a recreation site with a boat launch and campground at the south end.

Saul Lake (Map 27/F5)

This 25 hectare (62 ac) lake is located on the Sawmill Lake Forest Service Road and has a recreation site. It offers good fishing throughout the ice free season for small rainbow that are easily taken on a fly (shrimp or attractor patterns) or by a lake troll.

Saunier Lake (Map 4/F1)

On the good two-wheel drive Tuzo-Eugene Forest Service Road, this 5 hectare (12 ac) lake offers a small campsite with a cartop boat launch. Fly-fishing and bait fishing for small rainbow can be productive during the spring and fall.

Scot Lakes (Map 32/D7)

Accessed off the Egan-Bonaparte Forest Service Road (3700 Rd), Scot Lake covers 29 hectare (71 ac) and offers a recreation site with camping and a boat launch. There are nice shoals around the inflow and outflow streams where fly anglers can try their luck for rainbow trout. Nearby Little Scot Lake (to the northwest) also offers a recreation site with camping. The smaller lake is best fished in the spring and fall for average size rainbow.

Scott Lake (Map 28/C1)

This small, 30 hectare (74 ac), high elevation lake is located on a two-wheel drive road off of the Gorman Lake Road. The lake provides good fishing for rainbow trout up to 1 kg (2 lbs) throughout the spring and fall by fly-fishing. The lake has a recreation site.

Scuitto Lake (Map 22/F4)

Scuitto Lake is one of the larger, but shallower lakes in the Roche Lake area. The lake provides good fly-fishing for rainbow (last stocked in 2011) that are rumoured to grow up to 5 kg (10 lbs) in size. The lake has dark, nutrient-rich water, which warms in the summer resulting in an algae bloom and poor fishing. The late spring caddis hatch is the best time to fish. Most two-wheel drive vehicles should be able to access the lake from the north.

Sedge Lake [Bonanza Lake] (Map 33/B3) 🛶

This small lake is not named on our maps, although it lies between Long Island Lake and Emar Lake, south of Highway 24. The lake can be reached by portage from either lake and offers fair fishing for stocked rainbow trout up to 1 kg (2 lbs). Focus your efforts along the fringe area of the deep hole that is found in the middle of the lake.

Shadow Lake (Map 37/D1)

This Wells Gray Provincial Park lake is quite small and can be reached via a short trail off the east side of the Clearwater Valley Road. The lake is inhabited by numerous small rainbow trout that can be caught by fly-fishing or spincasting.

Shannon Lake (Map 9/F1) 🛶

Found in West Kelowna, Shannon Lake is stocked with rainbow and has been set aside as a kid's fishery. This lake is also a good ice fishing lake for perch and bass. The lake is accessed by the Shannon Lake Road and has a nice park to enjoy. Check the regulations for special retention limits and other restrictions.

Sharpe Lake (Map 32/C6) 🛶

Located northwest of Bonaparte Lake off the Eagan-Bonaparte Forest Service Road (3700 Rd), this 57 hectare (140 ac) lake is stocked annually with rainbow trout. There is a recreation site providing camping and a cartop boat launch along the west side of the lake.

Shea Lake (Map 7/E1) 🛶

The 25 hectare (62 ac) Shea Lake has a popular recreation site complete with a cartop boat launch. The lake offers good fishing for stocked rainbow with trolling being the preferred method.

Shelley Lake (Map 28/A3)

Shelley Lake is a hike-in lake along Deadman Trail. The high elevation 40 hectare (99 ac) lake offers good fishing for rainbow trout throughout the summer and fall.

Sheridan Lake (Map 32/B3) 🛶

One of the premier rainbow trout lakes in the province, Sheridan receives heavy fishing pressure year-round. The 1,659 hectare (4,099 ac) lake is highly productive due to an abundance of freshwater shrimp (scuds) that allow the rainbow trout to reach some impressive sizes (the odd trout over 8 kg/17 lb is landed). Trolling is the best method of fishing the lake with the spring chironomid hatch, the evening mayfly hatch in mid-June and the evening sedge hatch beginning in July being the best times to fish. In order to meet the needs of the large number of anglers using the lake, there are numerous resorts, boat launches, private residents and a nearby store with a café and a gas station. In addition, the lake is heavily supplemented, with nearly 300,000 rainbow stocked here each year.

Shumway Lake (Map 22/D4)

Home to an ice fishing derby in winter, this lake rests next to Highway 5A south of Kamloops. The long narrow lake is best trolled in summer for average size rainbow. Watch for the no fishing zone.

Shuswap Lake (Maps 24, 29, 30, 35)

This large, deep lake has 19 species of fish for the avid angler. The rainbow trout can reach 10 kg (22 lbs) with 2 kg (4 lb) fish being the norm rather than the exception. These big fish are more often caught in the winter and early spring when the surface water temperatures are cooler. Try trolling an Apex, Gypsy spoon or Lyman plug, working progressively deeper as the lake warms. There is also a fairly good population of kokanee as well as some lake trout (up to 10 kg/22 lbs) and Dolly Varden. Full facilities are found around the easily accessible parts of the lake. Anglers need special tags to keep any trout here; check the regulations for other restrictions.

Sicily Lake (Map 37/A5)

Located on Road 20 east of Clearwater, Sicily Lake is a good fly-fishing lake for rainbow trout up to 1.5 kg (3.5 lbs). Matching the hatch will provide the best results; however, popular fly patterns used on the lake include caddisflies, mayflies and leeches. Be sure to bring a floatation device, as the marshy shallow shoreline makes it all but impossible to have success from shore. There is a recreation site with a cartop boat launch available at the lake.

Sigalet Lake (Map 25/E6) 🛶

Off the Silver Hills Forest Service Road, this 25 hectare (62 ac) lake has stocked rainbow primarily caught by fly-fishing. There is also a small population of kokanee that occasionally are caught by trolling. There is no ice fishing allowed at the lake but there is a recreation site with a campground and cartop boat launch available.

Silence Lake (Map 38/C5) 🛶

Silence Lake makes a great weekend fishing destination due to its fairly remote location northwest of Clearwater along the Raft River Forest Service Road. Anglers will find rainbow trout that are stocked on a regular basis as well as a nice recreation site offering a boat launch and campsites.

Silver Lake (Map 9/C1)
Silver lake is stocked with rainbow trout, so it generally has good fishing for trout that grow up to 1 kg (2 lbs) in size. It is accessed by a good two-wheel drive road and has a small recreation site with a cartop boat launch and campground, in addition to a private forestry lodge. There is an electric motor only restriction on the lake.

Siwash Lake (Map 8/D1)
This 35 hectare (86 ac) lake has hit-and-miss fishing for rainbow trout up to 1 kg (2 lbs) with fly-fishing, spincasting or trolling in the spring or fall being your best bet. The high elevation lake has resort facilities and is accessed by a four-wheel drive road off the Whitehead Lake Road.

Six Mile Lake [Pat Lake] (Map 21/E1)
Located west of Cherry Creek not far from Highway 1 along the Six Mile Road, this small lake is known as Pat and Six Mile Lake. Regardless of the name, it is a popular destination for fly anglers looking for stocked rainbow trout. The watershed enhancements have improved the fishing, but anglers should be wary that the clear water makes the fish skittish and all the natural feed can make it hard to catch anything. However, the fish caught here are usually quite large. Check the regulations before heading out.

Skaha Lake (Map 3/G2–9/G7)
Located in the arid terrain of the southern Okanagan, this large lake is home to resorts, several campsites and beautiful beaches. The lake is best trolled for the kokanee and the big rainbow trout that are occasionally caught. There are also good numbers of smallmouth and largemouth bass, burbot and carp that can be caught by spincasting the shallow bays. Check the regulations for boating restrictions.

Skmana and Little Skmana Lakes (Map 29/D6)
Recently rehabilitated, these lakes have been restocked with rainbow and are ready for some great angling action. There is a recreation site at the lake, as well as a resort and trails to explore.

Skimikin Lake (Map 30/A7)
This 20 hectare (50 ac) lake has been rehabilitated to rid the waters of the illegally introduced yellow perch. Anglers should once again be able to catch stocked rainbow at this popular recreation lake that is easily accessed off the Skimikin Lake Road west of Tappen Valley. There is a recreation site and a host of trails in the area.

Skookum Lake (Map 27/C2)
This 19 hectare (47 ac) lake is best fished in the spring or fall for rainbow and kokanee. The shallow lake has some nice shoals for fly anglers to work, while trollers will want to stick to light gear.

Skunk Lake (Map 15/E7)
We are not sure if the name refers to the fishing or the little critters that frequent the area. Regardless, the 40 hectare (99 ac) Skunk Lake is a hike-in lake that is accessed by a 1.5 km trail from the Reservoir Lake Recreation Site. The lake was stocked in the past, but now the rainbow trout fishery is subject to possible winterkill.

Smith Lake (Map 33/C6)
This 20 hectare (50 ac) lake is reached by a short hike north of the Darlington Creek Forest Service Road. Fishing is best in the spring or fall for rainbow trout up to 1 kg (2 lbs).

Smith Lake (Map 37/F3)
Located within Wells Gray Provincial Park, just a short hike from Boundary Road, this small wilderness lake makes a great day trip for those seeking either rainbow or eastern brook trout. The rainbow trout population is supplemented with regular stocking. Check the regulations for special restrictions and retention limits before heading out.

Snake Lake (Map 28/E2)
This small, narrow lake is located southwest of Barriere in the cluster of four-wheel drive accessible lakes to the east of Westsyde Road. It is possible to launch small cartoppers to get at the stocked rainbow trout.

Snohoosh Lake (Map 27/C3)
This long, thin 91 hectare (225 ac) lake has a recreation site at the north end of the lake with a boat launch and camping as well as a private campground at the south end of the lake. The lake contains rainbow trout and kokanee.

Solco Lake (Map 4/D1)
Solco Lake is a good choice if you want to try your luck at a scenic, high elevation fly-fishing lake. The rainbow trout are usually small (20-25 cm/8-10 in), but offer good fly-fishing throughout the year.

South Lake (Map 17/D5)
South Lake is a short 500 metre hike from Postill Lake. The 25 hectare (62 ac) lake offers steady fishing for rainbow up to 1.8 kg (4 lbs) that can be taken on the fly during the open water season. Check the regulations for special retention limits and other restrictions.

South Barrière Lake (Map 34/C7)
The smallest of the three Barrière Lakes, this lake contains many rainbow trout caught by fly-fishing or trolling throughout the spring or fall.

Spa Lake (Map 24/A4)
There is a rustic campground with a cartop boat launch at this 77 hectare (190 ac) lake east of Bolean Lake. Spa Lake offers fair fishing from June through August given the elevation. Fly-fishing (wet or dry fly) can be quite productive for rainbow trout that can reach 1.5 kg (3 lbs) in size.

Spanish Lake (Map 24/A5)
Spanish Lake is a scenic 8 hectare (20 ac) lake with a fairly good fishery for stocked rainbow trout. It is best to fish the shallows anytime during the spring or fall. Access into the lake is difficult.

Spec Lakes (Map 17/F4)
Located in a mess of great fishing lakes southeast of Vernon, this trio of lakes offers fair fishing for rainbow. Lower Spec or Spec 1 is no longer stocked, but remains the most popular fishery for generally smaller fish. The productive lake produces an abundance of insects adding to the challenge. The middle Specs Lake is prone to winterkill and offers up the odd bigger fish, while the upper lake is the least fished. A canoe or pontoon boat to manoeuvre around in is recommended and camping is available.

Spukunne Lake (Map 8/C4)
This small lake offers some large rainbow trout (1 kg/2 lb fish are common) since the access is somewhat difficult and there is a one fish limit on the lake, as well as other restrictions. Access is limited by the washed out bridge on the Siwash Creek Road (at 8 km). The trout are stocked annually.

Square Lake (Map 23/F6)
Home to a recreation site, this 10 hectare (25 ac) lake has a steep drop-off and limited shoals making fishing a challenge here. It is too small to troll, so it is best to use long leaders if fly-fishing for the stocked rainbow trout. Check the regulations for special retention limits and other restrictions.

Stay safe. Life jackets and personal flotation devices are known to save lives; they only work when they are worn and fitted correctly.

St. Margaret Lake (Map 18/B6)
Set below Jubilee Mountain in Graystokes Park, this scenic 25 hectare (62 ac), hike-in lake has rainbow trout up to 1 kg (2 lbs). The high elevation lake is best fished in the summer and fall using a fly or small lure.

Stake Lake (Map 22/A5)
Stake Lake is a 25 hectare (62 ac) lake with a cartop boat launch north of Lac Le Juene. There are fair numbers of rainbow trout that grow up to 2 kg (4.5 lbs). The lake has an aerator to guard against winterkill and it is stocked fairly regularly. The mainstay of the lake is trolling, although fly anglers can produce using a caddisfly pattern in late May. For best results, cast near the shoals and drop-offs, which are easily seen through the clear water.

Star Lake (Map 33/D1)
Star Lake is located west of Clearwater off the Camp 2 Road. The lake contains good numbers of rainbow trout up to 1 kg (2 lbs). If you plan to fly-fish, try an attractor pattern such as a woolly bugger. There is a rustic camping area and boat launch along the north shore of the lake, but watch for the engine power restriction. The Star Lake Resort offers cabin and boats rentals. Ice fishing is popular here.

State Lake (Map 11/C5)
State Lake is a secluded, hike-in lake, tailor-made for fly-fishers. In fact, the lake is designated fly-fishing only. Check the regulations for other restrictions. The lake contains rainbow and is best fished in the early summer and in the fall. Remember, it is an uphill walk to get out.

Stevens Lakes (Map 38/B3–C2)

This series of seven lakes are located in the southern portion of Wells Gray Provincial Park. A very rough route from distant logging roads can be used to access the lakes. If you do reach the lakes, you can expect very good fishing for rainbow trout on the fly or by spincasting.

Stinking Lake (Map 26/G7)

This shallow lake offers good fishing for brook trout in the spring and fall. Try spincasting with bait and fishing near the bottom. Good access is provided along the Deadman-Cache Creek Road.

Strait Lake (Map 42/E6)

Strait Lake is another hike-in lake accessible form the much larger Murtle Lake. The hike is quite long, although you will be rewarded with fine scenery and good fishing for rainbow trout that can reach up to 1 kg (2 lbs) in size.

Streak Lake (Map 17/D3)

This 22 hectare (54 ac) lake is a long narrow lake with spotty fishing for small stocked rainbow trout. The lake is accessed off the King Edward Lake Road and is best fished in the spring or fall by trolling or fly-fishing.

Stringer Lake (Map 8/A4)

Located on a steep four-wheel drive road that winds up the grassy slopes to the east of Allison Lake, this lake has stocked rainbow trout that can grow up to 1.5 kg (3lbs) in size. There is a small recreation site on the lake.

Stukemapten Lake (Map 35/C5)

Easily accessed on the Humamilt Lake Road, this lake is usually trolled for rainbow trout that reach 2 kg (4.5 lbs), although recent reports indicate the lake is overrun with suckers. The best time to fish is in the late spring or early fall as the lake warms during the summer.

Stump Lake (Map 22/C7)

This large lake is located right next to Highway 5A and a rest area. It is known for being extremely difficult to fish because of wily fish and unpredictable winds that can play havoc with boaters. The lake does produce large rainbow (up to 5 kg/10 lbs), brook trout (up to 2 kg/4.5 lbs) and kokanee (up to 1 kg/2 lbs). Rainbow and kokanee are stocked heavily into the lake each year. Trolling is the mainstay of the lake, which offers picnic facilities, a boat launch and private camping facilities. Check the regulations before heading out.

Sugar Lake (Map 25/F6)

Sugar Lake has dollies that average 2-4 kg (4-9 lbs) as well as Gerrard-strain rainbow that reach similar sizes. These fish are best caught by trolling the lake, although fly-fishing can be successful if you concentrate on the river channel at the north end of the lake or the other creek/river inlets. The lake also has a plentiful supply of large whitefish and some kokanee and burbot. The developed lake offers everything from recreation campsites to a resort with cabins. Check the regulations for special restrictions.

Sulphorous Lake (Map 32/C1)

Squeezed between Hathaway and Deka Lakes, the clear waters of Sulphorous make for a great fishery. Anglers can find rainbow and lake trout, kokanee, and burbot. The rainbow and kokanee are stocked heavily each year. Covering 380 hectares (939 ac), the lake is a trolling lake as it is very deep. Spincasters and fly anglers can still work the near shore area including around the island at the middle of the lake or off the large shoal near the west end of the lake. For the kokanee a small silver lure is a good bet, while a silver spoon should get the rainbow interested. Traditionally there is a fishing derby held here in August. Check the regulations for the special restrictions and retention limits on lake trout here.

Summit Lake (Map 33/B4)

This Summit Lake is located south of Emar Lakes Provincial Park along rough secondary roads west of Thuya Lake. The 4.8 hectare (12 ac) lake is stocked with rainbow trout. Check the regulations before heading out.

Sunset Lake (Map 15/F7)

This small lake offers good fishing for rainbow trout that can grow up to 1 kg (2 lbs). The lake is reached by a well-developed trail, which allows you to pack a canoe into the lake. A trail also leads around the lake providing shore fishing opportunities, particularly on the western shores. It is best fished during the spring or fall by spincasting or fly-fishing.

Surprise Lake (Map 37/C6)

Surprise Lake lies to the west of the Grizzly Lakes and is accessible via the 156 spur road. It is recommended to travel the road with a high clearance vehicle. Fishing for rainbow trout is generally fair throughout the open water season.

Surrey Lake (Map 21/G7)

Surrey Lake is accessed by the rough Surrey Lake Forest Service Road, just off the Coquihalla Highway (Hwy 5). The lake has many small stocked rainbow trout that are best caught by fly-fishing with an attractor type pattern or by spincasting a small lure during the open water season. Ice fishing is also productive. Surrey Lake has a rustic resort offering cabins and campsites.

Sussex Lake (Map 21/G7)

Sussex Lake is accessed by the Surrey Lake Forest Service Road (two-wheel drive road), just off the Coquihalla Highway. Like Surrey Lake just up the road (and stream), the 20 hectare (50 ac) Sussex Lake has numerous small trout that rise quickly to a fly. There is a campsite.

Swan Lake (Map 24/D7)

Despite seeing regular stockings of spring catchable and yearling rainbow trout, the fishing at this 410 hectare (1,015 ac) lake is typically slow. There are also a few brook trout swimming in this shallow lake found north of Vernon. There is a commercial RV site as well as a hand launch area utilized by the local paddling club at this lake.

Ta Hoola Lake (Map 32/G2)

With recent road access, the fishing in Ta Hoola Lake is not as good as it once was. Regardless, there are still plenty of rainbow that grow up to 1 kg (2 lbs) in size.

Taurus Lake [Bull Lake] (Map 5/B2)

Taurus Lake is stocked with rainbow, which generally remain small. Trolling and fly-fishing both produce well on the reed-lined lake. There are two recreation sites on the lake and the one on the northwest corner has a cartop boat launch.

Taweel Lake (Map 33/B1)

This 440 hectare (1,087 ac) lake lies within the Taweel Park, but there are resorts that restrict road access. There is no public boat launch, but if you are interested in a resort-based fishing trip, the fishing can be good for rainbow trout up to 2 kg (4.5 lbs).

Taylor Lake [Gulliford Lake] (Map 3/F4)

This small lake, set below Orofino Mountain, is best fished by spincasting or fly-fishing for the many small stocked rainbow and brook trout that inhabit the lake. The lake is accessed by a rough four-wheel drive road off the Twin Lake Road. The lake suffers from drawdown in the summer so the spring and fall are the best times to fish. There is also excellent ice fishing for brook trout beginning in mid-December.

Teepee Lakes (Map 8/D2)

The Teepee Lakes, which comprise Friday, Saturday and Sunday Lakes, are a good choice if you want to stay at a rustic fishing resort and sample some good fishing. The lakes usually produce small rainbow throughout the spring and into the early summer by fly-fishing. A hike is required to reach Saturday and Sunday Lakes, while a private road from Osprey Lake leads to Friday Lake. Friday and Sunday lakes are stocked annually with rainbow. Check the regulations before heading out.

Telfer Lake (Map 35/A3)

Located just to the northeast of Adams Lake, Telfer Lake can be reached by the Gannett Lake Forest Service Road. The lake offers good fishing for rainbow trout that can reach 1 kg (2.5 lbs). The best areas to try are around the two creek mouths found along the lake.

Thalia Lake (Map 7/E3)

Thalia is one of the more popular lakes in the area. Perhaps it is the rumours of a 10 kg (22 lb) trophy being landed or maybe it is the fact that the lake holds good numbers of stocked rainbow. Regardless, trolling and fly-fishing (dragonfly nymph, leech or shrimp patterns) can be quite effective throughout the year.

Thelma Lake (Map 18/B4)

Thelma Lake lies within the Taweel Provincial Park and is best accessed by rough trail from Taweel Lake. The road access is gated. If you do find the lake, the fishing can be quite good for rainbow trout that can reach 1 kg (2 lbs). The trout are usually fairly aggressive and can be caught using flies, bait or lures.

Thirsk Lake (Map 8/G3)

This man-made lake offers fair fishing for small rainbow trout, primarily by trolling in the spring or fall. The lake has an electric motor only restriction and offers a recreation site with camping facilities. Drawdown is a problem in the summer.

Thone Lake (Map 11/D7)

Thone Lake a good fly-fishing lake for small stocked rainbow that is found about 14 km down the Thone Lake Forest Service Road, which leads east from the 27 km mark on the Christian Valley Road. There is a recreation site with a cartop boat launch on its western shores. Fly anglers can have a lot of fun during the late spring caddisfly hatch.

Three Mile Lake (Map 26/A3)

Found south of Clinton alongside Highway 97, this small lake has small brook trout. It is a deep-water lake that is best fished through the ice in winter. During the ice-free season, shore fishing is possible.

Three Valley Lake (Map 31/F4)

This 105 hectare (260 ac) lake lies right alongside the Trans-Canada Highway, just west of Revelstoke. The lake offers fair to slow fishing for rainbow, lake trout, bull trout, kokanee and whitefish mainly by trolling. It is one of the lowest elevation lakes in this region and fishing starts early, but slows down in the summer, picking up again in the fall. There is a good boat launch as well a resort and camping available at the roadside lake. Lake trout and Dolly Varden are catch-and-release.

Thuya Lakes (Map 33/B4)

Most anglers use the lodge as a base to explore this chain of lakes, which are found off the 2300 Road south of the Eakin Creek Road. There are a series of ATV accessible trails that connect the lakes, which hold nice sized rainbow trout. There is an electric motors only restriction on the main lake.

Tobe Lake (Map 32/G4)

An overgrown road/trail leads from the Machete Lake Road to the western shore of Tobe Lake. Due to the difficult access, few visitors make it into the remote lake. Fly-fishing can be good for rainbow trout that reach above average sizes.

Todd Lake (Map 22/G6)

Todd Lake is a narrow lake that lies alongside the two-wheel drive accessible Monte Creek-George Forest Service Road, just north of Pratt Lake. The lake holds fair numbers of rainbow trout.

Tortoise Lake (Map 32/G4)

Accessible by trail from Birch Lake, this lake offers the chance to catch a large rainbow in the 2 kg (4.5 lb) range. Unfortunately, squawfish compete for available food sources and the trout are not as plentiful as they could be. Casting off the rock bluff along the western shore is a good spot to try your luck. Alternatively, there are plenty of weed beds and shoals that line the lake.

Tranquille Lake (Map 27/G5)

Located on a rough two-wheel drive road north of Kamloops, this high elevation lake is considered a good option throughout the ice-free season for the abundant small rainbow and kokanee. Fly-fishing (Doc Spratley, leeches or small attractors), trolling (Willow Leaf and maggots) and spincasting (small lures) all work. There is a resort on the lake. Check the regulations for special retention limits.

Trapper Lake (Map 2/C7)

Trapper Lake is a great place to go if you want to try your luck at a small mountain lake. The challenging hike-in takes you through some rugged yet beautiful mountain country.

Trout Lake [Lusk Lake] (Map 3/E2)

This small lake is right next to Highway 3A and the brook trout that survive here can be quite picky. There is an electric motor only restriction.

Tsikwustum Lake (Map 35/C4)

This lake is found on the Rock Creek Main and covers an area of 123 hectares (305 ac). The lake holds rainbow trout up to 1 kg (2 lbs) that are best caught by trolling in the early summer or fall. It is possible to camp or launch small boats at the lake.

Tsintsunko Lake (Map 28/A3)

This high elevation lake offers reasonable fishing for small rainbow trout on a fly or by trolling throughout the summer months and into the fall. The lake is found along the Tsintsunko Lake Trail, which leads off the 4300 Road.

Tsotin Lake (Map 26/F7)

Tsotin Lake is located east of Cache Creek off the Deadman-Cache Creek Road. Anglers heading to this lake will find populations of eastern brook and rainbow trout. Both species are stocked on a regular basis to help sustain the fishery.

Tuc-El-Nuit Lake (Map 4/A4)

In the southern Okanagan, this warm water lake has good fishing for bass. The lake is easily accessed by a paved road and has an electric motor only restriction.

Tuloon Lake [Tintlhohtan Lake] (Map 33/C2)

This is another fine lake with a fishing lodge from which to base your efforts. The lake is inhabited by good numbers of rainbow trout that can reach 1 kg (2 lbs) in size. Dragonfly and leech fly patterns are two of the more popular fly patterns used at this lake.

Tumtum Lake (Map 39/D4)

Tumtum Lake can be found southeast of the town of Blue River via a long, dusty and often bumpy logging road. The lake is very deep and is best suited for trolling to help find the good-sized rainbow trout found in the lake. There are also a few Dolly Varden, but you may only retain one of these fish. The recreation sites are no longer maintained. There is a bait ban here.

Tunkwa Lake (Map 21/C3)

Perhaps the most popular fishery in the region, Tunkwa Lake has fair numbers of rainbow trout that can grow up to 3 kg (6 lbs). It is stocked heavily and is best fished using a fly or by trolling in the spring or fall since the lake is subject to drawdown in the summer. For patient fly anglers the early June damselfly hatch and the spring chironomid hatch are probably the best times to fish. Watch for the engine power restriction.

Tupper Lake (Map 21/C6)

Tupper Lake is accessed by a four-wheel drive road north of Cathaway Lake and offers good rainbow fishing throughout the spring and fall. It is best to use a fly (attractor type pattern) or by spincasting a small lure with bait for the stocked trout. There is a recreation site complete with a cartop boat launch (electric motors only) on the lake.

Twin Lakes (Map 3/E2)

Easily accessed off Highway 3A on the Twin Lake Road, this pair of lakes offers a decent fishery for brook trout as well as rainbow, kokanee and even carp. Nipit (the southern) Lake is stocked regularly with brook trout, rainbow trout and kokanee and is home to a resort and boat launch. Both lakes are best trolled, but are subject to an electric motor only restriction.

Tyner Lake (Map 14/B2)

Tyner Lake is found along a two-wheel drive road off the Skuhun-Pimainus Forest Service Road. It has a campsite with a cartop boat launch. The 24 hectare (59 ac) high elevation lake offers fairly good fishing for stocked rainbow trout that reach decent sizes. Fly-fishing and trolling are the preferred methods of fishing.

Vaseux Lake (Map 4/A3)

No powerboats are allowed on this 275 hectare (170 ac) lake on the Okanagan River south of Okanagan Falls. The lake is home to many species of fish, including kokanee, smallmouth and largemouth bass, rainbow trout, perch and carp. In fact, it is arguably the best largemouth bass fishing lakes in the province with lunkers that can top 4.5 kg (10 lbs). The scenic lake lies next to Highway 97 and offers a provincial park for camping. Check the regulations for special restrictions.

Fish love structure, mostly because it offers refuge from predators, cover for ambush feeding, great spots for resting against a current and temperature control in various climates.

Venables Lake (Map 20/D4)

This 40 hectare (99 ac) lake supports rainbow that can reach 1 kg (2 lbs). Trolling in the spring or fall is your best bet. A cartop boat launch is at the lake, which is accessed via the Venables Valley Road (two-wheel drive access).

Victor Lake (Map 31/G4)

Victor Lake is a blip on the Eagle River. It holds many of the same species as the Eagle River (cutthroat, lake and bull trout, kokanee and whitefish), but the prime reason most come here to fish is for the stocked rainbow. Victor Lake Park offers access to the lake and it is possible to hand launch a boat. Note that any lake or bull trout caught must be released.

Vidette Lake (Map 27/B2)

This 35 hectare (86 ac) lake is found at a relatively low elevation. Although this is a deep lake, fishing is still best during spring and fall. The lake is also a popular ice fishing location in winter. Both the small kokanee and average size rainbow are best caught by trolling (try deeper for the trout). There is a resort as well as a recreation site on this popular summer destination lake.

Walker Lake (Map 15/F7)

Walker Lake is a high elevation lake with good fishing for stocked rainbow throughout the open water season. There is no ice fishing allowed at the 16 hectare (40 ac) lake, which is accessed by a 1 km trail from the Reservoir Lake Recreation Site. Check the regulations for special restrictions and retention limits before heading out.

Wallensteen Lake (Map 23/G2)

Wallensteen Lake offers good fishing for small rainbow from June to October with August being the best time. Your best bet is to try fly-fishing during the evening using a float-tube, although trolling and bait fishing can also be productive. The 10 hectare (25 ac) lake has a recreation site with a campground and boat launch.

Walloper Lake (Map 22/A5)

Walloper Lake is a dark, nutrient rich lake with many small rainbow trout that can easily be caught. It is a popular family lake due to the good shore fishing opportunities. The lake is aerated in winter to prevent winterkill and ice fishing is not recommended. Picnicking, a wharf and boat launch facilities are found at the provincial park.

Wap Lake (Map 31/E5)

Wap Lake is accessed by a good two-wheel drive road south of Three Valley Gap. The lake is set in a scenic valley below the Monashee Mountains. The lake is best trolled for rainbow up to 2 kg (4.5 lbs) and Dolly Varden averaging 2-3 kg (4.5-6 lbs). For the dollies, it is best to fish in the fall, trolling a Krocodile or Flatfish. Casting from the old railbed next to the lake can also be successful. The lake offers a recreation site with a cartop boat launch.

Warren Lake (Map 29/A7)

Found southwest of Hyas Lake, Warren Lake has good fishing for stocked rainbow that occasionally reach 2-3 kg (4.5-6 lbs). There are private cabins on the 25 hectare (62 ac) lake and an option to launch a small boat. Check the regulations for special restrictions and retention limits before heading out.

West Badger Lake (Map 28/E3)

West Badger is located conveniently enough just a little west of Badger Lake, but it is best to access West Badger from its own access road that can be reached directly from Highway 5. Anglers heading to West Badger will find stocked rainbow trout.

West Lake (Map 37/D1)

Located within Wells Gray Provincial Park, this small wilderness lake receives regular stocking of rainbow trout. Anglers wanting to try their luck here will need to hike a short trail from the Clearwater Valley Road.

Whatshan Lake (Map 19/E3–E6)

A popular destination for local anglers, this relatively large (1,733 hectare/4,280 ac) lake is best trolled. Even though it is big and deep, the lake still produces better in spring for rainbow that grow up to 1.5 kg (3 lbs). The odd bull trout up to 5 kg (11 lbs) and even some small kokanee also roam the lake. There is camping, a boat launch and cabins on the lake.

White Lake (Map 30/C5)

White Lake is a popular recreational lake north of Salmon Arm. The lake offers fair to good fishing for stocked rainbow that can reach 6 kg (13 lbs). The primary method of fishing is trolling, although in the early spring and late fall, fly-fishing is particularly effective because of the many shoals that line the lake. Ice fishing is also effective using most bait beginning in late December after the ice thickens. Unfortunately, perch have been illegally introduced and may affect the trout fishery. Check the regulations for special restrictions.

Whitehead Lake (Map 8/F2)

Fishing here is pretty good for rainbow trout that can reach 1 kg (2 lbs). The high elevation lake is best trolled or fly-fished in the early summer, due to drawdown in the summer. The 50 hectare (125 ac) lake is stocked annually and has a recreation site with camping and boat launch facilities.

Whitewood Lake (Map 28/C3)

Located along the Jamieson Creek Forest Service Road (two-wheel drive access), the 15 hectare (37 ac) Whitewood Lake has a recreation site, complete with camping and boat launching facilities. The lake is fairly good for trolling and fly-fishing for rainbow that can reach 1 kg (2 lbs).

Wilgress Lake (Map 6/A4)

This small, popular lake rests alongside Highway 3 near a nice rest area. Despite constant fishing pressure throughout the entire year, the lake still produces well for small rainbow and brook trout by trolling or fly-fishing. Ice fishing can be productive at times. Rainbow are stocked annually.

Williamson Lake (Map 5/D2)

Williamson Lake is a small lake found at the end of the Sebastian Creek Forest Service Road and a short hike. The lake offers good fishing for stocked rainbow that can reach 2 kg (4.5 lbs) in size. This is a high elevation lake, and, like most of the lakes in and around the Christian Valley, has a small recreation site to camp at.

Willow Lake (Map 32/G3)

Willow Lake offers a good fishery for rainbow trout. The lake is best fished beginning in late May to early June. It is deep enough to troll.

Willowgrouse Lake (Map 28/A2)

Willowgrouse provides good fishing for rainbow up to 1 kg (2 lbs) by fly-fishing or spincasting. It is best fished in the spring and fall. The lake can be accessed along the Tuwut Lake Canoe Route or by the Masters Sub-Alpine Trek.

Wilma Lake (Map 17/E3)

Wilma is a small 11 hectare (27 ac) lake, located on a short trail off the Dee Lake Road. The lake is high enough to support fair fishing for small rainbow trout throughout the ice-free season.

Windy Lake (Map 28/A2)

Windy Lake is located just outside of Bonaparte Provincial Park on the Windy Lake Road (two-wheel drive access). The recreation site on the lake is popular with both hikers and anglers. The lake has fair fishing for stocked rainbow up to 1 kg (2 lbs) during the spring and fall. The preferred methods are trolling and fly-fishing. Fly anglers can try chironomids, mayflies or leeches.

Wolfe Lake (Map 2/D1)

The 28 hectare (69 ac) Wolfe Lake is located a kilometre to the west of Highway 3 on a two-wheel drive road that leads through the Indian Reserve. The lake offers a good early spring fishery for rainbow. Nearby Issitz can also produce well in the spring.

Wollaston Lakes (Map 17/E4)

The Wollaston Lakes are found south of Grizzly Lake off the rough Wollaston Forest Service Road. All three lakes offer nice rainbow trout fisheries, with the two smaller lakes located to the south of the main lake being stocked each year with rainbow to help their population.

Wood Lake (Map 17/B4)

Wood Lake is located in the Okanagan Valley south of Kalamalka Lake. The popular recreational lake is not only busy with boat traffic, but is also one of the highest-used kokanee fisheries in the province. Unfortunately, poor lake conditions have severely affected the kokanee populations and a shortened season with lower catch quotas has been implemented. Anglers can also find the odd rainbow trout along with a few carp. Ice fishing is popular here when the ice is safe. Check regulations before heading out.

Woods Lake (Map 23/D6)

Off the Ingram Creek Forest Service Road, Woods Lake is a clear lake that offers good sight fishing and trolling around the many shoals and drop-offs. The stocked rainbow can reach 1.5 kg (3 lbs). The lake has a cartop boat launch and camping at the recreation site.

Xenia Lake (Map 6/C3)

On the Miller Creek Forest Service Road, this 15 hectare (37 ac) lake is accessed by four-wheel drive vehicle or trail from Christina Lake. The lake has a scenic recreation site with a cartop boat launch and offers good fly-fishing for small rainbow. The remoteness of the lake and the decent fishing for the stocked rainbow make this lake a good choice.

Yellowhead Lake (Map 48/C2)

Yellowhead Lake is found off Highway 16 near the eastern entrance to Mount Robson Provincial Park. Anglers will find small rainbow trout, bull trout, kokanee and whitefish, as well as the odd lake trout that can reach 5 kg (11 lbs). There is a campground and boat launch at the west end of the lake.

Yellow Lake (Map 3/E2)

Fair numbers of brook and rainbow trout are found at this 35 hectare (86 ac) lake which is next to Highway 3A. The lake is stocked regularly with both species and is best fished in the early spring or late fall by trolling or fly-fishing since it suffers from algae bloom in summer and is also infested with perch. There are picnic facilities as well as an aeration system. Recently, kokanee have also started to be stocked into the lake. Check the regulations for special boating restrictions.

Young Lake (Map 32/A7)

This 252 hectare (622 ac) lake provides reasonably good fishing for rainbow trout up to 2 kg (4.5 lbs) and small kokanee by trolling. The narrow lake is best accessed from the north and is a relatively low elevation lake. The best times to fish are spring and fall.

Stream Fishing

Adams River (Map 29/F5)

The Adams is known worldwide for its incredible sockeye salmon run every fall. It also holds rainbow trout, Dolly Varden, whitefish, as well as Chinook, chum and Coho salmon, although the river is closed to salmon fishing. Unfortunately, this river is one that is easier to look at than fish. Guided trips for trout are offered by the First Nations (out of Quaaout Lodge) near the source, while the lower portions are protected by Roderick Haig Park. Your best bet is fly fishing an egg imitation or casting small spoons and spinners. The river is heavily regulated and it is best to double check regulations before heading out.

Allison Creek (Map 7/G4–8/B7)

Allison Creek offers fair fishing for small rainbow trout that can be caught by bait fishing or by fly-fishing the larger pools. The creek is best accessed below Allison Lake, as it parallels Highway 5A all the way from the lake to where it flows into the Similkameen River just east of Princeton.

Anstey River (Map 30/G1–36/A5)

Draining into the north end of the Anstey Arm of Shuswap Lake, this small river offers a catch and release fishery for rainbow and Dolly Varden. It is a remote river that has some fabulous pools for those willing to bushwhack their way in. Watch for bait bans.

Ashnola River (Map 2/D6–3/B4)

This river lines the north end of Cathedral Lakes Park and is easily accessed along a good two-wheel drive road (Ashnola River Road). The river has many pools that offer good fishing for small cutthroat and rainbow trout and mountain whitefish on a fly, by spincasting or by bait fishing. The spring closure does not apply to this river.

Asp Creek [China Creek] (Map 7/G6–8/B7)

Asp Creek can be accessed off the Snowpatch Road or the logging roads on the east side of the creek. The creek is located north of Princeton and offers good fishing for small rainbow using bait and hook in the many small pools along the length of the creek. The spring closure does not apply to this creek.

Blue River (Map 38/E1–43/A7)

Found near the town of Blue River, this river offers fair to good fishing for nice sized bull trout. The river is best fished in the spring or fall with lures or bait, although these fish will aggressively hit properly presented streamers.

Bonaparte River (Map 20/D1–26/A4)

The Bonaparte is a salmon-bearing river, but like a lot of the rivers this far upstream, there is no salmon fishing allowed. Instead, you can try your luck for the wild rainbow, which are plentiful (but no fishing is allowed below the falls at the fishway). It is a small shallow river with clear water that flows from Bonaparte Lake to the Thompson River. The river is heavily regulated.

Boundary Creek (Map 5/F1–E7)

Boundary Creek is a medium size creek that is easily accessed along Highway 3 and then along the Boundary Creek Road north of Greenwood. The creek sees heavy fishing pressure from travellers on Highway 3 but is still fairly good for rainbow and brook trout that can reach 1 kg (2 lbs) in size. The trout are usually smaller and fly-fishing is possible, although bait fishing is the preferred method.

Burrell Creek (Map 6/A1–12/C1)

This large creek is easily accessed on the Burrell Creek Forest Service Road and offers reasonably good fishing for small rainbow and whitefish by bait fishing or fly-fishing after the high water has subsided. In recent times, however, landslides have caused a severe reduction in the numbers of rainbow, making the fishing quite poor.

Camp Creek (Map 47/A6–A4)

This small creek can be reached off Highway 5 south of Valemount. It offers good fishing for bull trout and whitefish. The best time to try this stream is well after the spring runoff when water levels are at summer conditions.

Canoe River (Map 46/C4–47/B3)

Accessible via a rough logging road south of Valemount, this river provides fishing opportunities for rainbow trout, bull trout and whitefish. Bull trout in this river can reach up to 5 kg (11 lbs) in size and are best caught using lures, bait balls or larger streamer pattern flies.

Castle Creek (Map 45/B1–49/E4)

Castle Creek dumps into the Fraser River just northwest of the town of McBride. The creek offers fair fishing for generally small bull trout. Try the holes formed by the feeder creeks further from the highway.

Cherry Creek (Map 18/E1–25/G7)

Cherry Creek is a large creek to the east of Cherryville. It provides a good option for small dollies and rainbow trout by spincasting tiny lures or by bait fishing. The creek is easily accessed along the North Fork Forest Service Road from Cherryville.

Clearwater River (Map 33/F1–41/D7)

Running along the main corridor of Wells Gray Park, there is good access to the many pools that line this river. Of course, the easy access makes for some busy holes, especially during the popular salmon runs in late summer and early fall. The Chinook are the big draw here, with the main runs coming in August and early September. Some sockeye, Coho and chum can also be found in the system but their upstream migration is limited by the famous falls that line the river. However, there is fairly good fishing for rainbow, Dolly Varden and whitefish along its entire length. When targeting the rainbow, small dry flies resembling sedge and damsel flies are recommended. Check the regulations before setting out on your fishing adventure.

Coldwater River (Map 7/B4–14/D4)

The Coldwater River runs along the Coquihalla Highway north of the tollbooth and provides spotty fishing for small rainbow and larger dollies. The best fishing is in the lower reaches of the river, closer to Merritt. The river is large enough that fly-fishing and casting small lures can be effective. Check the regulations for special restrictions.

Copperkettle Creek (Map 11/B3–C4)

Most of the lower reaches of the Copperkettle Creek are inaccessible unless you are willing to bushwhack up the creek. Therefore, fishing tends to be quite good for small rainbow.

Fish exhibit different feeding habits between lakes and streams. In a stream fish wait for food to come to them, so look for merging streams, outsides of bends, back eddies, drop-offs and deep pools where food might collect.

Creighton Creek (Map 18/B2–D2)

This creek is easily accessed on the Creighton Valley Road east of Lumby and provides a good choice if you want to try bait fishing for small rainbow.

Deadman River (Map 21/B1–27/F2)

The Deadman has two distinct sections. Above the impressive Deadman Falls, it is a wild, beautiful river offering good fishing for rainbow up to 35 cm (14 in). Below the falls, the river flows through dry ranch country and the trout fishing is marginal. Although steelhead, Coho and Chinook run the lower reaches, these fragile runs are closed to fishing. Check for other restrictions as well.

Dore River (Map 49/A5–C2)

Surrounded by dynamic mountain scenery, the water flows quickly in the remote upper reaches of the Dore. Most of the fishing is found closer to McBride, where road access is good. Fishing is generally fair for small rainbow and bull trout. It is well advised to wait until the high water has receded before fishing.

Eneas Creek (Map 9/D3–E5)

This 19 km long creek flows through Garnet Lake and under Highway 97 before flowing into Okanagan Lake. Access to Eneas Creek is best along Garnet Valley Road, or off the aforementioned Highway 97. The creek contains brook and rainbow trout. Kokanee can also be seen spawning in late summer. This stream is exempt from the region wide spring closure.

Fraser River (Map 13/A2–C7; 49/A1–51/D7)

The Fraser is the mightiest of BC rivers, flowing from Mount Robson Provincial Park in the north to the Pacific Ocean in the south. North of Hope, the Fraser is a wild river with few access points. The portion of the Fraser River in Mount Robson Provincial Park offers good fishing for rainbow trout, bull trout and whitefish. The best areas are near creek mouths that flow into the Fraser. Other areas that provide decent results are the pools formed near Rearguard Falls and Overlander Falls. Watch for special restrictions, especially during the Chinook salmon run in the summer and early fall.

Gable Creek (Map 11/F6–12/A7)

Gable Creek is found in the Granby River Valley and is another small creek that can provide fairly good fishing for small rainbow after the high water has receded. The creek is easily accessed by the Gable Creek Forest Service Road along its entire length.

Granby River (Map 6/B6–19/B6)

Although the headwaters of this river are protected inside Granby Provincial Park, the mid and lower reaches of the river are easily accessed by the Granby River Road. It is a popular river with many large pools to cast a lure, fly or even sink some bait. The river contains small rainbow and brook trout as well as a population of whitefish and can be productive anytime during the summer. Check the regulations for closures.

Hayes Creek (Map 8/C7–D4)

The upper reaches of Hayes Creek are easily accessed along the Princeton-Summerland Road, whereas the lower reaches require bushwhacking to get into the good pools. The creek, which drains into the Similkameen River to the east of Princeton, provides reasonably good fishing for small rainbow best caught by bait fishing.

Hemp Creek (Map 37/F4–G2)

North of Clearwater, you can find this small creek off the Clearwater Valley Road in Wells Gray Provincial Park. There are plenty of small rainbow trout in this creek that are usually quite eager to take bait or flies. This creek is one of the few streams that is exempt from the region wide spring closure.

Holmes River (Map 49/D3–50/F3)

The Holmes River flows from the Continental Divide to the Fraser River southeast of McBride. Most of the river can be accessed via established logging roads. Fishing is quite good in some areas for rainbow trout, whitefish and bull trout. The months of June and July see some big bull trout that run in this river for spawning purposes.

Horsey & Small Creeks (Map 50/C5; 50/D5)

These fast flowing creeks cross under Highway 16 northwest of McBride. After high water, fishing can be good throughout most of the creeks for small rainbow trout and bull trout.

Inonoaklin Creek (Map 12/E1–19/A4)

Inonoaklin Creek is a large creek, which parallels Highway 6 to the west of Lower Arrow Lake. After the high water subsides, brook trout and rainbow up to 30 cm (12 in) can be caught by fly-fishing or using bait. The creek is closed to fishing below Galloping Creek.

Keremeos Creek (Map 3/C2–D4)

Keremeos Creek runs from the Apex Mountain Ski Area to Keremeos and eventually into the Similkameen River. The creek is easily accessed along Highway 3A, Green Mountain Road and the Keremeos Creek Forest Service Road and provides spotty fishing for small rainbow best taken by bait fishing.

Kettle River (Map 5/E7–19/B3; 6/A6–E6)

The Kettle River is approximately 150 km in length and offers a number of forest service sites where you can camp. The river is large enough that spincasting and fly-fishing is possible. Small rainbow are the mainstay of the fishery although there are brook trout and whitefish that take readily to bait and hook. There have also been a few brown trout pulled out of here. The best time to fish for the rainbow is in early spring before high water, whereas the best time to fish whitefish is during the winter season. This stream is exempt from the spring closure, but check the regulations for restrictions.

Kiwa Creek (Map 46/B2–50/C7)

The Kiwa Creek dumps into the Fraser River near Tête Jaune Cache. The fast flowing creek provides fair to good fishing during the summer and fall for small but plentiful rainbow and bull trout. Worms work for both species, while flies are more productive for rainbow.

Lawless Creek (Map 7/C4–D6)

Lawless Creek drains the slopes of Mount Thynne towards Tulameen where it flows into the Tulameen River. The creek is accessed along most of its lower reaches by the Lawless Creek Forest Service Road, but access to the upper reaches is by bushwhacking. As a result, there can be good fishing for small rainbow trout by bait fishing or fly-fishing.

Mahood River (Map 37/D4)

Only 5 km long, the Mahood River drains into the Clearwater River. It is possible to navigate the river on boat from Mahood Lake to the waterfalls or by trail. Fishing can be good for generally small rainbow by fly-fishing or spincasting lures. Check the regulations for special restrictions, including a bait ban and spring closure.

McKale River (Map 49/B1)

The McKale River is located northwest of McBride via Mountainview Road. The river offers fair to good fishing for rainbow trout, whitefish and bull trout. Fishing is best well after the spring runoff period.

McLennan River (Map 46/E1–47/A3)

You can access this river off Highway 5 between Tête Jaune Cache and Valemount. Fishing in the river is generally fair for nice sized bull trout and small rainbow trout. The river is best fished in the summer after the spring runoff period. Be sure to check the regulations before heading out, as there are special restrictions in place during the fall salmon season.

McNutty Creek (Map 2/G1–8/G5)

Draining southward into Hedley Creek north of Hedley, this small creek is noted for its particularly good fishing for small rainbow. Most of the creek is reached by the Stemwinder Mountain Forest Service Road system.

Mission Creek (Map 10/A1–18/B5)

Mission Creek flows from Mission Lake into Okanagan Lake. The stream is closed to fishing below the Gallagher Canyon Falls on the outskirts of Kelowna. The upper reaches of the creek are accessed off the Mission Creek Forest Service Road or the Graystokes Forest Service Road. The creek contains a number of sport fish, including rainbow and brook trout. Kokanee can also be seen spawning in early fall below the Gallagher Canyon Falls. In Mission Creek Regional Park a stocked trout pond for kids is found at Hall Road.

Moose River (Map 47/F1–51/D4)

The Moose River is a remote river flowing from the Continental Divide to the Fraser River just east of Moose Lake. Access to the upper reaches is limited to hikers with good navigational skills. Fishing in the river is fair to good in sections for generally small rainbow trout and whitefish, although the bull trout in the river can reach up to 2 kg (4.5 lbs) in size. Streamer pattern flies or lures work best for the larger bull trout.

Murtle River (Map 37/D3–42/A7)

This river travels through Wells Gray Provincial Park between Mahood Lake to the west and Murtle Lake to the east. The area closer to the west arm of Murtle Lake seems to offer the better fishing. There are numerous holes and pools found along this section that are ideal holding areas for nice sized rainbow trout. Fly-fishing can be very productive. This stream is a good option for those wanting to do some early stream fishing as it is exempt from the region wide spring closure.

Nicola River (Map 14/F3–20/D6; 15/B3–16/D4)

Nicola River is a large river draining into and out of Nicola Lake before eventually flowing into the Thompson River. The river is easily accessed along its entire course by either Highway 8 or Highway 5A. The river meanders along its length, providing many bends and pools to try spincasting, fly-fishing or bait fishing for rainbow, Dolly Varden, steelhead and salmon in the summer and fall. Check the regulations for special fishing restrictions.

North Thompson River (Maps 22, 28, 33, 34, 38, 39, 42, 43, 46)

The North Thompson River is a big river that starts in the mountains northwest of Blue River before eventually joining the South Thompson at Kamloops. Highway 5 parallels the river for the most part, providing good access throughout. It is well advised to bring a boat and drift down the river, although shore fishing is possible. Chinook salmon (from June until August) and Dolly Varden (year-round) get most of the angling attention, but there are rainbow and the other four salmon species run in the fall. Although exempt from the spring closure, check the regulations for special restrictions.

Okanagan River (Map 3/G2–4/A6)

Most of the Okanagan River flows in the United States but from Okanagan Falls south to Osoyoos Lake there are about 30 km of fishable waters. The river is easily accessed along Highway 97 and provides slow fishing for rainbow, but is becoming increasingly more popular for smallmouth and largemouth bass, which can get quite large. Check the regulations before heading out.

Otter Creek (Map 7/E6–G1)

Otter Creek is a large creek flowing southward along Highway 5A and eventually into the Tulameen River at Tulameen. The creek is easily accessed along the highway and the Coalmont Road. As a result, it receives a fair amount of fishing pressure and is not a particularly great producer. It is still possible to catch small rainbow on a fly, by spincasting or with bait throughout the summer months.

Pasayten River (Map 2/A5–A7)

This small river flows north across the border and into the Similkameen River at Similkameen Falls. The river is accessed by a forestry road and/or trails in the area. The river offers reasonably good fishing for small rainbow in the summer months.

Pass Creek (Map 5/G3–6/B4)

This small creek drains eastward into the Granby River north of Grand Forks. It is easily accessed by the Pass Creek Forest Service Road and offers reasonably good fishing for small rainbow from July to October by bait fishing or fly-fishing.

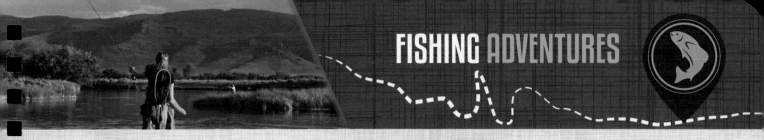

Paul Creek (Map 22/D1)

This creek drains Paul Lake and is open year-round for Authorised Anglers. This means that only youth (under 16) or disabled anglers and their companions (maximum two) may fish here. For most of its length, the stream runs parallel to Paul Lake Road offering good access and fishing for rainbow trout.

Peachland Creek (Map 9/B1–D3)

Peachland Creek is a small creek leading from Peachland Lake into Okanagan Lake at Peachland. The creek is easily accessed by a series of forestry roads and the paved Brenda Mines Road. Given the proximity to the Okanagan towns and the easy access, the creek is heavily fished. It still offers fair fishing for small rainbow. Watch for the no fishing zone below Hardy Falls.

When angling from the banks of a river remember to keep low and move slow, as fish may be spooked by your shadow.

Powers Creek (Map 9/F1–16/D7)

Powers Creek is a small creek that drains into the Okanagan Lake at Westbank. The creek is accessed by the Jackpine Forest Service Road in the upper reaches with the middle reaches of the creek being inaccessible except by a long hike. The creek offers fairly good fishing for small rainbow. Check the regulations for the no fishing zone below the Highway 97 bridge.

Quilchena Creek (Map 15/A3–B6)

This creek drains into Nicola Lake and is accessed by a good forestry road along its lower reaches. The creek provides good fishing for small rainbow, primarily by bait fishing. It is possible to fly-fish certain portions of the creek.

Rauch River (Map 46/B5–49/E4)

The Rauch River flows into the Fraser River northwest of Tête Jaune Cache. Road access is limited due to gates and/or private roads in the area. As a result, fishing in the river can be quite good for nice sized bull trout and whitefish. Whitefish readily take flies, while lures or streamer flies work best for bull trout.

Rendell Creek (Map 11/D4–F1)

Rendell Creek is accessed on its lower reaches by a good, gated forestry road. The upper reaches require some bushwhacking to find the better holes. Due to its limited access, good fishing for rainbow trout from July to October can be found. Bait fishing and fly-fishing are the preferred methods.

Robson River (Map 51/A6)

This dynamic river flows from the glacial fed Berg Lake south into the Fraser River. The river is quite scenic as the mighty Mount Robson dominates the landscape. Fishing in the river is generally fair in places for small rainbow trout, bull trout and whitefish. Watch for special restrictions on portions of the river.

Seymour River (Map 35/F6–39/F6)

Similar to nearby Anstey River, the Seymour River helps feed Shuswap Lake. The river offers a catch-and-release fishery for rainbow and Dolly Varden below the falls. There is also a bait ban.

Shingle Creek (Map 9/E6–F7)

Shingle Creek is a small creek draining into the channel between Okanagan Lake and Skaha Lake at Penticton. Do not expect good fishing, though. The entire length of the creek is easily accessed by either the Green Mountain Road or the Shingle Creek Road.

Shorts Creek (Map 16/D3–G3)

This small creek leads eastward into the Okanagan Lake and offers good fishing for small rainbow by bait fishing. Access is limited but some nice pools are found along the Short Creek Canyon Trail. Check the regulations for the no fishing zone downstream of the Westside Road bridge.

Shuswap River (Map 24/F1–25/C2; 25/C5–G3)

A combination of highways, paved roads and logging roads provide good access to this river, which provides fairly good fishing for rainbow, Dolly Varden and whitefish along its entire length. However, the river also contains all five salmon species, including Chinook up to 8 kg (20 lbs). The Chinook start running in June followed by large runs of sockeye in September, with Coho and chum lasting into early November. The salmon are a popular draw between Enderby and Mabel Lake, but can be found as far upstream as Shuswap Falls. Check the regulations before setting out on your fishing adventure.

Similkameen River (Map 1–3/F7)

Most of this river length is accessed by Highway 3, and despite easy access, still produces well for rainbow on a (dry) fly, by spincasting small lures or by bait fishing. There is a bait ban from April 1st to October 31st as well as a catch and release section for wild rainbow for 31 km south of the Highway 3 bridge at Princeton. A good whitefish fishery is offered in the winter season. This river is exempt from the spring closure.

Siwash Creek (Map 8/B2–D4)

Siwash Creek drains into Hayes Creek to the north of Princeton. A washed out bridge prevents vehicle access above the 8 km mark but anglers can access the upper reaches from the Siwash Creek Forest Service Road off of the Okanagan Connector (Hwy 97C). The creek offers good fishing for small rainbow on a fly or by bait fishing.

South Thompson River (Map 22/B2–29/F6)

This slow-moving river flows from Shuswap Lake to Kamloops. Fishing really heats up near the headwaters when the millions of sockeye salmon pass through on their way to the Adams beginning in late August. At this time fishing can be excellent for rainbow trout, Dolly Varden and whitefish, which all feed on the dislodged salmon eggs. The other salmon species are also found in the river, with Chinook showing up in early June and Coho and chum runs lasting into November. Drift fishing is popular on this river.

Summers Creek (Map 8/A3–B6)

Summers Creek flows southward from Missezula Lake into Allison Creek just north of Princeton. This small creek provides fairly good fishing for small rainbow and brook trout by fly-fishing or bait fishing.

Tête Creek [Sand Creek] (Map 46/C3–50/E7)

Tête Creek flows into the McLennan River near Tête Jaune Cache and offers good fishing near the confluence area for bull trout, whitefish and rainbow trout. Be sure to check the regulations before heading out, as there are special restrictions in place during the salmon run periods.

Thompson River (Map 13/A2–21/C1)

This large river is renowned for its excellent steelhead fishery. However, despite conservation measures, the fishing has declined. Still anglers come from around the world to try to hook into one of these mighty trout (some reach 13 kg/30 lbs) during the late fall (October to December). The pools around Spences Bridge are legendary. The most popular rainbow trout section of the river is between Kamloops Lake and Ashcroft. This section of river can be drift fished and provides some excellent (dry) fly-fishing for rainbow up to 1.5 kg (3+ lbs). Other species in the river include all five species of salmon (from early summer to November), sturgeon, Dolly Varden and whitefish. There are a number of provincial parks providing camping next to the river. Please check the regulations as the river is closely regulated.

Trépanier Creek (Map 9/E2–16/B7)

This small creek is found to the east of Okanagan Lake and is easily accessed by a logging road next to the Okanagan Connector. As a result, the creek is not particularly good but does have some small rainbow. No fishing is allowed from Highway 97 downstream to Okanagan Lake.

Trout Creek (Map 8/G2–9/F5)

Draining the Headwater Lakes, this creek has gained notoriety as forming a scenic backdrop for sections of the Kettle Valley Railway. Most of the creek is easily accessed along the Princeton-Summerland Road, the KVR or along the Trout Creek Forest Service Road. The best fishing is in the upper reaches where it is possible to catch good numbers of small rainbow and brook trout by bait fishing. No fishing is allowed downstream of the trestle of Trout Creek Canyon; upstream is exempt from the spring closure.

Tulameen River (Map 1/C2–8/A7)

The Tulameen flows from the Cascade Mountains before arcing past the town of Tulameen and spilling into the Similkameen River at Princeton. The 80 (50 mi) km long river contains a number of species, most notably rainbow and brook trout and mountain whitefish. Although most sections of the river are easily accessed, there are some remote, wild sections that offer excellent fishing. This stream is exempt from the spring closure, but watch for the bait ban between April 1st and October 31st.

West Kettle River (Maps 4, 5, 10, 11, 18)

For the most part, this large river is easily accessed along Highway 33. It extends approximately 90 km (55 mi) from the Big White Mountain area before joining the Kettle River at Westbridge. Despite its good access, the river still provides fairly good fishing for rainbow (catch-and-release only) that can reach 1 kg (2 lbs) in size but are usually quite small. Look for logjams or other structure. Bait fishing (between November 1st and March 31st only), casting small lures or fly-fishing weighted nymphs or dry flies can be a lot of fun. The stream is closed to all fishing during the month of August, but there is no spring closure here.

HUNTING
ADVENTURES

BC hunters enjoy possibly the widest variety of game animals anywhere on the continent and most of them can be found in the Thompson/Okanagan. This diversity of wildlife is made possible by the range of habitats – from riverbank to alpine and desert to rainforest.

Regardless of habitat, winter is normally the bottleneck for survival of wild animals and the intensity of winter weather will affect the hunting success during subsequent seasons. In general, winters in the latter part of the 20th Century and the first decade of the 21st are the mildest in a hundred years. As a result, most game populations are thriving.

The recent trend in hunter numbers is down, so combined with increased backroad access and strong game numbers, hunters now experience some of the best hunting ever. The ungulates in the deer family (deer, elk and moose) are the most popular species hunted, but keen hunters also pursue less common ungulates like mountain goats and mountain sheep in the Thompson and Okanagan Regions. Predator species are abundant with black bears being the most commonly sought of these game animals, but grizzly bear, cougar, wolf and coyote also interest many sportsmen.

Upland game birds of the Thompson Okanagan include four species of grouse, two partridges, ptarmigan, two kinds of pigeon, pheasants and turkeys. Some species such as chukar and turkey have very restricted ranges, but blue grouse and ruffed grouse can be found in any corner of the region. Waterfowl hunting is not particularly productive in this area. Ducks are not numerous and while Canada geese have reached nuisance numbers in some urban areas, unfortunately, many of the best hunting areas are closed by Municipal bylaws. Still, the birds are there and the seasons are long.

A person wanting to hunt in BC first needs a Hunter Number, which he can get after completing the Conservation and Outdoor Recreation Education course (see *bcwf.bc.ca/programs/core/index.html*). You then need a hunting licence and a species tag for each big game animal you intend to hunt. More details on licensing are at *env.gov.bc.ca/fw/wildlife/hunting/regulations/*. Some game animals are controlled through Limited Entry Hunting (*env.gov.bc.ca/fw/wildlife/hunting/resident/leh.html*), while non-resident hunters must be accompanied by a licensed guide.

Hunters looking for more of a challenge or wanting to extend their recreation may choose to hunt with archery equipment. In addition to being able to hunt with a bow in any open season, there are special bow hunting only times and places in the Thompson and Okanagan Regions.

GARMIN®

Big Game Species

The main big game species in the Thompson/Okanagan include deer, elk, moose and bear. In the winter, when hunting is slow, some sportsmen choose to go after the elusive cougar. Smaller game in the area consists mostly of birds, with waterfowl not being a big draw for hunters, although wild turkeys can be plentiful in some areas. The seasons for each species vary, as does the bag limit. Listed below is a summary of some of the main species to look for in the Thompson/Okanagan.

Bighorn Sheep

There are two sub-species of bighorn sheep in the Thompson/Okanagan: Rocky mountain (Ovis canadensis canadensis) and California (O. c. californiana), although they are genetically similar. Bighorn sheep are medium sized ungulates, with a stocky body. Adult rams may weigh 100 kg (220 lbs), while ewes reach weights of 60–75 kg (130–165 lbs). Both sexes sport a brown coat, a white belly and muzzle and a large, conspicuous white rump patch. Older rams carry a set of massive tapering horns that curve back, down and forward until the tip may protrude above the bridge of the nose. Rocky Mountain bighorns are generally larger animals and rams have a tighter horn curl than do their California cousins.

In Southern BC, bighorns are found where the arid climate promotes open grasslands, lightly forested, rocky slopes or treeless alpine meadows. Bighorns eat mostly grass and rely on keen eyesight to spot predators (including humans) so are found most often in wide open spaces. California bighorns in the Thompson /Okanagan Regions are more widely distributed, with pockets of abundance in the Ashnola River (WMU 8-03), the Okanagan Valley (WMU 8-09), Kamloops Lake (WMU 3-27, 3-28, 3-29) and the dry mountain slopes of the Fraser (WMU 3-31, 3-32). In the 1920s, Rocky Mountain bighorns were successfully introduced to Spence's Bridge (WMU 3-17) into what would normally considered California bighorn range.

Black Bear

Black bears (Ursus americanus) are the most common carnivore in the Thompson Okanagan and can be found in good numbers in almost any habitat, from river flat to mountain top. Adult male bears weigh up to 300 kg (660 lbs) and females about 200 kg (440 lbs). They get to that size by eating almost anything, from grass, roots and berries to freshly killed meat and rotting fish.

"Black" is the name, and black is the most common colour of the pelage (hair), but this animal can come in a variety of colours, from jet black through various shades of red and brown to bluish or pure white. There are both spring and fall hunting seasons for bears. In spring, the right habitat is just about anywhere that there is new green growth. Logged openings, recent wildfires and utility corridors are good areas to start. The south facing slopes of major river valleys green up quickly, so are a prime choice to hunt bears in the early season. By fall, bears are working hard to fatten up for winter hibernation and can be found anywhere where there is an abundance of food. Good places to start a fall bear hunt are wild berry patches or along streams, particularly those with spawning salmon.

Cougar

This largest member of the cat family in BC provides hunting recreation during the winter when little else is open. Cougars (puma concolor) are tawny coloured with lighter coloured hair under their chin, throat and belly. An adult male cougar is about the same size as an adult human although an adult female is usually less than 40 kg (90 lbs). Both sexes have a muscular tail that is about as thick as a man's wrist and can be almost as long as the rest of the body.

Cougars kill and eat a wide range of prey, but deer, particularly mule deer, are preferred, and their distribution and migration generally follows that of mule deer. Cougar hunters mainly use trained dogs to chase and tree the big cats. Pursuit only, a kind of "catch and release" hunting, is popular with some hunters. The hunting season is November to March, but January has the most reliable conditions with fresh, soft snow and the most productive hunting.

Elk

Rocky Mountain elk (cervus elaphus) are smaller than moose, but larger than any other member of the deer family in BC. A bull can weigh up to 350 kg (770 lbs) and a cow about 2/3 that weight. Their hefty body is primarily tan coloured, set off by darker coloured underparts, a creamy/orange coloured rump patch, a dark head and a heavy dark coloured mane. Mature bulls grow a spectacular set of antlers with a massive main beam and as many as 6, 7 or even 8 substantial tines.

Elk are not common in the Thompson Okanagan, but are found mainly across the south, around Princeton (WMU 8-04, 8-05, 8-06), the south Okanagan (WMU 8-01, 8-09) the Kettle (WMU 8-14) and Granby (WMU 8-15) River drainages. Elk are social animals, often found in small groups in summer. However, during the September/October rut, the biggest bull around will gather up a harem of up to 30 cows with whom he plans to mate and drives off all subordinate bulls. In rut, bulls make a characteristic loud vocalization called bugling which can be heard from mountain top to mountain top and is one of the most thrilling sounds in nature. Elk are normally secretive, so hunting elk often means using devices to duplicate bull or cow calls to attract the wary animals within shooting range.

Moose

Moose (Alces alces) are the largest member of the deer family, with adults standing 2 metres (over 6 feet) high at the shoulder and weighing 300–600 kg (650–1,300 lbs). They have a dark, almost black coloured body mounted on four long, slim legs with grey "stockings." Both sexes have a large elongated nose and usually a flap of long hair and skin called a "bell" hanging from their throat. Mature bulls grow palmated antlers with spikes around the edge of the palm, as opposed to the branching antlers of other BC deer. Yearling bulls may have antlers with only one or two points and are specifically targeted in the hunting regulations.

Moose can be found in any management unit in the Thompson Okanagan, but Princeton (WMU 8-04, 8-05, 8-06), Peachland (WMU 8-08), Shuswap (WMU 8-23), Merritt (WMU 3-12, 3-19, 3-20), Kamloops WMU 3-28, 3-29) and Clinton (WMU 3-30) produce higher than average moose harvests. Moose tolerate cold very well but suffer from summer heat. In summer and early fall they are more commonly found in cooler micro climates; near water areas and where they have access to high elevation spruce forests. Early in the hunting season, look for moose in cool forests and near to lakes and swamps. As summer wanes and the weather cools, moose can be found in forest openings such as those created by logging and forest fires. Lucky hunters may encounter a moose just driving logging roads. Other hunters increase their odds by using cow or bull calls, which can be especially effective during the rut (during mid-October).

Mule Deer

Deer in BC are either white-tailed (Odocoileus virginianus) or black-tailed (Odocoileus hemionus). The latter are further divided into mule deer and coastal black-tails. Coastal deer do not occur in Thompson Okanagan, but mule deer are the most widely distributed and most sought after big game animal in the region. Mule deer bucks weight about 100 kg (220 lbs) with does about 2/3 that weight. Both sexes have a grey/brown coat and oversized ears (hence the name) and a light cream coloured rump patch with a narrow, black tipped tail. Mule deer antlers are bifurcated, that is, continuously branched into two as they grow. When startled, instead of running, mule deer often move with a bounding leap called "stotting" in which all four feet spring the animal forward and come down together.

Mule deer can be found in every corner of the Thompson Okanagan with Princeton, Merritt, Kamloops Lake and Lillooet being some favoured hunting areas. These deer prefer generally open country and can be found in the alpine and in forest openings created by logging or forest fire. Hunters should be constantly glassing the hillsides with binoculars when hunting mule deer. Autumn snow forces these animals to lower elevation where they concentrate on south facing slopes for winter. Young mule deer can be remarkably unwary regarding humans but big mulie bucks can be shy, although even they become less cautious in the rut (during mid-November).

White-Tailed Deer

White-tailed deer are about 3/4 the size of mule deer with body and tail of pale brown hair and "normal" sized ears. They are wary animals and when alarmed, they usually run quickly away with their broad tail lifted to expose its white underside and broad white rump patch (hence the name). The bucks' antlers grow with separate tines rising from a main beam.

White-tailed deer are not widely distributed in this region, being absent from much of the Thompson (Region 3) areas, except around Salmon Arm and Merritt. However, in the Granby (WMU 8-15), Kettle (WMU 8-14), West Kettle (WMU 8-12) and Shuswap (WMU 8-23) River drainages, these deer are abundant. They prefer tighter cover and lower elevations than do mule deer and favour the edges of hayfields and riparian forests. Whitetails are alert and wary of humans so are often taken by hunters shooting from tree stands or ground blinds or other cover. There is a wide variety of calls, scents and rattles designed to mimic whitetail sounds and behaviours to lure a deer within shooting range. Hunter success is vastly increased during the rut (during late November).

Game Birds

Blue Grouse

The blue or dusky grouse is a game bird of the mountains and can be found in every corner of the Thompson Okanagan. It is the largest of our native grouse at about 1 kg (2 lbs) in size. The name is "blue" but the plumage is a subtle mix of several dark shades of black, grey and blue flecked with white. The dark tail feathers may have a thin white band at the tip. In spring mating season male blue grouse announce themselves with a low hooting sound. They then impress the females by raising neck feathers to expose a large halo of white feathers surrounding a brightly coloured (yellow, red or purple) bare neck patch called the cerival apteria. Females and chicks feed together through the summer, but by fall, the families break up and the birds spend the winter singly or in small groups.

Early in the hunting season, look for blue grouse in open dry Douglas fir forests or in old logging blocks. Later in the fall hunters have to follow these birds into their winter range, which are the higher elevation spruce, balsam and pine forests.

Chukar Partridge

If you like to scramble up steep, rocky, sun baked, cactus infested slopes, then chukar hunting is for you. These game birds are native to Asia, but were introduced to the dry interior valleys of Southern BC. They seem to have established best in the Thompson Valley from Kamloops to Lytton (WMU 3-27 to 3-30 and 3-17), but really keen hunters may be able to find them in the south Okanagan and Similkameen Valleys (WMU 8-01). Chukars are the size of a small chicken with a chunky grey-brown body, white and black bars on the wings and a striking black line from each eye that joins in a V in the middle of their chest.

To hunt chukars, the simple rule is: be ready! Their typical behaviour is to run uphill and fly down. They can run faster than you and hide in the tall grass, so a good dog is almost essential. When flushed, they burst from cover and fly quickly away, so only the most alert and practiced shot gunners are rewarded with this small but very tasty game bird.

Ruffed Grouse

Ruffed grouse are the most widespread upland game bird in the Thompson and Okanagan Regions. Found in all Management Units, they are about the size of a crow with reddish-grey coloured body and wing feathers and a broad black band near the tip of the tail. The "ruff" is a bunch of black neck feathers that can be raised and puffed out to create a collar that increases the male bird's apparent size and impresses the ladies. In spring, a male ruffed grouse announces his territory by "drumming" a beat with his cupped wings that starts slowly and increases to a maniacal drum roll.

In the fall, ruffed grouse are often found in groups of 5-10 birds called coveys. Favoured habitats are the moist forests of major river valleys and forests of mixed of conifer and aspen or cottonwood. You can also find them in brushy areas where forest has been disturbed by fire, logging or powerlines. These birds do not migrate latitudinally or altitudinally, so successful hunters revisit areas where they have seen ruffed grouse in past years.

Grouse use the element of surprise to evade hunters, exploding out of the brush without warning, so be ready for fast shooting. Keep your gun in both hands, with the muzzle near eye level, and be ready to switch off the safety in an instant.

Turkey

Wild turkeys are native to eastern and southern North America, but have been introduced to many sites in Southern BC. As their populations increase and hunting seasons open, turkey hunting has become quite popular in the Okanagan. They are one of the few game species open in the spring, with the added bonus of a fall season too. Weighing up to 10 kg (20 lbs), they are much larger than any other native game bird and there really is no mistaking them. There are no turkeys in the Thompson Region yet, but in the Okanagan they are found around Grand Forks and Christina Lake (WMU 8-15) and up the Kettle Valley (WMU 8-14, 8-12). Small numbers have been reported from the south and central Okanagan (WMU 8-01, 8-09, 8-10). Turkeys live mostly in the valley bottoms and hunter access to private land can be an issue.

Some turkeys are taken just cruising the logging roads, but success is significantly increased by hunters who learn the techniques and calls to lure them within shooting range. These big birds are wary making them challenging and exciting to hunt. Prospective hunters should be warned that there is a high risk of addiction to turkey hunting.

Okanagan Region WMU Highlights

Hunting success is entirely dependent on location. Whether you are new to the area or are a seasoned local looking to switch it up, the following quick summaries of each Wildlife Management Unit (the large green numbers and boundaries on our maps) should help you make the right choice.

WMU 8-01

In this management unit, the dry grasslands and vineyards of the southern Okanagan valley give way to forests of Douglas fir and pine as you climb to higher elevations. Private land limits hunting in the valley bottom, but on the slopes there are bighorn sheep and mule deer, with white-tailed deer in the brushy draws and moose in the higher elevation willow thickets.

WMU 8-02

This area is composed primarily of the high forested ridges between the south Okanagan and Similkameen Valleys. Mule deer abound and black bear are common, while this area is also known for good blue grouse hunting. There are limited entry options for bighorn sheep and mountain goat near Keremeos.

WMU 8-03

Encompassing the drainage area of the Ashnola River, most of this management unit is protected by a provincial park. Hunting is permitted in most areas, but access is limited. This is bighorn sheep country, with steep, open slopes and dry forest. Mule deer are frequently encountered.

WMU 8-04

With forests of lodgepole pine, Douglas fir and spruce, this area has seen extensive logging and is laced with logging roads. You can find mule deer, moose, black bear, cougar and occasionally elk in the logged openings. The mix of old and young forest also favours ruffed and blue grouse.

WMU 8-05

This is a large management unit encompassing the pine and spruce forests in the drainages of the Tulameen River and Otter Creek. There is plenty of logging road access for hunters to pursue mule deer, moose, black bear, cougar, elk and forest grouse. This is a productive area but sees high hunting pressure.

WMU 8-06

This area includes the excellent winter deer range near Princeton grading to the high elevation forests in the northern reaches. Look for moose in the logged openings and along the meandering streams. Logging also favours mule deer and grouse. It is also possible to hunt white-tailed deer near the ranchlands of Hayes Creek valley.

WMU 8-07

Primarily a dry mid-elevation plateau of mostly lodgepole pine, logging access into this management unit is relatively recent. As they brush in, the logged openings will provide hunters with chances for moose, black bear and mule deer.

WMU 8-08

There are numerous habitat types in this management unit, from grassland to alpine. Logging access is abundant and so is the hunting pressure. There are good areas for mule deer, moose, black bear and cougar, with white-tailed deer becoming increasingly common near Peachland.

WMU 8-09

This area includes the dry rocky slopes and ridges along the Okanagan Valley as well as the moist forests of the Okanagan highlands. Big game hunters can pursue both species of deer, elk, moose, bighorn sheep, black bear and cougar. There also good pockets of blue grouse.

WMU 8-10

Much of this management unit is mid elevation plateau, with numerous streams, lakes and swamps. There is a long history of logging, and thus extensive road development. Moose and mule deer are the primary hunted species, but white-tailed deer and a few elk are also found here.

WMU 8-11

This area includes the dry forests and ridges west of Okanagan Lake and is a popular hunting area thanks to extensive logging roads. This is a productive area for mule deer, cougar, black bear and moose.

WMU 8-12

This management unit captures the narrow valley bottom and forested slopes of the West Kettle River. Both species of deer are common, with whitetail near the hayfields and low valley slopes and mule deer on the steep rocky valley sides. The north end of the MU produces a few moose and small numbers of elk are taken in the southern end.

WMU 8-13

This is a small rather remote area in the headwaters of the Kettle River. Logging has opened the country for early season mule deer hunters and the valley bottom is a major migration route for white-tailed deer in October and November.

WMU 8-14

Cattle ranching is a major activity in the Kettle River and Boundary Creek Valleys and most of the valley bottom is private land. There are moose, elk and mule deer here, but this management unit is famous for whitetail hunting. There is also a small population of wild turkey. Hunters must be sure to get permission to hunt the private land.

Be sure to check the BC Hunting Regulations env.gov.bc.ca/fw/wildlife/hunting/regulations for the most recent rules and regulations regarding bag limits and season opening and closing dates.

WMU 8-15

With gentle farmland across the south, backed by steep forests and rugged mountains, this WMU can be a good choice for hunting white-tailed deer, elk and turkey. Two large provincial parks limit the access in the high country, but bighorn sheep can be seen along the highway between Grand Forks and Christina Lake.

WMU 8-21

A high forested plateau dominates this management unit with steep slopes along the north and east boundaries. Logging has opened much of the area for mule deer and black bear hunters.

WMU 8-22

Much of the land in this area is farmland and ranch land, most of which is private. Mule deer are abundant and white-tailed deer are common, so hunters with access to private land or who find areas of Crown land can enjoy excellent sport. At one time this management unit also provided excellent pheasant hunting, but while still open, it is now restricted by development and firearm bylaws.

WMU 8-23

This area includes the rolling farmland of the Shuswap Valley and the spectacular Monashee Mountains. This is one of the best bets in the region for white-tailed deer and provides good harvests of mule deer. Cougar, black bear, a few grizzly bear, moose and even mountain goat can also be found here.

WMU 8-24

This area is rugged and forested. Access is limited to those tributaries with logging roads. The relatively moist climate produces abundant vegetation for black bear and white-tailed deer and smaller numbers of moose and mule deer.

WMU 8-25

Steep forested slopes and the accompanying logging provides this management unit with habitat for black bear, mule deer, whitetail and a fair population of ruffed grouse.

WMU 8-26

Relatively gentle terrain and extensive private land limits the opportunities for hunting in this unit. Mule deer and black bear reward hunters, especially along the eastern boundary of the area.

Thompson Region WMU Highlights

WMU 3-12

This management unit is dominated by lodgepole pine forests, but includes low elevation grasslands and sub-alpine spruce forests, with streams and scattered wetlands throughout. Access is plentiful and hunters have excellent opportunities for mule deer, moose, cougar, black bear and forest grouse.

WMU 3-13

In this area, hunters find a wide diversity of habitats from low elevation grasslands through dry forest to alpine. Mule deer, cougar and black bear are abundant. This is a good choice for upland birds, including grouse and ptarmigan but sharp-tailed grouse are closed for conservation.

WMU 3-14, 3-15

These management units straddle the Fraser River and consist of steep, rugged habitats from low elevation dry sage-steppe to coastal transition forests and alpine. Access is somewhat limited west of the Fraser. Black bear are abundant and mule deer common. Elk are present and increasing, but not yet open for hunting.

WMU 3-16

Steep, rocky forested slopes and bare rocky peaks characterize this area. The terrain and provincial parks limit access, but hunters can find good numbers of mule deer and some of the best opportunities for mountain goat in the region.

WMU 3-17

This management unit holds a diversity of dry forest types from low elevation grassland to scattered alpine. This WMU is a good choice for bighorn sheep hunters because both sub-species are present, but mule deer and cougar are also plentiful. This area also provides a high harvest of black bear.

WMU 3-18

Covering a high elevation plateau with pine, spruce and sub-alpine fire forests along with dry forest and grassland habitat, this area is a good bet for blue grouse. Mule deer, black bear and cougar are considered abundant, while a moderate population of moose is available.

WMU 3-19

Ranging from low elevation grasslands through Douglas fir and lodgepole pine to sub-alpine forests, with scattered wetlands throughout, hunters will find mule deer and black bear in abundance. In fact, this is one of the best bets in the region for moose and black bear. Grouse are also plentiful.

WMU 3-20

Within this management unit much of the land consists of private ranches. Still, hunters find decent numbers of moose, mule deer and black bear. This is one of the few areas of the region where waterfowl hunters can do well for geese and ducks.

WMU 3-26

This area straddles the transition from dry to wet interior forest and has a wide variety of forested habitats and the accompanying logging. Mule deer and black bear are abundant, while moose are common. This is also one of the better bets for white-tailed deer in the Thompson Region and there is even a small population of bighorn sheep at Chase. Ruffed grouse are harvested in reasonable numbers.

WMU 3-27

Consisting of the dry grass and forest slopes along the south Thompson River and forested highlands along the North Thompson River, this management unit supports one of the strongest populations of bighorn sheep in the region. Mule deer and black bear are abundant and this area is also an excellent choice for ruffed grouse hunters.

WMU 3-28

This long narrow management unit captures the riparian forest of the North Thompson River with Douglas fir, pine and spruce forests rising to the west. This area has seen extensive logging and hunting pressure has increased with access. Regardless, mule deer, moose and black bear remain plentiful.

WMU 3-29

This is a dry area, with grasslands along Kamloops Lake and dry forests upslope. An excellent choice for mule deer and bighorn sheep hunters, black bear and cougar are also abundant. Bird hunters can pursue blue and ruffed grouse as well as chukar partridge.

WMU 3-30

This management unit includes the dry slopes of the south Thompson and Fraser and the gently rolling forested slopes of the Bonaparte Plateau. Mule deer and moose are abundant, while shot gunners will find good to excellent numbers of virtually every game bird available in the region. Both upland and waterfowl provide good sport.

WMU 3-31

The low elevation terrain is covered by grassland/sage-steppe habitats along the Fraser that transition through Douglas-fir forests and alpine on the Marble Range. There is also an extensive plateau of pine and spruce forest on the northern part of this management unit. There are good numbers of mule deer, bighorn sheep, cougar and black bear here.

WMU 3-32, 3-33

These management units consist of the steep forested slopes of the coastal/ interior transition. Rugged country rewards experienced hunters with excellent mule deer hunting. Mountain goat and bighorn sheep are also taken, while these areas are among the best choices in the region for blue grouse and ptarmigan hunting.

WMU 3-34, 3-35

These are two small units in the interior wet belt forests with small but huntable populations of mule deer, moose, mountain goat, cougar and black and grizzly bear.

WMU 3-36, 3-37

The lower elevations of these management units are mostly cedar-hemlock forests and river and lakeshore riparian habitats, while upslope areas are spruce and balsam forests and alpine. Hunters find pockets of mule deer, white-tailed deer, moose, cougar and black bear and occasionally mountain goat and grizzly bear.

WMU 3-38, 3-39

River riparian and Douglas fir forests at low elevations transition through spruce and balsam forest to alpine. There are populations of mule deer, moose, cougar and black bear and occasionally whitetail. This is a productive management unit for most forest grouse species.

WMU 3-40, 3-41, 3-42, 3-43, 3-44, 3-46

From the North Thompson River, these management units progress from cottonwood forests through Douglas fir forests then cedar-hemlock and spruce-sub-alpine fir forests to sub-alpine parklands and alpine. This is steep and rugged country but keen hunters find good numbers of mule deer, cougar, and black bear as well as fair numbers of moose, mountain goat and grizzly bear.

Lower Mainland Region WMU Highlights

WMU 2-1

This wildlife management unit's bounds are within Manning Provincial Park, which is closed to hunting.

WMU 2-17

This management unit is more interior than coast and encompasses the Coquihalla drainage. The area has a lot of deer (mule deer), but heavy snow-pack can have a negative impact on populations. There are also lots of black bear, and some good cougar hunting, but the limited number of backroads in this area can make access difficult. The drier interior climate offers better conditions for grouse, too.

Kootenay Region WMU Highlights

WMU 4-09

Covering the area around Rossland and Trail, this area offers some fair bird hunting for grouse and wild turkey. There are fair populations of both white-tailed and mule deer here.

WMU 4-14

Protecting the west side of the Lower Arrow Lake Valley, this long, thin management unit offers good habitat for grouse. It is one of only a few units in the southern Kootenay with a decent population of moose, and also supports fair numbers of deer.

WMU 4-15

Encompassing the mountains east of Lower Arrow Lake, there is good terrain for grouse hunting along with good populations of deer and elk. Persistent hunters can also find a few moose here.

WMU 4-32

West of Upper Arrow Lake, this region offers good opportunities to hunt grouse, as well as white-tailed deer.

WMU 4-37

This unit is made up of mostly inaccessible mountains. Historically, hunting has been limited by poor access.

WMU 4-38

As you move farther north, moose populations in the Kootenays improve. This is one of the northernmost units in the region and as a result, offers some of the best moose hunting. In addition, there are small populations of black bear, elk, mule deer and mountain goat.

WMU 4-39

This management unit has poor road access, which leads to low success rates in hunting. However, the unit does offer some of the best moose hunting in the Kootenays.

WMU 4-40

On the east side of Kinbasket Lake, this management unit is hard to access and rarely hunted.

Cariboo Region WMU Highlight

WMU 5–15

This management unit captures the uplands of the Quesnel Highlands and the western edge of the Cariboo Mountains. It is within the interior wet belt and supports forests of spruce, hemlock and cedar, similar to coastal rainforest, but is much more productive for game animals. Logging has opened the access and the new logging blocks provide very good moose habitat. Hunters also take decent numbers of mule deer and black bear here. In addition, this is the most productive area in the Cariboo for mountain goat hunting. Upland bird hunters can do well in this WMU hunting for spruce, ruffed and blue grouse.

Omineca Region WMU Highlights

WMU 7-1, 7-2, 7-3

The Rocky Mountains are dramatic rocky, snow-capped peaks that border the wide valley bottom of the northern reaches of the Fraser River. The climate is moist and cool, but there is a distinctly drier zone from McBride to Valemount. Spruce forests dominate both the valley bottoms and mid slopes of the mountains. Hunters find a wide variety of big game animals including moose, elk, mountain goats, both species of deer and both species of bear. There are decent, but not spectacular, levels of harvest for all these species. Elk and white-tailed deer may be managed aggressively to reduce conflicts with agriculture in management units 7-2 and 7-3.

WMU 7-4, 7-5

The North Cariboo Mountains are a rugged, cool and wet area, with cedar and hemlock forests in the valleys and spruce and sub-alpine fir on the mountain slopes. Moose, mule deer and black bear are found throughout the area. This is not a bad choice for grizzly bear hunting and there are also small numbers of elk and white-tailed deer harvested.

 **DID YOU KNOW?**

Our British Columbia GPS maps feature over 150 WMUs for hunters. Access smart backgrounds & searchable Wildlife Management Units (WMUs) featuring detailed topography with industry leading contour lines & relief shading.

Kayaking on Trapp Lake
©Tourism Kamloops/Kelly Funk

PADDLING
ADVENTURES

Thompson Okanagan rivers offer a bit of everything. Some rivers meander through the arid interior valleys and are perfect for a scenic canoe trip. Others plunge steeply down into those valleys and attract local and international kayakers looking for a challenge.

If you are a serious whitewater paddler, most small volume rivers are at their best in the late spring run-off. As the summer wears on, the volume of water decreases and the rivers slow down. But it is in summer that the famous Thompson River shines. The early season run-off covers nearly all the interesting features on the river. It is a fast, boring run. But as the water level drops, the river's teeth are revealed and kayakers and rafters begin to play on one of BC's premiere rivers.

For each river, we have included the put-in and take-out locations for the most popular runs on that river. Also included are short descriptions highlighting the route. We use a modified version of the International scale to grade rivers, where the overall paddle is the grade of the river, while class refers to the difficulty of specific features.

Flatwater or Lake Paddling enthusiasts have literally hundreds of lakes to choose from in the area. Rather than describe all the small lakes and ponds that make for nice day trips, we have limited our descriptions to the canoe routes, multi-day destinations and popular lakes. This region offers several fantastic paddling routes including a number of popular routes in Wells Gray Park. The Parks and Recreation Site sections of this book will show more waterbodies that are popular with paddlers and have facilities such as boat launches.

The only style of paddling not represented in this area is ocean paddling. But there are a number of large lakes (Adams, Arrow, Kamloops, Shuswap and Okanagan to name a few) that offer an experience similar to paddling the narrow fjords of the west coast without the salt water. Still, like the ocean, these big lakes are prone to strong winds and caution must be taken by paddlers heading out onto big water.

Below we have listed a few of the best-known areas for both types of paddling opportunities. Please note that the descriptions given in this book are very general and may not contain enough detail to navigate certain routes safely, especially rivers with higher ratings. We recommend that you check the current conditions with local canoeists/kayakers or local outdoor stores before heading out. It is also essential to scout rivers, since conditions can change daily.

PADDLING ADVENTURES

Lake Paddling

Clearwater/Azure Lake Route (Map 41/D6–F3)
The access point for this fabulous wilderness route is located in the heart of Wells Gray Park at the end of the Clearwater Valley Road. There is a self-registration station with a fee drop off box at the launching site. The trip up Clearwater Lake usually takes about two days to cover the 21 km (13 mi) to the north end. Along the way, you can choose from 33 tent sites scattered around the shores. Some of the more popular sites sport a sandy beach area for sun seekers. The scenery along the way is fantastic as the forested slopes of the lake give way to the mountain peaks of Mount Ray and Azure Mountain. To get to Azure Lake, paddle 3 km upstream, then make the 500 metre (1,640 ft) portage to Azure. The portage is well-established with ladders rendering canoe carts useless. In June and July the river can be quite challenging. Azure Lake is 20 km (12.4 mi) long with 21 campsites. The return trip to Rainbow Falls is 96 km (60 mi) and will take at least four days.

Christina Lake (Map 6/D3–E6)
Located about 20 km northeast of Grand Forks, the Monashee Mountains surround this warm lake. You can access the lake from the boat launch on East Lake Drive near the Texas Creek Campground of Gladstone Provincial Park. From here, most venture north to explore the quieter part of the lake, where there are many sandy beachfront campsites. There are pictographs on the rock face near the campground and several marine access campsites for extended outings.

Dee Lake Canoe Route (Map 17/D4)
The chain of lakes that includes Dee, Island, Deer, Crooked and Beaver Lakes can be strung together for an enjoyable overnight or longer canoe route. A dam at the south end of Crooked requires portaging over. Access points can be found at the resorts on Dee or Beaver, while camping and access can be found at recreation sites on both lakes as well as on Island Lake.

Emar Lakes Canoe Circuit (Map 33/B3)
This is an easy route to access as it lies off the south side of Highway 24, west of Little Fort. This short, small lake canoe route travels in a circle from Long Island Lake and back. The first and longest portage is about a kilometre, bringing paddlers to Chub Lake. The route continues over five more portages and four water bodies, including Emar Lake. Rustic camping opportunities exist on all the water bodies and wildlife viewing and fishing are popular pastimes in the area. The route can be done in a day, but it makes an ideal overnight trip. Although the portages are cleared at the beginning of each summer, this is a wilderness area and those exploring need to be self-sufficient. Parking can be found at both Janice Lake and Willowgrouse Lake.

Humamilt Lake (Map 35/D6–E6)
The 12 km (7.5 mi) long Humamilt Lake offers plenty for the paddler to see including tall rock bluffs, wetlands and old growth Douglas fir trees. Keep your eye out for beaver dams, as well. There are a number of small islands at the east end of the lake perfect for exploring. Paddlers can also check out the rocky narrows, barely a canoe length wide, for some unique rock formations. There are two other small lakes here, Momich and Stukemapten Lakes, that offer more exploration if time permits. A nice recreation site with six camping spots can be found at the west side of the lake, while an unofficial campsite can be found on the north end.

Kinbasket Lake (Map 44/D7–47/B3)
There are two main access areas to this large man-made lake. The northern access point can be found southeast of the town of Valemount via the East Canoe Forest Service Road. The access road travels along the eastern side of this glacier fed lake and passes by two forest recreation areas before reaching the Canoe Reach Marina Recreation Site. The southern access is located north of the settlement of Mica Creek, east of the Mica Dam. Kinbasket Lake is a large reservoir lake formed by a series of dams on the mighty Columbia River. You can literally spend days padding the lake. There are hundreds of kilometres of shoreline to explore. At low water levels the lake is not as pleasant to paddle.

Lower Arrow Lake (Maps 12/G7–19/G3)
The best time to canoe or kayak this 90 km (56 mi) long lake is July and August when the water is high. There are a number of public launches available, including Fauquier Provincial Park, Eagle Creek Regional Park in Edgewood and Syringa Provincial Park near Castlegar. A popular day trip is to put in at Deer Park and canoe or kayak across to the Natural Arch trail, then hike the 1.5 km to the spectacular rock formation.

Lupin Lakes Canoe Route (Map 33/B6)
This canoe route involves a six-hour paddle through six small interconnecting wilderness lakes. There are four short portages, with the last portage being uphill. For those who enjoy fishing, all the lakes have trout in them and there are a number of rustic places to camp along the lakes.

Mabel Lake (Map 25/D5–E1)
Stretching for 35 km (22 mi), this large and sometimes windy lake is a great destination for paddlers. In particular, the quieter north end offers several boat access beaches that make nice places to camp. There are also a few recreation sites and a provincial park on the lake that offer camping and boat launches. Alert canoeists might be able to view 200 to 400 year old pictographs on the rock surfaces around the lake, while those hoping to catch their dinner can land kokanee, Dolly Varden and rainbow trout. Boat traffic is heaviest around the resort area in the middle of the lake.

Moose Lake (Map 51/D7–47/F1)
Stretching along the south side of Highway 16 in Mount Robson Provincial Park, Moose Lake can be accessed from a boat launch at the southeast end of the lake. There are lots of areas to explore with great scenery, including Moose Marsh, but canoeists need to be aware of strong winds and sudden changes in weather conditions and plan accordingly.

Mud Lake (Map 43/B7)
Mud Lake and the Mud Lake Delta offer a unique paddling and wildlife viewing experience. The delta features floodplain wetlands, back channels and oxbow lakes and moose are known to frequent the area year-round, while grizzly bears are often seen here in the spring. There is no overnight camping or day-use area.

Murtle Lake Canoe Route (Map 38/D1–42/C5)
Set in the eastern range of Wells Gray Park, Murtle Lake is surrounded by fabulous mountain scenery. There are 19 camping areas ringing the lake. The first and only portage on this trip is 2.5 km (1.6 mi) long and a canoe cart will certainly cut down on the work. The portage ends at the eastern side of the Murtle Lagoon, where it is then a short paddle to Murtle Lake. The lake offers good fishing and there are a number of water-accessed trails. A backcountry pass is required for overnight trips. Due to an infestation of Mountain Pine Beetles, care should be taken when selecting campsites and where tents are pitched and canoes stored. Although the forestry service is working to clear deadfall, high winds are responsible for persistent and dangerous debris.

Okanagan Lake (Maps 9, 10, 16, 17, 24)
Stretching from Vernon, down past Kelowna to Penticton, this huge lake is best paddled in the morning or evening as it becomes quite choppy during the afternoon. There are numerous spots to put your canoe into the water and a multitude of islands (Rattlesnake Island of Okanagan Mountain Park being a great spot) and bays to explore. The park also offers a number of marine access campsites for overnight trips. With the number of motorized boats on this lake, paddlers need to be alert and prepared.

Osoyoos Lake (Map 4/B6)
Osoyoos Lake is a popular summer spot for water recreation including canoes, paddle-boards, jet skis and more. It also offers a great bird watching area at the northwest end in the Osoyoos Oxbows Wildlife Reserve. If you are looking for a paddle here, avoid the busier south end and head to the top of the lake to enjoy the reserve.

Shuswap Lake (Maps 24, 29, 30, 35)
When most people think of Shuswap Lake, they think of house boating. Add in the many water sport enthusiasts and you will see why canoeists do not find this lake all that peaceful. But with over 1,000 km (620 mi) of shoreline and 26 marine parks to explore, the big lake can be a good place to paddle in a sea kayak. Canoeists still venture out during early mornings and evenings.

Tuwut Lake Canoe Route (Map 28/A2)
While it is possible to cram all ten (or more, depending on your route) lakes of this circuit into one day, most people spread this enjoyable trip out over two or three days. This is not a developed paddle and access to Tuwut Lake is through an old clearcut off the Windy Lake Road. The carry down to the lake will take about twenty minutes and is by far the most difficult portage of the entire journey. There is no established circuit, although there are well-beaten animal/angler trails between the lakes. The close proximity of lakes makes it possible to shorten or lengthen the trip.

River Paddling

Adams River (Map 29/E5)
From Adams Lake to Shuswap Lake, the Adams River runs 14 km (8.7 mi) over the gravel beds where the famous Adams River sockeye spawn in fall. Most people put-in at the south end of Adams Lake and take-out at the Squilax-Anglemont Road Bridge (a total of 10 km/6 mi). However, Holding Road parallels the river for its entire length and you can put-in or take-out wherever you want to. This is a safe, popular, warm river, with a paddling season that runs from April to October. The Adams is a Grade II river that is a great place for beginners to cut their teeth on a bit of whitewater. There are also enough play holes and standing waves to keep experts interested, too. The only section that might cause problems for inexperienced kayakers is the 75 metre long (245 ft) Class III–IV Gorge, aka the Devil's Door, as well as numerous sweepers and log jams that are not always visible in advance.

Ashnola River (Map 2/F5–3/B4)
Located within Cathedral Provincial Park, this Class IV River can be run from snowmelt in the spring through early summer (May and June); sometimes later if the winter produced heavy snow. There are numerous put-in options with the furthest being 20 km up the park access road. The 12 km and 6 km markers offer good access locations too. The run is easily boat scoutable, but the river does become more difficult the further you head downstream. The section from 20 km to 12 km is the easiest. At the 12 km mark, a powerful tributary meets the river and the rapids become more active while the largest rapid, the Sabretooth, is found at the 6 km marker.

Barrière River (Map 28/E1–34/A6)
The Barrière River flows down a steady gradient over small rock beds and will prove to be challenging to the guided beginner kayaker or expert canoeist. The river peaks in June, but there is usually enough water in May and July to keep things interesting. From the Barrière Lakes Road Bridge to the bridge on Barrière Town Road, it is a 20 km/12.4 mi (3 hour) Grade II/IV route. It is possible to put-in farther upstream, at the North Barrière Lake Forest Road Bridge, for an extra 6 km/3.6 mi (1.5 hours) of paddling. This second put-in will take you through a short but challenging canyon section. Be aware, the river is notorious for sweepers, deadheads and logjams.

Canoe River (Map 46/F4–47/B3)
The Canoe River is accessible via a rough logging road off the west side of Highway 5, south of Valemount. The first put-in is found east of the Upper Canoe River Recreation Site where an old bridge once crossed the river near the power lines. The other access is located west of the recreation site about 8 km (5 mi) from the old bridge access. Look for a rough road track into the bush. In high water, this is a Grade IV river that can be quite treacherous. There is a short canyon, drops, ledges and chutes that will test even the most skilled paddlers. In summer, the river slows down to a Grade III run with some Class IV features. The main take-out for this route is at the crossing of Highway 5 over the Canoe River.

Clearwater River (Map 37/D3–F7)
Accessed from Clearwater River Road on the west side of the river, there are several different runs to look for. Be sure to scout ahead as it is possible to see most of the river from the road on the drive up.

Upper Clearwater River
This is a Class 2 route accessed from the end of the Clearwater River Road. This section of the river is mostly calm, but there are Class 2 whitewater sections. You will pass the impressive Whitehorse Bluff and a trappers hut with a natural rock fridge. There is a large beach at km 28 that offers a nice camping location and a possible take-out. Beyond the next take-out at km 24 the river gets much more challenging.

Sabretooth Canyon
This rollercoaster ride starts at km 24 of the Clearwater River Road. A few km of Class 1 warms you up for the Class 4+ Tooth, followed by the Batholith, a shallow swift section, which will lead you to into the S bend and a wave train that can rise up to 6 metres (20 ft) at high water. Beyond here a few smaller wave trains lead down to the commercial rafting lunch spot at km 19. The river then mellows to a Class 1 float down to the campsite at km 14.

Middle Canyon
This run is accessed from the km 14 campsite and starts with a couple km of Class 1+ rapids before the Class 3 rollercoaster ride to House Rock. Be sure to avoid the Grizzly and Whale Holes. After House Rock you will find the Shanes Demise and Sharks Fin Rapids, which are considered some of the best rapids on the river. Make sure you take-out at the boat launch, river right, before The Kettle!

The Kettle
This 1 km run features a Class 5/6 drop over Kettle Falls. Above this drop the run is still Class 4/5 and runnable at low water. It is possible to run the entire rapid at very low flows, but it is best to eddy out river right before the falls and walk around.

Lower Canyon
This popular Class 3/4 run is typically started at km 8 on the Clearwater River. You will hit Three Fingers followed by the Mosh Pit. The river then splits around an island and it is recommended to stay river left to hit the Wall. Following the Wall you will pass through the German Basher and M87 before reaching a large eddy on river right. This is Hole in the Wall and an alternative put-in to avoid the more difficult rapids upstream. It is found near km 6.5 on the Clearwater River Road. After Hole in the Wall the river widens and you will find play holes everywhere! Keep an eye out for waves called Easy Rider and Tsunami and be sure to hit Pink Mountain, the last major rapid. The take-out is river right just above the bridge in town.

Helmecken Canyon
The Helmecken Canyon is Class 5/6 and is the most difficult and isolated section of the Clearwater River. It should only be attempted at very, very low flows by expert paddlers. The run is found downstream of Baily's Chute on the Clearwater Valley Road and continues through to km 38 on the Clearwater River Road. The first and most difficult drop is Gattling Gorge, followed by a number of big drops before ending with the Flowerpot rapids.

Coldwater River (Map 7/B3–14/D4)
This appropriately-named river flows beside and occasionally under the Coquihalla Highway for 35 km (22 mi) from Juliet Creek to Merritt. Access is fairly good along the winding, fast moving Grade II/II+ river with one Class IV drop after the bridge near the 18 km mark. It is possible to break this river up into bite-sized pieces (common put-ins/take-outs are Larson Hill, Coldwater Interchange and Patchet Road) or to do it in one long run. The first section between Juliet Creek and Larson Hill is easy (Grade I) and is often skipped by kayakers looking for a bit more excitement. Watch for sweepers.

When paddling in a new area, plan an "escape" route - an alternative place to get off the water should environmental conditions dictate it.

Dore River (Map 49/A4–C2)
The Dore River is a wild and fast flowing river. The South Fork is a Grade IV–V glacial fed run with plenty of Class III–V rapids including the Sucker Punch, which is found near the end of the run. The put-in is found about 4 km up the South Dore Road, while the take-out is found at the first bridge. Scouting is essential and do not miss the take-out since there are a number of extremely difficult Class V rapids further down the river that most recreational paddlers should not run.

From the third bridge, the West Fork of the Dore River is a Grade IV–V run, depending on the water level. This stretch of whitewater will grab paddler's right from the start and rarely lets up as it winds through sharp channels and over countless boulders. Around the second bridge, the Dore River is much tamer, ranging from Grade II to Grade III in high water. But do not be lulled into thinking it is over, as the last section of the run bombs through a narrow canyon and ends with a spectacular Class V–VI cascade. Most paddlers will want to take-out well before the canyon, at the Highway 16 Bridge.

Eagle River (Map 30/F6–31/C4)

Eagle River and the Trans-Canada Highway play hide and seek as both river and road weave their way from Sicamous to Revelstoke. A popular, easy (Grade I–II) paddle is from the Last Spike Monument to Shuswap Lake, a distance of 29 km (18 mi). It will take about six hours to travel the full distance, but there are many good access points along the route to shorten the journey.

Fraser River (Map 13/A2–C7; 49/A1–51/D7)

From the Yellowhead Pass to Vancouver, the Fraser River is a 1,600 km (995 mi) run that rages through narrow gorges, cascades over a short waterfall, and meanders lazily across the province. Through the Fraser Canyon and especially through Hell's Gate, the river is best left to extreme kayakers or rafting companies.

The northern reaches of the river contain two sections. Above Moose Lake, the river is a scenic Grade II paddle. Below Moose Lake to Tête Jaune Cache, the river has sections of Grade V water, but you can avoid the worst of the rapids by taking out almost anywhere, while extreme kayakers can simply put in above them. In fall, paddlers can see spawning salmon that have travelled almost 2,000 km from the Pacific Ocean to the final inland barrier at Rearguard Falls, which should probably be avoided by paddlers.

Granby River (Map 11/G6–6/A1; 6/A2–B6)

Between Eight Mile Flats and the 52 km marker, the Granby is a Grade II route. Beginner and intermediate paddlers do not want to miss this take-out, as below the 52 km marker the river passes through a Class IV+ canyon. Experts who want to run the canyon can take-out at the Granby-Burrell Recreation Site. The lower section of river can be accessed by the North Fork Road and offers a Grade I paddle or float all the way into Grand Forks. Be wary of the odd sweeper and the many shallow sections.

Holmes River & Chalko Creek (Map 49/F1–E3)

To access the upper section of this route, take the Holmes/Beaver River Forest Road east off Highway 16 south of McBride. Near the confluence of the Chalko Creek and Holmes River there is a rough access road that travels 7.5 km north to the put-in. Chalko Creek is a Grade II–III run in low water and a Grade III–IV in high water. The amazing run ends about 7.5 km (4.7 mi) downstream, about 400 metres after the confluence with the Holmes River.

In low water the Holmes River portion is a Grade II–III run and in high water is at least a Grade III run. The river offers a long stretch of whitewater in its upper portion, while the lower portion is a mix of boulder gardens and a few tight channels. Be sure not to miss the take-out at the Beaver (Holmes) River Recreation Site off the east side of the river, unless you are ready for a Class IV–V, 5 metre (16 ft) drop.

Horsey Creek (Map 50/B5)

This Grade IV–V run has plenty of big drops and technical Class V–VI rapids. The rugged shoreline and volume of water makes portaging near impossible on most parts of this creek. The upper portion of the creek is home to the major Class V–VI rapids and during low water, the southern half offers Class III–IV rapids. Look for the access road to this creek off the east side of Highway 16, just south of the highway crossing over the creek. The take-out is found off the east side of Highway 16 where the creek crosses under the highway.

Kettle River (Map 5/C1–6/E6)

Draining the southeast portion of the Okanagan, the Kettle River is a gentle giant for the most part. It flows quickly down from Keffer Lake in the Monashee Mountains and through the Christian Valley before settling into the farmlands along Highway 3 west of Rock Creek. From Midway to Grand Forks it dips back and forth between Canada and the USA before eventually joining the Columbia River in Washington State. The Kettle is one of the cleanest, warmest rivers in BC and there are plenty of places to put-in and take-out.

McKale River (Map 49/B1)

The put-in for this route is found about 5 km up the McKale River Road, while the take-out is found at the Mountainview Road Bridge. This challenging run is regarded as a Grade III–IV run, depending on water levels, with non-stop rapids that are sure to test your physical endurance. There are plenty of Class III–IV rapids throughout the run with one particularly difficult Class IV–V drop about three quarters of the way along the route.

McLennan River (Map 46/E1–G2)

The McLennan Rivers travels between Crooked Creek Road and the Old Tête Jaune Cache, just northwest of Valemount. This trip is for experienced canoeists and can take between six and seven hours depending on water levels.

Mission Creek (Map 10/B1–17/C7)

Found in Kelowna, Mission Creek is a popular recreational retreat for local residents. The creek offers paddlers a chance to test their skills in a bit of whitewater during the spring with rock and boulder gardens, caves and a canyon. Above the Hollywood Road Bridge is a Grade II/III section, while below the bridge is an easy urban paddle through the heart of Kelowna. Go early (April to June) as there is not a lot of water in summer. Open canoes are not allowed during high water.

Nicola River (Map 14/E4–20/D6)

The Nicola flows from Nicola Lake west through Merritt and then north until it flows into the Thompson River near Spences Bridge. The upper river is mostly Grade I/II paddling with access points at the Voght Street Bridge in Merritt, the Sunshine Valley East Bridge, the N'Kwala Recreation Site and the Chief Joe Anthony Bridge. Between N'Kwala and Chief Joe is an 18 km (11 mi) Grade I run, with a couple Class II features, including a little headwall and mini canyon. Hazards along this portion of the river include sweepers, tight corners and blind channels. The take-out is accessed by turning left on Dot Ranch Cut-Off Road and following the dirt road that is found 1.3 km down the ranch road.

Beyond Chief Joe is a short Class II/III canyon that will challenge most kayakers. In fact, many do not go all the way to the Shackan Campground, preferring to take-out one bend after the canyon to do it again. Be sure to scout ahead. The last section is a long 27 km (17 mi) stretch of Grade II/III water that cuts through the scenic ponderosa pine dry belt below the Shackan Campground. Depending on rainfall, the paddling season can run from April to July and the trickiest section is near the Rattlesnake Bridge right before the Thompson. Some people take-out here, while others use the picnic area a kilometre downstream from the confluence with the Thompson. Good access is found along the whole route via the quiet Highway 8.

Remember that river conditions are always changing and advanced scouting is essential.

Pasayton River (Map 2/A7–A5)

The Pasayton River is a solid Grade II run and is quite challenging, especially in high water when there are only a few eddies. The put-in is found 20.7 km along the Pasayton River Forest Road, while the take-out is actually on the Similkameen River. Paddlers should park a second vehicle at the large gravel pull off on Highway 3, 2.5 km downriver from the Pasayton River Forest Road access bridge. You do not want to miss this take-out, as the Similkameen Falls are just around the corner.

Robson River (Map 51/A6)

This fantastic whitewater river is set in the beautiful wilderness of Mount Robson Park below Mount Robson, the highest peak in the Canadian Rockies. It features some of the best scenery—and some of the toughest paddling—in this region. The run is only 4 km (2.5 mi) long, but the Robson is a Grade IV–V river that will test even the best paddlers. There are three Class VI waterfall drops and a number of other rapids. To get to the put-in, kayakers hike 4 km up the Berg Lake Trail to a bridge over the Robson River where it flows out of Kinny Lake. The take-out is at the Berg Lake parking lot.

Seymour River (Map 35/G6)

The Seymour River is a secluded wilderness river with plenty of variety. It is 8 km (5 mi) from the bridge below Seymour Falls to the bridge to Silver Beach Park. The Grade II paddle has a Class III+ canyon to keep things interesting. The canyon needs advance scouting as there are usually sweepers or other obstacles. Expert kayakers can add to the length and difficulty of the run by starting upstream at the powerline. This section involves shooting a small, sometimes impassable canyon. Scouting is essential! There are also several Grade IV drops and a difficult portage around Seymour Falls (bring a rope). The best time to paddle is in July.

Shuswap River (Map 24/F1–25/C2)

Starting from Mabel Lake, the Shuswap starts out as a fast river, but soon tames as it flows through the farmland around Enderby where it is better known as a tubing river. Beyond Enderby, the river courses north and is not the best place to paddle or tube. The launches are well marked with adequate parking found off the Enderby-Mabel Lake Road.

Kingfisher Creek to Brandt Crossing Launch

The section, known as The Chuck, begins with a put-in at Kingfisher Creek and is best left to experienced paddlers. From Kingfisher Creek it is a 3 km (1.9 mi) Grade III (Grade IV at high water) run through boiling water, large waves, some holes and a few whirlpools. Advanced scouting is highly recommended, especially before tackling the Skookumchuck Rapids (The Chuck) where a large warning sign marks the take-out at the Brandt Crossing Launch. The season runs from March to October.

Brandt Crossing Launch to Cooke Creek Recreation Site

From The Brandt Crossing Launch, the next 7 km (4.3 mi) of the river are an easy Grade II paddle suitable for canoeists (no tubers please). The best time to paddle this section of river is after the spring runoff (late June). There is a signed portage just above Cooke Creek.

Cooke Creek Recreation Site to Trinity Valley Road Bridge

The section of the river offers a 20 km (12.4 mi) Grade II–III route best paddled later in summer. In high water, the route swells to a Grade III–IV paddle and should be left to expert paddlers only. An alternate access is found upstream at the Dale Launch. The take-out for this section is at the Trinity Valley Road Bridge.

Trinity Valley Road Bridge to Enderby

From the Trinity Valley Road Bridge, this section is 9 km (5.6 mi) in length and is rated a Grade I or II route. In summer this area is better known for tubing. Eby Launch and Belvidere Park provide alternate access points.

Enderby to Mara Lake

This 24 km (15 mi) easy Grade I–II paddle is better known for its nature viewing as it is a slow float. There is an alternate put-in/take-out at the Grindrod Bridge on Highway 97A, which is about 9 km (5.6 mi) from the take-out at Mara Lake.

Similkameen River (Map 2/A5–3/F7; 8/C7)

The Similkameen begins its long journey in Manning Park, then courses north to Princeton before looping southeast towards Osoyoos. South of the border, it spills into the south end of Osoyoos Lake. Highway 3 provides good access to most of the river.

Bridge on Placer Mountain Road to Princeton

Southwest of Similkameen Falls the river is often too shallow and loaded with debris to paddle properly. Most kayakers access the Upper Similkameen from the bridge on Placer Mountain Road. This is a long (40 km/25 mi), challenging paddle that should only be tried by experts after spring runoff. The difficult run is Grade III with numerous Class IV+ technical drops. The river mellows out after leaving the canyon and becomes a Grade II paddle. The Elk Ridge Outdoors Campsite, off Highway 3, provides an alternate access point.

Princeton to Bromley Rock Campground

This 20 km (12.4 mi) paddle has one section of easy Class II rapids near the take-out at Bromley Rock Campground. Most novices will enjoy the challenge of running these or will choose to take-out before the rapids.

Bromley Rock Campground to Pickard Creek Recreation Site

This is a 10 km (6 mi) Grade II route. There is a Grade III drop (at the Golden Dawn Cafe), which you may wish to portage around. The river is generally easy to paddle but watch for boulders throughout. The best paddling is from April–July. The take-out can be found at the Pickard Creek Recreation Site.

Lower Similkameen (Upper Section): Keremeos to the Red Bridge

The Lower Similkameen River begins as a Grade III paddle extending 9 km (5.6 mi). The put-in is found 12.7 km west of Keremeos and the route is best paddled in late June to early July. The take-out is at the Red Bridge.

Lower Similkameen (Middle Section): Red Bridge to Kobau Regional Park

This 6 km (3.7 mi) Grade III section of river beginning at the Red Bridge passes through Keremeos and ends in Kobau Regional Park. The route is best paddled in late June to early July as low water creates many hazards and shallow sections.

Lower Similkameen (Bottom Section): Kobau Regional Park to Chopaka Road Bridge

From Kobau Regional Park, this Grade II paddle meanders along the Lower Similkameen River for 19 km (12 mi) with some rapids. The best time to paddle this section is late June to early July. The section finishes at the take-out at the Chopaka Road Bridge.

Small River (Map 50/C6)

From the first bridge along the Small River Road, this portion of the Small River is rated Grade III–IV, with a number of Class III–IV rapids, as well as a Class IV–V boulder garden located just below the put-in. It can be easily avoided by putting in further downstream. The river is prone to logjams and debris along the run. It is best run during run-off.

Spius Creek (Map 14/A4)

The put-in for Spius Creek is just below Little Box Canyon, about 8 km south of the fish hatchery. Boats must be lowered down the steep bank by rope or driven down by a four-wheel drive vehicle. The twisting Grade II stream is a challenging paddle with numerous sweepers to watch out for. The biggest rapids are under the wood bridge and at a large rock studded left bend. Spius Creek flows into the Nicola River, where it is possible to take-out at the N'Kwala Forest Recreation Site.

Thompson River (Map 13/A2–20/C7)

The southwest Thompson River is one of the kayaking and commercial rafting hot spots in the province. This is not an area for the inexperienced (unless you are on a guided trip), but it is THE place for whitewater thrills. For intermediate paddlers with a strong roll, there are a couple of fast flowing sections to sample. Both routes offer a scenic paddle through dry ponderosa pine country. While this river is runnable at any level, it is most popular when the levels are relatively low in late summer and early fall.

From the Goldpan Campsite to the Nicoamen River is a 12 km (7.5 mi) Grade II/III route with plenty of turbulence and large waves but few rock obstacles. The biggest rapids are in the first few kilometres, including Frog Wave, a great play area near the start, Witch's Calderon, Cutting Board, which is left of the island, and Jaws. Jaws is located where the highway starts to move away from the river and it is possible to put-in here to avoid the big rapids. Below Jaws, the river begins to mellow and there are some sections of flatwater.

Continuing south to Lytton, the Thompson becomes more difficult to paddle as the water level and flow of the river increases. This second section extends 24 km (15 mi) and is rated as a Grade IV expert kayak route. The paddle is not technically difficult but is intimidating due to its large waves, rapids and holes. It is recommended that the route only be tried after a local has shown you the best line to take through the difficult sections.

Tulameen River (Map 7/D6–8/A7)

The Tulameen area is rich in history – from the gold mines to the historic Kettle Valley Railway stops, there are many sights and sounds to see along the way. The river is quite variable with many pools, rock and boulder gardens. Paddlers can start at the bridge about 7 km (4.3 mi) west of Tulameen and run through the canyon that features a series of Class II+ rapids before the easy float to Tulameen. The next stretch is the short section of Grade I water leading to Coalmont and the home of BC's oldest operating hotel. The final section is the 21 km (13 mi) Grade II route from Coalmont to Princeton. The Tulameenie Falls is a Grade IV+ drop that is particularly dangerous in low water and probably should be portaged (the portage is through an old railway tunnel). Below the falls, the river is mostly Grade I, with a few easy Grade II sections. Along the way, marvel at the hoodoos or stop and relax on the sandy beaches. The best time to paddle the route is in May or June, during spring runoff.

Upper Adams River Route (Map 34/G4–39/D4)

The Adams River can be accessed from a number of spots along its length. There are a number of bridges along the way, as well access at Tumtum and Mica Lakes. All these points double as take-out points, or you can paddle into Adams Lake. The river is quite remote and is truly a beautiful wilderness experience. Although most of the river is a peaceful paddle, rated little more than Grade I, there is a Grade IV+ section of whitewater in the canyon that is found about 45 minutes south of the Tumtum access point. This section features about half a dozen big drops and scouting is essential. Below Mica Lake, the river returns to its gentle nature although it still should not be attempted by novice paddlers.

Robson Peak, Berg Lake, and Berg Glacier
from Toboggan Falls in Robson Provincial Park

PARK
ADVENTURES

From glorious beaches to mountain retreats, the provincial and regional parks of the Southern Interior provide a perfect destination to get away from it all. Through these parks and recreation sites, outdoor enthusiasts can pursue pretty well every imaginable activity and see some of BC's most amazing scenery.

Provincial parks offer campers and day visitors a variety of options, from impeccably manicured RV-friendly sites on the shores of Okanagan and Shuswap Lakes to rustic, difficult to access sites located high in the mountains. No matter their size or location, most parks cater to people looking to pursue outdoor activities in a natural area. However, there are a few parks and protected areas that are set aside to protect ecologically sensitive habitats. Visitors are discouraged from visiting these select areas.

Campgrounds within provincial parks generally operate from early spring through fall. Some stay open all year. Almost all parks charge a fee that varies according to the facilities and services provided. In the Southern Interior, many of the popular campsites can be reserved (look for the █ symbol). Considering how busy these parks can be from the May long weekend through to the end of summer, reserving a site before you go is a great idea. To reserve your site, call Discover Camping at 1-800-689-9025 (604-689-9025 in Greater Vancouver) or visit *discovercamping.ca*.

The regional and city park system in the Southern Interior is also quite impressive and varied. Mostly providing day-use facilities, these are great places to visit for a picnic, a day at the beach or even a short hike through the woods. Combined with the provincial system, there are a staggering number of great places to get out and enjoy all the Thompson Okanagan has to offer.

To make things easier when planning a trip, we have added recreational symbols beside each park name. These symbols will not only show you the features of the park, but also give you an indication of some of the more popular activities pursued in the area. The description is intended to give you a good background on the park. We do not list all of the provincial or regional parks. The ones we left out generally do not offer much in the way of recreational appeal. However, if a site in missing that you feel should be included, please let us know. You can also find more information on the provincial park system through the impressive new government website found at *bcparks.ca*.

With over 1000 provincial parks to explore,

You'll never be lost for adventure.

Find yourself in BC Parks.

www.bcparks.ca

BRITISH COLUMBIA | BC Parks

Adams Lake [Bush Creek] Provincial Park (Map 29/D4)

This tiny, 56 hectare (138 ac) park is located on the southwest shores of Adams Lake at Bush Creek. The sitae offers 27 vehicle access and four walk-in campsites, hiking trails and all types of boating activities. Amenities include pit toilets and a rough gravel boat launch at this park. There are archaeological sites in this park and opportunities for swimming, waterskiing and windsurfing.

Adams Lake Marine Park (Map 29/E2–34/G5)

This marine park is made up of a few boat access campsites on Adams Lake. Poplar Point is a tiny 32 hectare (79 ac) park providing a stopover for boaters on the east side of the lake. Spillman Beach is one of the nicest beaches on Adams Lake and is boat access only, with room for a few picnic or overnight groups on the beach. Refuge Bay is a tiny site found on the northwest shore of the lake, providing one of the few secure boat landing sites.

Albas Marine Park (Map 35/F7)

Located on the western shores of the Seymour Arm, this small park is part of the Shuswap Lake Marine Park system. Although it can be accessed by road or water, the five campsites and pit toilets south of Blueberry Creek are only accessible by water. The park also has picnic facilities as well as a beach for sunbathers. A trail follows Celesta Creek to a series of waterfalls.

Allison Lake Provincial Park (Map 7/G4)

Located on Highway 5A, 28 km north of Princeton, this 23 hectare (57 ac) park is located on the south end of Allison Lake. The rustic campground has 22 campsites amongst the tall stands of aspen above the lake, while the separate day-use area provides a boat launch, pit toilets, picnic facilities and a nice swimming hole.

Antlers Beach Regional Park (Map 9/D3)

Antlers Beach is located on Okanagan Lake, next to Hardy Falls Regional Park. The park is located just off Highway 97 and Hardy Road in Peachland. This park offers a natural beach, a swimming area, and shaded picnic area. Across the lake from the park is Squally Point, where Ogopogo is rumoured to live.

> *Each year dozens of forest fires are started by human negligence. Be sure your fire is completely out and cool to the touch before moving on.*

Anstey Hunakwa Provincial Park (Maps 30/G1, 31/A1, 35/G7, 36/A7)

This 6,587 hectare (16,270 ac) park extends from the shores of Hunakwa Lake to the surrounding mountain peaks and old growth forest. The best access is provided from the north end of Anstey Arm, which is accessible by boat and offers sandy beaches, swimming, trails and access to fishing holes. Backcountry camping is permitted in the park as well.

Arrow Lakes Provincial Park (Map 12/E1–19/F6)

Both of these lakes are popular with recreational boaters and have endless bays and sandy beaches to explore. Only the Lower Arrow Lake is found in this book and provides a couple of popular day-use areas. The Eagle Creek site is located south of Edgewood on the western shores of the Lower Arrow Lake and provides a picnic area, sandy beach and boat launch. The Fauquier site is situated off Highway 6 on the eastern shores of the Lower Arrow Lake and has a boat launch, picnic area and beach. This park also offers RV accessible campsites on a first-come, first-served basis.

Arrowstone Provincial Park (Map 26/E6)

Located in the foothills northeast of Cache Creek, this 6,203 hectare (15,320 ac) wilderness park preserves one of the largest undisturbed valleys in the southern interior, with large stands of old growth Douglas fir. Activities include backcountry camping (no facilities provided), nature and wildlife viewing, hunting, fishing and cross-country skiing.

Bear Creek Provincial Park (Map 16/G6–17/A6)

Found close to Kelowna on the Westside Road, this is one of the busiest campsites in the Okanagan. It has a total of 122 reservable campsites with accessible washrooms, showers, sani-station, playground, large picnic area and a sandy beach that stretches nearly half a kilometre. Park activities include biking, fishing, hiking, paddling, swimming, wildlife viewing and wind-surfing. The longest trail in the park is a 5 km trek along the scenic Bear Creek Canyon, which has been carved into the bedrock by Bear Creek cascading onto the cottonwood lined delta. Campers are recommended to make reservations.

Bedard Aspen Provincial Park (Map 20/B3)

This 173 hectare (427 ac) park is accessed only by trail. The centerpiece of the park is Bedard Lake and most people hiking in also bring fishing gear. There are no developed facilities, but hunting and backcountry camping are possible.

Bertram Creek Regional Park (Map 9/G2)

This 18 hectare (44 ac) park is found along the eastern shores of Okanagan Lake along Lakeshore Road just past Cedar Creek Winery. This day-use park provides a swimming beach, hiking paths, canoeing and boating opportunities. There is also an amphitheatre, playground, BBQ facilities and washroom facilities at this park.

Blue Earth Lake Provincial Park (Map 20/B4)

This 705 hectare (1,740 ac) park is only accessed from the Blue Earth Lake Forest Road to the east. There are a few rustic vehicle access campsites at the first lake and two more at the second lake along with pit toilets and a rough boat launch for smaller boats. Activities here include fishing, hiking, hunting and mountain biking.

Blue River Provincial Parks (Map 43/A7–A6)

These parks, Blue River Pine and Blue River Black Spruce, were established to help protect a portion of the wetland habitats around the Blue River and Thompson Rivers confluence. Both the Blue River and Thompson River offer fishing opportunities. There are no established campsites in the park, although wilderness camping is possible. The Black Spruce Area makes up the majority of the park and is 175 hectares (432 ac) in size. This section provides canoe/kayak access to the Thompson River. The 26 hectare (64 ac) Pine Area lies just to the north of the much larger Black Spruce area and is only accessible by canoe from along the Thompson River or by snowshoe in the winter.

Bonaparte Provincial Park (Map 27/G1–28/A2)

This 11,811 hectare (29,175 ac) park encompasses the highlands of the Bonaparte Plateau. Road access is limited and requires a long drive along logging roads up Jamieson Creek. Instead, most people get into the park by floatplane, horseback, or on foot. Within the park are numerous fishing lakes, including four fly-in fishing resorts, together with several hiking trails and a canoe route. There is backcountry camping and an old recreation site at Windy Lake, as well as two cabins maintained by the snowmobile association.

Boundary Creek Provincial Park (Map 5/E6)

Nestled beside Boundary Creek to the south of Greenwood, this provincial park is easily accessed off Highway 3. There are a total of 18 campsites located in a semi-open area, which are primarily used as a stopover. The campground provides an opportunity to fish the creek or explore for remains of old mining activities.

Brent Mountain Protected Area (Map 9/C7)

This protected area encompasses a 4,344 hectare (10,730 ac) section of alpine area around Mount Brent. There are a number of established trails in the area, including one to the top of Brent Mountain and another along Shatford Creek. Hikers, horseback riders, cross-country skiers and snowmobilers all frequent the area. The trailhead is approximately 4 km from the closed bridge on the Shatford Creek Forest Service Road. There are pit toilets at the lookout.

Bridge Lake Provincial Park (Map 32/E3)

Located just off Highway 20, this tiny park helps protect a scenic point at the southern end of Bridge Lake. The park is home to 13 drive-in campsites and 3 walk-in sites, pit toilets, a boat launch and a day-use area. There is also a 2 km hiking trail that circles the park and provides nice views of the lake and the surrounding area. The main attraction of the park is the fabulous fishing in Bridge Lake.

Bromley Rock Provincial Park (Map 2/E1)

Bromley Rock is a striking rock bluff along the Similkameen River east of Princeton. The park is found right next to Highway 3. It is open year-round (with full services from mid-April to mid-October) and offers 17 rustic campsites, 9 of which are reservable, and a separate picnic area, both with accessible pit toilets. There is good access to the large fishing and swimming holes of the Similkameen River and good paddling in the area. Tubing from here to Stemwinder Provincial Park is a popular summer pastime.

Caligata Lake Provincial Park (Map 38/B6) 🏔️⛺🚵🚤🌲🚻

Encompassing the magnificent mountain basin that is home to Caligata Lake, this 153 hectare (378 ac) park can be reached off Saphats Creek Forest Service Road north of Clearwater. During the spring/summer season, visitors often marvel at the wildflowers. The area is also becoming increasingly popular in the winter with backcountry skiers. Although there are no facilities at this park, backcountry camping is permitted.

Castle Rock Hoodoos Provincial Park (Map 27/B5) 🚻🚻

At only 34 hectares (84 ac), this park is set aside to protect a series of Hoodoos in the Deadman Valley. The area has no infrastructure or trails and visitors are asked to keep off the sensitive formations. Located approximately 75 km northwest of Kamloops, this area is inundated with wood ticks from March until June. Hunting is permitted in the park as well.

Cathedral Provincial Park and Protected Area (Map 2/D5–3/A7) 🎿⛺🚂🛶🏊🚵🚴🚣🏇🚤🚻

This 33,077 hectare (81,700 ac) wilderness park (plus 353 hectares/872 ac of protected area) offers some of the best hiking and backpacking in the region with its jagged mountain peaks, turquoise lakes, alpine meadows and the ever popular Stone City. Most people travel to the core of the park around Quiniscoe Lake, set up camp (or stay at the Cathedral Lakes Resort) and spend a few days or weeks making day-trips. The shortest of three hikes into the core area is a 16 km hike from the Lakeview Trailhead, but many prefer to use the resort's four-wheel drive jeep service (250-226-7560). Camping within the park's core area is restricted to sites near Lake of the Woods and Quiniscoe Lake. There are also a couple drive-in campsites along the Ashnola River Road. The Lakeview Trailhead Campground is found near the footbridge spanning the Ashnola River, while the Buckhorn Campground is two kilometres further along the Ashnola River.

Chasm Provincial Park (Map 26/B1) 🚂🚵🚴🏇🚻

The Chasm is a dramatic canyon cut through colourful bands of lava where Chasm Creek flows into the Bonaparte River Valley. It is 8 km long, 600 metres (1,950 ft) wide and 300 metres (975 ft) deep. Facilities include pit toilets and a lookout at the day-use area, but no picnic tables. Hunting and horseback riding are permitted in this park.

Christie Memorial Provincial Park (Map 3/G2) 🚂🚣🛶🏊🚵🚴🚤🚻

On the south shore of Skaha Lake at the town of Okanagan Falls, this year-round 3 hectare (7 ac) provincial park offers a day-use facility and a beach. It is a popular spot for swimming, picnicking, canoeing and fishing in the summer months.

Christina Lake Provincial Park (Map 6/E6) 🚂🚣🛶🏊🚤🏊🚤🚴

This is a popular sandy beach and day-use picnic site on the south end of Canada's warmest recreation lake. Watersports are the name of the game here with swimming, canoeing and waterskiing opportunities available. There are plenty of picnic tables set back from the beach, toilet facilities and the park is wheelchair accessible. There is also a public boat launch and marina facilities within the vicinity of the park.

Cinnemousun Narrows Provincial Park (Map 30/F3) ⛺🚣⚓🚂🛶🏊🚴🚵🚤🚻

This popular water access only park is located on the shores of Shuswap Lake where the four arms of the big lake meet. On the northern side of the lake there is a small camping area containing 4 sites and a docking wharf. On the southerly side is a 24 site camping area with pit toilets, two shelters, docking wharf and a beach suitable for swimming or sunbathing. A 1.5 km hiking trail leads from the campground to a vantage point overlooking the lake.

Coldwater River Provincial Park (Map 7/B3) 🚵🚴🚤🚻

This is one of the least publicized and least used parks in the province, especially considering its proximity to a major highway. Access to this day-use park is off the Coquihalla Highway, about 50 km south of Merritt. There is good fishing in the Coldwater River and it makes a nice stop for hikers and cyclists doing the Trans Canada Trail.

Conkle Lake Provincial Park (Map 4/G4) 🎿⛺🚂🚣🛶🏊🚤🚴🚵🚤🚣🚻

Located on a rough two-wheel drive road (Johnstone Creek West Road or Conkle Lake Road) in the Okanagan Highland east of Osoyoos, this rustic 587 hectare (1,450 ac) provincial park has a total of 34 non-reservable campsites together with pit toilets, 2 group sites, a few walk-in tenting sites

above the area as well as a cartop boat launch, day-use area and a sandy beach. In addition to fishing and water based activities, hiking trails circle the picturesque lake and leads west from the campground to the scenic falls.

Coquihalla Summit Recreation Area (Map 7/A5) ⛺🚂🚵🏇🚤🏊🚴⛷️🚻

Near the summit of the Coquihalla Highway (Hwy 5) is a lovely picnic area with views of Zopkius Ridge and Needle Peak. The 5,750 hectare (14,205 ac) park also offers hiking, hunting and winter activities. It is possible to explore the sub-alpine terrain around the rest area, fish at Falls Lake or challenge the many surrounding peaks. Backcountry camping is permitted year-round.

Cornwall Hills Provincial Park (Map 20/C2) 🚵🚴🏇🚤🚻

To the west of Ashcroft, this undeveloped day-use park can be accessed by the Cornwall Lookout Road. The summit of Cornwall Hill is a popular launch for hang gliders. There are also a number of unmarked trails for hiking and biking through the meadows and rare Englemann Spruce in the 1,235 hectare (3,050 ac) park. Hunting is also permitted in the park.

Darke Lake Provincial Park (Map 9/C3) 🚵🚴🏇⛷️🚤🚻🚤

This 1,470 hectare (3,630 ac) provincial park is located off a gravel road northeast of Summerland and is a popular retreat for trout fishing. Campers will find five rustic campsites as well as pit toilets. The park is open year-round and is popular with snowmobilers in the winter. Hunting and horseback riding are also permitted in this park.

Dunn Peak Protected Area (Map 33/E3–34/A5) 🚵🚤🚴🚣🚻🚤

This remote 19,353 hectare (47,800 ac) area is extremely rugged, but very beautiful. It preserves the towering Dunn Peak and most of the Dunn Mountain Range. Hiking, fishing, nature observation and rock climbing are the main attractions here. In the winter, the area provides excellent alpine skiing and snowshoeing opportunities.

Dutch Lake Park (Map 33/F1) 🚂🚣🏊🚤

This small park is found within the town of Clearwater off the north side of Highway 5. The park encompasses the quiet Dutch Lake and makes a fine spot to stop and have a summer picnic, fish, swim, canoe or kayak. There is also a full service beach house and wharf along the 10.5 hectare (26 ac) shoreline of the park.

E.C. Manning Provincial Park (Map 1) 🎿⛺🏕️🚂🛶🏊🚴🚵🏇🚤🚣🚴🚴🚤🚻

Adding the Cascade Recreation Area to the northwest has expanded this four season outdoor paradise to 83,671 hectares (206,755 ac) of rugged mountains, valleys, meadows, lakes and rivers. Trails of all shapes and sizes, lakes for canoeing and fishing, wildlife for viewing and slopes for downhill and cross-country skiing in winter are just some of the features of the park. Highway 3 runs through the park, providing easy access. Campers will find four campgrounds in the park. Lightning Lake Campground is the most popular site with 143 reservable sites and yurts, while Coldspring, Hampton and Mule Deer Campgrounds, with 212 sites between them. There are also three reservable group campsites: Lone Duck I and II and Cambie Creek. Trail users will also find 10 designated areas with 55 backcountry campsites ranging from three to 10 tent pads. Day visitors will find seven sites around the park including West Gate, Sumallo Grove, Lightning Lake and the popular Sub-Alpine Meadows area.

Eakin Creek Parks (Map 33/C4) 🚵🚴🚤🚻🚤

Both parks are found west of Little Fort off the south side of Highway 24. The Canyon site offers a short trail to a scenic waterfall and is only 10 hectares (25 ac) in size. The undeveloped Floodplain site is 126 hectares (311 ac) in size and features ancient cedar and cottonwood trees. Bird watching is a popular activity in summer, while ice cave exploration, cross-country skiing and snowshoeing are possible during the winter.

Echo Lake Provincial Park (Map 18/D2) 🚣🚂🚤🏊🚵🚴🚤

Located on the Creighton Valley Road to the east of Lumby, this quiet provincial park has a day-use area ideal for paddlers, fishermen, swimmers and sunbathers. There is a wharf and open area next to the lake that is a short walk from the road. A resort with boat launch, cabins and other amenities is also found on the lake.

Elephant Hill Provincial Park (Map 20/E1) 🚵🚤🚻

This park protects a pair of prominent hills in a naturally dry grassland area, which are home to rattlesnakes. The grasslands are closed to vehicle traffic and no camping or day-use facilities are provided. There are random trails in the 979 hectare (2,420 ac) park along with abundant wildlife. Hunting is permitted in the park.

Ellison Provincial Park (Map 17/A3) [icons]
Southwest of Vernon, this 200 hectare (494 ac) provincial park is comprised of a rocky forested shoreline with two sheltered bays on Okanagan Lake. It is accessed along the Okanagan Landing Road and it provides 71 campsites, 51 of which are reservable, together with a large day-use area, playground and washrooms with showers. This is also Canada's first freshwater underwater diving park. The mooring facilities, developed beaches (including a separate doggie beach) and over 6 km of easy hiking trails make this a fine destination park. A public boat launch is found north of the park.

Emar Lakes Provincial Park (Map 33/B3) [icons]
This 1,604 hectare (3,960 ac) park encompasses a series of small lakes that are easily accessed off Eakin Creek Road to the south. The park is very popular during the spring through fall with anglers, hunters, swimmers, canoers and nature enthusiasts, while the winter draws cross-country skiers and snowshoers. The lakes can also be strung together into a peaceful canoe circuit. Rustic camping with picnic tables and pit toilets is possible at Long Island Lake.

Enderby Cliffs Provincial Park (Map 24/F3) [icons]
This 2,277 hectare (5,625 ac) day-use park protects the prominent rock cliffs that tower 1,200 m (3,940 ft) above the valley floor. There are a few popular trails in the area including one that leads to the scenic cliffs and another that runs past Reeves Lake, a popular walk-in fishing destination. Hunting is also permitted in the park.

Eneas Lakes Provincial Park (Map 9/B2) [icons]
Well off the beaten track in the mountains east of Peachland, the four small lakes within this 1,036 hectare (2,560 ac) park are ideal for fishing throughout the ice-free season. It is possible to launch a boat at the lakes, camp in one of the many clearings (there are four levelled spots), hike/bike one of the rough trails or stay in one of the cabins at the north end of Tuch Lake. The park is accessed by the Eneas Lakes Road, which has been deactivated and is very rough four-wheel drive road.

Epsom Provincial Park (Map 20/D4) [icons]
Located on the west bank of the Thompson River north of Spences Bridge, this 102 hectare (252 ac) park provides access to the river, mostly for anglers. There is no road access to the park, so anyone wishing to visit must scramble down to the river from Highway 1 along a rough trail. Be careful crossing the railway tracks and watch for wood ticks in the spring. Hunting is permitted in this park.

Finn Creek Provincial Park (Map 39/A3) [icons]
This small 303 hectare (748 ac) provincial park contains a portion of lower Finn Creek and a number of islands along the North Thompson River. Paddling is possible here and an old trail system can be picked up off the west side of Highway 5 for hiking and wildlife viewing. The trails meander along the side of Finn Creek leading from the highway to the Thompson River. In winter, visitors backcountry ski and snowshoe in the area, while the park is used as a staging area for snowmobilers running up Groundhog Mountain.

Fintry Provincial Park and Protected Area (Map 16/E3–17/A3) [icons]
North of Kelowna, this is a popular destination due to its location on the western shores of Okanagan Lake. The 361 hectare (892 ac) park (and 523 hectare /1,290 ac protected area) was developed on the former Fintry Estate Heritage Site, a social and economic centre in the 1800s for the Hudson Bay Company. There are a total of 100 campsites between three locations, 70 of which are reservable, washrooms with showers, a playground as well as a day-use area, three group camping areas and a beach. Trails lead through the park and up the 400 stairs to Short Creek Falls. It is possible to continue into the canyon along the Shorts Creek Canyon Trail. There is scuba diving here along with a variety of water sports. Hunting is permitted in the protected area above the highway.

Gladstone [Texas Creek] Provincial Park (Maps 6, 12) [icons]
On the north end of Christina Lake, Gladstone encompasses a large chunk of the Selkirk Foothills. Most of the 39,387 hectare (97,285 ac) park is pristine wilderness, which is seldom visited except where the park can be reached by boat on Christina Lake. The access points to the park include Lynch Creek/Mount Faith Trails to the north, Highway 3 to the south and the Deer Point/Sandner Creek Trails at the north end of Christina Lake for hiking, biking and horseback riding. Seven boat access only marine sites line Christina Lake providing camping and beach facilities, while the recently upgraded Texas Creek Campground provides 62 vehicle accessible, reservable campsites and

washroom facilities with showers. There is a boat launch near the entrance to the campground and ancient pictographs can be found a short paddle north. Hunting is permitted in the park.

Goldpan Provincial Park (Map 20/C7) [icons]
Located right next to Highway 1 (and between two busy railroads), the park's day-use area is open year-round and is popular with people who wish to explore the Thompson River for fishing or paddling opportunities. There are 14 non-reservable campsites with picnic tables and toilet facilities at the park. Wildlife viewing opportunities exist as well.

Granby Provincial Park (Maps 11, 12, 18, 19) [icons]
This remote provincial park is assessed by the Granby Wilderness Trail to the south or the Mount Scaia Road to the north. The 40,845 hectare (100,885 ac) park is a pristine area that was established to preserve important Grizzly Bear habitat as well as the headwaters of the Granby River and several adjacent basins. Wilderness camping, fishing, horseback riding and hunting are some of the recreation pursuits available. In winter, backcountry skiing and snowshoeing are possible. The Mount Young Cabin is the only functioning public accessible cabin in the park. Be advised that trail maintenance is minimal and fallen trees and/or trail wash-outs are common.

[play button icon]

> *It is ideal to carry a water filter, iodine tablets, or boil water for a minimum of 10 minutes before consuming, as many waterbodies carry the bacteria commonly referred to as Beaver Fever.*

Graystokes Provincial Park (Map 18/B4–C7) [icons]
Graystokes Protected Area was established in 2001 to protect 11,958 hectares (29,535 ac) of lakes, swamps, meandering streams and meadows that are prime habitat for moose, mule deer and white-tailed deer. The area has been a popular snowmobile destination for years and there are established trails and warming cabins. Cross-country skiing and snowshoeing are also possible. When the snow clears, the lakes and former forest service campsites make fine fishing destinations. Please note that motorized access is not permitted in summer. Hunting is also permitted in the park.

Greenstone Mountain Provincial Park (Map 21/F3) [icons]
Off the Dominic Lake Forest Service Road, this 124 hectare (306 ac) park encompasses Greenstone Mountain and a former forestry lookout. The park also contains Kwilalkwila Lake and many informal trails, which connect to an extensive bike/ATV trail system outside the park. Hiking, fishing and horseback riding can be done in the warmer months, while snowshoeing and snowmobiling are favourites in the winter.

Harbour Dudgeon Lakes Provincial Park (Map 35/D2) [icons]
This fairly remote 375 hectare (926 ac) park protects a portion of the western shorelines of the two Harbour Lakes as well as some important wetland areas. The forested valley is surrounded by Mount Cunningham to the west and the Seymour Range to the east. You will need to bushwhack through the forest to find the lakes, but once there you are rewarded with fantastic fishing, swimming and canoeing opportunities. Snowshoeing is possible in the winter.

Hardy Falls Regional Park (Map 9/D3) [icons]
Hardy Falls is found just off Highway 97 in Peachland at Hardy Road. From the parking lot, a short 15 minute trail follows Deep Creek to the falls. There is a picnic area and benches along the trail, providing visitors with excellent birdwatching opportunities, while September sees kokanee spawning in Deep Creek.

Harry Lake Aspen Provincial Park (Map 20/A1) [icons]
Located to the south of Highway 99, 40 km west of Cache Creek, this park preserves 330 hectares (815 ac) of grassland and aspen forest around Harry Lake. Activities around the lake include hiking and mountain biking, while nature enthusiasts will love the wildflower bloom in July and August. Road access is limited and there are no camping or facilities provided. Hunting is permitted in this park.

PARK ADVENTURES

Haynes Point (sẁiẁs) Provincial Park (Map 4/B7)

Near Osoyoos, this popular 38 hectare (94 ac) provincial park campsite is located on a narrow sandy spit on Osoyoos Lake. Now managed by the Osoyoos Indian Band as an ancient burial ground was discovered there in 2014, there are 41 reservable campsites. This is a great destination for swimming, canoeing and waterskiing. There are also day-use facilities, a boat launch, pet beach and wildlife viewing platform on the marsh.

Herald Provincial Park (Map 30/D7)

This popular 79 hectare (195 ac) park on the Salmon Arm of Shuswap Lake has 119 campsites, 108 of which are reservable, washrooms with showers and sani-station as well as an impressive beach, boat launching facilities and large day-use area. A number of trails including the short trail to Margaret Falls are found within the park. Remains of the old homestead owned by the Herald Family, who donated the land for the park, can also be seen. Watersports including scuba diving, windsurfing and waterskiing along with fishing are the primary attractions to the busy park.

High Lakes Basin Provincial Park (Map 33/A5)

This remote provincial park lies north of Bonaparte Lake and encompasses three high elevation lakes containing wild trout. There is no road access into the park, but it is possible to bushwhack in or horseback ride from the logging roads north of Caverhill Lake. There are some rustic, user-maintained campsites in the 560 hectare (1,385 ac) park. Hunting is permitted in the park.

Holliday Creek Arch Protected Area (Map 49/G4)

The Holliday Creek Arch area is a Class A provincial park and the namesake feature is a natural arch carved away over the centuries by the Holliday Creek. A steep, rustic trail leads into the 395 hectare (976 ac) park where mountain goats and the impressive 80 metres (260 ft) wide by 18 metres (60 ft) high stone arch can be seen. The trail up to the arch is not maintained and very difficult to negotiate. Hunting is permitted in this park.

Inkaneep Provincial Park (Map 4/A4)

This provincial park is located 6 km north of Oliver on Highway 97 next to the Okanagan River. The small park provides seven non reservable rustic campsites nestled in large cottonwood trees a short walk from the Okanagan River with pit toilets. Visitors can canoe, fish, hike or enjoy the abundance of flora and fauna in the 21 hectare (52 ac) park. Bird watching is popular here.

Jackman Flats Provincial Park (Map 46/F1)

The Jackman Flats are an ecological paradox, as the area hosts both wetlands and arid sand dunes. There is a small parking area where a trailhead leading to a series of easy interconnecting loops can be enjoyed year-round, along with a day-use area with picnic tables and toilets in this 615 hectare (1,520 ac) park. Hunting and horseback riding are permitted.

Jewel Lake Provincial Park (Map 5/F4)

This 3 km long lake provides a great rainbow trout fishery. The park boasts a nice beach and can make a great camping destination. There are 26 non reservable campsites, some of which are double spots, with a cartop boat launch, picnic tables and accessible pit toilet facilities.

Johns Family Nature Conservancy Regional Park (Map 9/G2)

Now covering 403 hectares (995 ac), the Cedar Mountain portion is the only part open to public use until a user plan is implemented. In Cedar, the remnants of the 2003 Okanagan Mountain Fire are still evident on hiking/biking trails and through interpretive programs, while Kelowna Crags make an interesting geological formation that is popular with climbers. To find the park, take Lakeshore Road to Chute Lake Road. The parking lot is about 3 km from the start of the gravel road.

Johnstone Creek Provincial Park (Map 5/A6)

This small 38 hectare (94 ac) provincial park is found on Highway 3, just east of the turnoff to Conkle Lake Provincial Park. There are 16 non reservable campsites and pit toilets in a forested creek draw providing plenty of shade in the heat of the summer. The park is used mainly as a stopover for travellers along Highway 3 and features a short trail.

Juniper Beach Provincial Park (Map 20/G1–26/G7)

On Highway 1 between Cache Creek and Kamloops, Juniper Beach offers 32 campsites with electrical hook-ups, 15 of which are reservable, on the shores of the Thompson River. It is open from February to November and amenities include pit toilets, showers, small boat launch and a sani-station. The 260 hectare (642 ac) park offers bird watching, fishing, paddling and swimming opportunities.

Kalamalka Lake Provincial Park & Protected Area (Map 17/C2)

Located just south of Vernon is a 4,209 hectare (10,395 ac) provincial park and protected area on the northeast shore of Kalamalka Lake and the higher elevated area. Surrounded by grasslands dotted with ponderosa pine, the most popular destination is the beach at Cosens Bay, which is trail or boat access only. The main trailhead is found at the end of Kidston Road. There are several other day-use areas with picnic tables and pit toilets as well as a variety of rare and endangered wildlife in the park including rattlesnakes. Horseback riding and hunting are also permitted in the park.

Kalamoir Regional Park (Map 9/G1)

Situated along the shoreline of Okanagan Lake in West Kelowna, this 27 hectare (67 ac) park features a beach and trail system along the lakeside and through stands of old growth forest. A dog beach, picnic tables and toilet facilities are also found here.

Kaloya Regional Park (Map 17/B4)

This small 3.7 hectare (9 ac) park at the south end of Kalamalka Lake offers a swimming area, playground, wedding arbour/gazebo, covered picnic area, a lily pond and protected boat beach. Birdwatching is also a popular activity as there are a number of benches and walking trails for viewing. The park is found in Oyama at the end of Trask Road.

Kekuli Bay Provincial Park (Map 17/C2)

Found on the west side of Kalamalka Lake, 11 km south of Vernon, there are 69 campsites, 50 of which are reservable, including four sites with 30 amp electrical hook-ups. The boat launch is equally as popular, while visitors can visit a small beach along with a trail through the grasslands around the campsite. Washrooms with showers, day-use picnic facilities and a playground add to the amenities.

Kentucky-Alleyne Provincial Park (Map 14/G7–15/A7)

This 144 hectare (356 ac) park is located south of the Okanagan Connector in the rolling grasslands and dry open forests typical of the cattle country of this region. The park is also an ideal place to sample a few mountain lakes for stocked rainbow trout or explore a few trails. There are 58 rustic campsites, 10 of which are reservable, a boat launch, group campsite, pit toilets and a 4 km trail that circles Kentucky Lake.

Keremeos Columns Provincial Park (Map 3/E3)

This undeveloped 57 hectare (141 ac) park is requires a long hike to access. The trail crosses through the dry sagebrush country as you climb steeply to the columns, which, strangely enough, are outside of the park boundaries. In the spring, the Lewisia blossoms are in full bloom. Please obtain permission to cross the private property en route.

Kettle River Recreation Area (Map 5/B5)

To the north of Rock Creek on Highway 33, this park has been expanded and now includes washrooms with showers and a nice adventure playground for kids. In addition to the 113 campsites, 83 of which are reservable, set in a semi-open ponderosa pine forest next to the river, the 179 hectare (442 ac) park features a scenic picnic area that is popular with anglers and swimmers. The old Kettle River Railway, now part of the Trans Canada Trail, bisects the area and can be explored by mountain bike or by foot. Other activities in the area include tubing or fishing the river, and in the winter, many use the area to cross-country ski or snowshoe. The park was ravaged by a wildfire in August 2015 but is expected to reopen in the spring of 2016.

Kickininee Provincial Park (Map 9/F6)

On the western shores of Okanagan Lake about 8 km north of Penticton, this small provincial park provides day-use facilities at three different locations along the lake– Kickininee, Soorimpt and Pyramid. Each site is easily accessed off Highway 97 and all three have picnic tables and accessible pit and flush toilet facilities. There is a boat launch at the Soorimpt site.

Kingfisher Creek Provincial Park (Map 31/B6)

Protecting a remote 440 hectare (1,085 ac) section of the Hunters Range, this park is an extension of the Kingfisher Creek Ecological Reserve. There is an old trail and cabin found at Twin Lakes in the southwest part of the park, while hikers, horseback riders, wildlife enthusiasts and snowmobilers can all explore the surrounding mountain range.

Kopje Regional Park (Map 17/A4)
This 3.2 hectare (8 ac) lakefront park on Okanagan Lake is also home to the Gibson Heritage House. There is a swimming and picnic area, as well as a playground, ball diamond and large field area. Nestled in scenic Lake Country, this is a great place to take the kids for an afternoon at the beach.

Lac Du Bois Grasslands Protected Area (Maps 21, 22, 27, 28)
Lac Du Bois is a land of open grasslands, dry forests and grand cliffs and canyons. The park is bisected by the Lac du Bois Road and preserves a series of small lakes in addition to the 15,712 hectares (38,810 ac) of grassland. There are few facilities in the area but there are a variety of trails to explore for hikers, mountain bikers and nature enthusiasts. Some camping is available at the old Watching Creek Recreation Site (off the Tranquille-Criss Creek Road) but there are no specified campsites. In the fall/winter months the area is used by hunters and snowshoers. California Bighorn Sheep can be spotted in this area at the Dewdrop Cliffs.

Lac Le Jeune Provincial Park (Map 22/A5)
Lac Le Jeune Provincial Park is situated not far from the Coquihalla Highway (Hwy 5) south of Kamloops. There are a total of 144 campsites, 91 of which are reservable, with wheelchair accessible pit and flush toilets, a sani-station, playground, boat launch and a large picnic area. The park is extremely popular for boating, swimming and fishing in the summer months, while the cross-country ski trails can also be hiked and biked.

Lions Regional Park (Map 3/G2)
Found at the south end of Skaha Lake, this small beachfront park offers a number of picnic tables for enjoying the scenic rolling hills and lake.

Mabel Lake Provincial Park (Map 25/D5)
This 187 hectare (462 ac) provincial park is found on the eastern shores of Mabel Lake, just after the pavement ends on Mabel Lake Road. The campground is very popular and often full in the summer. There are a total of 84 campsites, 36 of which are reservable and a large amount of accessible flush toilets. In addition there is a sani-station and playground, a large day-use area, a boat launch and a nice sandy beach. Mabel Lake makes an ideal destination for summer camping and boating as well as a good year-round fishing destination.

Manitou Regional Park (Map 9/G5)
Found along Okanagan Lake in the peaceful community of Naramata, this urban park has a beach, picnic area and playground. This park offers spectacular views of the lake and the surrounding hills and makes for a great spot for family gatherings.

Manning Provincial Park (Map 1)
See E.C. Manning Provincial Park

Mara Lake Provincial Park (Map 24/F1)
At 5.9 hectares (15 ac) in size, this small provincial park is located on the eastern shores of Mara Lake and offers a nice beach for picnickers or sunbathers as well as a boat launch and accessible flush and pit toilets throughout the park. Note that this is a day-use park only; no overnight camping is permitted, and mooring of boats overnight is not allowed.

McConnell Lake Provincial Park (Map 22/B4)
McConnell Lake is noted for big rainbow trout, which means it sees a lot of action from anglers. There is a small gravel boat launch suitable for small boats or canoes (no motorized boats allowed) along with a rustic day-use are with picnic table and pit toilet. The 102 hectare (252 ac) park is also a good place to hike, bike or cross-country ski.

Mill Creek Regional Park (Map 17/C6)
This park is found in the Ellison area, east of the Kelowna Airport. A trail system follows the scenic creek through to a nice waterfall. Picnic tables, toilet facilities and wildlife viewing are all available within this dog friendly park.

Mission Creek Regional Park (Map 10/A1–17/C7)
One of the largest and most developed regional parks in the Central Okanagan, this 92 hectare (227 ac) park is home to the Environmental Education Centre for the Okanagan, where you will find the Xeriscape and Compost Education Garden. There are over 12 km of trails in the park, a stocked trout pond, good opportunities to watch birds and a chance to see kokanee spawn in September and October. Mountain biking is permitted on the Greenway and along the fire road between Hall Road and the Greenway.

Momich Lakes Provincial Park (Map 34/G5–35/B5)
Momich Lakes are located on the eastern slopes of Adams Lake. The park covers 1,648 hectares (4,070 ac) and marks the northern extension of the larch tree. The user-maintained 20 unit Momich River Campsite with pit toilets is found next to Adams Lake, while the former recreation site on the west end of Momich Lake also has campsites. The site on the east side of the lake is closed indefinitely. All lakes in the area provide reasonably good fishing and canoeing and there is scuba diving in Adams Lake. Hunting is permitted in the park.

Monck Provincial Park (Map 15/A3)
Located on the northern shores of Nicola Lake in the heart of cattle country, Monck Park is open from March to November and contains 120 campsites, 72 of which are reservable, with accessible flush toilets, a sani-station, playground, boat launch as well as a large picnic area with over 40 picnic tables and a beach. Trails lead up the mountainside to volcanic outcroppings or to the second beach and some First Nations pictographs, but the focus of the park is on watersports on Nicola Lake.

Monte Lake Provincial Park (Map 23/C5)
Next to Monte Lake and Highway 97, this small 8 hectare (20 ac) provincial park provides access to a popular lake. There are no facilities, but camping is available at a private campground nearby and a rustic boat launch is found near the north end of the lake.

Mount Robson Provincial Park (Maps 47, 48, 50, 51)
Mount Robson Provincial Park was designated as a part of the Rocky Mountains World Heritage Site in 1990. The park protects 224,866 hectares (555,420 ac) of breathtaking natural terrain and is a testament to British Columbia and Canada's natural splendour. The massive 3,954 metre (12,972 ft) Mount Robson is the cornerstone of this park which also protects the headwaters of the mighty Fraser River. From alpine fed lakes to wild mammals like the grizzly bear, there are many sights and sounds to enjoy. In fact, a truly spectacular natural phenomenon can be witnessed every August and September at Rearguard Falls. The falls are found just west of the park boundary and mark the furthest migration of spawning salmon from the Pacific Ocean, over 1,200 km away. There are 3 separate vehicle access campsites: Robson Meadows with 125 sites, Robson River with 19 sites and Lucerne with 36 sites. There are also over 98 reservable backcountry sites, as well as 2 boat launches, two group campsites, two picnic areas, pit toilets, a playground, shower facilities and a sani-dump station. For more details on this spectacular mountain park, see the Canadian Rockies Backroad Mapbook.

Mount Savona Provincial Park (Map 21/D2)
Encompassing a former forest service lookout, it is possible to drive to the summit along a rough four-wheel drive road. Visitors to the area can hike, mountain bike or hunt, while nature lovers will find an abundance of flora and fauna within the 382 hectare (944 ac) park. There are no facilities within the park, but backcountry camping is allowed.

Mount Terry Fox Provincial Park (Map 46/G1–51/A7)
Named after the national hero, this park is just one of the lasting legacies of this great Canadian. The park itself encompasses 1,930 hectares (4,765 ac) but the peak is more often viewed from Highway 16 than visited. There are picnic tables and outhouses available at the viewpoint, but for a closer and more intimate experience, there is an established trail that traverses towards the mountain. The trailhead can be found off the east side of Highway 5, just south of the railway tracks.

Mud Lake Delta Provincial Park (Map 43/C7)
Just east of Mud Lake off Highway 5, this park helps protect 500 hectares (1,235 ac) of important wetland habitat. Moose and waterfowl frequent the wetlands and can be seen by canoeists and nature enthusiasts who venture in on foot or on snowshoe. Hunting is permitted in the park.

Myra-Bellevue Provincial Park & Protected Area (Map 10/B1–C3)
The highlight of this 7,829 hectare (19,340 ac) park is the spectacular Myra Canyon section of the Kettle Valley Railway and its trestles and tunnels. The famous trestles have been restored and make an incredible hiking and biking destination. In addition to this popular section of the park, there are other highlights and trails to explore such as Angel Springs and Little White Mountain. Snowmobiling and hunting are permitted in the park.

Naramata Wharf Regional Park (Map 9/G5)
Found along the Naramata Waterfront, there is a short walking trail, benches and picnic tables at this small regional park. As the name implies, there is a boat launch and wharf to help access the lake.

Nickel Plate Provincial Park (Map 3/B1)
Nickel Plate Provincial Park is located just north of Apex Mountain. The park is known for its backcountry camping, biking, hiking and fishing opportunities. In the winter, there are several kilometres of maintained cross-country ski, snowshoe and snowmobile trails. The 105 hectare (259 ac) park also features a boat launch on the lake. Hunting is permitted in the park.

Niskonlith Lake Provincial Park (Map 29/C7)
Located approximately 8 km from Chase on the Niskonlith Lake Road, this 238 hectare (588 ac) park offers 29 rustic non reservable campsites, pit toilets and a cartop boat launch on the eastern shore of the lake. Activities in the area include canoeing, hiking, mountain biking, scuba diving, swimming and windsurfing in the summer, while winter enthusiasts use this park for cross-country skiing and snowshoeing.

North Thompson Oxbows Provincial Park (Maps 28/C6; 42/G1; 43/B1)
Ranging from the Jensen Island site in the south to the Manteau and East sites in the north, this 515 hectare (1,272 ac) park protects important features along the North Thompson River. Access is limited to this park, however visitors can paddle the North Thompson River and look for wildlife.

North Thompson River Park (Map 33/E1)
Near the confluence of the Thompson River and Clearwater River, this small 126 hectare (311 ac) park is located off Highway 5 just west of the town of Clearwater. The park offers 60 vehicle access campsites, 53 of which are reservable, a playground, pit toilets and a day-use area next to the scenic Thompson River. Visitors can explore four easy trails or try their luck fishing in the Thompson River.

Okanagan Centre Safe Harbour Regional Park (Map 17/A5)
As one might gather from the name, this regional park provides a safe area for boaters during storms. There are two recently refurbished docks, for emergency and pedestrian use, a swimming beach, pit toilets and a popular boat launch. Scuba diving groups sometimes use the beach and lake area to the left of the boat launch.

Okanagan Falls Provincial Park (sx̌ʷəx̌ʷnitkʷ) (Map 3/G2)
Located south of Skaha Lake in the heart of the Okanagan, sx̌ʷəx̌ʷnitkʷ (pronounced "sxwexwnitkw" or "s-wux-wux-neet-kw") park is a tiny 2 hectare (5 ac) park now managed by the Osoyoos Indian Band. Found off Highway 97, the park has 25 non reservable campsites and pit toilets. The area is a popular spot for wildlife viewing, especially for bats.

Okanagan Lake Provincial Park (Map 9/E4)
With 168 campsites right on or overlooking Okanagan Lake between two locations, this is a popular summer vacation getaway. Campers will find 88 sites at the South campground, 60 of which are reservable, and 80 sites at the North campground, all of which are reservable, as well as front country marine camping. The 98 hectare (242 ac) park is located on the western shores of Okanagan Lake north of Summerland, in a ponderosa pine/sage brush ecosystem. The campground is open year-round and there is a picnic area, playground, washrooms with showers, over a kilometre of sandy beaches, hiking trails, sani-station and a boat launch. Be wary of rattlesnakes in the area.

Okanagan Mountain Provincial Park (Map 9/F3)
Covering 11,038 hectares (27,265 ac) from the lakeshore to the dry pine forest surrounding Okanagan Mountain, this park features 24 km of multi-use trails, a cabin at Divide Lake, day-use areas and numerous backcountry campsites and lakes. The park provides excellent opportunities for hiking, horseback riding, mountain biking and fishing. Alternatively, there are six marine campgrounds with pit toilets set in secluded bays with sandy beaches that are ideal for boaters or paddlers exploring Okanagan Lake. First Nation pictographs are found at Commando Bay and south of the park. Remnants of the 2003 fire are still very evident and caution is needed when travelling through burned areas. Hunting is permitted in this park.

Oregon Jack Provincial Park (Map 20/B3)
Easily accessed on the Hat Creek Road, this undeveloped 233 hectare (576 ac) park preserves the Notch, a spectacular limestone canyon and falls on the Oregon Jack Creek drainage. A First Nations pictograph can be seen in the canyon, while hunters frequent the area in fall.

Osoyoos Lake Regional Park (Map 4/B6)
Located along Osoyoos Lake near the American border, this park features a picnic area and a beautiful beach. It is not as busy as the city park near the heart of town, but does provide good swimming, fishing and canoeing opportunities.

Otter Lake Provincial Park (Map 7/E6)
In the Tulameen Valley northwest of Princeton, Otter Lake provides two separate areas to visit. The 45 site (36 reservable) lakeside camping area is found near the north end of the lake and has pit toilets, while the day-use facility, boat launch and developed beach area are found at the south end of the lake. The 51 hectare (126 ac) park is less developed than other provincial parks so you should expect a more rustic camping experience.

Painted Bluffs Provincial Park (Map 27/E7)
Protecting a small but geologically significant site on the north shore of Kamloops Lake, this park is rarely visited. This 100 hectare (247 ac) site gets its name from the distinctive multi-coloured rocks and soils on the bluff. It is possible to visit by boat or canoe as well as on foot, but most people enjoy the view of the bluffs from the highway viewpoints across Kamloops Lake. Hunting is permitted in this park.

Paul Lake Provincial Park (Map 22/F1)
Nestled in a mixed forest just northeast of Kamloops, Paul Lake, at 728 hectares (1,800 ac), has a large beach and day-use area, as well as a campground with 90 sites, 47 of which are reservable, pit and flush toilets, open air showers, a group campsite, playground, sani-station and boat launch. There are seven kilometres of hiking trails, including a popular trail to the top of Gibraltar Rock and plenty of watersports to enjoy. This is a popular getaway for locals from Kamloops.

When front country camping, food must be stored safely in your vehicle. Picnic tables and the surrounding areas must be free of food scraps and dishes are not to be left out.

Pennask Lake Provincial Park (Map 15/G6)
Most of the rainbow trout caught in the Southern Interior were gleaned from eggs from Pennask Lake, so, as you might expect, this is a great fishing lake. However, access to this 244 hectare (603 ac) park is not easy. In addition to the main campsite with 25 non reservable rustic spots, there are several canoe access camping areas. The nearby Pennask Creek Park helps protect the spawning stream and is not intended for public use.

Pillar Provincial Park (Map 23/E3)
This tiny 2 hectare (5 ac) provincial park takes its name from the feature that it was set aside to protect, a pillar of conglomerate stone. There is a short but steep trail to reach the pillar and pit toilets.

Porcupine Meadows Provincial Park (Map 27/G4–28/A4)
This park is mostly comprised of wetlands with some patches of old growth forest. The 2,704 hectare (6,680 ac) area is designated mostly for conservation and recreation is limited. Hikers, horseback riders, hunters, snowshoers and snowmobilers do frequent the area. There is an old pack trail leading past several small lakes to Porcupine Ridge and an old forestry lookout.

Pritchard Provincial Park (Map 23/C2)
One of the few spots along the Thompson River between Chase and Kamloops that is not under private ownership, this 15 hectare (37 ac) provincial park gives the public access to the foreshore for birding and paddling.

Pukeashun Provincial Park (Map 30/C1–35/C7)
Although quite remote, this 1,779 hectare (4,395 ac) park is accessed by ATV and by foot into the high elevation pass and lake with both sub-alpine and alpine areas. In winter, the area is visited by backcountry skiers and snowmobilers. The rest of the year backcountry camping and hunting are possible.

Pyramid Creek Falls Provincial Park (Map 43/C3) 🏕️🚻🏔️
While Pyramid Creek Falls is spectacular, there are no trails or roads into this 13 hectare (32 ac) park. The best viewing area, without bushwhacking in, is from Highway 5. Hunting is permitted in the park.

Raymer Bay Regional Park (Map 16/G7) 🏕️🏊🚣🏖️🛶🚻
This 6.8 hectare (17 ac) park is popular in the summer and features a nice beach and swimming area. The park is located on Westside Road, just before Bear Creek Provincial Park and has no facilities or campsites other than a gazebo. No dogs are allowed.

Rearguard Falls Provincial Park (Map 50/G7) 🥾🚶🐟🚻
This small 48 hectare (119 ac) provincial park is little more than a viewing area over Rearguard Falls, a natural barrier to salmon spawning upstream. This marks the farthest point most Chinook can spawn up the Fraser, a distance of 1,200 km from the Fraser estuary. Surprisingly, a few salmon still have the energy to battle their way up and over the falls to the gravel beds above. Visitors can fish, hike or snowshoe at the park.

Reiswig Regional Park (Map 17/B4) 🏕️🏖️🚣🏊🛶
This small park has a swimming beach, a picnic area and a field with a running track. Watersports include paddling and boating. Together with the city run Beasley Park, which has a covered picnic area and playground, this is a popular year-round recreation area.

Roche Lake Provincial Park (Map 22/F5)
🏕️⛺🚤🏊🚣🥾🚵🏇🐟⛷️❄️🐟🚻🛶
Roche Lake is the largest of seven world-class fishing lakes in this 2,041 hectare (5,040 ac) park. Road access is limited but there are many informal multi-use trails for hiking, horseback riding and mountain biking in the warmer months, or cross-country skiing and snowmobiling in the winter. There are 75 non reservable rustic campsites with pit toilets on Black, Horseshoe and Roche Lakes and a group campground at Roche Lake North. A boat launch and resort is also found on the bigger lake. Hunting is permitted in this park.

Rock Ovens Regional Park (Map 9/G4) 🥾🚵🏇🚻
Found near the Adra Tunnel, where Elinor Road crosses the Kettle Valley Railway, this regional park protects two sets of rock ovens that were built to feed workers during the construction of the Kettle Valley Railway back in 1911 and 1915. It is a popular stop for travellers, mostly bikers and hikers, on the Trans Canada Trail.

Roderick Haig-Brown Provincial Park (Map 29/E5)
🏕️🚣🥾🏇🚵⛷️🐟🚻♿
Named after the famous poet/author/fly fisherman, this provincial park protects 1,076 hectares (2,660 ac) of land on both sides of the Adams River. The main attraction to the area is the incredible display of spawning sockeye in October (peak years occur every four years; the next one will be in 2018). The park also hosts 26 km of multi-use trails, one of which is wheelchair accessible, along with an accessible wildlife viewing platform at Salute Plaza, pit toilets and whitewater paddling opportunities.

Rose Valley Regional Park (Map 16/G7) 🥾🚵🐟🚻
Rose Valley is a 250 hectare (618 ac) regional park that has been left in its natural state. Hiking and biking along with birdwatching are the most common activities, although fishing is possible.

Scenic Canyon Regional Park (Map 10/C1) 🥾🚻
Part of the Mission Creek Greenway, this 89 hectare (220 ac) park features old placer mining areas and rock ovens used by Chinese labourers. There are hiking paths that begin at the end of Field Road and meander through forests of mature stands along KLO Creek. This park is located adjacent to Gallagher's Canyon Golf Course.

Shannon Lake Regional Park (Map 9/F1) 🏕️🥾🏊🚻
Located in West Kelowna, this pretty park is not only a popular birdwatching area, but the picnic area is a popular place for couples to get married. A gravel path leads through a natural forest setting alongside the lake and is dog friendly. There is a floating dock and a fishing program for children 15 and under.

Shuswap Lake Marine Provincial Park (Maps 30, 35)
🏕️⛺⚓🚻🏖️🚣🏊🚤🛶🥾🐟🚻♿
Covering over 1,000 kilometres of shoreline, Shuswap Lake is a large lake with beautiful beaches found at most of the 24 marine sites around the four arms of the lake. The many parcels of the park cover 896 hectares (2,215 ac) with campsites located at Anstey Beach, Anstey View, Four Mile Creek, Horseshoe Bay, Marble Point, Encounter Point, Two Mile Creek and more. Albas and Cinnemousun Narrows are the most used sites. There are multiple boat launches around the lake as well as pit toilets at most sites. Marine activities include fishing, scuba diving, swimming, waterskiing, windsurfing and even paddle boarding.

Shuswap Lake Provincial Park (Map 30/A5)
🏕️🚻🏖️🚣🏊🚤🚣🐟🥾🚵🏇⛵🛶📷☕♿🚻
While this park is a mere 149 hectares (368 ac), it is the largest and most popular campground in the Thompson District. There are 274 reservable campsites in addition a playground, picnic area, boat launch, washrooms with showers and sani-station. It is a great place to bring the family as there is a large beach (including a separate pet beach), trails and even stores just outside the gates. If you have a boat, it is highly recommended that you visit Copper Island, which is part of the park. This island is one of the better areas to fish in the big lake and it has a nice hiking trail in addition to sheltered mooring for day-use. Be sure to reserve a campsite well in advance.

Shuswap River Islands Provincial Park (Map 25/A3) 🚣🛶🚻
Protecting a 185 hectare (457 ac) stretch of river, this park is mostly used by paddlers and anglers. The Dale Canoe Launch is found just upstream of the park, but it is possible to access the river from the Mabel Lake Road as well.

Silver Beach Provincial Park (Map 35/F6) 🏕️🚻🏖️🚣🏊🚤🐟🥾⛵🛶🚤
This 130 hectare (321 ac) provincial park is found at the north end of the Seymour Arm, where once a gold rush town called Ogden City stood. The campground is located next to a beautiful beach on the Seymour River estuary and has 35 non reservable campsites along with a boat launch, picnic area and pit toilets. If approaching by boat, it is safest to proceed from the east as the sandbars in front of the main beach can be cause serious problems.

Silver Star Provincial Park (Map 24/F6) 🎿🥾🚵🏇🏂⛷️🚠🛶📷🚻
This year-round 5,573 hectare (13,765 ac) provincial park is set in the mountains northeast of Vernon and is easily accessed by the Silver Star Road. The elevation changes quite dramatically from valley to peak, making for a refreshing escape from the Okanagan heat. While the area is best known for the Silver Star Ski Resort, which has accommodation and food services, there are also cross-country skiing at Sovereign Lake, lift assisted mountain biking, snowshoe and snowmobile trails as well as horseback riding. The Trinity/Ricardo Trail network continues north from the park towards Salmon Arm offering spectacular views of the Okanagan Valley and Monashee Mountain Range.

Skihist Provincial Park (Map 13/B2) 🏕️🚻🏖️🥾🚵🐟♿🚻
Used primarily as a stopover by travellers on the Trans-Canada Highway (Hwy 1), there are 56 non reservable campsites set back into the ponderosa pine forest above the Fraser River with accessible pit and flush toilets. The 386 hectare (953 ac) park is also a popular base camp for visitors enjoying river rafting, fishing and exploring the Thompson River area. About 8 km of trails lead from the campground and provide great views of the Thompson Canyon and a chance to see mountain goats or elk in the surrounding hills. A sani-station is available.

Skookumchuck Rapids Provincial Park (Map 25/C2) 🚣🛶🚻
This 71 hectare (175 ac) park is located 20 km east of Enderby and protects a 3 km long canyon along Shuswap River. It is a popular destination for anglers and whitewater paddlers, but paddlers need to heed the take-out notice at the west end of the park.

Small River Caves Provincial Park (Map 50/E4) 🚻🕳️
At 1,818 hectares (4,490 ac), this park protects an area around the Small River cave complex. Not only is this area hard to reach, but the caves are very dangerous and should only be explored by highly experienced cavers. If you don't know what you're doing, don't go.

Steelhead Provincial Park (Map 21/C1)
🏕️🚻🏖️🚣🏊🚤🥾🚵🐟☕♿
Steelhead is located on the southwest shore of Kamloops Lake, near Savona and the mouth of the Thompson River. It is a popular fishing destination with 44 non reservable campsites, 10 of which have power hook-ups, washrooms with showers, a day-use area with 10 picnic tables, trails and a large beach area. Although there is a boat launch for cartop boats, the public boat launch in Savona better serves bigger boats.

Stemwinder Provincial Park (Map 2/G2) 🏕️🚻🏖️🥾🚵🐟♿🚻
This tiny 4 hectare (10 ac) park is located on Highway 3 just west of Hedley. It has 26 campsites, 14 of which are reservable, accessible pit toilets, as well as a picnic facility next to the Similkameen River. Test your luck fishing or soak up some rays along the shoreline. Note that the fast running Similkameen River can be dangerous to swim in.

Sun-oka Beach Provincial Park (Map 9/F5)

The park name comes from the contraction of Sunny Okanagan. Appropriately, this 30 hectare (74 ac) park boasts one of the best beaches in the province and day-use facilities with about 90 picnic tables, flush toilets, change rooms and a playground. Found about 6 km south of Summerland, it is very popular with sunbathers, scuba divers and also sports a playground.

Taweel Provincial Park (Map 33/B1–37/A7)

Access into the 4,558 hectare (11,260 ac) Taweel Provincial Park is limited since the access road to the southeast shore of Taweel Lake is privately owned and controlled by the resorts on the lake. This helps maintain the good fishing in the local lakes. Although there are no facilities at this park, wilderness camping is permitted. Rough trails lead from Taweel Lake to many of the smaller lakes, such as Johnny Lake and Doris Lake. Be sure to respect the private property of the cabins and resorts on Taweel Lake. Hunting is permitted in this park.

Traders Cove Regional Park (Map 17/A6)

This 13.5 hectare (33 ac) lakeshore park is a popular destination in summer with two swimming areas, a sand beach, canoeing and fishing. There are also buoys where boats can tie up.

Trepanier Provincial Park (Map 9/C1–16/C6)

Protecting 2,884 hectares (7,125 ac) of land around Trepanier Creek, most of the recreational activity occurs around Cameron Lake where there is a small campsite. There is also camping and fishing at Lacoma Lake, which is accessed by a fairly long 11 km trail from the south. Hunting is permitted in the park.

Tsintsunko Lakes Provincial Park (Map 28/A3)

Located on the Bonaparte Plateau, this 333 hectare (823 ac) park protects a series of interconnected lakes and wetlands. There are no facilities, but there are a number of trails throughout the park, mostly used by hikers and snowshoers accessing the decent fishing holes for day-use. Hunting is also permitted in the park.

Tunkwa Provincial Park (Map 21/C3)

Tunkwa and Leighton Lakes offer some of the best recreational fishing in the province, so this park sees a lot of anglers. However, the 5,100 hectare (12,595 ac) park offers much more than just fishing. There are 275 non reservable campsites spread around both lakes, a group campsite, boat launch, pit toilets and day-use area. Activities include horseback riding and hunting, and, in the winter, cross-country skiing and snowmobiling. Wildlife viewing is also good here.

Upper Adams River Provincial Park (Map 34/G4–39/D3)

With 5,733 hectares (14,160 ac) of protected terrain, this long narrow park helps preserve over 65 km of important river floodplain. The park stretches from just north of Adams Lake to near Tumtum Lake, and access is difficult. There are two designated vehicle accessible campsites in this park, one at the southeast end of the lake and the other on the southwest end of the lake, with pit toilets and a car top boat launch. Hunting is permitted in the park.

Upper Seymour River Provincial Park (Maps 35, 36, 39, 40)

Set aside to protect the headwaters of the Seymour River, which drains into the Seymour Arm of Shuswap Lake, this 10,672 hectare (26,360 ac) park protects the flora and fauna of the northern Columbia Mountains. The upper portion of the park is pristine wilderness, with high glaciers and alpine tundra that are popular with heli-hiking, skiing and fishing operators. Grizzly bear and mountain caribou call the area home, while fishing for native bull and rainbow trout is popular.

Upper Violet Creek Provincial Park (Map 24/E1–30/E7)

This 124 hectare (306 ac) park is located 12 km southeast of Salmon Arm along the southeast edge of the Larch Hills. The park protects the creek as it flows into Mara Meadows Ecological Reserve. The Larch Hills Cross-Country Ski Trails are found partially within the park.

Vaseux Lake Provincial Park (Map 4/A2)

This small provincial park is located on the shores of Vaseux Lake to the south of Okanagan Falls. There are 12 non reservable campsites, accessible pit toilets and a day-use area together with a developed beach and wildlife centre at the park. The primary attraction is the wildlife sanctuary, which contains an abundance of waterfowl as well as Canada's largest herd of California bighorn sheep. The lake provides decent fishing year-round. Winter camping is permitted; however the gate is locked so you have to walk in.

Victor Lake Provincial Park (Map 31/G4)

Located near Highway 1 to the southwest of Revelstoke, this 15 hectare (37 ac) park has poor access and no developed facilities. It is a beautiful lake found near Eagle Pass that does hold trout. The lake is also popular for paddlers.

Walloper Lake Provincial Park (Map 21/G5–22/A5)

Accessed off Exit 336 from the Coquihalla Highway (Hwy 5), Walloper Lake Provincial Park provides a day-use area for fishermen and picnickers. There is a fishing wharf, picnic tables and pit toilets at the 55 hectare (136 ac) park. Please avoid crossing the private property surrounding the park. No overnight camping is permitted.

When available, choose an existing site to reduce your impact on our parks' fragile ecosystems. Otherwise, choose rock, gravel, dry grass, or snow for a camping surface to minimize signs of your presence.

Wells Gray Provincial Park (Maps 37, 38, 41, 42, 45, 46)

From massive glacial fed lakes to towering mountain alpine peaks, Wells Gray offers visitors the chance to experience a truly wild part of the province. The 541,516 hectare (1,337,545 ac) park is home to a variety of large mammals, such as deer, moose, bear, mountain goat and caribou and offers adventurists countless hiking trails, backcountry camping and a number of excellent paddling routes. The main area of the park is called the Corridor, which is the route in along the Clearwater Valley Road. Here you will find 155 campsites across four maintained campgrounds (Mahood Lake, Pyramid and Clearwater Lake and Falls Creek) and a number of hiking trails, including the ever-popular Helmcken Falls Rim Trail. Dawson Falls, Bailey's Chute and other falls are featured along the Clearwater River. There are also group campsites, several day-use areas, pit and flush toilets, a playground and a few rustic cabins throughout the park.

From the main campground and boat launch at the west end of Mahood Lake, it is possible to find three boat access campsites and some big trout. The Clearwater/Azure area is a popular destination with paddlers, anglers and boaters and features 12 water access campsites. Murtle Lake is the largest canoe-only lake in North America. There is a 2.5 km portage into the lake, which has 20 rustic campsites scattered along the shores. Other popular areas to explore are Spahats Creek, Clearwater River and Trophy Mountain.

White Lake Provincial Park (Map 30/C5)

White Lake is one of the busiest fishing lakes in the province. There is a rustic campsite with room for about 10 vehicle units that can be busy throughout the year. The 266 hectare (657 ac) park is open year-round unless the snow makes the access road impassable. Painted turtles call this park home so please be careful.

Wire Cache Provincial Park (Map 39/A6)

Helping preserve a set of old river bends, this park encompasses 50 hectares (124 ac) of the North Thompson River shoreline. The wetland habitat with old growth cedar, birch, cottonwood, spruce and dogwood stands make the perfect hunting conditions for moose and deer. Canoeing, kayaking and fishing are also possible in this day-use park.

Wrinkly Face Provincial Park (Map 17/C5)

Located above Lake Country off the Beaver Creek Road, this 43 hectare (106 ac) park is set aside to protect a series of meadows at the top of a basalt cliff. The High Rim Trail is a main recreational feature here, providing 55 km of moderate trail for both hikers and horseback riders to explore. For experienced climbers, the southwest side of Wrinkly Face offers mountaineering opportunities. It is a 3.25 hike to the park from Beaver Lake Road trailhead. Hunting is permitted in this park.

Yard Creek Provincial Park (Map 31/B5)

Yard Creek is located on the south side of Highway 1 northwest of Sicamous. It has 65 RV accessible campsites that are managed by the regional district, a covered picnic area, sani-station, pit toilets as well as several short hiking/cross-country ski trails. Snowmobilers use the 175 hectare (432 ac) provincial park as a staging ground to access the Cariboo Lake area in the winter. The park is also popular with bird watchers.

B.C.'s Backcounty Playground

With over 1300 sites and 800 trails for you to explore.

Check out website for information on locations, activities, and facilities.

www.sitesandtrailsbc.ca

BRITISH COLUMBIA | Recreation Sites and Trails BC

RECSITE
ADVENTURES

While it is true that you can erect a tent most anywhere that suits your fancy on public land, many of the best sites have already been discovered and at least partially developed into camping areas.

While provincial and national parks capture the lion's share of attention, there is a host of sites that have been developed by the BC Forest Service, or by various forestry companies, as a base from which to explore the wilderness of BC. They are often remote and beautiful locations – lakes, rivers and mountain areas – that are often less crowded and more rustic than provincial park campsites.

Recently, these sites were transferred to the new Ministry of Tourism, Sports and the Arts and are now simply called Recreation Sites. There are many great improvements happening to these sites – many have been enhanced and upgraded to rival or outshine provincial parks. These sites are considered Managed Recreation Sites and they come in two flavours: with fees and without. While the majority of sites are free, a minimal fee (approx. $10-$16/night) is charged at sites where increased levels of service are provided (from May to October). Some of these sites are gated in the off season. Those sites that currently charge fees are marked with a **S** symbol.

On the other hand, there are still many user maintained, free-to-use sites. These sites range from rustic backcountry sites with few, if any, amenities to well-developed sites with picnic tables, fire rings and pit toilets. User maintained is a key concept. It is your responsibility to care for these sites, and if you pack it in, you pack it out.

Below we have listed the majority of sites in the Thompson Okanagan Region in alphabetical order. Those missing are usually day-use sites or trail access areas. We have given a brief description of the area and included symbols for popular activities. Although we have listed the number of campsites that are found at these sites, these are often just a rough estimate, and more groups can, and often do, squeeze in.

Accessing some of these sites can be quite the challenge; long, four-wheel drive only roads that are sometimes unmarked are par for the course. Other sites are found along active logging roads. Be careful when travelling along these roads, and watch out for industrial vehicles. If possible, check ahead with the Ministry of Forests (see back of book for contact information) or with the logging companies regarding current activity. The new ministry recreation site website (*sitesandtrailsbc.ca*) is also a great resource.

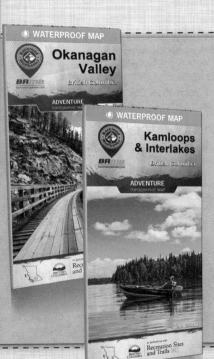

Abbott Lake Recreation Site (Map 14/B1) 🏕🏖🎣🚽
Located northwest of Merritt, Abbott Lake is found off the Tyner Forest Service Road and has three campsites in a semi-open area on the northeast side of the lake. The road in is rough and suitable only for four-wheel drive vehicles.

Aileen Lake Recreation Site (Map 17/E4) 🏕🏊🏍🚽🛶🚶
This two unit site is accessed by the very rough four-wheel drive only Dee Lake Road. There is a cartop boat launch at this recreation site, allowing easy access to Aileen Lake, as well as many other lakes in the area.

Allan Lake Recreation Site (Map 33/C7) 🚵🏕🏖🏊🎣🚽🛶
The turn off to Allan Lake Recreation Site is found approximately 45 km down the Jamieson Creek Forest Service Road. This site has six campsites, picnic facilities and a cartop boat launch. The lake is popular with anglers as the high elevation on the Bonaparte Plateau is a nice spot to escape the summer's heat.

Allendale Lake Recreation Site (Map 4/D1) 🏕🏖🎣🚽
Allendale Lake is located on a rough two-wheel drive suitable spur road off the Okanagan Falls Forest Service Road, east of Okanagan Falls. The recreation site offers a six unit campground and cartop boat launch.

Andy's Lake Recreation Site (Map 7/C3) 🏕🏖🏊🎣🏍🚽🛶
This recreation site sits in an opening next to the lake, a short walk from the Thynne Mountain Road. The two unit campsite is used by anglers and snowmobilers.

Antler Lake Recreation Site (Map 21/C7) 🏕🏖🚶🏍🚽🛶
This recreation site is located south of Logan Lake and north of Dot Lake, and can be accessed by various four-wheel drive roads. Antler Lake is small, with two tent sites on the lake and one a short distance away. There is a boat launch, picnic tables and toilet facilities here.

Apocynum Recreation Site (Map 13/A6) 🚵🏕🏖🏊🏊🚶🚽🛶⑤
Recently upgraded and upsized, this popular site is found 16.5 km along the Nahatlatch River Forest Service Road. There is space for 16 groups at the site, which is RV accessible. Whitewater paddling, fishing, hiking and hunting are popular pastimes in the area as the Nahatlatch River and Provincial Park are within close proximity. Like most recreation sites, this campsite is available on a first-come, first-served basis and no firewood is available for sale.

Arlington Lakes Recreation Site (Map 10/G4) 🚵🏕🏖🏊🏊🚶🏍🛶⑤
These three lakes are found 3 km off Highway 33, about 24 km south of the Big White turnoff. The picturesque recreation site sits on the southernmost lake, with good fishing and easy access to the Kettle Valley Railway. There are 23 campsites split between three camping areas, with the northwest site popular for hikers doing the Trans Canada Trail. This is a maintained site and fees do apply.

Arthur Lake North Recreation Site (Map 24/A4) 🚵🏖🏊🎣🚽
This forested site is found in the Spa Hills east of Bolean Lake and has three campsites. It is accessed off the two-wheel drive Bolean Lake Road and has a rough cartop boat launch.

Badger Lake Recreation Site (Map 28/E3) 🚵🏖🏊🎣🛶⑤
Badger Lake is a popular trout fishing destination. There are 17 campsites and a cartop boat launch. The two main access points are either via the Knouff Lake Road off of the Sun Peaks Road or Orchard Lake Road off of Highway 5 (between Vinsulla and McLure).

Baird Lake Recreation Site (Map 25/B3) 🏕🏖🏊🎣🛶🚽
Located approximately 4 km west of Mabel Lake, this timbered site has seven campsites, a boat launch, picnic tables and toilet facilities. The road starts to deteriorate shortly after Hidden Lake, making this site more suitable for four-wheel drive vehicles.

Bardolph Lake Recreation Site (Map 17/F1) 🏕🏖🏊🎣🏍🛶🚽
Located in the Vernon Hills Interpretive Forest, this site offers three tenting pads and a cartop boat launch on the north end of the lake. The access into the lake is quite rough.

Barnes Lake Recreation Site (Map 20/E2) 🚵🏕🏖🏊🎣🏍🛶
This site is located 2 km north of Highway 97, southeast of Ashcroft. Set in an open range next to the lake, the RV accessible site receives heavy use throughout the year. Barnes Lake is a popular rainbow trout lake.

Bear Lake Recreation Site (Map 17/E3) 🏕🏖🎣🏍🛶🚽
There are three campsites together with a rough cartop boat launch at this site on Bear Lake. It is accessed by a four-wheel drive road east of King Edward Lake.

Beaver River Recreation Site (Map 49/E3) 🚵🏖🚽🛶🚽🏕
Found off the Holmes River Forest Service Road south of McBride, this site is close to the highway and is a popular pull-off for weary travellers. The site offers ten camping/picnic sites along the eastern shore of the river. A short trail leads east from the recreation site to Beaver River Falls.

Becker Lake Recreation Site (Map 17/E1) 🏕🏖🏊🚶🏍🛶🚽🚶
The Becker Lake Recreation Site has seven campsites in two different areas on the north side of the lake and a rough boat launch. Becker Lake is part of the Vernon Hill Interpretative Forest and there are several trails in the area to explore if you are not into fishing. Access this recreation site via Becker Forest Service Road.

Big OK Lake [Island Lake] Recreation Site (Map 20/G5) 🏕🏖🏊🎣🏍🛶
This high elevation lake is popular with fly-fishers. The recreation site features seven campsites and a cartop boat launch. The route in via the Highland Valley Copper Mine is no longer open, so access this lake via Laura Lakes Road (four-wheel drive recommended).

Billy Lake Recreation Site (Map 21/C6) 🏕🏖🏊🎣🚶🛶
Billy Lake is found southwest of Logan Lake and can be reached by four-wheel drive vehicle along the Pimainus Lake Forest Service Road. There are four campsites in a semi-open area next to the lake, a cartop boat launch, picnic tables and toilet facilities.

Bisson Lake Recreation Site (Map 18/E4) 🏕🏖🏊🛶🚽🚶
Located on a rough four-wheel drive spur road off of the Kettle Valley Forest Service Road near Highway 6, this small lakeshore recreation site has a cartop boat launch, picnic tables, toilet facilities and four campsites.

Blackwell Lake Recreation Site (Map 22/G6) 🏕🚶🛶
Located southeast of Roscoe Lake Provincial Park, Blackwell Lake is accessed by a 3 km trail from Pratt Lake to the north. Although there are no designated campsites, Blackwell makes a fine overnight walk-in camping destination for anglers.

Bleeker Lake Recreation Site (Map 22/E5) 🚵🏖🏊🎣🛶
In the Roche Lake area, off of the Bleeker Lake Forest Service Road, this small site hosts five campsites and a boat launch for good fishing opportunities.

Bluejoint Creek Recreation Site (Map 12/B6) 🚵🏖🛶🚽
Located on West Burrell Forest Service Road, this small site is set in a clearing at an old sawmill site next to Bluejoint Creek. This site is rarely busy and offers two spacious campsites that are ideal for larger groups.

Bluey Lake Recreation Site (Map 8/A1) 🏕🏖🏊🎣🛶🚶
This popular fishing lake has seven small campsites shaded by Douglas fir forest. Located south of Kentucky-Alleyne Provincial Park, access is off Highway 97C via the Loon Lake exit.

Bob Lake West Recreation Site (Map 21/G7) 🏕🏖🏊🎣🛶🚽
Located on the western shore of Bob Lake, this site has three campsites located on a difficult to find four-wheel drive road. This is a popular destination with anglers, campers and boaters in the summer and for hunters in the fall.

Bob's Lake Recreation Site (Map 15/D7) 🚵🏖🏊🎣🏍🛶
This small recreation site has two campsites situated on the northwest of the lake. In late 2010, the area was logged extensively to remove pine beetle infected trees, leaving a wide open and windy site. Located on the Elkhart Road just north of the Coquihalla Connector (Hwy 97C), Bob's Lake has easy access to other recreation sites in the area including Elkhart, Paradise and Island Lakes.

Bog Lake Rec Site (Map 7/A2) 🏕🏖🏊🎣🛶
Located just southwest of Bonaparte Lake, this is a popular destination for campers and anglers. There are several access roads that lead into the three-unit site (most notably from North Bonaparte Road and Bog Lake North Road), and there is a boat launch, picnic tables and toilets.

Bolean Lake Recreation Site (Map 23/G4) 🚵🏖🏊🎣
Bolean Lake is a popular fishery that is easily accessed by the Bolean Forest Service Road north of Falkland. The recreation site is located just past the fishing lodge. There are five campsites next to the lake and a good cartop boat launch.

Bonaparte Lake Recreation Site (Map 32/E7)

Although there are several resorts around this popular lake, many visitors prefer to use this four unit recreation site in an open grassy area on the northwest end of the big lake. Most visitors take advantage of the good gravel boat launch to try their luck fishing, or spend an afternoon exploring the shoreline in a canoe.

Bonaparte River Recreation Sites (Map 26/E1)

Located east of Highway 97 and Chasm Provincial Park on the Clinton-Loon Lake Forest Service Road (3400 Rd), there is a pair of sites (Bonaparte River Bridge and Bonaparte Suicide Crossing) here. Offering a total of three campsites, the sites are used by anglers and hunters exploring this part of the Bonaparte River.

Boot Lake Recreation Site (Map 15/D7)

Boot Lake is found on a four-wheel drive road north of the Coquihalla Connector (Highway 97C) at the Elkhart Road Exit. There are a total of four forested campsites at an elevation of 1,485 metres (4,870 ft), providing a refreshing climate in the heat of summer. This site features a cartop boat launch, picnic tables and toilet facilities.

Bose Lake Recreation Site (Map 21/B5)

This small recreation site is comprised of five campsites together with a car-top boat launch at the south end of Bose Lake. A four-wheel drive vehicle is required to access the campsite, which is used mostly by fishermen and canoers in the summer and snowmobilers in the winter. An interesting side trip is to visit the Bethlehem Copper Mine to the south.

Boss Lake Recreation Site (Map 7/E1)

Boss Lake is one of three very popular lakes in the Voght Valley. The large 25 unit site has good road access and can accommodate RVs of any size, making it a very popular destination. It also has two docks and a boat launch. The lake can be reached by Voght Valley Road.

Botanie Lake Recreation Site (Map 20/A7)

Located north of Lytton, this site has three wooded camping areas. Access is along Botanie Creek Road, which is suitable for RVs. This site is very popular in the winter for snowmobiling, snowshoeing and tobogganing, and has an enclosed shelter for warming up. Please note most of the land around the recreation site is an Indian Reserve and access may be restricted.

> Be sure to visit sitesandtrailsbc.ca for the latest information on fees, closures and upgrades to the recreation site you plan to visit.

Bouleau Lake Recreation Site (Map 16/E1)

On the east side of the medium sized lake is the Bouleau Lake Recreation Site, which has two campsites and a good cartop boat launch. At the west end of the lake system and next to the smaller lake is the Little Bouleau Lake Recreation Site. Find this lake along the Bouleau Lake Forest Service Road.

Bowman Point Recreation Site (Map 12/E5)

In a sheltered anchorage on the Lower Arrow Lake, this small, two unit treed site is accessed by boat only. Depending on the level of the lake, there are as many as five mooring buoys. Fishing, swimming and boating are the primary attractions. Sailboats frequent the area.

Brenda Lake Recreation Site (Map 15/G7)

There are four campsites in this small site on the shores of Brenda Lake, with a new boat launch, picnic tables and toilet facilities. This lake is popular with anglers and easily accessed, however, snow can linger into June due to the high elevation. Brenda Lake is located about 30 km northwest of Peachland and can be accessed via the road to Brenda Mines.

Brennan Creek Recreation Site (Map 29/E1)

Formerly called Sandy Point, this site is located on the western shores of Adams Lake south of Brennan Creek. It is a larger site with space for about 20 units, a boat launch and a sandy beach. Access to this site is along the Adams West Forest Service Road and there is a fee to camp here.

Browne Lake Recreation Site (Map 10/E1)

Browne Lake is to the north of McCulloch Reservoir/Hydraulic Lake outside of Kelowna. The six unit semi-open site features a boat launch and fishing opportunities at the three small lakes. There are also many trails to explore in the area.

Bruer Creek Recreation Site (Map 18/E5)

Found at the junction of Bruer Creek and Kettle River, this roadside site can be a little noisy when the logging trucks are running the Kettle River Forest Service Road. There is only one campsite here used mostly by fishermen and hunters.

Brunette Lake Recreation Site (Map 17/E4)

Brunette Lake is accessed by the rough two-wheel drive Brunette Main leading south from the Dee Lake Road at Doreen Lake. There is a rough cartop boat launch as well as a few tenting pads, but the site is mainly used by day-trippers. This area is also a favourite spot for nature study.

Buck Lake Recreation Site (Map 8/B2)

Buck Lake is located on the Shrimpton Creek Forest Service Road south of the Loon Lake Exit on the Coquihalla Connector (Hwy 97C). There are ten campsites on the northern shore as well as a boat launch, picnic tables and ATV trails for visitors to enjoy.

Buck Lake Recreation Site (Map 11/A5)

This small site has three campsites set in the forest that surrounds Buck Lake. The site is accessed along a rough four-wheel drive road set below China Butte in the hills dividing the Kettle River and the West Kettle River. Toilet and picnic table facilities as well as a cartop boat launch are offered.

Burnell Lake Recreation Site (Map 3/G4)

This is an open site with space for eight campsites next to the lake. The popular site is used mainly by fishermen and provides a cartop boat launch as well as toilet and table facilities. There is also a trail around the lake for hiking and ATV opportunities, as well as a day-use area for picnicking. This lake can be found along Sawmill Burnell Lake Forest Service Road.

Cabin Lake Recreation Site (Map 13/F6)

This is a small four unit site accessed along Miner Forest Service Road by high centered four-wheel drive vehicles only (no off-highway recreational vehicles are allowed at this site). Hikers accessing the Heather Basin Trail frequent the area. This area is also utilized for camping and fishing in the summer and snowmobiling in the winter. It is also a First Nations cultural site used on occasion for tribal gatherings.

Calling Lake Recreation Site (Map 20/G6)

Found south of Big Ok Lake, Calling Lake is usually a quieter place to visit. There are four campsites that are accessed from the northwest off the Laura Lakes Road, which can be quite rough. This site provides excellent fishing and camping opportunities, as well as a base camp for hunters in the fall months.

Campbell Lake Recreation Site (Map 22/F4)

On the southwest side of Campbell Lake, there are 31 campsites and a nice day-use area next to a small bay. Access into the lake is generally good via the Scuitto Creek Forest Service Road. The site is popular with anglers and boaters. There is a gravel boat launch for small trailered boats.

Canoe Reach Marina Recreation Site (Map 47/D5)

A well-developed marina facility providing boat access and moorage on the north end of Kinbasket Reservoir, this site has 17 campsites with picnic tables and toilet facilities. Between June and mid-September there is a fee to camp here. Access is 21 km south of Valemount on the gravel East Canoe Forest Service Road.

Canyon Creek Recreation Site (Map 11/C7)

Canyon Creek is a popular destination for anglers and swimmers. There are two campsites set in the forest and a nice swimming hole with a sandy beach on the Kettle River. The recreation site is 32 km along the paved Christian Valley Road and can be accessed by smaller RVs and trailers.

Canyon Flats Recreation Site (Map 11/C7)

This large well used site on the banks of the Kettle River is found at the 31 km mark on the paved Christian Valley Road. Although the site only has three developed sites with tables and toilets, it is suitable for large groups and RVs. Visitors will appreciate the deep swimming hole and sandy beach found about 200 metres downstream.

Caribou Lake Recreation Site (Map 19/F1)

Accessed off the Caribou Lake Forest Service Road from the east or the Whatshan Forest Service Road to the south, this is a popular three unit, semi-open lakeshore site set between two marshy lakes. There is a cartop boat launch (electric motor only) and the lake is stocked. This area is also popular for ATVing in the summer and snowmobiling in the winter.

Cascade Beach Recreation Site (Map 25/D4)

Found about 15 km along the Mabel Lake Forest Service Road, on the eastern shores of the beautiful lake, this site has a couple of different locations, with five nice lakeside campsites between them. This site is walk-in only and has easy access to beautiful beaches and a scenic waterfall. Swimming, fishing, hiking and mountain biking are a few of the recreational opportunities here.

Chain Lake West Recreation Site (Map 8/E3)

Chain Lake is a popular destination next to the Princeton-Summerland Road. The large site has 31 campsites in a semi-open location next to the lake. Good road access makes this a favourite site with RVs and larger trailers. Visitors can launch a small boat onto the lake or explore the Kettle Valley Railway trail.

Charcoal Creek Recreation Site (Map 23/E2)

The Charcoal Creek site is located on a large, grassy bench above the creek. It is a good group site with four individual campsites that is easily accessible off the Chase-Falkland Road (RV friendly). Charcoal Creek provides excellent fly-fishing opportunities.

Chase Creek Recreation Site (Map 23/E3)

Located a few kilometres to the north of Pillar Lake on the Chase-Falkland Road, this site is set in a forest alongside Chase Creek. There is good road access to the three campsites with picnic tables.

Cherryville Recreation Site (Map 18/E1)

This ten unit open site is on the banks of the Shuswap River. The RV and group friendly recreation site provides a beach for sunbathing as well as picnic tables. This site is easily accessed along the Sugar Lake Road and is popular with anglers on the Shuswap River. A newly developed boat launch provides easy access for fishing and paddling.

Chute Lake Recreation Site (Map 10/A3)

Found at the south end of the lake near the Chute Lake Resort, this is a popular place for fishermen, bikers and hikers travelling along the Kettle Valley Railway between Penticton and Kelowna. This small, rustic site has space for four camping groups and is managed without fees.

Clark Lake Recreation Site (Map 11/B5)

It is a 2.2 km hike from the 7 km mark of the Lassie Lake Forest Service Road to this small site on the northeast shores of Clark Lake. The trails and campsite are mostly used by anglers. Many other small backcountry lakes can be accessed by a network of trails stretching out from the campsite.

Cleo Lake Recreation Site (Map 11/B5)

This hike-in campsite is found in the hills above the Christian Valley. The Cleo Lake site is a small, open campsite that is found along a 2.5 km trail past Joan Lake from the 6.5 km mark on the Lassie Lake Road.

Clifford Lake Recreation Site (Map 7/E3)

The second of a series of small fishing lakes found north of Youngberg Road near Thalia Lake, Clifford Lake offers five nice campsites that are somewhat hidden from the main road. Activities here include fishing, ATVing, canoeing and nature studies. This site is accessed via Pike Mountain Forest Service Road.

Coldscaur Lake Recreation Sites (Map 37/B7)

There are two sites on this long, narrow lake accessed off TFL 18 Road 2, west of Clearwater. The more popular site is found at the north end of the lake and offers a decent boat launch and around 13 campsites. The southern site is much smaller with only about five campsites and cartop boat access. While in the area, be sure to visit the nearby trail that leads from the western end of the lake to an impressive rock bridge.

Community Lake Recreation Site (Map 28/F5)

Community Lake offers room for nine campsites and has a boat launch together with a wharf. Fishing is the primary attraction to the site, but snowmobiling is also popular in the winter. This site is located off Knouff Lake Road.

Cooke Creek Recreation Site (Map 25/B2)

This site is located along the paved Enderby-Mabel Lake Road on the banks of the Shuswap River. The area is particularly popular during the late summer and fall when the Chinook and sockeye salmon are running. There is a fish hatchery and hiking trails in the area. There are eight RV accessible campsites available at this site, which is managed with fees.

Copper Creek Recreation Site (Map 2/A5)

This small site is located 500 metres from Highway 3 on the Placer Mountain Forest Service Road. There are a total of five campsites in a semi-open location next to the creek. RVs can access the site so it makes a good stopover for travellers on the Hope-Princeton Highway (Hwy 3). There is a fee to camp here.

Copper Kettle Lake Recreation Site (Map 11/C3)

This small campsite is located at the end of a 3 km trail leading from around the 66 km mark on the Kettle River Forest Service Road. This mountain lake provides good fishing as well as a rustic tenting area at the south end.

Cottonwood Beach Recreation Site (Map 25/D2)

This popular 37 unit recreation site is located on the eastern shores of Mabel Lake, which is nestled on the northern edge of the Okanagan to the north of Lumby. The site has a good cartop boat launch as well as a sandy beach for swimming and beach activities. Easily accessed off the Mabel Lake Forest Service Road, the site is managed with fees and has seen a recent expansion in 2013. ATVing is popular among the many roads that lead up the mountains around the lake.

Crescent Lake Recreation Site (Map 8/G2)

Crescent Lake is located a few kilometres to the east of the Headwater Lakes on the Peachland Forest Service Road (good two-wheel drive access). It offers room for five or more groups on the dam in an open, exposed area. It is not particularly beautiful but it does provide good fishing for rainbow.

Crump Recreation Site (Map 9/C5)

Thanks to the Summerland ATV Club, the Crump Recreation Site is now proudly displaying its sign again. Found 3 km west of the pavement on the Summerland-Princeton Road, the site is ideal for ATVers, bikers, horse riders and campers in general. The site rests next to the decommissioned KVR Railway Line, which is part of the Trans Canada Trail. There are literally hundreds of miles of trails of all types in the area. The site itself has two large group sites along with ample parking. You will need to bring your own water.

Crystal Lake Recreation Site (Map 32/D4)

Not far from Highway 24 via the North Bonaparte Road, this site is situated along the northern shore of the lake. The 12 vehicle units along with a cartop boat launch can be used as a base to explore the many lakes in the area.

Cup Lake Recreation Site (Map 11/B5)

Cup Lake is found off the Lassie Lake Forest Service Road (two-wheel drive access) rising out of the Christian Valley. It has two heavily treed campsites located in a clearing next to the lake and offers picnic tables and toilet facilities plus a wharf for casting.

Dairy Lake West Recreation Site (Map 21/E3)

Located along the Duffy Lake Forest Service Road (two-wheel drive access), this site has four campsites and a cartop boat launch. A separate site is also found at the north end of the lake, but is more difficult to access. Found close to Kamloops, this site is a popular day-use site for anglers, while trail enthusiasts can find an elaborate off road riding area around nearby Greenstone Mountain.

Damer Lake Recreation Site (Map 17/D3)

There is space for three groups at this site, which is accessed north of Oyama Lake on a rough road. Visitors will find a rustic cartop boat launch on the highly fluctuating lake. The Kalamalka Lookout and the High Rim Trail are nearby.

Damfino Creek Recreation Site (Map 11/D3)

Located on the Damfino Creek north of the Christian Valley, there is room for three campsites on either side of the creek. There is good access is off the Kettle River Forest Service Road for RVs and larger units.

Dardanelles Lake Recreation Site (Map 22/F7)

This recreation site has space for four groups and is found off Dardanelles Forest Service Road. The typical users of this site are anglers and hunters, but the area also hosts nature enthusiasts and a few ATVers.

Davis Lake Recreation Site (Map 7/E1)

Davis Lake is perhaps the most popular lake in the Voght Valley. There are 46 campsites set in a semi-open forest with good road access that makes the site ideal for RVs. Two boat launches provide access to the lake. Enjoy fishing along the wharf, canoeing and ATVing in the surrounding area. Fees are collected from early May to mid-October. Davis Lake is found off of Vogt Valley Road.

Deadman Lake Recreation Site (Map 7/G3)
Deadman Lake is located west of Highway 5A on a four-wheel drive road off the Hornet Forest Service Road. There are a total of three semi-open campsites next to the small fishing lake. Hunters use the area in the fall.

Deadman Lake Recreation Site (Map 27/C2)
Deadman Lake is found in the eerily named valley north of Kamloops Lake and Savona. Accessed along the Deadman Vidette Road, 47 km north of Highway 1, this site has four treed campsites and facilities such as tables and a cartop boat launch. Fishing, swimming and canoeing are possible in the lake.

Deer Lake Recreation Site (Map 33/B3)
Deer Lake is a small but popular fishing lake in the Nehalliston Plateau north of Highway 24. The six unit site is often full, especially on weekends, as the area is a hotspot for fishing, ATVing and canoeing. In the winter, the area is very popular for snowmobiling.

Fees are generally quite reasonable (approx. $10-$16/night) compared to provincial parks or private sites, and are usually collected from May to the end of September. In the off season some sites are gated.

Dennis Lake Recreation Site (Map 29/C6)
Found on a rough side road off the McGillivray Lake Forest Service Road, this small site has two campsites and a cartop boat launch. This site is popular with anglers and canoers as there is easy access to the lake.

Dennis Lake Recreation Site (Map 39/A4)
Dennis Lake is a headwater lake of the Mad River and is home to a small two unit recreation site set in the trees. The main attraction of the lake is its quality fishing opportunities. Access is via the Mad River Forest Service Road.

Dewdney Recreation Site (Map 8/C7)
Dewdney is the closest site to Princeton on the Old Hedley Road. The good road access and open setting under Ponderosa pine trees allows room for about six RVs or campers. Visitors can test the waters with a fishing line or on a canoe or explore the surrounding area for Indian pictographs.

Doreen Lake Recreation Site (Map 17/E3)
This site is found at the south end of Doreen Lake off the Dee Lake Road. There is room for 10 units, along with a rustic boat launch for those looking to fish the fly-only lake. The good roadside access makes this recreation site popular with hunters and fishermen.

Dot Lake Recreation Site (Map 21/C7)
Found just southeast of Chataway Lake on a two-wheel drive spur road off the Aberdeen Road, this site has five campsites in a small treed area. There is a cartop boat launch for fishing and canoeing as well trails in the surrounding area. The area is also used in the fall by hunters.

Double Lakes Recreation Site (Map 37/A6)
Northwest of Clearwater, the Double Lakes Recreation Site is located on Road 20. The site is quite popular with anglers as there are two shoreline campsites, along with picnic tables and a rough boat launch onto the lake.

Downie Creek Recreation Site (Map 36/E3)
This site is on the Downie Arm of Lake Revelstoke. Downie Creek's claim to fame is that it is the best boat launch on Lake Revelstoke. There are 22 sites here, suitable for big trailers and recreation vehicles. Access is 72 kilometres north of the Trans-Canada on Highway 23.

Duffy Lake Recreation Site (Map 21/E3)
Located off the Dairy Lake Forest Service Road, this site is set below Greenstone Mountain. There are 52 campsites together with a boat launch for anglers to test their luck. This site has a wide network of ATV and dirt bike trails that are popular with snowmobilers in the winter.

Dunn Lake North Recreation Site (Map 33/D4)
At the north end of Dunn Lake, this semi-open, grassy site has room for six groups of campers. Access is good off the Dunn Lake Road, but you will need to cross the river via ferry at Little Fort. The area used by horseback riders, anglers and canoers in the summer and snowmobilers in the winter.

Dunsapie Lake Recreation Site (Map 28/C1)
This site is located on the Jamieson Creek Forest Service Road and receives heavy use throughout the summer months. It has three sites as well as a cartop boat launch.

East Barrière Lake Recreation Site (Map 34/B7)
This is a large 16 unit site set in a forested area on the northwest shores of the lake. The site is easily accessed on the East Barrière Road and offers full facilities including an improved boat launch and picnic tables. Fishing is popular here, as is boating, canoeing or just going for a swim at the site's open sandy beach. Hikers can follow the East Barrière Lake Trail along the shore of the lake.

East Maury Lake Recreation Site (Map 37/C4)
Found north of Clearwater off Road 9, the site lies on the north end of the lake providing three campsites along with a gravel boat launch and picnic tables. The site can be quite busy during the summer months.

Edith Lake Recreation Site (Map 22/C4)
Edith Lake's close proximity to Kamloops makes it a very popular location. Camping and day-use facilities lend to the popularity of this spot as a great fishing lake. The recreation site provides 12 campsites, with fees in effect from spring through fall, along with three boat launch areas and a couple of day-use areas. A new dock has been recently added. This site is found along Edith Lake Road.

Edwin Lakes Recreation Site (Map 17/F3)
Edwin Lakes are located on a fairly good road off the Aberdeen Lake Forest Service Road. There are three lakeshore camping pads together with a cartop boat launch.

Eight Mile Flats Recreation Site (Map 11/G7)
Eight Mile Flats is located at an old bridge site and provides good access to the Granby River. The small site is located on a rough two-wheel drive road off the Boulder-Traverse Creek Forest Service Road and on the opposite side of the river from the Granby Forest Service Road. This site only offers one campsite with a table and toilet. Visitors should also note the water is quite shallow and fast and not recommended for swimming.

Ejas Lake Recreation Site (Map 37/B5)
There are three camping units at this site, which is set along the western shore of Ejas Lake along Road 9. Picnic tables and a cartop boat launch are also available at the lake.

Elbow Lake Recreation Site (Map 25/B2)
Currently closed due to no road access (check sitesandtrailsbc.ca for updates), this single unit site offers access to the small, shallow Elbow Lake. Located off the Cooke Hunter Forest Service Road to the west of Mabel Lake, access is very rough and slow at times; a four-wheel drive vehicle is recommended.

Elkhart Lake Recreation Site (Map 15/D7)
This recreation site can be found along Paradise Lake Road, which if found north of the Coquihalla Connector (Highway 97C) at the Elkhart Road Exit. There is room for three units on the west side of the lake. It is possible to haul a canoe or small boat to the lake. This area is favourite spot for hunters in the fall.

Evely [Okanagan] Lake Recreation Site (Map 17/A2)
The former Okanagan Lake site was renamed after the former forest service employee. There are 50 popular sites here, many with their own beach access, a separate day use area, trails and a rustic boat launch. The site is managed with fees from the beginning of May to mid-September. Access is off Westside Road past Fintry Provincial Park, 34 km north of Kelowna.

Face Lake Recreation Site (Map 21/F4)
Located northeast of Logan Lake, this small two unit campsite is set in a forested area at the north end of Face Lake. There is a cartop boat launch for anglers and canoeists and decent access from Highway 97C along the Paska Lake Road (four-wheel drive only). During winter the road network is often utilized by snowmobilers.

Fir Flats Rec Site (Map 13/A6)
This 6 unit site is located along the Nahatlatch River, 18 km up the Nahatlatch Forest Service Road northwest of Boston Bar. A great destination for those interested in hiking, fishing and hunting, this site is available on a first-come, first-served basis and is open year-round (weather permitting).

Fishtrap Creek Recreation Site (Map 28/D2)
This recreation site is primarily used as a staging area for horseback riders in the Fishtrap Mountain area. In the fall, the site is popular with hunters. There are six campsites at this easily accessible recreation site off of Westsyde Road.

Flyfish Lakes Recreation Sites (Map 17/E4)
As the name implies, fly-fishing is the name of the game here. Flyfish No. 1 is accessed by a short hike, while Flyfish No. 2 is accessed by a four-wheel drive branch off the Dee Lake Road. There are three campsites on No.1 and four campsites on No. 2, along with a good cartop boat launch and a trail leading south to tiny Ruth Lake.

French Lake South Recreation Site (Map 32/D2)
French Lake is a hidden lake found just east of the Windy Mountain Forest Service Road (1900 Road). The rough road access and lack of facilities makes this site a more popular day-use area for anglers. There is a well-used boat launch area and room for a couple of campsites.

Frog Falls Recreation Site (Map 31/F5)
Only about 4 km from the highway off the Wap Lake Forest Service Road, this small four unit site is located in a dense forest near Frog Falls on Wap Creek. A short hike leads to the scenic falls.

Gable Creek Recreation Site (Map 12/A7)
Found at the bottom of a steep hill on the Gable Creek Forest Service Road, this site is located in a scenic gorge created by Gable Creek and the Granby River. Anglers and hunters primarily use the forest service site which has two large sites, picnic tables, pit toilets and plenty of room for RVs or bigger units.

Gannett Lake Recreation Site (Map 35/A3)
Set at the base of Gannett Mountain, this high elevation lake makes a fine summer fishing destination and is popular with hunters in the fall. The recreation site is accessible via the high clearance two-wheel drive Gannett Lake Forest Service Road northeast of Adams Lake. There are three campsites available in an open area along with a gravel boat launch.

Gillis Lake West Recreation Site (Map 14/B7)
The Murray Lake Road to the west of Kingsvale accesses this site on the western side of the lake. Visitors will find five treed sites as well as a boat launch for anglers testing their luck. This area is known for its wildlife viewing and nature study.

Glimpse Lake North Recreation Site (Map 15/D2)
Found on the north side of Glimpse Lake, along Lauder Road, this 17 unit site is set under a Douglas fir stand. This site is managed with fees since it is popular with anglers and hunters. The road in to the site is in good shape and is passable by RV.

Glimpse Lake Southwest Recreation Site (Map 15/D2)
This recreation site is found at the southwest corner of Glimpse Lake. The road in is slightly rougher than the northern site, but is still two-wheel drive accessible. There are eight campsites available here. For access, take the Douglas Lake Road off Highway 5A to Lauder Road, then follow that road north to the lake.

Goose Lake Recreation Site (Map 33/B3)
This six unit recreation site is easily accessed from Highway 24. Containing sites on both the shoreline and in the trees, there is a small cartop boat launch and easy access to several other fishing opportunities in the area.

Goose Lake North Recreation Site (Map 7/E3)
The smaller of the two sites on Goose Lake, there are three campsites set away from the water. This site is popular with fisherman wanting easy access to other nearby lakes.

Goose Lake South Recreation Site (Map 7/E3)
Located on the southeastern shore of Goose Lake, this site has nine open campsites set under a stand of Douglas firs. This area is popular with anglers and nature enthusiasts in the summer and hunters in the fall months. A boat launch, picnic tables and toilet facilities are available. Goose Lake is found off the Pike Mountain Forest Service Road.

Gordon Bay Recreation Site (Map 34/G4)
This small site is the northernmost site on the Adams Lake and accessible by road or water. There is a nice beach and a rustic boat launch onto the lake. Swimming, canoeing, boating and fishing are the most common activities here.

Gordon Lake Recreation Site (Map 14/B2)
This site is found on a four-wheel drive road off the Tyner Forest Service Road. There are four campsites set in the trees next to the lake. A cartop boat launch is available for anglers and canoers.

Gorman Lake Recreation Site (Map 33/C7)
This is one of a series of popular fishing lakes east of Bonaparte Lake. The two unit campsite is found in an open, grassy area and is used mostly by anglers. This site is located between Bonaparte Lake and Highway 5 along the Gorman Lake Forest Service Road.

Graffunder Lakes North Recreation Site (Map 34/E2)
Accessible via Road 2 from Vavenby to North Adams Lake, this recreation site only has one large unit. Easy access to the lake makes this site a popular spot during the summer months with both campers and day trippers.

Granby-Burrell Recreation Site (Map 6/A1)
This semi-open campsite is used mainly by river fishermen in the summer and hunters in the fall. There are three official sites, but there is plenty of room to accommodate more campers or day visitors. The RV accessible site is located right at the 28 Mile Bridge and is very popular due to the paved road access to the bridge.

Granite Creek Recreation Site (Map 7/F7)
This site is found 18 km northwest of Princeton by following the signs through Coalmont. Its good access and proximity to the scenic Tulameen River and the Kettle Valley Railway makes it a very popular forest service site. There are 21 RV accessible campsites together with a picnic facility and a cartop boat launch. The site is often used as a staging area for paddlers as well as ATVers and snowmobilers.

Grizzly Lake East Recreation Site (Map 37/C6)
This small site at the base of Grizzly Mountain is found west of Clearwater on Road 5. The two unit site is used mostly by anglers and day trippers and has a cartop boat launch.

Gump Lake Recreation Site (Map 21/C6)
Gump Lake is one of a mess of lakes southwest of Logan Lake that offer good fishing. This 20 hectare lake is known for its large rainbow trout population, but the rough access along Highmont Road (a four-wheel drive vehicle is recommended) limits visitors. There is only space for one group at the recreation site.

Be careful when travelling on backroads and watch out for industrial vehicles in active logging areas.

Gwen Lake Recreation Site (Map 14/E6)
Although found close to the Coquihalla Highway, access into Gwen Lake (via Comstock Road) is rather rough and not recommended for RVs. The recreation site is situated in the trees next to the west side of the lake and has two campsites.

Haddo Lake Recreation Site (Map 17/F4)
Haddo Lake is a man-made reservoir that sees its water levels fluctuate dramatically. This being said, it still offers decent fishing throughout the spring and fall. On the north end of the lake, there are four campsites as well as a good boat launch. Haddo Lake is accessed along Beaver Lake/Dee Lake Roads, about 36 km northeast of Winfield or southeast of Vernon off the Aberdeen Lake Forest Service Road.

Hammer Lake North Recreation Site (Map 32/E7)
This site is found off the Egan-Bonaparte Forest Service Road (3700 Rd) and offers 11 campsites with a boat launch. In addition to fishing or paddling around the lake, ATV and snowmobile trails are readily accessible in the area. Boaters should note the electric motor only restriction.

Harmon Lake Recreation Sites (Map 14/F6)
The Kane Valley is extremely popular with fishermen and finding a camping area anywhere is often difficult. This is particularly true here. There are two separate sites totalling 45 campsites, 32 at Harmon Lake East and 13 at Harmon Lake West. The site offers an interpretive trail, a boat launch, canoeing, fishing, mountain biking and cross-country skiing in the winter. Located south of Merritt, Harmon Lake is found along Kane Valley Road.

Harper Lake Recreation Site (Map 23/D1)
This small site is accessed off of Harper Lake Road (staying right at the junction at km 3). The fishing at the lake remains fairly good throughout the spring and fall. The seven unit site has toilet and table facilities for the overnight camper and a boat launch for fishermen.

Hatheume Lake South Recreation Site (Map 15/G6)
There are 12 forested campsites and a boat launch at this recreation site. The lake is stocked with rainbow trout and is popular with anglers interested in a good catch and release fishery. Hatheume Lake is reached by the Sunset Interchange on the Coquihalla Connector (Highway 97C); follow the signs to the resort for about 21 km from the highway.

Headwater Lakes Recreation Site (Map 9/A2)
This seven unit site is located in the centre of the Headwater Lakes at Headwater Lake #3. The site is accessed by the old Brenda Mine Site road, about 27 km west of Peachland. It provides a quiet, scenic camping spot for individuals wishing to try their luck fishing at one of the four Headwater Lakes. Access to this recreation site is a little rough so RVs should not try to reach this site. There is also a resort and cross-country ski trails in the area.

Heffley Lake Recreation Site (Map 28/F6)
This lake is found on the paved Sun Peaks Road. The popular 19 unit recreation site is often full of RVs and other large units throughout the summer months. Canoeing, swimming and fishing are the main pastimes in the spring through fall. Ice fishing is also popular as the lake can be accessed year-round. There is a cartop boat launch and picnic tables at the recently enhanced site.

Helmer Lake Recreation Site (Map 14/F1)
This scenic eight unit site on the south side of Helmer Lake is easily accessed from Exit 315 on the Coquihalla Highway (Hwy 5). There are endless roads and trails and a great snowmobile system to explore for those not interested in fishing.

Herman Lake Recreation Site (Map 30/D5)
This is a small, single timbered site near Herman Lake that has a boardwalk built along the marshy shoreline of the lake. The area also has hiking trails that circle the lake that allow you to see plenty of waterfowl. The recreation site is easily accessed on the Bastion-White Lake Forest Service Road from the west.

Hidden Lake Recreation Site (Map 25/B3)
There are a total of 47 campsites surrounding this beautiful lake, a good boat launch and several old roads in the area to explore year-round. The lake is easily accessed off of the Hidden Lake Forest Service Road allowing for RVs to reach the fee based site.

High Lake Recreation Site (Map 17/D3)
High Lake is accessed by either the Oyama Lake or the King Edward Lake Forest Service Roads. Whichever way you choose, you will have to park beside the cattle guard and walk a short distance along a rough trail to the lake. There is room for a few tents at this small lake.

Hihium Lake South Recreation Site (Map 26/G3)
Follow Chasm Road to the Clinton-Loon Lake Forest Service Road (3400 Rd) from Highway 97 for 37 km, then turn onto Hihium Road to find this 17 unit recreation site at the southeast end of Hihium Lake. This lake has excellent fishing for rainbow trout, but note the engine size restriction of 7.5 kW (10 hp) on the lake. Despite the drive from the highway, the site is suitable for RVs and trailers.

Holiday Lake Recreation Site (Map 25/C1)
This site is located on the shores of a marshy lake, which offers reasonable fishing during the spring and fall. To reach the lake, follow the Mabel Lake Road east from Enderby to the Beattie Forest Service Road leading north. Look for the fork to Holiday Lake at the Holiday/Noreen junction. This site has room for one group. Access to this site can be difficult, and four-wheel drive is recommended.

Holstein Lake Recreation Site (Map 25/D7)
This site is accessed by a rough four-wheel drive spur road off the Silverhills Forest Service Road. The recreation site has two treed campsites as well as a rough cartop boat launch. Nature enthusiasts flock to this area as it is a prime spot for bird watching and wildlife viewing.

Honeymoon Bay Recreation Site (Map 34/F6)
Honeymoon Bay offers 13 campsites on the western shores of Adams Lake, accessed by Adams Lake West Forest Service Road. The sites are set in the forest and there is a nice sandy beach on the lake and a concrete boat launch available. This is a fee based campground, charging Thursday through Sunday, May to September. We have yet to see any newlyweds vacation here.

Hoodoo Lake Recreation Site (Map 5/B1)
There are two campsites located in an opening next to the lake. Hoodoo Lake is accessed at the 14 km mark of the Waddell Creek Forest Service Road and there is a cartop boat launch for fishermen and paddlers. To the south Moore and Pete Lakes also offer small areas to camp at.

Hook Lake North Recreation Site (Map 8/A2)
In addition to the four unit campsite at the north end of Hook Lake, there is a boat launch, picnic tables and toilet facilities here as well. Hook Lake is found west of Missezula Lake and is accessed by taking the Dillard Creek Forest Service Road from Highway 5, then the Ketchan Forest Service Road.

Horse Creek Recreation Site (Map 47/D5)
Horse Creek flows into the northeast side of Canoe Reach on the Kinbasket Reservoir about 21 km south of Valemount on East Canoe Forest Service Road. There are 22 RV accessible campsites, a boat launch, picnic tables and toilet facilities at this fee based recreation site.

Horseshoe Canyon Recreation Site (Map 3/A5)
Horseshoe Canyon is located 15 km along the Ashnola River Road and offers room for five units. The site is primarily used as a stopover for visitors heading into Cathedral Provincial Park or for fisherman, hikers and hunters in the Ashnola River area. There is a fee charged from mid-May to mid-September.

Howe Creek Recreation Site (Map 11/G6)
Located 4 km up the Granby Bluejoint Forest Service Road, this is a large, open campsite on the west side of the Granby River. This site features four campsites, picnic and toilet facilities and is known for its excellent fishing. Small RVs can access the site.

Humamilt Lake Recreation Sites (Map 35/E6)
Humamilt Lake is a long narrow lake in the hills between Adams and Shuswap Lakes. There are three separate recreation sites, one at the west end of the lake and one at the east end of the lake along with a day-use only site on the north side. The western site has six campsites while the eastern side has two sites; both are accessed by the Seymour Arm Forest Service Road to the south. Both sites also have boat launches and picnic facilities.

Hyas Lake South Recreation Site (Map 29/A7)
Hyas Lake has a four unit recreation site found at the south end of the lake. The site is accessible by two-wheel drive vehicle along Hyas Lake Road and is mostly used by anglers looking for rainbow trout. There is a short, boat accessible angler trail to Hadlow Lake from the north end of the lake.

Hydraulic Lake Recreation Site (Map 10/E2)
The lakes in this area are collectively known as the Hydraulic Lakes. This enhanced site is located on the north end of McCulloch Lake and offers 18 RV friendly forested campsites and a cartop boat launch. Along with good fishing and canoeing, there is a resort in the area, a 3 km hiking trail, a series of cross-country trails and the famed Kettle Valley Railway. Hydraulic Lake is accessed along Hydraulic Lake Road, about 35 km southeast of Kelowna. There is a fee to camp here.

Ideal Lake Recreation Site (Map 17/F5)
Ideal Lake is a popular fishing hole accessed by Philpott Forest Service Road, then Ideal Lake Forest Service Road. The recreation site has room for seven groups of campers and is set in a forest at the south end of the lake. There is a boat launch as well as table and toilet facilities.

Idleback Lake Recreation Site (Map 10/D6)
This site offers 18 forested RV friendly sites to the east of Penticton. Reached off the Okanagan Falls Forest Service Road, there is a trail around the lake, a cartop boat launch and picnic facilities. Idleback Lake is a fly-fishing only lake and is restricted to electric motors only.

Isintok Lake Recreation Site (Map 9/B5)
Reached by McNulty Forest Service Road, this six unit forested site has toilet and table facilities as well as a cartop boat launch. The recreation site is set beneath Isintok Mountain and next to the lake providing a beautiful setting. It is used primarily by fishermen and hunters.

Island Lake Recreation Site (Map 15/D7)
This Island Lake is known as a trophy trout fishing lake and visitors will find about eight campsites together with a cartop boat launch. In the winter this area is a favourite spot for snowmobiling. Island Lake is accessed by Paradise Lake Road about 8 km from the Coquihalla Connector (Highway 97C) at the Elkhart Road Exit.

Island Lake Recreation Site (Map 17/E4)
Island Lake has seven official sites (though more people often camp here) as well as a good boat launch. This high elevation lake makes a fine paddling and fishing destination, although water levels fluctuate. The site is well maintained and RV friendly. Island Lake is accessed by Beaver Lake Road, then Dee Lake Road, approximately 20 km northeast of Winfield.

Isobel Lake Recreation Site (Map 28/B6)
There are 19 campsites and two day-use areas found here. This site offers an extensive trail network along with canoeing and fishing for stocked rainbow trout. ATVs and other off highway vehicles are not permitted here. The site is found along the Lac Du Bois Forest Service Road and there is a fee to camp from May to mid-October.

Italia Lake Recreation Site (Map 37/B5)
Italia Lake is one of the bigger lakes in the area and is easily accessed off the busy Road 20. There two-units available at the south end of the lake as well as picnic tables and a gravel boat launch.

Jackpine Lake Recreation Site (Map 16/D7)
Jackpine Lake is found off the Jackpine Forest Service Road, which in turn is found along the Bear Main Logging Road near Lambly Creek and offers eight open campsites next to the lake. The site is used by fishermen as well as prospectors interested in exploring the surrounding area, including the gold mine nearby. There is a fee to camp here from mid-May to mid-September.

James Lake Recreation Site (Map 17/D6)
This ten unit site rests in a semi-open area along the shoreline. The reservoir lake offers decent fishing and has a cartop boat launch, while ATVers can enjoy the plethora of old roads and trails in the area. From Highway 33 turn onto Goudie Road, then James Lake Forest Service Road to reach this recreation site.

Jimmy Lake Recreation Site (Map 23/C7)
The access into Jimmy Lake is good, but you will have to come in from the north off the Ingram Creek Forest Service Road as the access from the Douglas Lake Road is gated. Jimmy Lake has five campsites with a good cartop boat launch. RVs are best to stay in the upper field area.

Joan Lake Recreation Site (Map 11/B4)
This is a small walk-in site next to the scenic Joan Lake. The nice sandy beaches make this a fine destination in summer. To reach the lake, it is an easy 1.5 km walk from the 6.5 km mark on the Lassie Lake Forest Service Road.

Take care of the areas we love by taking all garbage with you and leaving only footprints.

Johnny Lake Recreation Site (Map 7/E3)
This site offers four campsites with a boat launch on the forested south end of the lake. The lake has good fishing and is popular for canoeing and nature viewing. Access from the east and Highway 5A is by a rough and narrow road off the Pike Mountain Forest Service Road (turn right at the 1 km mark). From the west follow Youngsberg Road from Coalmont Road and the Otter Valley.

Johnson Lake East Recreation Site (Map 29/D1)
This is a 12 unit site located at the eastern end of the lake (on the opposite side of the lake from the resort). It has a cartop boat launch, picnic tables and toilet facilities. Used primarily by anglers, this site is also a popular canoeing and kayaking lake due to the clearness of the water. Access is along the Johnson Lake Forest Service Road and there is a fee to camp here.

Jolly Creek Recreation Site (Map 4/G6)
An open, grassy site is found a short distance from Highway 3 near Bridesville. The recreation site is easily accessed by cars and RVs and sees a lot of day-use in the summer. An old road in the area leads past old prospector cabins and mining artefacts.

Joyce Lake Recreation Site (Map 23/F3)
This site has seven campsites and a good cartop boat launch on the shores of Joyce Lake. The site is easily accessed by the Chase-Falkland Road off Highway 97 near Salmon Arm. In winter, the Spa Hills to the east offer a fine snowmobiling destination.

Kaiser Bill Lake Recreation Site (Map 17/D3)
Kaiser Bill Lake is located on a four-wheel drive road off the King Edward Lake Forest Service Road. The recreation site has two campsites together with a rough cartop boat launch and toilet facilities. This area abounds with wildlife making it a great spot for nature study enthusiasts.

Kane Lake Recreation Site (Map 14/F6)
The Lower Kane Lake offers a scenic, but busy site next to the bulrushes on the south side of the lake. There is room for ten campsites and boat launches are scattered around both lakes. These lakes are RV accessible and receive heavy use during the summer primarily by fishermen. There is also an excellent trail system in the area. This site is reached by Kane Valley Road, about 9 km from the Coquihalla Connector (Highway 5A).

Kathy Lake Recreation Site (Map 25/D7)
Kathy Lake is easily accessed by the Silver Hills Road and offers three user maintained sites next to the lake. There is a cartop boat launch for anglers and paddlers to use.

Kettle Bench/Canyon Recreation Site (Map 11/C6)
Located at km 41 on the Christian Valley Road, this four unit site is a favourite fishing, camping and swimming hole. A scenic waterfall, cliffs and deep water attract a lot of day visitors for diving and swimming. The site is also popular with anglers and tubers in summer.

Kettle River Recreation Site (Map 18/D6)
Easily accessed along the Kettle River Forest Service Road, this eight unit site rests next to the river. The flat, open site is good for group camping.

Kettle River Crossing Recreation Site (Map 11/D1)
A small, open grassy site next to the Kettle River, this site is found at the 80 km mark on the Kettle River Forest Service Road. This area is typically used by anglers in the summer and hunters in the fall months. Despite the long bumpy road, small RVs and trailers can access the site. There is room for two groups of campers here.

Kidney Lake Recreation Site (Map 31/D7)
This scenic mountain lake receives steady use by fishermen during the spring and summer months. A rough boat launch, picnic tables and toilet facilities are available at this treed, two unit campsite. Access is along Mabel Lake, Kidney and Bottom Forest Service Roads and may require a four-wheel drive vehicle.

King Edward Lake North Recreation Site (Map 17/D3)
One of many good fishing lakes in the area, King Edward Lake has a cartop boat launch for anglers to use. Campers will find room for two vehicle units on the western shores of the popular lake. This site is found off of King Edward Lake Forest Service Road.

Kitty Ann Lake Recreation Site (Map 37/A5)
This small recreation site sits on the eastern shore of Kitty Lake in the shadows of the scenic Rioux Mountain. There are four campsites available with picnic tables and a gravel boat launch. To reach Kitty Ann Lake take Road 2 out of Clearwater for 29 km, then Road 20 for 8 km and take a left.

Kump Lake Recreation Site (Map 7/G3)
Found just off Highway 5A in the popular Pike Mountain area, there are seven semi-open sites on the south side of the Kump Lake and another four on the west side of the lake. In addition to fishing and hunting, this is a popular dirt biking area.

Lambly Lake Recreation Site (Map 16/E6)
Located on the east side of Lambly Lake at the 24 km mark of the Bear Creek Forest Service Road, this 17 unit site has been recently upgraded and offers a pair of boat launches for electric motors only. The lake is part of the Westbank watershed, but remains a good fishing and canoeing lake.

Lassie Lake Recreation Site (Map 11/B4)

There are seven campsites in the thick forest of larch trees towering over the weedy shores of Lassie Lake. The site receives heavy use during the summer and fall and offers a gravelled boat launch for easy access to fishing, canoeing and kayaking. In the fall this area is a hotspot for hunters. This site can be accessed by Trapping Creek, Beaverdell-State or Kettle River-State Forest Service Roads.

Lastcourse Lake Rec Site (Map 7/B2)

Located southwest of Bonaparte Lake, this rec site has room for one unit. To reach it, turn east onto 70 Mile-Green Lake/North Bonaparte Road off Highway 97. At the 3240 km marker, turn right onto the Eagan-Bonaparte Forest Service Road. Stay on this road for a while until you reach the Clinton Upper Loon Lake Road (3300 Rd), which leads to the short access trail.

Latremouille Lake Recreation Site (Map 33/B3)

This rustic, treed site sits on a popular fishing lake. It consists of nine campsites spread along the water's edge with some above, away from the water. There is a rough, cartop boat launch and two outhouses. Traveling west from Little Fort on Highway 24, the access road to the lake appears at about 16 km.

Lawrence Lake Recreation Sites (Map 37/B5)

There are actually two sites on this small lake found west of Clearwater. Each site is quite small with the eastern site providing two campsites and a gravel boat launch. The western site has just one treed site and a boat launch. To reach the sites, take Road 20 off of TFL 18 Road 2 from Clearwater.

Lightning Lake Recreation Site (Map 13/F6)

This campsite is found in a heavily forested area along the northern shore of the small mountain lake. There is room for about four units on this site, which is popular for fishing and hunting in the summer and fall or snowmobiling in the winter months. A four-wheel drive vehicle is required to access the lake as the road is very rough as you proceed down Miner Forest Service Road.

Lily Lake Recreation Site (Map 14/C5)

Located on the rough Lily Lake Road, this recreation site offers three campsites in a semi-open area next to the lake. There is a cartop boat launch together with a day-use area. Fishing is the primary attraction to this site, although nature enthusiasts gather for bird watching and wildlife viewing.

Link Lake Recreation Site (Map 8/E3)

Link Lake is one of a series of popular lakes found on the Princeton-Summerland Road and next to the Kettle Valley Railway trail. This lake offers 10 RV accessible campsites (with applicable fees on all days) and a cartop boat launch. This site is found just off the Princeton-Summerland Road, 42 km northeast of Princeton.

Little Bouleau Lake Recreation Site (Map 16/E1)

Found west of the bigger lake, off Granite Creek Road, Little Bouleau Lake also hosts a recreation site. The single unit site offers a decent boat launch and a little more solitude than the Bouleau Lake site. There is good road access and room for smaller trailered units. The site is used by anglers, hunters and canoeists.

Little McGillivray Lake Recreation Site (Map 29/B6)

Little McGillivray is accessible via a four-wheel drive road and offers three campsites and a cartop boat launch. In the summer the area is a favourite for biking and in the winter for cross-country skiing. The small lake is particularly swampy around the edges and a boat is necessary if you want to fish it. Mosquitoes abound in the area.

Little Scot Lake Recreation Site (Map 32/C7)

The small recreation site is located on the north end of Little Scot Lake next to the Egan-Bonaparte Forest Service Road (3700 Rd). Access to the site is good and small RVs often fill the three spaces available.

Lodestone Lake Recreation Site (Map 7/D7)

Lodestone Lake is located on the rough Lodestone Lake Forest Service Road on the outskirts of Princeton. The site, which is located in a semi-open forest, has two campsites and is used by fishermen and as a stopover for hikers and horseback riders on the Hope Brigade Trail.

Lodgepole Lake Recreation Site (Map 22/A4)

On the Chuwhels Mountain Road, this small nine unit recreation site is used primarily by fishermen or visitors to the Chuwhels Mountain Motorcycle Trails. Access is best left to four-wheel drive vehicles, but the sites are right on the water allowing easy access to Lodgepole Lake. The site has a rough boat launch, picnic tables and toilet facilities.

Lodwick Lake Recreation Sites (Map 7/F3)

This is a popular lake for fishing, hunting and camping and can be accessed via the Pike Mountain Forest Service Road off Highway 5A to the east or the Youngsberg Road from Coalmont Road to the west. The north side offers five campsites in a heavily treed area, while the south end features four campsites in a more open setting. Both recreation sites have boat launches, picnic tables and toilet facilities.

Lolo Lake Recreation Site (Map 33/D1)

Found by taking Road 2 out of Clearwater, this two unit recreation site comes complete with picnic tables and a gravel boat launch. The easy access and close proximity to Clearwater make this recreation area a busy place during the summer months.

Loon Lake Recreation Site (Map 17/E4)

This small site has one campsite and is accessed by a rough four-wheel drive road leading south from the Dee Lake Road to the east of Doreen Lake. There is a rough cartop boat launch on Loon Lake for easy access to fishing and canoeing opportunities.

Loosemore Lake Recreation Site (Map 7/G3)

Loosemore Lake is a small fishing lake sandwiched between the Otter Valley and Highway 5A along Hornet Forest Service Road. There are three campsites at the north end of the lake, a boat launch, picnic tables and toilet facilities.

Lost Horse Lake Recreation Site (Map 33/A2)

This four unit recreation site is found in the Nehalliston Plateau north of Highway 24 and accessed off the Taweel Lake Forest Service Road. The site features picnic tables and toilet facilities and is mostly used by anglers and motorized trail bike riders in the summer. In the fall, the area is a gathering spot for some good hunting, while snowmobilers frequent the area in winter.

Lundbom Lake West Recreation Site (Map 14/G4)

On the western side of Lundbom Lake off Lundbom Lake Road, this site offers 26 campsites, a boat launch, picnic tables and toilet facilities. This site is popular with the horseback riding crowd and corrals fill quickly, so it is recommended that you bring your own portable corral in case it is full. This is also a fee based site from May to mid-October.

Lundbom Lake East Recreation Site (Map 14/G4)

The eastern site on Lundbom Lake, this is a 26 unit fee based campsite. There is a plethora of activities here, with a boat launch, beach activities, horseback riding, swimming, nature study and ATVing. Located east of Merritt, access is off the Coquihalla Connector (Highway 97C) via Lundbom Lake Road.

MacDonald Lake Recreation Site (Map 16/A7)

MacDonald Lake is found next to Brenda Lake and best accessed from the Coquihalla Connector (Hwy 97C) off the Sunset Forest Service Road. The three unit recreation site is RV friendly and has a cartop boat launch, picnic tables and toilet facilities.

Madden Lake Recreation Site (Map 3/G3)

This recreation site on Madden Lake is found northwest of Oliver and just south of Ripley Lake along the Sawmill/Burnell Forest Service Road. This site is in an open area and has room for nine units next to the lake. In addition to a cartop boat launch there is a trail around the lake.

Marquart Lake Recreation Site (Map 14/F4)

Found close to the Coquihalla Connector, this is a popular place for travellers to stop for a picnic. There are 13 units split between two sites on this lake. The western site has three walk in spots for tenting, while the eastern side has 10 RV friendly campsites, picnic tables, toilets and a boat launch. Access can be found along Lundbom Lake Road and fees are charged for camping from May to mid-October.

Marshall Lake Recreation Site (Map 5/G5)

On the Phoenix Road, this recreation site is an excellent staging ground for year-round recreation adventures. In the summer, you can try fishing the lake, exploring the abandoned mines, mountain biking or hiking. In the winter, Phoenix Hill provides downhill skiing and the Marshall Lake Trails offer great cross-country skiing, snowshoeing and even snowmobiling. Recently the dam on the lake has been deactivated, significantly lowering water levels.

Mayson Lake Recreation Sites (Map 28/B1; 33/B7)

Mayson Lake is a large, scenic lake just south of Bonaparte Lake ideal for wildlife viewing and fishing. The main site is provides four campsites as well as a cartop boat launch. At the north end of the lake, another six site area offers horseback riders a chance to camp and ride in the area. Access is found along the Jamieson Creek Forest Service Road and a four-wheel drive vehicle is recommended.

McCulloch Reservoir Lake Recreation Site (Map 10/E2)

Located towards the south end of the popular McCulloch Lake, this 12 unit treed site marks the beginning of McCulloch Canoe Route. In addition to a place to launch a boat, there are toilet and table facilities as well as a hiking trail leading to the Hydraulic Lake Site. There is also a series of cross-country ski trails and the Kettle Valley Railway/TCT in the area. The RV accessible site is managed with fees and is accessed along McCulloch Road.

McGillivray Lake West Recreation Site (Map 29/B6)

With good road access off the McGillivray Lake Forest Service Road beginning at the west end of Niskonlith Lake and plenty of recreational activities in the area, this site can be busy. Unfortunately, the swampy nature of the lake also attracts many voracious mosquitoes during wet season along with leeches along the edges of the lake (anglers take note). The recreation site offers three campsites and a cartop boat launch.

Missezula Lake North Recreation Site (Map 8/A2)

Located on the northern shores of the lake, this site has 10 campsites in a forested setting with a cartop boat launch for anglers, canoers, swimmers and boaters. The scenic lake is found east of Highway 5A off the Dillard Creek Forest Service Road. Nature enthusiasts will find the area teeming with wildlife.

Mohr Creek Recreation Site (Map 11/E1)

Located along the Kettle River Forest Service Road, this is a single unit site right next to Mohr Creek and is a perfect spot for overnight camping or spending the day picnicking along the shores of the creek.

Moira Lake South Recreation Site (Map 37/D5)

Moira Lake is one of a mess of lakes found south of Mahood Lake and northwest of Clearwater. The area is popular with anglers and this lake is no exception, with a good gravel boat launch and five campsites set in a semi-open area. This site is accessed by Road 2 and Road 6.

Monashee Kettle River Recreation Site (Map 18/G4)

This is a small open campsite next to the Kettle River that is used primarily by river fishermen or as a stop-over for visitors on Highway 6. The recreation site is easily accessed off the Keefer Lake Forest Service Road and has room for two or more units with hiking, picnicking and nature study opportunities.

Moore [Bullman] Lake Recreation Site (Map 17/D5)

This Moore Lake is also known as Bullman Lake due to the small stream that flows into and then out of the lake. Found north of Postill Lake Road, visitors will find four campsites and a rough boat launch at this lakeside recreation site. The lake levels usually drop during late summer from irrigation drawdown.

Moose Lake Recreation Site (Map 32/B6)

This small recreation site is located on the Egan-Bonaparte Forest Service Road (3700 Rd) at the northwest end of the lake. It has a boat launch, picnic tables and toilet facilities as well as space for about three vehicles.

Moose Lake Recreation Site (Map 37/B7)

To find this small lake, follow the Camp 2 Road west from Clearwater to Road 10. Not far down Road 10, look for the turnoff to the small lake and a large single lakeside campsite. Visitors will find a picnic table, an outhouse and a gravel boat launch.

Morrissey Lake Recreation Sites (Map 29/C6)

Located close to the Sun Peaks ski resort, these recreation sites are used primarily by anglers in the spring through fall and snowmobilers and cross country skiers in winter. The sites are reached by the Morrissey Lake Forest Service Road either from the Sun Peaks or Chase Road side. The western shore three timbered sites with a cartop boat launch, while the eastern site has four campsites and a cartop boat launch.

Murphy Lakes West Recreation Site (Map 7/C6)

There are five sites the west end of the lake, which is popular with fishermen and hikers. In the fall, the area can be busy with hunters and ATVers. Located west of Tulameen, access is south of the Lawless-Britton Forest Service Road via Grasshopper Road. It is about an 800 metre walk from the campsite to the lake.

Murray Creek Recreation Site (Map 20/B5)

Located on the Murray Creek Forest Service Road west of Spences Bridge, this is a small four unit semi-open site, which requires a four-wheel drive to reach. The recreation site is next to Murray Creek and is used primarily by hunters in the fall, although the nearby Onion Lake/Monkey Wrench Riding Area does attract dirt bikers in the summer.

Murray Lake Recreation Sites (Map 7/B2)

In total there are 12 campsites at two sites on the lake, nine at the north and three at the south, with the primary users being fishermen and canoers in the summer and hunters in the fall. Both sites offer decent boat launches, with the northern site being a bit bigger and easier to access if you are hauling a trailer. A new, less steep access to the site has been made via the Juliet Creek and Bottletop Roads from the Juliet Exit off the Coquihalla Highway (Hwy 5).

> Mosquitoes can carry West Nile disease, so use recommended types of mosquito repellents and appropriate clothing.

Mystery Lake Recreation Site (Map 42/G7)

Found along the North Blue Forest Service Road, this recreation site receives low use despite the picturesque setting next to Mystery Lake. The two treed campsites are equipped with picnic tables and there is also a small boat launch available at the lake. The access road is quite rough and should be travelled in a four-wheel drive vehicle.

N'Kwala Recreation Site (Map 14/A3)

This 20 unit site is found on the Nicola River and is a popular put-in or take-out for canoeists and kayakers exploring the river. Activities in the area include hiking, biking, horseback riding and wildlife viewing. This site is found off of Highway 8 about 20 minutes west of Merritt.

Nahatlatch River Recreation Site (Map 13/A6)

This is a quiet, six unit site on the south side of the Nahatlatch River. Access is along the rough Nahatlatch Forest Service and Power Puff Roads and requires a four-wheel drive vehicle. Access to this site early in the year is dependent on snow and water levels.

Needa Lake Recreation Site (Map 32/E1)

At about the 1960 km mark of the Windy Mountain Forest Service Road (1900 Road), a branch road leads to this site. There are six campsites ideal for small trailers or campers. A steep cartop boat launch and picnic tables are also available at the popular fishing hole.

Nellie Lake Recreation Site (Map 35/F7)

Nellie is a small lake just north of Albas Park near Salmon Arm. The four unit recreation site contains picnic tables, toilet facilities and a rough boat launch. Visitors generally come for fishing, boating and lazing on the beach. This site is found near the 33 km mark of Seymour Arm Forest Service Road and can be accessed by small RVs.

Nevertouch Lake Recreation Site (Map 11/D1)

Following the forest fire of 2007, the two separate sites at the north end of the lake have been reconstructed to provide a total of 15 campsites. The five unit site and boat launch on the northwest side of the lake is only suitable for smaller RVs and campers. The 10 unit site at the north end is suitable for large RVs, but boat launching is limited to cartoppers only. There is limited tree cover due to the fire. This site is found up the Christian Valley on the Nevertouch Forest Service Road.

Nickle Plate Lake Recreation Site (Map 3/B1)

On the boundary of Nickle Plate Park, this four unit site is set in an opening next to the lake and sports a cartop boat launch. The lake is a popular fishing destination and there are a series of good trails to explore in the area. The site requires a four-wheel drive vehicle to reach along Nickel Plate Forest Service Road.

Nicklen Lake Recreation Sites (Map 17/G3)

Nicklen Lake is the water source for local residents and the water levels fluctuate significantly here. Access into the area is good (RV friendly) along the Goat Mountain Forest Service Road. There are 12 campsites split evenly between the two sites (east and west). Each site also sports good boat launches, picnic tables and toilet facilities. Fishing and nature viewing are popular here.

Noisy Creek Recreation Site (Map 25/D1)

Most of the activities at this site on the western shores of Mabel Lake are focused around the lake and at the nice sandy beach. There is a boat launch and 63 nicely spaced campsites at this popular fee-based recreation site. There is a plethora of activities to partake in at this site including swimming, fishing, boating, hiking and canoeing. This site is accessed by a branch road off of Three Valley Gap Forest Service Road.

Noreen Lake Recreation Site (Map 25/C1)

This small timbered site provides space for one unit on Noreen Lake. There are many activities in the area such as fishing, canoeing and motorized trail riding in the summer, plus hunting in the fall. This site has a boat launch, picnic table and toilet facilities. Access is along a rough spur road off the Beattie Forest Service Road.

North Barrière Lake Recreation Site (Map 34/B5)

Formerly called Vermelin Creek, this site has been recently upgraded and has become a family favourite. New amenities include 25 campsites (including one group site) and a large boat launch. The area provides for an array of recreation activities, particularly beach and water activities in the summer months. The lake is also popular for fishing and is accessed by North Barrière Lake Forest Service Road.

Nugget Lake Recreation Site (Map 23/C7)

To the south of Jimmy Lake, Nugget Lake is found on a rough four-wheel drive road that is better left to hikers or ATV riders. There are five user maintained campsites at the lake together with a place to launch small boats or canoes.

Old Hedley Road Recreation Sites (Map 2/F2)

These sites, found on Old Hedley Road, are situated on the Similkameen River in a semi-open Ponderosa pine forest. Both sites have room for RVs, good access to the river and are managed with fees. The east site is slightly larger, with 14 campsites, while the western site offers 12 spots.

Osprey Lake North Recreation Site (Map 8/E3)

Located near the Kettle Valley Railway, this is a popular fee based site found along the Princeton-Summerland Road northeast of Princeton. The 11 unit site is mainly used by campers and boaters, but hiking and mountain bike enthusiasts also enjoy the area's many trails. Snowmobilers call this place home in the winter.

Oyama Lake Recreation Site (Map 17/D3)

Located in a popular recreational area between Lake Country and Vernon, this small five unit site is used primarily by anglers and canoers. Oyama Lake is a reservoir so water levels will fluctuate significantly at times. There is a boat launch, picnic tables and toilet facilities at this site, which is accessed by a rough four-wheel drive route off the Oyama Lake Road.

Paradise Lake (Map 15/D7)

This two unit recreation site is a popular location for a vast array of activities and is found along Paradise Lake Road to the north of the Coquihalla Connector (Highway 97C) and the Elkhart Road Exit. The area is mainly used by anglers and canoers as there is a boat launch and a dock available. This site is very near to Island Lake and both have excellent beaches and swimming areas.

Paska Lake Recreation Site (Map 21/F5)

This enhanced recreation site has 49 RV friendly campsites that are extremely popular in the summer. The site is set in a semi-open area and offers a car-top boat launch, picnic tables and toilet facilities. Paska Lake is accessed by Paska Lake Road off of Meadow Creek Road, about 48 km southwest of Kamloops and is managed with fees.

Pass Lake Recreation Site (Map 28/A6)

Located on the shores of Pass Lake, this scenic 13 unit site is extremely popular with fly fisherman. Other activities in the area include hiking, canoeing and wildlife viewing. The site has a boat launch, picnic tables and toilet facilities and is easily accessed off the Lac Du Bois Road. There is a fee to camp here from May to mid-October.

Peachland Lake Recreation Site (Map 9/B1)

Peachland Lake is a pretty lake with a little island in the middle. RVs and other campers will find good access from the Brenda Mine Road and room for about eight units in an open area on the eastern shores of the lake.

Pendleton Lake Recreation Site (Map 37/A3)

This site provides access to the Pendleton Lake, but may require a four-wheel drive vehicle to negotiate the last section of road. The recreation site lies along the western shore of the lake and is home to three treed campsites complete with picnic tables. A rough boat launch provides access to Pendleton Lake. Access is via Pendleton Lake Forest Service Road, which branches off from the Spanish Creek Forest Service Road (7000 Rd).

Pete Lake Recreation Site (Map 5/A1)

This small lake offers three treed sites with tables and a toilet and is found about 2 km up the Pete Lake Forest Service Road, which in turn is found at the 9 km mark on the Waddell Creek Forest Service Road. Suitable for larger RV's, access can be a bit rough. There is a boat launch at the lake that offers good fishing in spring and fall.

Peter Hope Lake North Recreation Site (Map 15/D1)

There is room for 28 vehicle units at this forest service site, set on the northern shores of Peter Hope Lake. The site is very popular with anglers looking for large rainbow trout and provides a boat launch, picnic tables and toilet facilities. Nature enthusiasts will find the area teeming with wildlife. This lake is found along Peter Hope Lake Road off of the old Kamloops Highway (Hwy 5A). There is a fee to camp here.

Phinetta Lake Recreation Site (Map 32/G4)

Accessed off the Eakin Creek Road near the summit of Highway 24 west of Little Fort, there are four sites on the lake. One is located at the north end and the other camping area and boat launch are located at the east end of Phinetta Lake. The recreation site is a popular location for fishing or picnicking for highway travellers.

Pickard Creek Recreation Site (Map 2/F1)

Located on the Old Hedley Road, which starts about 6 km west of Hedley along Highway 3, this site is a popular destination with paddlers on the Similkameen River. Camping and swimming are also popular at the 16 unit RV accessible site.

Pimainus Lake East Recreation Site (Map 20/G6)

Located on a two-wheel drive road (Pimainus Lake Road) south of Highland Valley, this recreation site has three campsites next to the lake. The area is popular throughout the year with fishing, paddling and snowmobiling being the primary recreation pursuits. In the fall, the area transitions into prime hunting territory.

Pinaus Lake Recreation Sites (Map 23/F5)

Pinaus Lake is a popular destination for fishers, canoers and hunters. The main site offers eight campsites along with a good boat launch set in a forest on the north shore of the lake. There is also a recreation site on the east side of the lake, but it is day-use only. The best access is from the Ingram Creek Forest Service Road, which branches south of Highway 97 to the east of Westwold. The access is good enough to allow RVs into the area when the roads are dry.

Pinnacle Lake Recreation Site (Map 15/G6)

This small, five campsite recreation site is set in a forested area next to a small lake. Fishing is popular here and at the surrounding lakes. This site features a subalpine hiking trail, a boat launch, picnic tables and toilet facilities. The lake is found along Hatheume Forest Service Road.

Plateau Lake Recreation Site (Map 15/D1)

Found in the hills west of Stump Lake, Plateau Lake offers six campsites and access to the lake via a rough boat launch. This site is popular with fly anglers as the shoals and weed beds provide perfect casting areas. Access into the lake requires a four-wheel drive vehicle following the road from Peter Hope Lake.

Postill Lake Recreation Site (Map 17/E5)

The recreation site is located along the Postill Lake Road, not far from the resort. With good road access, it is a popular area with five official sites, but room for more. There is a cartop boat launch for anglers and paddlers, while a series of ski trails provide excellent hiking and biking in the summer.

Potlatch Creek Recreation Site (Map 44/D7) 🏕🚻⛴🎣🛶🚣🎿
There are 14 campsites at this large, open site found at the 2.5 km mark of Red Rock Forest Service Road northeast of Mica Dam on Kinbasket Lake. The area is popular with anglers and is one of the few boat launches in the area (if the water is high). Besides fishing, boating and kayaking is popular here.

Pratt Lake Recreation Site (Map 22/G6) 🏕🚻⛴🎣🐟
Pratt Lake is accessed along Pratt Forest Service Road and has seven campsites together with a boat launch for easy access to the lake. This site is used primarily by anglers and boaters.

Pressy Lake Recreation Site (Map 32/A5) 🏕🚻⛴🎣🚲🛶🚣
This is a small campsite, with space for three vehicles, located on the northeast end of this long narrow lake. The access is good enough for small RVs and there is a boat launch on the lake. Access to this recreation site is along North Bonaparte Road, then along South Green Lake Road. Note the engine size restriction on the lake.

Prosser Lake Recreation Site (Map 7/G3) 🏕🚻⛴🎣🛶🚣🎿
Prosser Lake has three campsites, a boat launch, picnic tables and toilet facilities. Anglers are the main visitors to this site in the summer, while hunters gather in the fall. This area is also a favourite with nature enthusiasts. This site is located on a rough four-wheel drive access road off the Hornet Forest Service Road north of Princeton.

Rampart Lake Recreation Site (Map 8/B4) 🏕🚻⛴🎣🛶🚣🎿
To the north of Princeton, Rampart Lake is found off the Hombrie Mountain Road to the south, a branch of the Jura Road. There are seven campsites at the south end of the lake as well as a cartop boat launch for anglers. This area is a great spot for nature study and hunting as well.

Red Bridge Recreation Site (Map 3/E4) 🏕🚻🎣🦌🐕🛶🚣🚸
Named after the easily identified landmark signalling the start of the Ashnola River Road, this site is found 8.6 km down the road. The 11 unit site is primarily used as a stopover for visitors heading into Cathedral Provincial Park or for anglers, hikers and hunters in the Ashnola River area.

Reflector Lake East Recreation Site (Map 37/D6) 🏕🚻⛴🎣🚲🛶🚣
This small three unit site is found along the rough Road 5 northwest of Clearwater. Fishing is popular here, as is hunting in the fall. There is a boat launch for easy access onto the lake.

Reservoir Lake Recreation Site (Map 15/E7) 🏕🚻⛴🎣🐟🚣
Reservoir Lake is located east of Paradise and Island Lakes off the Coquihalla Connector (Highway 97C) between Kelowna and Merritt. This site, accessed by the four-wheel drive Pattison Lake Forest Service Road leading north from the Sunset Exit, has a total of four sites in a semi-open area next to the lake. The cartop boat launch can be used by anglers and canoeists.

Rickey Lake Recreation Site (Map 7/E3) 🏕🚻⛴🎣🛶🚣
Part of a series of good fishing lakes next to Youngberg Road and Thaila Lake, Ricky Lake offers two small camping areas with five sites between them. Suitable for mid-sized trailers and fifth wheels, there is also a cartop boat launch to aid anglers.

Ripley Lake Recreation Site (Map 3/G3) 🏕🚻⛴🎣🐟
Ripley Lake is located to the north of Madden Lake on a rough secondary road west of Oliver. The seven unit site provides picnic tables and a rustic boat launch for canoeing and fishing.

Robertson Lake Recreation Site (Map 7/F3) 🏕🚻⛴🎣🛶🚣
Robertson Lake is a small fishing lake found west of Highway 5A along the Pike Mountain Forest Service Road. There are two semi-open campsites at the lake plus a boat launch, picnic tables and toilet facilities. Activities at this site include fishing in the summer and hunting in the fall.

Rocky Point Recreation Site (Map 34/G5) 🏕🚻🎣⛴🎣🛶🚣🚸
Rocky Point is named for its rocky beach that juts out into the northwest shores of the Adams Lake. The scenic site offers space for five units as well as a cartop boat launch. It is found around the 63 km mark of the Adams West Forest Service Road (good two-wheel drive access).

Roscoe Lake Recreation Site (Map 21/B7) 🏕🚻⛴🎣🦌🐟🛶🚣🎿
Roscoe Lake is found in a popular recreational area northwest of Chataway Lake along the Skuhun-Roscoe Forest Service Road. There are six campsites at the south end of the lake together with a cartop boat launch. A hiking trail leads around Roscoe Lake and over to Knight Lake.

Rosemond Lake Recreation Site (Map 24/F1) 🏕🚻⛴🎣🐟
Rosemond Lake is really an extension of Mara Lake, but access is through Larch Hills and the Rosemond Forest Service Road to the west. On the western shores of the lake is a small recreation site, which provides two campsites as well as picnic tables.

Ross Moore Lake Recreation Site (Map 22/B5) 🏕🚻⛴🎣🥾🚴🛷🐟
This small site is very popular with fly fishers and trollers alike and is accessed by a rough secondary road off of Long Lake Road off Highway 5A near Stump Lake. There are four campsites and a boat launch.

Sago Creek Recreation Site (Map 11/B6) 🏕🚻🥾🛶🚣
This is a small, pretty site with space for three groups, located next to Sago Creek at the 18 km mark of the Beaverdell-State Creek Forest Service Road. It is used primarily as a staging ground for hikers to the Collier Lakes.

Sandrift Lake Recreation Sites (Map 11/C4) 🏕🚻⛴🛶🚣
These are a trio of small lakes in the Christian Valley. The second lake offers three small semi-open campsites, while the lake site has one campsite with tables and a toilet. Fishing is good in spring and fall. Access is found around the 11 km mark of the Christian-Trapping Forest Service Road.

Sandy Bend Recreation Site (Map 11/D2) 🏕🚻🎣🛶🚣🎿
This site is only half a kilometre south of the Kettle River Crossing Site and is a small semi-open site next to the Kettle River, which offers a sandy beach and a good swimming hole. The user maintained site is located at the 79 km mark on the Christian Valley Road/Kettle River Forest Service Road.

Saskum Lake Recreation Site (Map 34/D4) 🏕🚻⛴🎣🎣🐟
This 11 unit site at the north end of Saskum Lake is easily accessed along the Saskum Lake Forest Service Road. The recreation site provides a sandy beach for sun tanning and swimming plus a cartop boat launch for easy access to some great fishing.

Saul Lake Recreation Site (Map 27/F5) 🏕🚻⛴🎣🚲🐟🚣
Saul Lake is a popular year-round destination. Anglers test their luck during the open water season and through the ice, while ATVers and snowmobilers can explore the elaborate series of old roads and trails in the area. The recreation site offers a single campsite with a cartop boat launch on the western shores of the lake and is best accessed via Sawmill Lake Forest Service Road.

Saunier Lake Recreation Site (Map 4/F1) 🏕🚻⛴🎣🐟
The user maintained site at Saunier Lake has two small campsites set in the dense forest on the shores of the lake. There is also a cartop boat launch. The site is found at about the 8 km mark on the Tuzo-Eugene Forest Service Road (good two-wheel drive access).

Scot Lake North Recreation Site (Map 32/D7) 🏕🚻⛴🎣🎣🚲🐟🚣
A popular fishing spot, Scot Lake is easily accessed off the Egan-Bonaparte Forest Service Road. The site provides four campsites and a boat launch at the north end of the lake. There is also a small, sandy beach on the lake.

Scott Lake Recreation Site (Map 28/C1) 🏕🚻⛴🎣🐟🚣🚸
This small recreation site has three campsites together with a cartop boat launch. The site is located on the east end of the lake in a forested area. Access is off the Gorman Lake Forest Service Road on the Bonaparte Plateau.

Sharpe Lake West Recreation Site (Map 32/C6) 🏕🚻⛴🎣🎣🚲🐟🚣
Sharpe Lake is found on Sharpe Lake Road, off of the Egan-Bonaparte Forest Service Road. The site offers space for two units and a cartop boat launch. This is a popular spot for fishing, canoeing, trail exploring and hunting.

Shea Lake Recreation Site (Map 7/E1) 🏕🚻⛴🎣🥾🚲🐟🚸
This site can be busy on weekends throughout the summer. There are ten sites located on the north end of the lake in a semi-open forest. Activities include hiking, motor biking, canoeing and fishing. There is a small boat launch, picnic tables and toilet facilities available here. Shea Lake is found off the Shea Lake Forest Service Road, branching north from the Voght Valley Road.

Sicily Lake South Recreation Site (Map 37/A5) 🏕🚻⛴🎣🎣🚲🐟🚣
Easily accessed from Road 20, there is an undeveloped site at the north end of the lake and a fully developed site along the southern shore. The southern site also offers a gravel boat launch and six treed campsites. To reach the southern site, take TFL 18 Road 2 from Clearwater, turn right onto Road 20, and travel about 11 km to the site.

Sigalet Lake Recreation Site (Map 25/E6)

Anglers often seek out Sigalet Lake since it has a reputation of being a good fly-fishing lake. In addition to the two campsites there is a cartop boat launch at this forest service site. The access road into the lake is narrow and best left to four-wheel drive vehicles. From Mabel Lake Road turn east onto Squaw Valley Road, then Jack Creek Road followed by Ireland Forest Service Road to reach this site.

Silence Lake Recreation Site (Map 38/C5)

The Silence Lake Recreation Site is home to three or more campsites set along the southwest shore of the lake. The campsite is rarely full due to the rough four-wheel drive access off the Raft River Forest Service Road. There is a short trail from the main camping area to another campsite.

Silver Lake Recreation Site (Map 9/C1)

Located in a spruce/Lodgepole pine stand next to the lake are six campsites and a cartop boat launch. The site is found via Brenda Mines and Silver Lake Forest Service Roads. The Peachland Cross-Country Ski Trails provide year-round trails to explore. This site is used in the summer by anglers, canoers and horseback riders, and in the winter by cross-country skiers.

Never drive Off Highway Vehicles like ATVs and dirt bikes on main haul roads.

Silver Lake Recreation Site (Map 13/F6)

Located in a spruce tree stand next to the lake, this site has two campsites and a cartop boat launch. The site is found on a four-wheel drive road off of Spius Creek Road and is a favourite for its hunting, fishing, canoeing and snowmobiling opportunities.

Silvertip Falls Recreation Site (Map 38/A6)

A high clearance two-wheel drive or four-wheel drive vehicle is recommended to access this semi-open two unit site via Road 80. The short trail from the campsite area to Silvertip Falls is quite scenic and is a favourite for nature enthusiasts.

Skimikin Lake Site (Map 30/A7)

This semi-open site is easily accessed via the paved Skimikin Lake Road northwest of Salmon Arm. The 36 unit RV friendly site is managed by the local horseback riding club with many horse-friendly features. The trails are also quite popular with hikers, ATVers, cross-country skiers and snowmobilers. Anglers will be happy to note that the lake is once again stocked with trout.

Skmana Lake Recreation Site (Map 29/D6)

This is a small open site with three tenting sites accessed by the Loakin-Bear Creek Forest Service Road. This area is a perfect place for non-motorized adventurers with an extensive local trail network suitable for hiking, mountain biking and cross-country skiing. Anglers and boaters also use this popular area.

Skwaam Bay Recreation Site (Map 29/C3)

On the western shores of Adams Lake, Skwaam Bay is a popular four unit site. Access off the Adams West Forest Service Road is steep with a limited turn-around so it is not recommended for RVs. There is a cartop boat launch, beach and picnic tables at the recreation site making it a perfect spot for swimming or lazing in the sun.

Skyline Lake Recreation Site (Map 34/E1)

Skyline Lake is found via a rough access road from the Vavenby Adams Forest Service Road. The recreation site receives low use and offers four campsites in a recently reforested area. Anglers often try their luck in this secluded lake.

Snohoosh Lake North Recreation Site (Map 27/C3)

Found in the forest at the north end of the narrow Snohoosh Lake is a two unit campsite. This recreation site also offers a cartop boat launch and is easily accessed at km 43 on the Deadman Vidette Road.

Snowshoe Lake Recreation Site (Map 19/D6)

On a four-wheel drive road off Highway 6, there is a small three unit treed and grassy site next to Snowshoe Lake. There is a rough boat launch for electric motor only boaters interested in fishing. In the winter, the area is a haven for the snowmobile crowd.

Sock Lake Recreation Site (Map 37/F6)

Sock Lake is found just outside the boundary of Wells Gray, about 15 km down Road 1. The two unit site is used by anglers in the summer and hunters in the fall. There is a boat launch, picnic tables and toilet facilities.

Solco Lake Recreation Site (Map 4/D2)

There are six campsites at this site, found on the Solco Lake Branch Road (rough two-wheel drive access). The site has a boat launch, which is used mostly by anglers. There are several trails in the vicinity as well.

South Barrière Lake Recreation Site (Map 34/C7)

Located on the South Barrière Lake Forest Service Road, this two unit site is found at the west end of the pretty lake. There is a cartop boat launch for easy access to the lake, which is used mainly by anglers and canoers.

Spa Lake Recreation Site (Map 24/A4)

There are two campsites and a rustic cartop boat launch at this site on the shores of Spa Lake. Access is via Spa Road, which is a spur road off the Bolean Lake Road past the Arthur Lake Recreation Site.

Spanish Lake Recreation Site (Map 24/A5)

This scenic lake is set below Mount Connaught and has five campsites together with a good cartop boat launch. Skiing in the winter and mountain biking/hiking or fishing in the summer are the attractions to the area. This site is accessed by Silvernail Road, 6 km from Highway 97. The last section of the drive can be rough and muddy after rain.

Specs Lakes Recreation Site (Map 17/F4)

Specs Lakes are accessed by a four-wheel drive road found at the 24 km mark of Aberdeen Lake Forest Service Road. There are nine campsites ideal for fishermen or paddlers who want to explore a chain of small lakes to the east of Grizzly Lake. The cartop boat launch at the site is very rough.

Sprague Bay Recreation Site (Map 44/E6)

Sprague Bay is located where all three arms come together on Kinbasket Lake, near Mica Dam. Access is via the two-wheel drive accessible Branch 11 off of Red Rock Forest Service Road. The 13 unit campsite is a popular place to launch bigger boats onto Kinbasket and is used year-round, at any water level. Other activities in the area include kayaking, fishing and hunting. There is also a short hiking trail that leads to the historic Boat Encampment Monument.

Square Lake Recreation Site (Map 23/G6)

Just past Pinaus Lake on the Pinaus Lake Road, this user maintained site has seven campsites. There is a rough cartop boat launch at the site together with toilets and tables.

St. Anne's Meadow Recreation Site (Map 12/B6)

St. Anne's Meadow is a large, grassy field overlooking Burrell Creek that offers a secluded summer camping area. Although there are only two picnic tables, there is room for several groups in the area. The recreation site is found 7.5 km up the deteriorating West Burrell Creek Forest Service Road.

State Creek Recreation Site (Map 11/C5)

This is a large, semi-open, grassy and RV friendly site found at the 46 km mark on the Christian Valley Road/Kettle River Forest Service Road.

State Lake Road Recreation Site (Map 11/C4)

This single semi-open site is mostly used by anglers and marks the beginning of the 1.5 km trail to State Lake. There is also a small camping area with table and toilet at the north end of the lake. This site is found 9 km up the Christian-Trapping Creek Forest Service Road.

Stevens Creek Recreation Site (Map 19/E3)

At the north end of Whatshan Lake, this is a medium sized, 13 unit site set in the forest of large white pines overlooking Whatshan Peak and the Pinnacles in the distance. A separate day-use area offers picnicking and a nice beach leading to the warm, sandy bottomed lake, while the boat launch provides fishing and canoeing opportunities. The area is also popular for ATVing. Access is along the Whatshan Forest Service Road.

Stoney Lake Recreation Site (Map 7/F3)

Yet another lake in the cluster of fishing lakes northwest of Pike Mountain, Stoney (or Stony depending on what map you look at) Lake has three treed sites located on the south side of the lake. In the summer, the area is great for fishing and canoeing, while in winter, this site is used by snowmobilers.

Stony Lake Recreation Site (Map 25/C1) 🏕🚵🎣🏁

There are several camping pads located on the forested shoreline of Stony Lake, which is located just northeast of Holiday Lake on a four-wheel drive spur road off the Beattie Forest Service Road. The recreation site is a good choice for a secluded weekend getaway as the poor access road limits the number of visitors.

Streak Lake (Map 17/D3) 🏕🍽🏊🚵🎣🏁👣

Part of the series of fishing lakes with recreation sites in the hills southeast of Vernon, this is a four unit campsite. There is a cartop boat launch, picnic tables and toilet facilities here. Located off Highway 6, the King Edward Forest Service Road into the site itself is very rough (four-wheel drive recommended).

Stringer Lake Recreation Site (Map 8/A3) 🏕🍽🛶🎣🚵🎣🏁

To the north of Princeton, this site is located on a rough four-wheel drive road starting at the 14 km mark of Dry Lake Road. There are two campsites with a boat launch that are used primarily by fishermen in the summer. In the winter, the area is popular with snowmobilers.

Stump Lake Recreation Site (Map 22/C7) 🏕🍽🏊⛵🎣🏁🛶

Stump Lake is a large lake found alongside Highway 5A south of Kamloops on Planet Mine Road. The recreation site is found on the other side of the lake on a steep grassy hillside that is not recommended for large camper trailers. There are four sites here that are usually full on weekends. This area is a favourite of the windsurfing and waterskiing crowd.

Sugar Creek Recreation Site (Map 25/F5) 🏕🍽🏊🛶⛵🚵🎣🏁S

The Sugar Creek Recreation Site is located on the eastern shores of Sugar Lake around the 17 km mark of the Kate Creek Forest Service Road. The site has room for 17 vehicle units together with a nice beach and a cartop boat launch. The site is managed with fees, but is not suitable for trailers or large RVs as the access road is rough and extremely hard to turn around on.

Sugar Lake Sites (Map 25/F5) 🚻🍽🛶🏊⛵🎣🚵🎣🏁S

There are four separate sites on the western shores of Sugar Lake (1 Mile, 2 Mile, 3 Mile and 9 Mile), a popular fishing destination north of Cherryville and Highway 6. Access into the area is suitable for a small RV or trailer along Sugar Lake Road. Two Mile is the largest site with room for 50 units in the open area. Activities here include swimming, boating, ATVing and nature study.

Sullivan Lake West [Knouff] Recreation Site (Map 28/F4)
🚻🍽🛶⛵🎣🎣

Located at the northeast end of the lake and easily accessed from the Knouff Lake West Forest Service Road, this recreation site is small in size but big on fishing. There are four designated campsites with little room for overflow and a boat launch.

Sunshine Bay Recreation Site (Map 12/F5) 🏕⚓🍽🛶🏊⛵🎣🎣

On the eastern shores of the Lower Arrow Lake, this small, popular recreation site is accessed by boat or four-wheel drive vehicle along Sunshine Bay Forest Service Road. Providing four campsites under an impressive pine stand, this area is known for its excellent fishing (at the mouth of Sunshine Creek), hiking, swimming and ATVing. During low water, a nice beach is exposed and there is plenty of shade for campers. Mooring buoys are available for boaters and there is a boat launch, picnic tables and toilets.

Sussex Lake Recreation Site (Map 21/G7) 🏕🍽🎣🎣🏁

This three unit site is primarily used for fishing and hunting, and has recently been logged to prevent the spread of mountain pine beetle. Four-wheel drive is recommended to access this site, which is found off of Surrey-Sussex Lake Road not far from the Coquihalla Highway (Hwy 5).

Sutter Creek Recreation Site (Map 1/B1) 🚻🍽🥾🚵🏁🎣

This site is found on the Tulameen River Forest Service Road in a quaint little area next to the creek, near km 34. There are three campsites within a fairly open area not far from nearby Vuich Falls Recreation Site. Hiking to Treasure Mountain, ATVing, wildlife viewing and hunting are popular pastimes.

Swalwell Lake Recreation Site (Map 17/D4) 🚻🍽🛶⛵🥾🏃🎣

Just to confuse you, they called the site Swalwell, which is the official, though rarely used name of Beaver Lake. This well maintained site offers a park-like setting for 10 groups next to the fine fishing and paddling lake. In addition there is a series of trails for hikers and skiers as well as a boat launch. Access along Beaver Lake/Dee Lake Road is rough, but it is possible to bring in RVs.

Tahla Lake Recreation Site (Map 7/E1) 🚻🍽⛵🚵🎣🏁🏍S

Tahla Lake is the quietest of the four lakes in the Voght Valley, but still sees its share of visitors. The small, managed recreation site has four campsites at the south end of the lake. The area is popular with anglers, motorized trail bikes and ATVs. This site is found along Voght Valley Road.

Taite Creek Recreation Site (Map 12/F1) 🏕🍽🏊🛶⛵🎣

Near Applegrove on Lower Arrow Lake, this site has space for five campsites amongst a stand of mature trees and plenty of room to camp on the beach. At low water, there is a nice beach with lots of sun for water enthusiasts. To reach this site turn off Highway 6 onto Applegrove Road for around 10 km and turn right just before the bridge over Taite Creek. The access road is not recommended for RVs.

Taurus [Bull] Lake Recreation Site (Map 5/B2) 🚻🍽🛶⛵🎣🎣🏁

Taurus Lake is a popular fishing lake with 12 campsites divided between the west and east side of the lake. The west side offers five sites suitable for all types of RVs, pit toilets and two boat launch sites. The east side is steeper with a large camping area featuring a table, toilet and steep boat launch. The lake itself is reed-lined and has a muddy shoreline broken up by sandy beaches that offer good swimming opportunities. To reach the lake turn onto Taurus (Bull) Lake Forest Service Road off of Highway 33, then take a right at the junction at 6 km and another right at a junction 1 km further.

Thalia Lake South Recreation Site (Map 7/E3) 🚻🍽🛶⛵🎣🏁🏍

Located at the south end of Thalia Lake, this campsite has space for seven groups. The site features two undeveloped boat launches, picnic tables and toilets. The campsites are not recommended for large RVs or fifth wheels due to the rough access via the Pike Mountain Forest Service Road off Highway 5A to the east or the Youngsberg Road from Coalmont Road to the west. Fishing and canoeing are popular on the lake.

Third Lake Recreation Site (Map 20/F7) 🚻🍽🏊🛶🎣🏁

Found west of the more popular Pimainus Lake, Third Lake often makes for a quieter retreat. There is room for four groups in the area on the northwest shore of the lake. Summertime provides great fishing and canoeing, while the fall provides a haven for hunters. Third Lake is accessed by Aberdeen Road which turns into Skuhun-Pimainus Forest Service Road.

Thone Lake Recreation Site (Map 11/D7) 🚻🍽🛶⛵🎣🎣🏁

There are seven small campsites, which are extremely popular during the summer with fishermen and in the fall with hunters. The recreation site is accessed about 14 km down the Losthorse-Thone Lake Forest Service Road. This good two-wheel drive road leads from the Christian Valley Road at around the 27 km mark.

Three Sisters Creek Recreation Site (Map 20/B3) 🏕🚵🏁🎣

This is a small site with one open, grassy campsite and toilet that makes an ideal location for those visiting nearby Cornwall Hills Provincial Park. Hang-gliding is a popular activity in the area. The site can be found about 15 km up Oregon Jack Road. Be aware of extremely slick conditions on this road during wet weather; a four-wheel drive vehicle is recommended. Visitors are asked to stay away from the nearby creek as it is the water source for a local community.

Tranquille Crossing Recreation Site (Map 27/G7) 🚻🍽🥾🚵🎣🏁🎣

Found just beyond the Lac Du Bois Grasslands Provincial Park on the well maintained Tranquille-Criss Creek Road, the Tranquille Crossing Recreation Site is the first and smaller of the two user maintained sites in the area. If this site is full, nearby Tranquille Meadow may have room. The Watching Creek Trail is a short drive to the east and well worth visiting if in the area.

Tranquille Meadow Recreation Site (Map 27/F7) 🚻🍽🛶🚵🎣🏁🎣

Certainly a contrast in campsites, Tranquille Meadow is a big RV friendly site with room for about 50 units. It is the busier of the two user maintained sites in the area (Tranquille Crossing is a much smaller site to the east) and is often used by people explore the series of roads and lakes north of Kamloops Lake.

Trout Creek Crossing Site (Map 9/C4) 🚻🥾🛶🏁🎣🎣

Found next to Trout Creek, the Princeton-Summerland Road and the Kettle Valley Railway is a small three unit campsite. Despite the nice forested setting and good road access, this site is not as busy as others in the area.

Tsikwustum Creek Recreation Sites (Map 34/G5) ⛏🏕🏊🛶🎣🚤🚻🚽
These sites on the eastern shores of Adams Lake are located around the outflow of Tsikwustum Creek. Both sites are accessible by RVs along the Adams East Forest Service Road. On the north side of the creek is a medium sized seven unit site located in an opening next to Adams Lake. It has a good boat launch together with picnic tables and toilet facilities. On the south side of the creek is a small three unit treed site with a beach for swimming access.

Tupper Lake Recreation Site (Map 21/C6) ⛺🏕🛶🎣🚲🚽🚻
There are three campsites and a cartop boat launch at this small lake southwest of Logan Lake. Accessed by the four-wheel drive Highmont Road, the area is used mainly by fishermen and ATVers. The area surrounding Tupper Lake has a rich mining history.

Tyner Lake Recreation Site (Map 14/B2) ⛺🏕🛶🎣🚽🚻
Tyner Lake is found on the Pamainus Forest Service Road and has six sites set in the forest next to the lake. There is a cartop boat launch for anglers and paddlers to explore the lake. Hunters flock to the area in the fall.

Upper Canoe Recreation Site (Map 46/G4) ⛏🏕🎣🚽🚻
This campsite with space for two units is found about 6 km from Highway 5 on the Upper Canoe Forest Service Road. The site is occasionally used by paddlers as well as hunters.

Vidette Lake Recreation Site (Map 27/B2) ⛏🏕🛶🎣🚽🚻
Just north of Deadman Lake, Vidette Lake is a narrow waterbody offering anglers a chance to test their luck. The small site has two campsites and a cartop boat launch. Access can be found at 52.7 km on the Deadman Vidette Road off the Trans-Canada Highway, west of Savona.

Vinson Lake Recreation Site (Map 8/B2) ⛺🚶🎣
Vinson Lake is primarily a day-use area, but some overnight camping does occur. This site is popular with anglers and is located on the Schrimpton Forest Service Road about 4 km past Buck Lake Recreation Site.

Vuich Falls Recreation Site (Map 1/B1) ⛏🏕🚶🚲🚽🚻🚻
Located about 34 km down the Tulameen River Forest Service Road, this three unit site provides access to a lookout over the cascading waters of Vuich Creek. It is a small forested site that is used primarily by hikers in the summer and hunters in fall.

Wallensteen Lake Recreation Site (Map 24/A2) ⛺🏕🛶🎣🚤🚽🚻
Mostly hunters and fishermen use this small two unit lakeshore site, which has a cartop boat launch, picnic tables and toilet facilities. The area also comes alive in winter as snowmobilers follow the endless road system around Fly Hill.

Wap Lake Recreation Site (Map 31/E5) ⛏🏕🛶🎣🚶🚽🚻
This is a small timbered site found on the beautiful little lake. Although there is a site on the east side as well, the camping is limited to one or two spots at the west end of the lake. That being said, the activities here are quite extensive with beach activities, fishing and canoeing available. There is also a rough boat launch on the western shore, but use caution when entering or leaving the area as the sites are accessed via an active logging road (Wap Lake Forest Service Road).

White Lake Recreation Site (Map 37/A7) ⛏🏕🛶🎣🚤🚽🚻
The recreation site is located at the northwest end of the lake and is home to two small campsites with picnic tables and a boat launch. The logging truck traffic on Road 10 can take away from the experience, especially during weekdays.

Whitehead Lake Recreation Site (Map 8/F2) ⛺🏕🛶🎣🚽🚻
Whitehead Lake is located in the hills above Osprey Lake along a series of logging roads between the Princeton Summerland Road and the Coquihalla Connector (Highway 97C). The recreation site is located in the trees next to the lake and has toilet and table facilities as well as a cartop boat launch, but only one large camping area. Whitehead Lake offers good trout fishing, but it is a domestic reservoir for Summerland and is subject to water fluctuations.

Whitewood Lake Recreation Site (Map 28/C2) ⛏🏕🛶🎣🚽🚻
Accessed at 27 km on the Jamieson Creek Forest Service Road north of Kamloops, this five-unit site allows visitors to haul in a small RV. In addition

to a cartop boat launch, visitors have a choice of either camping in the open or under the trees.

Willard Lake Recreation Site (Map 20/E2) 🏕🎣🛶🚶🚲🚽
Located on the Barnes Lake Road southeast of Ashcroft, this site is located in an open range next to the lake. This is a day-use only area with outhouses. Activities in the area include fishing (ice fishing and open water fishing) as well as hiking and biking.

Williamson Lake Recreation Site (Map 5/D2) ⛺🏕🛶🎣🚽
This is a small lake popular with canoers and anglers featuring a boat launch and four campsites. From Highway 43 turn onto Kettle River East Forest Service Road for 7 km, then onto Sebastian Creek Forest Service Road for 3 km to access this site. A four-wheel drive vehicle is recommended.

Windfall Lake Recreation Site (Map 28/B1) ⛏🏕🛶🎣🐴🚶🚲🚽🚻🚻
This small lake is found along the Jamieson Creek Road (rough two-wheel drive access) not far from Bonaparte Lake. The high elevation forested recreation site offers three campsites as well as a cartop boat launch for anglers and paddlers. There is a series of horseback trails along with ATVing and snowmobiling in the area.

▶

> *In the backcountry, all food and other scented items should be properly stored in a bear cache or in a pack that is hung from a tree at least 5 metres (15 ft) from the ground. Keeping a clean campsite will ensure a fun and bear free camping adventure.*

Windy Lake Recreation Site (Map 16/B6) ⛺🏕🛶🎣🚶🚽🚻
Windy Lake is found high in the hills west of Kelowna along the good two-wheel drive Bear Creek Forest Service Road. The five unit forested site provides access to a popular fishing hole and offers a boat launch, picnic tables and toilet facilities.

Windy Lake Recreation Site (Map 28/B2) ⛺🏕🛶🎣🚶🚽🚻
Found on the Bonaparte Plateau, Windy Lake can live up to its name. Luckily, the five-unit campsite is set in a dense forest. Skoatl Point Trail and Tuwut Lake Paddling Route are found nearby. Access can be found along the Windy Lake Road off the Jamieson Creek Forest Service Road.

Winnifred Creek Falls Recreation Site (Map 18/D6) ⛏🏕🚽🚻
This site is set next to a small creek and some scenic falls and has room for one group. The area is popular with hunters and is located along the Kettle River Forest Service Road about 6 km south of the Bruer Creek Junction.

Woods Lake North Recreation Site (Map 23/D6) ⛏🏕🛶🎣🚶🚲🚽🚻
Woods Lake is accessed by a spur road leading from the Ingram Creek Forest Service Road to the south. The 17 RV friendly sites are spread over two sites – one open and one treed. There is a cartop boat launch for anglers and canoeists. ATVers frequent the area.

Yellowjacket Creek Recreation Site (Map 47/D5) ⛏🏕🛶🚤🚽🚻💲
Located about 19 km south of Valemount on the active Canoe East Forest Service Road, this ten unit recreation site is used mostly by people who are just looking to camp, but is also frequented by anglers. The reach is sometimes used for canoeing and kayaking, but caution must be exercised on the big water of Kinbasket Lake.

Zum Peak Recreation Site (Map 7/A4) ⛺🏕🚶🎣🚽🏂🚽🚻
Although it is possible to camp at the trailhead to Little Douglas Lake, many prefer to camp next to the lake, which is set below the towering Zum Peak. The high elevation lake is a nice summer getaway for anglers or hikers and is a prime spot for cross-country skiing in the winter. Smaller trailers and truck campers should find access relatively easy, but the two unit site is not suitable for large motorhomes or fifth wheels. Take Exit 228 off the Coquihalla Highway (Hwy 5) and continue on Upper Coldwater Road for 7 km to access this rec site.

TRAIL ADVENTURES

From the world famous Kettle Valley Railway to the dramatic peaks of Cathedral Park and Wells Gray Park, trail users in the Southern Interior are blessed with plenty of variety. The rolling grass covered hills of the Central Interior are riddled with trails and old roads to explore. There are also destination-oriented trails leading to fishing lakes, mountain vistas, waterfalls and more.

We have included information on the majority of trails and routes in Southern BC. To help you select the trail that best suits your abilities, we have included information on elevation gain, return distance and special features wherever possible. Unless otherwise noted, distances and times are for round trip hikes. Also included in each description is a symbol to indicate what the trail is used for: mountain biking, hiking, horseback riding, etc. Although there is a separate section for motorized trail users (ATVers and motorbikers), these users will still find many multi-use trails open to motorized traffic. Watch for the symbol.

Hiking trails are usually tagged with one of the following descriptors: An easy trail has gentle grades and is suitable for family excursions. A moderate trail can involve a long, steep hill, some scrambling and is probably enough to tax most users. Just because they are not considered difficult, does not mean that they are not challenging. Do not overestimate your ability, or underestimate the difficulty of the trail. Only experienced trail users should consider difficult routes. These trails are often rough and/or unmarked.

This area is hot and dry. Bring along plenty of water. Higher elevation trails and routes (over 1,000 metres/3,000 ft) might have a limited season due to late season snow. Remember, our maps are designed only as a general access guide and are not intended to navigate you through a hidden mountain pass or across an expansive ridge network. If you are travelling on unmarked trails, we recommend that you have mountaineering knowledge and are equipped with a topographic map and compass.

Also note that wildfires new and old have raged through areas covered in this book. From the 2003 Okanagan Mountain Park to the 2009 West Kelowna and area trails, the damage is hard to predict. Some trails will remain closed for years, while others are open but users need be wary of the hazards. Thankfully, the world famous trestles in Myra Canyon have been restored and initiatives like the Shuswap and South Okanagan Trail Alliances and BC Horse Council are growing the trail opportunities out there.

Despite the wealth of trails listed below, this still only represents a fraction of opportunities for outdoor adventurers. If you are planning on getting off the beaten path, be careful. The Coast Range is very rugged terrain.

DID YOU KNOW?

OUR BC GPS MAPS FEATURE 36,000 KM OF MULTI-USE TRAILS

 1000s OF TRAILS

Thousands of clearly marked multi-use and motorized trail systems (ATV, hiking, mountain biking, horseback riding, cross-country skiing, snowshoeing, snowmobiling, and more).

 ACTIVITY POI'S

Thousands of searchable POIs with descriptions, including campsites, recreation sites, boat launches and canoe access, fish species, trailheads, scenic viewpoints, and more.

CUSTOMIZE YOUR MAP

Add your own waypoints and create your own routes for a map that's all your own.

 backroadmapbooks.com/gps-maps

Allan Creek Alpine Area (Map 47/B6) 🚶🏕️

Best known for its snowmobiling, the Allan Creek area is also popular with locals looking to hike in the alpine. The trailhead is the snowmobile parking area off of Highway 5, about 37 km south of Valemount. Follow the road as far as you can drive (about 12 km) and hike from there.

Allison Lake Trail (Map 7/G4) 🚶🎣

Found along the western side of Allison Lake, this 2.1 km (1.3 mi) easy trail is a nice place to stretch your legs while traveling along Highway 5A.

Albas Falls Trail (Map 35/F7) 🚶🏕️

Within Albas Park, this 3 km (1.8 mi) trail leads from the shores of the Shuswap Lake up both sides of Celista Creek past five gorgeous waterfalls as well as a waterwheel and flume. The park is accessed off the Seymour Arm Forest Service Road or by boat.

Anarchist Mountain Trails (Map 4/D6) 🚶🚴‍♂️⛷️🏕️

Anarchist Mountain is a prominent peak near the US border and east of Osoyoos Lake. The trails – or rather, network of old roads – wrap their way around the mountain. Hikers are free to leave the beaten trail and make their way to the top through mostly open grassland and open ponderosa pine forest. About 36 km (22 mi) of trails climb 240 m (790 ft) up Anarchist Mountain.

Angel Springs Trail (Map 10/C2) 🚶🚴‍♂️🎣🏕️

From the one kilometre mark on Little White Forest Service Road, a signed trail leads left (park on the right). The hike is 6.4 km (4 mi) return with an elevation gain of 300 m (985 ft). Hike 1.4 km on a steady uphill grade until you reach the junction with Myra Bailout Trail. The Angel Springs Trail forks left and is fairly level until the last 600 metres when it narrows and descends steeply into a deep canyon, where you will see Angel Springs and the unique tufa deposits.

Anstey Peaks Trail (Map 31/B2) 🚶🏕️

This 15 km (9 mi) round trip trail climbs 1,235 m (4,050 ft) as it makes its way past a couple of sub-alpine lakes to several peaks connected by a long ridge. Some bushwhacking is necessary and the jagged peaks require a bit of scrambling. This trail provides great views of the surrounding mountains.

Apex Mountain Resort (Map 3/C2) 🚶🚴‍♂️🏕️

There is a lot of hiking/biking to be had at this resort. For the ambitious, it is possible to walk up to the top of Apex on the gentle slope of Grandfather's Run. This route features breathtaking scenery and meadows of alpine flowers. If you are feeling lazy, take the lift to the top and walk or bike down via the numerous downhill and cross-country trails ideal for biking. Last count, there were over 150 km (90 mi) of riding in the Apex area, 30 km (18 mi) of which is lift accessed.

Avalanche Pass Trail (Map 49/A5) ⛺🚶🏕️

This challenging backcountry trek covers about 26 km (16 mi) return, climbing over 940 m (3,085 ft). The trailhead is located at the end of the South Dore Forest Service Road. The route traverses into the sub-alpine then over Avalanche Pass before descending down to Cariboo Lake. At the pass, be prepared for snow any time before mid-August.

Aylmer Lake Trail (Map 29/D7) 🚶⛷️🎣🏕️

From top of the switchback on Neskonlith Lake Road, an old road leads 9.5 km (5.9 mi) through a dry hillside and then a second growth forest to the lake. The marshy lake is not open to fishing, as it is used to rear brown trout for stocking elsewhere. Also in the area are a series of interconnecting cross-country trails through open rolling terrain. During the early summer the Neskonlith Meadows are teaming with wildflowers. Ask permission to cross the Indian Reserve before heading out.

Badger Trail (Map 6/E5) 🚶🚴‍♂️🏕️

The Badger Trail is an easy hike/bike overlooking Christina Lake. There are some rocky steps near the southern end of the trail as well as a few steep sections that bikers should be wary of. The trail is just over 2 km long, but side trails, including one to Mary's Lookout can extend your outing.

Baldy Mountain Trail (Map 33/F4) 🚶🚴‍♂️🐎⛷️🏕️

From 1916 to 1939 the Windpass Gold Mine was located on Baldy Mountain. Remnants are still visible as you make your way up the mountain to the site of an old forestry lookout. Indeed, the trail, such as it is, is the access road for the former lookout tower and is quite easy to hike, although it is a fairly relentless 380 m (1,250 ft) climb to the top, over a distance of 10.5 km (6.5 mi).

Balmoral Bluff Trails (Map 30/B5) 🚶🚴‍♂️🐎⛷️🏕️

From the signed trailhead on Balmoral Road, this trail system connects with the Blind Bay Lookout to the north and White Lake to the east. The Balmoral Bluff Trails are a series of short loops that allow trail enthusiasts to enjoy a short forest walk to a nice viewpoint. The Blind Bay Lookout Trail follows the upper trail and leads 6.5 km (4 mi) north to the impressive lookout of the South Shuswap area. It is possible to make your way down the steep 1 km trail to the MacArthur Heights trailhead off McBride Road. The Blind Bay to White Lake Trail is the lower connector trail that extends about 8 km (5 mi) one-way to the White Lake Lookout. The trail gains about 310 m (1,015 ft) before dropping another 235 m (770 ft) down to the White Lake Road trailhead at the west end of the lake. A two car system is recommended if doing the entire trail.

Banbury Trails (Map 2/G2) 🚶🏕️

These old roads and trails lead through old mining sites where you will pass old shafts and building. The trail runs along the side of Henri Creek and is quite steep. To get here, follow Highway 3 for about 8 km west of Hedley, then turn south over the Similkameen River for 4 km.

Barnes Creek Trail (Map 19/C3) 🚶🐎🏕️

This 8 km (4.8 mi) trail climbs 460 m (1,150 ft) as it heads into the South Pinnacles of the Monashee Mountains and links up with the Vista Pass Trail at the pass. The trailhead is found off the Keefer Lake Road on a four-wheel drive road. This is a very scenic route popular with both hikers and equestrian riders.

Bastion Cliffs & Mountain Trail (Map 30/C7) 🚶🚴‍♂️🐎⛷️🏕️

This challenging 36 km (22 mi) return trek from the parking lot near the junction of the Sunnybrae-Canoe Point Road and the Bastion Mountain Road takes you along an old logging road then a trail near the top of the mountain for a good view of Shuswap Lake. Hikers often drive/ATV up the road to reduce the length of the hike as well as decrease the 800 m (2,625 ft) of elevation gain. The Bastion Cliffs are a short 1 km (0.6 mi) side trip. A scenic trail leads from the road to the edge of the cliffs for a great view of Shuswap Lake and the surrounding mountains. The trail may be closed during fire season.

Battle Bluff Trail (Map 21/G1) 🚶🏕️

Found just west of Lac Du Bois Provincial Park on Frederick Road, this trail starts on an old road and leads to the bluff overlooking Kamloops Lake. It is 2 km (1.2 mi) one-way with most of the 110 m (360 ft) elevation gain happening in the last half kilometre.

Bear Creek Park (Map 16/G6–17/A6) 🚶🚴‍♂️🏕️

The most popular trail in this park is the 5 km (3 mi) route along the scenic Bear Creek Canyon, climbing 480 m (1,575 ft). Great views over Okanagan Lake and a few bridge crossings add to the experience. Other trails circle the campground offering a nice leisurely stroll.

Becker Lake Trails (Map 17/E1) 🚶🚴‍♂️🚵

Several trails are found in and around Becker Lake and the Vernon Hill area. Most follow old roads and are popular with hikers, bikers and ATV enthusiasts. Many hikers prefer to loop around the lake on what can be a 5.75 km (3.6 mi) up and down loop. The trail has minimal elevation gain.

Beaven Mountain Trail (Map 19/B1) 🚶🏕️

Accessed off South Fork Road east of Lumby, this steep 7 km (4.3 mi) trail climbs 700 m (2,295 ft) to the top of Beaven Mountain. Although well developed, there are rough sections along the trail. Be careful, this is Grizzly bear country.

Belle Mountain Trail (Map 49/B2) ⛺🛶🚶⛷️🎣🏕️

Belle Mountain is a popular multi-use recreational area west of McBride. From the parking area and cabin, at the 5 km (3 mi) mark, there are two options. To access the scenic alpine area around the summit, continue along the road. The complete route is about 25 km (15.5 mi) in length. The other option is to hike or ski the extensive, lower elevation trail system. The trail system offers over 18 km (11 mi) of easier trails. The system traverses through a mix of wooded and open areas, with a number of fine viewpoints of the valley below.

Berg Lake Trail (Map 51/B4–B5) ⛺🚴‍♂️🐎⛷️🎣🏕️

The Berg Lake Trail is a world-renowned trail system that provides access to the beautiful backcountry of Mount Robson Park. The trailhead can be found at the end of the Kinney Lake Road, which is located near the park visitor centre off the north side of Highway 16. From the trailhead, the trail follows the Robson River past Kinney Lake. Mount Robson dominates the landscape as the route travels through the scenic Valley of a Thousand Falls to the beautiful Berg Lake. Along the trail, there are a number of campsites to base camp

from as well as several side routes to explore. Overall, the Berg Lake Trail is a moderate journey that traverses over 21 km (13 mi) one-way and gains 800 m (2,625 ft). Reservations are now required and can be made through *discovercamping.ca* starting in January. Anyone planning to attempt this trip should have adequate backcountry experience.

Birk-Leone Loop (Map 33/G6)
The Birk-Leone Loop is a long trail that climbs 540 m (1,770 ft) into the sub-alpine south of Dunn Peak Provincial Park. The 27 km (17 mi) trail is best done as an overnighter, although it has been done in a very long day. The popular horse trail should be left to experienced backcountry travelers.

Black Knight Mountain Trail (Map 17/C7)
To reach this forestry lookout at 1,280 metres (4,160 ft), you can either hike or mountain bike to the top. It is about an 11 km (6.8 mi) return trip from the gate at Pyman Road (this road is gated at the gravel pit; this gate is not always locked but you risk being locked in without notice) with a total gain of 500 m (1,640 ft). Like most other lookouts, the view of the surrounding country is fabulous. Mountain bikers often descend along the challenging single track trail found near the top.

Blackwell Lake Trail (Map 22/G6)
From the Pratt Lake Recreation Site, this trail extends 4.5 km (2.8 mi) one-way to scenic Blackwell Lake. The trail also passes by two smaller lakes and is popular with anglers. There is a 165 m (540 ft) elevation gain.

Blue Grouse Mountain Trails (Map 16/G6)
It is 13 km (7.9 mi) return from the Grouse Mountain No 1 sign to the top, at 1,250 m (4,100 ft), making for a total climb of 720 m (2,360 ft). Once you reach the top, there is an excellent view of Okanagan Lake and Kelowna. There are also a series of mountain bike and ATV trails in the area.

Blueberry Trail (Map 50/D2)
The trailhead for this trail is located near the 44 km mark of the Holmes River Forest Service Road. The trail is a remote route that stretches 12 km (7.5 mi) into the alpine and continental divide area of the Rockies, climbing 920 m (3,020 ft). Horseback riders are the primary users of this difficult trail.

Blue Mountain Trail (Map 9/F6)
To the west of Penticton, it is possible to hike or mountain bike about 18 km (11 mi) return along an old access road to the transmitter and summit of Blue Mountain, making for a 900 m (2,955 ft) gain in elevation. At 1,400 metres (4,595 ft), the view is excellent. The trailhead is located by driving along Bartlett Road to Rifle Range Road. Give yourself a few hours on bike, or the better part of a day on foot.

Blue River Trails (Map 43/A7)
The Blue River Trails area is located in the east end of town, near the junction of the Blue and Thompson Rivers. The trails are used for hiking and biking during the summer and cross-country skiing in winter months. You can explore over 22 km (13.5 mi) of easy to moderate trails in a number of interconnected loops. The more scenic trails skirt the river shores.

Bluenose Mountain Trail (Map 17/F2)
This loop trail is a 4.4 km (2.7 mi) scramble from the signed trailhead on Aberdeen Lake Road. The trail takes you steadily upward through a timbered slope, then over 3 summits gaining 250 m (820 ft) along the way. From the highest summit at 1,270 metres (4,165 ft) there is a good view of the Coldstream Valley. Please note that the middle peak is privately owned.

Bob's Lake–Elkhart Lake Trail (Map 15/D7)
This 6 km (3.6 mi) hike links Bob's Lake with Elkhart Lake to the south. Both lakes offer wilderness camping and good fishing opportunities.

Bonaparte Provincial Park (Map 27/G1–28/A2)
Bonaparte Provincial Park makes a great wilderness location with a number of outdoor recreation opportunities. A number of multi-use trails travel throughout the park, including the epic 24.5 km (15 mi) Masters Subalpine Trek. The Deadman Trail is a popular route, with Shelly Lake being a good stop en route for anglers. The Heller Lake Circuit, accessible from Deadman Creek Road, offers several days' worth of exploring with many lakes along the way. Traveling to Mollimarn Lake is a 4.6 km (2.8 mi) one-way trail while the Skoatl Point Trail spans 12 km (7.5 mi) leading to a dramatic volcanic cone with a panoramic view of the surrounding lakes and forest. The latter route will take about four hours.

Border Lake Trail (Map 2/C7)
Border Lake Trail is one of a series of rugged mountain trails between Manning Provincial Park and Cathedral Park. This particular trail leads 10 km (6 mi) from Trapper Lake to Border Lake, climbing 360 m (1,180 ft). Hikers and equestrians use the trail primarily to access the fairly good fishing lake. Of course, you first have to get to Trapper Lake, which is accessed by a 20 km (12 mi) trail or a very rough four-wheel drive road.

Botanie Mountain Trail (Map 13/A1–20/A7)
The length of the hike really depends on how far you can drive along the old lookout road leading from the Botanie Valley Road. If you do not have a four-wheel drive vehicle then you will have to hike about 18 km (11 mi), climbing 1,425 m (4,675 ft) to the lookout. Along the way you will pass open meadows with wildflowers (in July) along with great views of the Stein Valley, Thompson River and Fraser River. The hiking season runs from June to October.

Boulder Mountain Trail (Map 49/C3)
This trail begins by following the old lookout tower access road through some old growth cedar and hemlock. The route turns to a footpath that passes by an old forestry cabin before breaking through the tree line to a scenic open area. The difficult hike covers 7.5 km (4.6 mi) and gains about 1,200 m (3,935 ft) along the way.

Brent Mountain Trails (Map 9/C7)
The Brent Mountain area provides a series of trails leading into a rolling alpine area with panoramic views of the Coast and Monashee Mountains. From the south, the Mount Brent Trail climbs 445 m (1,460 ft) to the old fire lookout at the top of Mount Brent, and is a 10 km (6 mi) round trip. Alternately, the Sheep Rock Trail is a 13 km (8 mi) round trip that climbs 480 m (1,575 ft) to a scenic lookout at Sheep Rock. The Brent Mountain Connector bridges the two peaks over a distance of 2 km. Both routes are found off the Apex Road along the Shatford logging road. The Sheep Rock trailhead is just past the Shatford Creek Bridge about 2.3 km along the road, while the Mount Brent trailhead is about 4 km down the road. From the east, it is possible to access the area from most drainages (June, Skulaow or Shingle Creek Trails). The Isintok Trail provides access from the north.

Bryden–Pement Lakes Trail (Map 23/F1)
Depending on the distance you can drive up the Charcoal Creek Forest Service Road branch road, there are about 7 km (4.3 mi) of easy trails leading along Blanc Creek to two small lakes, with an elevation gain of around 60 m (200 ft). Found in the rolling Ptarmigan Hills, the multi-use trail system makes a fine overnight fishing destination.

Bundschu Trail (Map 6/D6)
This trail is accessed by turning off Highway 3 onto Gilpin Forest Service Road 6 km east of Grand Forks. The low elevation trail runs parallel to Highway 3 through Gilpin Grasslands Provincial Park for a 10 km (6 mi) return distance. This is one of the first trails in the area to be rideable in the spring and has minimal elevation gain.

Burnt Basin Trail (Map 6/F4)
Accessed from the Lafferty Gravel Pit area on Highway 3 north of Christina Lake, the trailhead is actually found 9 km up the Josh Creek Forest Service Road. From the end of the steep road, a fast downhill mountain bike trail can be found. The trail leads 7.3 km (4.5 mi) back to the highway, making a nice 16 km loop if you ride the road to the top. The trail loses 750 m (2,460 ft) in elevation.

Bush Lake Interpretive Forest (Map 22/B4)
Found on Goose Lake Road, hikers will enjoy the short, easy loop trails that display interpretive forest practices. Also in the area is a network of rewarding mountain bike trails. For the advanced rider, Quickdraw heads east (left) from the parking lot and eventually loops back after a grueling 11.5 km (7 mi). This single track trail offers several hills, technical sections and mud. Trappers Line is an easier and shorter 5.5 km (3.4 mi) loop starting at the back of the parking lot. This trail combines single track and old roads.

BX Creek & Falls Trail (Map 24/D7)
The BX Creek Canyon is a melt-water channel from the last ice age that has carved through layers of the earth revealing glimpses into the Okanagan Valley's formation. From Tillicum Road, just off Silver Star Road, the trail leads you to a viewpoint overlooking the spectacular falls over a distance of 2.8 km (1.7 mi) and an elevation gain of 120 m (395 ft). You can also branch off and follow a steep, short trail that takes you to the bottom of the falls. The southern trailhead is located at the bottom of the switchbacks on Star Road.

Cabin Lake Trails (Map 13/F6) 🚶‍♂️🏕️🎣🐎⛵🏞️

To reach Cabin Lake, you can use a four-wheel drive vehicle, ATV or walk along the rough Cabin Lake Road (7 km/4.3 mi) gaining 215 m (700 ft) to the lake. Hiking time is about four hours. Given the elevation (1,860 m/6,100 ft), the best time to sample the area is in June through September. From the lake, it is possible to access the alpine Stoyoma Mountain along the moderate 7 km (4.3 mi) trail gaining 420 m (1,375 ft). Another alternative is to access Heather Basin to the west via a 15 km (9.3 mi) hike along an alpine ridge. This difficult route leads past an old aircraft wreck. Another option is to hike to Lightning Lake, which involves a steep 5 km (3 mi) excursion along an old road.

Camel Hump Trail (Map 18/C2) 🚶‍♂️🏞️

From the Creighton Valley Road, take the road marked "R.V. Schmidt Channel" and follow it past Clier Lake to the signed trailhead. From there, the hike leads 6 km (3.6 mi) on a well-developed trail up the gently sloping southern side of The Hump. The elevation gain is 300 m (985 ft) to the summit at 1,330 metres (4,365 ft).

Canoe Mountain Trail (Map 47/B4) 🚶‍♂️🎿🐎🏞️

Look for a rough access road off the east side of Highway 5, about 15 km south of Valemount. The road gets very rough very fast and requires a four-wheel drive vehicle to travel any significant distance. Once you find a suitable parking area, follow the access road as it ascends towards Canoe Mountain. From the top you will be rewarded with panoramic views of the surrounding countryside, including a fabulous view of Kinbasket Lake. For the more adventurous, you can continue east along the alpine to the peak of Mount Thompson, which stands 2,591 metres (8,500 ft) above sea level. This route is moderate in difficulty and covers over 20 km (12.5 mi) from the beginning of the access road, gaining 1,840 m (6,040 ft) in elevation.

Carrot Mountain (Map 9/E1–16/F7) 🚶‍♂️🎿🏞️

Carrot Mountain is reached by hiking along Smith Creek Road from the gate (along the deactivated Mount Swite Forest Service Road) and then picking a place to scramble up the hillside to the top of the mountain, making for a 7 km (4 mi) trip with an elevation gain of 700 m (2,295 ft). Once you reach the top at 1,525 metres (5,000 ft), you will be rewarded with a view of the McDougall Creek and Powers Creek Valleys. An alternative route is to scramble up the mountain from the road paralleling McDougall Creek.

Cathedral Park Trails (Map 2/D7–3/G5) 🏕️🚶‍♂️🎣🐎⛵🏞️

This is truly one of the best backcountry parks in the province, with spectacular rock formations, great views, good fishing, plentiful wildlife and unbelievable rock climbing opportunities. To reach the northern boundary of the park, follow the Ashnola River Road west of Keremeos. Upon reaching the park, there is a private road (gated) to the Core Area (at 2,330 m/7,645 ft) but you will have to hike into the sub-alpine unless you pay to be transported in. If you choose to reach the Core Area by foot, you can take one of three routes: the Lakeview Trail, the shortest of the three at 16 km (9.8 mi). It will take about seven hours climbing 1,300 m (4,265 ft) in elevation, the Wall Creek Trail, at 20 km (12.5 mi) trip gaining 1,100 m (3,610 ft), or the daunting 28 km (17 mi) Ewart Creek Trail, which gains 1,740 m (5,710 ft). Allow at least ten hours to complete the hike in. These distances are for one-way trips. Once you reach the Core Area, there are plenty of areas to camp, or you can stay at the lodge. From here there are a number of trails to explore.

Trails accessible from the Core Area include the Stone City Trail, which features views of unique quarts monzonite formations known as the Devil's Fenceposts, as well as the Diamond Trail, an intermediate trail that offers great views of the Ashnola Corridor. In poor weather take the Goat Lake Trail, which stays in the valley bottom with minimal elevation gain. Anglers will want to take the Ladyslipper Lake Trail, which will lead them to one of the best fishing spots in the park. For those looking for a workout and stunning views, the Lakeview Mountain Trail climbs to the highest point in the park and usually takes 10 hours to conquer. The Pyramid Loop Trail is an easy, short trail that features bridges and boardwalks criss-crossing through marshland and over creeks.

Diamond Trail (Map 2/F6)

This 8 km (5 mi) hike leads around Scout Mountain gaining 225 m (740 ft). Allow four hours as the trail winds up through clusters of flowers over rock bluffs and past a small rock glacier where the rocks are slowly moving and pushing into the soil. The Diamond Trail offers great views of the Ashnola Corridor. Along this route, Scout Lake is a shorter destination that only requires a 3 km (1.8 mi) hike gaining 125 m (410 ft).

Quiniscoe Mountain (Map 2/F7)

Towering above Glacier Lake, the plaque atop the mountain is a positional marker that once aided in mapping the area. The well-marked route covers 8 km (5 mi) as you hike past Glacier Lake over steep terrain. You will gain 500 m (1,640 ft) along the way.

Rim Trail (Map 2/F7)

From the core area, the trail to Glacier Lake is the quickest way into the alpine. However, it is fairly steep, gaining 200 m (655 ft) in 3 km (1.8 mi). Beyond the lake, Pyramid Mountain is accessed via a steep trail that climbs 475 m (1,560 ft) over 7 km (4.3 mi) from the lodge. Allow about 3.5 hours to hike this one, or extend your trip along the Rim Trail. The Rim Trail links all the surrounding peaks, including Quiniscoe Mountain, which towers above Glacier Lake and Red Mountain along a difficult route.

Stone City (Map 2/F7)

One of the highlights of the park, these quartz monzonite formations that have been eroded by the action of wind over millennia are often referred to as the Devils Fenceposts. The Giant Cleft that is featured here was formed when softer basalt rocks eroded, leaving a split in the granite. The 12 km (7.3 mi) hike takes you past Glacier Lake gaining 500 m (1,640 ft). Allow 7–8 hours for this hike.

CATHEDRAL PARK TRAILS	MAP	DIFFICULTY	LENGTH	ELEVATION GAIN	BIKE	CABIN	CAMP	FISH	HIKE	HORSE	MOUNTAINEER	SKI	SNOWSHOE	VIEW
Centennial Trail	Map 2/D6	Moderate	12 km (7.3 mi)	1,080 m (3,545 ft)					•					
Diamond Trail	Map 2/F6	Moderate	8 km (5 mi)	250 m (820 ft)					•					•
Ewart Creek Trail	Map 2/D7–3/G5	Difficult	28 km (17 mi)	1,740 m (5,710 ft)	•		•		•	•		•		•
Glacier Lake Trail	Map 2/F6	Moderate	3 km (1.8 mi)	200 m (655 ft)					•					•
Goat Lakes Trail	Map 2/F7	Easy	5 km (3 mi)	150 m (490 ft)				•	•					•
Ladyslipper Lake Trail	Map 2/F7	Easy	3.5 km (2.2 mi)	200 m (655 ft)				•	•					•
Lakeview Mountain Trail	Map 2/G6	Moderate	6 km (3.7 mi)	600 m (1,970 ft)					•					•
Lakeview Trail	Map 2/D7–3/G5	Difficult	16 km (9.8 mi)	1,300 m (4,265 ft)			•		•	•				•
Pyramid Loop Trail	Map 2/F6	Easy	2 km (1.2 mi)	30 m (100 ft)					•					•
Quiniscoe Lake Trail	Map 2/F6	Easy	2 km (1.2 mi)	minimal					•	•				•
Quiniscoe Mountain Trail	Map 2/F7	Moderate	8 km (5 mi)	500 m (1,640 ft)					•					•
Red Mountain Trail	Map 2/F7	Difficult	5 km (3 mi)	250 m (820 ft)					•					•
Rim Trail	Map 2/F7	Difficult	30 km (19 mi)	500 m (1,640 ft)					•					•
Scout Lake Trail	Map 2/F6	Easy	3 km (1.9 mi)	60 m (195 ft)					•					•
Stone City Trail	Map 2/F7	Moderate	12 km (7.3 mi)	500 m (1,640 ft)					•					•
Wall Creek Trail	Map 2/D7–3/G5	Difficult	20 km (12.5 mi)	1,100 m (3,610 ft)	•		•		•	•		•		•

Centennial Trail (Map 1/A6–3/D6)

In the Okanagan region, the trail extends from Manning Park to Joe Lake near Keremeos offering a fantastic wilderness trek for experienced mountaineers or horseback riders. The trail leads past alpine lakes, rugged peaks and panoramic viewpoints. The best part of the trail is the 26 km (16 mi) section that connects Manning and Cathedral Provincial Parks. From the Monument 83 Trail in Manning Park, the Pasayten River Trail heads east. This trail requires a dangerous river crossing over the Pasayten River. After the river, the trail leads along a series of logging roads and eventually into the pristine wilderness near Trapper Lake. From the lake, the trail follows along Easygoing Creek, through Cathedral Provincial Park and on to Joe Lake. The last section will require good route finding skills.

> *By drinking plenty of water and knowing your limits, heat stroke/exhaustion can be easily avoided.*

China Ridge Cross-Country Ski Trails (Map 7/G6–8/A7)

Located west of Princeton at the old Snowpatch Ski Hill, there is a 40 km (25 mi) network of ski trails that follow old roads and skid trails through open timber, some cut blocks and across natural grassy slopes. In summer, about 30 km (19 mi) of the trails are popular with mountain bikers. The trails are at around 1,200 metres (3,935 ft) in elevation and offer the occasional view of the Tulameen River Valley.

Christina Crest Trail (Map 6/G4–G6)

While the area around Christina Lake is thick with trails, including the trails in Gladstone Provincial Park, they are for the most part low elevation routes. This difficult 20 km (12 mi) trail is the exception that proves the rule, climbing 550 m (1,800 ft) into the rugged alpine east of Christina Lake. The trail starts along an old road from the Santa Rosa Summit, making its way north to Mount St. Thomas. Near the end of the trail, it splits, with one fork dropping down to the Bonanza Creek parking area and the other heading to the mountain peak.

Clapperton Falls Trail (Map 14/G2)

This trail extends 6 km (3.6 mi) along an old road and undeveloped trail from Mill Creek Road to the falls gaining 100 m (330 ft) along the way. It is an easy hike and is best visited in March through October.

Clark-Maloney Lake Trail (Map 11/B5)

This is a 9 km (5.5 mi) one-way circuit that climbs 120 m (395 ft) as it leads past three wilderness lakes, with rustic Forest Service campsites at two of them. The trailhead is found 5.2 km along the Lassie Lake Road. The lakes provide some fairly good fishing in the spring and fall.

Clearwater River Trail (Map 37/F5–F7)

The Clearwater River Trail leads 18 km (11 mi) along the eastern bank of the river north to the Canyon Creek Trail, gaining 220 m (720 ft) in elevation. You can find the trailhead off the north end of Dutch Lake Road in the town of Clearwater. The beginning of the trail is quite easy and progressively becomes more challenging as the remoteness of the route increases further from town. Although the trail is not groomed in winter, it is a popular ski route.

Clemina Creek/Dixon's Glacier Trail (Map 47/E7)

While this area is a popular snowmobiling area, hikers love exploring this region, too. The trailhead is near the 19 km sign on Clemina Road. Watch for a trail that leads down to a creek. The warming hut is only a short walk away; from here you can hike to a viewpoint over Dixon's Glacier in a couple hours. From here, there are several small lakes and some alpine ridges to explore, making for a total distance of 7 km (4 mi) and an elevation gain of 680 m (2,230 ft).

Collier Lakes Trail (Map 11/B6)

This trail takes you 5 km (3 mi) return, with an elevation gain of 160 m (525 ft), to two wilderness lakes through rolling hills and a park-like setting. The trailhead is at the Sago Creek Forest Service Site, which is 18 km along the Beaverdell–State Creek Forest Service Road. The Collier Lakes are popular fishing lakes with rustic backcountry camping areas.

Cooke Creek Trail (Map 25/B3)

The trailhead to this hike is found along the Enderby-Mabel Lake Road at the Cooke Creek Forest Service Site. It is a 3 km (1.8 mi) easy walk along the Shuswap River and Cooke Creek through an interpretive forest and hatchery.

Copper Island Trails (Map 30/A5)

This island, which is part of the Shuswap Lake Provincial Park, receives heavy use in the summer by boaters on the big lake. Circling the island is a scenic 2.3 km (1.4 mi) trail that climbs up an over the summit, climbing about 455 m (1,495 ft). The attraction to the island is not only the sheltered waters and beaches but also the wide variety of plant life and animals that frequent the island.

Copper Kettle Lake Trail (Map 11/C3)

The Copper Kettle Lake Trail begins near the 66 km marker on the Christian Valley Road and leads 3 km (1.8 mi) one-way over fairly steep terrain (with an elevation gain of 240 m/790 ft) to Copper Kettle Lake. The lake offers reasonably good fishing and a wilderness campsite.

Coquihalla Mountain Trail (Map 7/A6)

Access this trail by the Tulameen Forest Service Road. This 14.5 km (9 mi) loop will lead you through forest and colourful alpine meadows, amid many sparkling blue tarns, before the scramble to the top of Coquihalla Mountain. Be careful of loose rocks around the summit. The 1,470 m (4,820 ft) climb will grant spectacular views of Flatiron, Needle, and Jim Kelly Peaks. In season, the area is abundant with blueberries, so be aware of bears looking for a snack.

Coquihalla Summit Recreation Area (Map 7/A5)

A series of trails are found near the old tollbooth and Boston Bar Summit Rest Area on the Coquihalla Highway (Hwy 5). These high elevation routes are best travelled from July to October and give experienced hikers a chance to explore the dramatic peaks and fantastic views.

Falls Lake Trail

This trail begins off the short road leading from Exit 221 of the Coquihalla Highway. From the parking lot, it is a nice 1.5 km return walk to the small mountain lake. The lake provides good fishing for small rainbow trout and a nice camping area. East of the main trail is Bridalveil Falls, but accessing the falls requires bushwhacking along the creek. (An easier approach is along the old KVR railgrade).

Little Douglas Lake Trail

The Little Douglas Lake Trail is a 1.5 km long and leads from the Zum Peak Recreation Site on the Upper Coldwater Forest Service Road to a small mountain lake. This lake also provides fishing for rainbow trout and a nice camping area.

Needle Peak Trail

Beginning across the highway, from the Boston Bar Summit Rest Area, a very strenuous hike climbs 855 m (2,800 ft) up the back side of the Needle. The reward for this difficult 13 km (8 mi) trip is the great view from the top, at 2,105 m (6,905 ft). This hike should only be attempted by experienced hikers.

Thar Peak Route

This trail begins from the Boston Bar Rest Area and follows the gas pipeline before heading upwards along a faint trail to the peak. The trail leads up the back of the mountain and provides a phenomenal view when you reach the summit. Although you only travel 10 km (6 mi), you should allow five hours return as you climb 1,100 m (3,610 ft) in total to the peak, at 1,920 m (6,300 ft).

Vicuna & Guanaco Peaks

These peaks can be accessed from the Zupkios Rest Area. From here it is a 10 km (6 mi) climb to Guanaco Peak. Alternately, four-wheel drive or two-wheel drive vehicles with good clearance can take the Upper Coldwater Forest Service Road to a closer starting point. The end of the road will bring you within 3 km (1.9 mi) of Guanaco Peak, but from here it is still a steep climb of 860 vertical meters (2,820 ft) to the peak. From Guanaco it is a short 1.4 km trek across the saddle to Vicuna peak. Both peaks are impressive in their own right, sitting atop massive rock shelves and towering over their surroundings.

Yak-Nak-Thar Loop

Yak, Nak and Thar peaks are all similar height (2,020 m/6,630 ft, 2,000 m/ 6,560 ft and 1,920m/6,300 ft respectively) so expect minimal elevation gain (but some sections of scrambling) after reaching the Yak summit – an initial 840 m (2,760 ft) gain from the starting point near the Zupkios Rest Area. The 9.8 km (6 mi) loop makes for a reasonable day trip or a scenic overnighter. In winter this area offers some excellent skiing lines.

Yak Peak Trail

Yak Peak is the dramatic peak rising above the Coquihalla Highway near the Coquihalla Summit truck brake check. After pulling off at the Zupkios Rest Area, access this trail by walking about 900 meters east along the highway. A left turn will take you through a marsh and into the forest before opening up into boulder fields and an impressive granite slab characteristic of the Coquihalla peaks. There is a false summit before the true peak, so keep pressing on for the full Yak Peak experience. Round trip for this trail is 4.4 km (2.7 mi) with an elevation gain of 840 m (2,760 ft).

Zoa Peak Trail

This is the easiest of the Coquihalla peaks to summit, an 8.6 km (5.2 mi) round trip with 720 m (2,360 ft) in elevation gain. Access this trail from the start of the Thar Peak Trail, not far from Falls Lake turnoff from Highway 5. The trail passes through a gradually thinning forest onto the ridge up to Zoa. Lush meadows and colourful wildflowers make up much of the scenery on this leisurely hike, and from Zoa Peak you will have an excellent view of the surrounding larger summits. Branching form this trail is a difficult day-long route to Zopikos Ridge, the dramatic rock face seen from the highway.

Zupjok-Alpaca Ridge

Access this peak from the Zopkios Rest Area. From here it is a 5 km (3 mi) climb to Zupjok Peak, gaining 680 m (2,230 ft) in elevation. Much of this route follows an old service road before a flagged route takes you through the bush to the peak. From Zupjok Peak your journey turns into a spectacular ridge walk as you make your way to Llama and Alpaca Peaks. The distance from Zupjok to Alpaca is 4.5 km (2.8 mi) with only a 250 m (820 ft) increase in elevation. This trek along the ridge is the highlight of the 19 km (12 mi) round trip, and a tremendous payoff for the initial climb.

Cotton Belt Trail (Map 35/G4–36/A3) 🥾🏕️

This hard to follow trail gets its name from the old Cotton Belt Mine on Mount Grace. A moderate 13 km (8 mi) trail climbs 1,040 m (3,410 ft) from the valley bottom to the alpine meadows and is best tackled in July–October. At the old mine, you can explore the remains of several mine shafts and old cabins. Further along the alpine meadows are filled with wildflowers and are dotted with small lakes. The trailhead is marked by a sign on a stump together with blue markers in nearby trees. Be cautious of grizzly bears that frequent the area.

Cougar Canyon Rim Trail (Map 17/C3) 🥾🚴🏕️

Just north of Oyama, the trail extends along the powerline to a scenic canyon for a spectacular view of Kalamalka Lake. Due to private property, the trail system is best accessed from the Cosens Bay Trail in Kalamalka Provincial Park. This route is 18 km (11 mi) and climbs 280 m (910 ft). It is best tackled in the spring when the wildflowers are blooming and the heat of the summer has not set in. The powerline is very popular with mountain bikers.

Crater Mountain Trail (Map 3/A4) 🏔️🥾🚴🏕️

This trail follows the old road to the top of Crater Mountain at 2,290 metres (7,515 ft) where you will have a great view of the surrounding countryside. The length of the hike will depend on how far you can drive along the Crater Mountain Road. From the Ashnola River Road it is 11 km (6.7 mi) one-way, climbing 1,140 m (3,740 ft). The deactivated road has a gate at the bottom, which is usually open and the road is ditched several kilometres up.

Crook Lake Trail (Map 6/A6) 🥾🚴🎣🏕️

This multi-use trail can be accessed off Highway 3 just west of Grand Forks, and can be rough in spots. The trail runs up Hardy and Eagle Mountains, and can be done as a loop from Reservoir Road. A viewpoint near the top provides views of the Grand Forks Valley and the Santa Rosa Summit.

Crowfoot Mountain Trail (Map 30/B4–C3) 🏔️🥾🚴🏂⛷️🚵🏕️

This trail, accessed off the forest service road at the end of Garland Road (continue north to the 'Sheep Trail' sign), leads 8 km (5 mi) one-way along an old road to the endless alpine meadows of Crowfoot Mountain. It is an additional 6 km (3.7 mi) to Mobley Mountain. The trail provides great views of the Shuswap high country as it follows the remains of the Old Big Bend Gold Rush Trail built in the 1800s, gaining 1,750 m (5,740 ft) in elevation along the way. The multi-use trail is very popular with ATV enthusiasts in summer and snowmobilers in winter.

Crystal Lake Trail (Map 11/A7) 🏔️🥾🎣

Crystal Lake is a small lake, accessed by a 2 km (1.2 mi) one-way hike from a rough four-wheel drive road off the Boyer Creek Forest Service Road to the south, with an elevation gain of 40 m (130 ft). Add another 4 km (2.4 mi) if you cannot make it to the end of the road. The lake can also be reached by bushwhacking along an old trail from the north. Crystal Lake makes a good overnight fishing destination.

Crystal Lake Trail (Map 32/D4) 🥾🎣🏕️

This easy 12 km (7.5 mi) trail begins from the west side of the lake at the Crystal Waters Guest Ranch. Be sure to check in with the ranch before heading out. The circle route travels around the lake through mixed timber and past a few other smaller lakes. The trail eventually reaches the North Bonaparte Road on the east side of the lake. You can return the way you came or continue along the road.

Cusson Lake Trail (Map 19/C1) 🥾🎣🏕️

Found off the Monashee Lake Trail, this remote lake offers good fishing in a sub-alpine setting. The moderate 10 km (5 hour) return hike follows the creek to the lake.

Deep Lake Loop (Map 28/C7) 🥾🐴🐎

Another in a series of trails found in and around Lac Du Bois Provincial Park, this trail starts off Westsyde Road at the end of Ida Lane. From here it is a 5 km (3.1 mi) trail that loops around Deep Lake overlooking the North Thompson River Valley. The trail climbs over 110 m (360 ft).

Deer Point Trail (Map 6/D4) 🏔️🥾🚴🎣🏕️

From the Texas Creek Campground, this 10.5 km (6.5 mi) hike climbs 180 m (590 ft) as it takes you along the eastern shores of Christina Lake. The moderate trail is initially steep and involves traversing over rolling terrain along an old roadbed, which was partly completed in the early 1900s. Popular destinations include the campsites at Deer Point (6 km one-way) and Troy Creek. It is possible to connect with the Sadner Creek Trail at the north end of the lake but you will have to obtain permission in order to cross private property.

Denison Lake Trail (Map 18/C3) 🏔️🥾🎣

This easy 4.3 km (2.7 mi) trail begins on the Bonneau Forest Service Road before leading up an old road and then a well-marked trail to the lake. The elevation gain is 200 m (655 ft) to the lake at 1,500 metres (4,920 ft), where rustic camping and fishing are possible.

Dewdney Trail – Cascade Recreation Area (Map 1/B4–F3) 🏔️🧍🥾🐴🏕️

Originally constructed in 1860 by Edgar Dewdney, this was one of the first trade routes linking the coast with the interior. The longest surviving section is found in the Cascade Recreation Area section of Manning Park, beginning at the parking lot on Highway 3. The trail extends 36 km (22 mi) to the Paradise Valley, gaining 1,130 m (3,700 ft) along the way. It is possible to trek over the divide into the Whipsaw Creek Forest Service Road. The trail is a popular horseback destination with its panoramic views of the valleys and mountains. There is wilderness and horse camping available along the way, as well as a cabin and the remains of the old Evans family cow camp.

Dewdney Trail – Christina Lake to Rossland (Map 6/E6–G6) 🏔️🥾🚴🐴🏕️

Between Christina Lake and Rossland portions of this historic pack trail have been restored. The West Dewdney Trail begins off of Santa Rosa Road near Christina Lake and follows a mix of trails and logging roads as it climbs past the former Trout Creek Recreation Site and the Santa Rosa Summit to the Santa Rosa Recreation Site. This trail is about 26 km (16 mi) long, with an elevation gain of 1,020 m (3,350 ft), but private lands, logging and powerline clearing have virtually eliminated the middle section of the trail. Mountain bikers are advised to climb via the Old Cascade Highway.

Dewdrop Trail (Map 21/G1) 🥾🚴🏕️

This 6 km (4 mi) one-way trail is accessed off Frederick Road outside of Kamloops. This is a moderate trail with some steep climbs and excellent views of Kamloops Lake and the surrounding valley. Wildlife viewers can keep an eye out for bighorn sheep that frequent this area.

Dixon Dam (Map 24/E7) 🚴

Found off the Silver Star and Tillicum Roads, the bike route around Dixon Dam offers a moderate 8 km (4.9 mi) loop that climbs 340 m (1,115 ft). From Dixon Dam Road, you climb along the steep road to above the dam. From here a technical single track trail will eventually lead you back to the gravel road.

Dunn Peak Trail (Map 34/A3)

There was a way to access Dunn Peak from the west, but the trail has fallen out of use and is all but impossible to find. Instead, most hikers will follow the forestry trail off the Harper Creek Forest Service Road in the east. This difficult 7.9 km (4.9 mi) hike will lead you up 400 m (1,310 ft) to Dunn Peak.

Dunster Trail (Map 49/G5)

Follow the Dunster-Croydon Road off the south side of Highway 16 to get to the Dunster Trailhead. The trail is a steep, moderate 6 km (4 mi) one-way trek that climbs 1,140 m (3,740 ft). There is a small cabin at the lake.

Eagle Creek Trail (Map 12/E1–B1)

The trailhead is found on the Burrell Creek Forest Service Road southwest of Edgewood. The moderate pack trail extends for 40 km/25 mi (2–3 days), gaining 1,320 m (4,330 ft) along an old trail north of Eagle Creek into the foothills of Gunwad Mountain and Granby Park. From the Mount Young Cabin, rustic routes join the various alpine peaks in the area. The Hopp Cabin in the north is rat infested, while others in the area are private guide outfitter cabins.

Eagle Crest Cliffs (Map 18/C2)

The trailhead for this hike is found at the Cozy Cabins Nature Resort, 19 km east of Lumby on the Creighton Valley Road. The trail climbs about 460 m (1,510 ft) to the top of the cliffs, where you can look down at the valley below.

Eagle Pass Mountain Trail (Map 31/E2)

An old forestry lookout can be accessed along a steep, difficult 5 km (3 mi) trail, gaining 840 m (2,775 ft). The trail winds up the timbered slope, eventually breaking out on the seemingly endless alpine. A second trail leads to Twin Lakes. The trailhead is found off the left fork at 8.8 km along the Crazy Creek Forest Service Road. It is also possible to follow an undefined route northeast to Mount Copeland for a very challenging 25 km (15 mi) one-way trek. You will need a compass and topographic maps as well as good route finding skills to follow the ridges and valleys between Hiren Creek and Eagle Pass Mountain. Given the elevation, the best time to hike the area is in mid-summer in order to avoid snow.

Eagle River Nature Park (Map 31/B5)

Five flat, easy nature trails lead through a beautiful old growth forest along the Eagle River and Yard Creek. In total there are about 6 km (3.7 mi) of trails to explore. The attraction to the park is the wildflowers, giant cedar trees and salmon spawning in the fall.

Eagle Valley Trail (Map 49/A5)

At the 14 km mark of the South Dore Forest Service Road, a deactivated logging road branches east to the Eagle Valley Trailhead. It is a moderate 12 km (7.5 mi) return trip gaining 485 m (1,590 ft). In addition to providing access to a moraine and glacier area, there is a backcountry hut available for overnight use. Cabin bookings are possible through the Ozalenko Alpine Club at 250-569-2596.

Eileen Lake Trails (Map 29/A6)

The Eileen Lake Trail is a 10 km (6 mi) trail that starts at Eileen Lake and loops south, returning back to the lake, gaining 120 m (390 ft) along the way. To get to the trailhead, take the North Barrière Lake Road to the Birk Creek (3300) Road turnoff and follow this road to a parking lot at km 5. The actual trailhead is 1.5 km past here.

Ellis Creek Trails (Map 10/A7)

The Ellis Creek Demonstration Forest is a 2,000 hectare patch of woods to the east of Penticton on the north banks of Ellis Creek. There are a number of easy trails here, including the 1.5 km (0.9 mi) Canyon View Interpretive Trail, the 4 km (2.4 mi) Ellis Ridge Trail and Carmi Ski Trails. There are also 24 km (15 mi) of ski trails, although some places are quite boggy in summer.

Ellison Park Trails (Map 17/A3)

Ellison Provincial Park is home to several small trails that make up 6 km (3.6 mi) of easy walking trails. The nature loop is a scenic trail that leads up through an open hill dotted with Ponderosa Pine trees to grassy openings overlooking Okanagan Lake. Shorter trails lead down to the beaches and protected bays of the big lake.

Embleton Mountain Trail (Map 28/F6)

The trailhead to this challenging 9.5 km (5.9 mi) hike begins at the Heffley Lake Recreation Site on the Sun Peaks Road. Expect to take about four hours as you climb 480 m (1,575 ft) to the summit.

Enderby Cliffs Trail (Map 24/E3)

The Enderby Cliffs tower high above the town of Enderby, offering breathtaking views of the Shuswap Valley and the North Okanagan. The fairly strenuous trail starts about 3 km from the Mable Lake Road at the end of Brash-Allan Road and has recently been upgraded. There are several new vantage points along the 6.5 km (4 mi) return hike, which climbs 700 m (2,295 ft) and features many wildflowers in June. Please stay on the trail!

Estekwalan Mountain Trail (Map 23/E4)

Estekwalan Mountain Trail is accessed off Rob Roy Forest Service Road from Falkland Dump Road. This is a difficult 7.25 km (4.5 mi) loop trail gaining 575 m (1,885 ft) to the height of land at 1,550 metres (5,085 ft). The lower sections of the trail are well developed, but scrambling is required to reach the ridge and open alpine. The route may be longer depending on whether you can drive to the trailhead.

Fawn Lake Trail (Map 32/A3)

This easy 26 km (16 mi) out-and-back trail is used mostly by mountain bikers and horseback riders in the summer. The elevation change is only about 70 m (230 ft). Look for the trailhead about 2 km along Fawn Creek Road.

Fred Laing Ridge (Map 40/D1–45/D7)

This alpine trail starts at a radio tower and heads to Gorge Lake. From the tower it is a 4 km return hike with there are good views of the surrounding area, including over Mica Dam. There is an old snowmobile cabin along the trail, and rustic campsites at the tarn and just below the ridge. From Gorge Lake, it is highly recommended to head up onto Fred Laing Ridge itself. From the ridge you can see all the way to Mount Robson, over 130 km away.

Giant's Head Mountain Trail (Map 9/F5)

A 2 km (1.2 mi) one-way hike starts from the gate at the end of Milne Road and climbs 320 m (1,050 ft) to the top of this landmark above the city of Summerland. When you reach the summit at 845 metres (2,770 ft), a number of short easy walks are available to enjoy the view of Summerland and Okanagan Lake. The ride up the lookout road is popular with bikers.

Goat Lookout (Map 11/A7)

It is possible to drive to within a kilometre of the flat-topped rock known as Goat Peak, but the road is rough. Without a four-wheel drive vehicle the hike will be longer and more challenging than the 500 metre trek, which gains 80 m (260 ft) in elevation. The trail is well-marked and offers an excellent panorama view once you reach the lookout at 1,740 metres (5,710 ft).

Godey Creek Trails (Map 14/E4)

Located right behind the Merritt Travel Information Centre, there are 5 km (3 mi) of easy trails climbing 60 m (200 ft) to a view over the valley and a picnic table. Mountain bikers also explore this network.

Golden Mile Trail (Map 3/G5)

A new concept in hiking! This 10 km (6 mi) easy trail connects a trio of wineries and a historic stamp mill west of Oliver. Stop in at each winery for a tour and some sampling; how long it takes you to complete this trail depends on how long you want to spend at each winery. The trailhead is at the Tinhorn Creek Winery.

Gorge Creek Trail (Map 31/C4)

From the Last Spike Monument off Highway 1, an easy 2 km (1.2 mi) trail leads along both sides of Craigflower (Gorge) Creek through an old growth forest and past three small falls. The scenic trail is well-marked and is a good choice for a family outing.

Granby River Trail (Map 11/G5)

The trailhead is found off the Bluejoint Mountain FSR. From here it is a short jaunt to the Traverse Creek Recreation Site along an old road. This is an easy overnight trip, covering 25 km of relatively level trail along the Granby River and entering the south end of the Granby Provincial Park, climbing 220 m (720 ft). The trail provides access to fishing pools, old-growth cedar trees, sandy beaches and views of the canyon. Although the first part of the trail is open to bikers, beyond the park boundary only horseback riders and hikers are allowed. It is possible to continue north through the park to access the alpine peaks that lead to the headwaters of the Granby and the Mount Scaia access road.

Grasslands Community Trail (Map 28/B7)

Best accessed from the north trailhead off McQueen Lake Road in Lac Du Bois Provincial Park, this trail links with the trails around Deep Lake and the trailhead off Westsyde Road at the end of Ida Lane. All told, you lose 540 m (1,770 ft) over 13 km (8 mi) if travelling south.

Graystokes Provincial Park (Map 18/B4–C7) 🏕️👤🚴‍♂️🐎🥾🛶

Characterized by gently rolling hills, the Graystokes Plateau is dotted with a number of lakes interwoven with an extensive complex of swamps and meadows. The plateau plays a vital role in providing mid and late summer range for wildlife once vegetation in the Okanagan Valley bottom has dried up. The area is a maze of old ATV trails. This is now closed to motorized vehicles (except snowmobiles in winter), but the trails remain open to hikers, horseback riders and bikers looking to explore the area. The Buck Hills Trail in the north and Mount Moore Trail in the south are two of the more established hiking trails.

Great Northern Railway Trail (Map 3/D4) 🚴‍♂️🛶

This trail runs from the Ashnola Road bridge in the west of Keremeos to Becks Road in the east, passing through the centre of town along the way. The trail runs parallel to Highway 3 and the Similkameen River for a one-way distance of 7 km (4 mi).

Green Tunnel Trail (Map 6/E5) 🚴‍♂️🛶🐎

Watch for the trailhead for this 7 km (3.6 mi) trail at the 7 km mark along the Old Cascade Highway/Santa Rosa Road. The route is actually an old road from the main road to Fife. There are some good views along the moderately difficult trail.

Grey Canal Historic Trail (Map 24/D7) 🚴‍♂️🛶🥾

The Grey Canal Historic Trail is a 3.5 km (2.1 mi) trail that follows an old irrigation ditch and provides magnificent views over the entire North Okanagan Valley. The trailhead parking lot is on the west side of Silver Star Road, just below the Silver Star Foothills subdivision. It is also possible to link up with the BX Creek Trail.

Greyback Mountain Trail (Map 10/C4) 🚴‍♂️🥾

The trailhead is located on the Greyback Road (R202 Road) and leads 3 km (1.8 mi) one-way to the top of Greyback Mountain at 2,134 metres (7,000 ft), making for a climb of 320 m (1,050 ft). The trail is undeveloped and hard to follow as it dissects the timber and reaches the treeless alpine region where great views of the surrounding area are provided.

Gypsum Mountain Trail (Map 21/C7) 🚴‍♂️🥾

Gypsum Lake is found off the Aberdeen Road south of Dot Lake. It is a fairly easy 4 km (2.4 mi) hike climbing only 80 m (260 ft) to the summit of Gypsum Mountain at 1,546 metres (5,070 ft).

H.B.C. Brigade Trail 1849 (Map 1/A2–7/D7) 🏕️🚴‍♂️🐎🥾

This historic trail east of Hope is seeing some significant upgrades by the Back Country Horsemen Society of BC. The 48 km (30 mi) trail makes its way from the Peers Creek Forest Service Road over towards the Whatcom Trail. Due to the distance and elevation gain of almost 1,570 m (5,150 ft), this trail is best travelled on horse. Along the way there are several designated campsites complete with food caches and toilets.

Haines Creek Trail (Map 24/B3) 🚴‍♂️🛶🐎🥾🏍️

Found south west of Salmon Arm near the community of Silver Creek, this is a popular multi-use trail. This trail goes through forest and along the creek drainage. Climbers use this trail to access the crags in the area. Motorbikers and other OHV users frequent the area.

Hamilton Lookout Trail (Map 15/C4) 🚴‍♂️🛶🚵‍♂️🥾

From the Douglas Lake Road, an 11 km (6.7 mi) moderate hike leads along an old driveable forestry lookout road. You will gain 600 m (1,970 ft) to the top at 1,508 metres (4,950 ft) where there is an excellent view of the dry Douglas Lake range country.

Harry Lake Trail (Map 3/C6) 🚴‍♂️🐎🥾

The trailhead for this 5 km (3 mi) trail is actually located at Joe Lake, which is 15 km (9 mi) from the nearest road, making for a 40 km (24 mi) out-and-back trip. The terrain is very rough, crossing over high mountain passes and through thick forests.

Hayman Lake Trail (Map 16/G7) 🚴‍♂️🛶🛶🥾

This is a 12 km (7.3 mi) return hike up the McDougall Creek Valley following a well-marked trail then an old road network climbing about 780 m (2,560 ft) to the lake. The trail begins at the cattle guard on the Bartley Road. Once you are there, you can enjoy the fine view of Kelowna or try your luck fishing. If need be, you can drive up the deactivated McDougall Creek Forest Service Road to reduce the hiking distance.

Headwater Lakes Ski Area (Map 9/A2) 🚴‍♂️🛶🎿🛶🛶

At the Headwaters Fishing Camp, which is accessed off the Peachland Forest Service Road, three easy cross-country ski trails dissect the Lodgepole pine forest around the lakes. Headwaters Lake Trail is a 4 km (2.4 mi) loop circling the main lake. Camp Trail is a short one-kilometre loop near the fish camp, while June Lake Trail is the longest loop covering 6 km (3.6 mi). This trail starts along the Headwaters Lake Trail but extends onto a smaller lake.

Hedley Creek Trail (Map 3/A2) 🚴‍♂️

The Hedley Creek Trail is found just north of Hedley and is a nice walk beside and often through the creek. The 3 km (2 mi) trail has an elevation gain of 300 m (985 ft) and takes you up the steep walled canyon where old mine shafts and pieces of an old flume can be seen. It is possible to link with Nickel Plate Lake via the challenging Twenty Mile Creek Trail.

Hiren Creek Trail (Map 31/G2) 🏕️👤🚴‍♂️🐎🚵‍♂️🥾

It is a 20 km (12.5 mi) 6–7 hour hike along an abandoned mining road that accesses sub-alpine terrain and several mountain lakes. Once you reach the old mine site, you can scout the old workings or try your luck fishing at Hiren Lakes, which can be accessed by climbing to the pass at 2,300 m (7,545 ft) elevation. The trail is shared with mountain bikers and horseback riders and requires an elevation gain of 525 m (1,725 ft) from the trailhead at the end of Copeland Mine Road (see our Kootenay Rockies Mapbook).

Holliday Creek Trails (Map 49/G4) 🚴‍♂️🥾

Northwest of Tête Jaune Cache, look for the Holliday Creek Rest Area off the east side of Highway 16. There are three different trails accessible in the area, but all have washouts to skirt around. The most popular destination is the Natural Arch, which is found up the western ridge. The Baker Ridge Trail traverses up along the western ridge of the creek, while the Groeneveld Trail follows the eastern ridge. Overall, there are about 10 km (6 mi) of trails to follow. However, be advised that the trail up to the Holiday Creek Arch is in very bad shape with windfall, washouts and several areas where detours are required. Travel is not recommended unless you are prepared for these conditions.

Hope Pass Trail (Map 1/C4–E4) 🏕️👤🚴‍♂️🥾

Starting at the Cayuse Flats Parking Lot on Highway 3, this trail climbs 1,050 m (3,445 ft) over a one-way distance of 23.5 km (14.5 mi). The trail passes over many creeks and, though originally a horse trail, it is now impassible for horses. Much of the trail parallels the Skaist River en route to the pass and the alternate trailhead on a branch road off the Whipsaw Creek Forest Service Road. Near the end of the route, there is an interesting side route to Dick's Cabin on top of Skaist Mountain. As an alternate, you could loop back along the Grainger Creek Trail and camp at Nicomen Lake.

Horsey Creek Trail (Map 50/C4) 🚴‍♂️🛶🐎🚵‍♂️🛶🛶🥾

Northwest of Tête Jaune Cache, the Horsey Creek Route is actually the Horsey Creek Road, which is accessible off the east side of the highway. From the highway, the road heads 20 km (12.5 mi) one-way into the Horsey Creek Valley. The moderate route crosses the creek in a few areas and although the bridges have been washed out, they have since been replaced with much smaller ones for bikers and hikers. The route passes through some scenic forested terrain, interrupted occasionally by signs of past logging practices. Near the uppermost portion of the route, you will find nice views of the various mountain peaks and glaciers.

Hunakwa Lake Trail (Map 30/G1) 🚴‍♂️🛶

At the north end of the Anstey Arm of Shuswap Lake, look for the small trailhead sign on the west corner of the bay by the creek. This easy 1.5 km one-way trail takes anglers and nature enthusiasts through an old growth cedar and cottonwood forest to the south end of Hunakwa Lake.

Hunter's Range Area (Map 24/G1–31/C6) 🚴‍♂️🛶🚵‍♂️🛶🥾

Northeast of Enderby, this is a popular snowmobile area following an old sub-alpine road network. With over 240 km (146 mi) of trails, there is a lot to see and do up there. During the summer, this high elevation area is accessible by vehicle and provides hiking on undeveloped trails with spectacular displays of wildflowers. A popular destination is Mount Mara and its extensive alpine meadows.

Hyde Mountain Trail (Map 30/F6) 🚴‍♂️🛶🛶🥾

Near Sicamous, this new trail climbs the north slope of Hyde Mountain offering fantastic views of Shuswap Lake and area. The return trip is 14 km (8.7 mi) with an elevation gain of 470 m (1,540 ft) from the trailhead on the 112 Forest Service Road. For the more adventurous, it is possible to continue southwest towards Salmon Arm along the epic 38 km (24 mi) long Larch Hills Traverse.

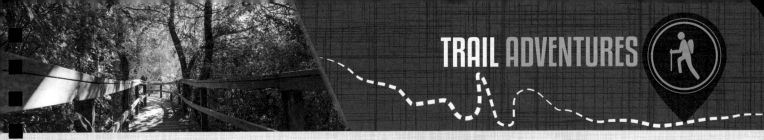

Illal Meadows Trail (Map 7/B6)
From the end of the road leading up Illal Creek, this 6.2 km (3.9 mi) one-way trail climbs steadily to the scenic meadows above Illal Creek. The trail gains 665 m (2,180 ft) and can be used to access Jim Kelly Peak or the northwest ridge of Coquihalla Mountain.

Inks Lake Area (Map 22/B3)
Found off the Coquihalla Highway, Inks Lake Road accesses a large network of trails popular with both mountain bikers and off-road enthusiasts. Following the first road left will give access to some single track trails. Several options are available including making your way south to Timber Lake Road. This difficult trail climbs 650 m (2,135 ft) over 21 km (13 mi) return. Reggie's Roost is another popular route that is found 7.5 km (4.6 mi) down the first road left. It is a moderate single track trail that links back with the Inks Lake Road.

Iron Mountain Trail (Map 14/E5)
From the top of Iron Mountain Road, a steep, technical mountain bike trail leads down to the Fox Farm Road, which can be accessed south of Merritt on the Coldwater Road. Unless you have legs of Iron, you will want to arrange for a shuttle to the top of the mountain.

Irrigation Canal Trail (Map 4/A4–6)
This route follows an old irrigation canal, created in the 1920s, which was used to transport water to the US border. The easy route offers nice views and leads about 10 km (6 mi) from Fairview/350 Avenue in Oliver towards Osoyoos.

Isobel Lake Trails (Map 28/B6)
It is an easy 3 km (1.8 mi) walk around Isobel Lake, with interpretative signs describing the ecology of region. If you wish a longer hike/bike, you can continue on the 10 km (6 mi) of cross-country ski trails in the area. Another alternative is to bike down the roads next to Dairy Creek from Isobel Lake to Westsyde Road. Along the way, you will cross several trails and roads (stay right at all intersections). This moderate ride is 15 km (9.3 mi) long.

Jackman Flats Trails (Map 46/F1)
North of Valemount off the west side of Highway 5, there is a parking area leading to series of easy, interconnecting loops leading around both wetlands and arid sand dunes. In total, there are about 12 km (7 mi) to explore. Across the highway a more challenging trail leads to Mount Terry Fox Park.

Jewel Lake Trails (Map 5/F4)
From the Jewel Lake Lodge at the south end of the lake, three short loop trails (up to 5.8 km/4.9 mi long) lead through the forest and to an old mine site (at the end of the Roderick Dhu Trail). These trails are well-marked and groomed in winter for skiing. In summer, they provide an enjoyable outing for hikers and bikers.

Joan-Cleo Lake Trail (Map 11/B4)
The trail to this pair of wilderness fishing lakes involves an 8 km (5 mi) return hike that will take two hours if you were just to walk there and back. However, most people will spend a few hours fishing or even spend the night at one of the Forest Service campsites. The trail has minimal elevation gain and is not too strenuous. The trailhead is found at 6.8 km on the Lassie Forest Service Road.

Joe Lake Trail (Map 3/C6)
Although this is the terminus of the historic Centennial Trail, the access from the west will require extensive route finding skills. A good trail has been cut from the end of the Susap Creek Forest Service Road to the lake where well-kept cabins and good fishing can be found. It is a difficult trail covering about 15 km (9 mi) with an elevation gain of 1,120 m (3,675 ft). The sheep trails make exploring the surrounding area a delight.

Johnson Lake Trails (Map 29/C1)
There are eight interlocking loop trails north of Johnson Lake, offering over 58 km (36 mi) of hiking and horseback riding. Many riders stay at Johnson Lake Resort or at the recreation site. The trails lead as far north as South Barrière Lake. The longest trail is the 23 km (14 mi) Johnson Lake Loop trail.

Joss Mountain Trails (Map 31/F6)
From the end of Branch 5 of the Three Valley Gap/Wap Lake Forest Service Road, it is about 3 km up to the summit. The 700 m (2,295 ft) climb is rewarded with great views of the Monashee Mountains and Blanket Glacier. An alternate route is found about 12 km up the rough four-wheel drive South Pass Forest Service Road. This 7.5 km (4.7 mi) one-way route leads through the alpine pass before branching west at the lake to the recently rebuilt lookout. Mountaineers can traverse the scenic ridge south to the Tsuius Mountain Trail system or link to Greenbush Lake to the east. Beware of grizzly bears in the alpine area.

Jubilee Mountain Trail (Map 5/F5)
Behind a tall red building on Togo Street in Greenwood is the trailhead for this trail that switchbacks past an old mine shaft on its way up the west ridge above Greenwood. The climb is fairly easy to the top of Jubilee. The trail splits at the 1.5 km mark (0.9 mi). Keep left.

July Mountain Trail (Map 7/A4)
A nice trail leads from a branch road off of Juliet Creek Forest Service Road, following North July Creek up to Drum Lake. More ambitious hikers can continue onto the top of July Mountain along the northern ridge, making for a 9.5 km (5.9 mi) return trip and an elevation gain of 715 m (2,345 ft). Camping is possible at Drum Lake.

Juniper Ridge Trail (Map 22/D2)
A popular hiking trail above the Juniper Ridge area of Kamloops, this trail is about 6.2 km (3.9 mi) one-way, with an elevation gain of about 250 m (820 ft). Trailheads are found along Coldwater Drive to the west or Cheakamus Drive in the east, with four-wheel drive/ATV access available via the old road leading west from Rose Hill Road.

Kalamalka Lake Park (Map 17/D2)
This park offers several multi-use trails. The main trail, from the gate on Cosens Bay Road, leads 6 km (3.6 mi) along the road to the beautiful sandy beach. Alternatively, you can try the 8 km (4.9 mi) easy walk up the gently sloping road to Deep Lake, which will take you through Bear Valley and outside the park. Also, there is an extensive network of trails through the dry grassland of the park. Bring water, stay on the trails and watch for rattlesnakes. Mountain bikers usually explore the single track trails found east of the Coldstream Trail. Rattlesnake Hill Trail is a popular but challenging trail, with a tough climb and fast technical descent. Allow 1 hour to bike the 9.5 km (5.9 mi) loop, which starts at the Cosens Bay Gate.

Kamloops Bike Ranch (Map 22/D2)
The Kamloops Bike Ranch mountain bike park is the most technically challenging municipal bike park in the country. It features downhill trails, a jump park and a BMX track. The 26 hectare park is found behind the Valleyview Arena off Highland Road.

Kane Valley Ski Trails (Map 14/F6)
In addition to over 50 km (31 mi) of ski trails cum hiking/biking/ATVing trails in the summer, there is an additional 2.5 km (1.5 mi) stroll through the demonstration forest near Harmon Lake. The trails follow old roads through open timber and across sloping meadows. Deer are frequently seen in the area.

Kelowna Crags Trail (Map 9/G2–10/A2)
You can hike or bike to the bottom of these 100 metre high (330 ft) basalt cliffs, which are made up of several fascinating columns. A trail also leads up to the cliff top at the north end. Depending on where you left your car, it is about a 6.5 km (4 mi) walk. The view from the top, at about 760 metres (2,500 ft), is beautiful.

Kentucky Lake Trail (Map 15/A7)
There is a 4 km (2.4 mi) easy walk that follows a well-marked trail around Kentucky Lake with minimal elevation gain. The trail leads through old growth timber and is ideal for wildlife viewing and to access the lake for fishing.

Keremeos Columns Provincial Park (Map 3/D4)
This popular 4 km (2.4 mi) hike begins at the second gate on Liddicoat Road north of Keremeos. The hike gains 210 m (690 ft) in elevation through an open sage brush range along an old road eventually leading to a series of basalt pillars that are over 100 metres (330 ft) tall. To reach the columns, it is necessary to obtain permission to cross private property. Watch for rattlesnakes and bring water.

Kettle River Trails (Map 5/B6)
A vast network of backcountry roads and trails are found in the scenic hills north and east of Rock Creek. In all there are over 120 km (74.5 mi) of trails that are mostly used by hikers, bikers and horseback riders. The main trailhead is found at the Rock Creek Fall Fair Grounds where camping and showers are available. The steeper southern trails are closed to motorized vehicles and provide nice views over the Kettle River Valley and town. ATVers can access the upper trails at the 3 km mark of the Riverside Road north of Rock Creek. Note: The Kettle Valley Wildlife Association operates an active Rifle Range near the trailhead so keep to the trails and obey all signage in this area.

Kettle Valley Railway/Trans Canada Trail (Maps 1–6, 7–10, 12)

The Trans Canada Trail/Kettle Valley Railway or KVR runs 550 km (335 mi) from Midway to Hope. There are also lesser-travelled spur lines south to Osoyoos, north to Merritt and south of Princeton. The route can be split up into day trips or completed in a few days to a week. Most people do the route from east to west to take advantage of the elevation loss.

Boundary Subdivision (Map 5/D7–12/G7)

This stretch runs for 162 km (99 mi) between Midway and Robson. The route includes the popular section from the old Eholt Station down to Grand Forks as well as the route up and over to Arrow Lake and Robson from Christina Lake. There are ten trestle crossings together with seven tunnels, including one over one kilometre long that requires a light in this section.

Carmi Subdivision (Maps 4, 5, 9, 10)

The Carmi section extends 215 km (130 mi) from Midway to Penticton, climbing 600 m (1,970 ft) over 125 km (76 mi). The trail levels out and begins one of its steepest descents from the old Carmi Station into Penticton. The section from Myra Canyon to the Adra Tunnel is one of the most picturesque and popular sections of the KVR featuring wood trestles and tunnels.

Osoyoos Subdivision (Maps 3, 9)

This portion of the KVR is 58 km (35 mi) long and takes travelers from Penticton to Osoyoos through the rural orchards and vineyards and along Skaha and Osoyoos Lakes. Some sections of the route are quite difficult to follow and cross private property so you may need to divert along the busy Highway 97.

Princeton Subdivision (Maps 7, 8, 9)

This subdivision extends 175 km (107 mi) from Penticton to Brookmere, climbing 700 m (2,295 ft) over 60 km (36 mi) from Penticton to Osprey Lake. You will pass through the Penticton Indian Reserve, which is private land, before crossing the Trout Creek Bridge. From Osprey Lake, the route begins its descent into Princeton. The last 65 km to Brookmere climbs gently (400 m/1,310 ft in total) and includes the popular Tulameen Canyon section.

Copper Mountain Subdivision (Maps 2, 10)

This subdivision is 21 km (13 mi) long and heads south from Princeton. This trail climbs 300 m (985 ft) to the mine but it is mostly impassable due to private residences and the deterioration of the trail. The section from Princeton to Smelter Lakes is mostly passable.

KVR & TCT Trails:

Trail	MAP	DIFFICULTY	LENGTH	ELEVATION GAIN	ATV	BIKE	CAMP	FISH	HIKE	HORSE	SKI	SNOWMOBILE	SNOWSHOE	VIEW
BOUNDARY SUBDIVISION (TCT)	5/D7–12/G7		162 km (99 mi)				•							
Midway to Greenwood	5/D7-F5	Easy	14 km (8.7 mi)		•	•	•	•	•	•				•
Greenwood to Eholt	5/F5-G4	Easy	14 km (8.7 mi)		•	•	•	•	•	•				•
Eholt to Grand Forks	5/G4-6/B6	Easy	23 km (14 mi)		•	•	•	•	•	•				•
Grand Forks to Christina Lake	6/B6-E6	Easy	23 km (14 mi)		•	•	•	•	•	•				•
Christina Lake to Robson (Castlegar)	6/E6-KRBC	Easy	88 km (55 mi)		•	•	•	•	•	•				•
CARMI SUBDIVISION (TCT)	4, 5, 9, 10		215 km (131 mi)	600 m (1,970 ft)										
Midway to Rock Creek	5/B6-D7	Easy	18 km (11 mi)		•	•	•	•	•	•				•
Rock Creek to Westbridge	5/B4-B6	Easy	15 km (9.3 mi)		•	•	•	•	•	•				•
Westbridge to Beaverdell	10/G7-5/B4	Easy	35 km (22 mi)		•	•	•	•	•	•				•
Beaverdell to McCulloch Lake	10/E2-G7	Easy	53 km (33 mi)		•	•	•	•	•	•				•
McCulloch Lake to Myra Canyon	10/C2-E2	Easy	14 km (8.7 mi)			•	•	•	•	•				•
Myra Canyon to Chute Lake	10/A3-C2	Easy	36 km (22.5 mi)			•	•	•	•	•				•
Chute Lake to Penticton	9/G6-10/A3	Easy	44 km (27 mi)			•	•	•	•	•				•
OSOYOOS SUBDIVISION (KVR)	3, 4, 9		58 km (35 mi)											
Penticton to Skaha Lake	9/G7	Easy	4 km (2.5 mi)			•		•	•	•				•
Skaha Lake to Kaleden	9/G7-3/G1	Easy	7 km (4.3 mi)			•		•	•	•				•
Kaleden to Okanagan Falls	3/G1-G2	Easy	5 km (3 mi)			•		•	•	•				•
Okanagan Falls to Oliver	3/G2-4/A4	Easy	19 km (12 mi)			•		•	•	•				•
Oliver to Osoyoos	4/A4-B7	Easy	23 km (14 mi)			•		•	•	•				•
PRINCETON SUBDIVISION (TCT)	7, 8, 9		170 km (106 mi)	700 m (2,295 ft)										
Brookmere to Tulameen	7/C2-E6	Easy	43 km (27 mi)		•	•	•	•	•	•				•
Tulameen to Coalmont	7/E6-F6	Easy	6 km (3.7 mi)		•	•	•	•	•	•				•
Coalmont to Princeton	7/F6-8/B7	Easy	19 km (12 mi)		•	•	•	•	•	•				•
Princeton to Osprey Lake	8/B7-F3	Easy	50 km 31 mi)		•	•	•	•	•	•				•
Ospery Lake to Summerland	8/F3-9/F5	Easy	52 km (32 mi)		•	•	•	•	•	•				•
NICOLA, KAMLOOPS & SIMILKAMEEN RAILWAY (KVR)	2, 7, 14		68 km (42 mi)	300 m (985 ft)										
Copper Mountain Subdivision	2/B1-A2	Easy	21 km (13 mi		•	•	•	•	•	•				•
Merritt Subdivision	7/C2-14/E4	Easy	47 km (29 mi)		•	•	•	•	•	•				•
COQUIHALLA SUBDIVISION (TCT)	7		87 km (53 mi	100 m (330 ft)										
Hope to Coquihalla River	7/A5-A6	Easy	9 km (5.6 mi)			•	•	•	•	•				•
Coquihalla River to Juliet	7/A6-B5	Easy	54 km (33.5 mi)			•	•	•	•	•				•
Juliet to Brodie	7/B5-B3	Easy	9 km (5.6 mi)			•	•	•	•	•				•
Brodie to Brookmere	7/B3-C2	Easy	15 km (9.3 mi)			•	•	•	•	•				•

Merritt Subdivision (Maps 7, 14)

It is 47 km (29 mi) from Brookmere to Merritt along this section of the KVR. The gentle decline combined with the scenic route through the Coldwater River Valley and Canyon makes this a pleasant route.

Coquihalla Subdivision (Map 7)

This is an 87 km (53 mi) section between Brookmere and Hope. After a gentle climb to the Coquihalla Summit the route loses 1,000 m (3,280 ft) over 50 km. From the Coquihalla Summit to the old Jessica Station, the official route is re-routed along the Trans Mountain Pipeline Road. Past Jessica, there are a few sections where you are forced to travel on the Coquihalla Highway.

Kiwa Creek South Trail (Map 50/C7–46/B2)

West of Tête Jaune Cache, the Kiwa Creek South Trail follows the old road for 14 km (8.7 mi) one-way deep into the heart of the Cariboo Mountains, with an elevation gain of 400 m (1,310 ft). Ardent bushwhackers can continue on to the magnificent Kiwa Glacier and the small lake that is formed below it.

Knight Lake Trail (Map 21/B7)

Knight Lake is a sheltered treed lake with good fishing potential if you can bring in a boat to work past the muddy shoreline surrounded by lily pads. From the western shore of Roscoe Lake, a 2 km (1.2 mi) easy walk follows a flat, well-marked trail.

Knox Mountain Trails (Map 17/A7)

Cyclists, hikers and joggers looking for a scenic but challenging trail close to downtown Kelowna use these trails. From the end of Ellis Street, the paved access road climbs 300 m (985 ft) to the top. Enjoy the view before following any number of routes down. The options include going down the steep face, circling around the backside to Paul's Tomb or venturing down to Clifton Road where you can follow the roads back to the start.

Lac Le Jeune Ski Trails (Map 22/A5)

This network of trails and old roads circle the lake and are well used throughout the year. The entire network is about 73 km (45 mi) long with many of the trails being moderate in difficulty because they have steep long climbs and are not maintained. A popular option is to circle the lake along the 8 km (5 mi) Gus Johnson Trail. It is also possible to link up with the Home Ranch and Stake Lake Trails in the area.

Lacoma Lake Trail (Map 9/C1–16/C6)

This moderate trail runs 11 km (6.7 mi) from a parking lot at Clover Creek off Trepanier Bench Road to the south. The first half of the trail follows an old road and is bikeable. The second half of the trail was not designed for bikes and has some steep sections as it climbs 200 m (655 ft) to the lake.

Larch Hills Traverse (Map 24/E1–30/F6)

This 38 km (24 mi) trail goes through the high countryside between Salmon Arm and Sicamous and is described by many as epic. Those not wanting to do all 38 km at once can do shorter circuit sections while others break it up into an overnighter. Currently there are two huts found along the route, but more are being planned. Within the nearby area there are over 150 km (92 mi) of trails. These include the traverse, cross-country ski trails as well as other hiking, equestrian and biking trails.

Leighton Lake Trails Map (21/C3)

The main trail circumnavigates Leighton Lake, starting and ending at the Tunkwa Campground and connecting with the two other campgrounds found around the lake. The easy 4.3 km (2.7 mi) trail leads past grasslands, wetlands and forest ecosystems. A shorter trail is found at the western side of the lake and leads to Bluff Hill, which provides great views out over Tunkwa Lake. This trail is 1.2 km (0.75 mi) one-way.

Little Lost Lake Trail (Map 50/F7)

Off the north side of Highway 16, the trailhead to this route can be found almost opposite the parking area for the popular Rearguard Falls. The Little Lost Lake Trail is a fairly easy hike that climbs about 3 km (1.9 mi) to the shore of the small lake. To extend your hike, there is a loop trail around the lake as well as a steep side trail to a scenic waterfall.

Little Mountain Park (Map 24/C1)

In the heart of Salmon Arm, this popular area offers 8 km (4.9 mi) of easy hiking trails that are set in a figure 8 leading to the top of Little Mountain. The trail network is also used by joggers, mountain bikers and cross-country skiers and offers an excellent view of Salmon Arm. The trails are accessed from the east end of Okanagan Avenue or from 10th Avenue S.E.

Little Nipple (Map 10/F5)

If you want to reach the Little Nipple, you will have to bushwhack from the Wilkinson Creek Forest Service Road to the top, at 1,764 metres (5,785 ft). You will be rewarded with a spectacular view of the Kettle River Valley. This is a difficult route.

Lisa Road Trail (Map 23/F3)

This old logging road will take hikers about 60 minutes to get to the end of (a bit less to return). There are great views of the surrounding area, with a small pond and wildflowers when in season.

Remember the golden rule of outdoor recreation: leave only footprints, and take only photographs.

Logan Lake Cross-Country Trails (Map 21/D5)

Accessed off Breccia Drive, which is reached from Chartrand Avenue in Logan Lake, this 36 km (22 mi) ski system allows for fine hiking and even better mountain biking during the warmer months. The trails are well marked and graded according to difficulty.

Lower Granby-Wolf Trail (Map 6/A1–12/A7)

This easy 5 km (3 mi) one-way trail begins approximately a kilometre past the 28 Mile Bridge on the Granby Forest Service Road. The signed trail follows an old trappers trail next to the Granby River to the Gable Creek Recreation Site. It provides access to fishing holes and is a pleasant walk.

Lower South Slopes/Crawford Trails (Map 10/B2)

This is Kelowna's most popular and largest mountain bike trail network with over 80 km (49 mi) of trails to explore. The area is found south of Kelowna, at the end of Stewart Road East (follow the signs to the parking lot). Pick any old road to ride up and then enjoy the single track trails that take you back down. The powerlines make an excellent landmark, but signs are being erected in the area. One of the most popular routes is the Flamingo Flats Circuit, which covers about 15 km.

Lower Westridge Trail (Map 46/G3)

Better known as a snowmobile trail, some people hike this trail, too, which gains 450 m (1,500 ft) in 5 km (3 mi). The trail can be accessed from km 13 on the West Ridge Forest Service Road, or from a point 2 km from the Cranberry Lake Road junction on the McLennan Forest Service Road. Most people leave a vehicle here and do this hike as a shuttle, as it is about five hours one-way.

Luca's Plateau Trail (Map 32/E3)

From Cabin 7 in Lac Des Roches Resort, this 4.4 km (2.7 mi) return trail leads to a vantage point over the lake. The trail climbs about 90 m (295 ft) and offers a chance to see wildlife in Moose Hollow or the aspen grove at the top. Be sure to ask the resort for access permission to the trailhead.

Lucille Mountain Trail (Map 49/B3)

In McBride, Samson Road leads to the Lucille Mountain Forest Service Road, which eventually accesses an old logging area. The trailhead is located on the east side of the upper cut blocks. The moderate route travels 3.4 km (2 mi) one-way into the alpine area of Mount Lucille, gaining 560 m (1,835 ft) along the way.

Lundbom Lake Trails (Map 14/G4)

The open grasslands around Lundbom Lake offer a series of mountain bike trails that can be enjoyed by hikers, bikers and horseback riders. Visitors will find fun rolling terrain and great views, especially over Tent Lake, on trails such as Coco Bonk, Tent Lake, Hogsback, Wounded Knee and Déjà Vu. The Coco Bonk Trail starts just before the cattleguard at Lundbom Lake; turn left and park just up this road.

Lumby Salmon Trails (Map 17/G1)

If you were to string together all the trails along Bessette and Duteau Streets, including the need to backtrack from one trail to another, (or more likely, connect via streets) you would be covering about 8 km (3.6 mi). The trails are most active in the late summer and early fall during the Coho and Chinook salmon spawn. The town of Lumby holds several events related to the cycle of spawning salmon during the year. Visit *lumby.ca/salmontrails* for more information.

Manning Provincial Park (Map 1)

Trails cut through all reaches of this fine destination park allowing people to explore the rugged mountains, meadows, lakes and rivers that you rarely see from the highway. Trail users will find designated areas for backcountry camping, while closer to the highway there are many short loop trails to explore. A number of trails run through Manning's picturesque and delicate sub-alpine meadows, including Bonnevier, Grainger Creek and Heather/Three Brothers Trails. Monument 78 and 83 Trails take hikers right up to the Washington border and the start of the Pacific Crest Trail, which stretches all the way to Mexico. The highest peak in Manning Park is accessed along the Frosty Mountain Trail, which passes Windy Joe Mountain on the way up. A number of lakes, with some decent fishing, are accessible along the Lightning Lakes Chain Trail and the Poland Lake Route. From Lightning Lakes, Skyline I and II Trails provide access to Camp Mowich and the Skagit Valley.

Bonnevier Trail (Map 1/F5)

Originally built as a packhorse route in the early 1900s, this is a difficult trail that is best hiked from west to east. You will lose more elevation than you gain in this direction (about 950 m/3,115 ft). The trail starts 7 km (4.3 mi) along the Heather Trail. Head east and follow the trail downhill to McDiarmid Meadows. The total distance hiked is 25 km (15.5 mi) one-way and can be done as a shuttle trip in a long day. Water is available at the 9 km mark.

Grainger Creek Trail (Map 1/C4)

In order to reach the Grainger Creek trailhead, you have to hike 6 km (3.7 mi) along the Hope Pass Trail. At the junction of Grainger Creek and the Skaist River, the Grainger Creek Trail swings east up the valley climbing steadily for 11 km (6.7 mi) to the western end of Nicomen Lake. The trail gains 800 m (2,625 ft) to the lake, which has a lovely camping area at its northern end. This trail can also be reached by hiking the Heather Trail to Nicomen Lake.

Heather/Three Brothers Trail (Map 1/E6–D4)

This is the main trail through Manning Parks' vast sub-alpine meadows. In mid-July to August, the sub-alpine are notorious for their amazing display of colourful wildflowers. To get here, you will have to drive up to the trailhead. Fortunately, the road leads all the way up to the sub-alpine, meaning you will only gain 290 m (950 ft) to the Nicomen Ridge overlooking Nicomen Lake. The trail is 21 km (13 mi) one-way, but it is possible to add the steep, 1 km side trail up to the top of the First Brother to the venture. Please remember that these sub-alpine meadows are extremely fragile.

Monument 78 Trail (Map 1/E7)

This is one of several trails that offer a chance to hike into Washington State via the Pacific Crest Trail. From the Monument 78/83 parking lot, it is a 12 km (6.7 mi) one-way hike, climbing about 200 m (655 ft) through several meadows. From the monuments near the USA border, it is possible to connect with Monument 83 through Washington State. Wilderness camping is available 500 metres south of the monument.

Poland Lake Route (Map 1/C6)

This trail is an easy 8 km (4.9 mi) one-way hike from the gate at Strawberry Flats to Poland Lake. Although the climb is gradual, you will still gain 435 m (1,425 ft) in elevation along the way. The area is a popular cross-country ski destination and the backcountry campsite sees a lot of use in the summer. From the lake, it is possible to hike 9 km (5.5 mi) one-way to Allison Pass on Highway 3 rather than return to Strawberry Flats. If you choose this alternate route, the hike will lead you along an unmaintained trail (Memaloose Trail). It is a good idea to have a vehicle waiting for you.

Three Falls/Strawberry Flats Trail (Map 1/C7)

Beginning at the Strawberry Flats parking lot, this is a rather scenic 9 km (5.5 mi) return hike. The trail is wide and well used at the beginning as it leads to the downhill ski area. From there, the trail is less used and continues on to Shadow Lake, Nepopekum Falls and eventually Derek Falls. For the most part, the trail follows Nepopekum Creek gaining 125 m (410 ft) in elevation along the way.

MANNING PARK TRAILS	MAP	DIFFICULTY	LENGTH	ELEVATION GAIN	BIKE	CABIN	CAMP	HIKE	HORSE	INTERPRETIVE	SKI	SNOWSHOE	VIEW
Beaver Pond Nature Trail	1/E7	Easy	0.3 km (0.2 mi)	Minimal				•		•			
Bonnevier Trail	7/D4-F4	Difficult	25 km (15.5 mi)	950 m (3,115 ft)			•	•					•
Canyon Trail	1/E7	Moderate	2 km (1.3 mi)	50 m (165 ft)				•		•			•
Dewdney Trail	1/B4–F3	Moderate	36 km (22 mi)	1,130 m (3,700 ft)	•	•	•	•					•
Dry Ridge trail	1/E6	Moderate	0.3 km (0.2 mi)	50 m (165 ft)				•		•			•
Engineers Loop	6/D2 (VCBC)	Moderate	0.5 km (0.3 mi)	200 m (656 ft)				•		•		•	
Frosty Mountain Trail	7/C6-C7	Difficult	27.5 km (17 mi)	1,205 m (3,950 ft)		•	•	•			•	•	•
Ghost Pass Trail	6/D2 (VCBC)	Difficult	9.1 km (5.6 mi)	775 m (2,545 ft)				•					•
Grainger Creek Trail	7/B2	Difficult	11 km (6.8 mi)	800 m (2,625 ft)			•	•					•
Heather/Three Brothers Trail	7/D5-B2	Moderate	21 km (13 mi)	290 m (950 ft)			•	•					•
Hope Pass Trail	1/C4	Moderate	23.5 km (14.5 mi)	1,050 m (3,445 ft)	•		•	•	•				•
Lightning Lakes Chain Trail	7/B7	Easy	12 km (7.3 mi)	25 m (80 ft)	•		•	•					•
Memaloose Trail	7/A5	Moderate	9 km (5.5 mi)	420 m (1,380 ft)	•			•					•
Monument 78 Trail	7/D6-D7	Moderate	12 km (6.7 mi)	200 m (655 ft)			•	•	•				•
Monument 83 Trail	7/E6-F7	Difficult	16 km (9.9 mi)	850 m (2,790 ft)	•	•	•	•	•				•
Mount Outram Trail	6/D2 (VCBC)	Difficult	8.2 km (5 mi)	1,675 m (5,495 ft)				•					•
North and South Gibson Trails	7/B6	Easy	7.6 km (4.6 mi)	125 m (650 ft)				•				•	•
Pacific Crest Trail	7/D6-D7	Difficult	4,300 km (2,700 mi)	4,010 m (13,155 ft)			•	•					•
Paintbrush Nature Trail	1/E6	Easy	1.5 km (1 mi)	Minimal				•		•			
Poland Lake Trail	7/A5	Easy	8 km (5 mi)	435 m (1,425 ft)	•		•	•	•				•
Rein Orchid Trail	1/E7	Easy	0.5 km (0.3 mi)	Minimal				•		•			
Rhododendron Flats	1/A4	Easy	500 m (0.3 mi)	Minimal				•		•			
Skagit Bluffs	6/F3	Easy	5.6 km (3.5 mi)	80 m (260 ft)				•		•			•
Skyline I Trail	6/G6-7/C6	Moderate	17 km (10.5 mi)	560 m (1,840 ft)			•	•					•
Skyline II Trail	6/F6-G6	Difficult	8.5 km (5.3 mi)	1,080 m (3,545 ft)			•	•					•
Three Falls/Strawberry Flats Trail	7/A6	Moderate	4.5 km (2.8 mi)	125 m (410 ft)				•	•		•		•
Whatcom Trail	1/C2	Difficult	13 km (8 mi)	1,080 m (3,545 ft)			•	•					•
Windy Joe Mountain	7/D6	Moderate	7.5 km (4.7 mi)	655 m (2,150 ft)	•		•	•	•		•		•

Mara Hill Trails (Map 22/A1)
From Tranquille Road, this trail climbs to the top of Mara Hill in Lac Du Bois Provincial Park for a fine view of Kamloops and the lake. It is just over 3.5 km (2.2 mi) one-way to the top, climbing over 675 m (2,215 ft). An alternate route leads from the north off the old road leading west off Lac Du Bois Road. From here it is about 4 km to the top climbing about 325 m (1,065 ft). Yet another option is found further west on the Tranquille-Criss Creek Road. This loop trail is 3.8 km climbing 160 m (525 ft).

Margaret Falls Trail (Map 30/D7)
From Herald Provincial Park, this easy 1 km walk takes you through a creek draw (Reinecker Gorge) with old growth cedar and moss covered canyon walls to a beautiful cascading waterfall. The trail is very popular and well-maintained (wheelchair access). If you want to get away from the crowds, try exploring the easy walking trails that meander along the creek to the Shuswap Lake and along the beach through Herald Park.

Mark Berger Traverse (Map 19/C1)
A difficult 27 km (17 mi) route, the Mark Berger Traverse takes about three and a half days to complete and is mostly unmarked, leading along a series of alpine peaks and narrow ridges. The trail connects the Twin Lakes and Monashee Lake Trails and features panoramic views. Be careful, this is grizzly bear country.

Marshall Lake Trails (Map 5/G5)
Easily accessed on a good two-wheel drive road (Phoenix Road) off Highway 3A, there are 17.5 km (11 mi) of cross-country skiing trails that can be used in summer by horseback riders, mountain bikers and hikers. The area surrounding the ski trails is rich with a history of old gold mines and the remains of an old gold rush town. Look for the Phoenix Forest Trails (see page 154) to help explore the area. Be careful when exploring these old mine works and please stay out of private property in the area.

Mary's Lookout Trail (Map 6/E5)
Accessed from the Texas Creek Campsite or McRae Road, the Mary's Lookout Trail is a nice side trail to the Badger Trail. This hiking only route is much steeper and makes for a nice loop trail of almost 4 km (2.5 mi) when combined with the Badger Trail.

Masters Subalpine Trek (Map 27/G5–32/G7)
This difficult four to five day trek extends for 24.5 km (15 mi) through the sub-alpine terrain and past numerous wilderness lakes and meadows of the Bonaparte Plateau. The main access points are from the Tranquille Lake Resort to the south or from around the 63 km mark on the Jamieson Creek Road to the north. Along the route are several cabins, which you can overnight in, as well as many remote fishing lakes. There is an overall elevation gain of 420 m (1,380 ft). The trail is very isolated and wanders through vast stretches of unspoiled wilderness. Hikers should come prepared with topographic maps and compass and should also be bear aware.

Mayson, Bogmar, Allan & Scott Lake Trails (Map 33/B7)
This network of eight trails is used to access a series of lakes just southeast of Bonaparte Lake. All told, there are about 31 km (19 mi) of trails here, ranging from half hour jaunts to overnighters. Best traveled from June to September, the trails are mostly easy and used by horseback riders and anglers. Some sections can be boggy. Note that there may be active logging in the area.

McBride Peak & Teare Mountain Trail (Map 49/D2)
McBride Peak is the prominent mountain peak located northeast of the town of McBride. A road to the lookout is found shortly along Mountainview Road. If you do not have a four-wheel drive vehicle, it is possible to hike or cycle up the steep road, which switchbacks up to the alpine. The trek up the mountain is a moderate 10 km (6 mi) one-way grunt to a lookout, with an elevation gain of 1,380 m (4,530 ft). For your efforts, you are rewarded with breathtaking mountain scenery. Beyond the lookout, it is also possible to continue to the southern slopes of Mount Teare. This deteriorating 10 km (6 mi) extension is preferred by the equestrian crowd.

McCulloch Ski Trails (Map 10/E2)
Located on the McCulloch Road (good two-wheel drive access), this is a series of 45 km (28 mi) trails towards the north end of McCulloch Lake. The trails are well marked by the local ski club and can be used by hikers and bikers in the summer.

McDougall Rim Trails (Map 16/F7)
The McDougall Rim Trail is one of the more popular in the Kelowna Area, but is relatively hard to find. Follow Bartley Road out of West Kelowna to the McDougall Rim Trail sign. Depending on what route you choose, the circuit

is over 15 km (9 mi) long as you access the area around Hayman Lake, Mount Swite and Carrot Mountain. Due to 600 m (1,970 ft) elevation gain to Hayman Lake, mountain bikers will find this quite strenuous and challenging. The valley and lake views make it all worthwhile.

McKinney Ski Trails (Map 4/E5)
Better known as a cross-country ski area (see Winter Recreation), there are 4 km (2.4 mi) of hiking trails here as well. There are some views of Mount Baldy.

McKirdy Hut and Meadows Trails (Map 47/B2)
Hikers will climb 765 m (2,500 ft) in a mere 3.2 km (2 mi) to reach the timberline from the end of the access road. Once you get to the alpine, you are free to wander all over the place, making it hard to put a total distance on this route. A popular destination is the YORA McKirdy Cabin. Registration and a small fee are required. Call 250-566-4225 for information.

McKirdy Summit/McKirdy Creek Trails (Map 47/B3)
From the north end of the Selwyn Traverse, hike along this trail for 4.3 km (2.8 mi) to the McKirdy Summit Trail junction. From here, the trail climbs 1,500 m (4,920 ft) in 3.7 lung-busting kilometres to the 2,600 metre (8,530 ft) summit. It will take a full day to climb to the top and back.

Mica Mountain Trail (Map 46/D2)
Just west of Tête Jaune Cache, you can find the trailhead off the Sand Creek Forest Service Road at the 6 km mark. This moderate trail ascends to the alpine of Mica Mountain and is about 5 km (3.1 mi) one-way, with an elevation gain of 820 m (2,690 ft). The view at the top is quite impressive as you can see Mount Robson in the distance. Along the way, you can also explore an old mine site.

Midway Village Trail (Map 5/D7)
Recently upgraded, there are now about 15 km (9 mi) of hiking and biking trails in the area. The trails are well marked and mapped and provide some scenic viewpoints of the Kettle Valley, Baldy Mountain and the Kettle River leading south into the USA. Options include an easy flat 4.6 km loop on the north side of the Kettle River that links Midway with the Trans Canada Trail system. More advanced mountain bikers will prefer the trails on the hillside south of town between the river and the USA border. These trails start of Myers Creek Road East and feature nice views and a 350 m (1,150 ft) elevation gain. Camping and shower facilities are available in summer at Frank Carpenter Park (fees applicable).

Mission Creek Greenway (Map 10/A1–17/C7)
One of the most popular trails in Kelowna, the Mission Creek Greenway follows Mission Creek from Lakeshore Road to just below Gallagher's Canyon, a total distance of 16.5 km (10 mi). It really is an oasis away from the city offering everything from lush forests to fine viewpoints and kokanee spawning areas (in fall). The lower section (southwest of Springfield) is paved and quite easy to follow, while the gravel upper section is a bit more challenging. Phase III is already in progress and will continue the trail upstream, well away from the city.

Monashee Lake Trail (Map 19/C1)
The trail to the beautiful glacier-fed Monashee Lake is one of the main access routes into the Pinnacles area. The Pinnacles are a spectacular destination with towering spires that provide lots of options for rock climbers. To the lake, the trail climbs 700 m (2,295 ft) over 4.5 km (2.7 mi) but it is possible to continue north on the Mark Berger Traverse or the seldom used Cusson Lake Trail. The trail is marked by red diamonds and is best left to the experienced hiker.

Monck Park Trails (Map 15/A3)
Within Monck Provincial Park is a well-developed 5 km (3 mi) interpretive loop trail with three trailheads. The trail explores the shores of Nicola Lake and leads up to an ancient volcanic outcropping and Indian pictographs on the slopes above the lake. An additional 1.3 km loop was opened in 2005. This section is best walked from the upper end and contains some steep climbs.

Moonscape & Peter and Paul Peaks Trails (Map 22/D2)
Moonscape is a popular biking route located on the Kamloops Indian Reserve amidst the dramatic looking hoodoo formations and sagebrush north of the Thompson River. Instead of continuing up the peaks, you cut east along a sandy old road and single track. The complete loop covers 12 km (7.3 mi). Hikers prefer to follow the 2 to 3 hour trail up to Peter and Paul Peaks for a great view of Kamloops. A permit (acquired from the Indian Band) is required before setting out. The trailhead is on Shuswap Road, just east of Highway 5.

Moul Creek Trail (Map 37/F5) 🥾🚵📷
The Moul Creek Trail is located off the west side of the Clearwater Valley Road approximately 21 km north of the town of Clearwater. The easy 1.5 km trail traverses through a cattle-grazing area before reaching the scenic waterfall along Moul Creek.

Mount Baldy Area (Map 4/E4) 🥾🚵📷
If you want a great view along with splendid wildflowers in season (July-August) then hike up the ski lift at Mount Baldy. You climb roughly 540 m (1,770 ft) to the top at 2,304 metres (7,560 ft) where you get a true feel for the vast wilderness of the south Okanagan.

Mount Boucherie (Map 9/G1) 🥾📷
To reach the top of this 762 metre (2,500 ft) mountain, simply drive along Boucherie Road to the base of the mountain. From the road it is a 5 km (3 mi) return scramble to the top where there is an excellent view of Kelowna. Trails also lead up and around the mountain from the arena found off Ross Road from Highway 97.

Mount Campbell Trails (Map 9/G6–10/A6) 🚵🚶📷
One of the easiest mountain bike trail systems to access from Penticton, these trails are mostly moderate to difficult. There are a lot of uphill climbs and steep, fast descents on smooth trails. The trailhead is found at the municipal dump.

Mount Dilworth Trails (Map 17/B7) 🥾📷
Just northeast of downtown Kelowna on Longhill Road, a series of trails are found along Mount Dilworth. The trails lead across, up and over the mountain, which offers a fine view from the summit at 635 metres (2,085 ft). Depending on your route, the hike can range from 3 to 10 km (1.8–6 mi) in length.

Mount Drought Trail (Map 9/E1) 🥾📷
The trailhead to this hike is found 2.5 km south of the Gorman Sawmill on Highway 97. The trail is 6 km (3.6 mi) long and climbs 360 m (1,180 ft), starting out along an old road before leading right along the powerline and to a scramble uphill to the summit. From the top, an excellent view of the Peachland area is offered. An alternate route up starts at the end of Morning-side Drive off Glenrosa Road. This trail climbs about 340 m (1,115 ft) over the 4.5 km (2.8 mi) one-way trek.

Mount Dufferin Trails (Map 22/B2) 🥾🚵📷
Dufferin Hill is a popular and easily accessible hiking/biking area in Kamloops. From the Kenna Cartwright Park trailhead on Hillside Drive, follow the road up to the tower (about 2 km). At the top, a couple of moderate trails will give you a wide variety of options. It is possible to make your way north to Mission Flats Road or to loop back on the Old Race Course Loop, which starts from the second switchback. This moderate 9 km (5.5 mi) loop returns you to the tower road.

Mount Faith Trail (Map 6/B2–D1) ⛺🥾🚵🐕📷
From the end of Lynch Creek Forest Service Road, this old horse trail leads 36 km (22 mi) return to the top of Mount Faith within Gladstone Provincial Park, encompassing an overall elevation gain of 1,540 m (5,050 ft). Once a popular route, the trail is slowly fading away, but can still be followed if you know where to look. Hikers will need at least two days to track their way up.

Mount Fowler [Grizzly Mountain] (Map 30/E2) 🏔🥾🚵🚴📷
Also known as Grizzly Mountain, this trail is found north of St. Ives. Look for the Forest Service Road #1025 branching left off the Seymour Arm Forest Service Road, about 4 km after the pavement ends. At km 10.4 of the 1025, there is a parking area at the junction. From here a trail leads through alpine meadows with panoramic views of the surrounding area over a return distance of around 10 km (6 mi), with a 565 m (1,855 ft) elevation gain. Experienced hikers can continue west to link up with the Crowfoot Mountain trail system.

Mount Harper Trails (Map 22/F1) 🥾🚵🚶🏔📷
Found east of Kamloops, off the Paul Lake Road, is a 14 km (8.5 mi) cross-country trail system. These trails are found on the north side of Mount Harper, around the downhill area. Hikers and bikers can follow these trails in summer. For advanced cyclists, the downhill ski trails feature some seriously technical riding.

Mount Henning Trail (Map 7/C4) 🥾🏔🚶📷
This area is easily accessed from the Britton Creek Rest Area off the Coquihalla Highway (Hwy 5). An 8 km (5 mi) hike/bike leads along an old road to a viewpoint and then along a faint trail through some alpine meadows to the base of Mount Henning. Overall, the elevation gain is 550 m (1,805 ft) to the summit at 1,818 metres (5,965 ft). Most hikers return to the parking lot by way of another faint trail passing by an old mining camp and then leading along the old road. Another option is to hike the 7.5 km (4.6 mi) trail that leads through the sub-alpine between Thynne Mountain and Mount Henning. In the winter, the area becomes an extensive series of snowmobile trails.

Mount Ida Trail (Map 24/C2) 🥾📷
This is a popular hiking area south of Salmon Arm. The main trail starts from the Mount Ida Forest Service Road (825 Road) and leads 13 km (7.9 mi) return to the two scenic viewpoints. The moderate trail is fairly steep and requires climbing 1,100 m (3,610 ft). To reduce the hike to 6 km (3.6 mi) return, it is possible to drive the four-wheel drive road to a saddle set below the two summits. From the top, you will get an excellent view of the surrounding valley and mountains. Mountain bikers should note that the West Peak Trail is not rideable while the steep demanding East Peak Trail may require some dismounting.

> *It is always a good idea to carry a map, compass and a GPS device, and to research your route ahead of time.*

Mount Kobau Trails (Map 3/F5) 🥾🚵📷
At the top of the Richter Pass on Highway 3, the Mount Kobau Forest Service Road takes off to the northwest and eventually leads to the top of the mountain at 1,870 metres (6,135 ft). Below the summit is a parking lot with toilet facilities, picnic tables and two marked trails. From here, you can either hike the old access road for the fire lookout for 1.5 km to the top for a great view of the Osoyoos area, or you can hike through the forest below Mount Kobau. This 5 km (3 mi) loop is called the Testalinden Trail.

Mount Mara Lookout (Map 31/A7) 🥾📷
Offering fantastic views of Mabel and Shuswap Lake as well as the Monashee Mountains, the lookout tower on Mount Mara is a great destination. It is found just beyond the 17 km marker on the Owlhead Creek Forest Service Road outside of Sicamous. The moderate 16 km (10 mi) return hike requires a steep climb near the summit, where wildflowers dot the alpine meadows. The easier 6 km (3.6 mi) route is found at the end of the deteriorating four-wheel drive Mount Mara Road to the south.

Mount Moore Trail (Map 18/C7) 🥾🚵🐎🚶🏔📷
A 12 km (7.3 mi) hike follows an old pack trail from the Okanagan Falls Forest Service Road to the top of Mount Moore, with an elevation gain of 180 m (590 ft). Expect to take about four hours. From the top is an excellent view of the Kettle River Valley. The trail is well developed and is used by mountain bikers, horseback riders and hikers in summer and snowmobilers in winter.

Mount Nelson Trail (Map 25/E4) 🥾📷
Mount Nelson sits in the high alpine area to the east of Mabel Lake. Although not well known, there is a 9.5 km (5.9 mi) one-way trail up the mountain. You gain roughly 620 m (2,035 ft) in elevation from the end of Taylor Creek Forest Service Road.

Mount Nkwala Trail (Map 9/F6) 🥾📷
From West Bench northwest of Penticton, follow Sage Mesa Drive to the trailhead that is south of the Pine Hill Golf Club and near the sign saying "A West Bench Irrigation District." The steep trail to the top of the mountain, at 1,020 metres (3,345 ft), is 13 km (7.9 mi) long and is well marked (blue stakes), gaining 300 m (985 ft) of elevation along the way. From the summit, there is a panoramic view of the Okanagan Valley.

Mount Roderick Dhu Trail (Map 5/F4–F2) 🥾🚵🐎🚶🏔📷
The start of this trail can be found next to a large trail map and registration box on Jewel Lake Road, about 9 km from the junction with Boundary Creek Road. The trail up to the Roderick Dhu summit is around 6 km (4 mi) in length, with an elevation gain of 700 m (2,297 ft). The route follows an old road to a former forestry lookout and an old cabin. Here you can enjoy the nice views of Jewel Lake, Phoenix Mountain and the surrounding area. An undefined route continues north along the ridge to Almond Mountain.

Mount Robson Park Trails (Maps 47, 48, 50, 51) 🏕️🥾🚵🐴🏃⛷️🛶🔭

Mount Robson is one of British Columbia's oldest and best-known provincial parks and is home to one of BC's oldest and best-known hiking trail, the Berg Lake Trail. This multi-day trail follows the Robson River and the Valley of a Thousand Falls on its way to Berg Lake, with many side trails and wilderness campsites along the way. There are also a number of additional trails in the park. Easy nature trails that stick close to park campsites include the Fraser River Nature Trail and the Labrador Tea Trail, among others. Hikers looking for more of a challenge can take the Snowbird Pass Route, which is mostly unmarked and leads to spectacular glacial scenery, or the Moose River Route, which can take several days to complete. Mount Fitzwilliam Trail offers several backcountry campsites and majestic views following a steep ascent, while the Yellowhead Mountain Trail is a moderate trail with lots of alpine to explore. Be sure to check out the Canadian Rockies Backroad Mapbook for more details on this and other fabulous parks in the Rockies.

Kinney Lake Trail (Map 28/D3) 🏕️🥾🚵🐴🏃🛶🔭

The Kinney Lake Trail begins from the Berg Lake Trail parking area. En route, the trail traverses through old growth cedar along the Robson River and past Knowlton Falls. At Kinney Lake, you are rewarded with a spectacular view of Canada's tallest mountain, Mount Robson. The return trip for this moderate trek is over 10 km (6 mi). This is also the trail to Berg Lake and hikers can wander past the lake to extend the trip.

Moose River Route (Map 29/C3–35/G7) 🏕️🥾⛷️🔭

This difficult backcountry route travels through the heart of Mount Robson Park. The route stretches from Highway 16, east of Moose Lake, all the way to Jasper National Park, deep in the Rocky Mountains. From Highway 16, the route follows along the lush forested shoreline of Moose River eventually breaking into the alpine near Moose Pass on the border of Jasper Park. Depending on how far you wish to travel, this trek could take several days. All travellers should have good maps, compass and the skills to use them. Since the trail can be challenging to follow at times, only experienced and well-equipped hikers should attempt this route.

Mount Fitzwilliam Trail (Map 29/F6) 🏕️🥾⛷️🔭

The trailhead to the Mount Fitzwilliam Trail is located across from the Yellowhead boat launch area on the south side of Highway 16. This scenic mountain route ascends quickly into the backcountry of Mount Fitzwilliam. About half way along the trip, you will find a cluster of backcountry campsites available for overnight use. As you approach the alpine, fantastic views of the Rockies and the Robson Valley can be enjoyed. There are also backcountry campsites available in the alpine areas. In total, the trail to the alpine and back is a 22 km (13.7 mi) journey and is regarded as moderate in difficulty.

Mount Shields Trail (Map 6/G1) 🥾🔭

Off Summs Road, this 8 km (4.8 mi), four hour moderate hike leads to the summit of Mount Shields at 1,789 metres (5,870 ft). The view of the Lower Arrow Lake is fabulous.

Mount St. Thomas Trail (Map 6/G4) 🥾🐴🚵🏃⛷️🔭

There is a road that runs up to near the top of Mount St. Thomas from the parking area at Bonanza Creek Recreation Area. This is a popular year round destination as it is one of the only routes in the area to lead into alpine terrain.

Mount Rose-Swanson Trail (Map 24/C5) 🥾🚵🐴🔭

The trailhead to this well-marked trail system is found at the end of Camberlaine Road to the south of the Salmon River Road. It is considered an easy climb despite gaining 300 m (985 ft) over 10 km (6 mi) to the summit of two mountains. The main attraction to the area is the great view of Armstrong from the top.

Myra Canyon (Map 10/C2) 🥾🐴⛷️🏃🚵🔭

The most popular destination on the very popular Kettle Valley Railway cum Trans Canada Trail route, the trestles have been restored from the devastating fire in 2003. An easy 13 km (7.9 mi) hike or bike can be accessed from either the Little White or Myra Forest Service Roads. In all you will cross up to 18 trestles and through two tunnels, with stunning views of both Myra Canyon (the railway snakes along both sides of the canyon) and the city of Kelowna. It is easy to extend your hike/bike in either direction along the former railway/TCT.

N K & S Railway Trail (Map 14/F3–20/D6) 🥾🚵🐴⛷️🏃🛶🔭

This old railbed covers 75 km (45 mi) from Nicola to Spences Bridge and if followed east to west it is all downhill. From the ginseng farm west of Nicola this beautiful route descends along the scenic Nicola Valley. While the railbed is still fairly unbroken (even the eight bridges over the Nicola are still in good condition), there are three Indian reserves on the route that must be routed around, or permission gained to cycle through. The name is an acronym for the Nicola, Kamloops & Similkameen Coal & Railway Company who originally built the railway line.

Natural Arch Trail (Map 12/F7) 🥾🔭

This impressive 20 metre (65 ft) high, 44 metre (144 ft) long natural archway requires a boat to access the trailhead. From the lake it is a 4.5 km (2.8 mi) steep hike to the arch found 250 m (815 ft) above the Lower Arrow Lake.

Nickel Plate Cross-Country Trails (Map 3/B1) 🏕️🥾🚵⛷️🏃🛶🔭

The Nordic Centre is home to 50 km (30 mi) of ski trails that provide excellent hiking/biking trails after April. In particular, the Okanagan Vista Trail offers a nice 8 km (4.9 mi) loop whereas the Burn Perimeter Trail is a 12 km (7.2 mi) loop. Both trails are best hiked in the late summer, as they are boggy in the earlier part of the season.

MOUNT ROBSON TRAILS

	MAP	DIFFICULTY	LENGTH	ELEVATION GAIN	BIKE	CAMP	FISH	HIKE	HORSE	INTERPRETIVE	SKI	SNOWSHOE	VIEW
Berg Lake Trail	51/A6-B4	Moderate	800 m (2,625 ft)	21 km (13 mi)	•	•		•			•	•	•
Fraser River Nature Trail	51/A6	Easy	Minimal	2 km (1.2 mi)		•		•					•
Hargraves Lake Route	51/B5	Moderate	280 m (920 ft)	2 km (1.2 mi)				•					•
Kinney Lake Trail	51/A6	Moderate	160 m (525 ft)	5 km (3.1 mi)	•	•	•	•			•	•	•
Labrador Tea Trail	48/C2	Easy	Minimal	2.5 km (1.6 mi)				•		•			
Moose River Route	47/F1-51/C3	Difficult	980 m (3,215 ft)	n/a		•		•			•	•	•
Mount Fitzwilliam Trail	48/C2	Moderate	900 m (2,950 ft)	11 km 6.8 mi)		•		•			•	•	•
Mumm Basin Route	51/B4	Moderate	400 m (1,310 ft)	5 km (3 mi)				•					•
Overlander Falls Trail	51/A6	Easy	40 m (130 ft)	5 km (3 mi)				•					•
Portal Lake Trail	48/D1	Easy	Minimal	2 km (1.2 mi)				•					•
Robson River Trail	51/A6	Easy	Minimal	1 km (0.6 mi)				•					•
Snowbird Pass Route	51/B5	Difficult	780 m (2,560 ft)	22 km (13.7 mi)				•					•
Swift Current Creek Trail	50/G6	Easy	260 m (855 ft)	4 km (2.5 mi)				•			•	•	•
Toboggan Falls Route	51/B4	Moderate	360 m (1,180 ft)	6 km (3.7 mi)				•					•
Viewpoint Field Walk	51/A6	Easy	Minimal	1 km (0.6 mi)				•					•
Yellowhead Lake Trail	48/C2	Easy	Minimal	2.5 km (1.6 mi)		•		•		•			
Yellowhead Mountain Trail	48/C2	Moderate	800 m (2,625 ft)	8 km (5 mi)				•					•

North Thompson River Park (Map 33/E1) 🚶‍♂️🏊‍♂️🚻

The North Thompson River Park is located just south of the town of Clearwater off Highway 5. The park lies along the shore of the beautiful river providing a great place for a weekend camping excursion. There are three interconnecting trails visitors can explore from the day use and campground areas. The easy trails make up about 3.6 km (2.2 mi) in length.

Okanagan High Rim Trail (Map 17/E7–D2) 🏕️🚶‍♂️🐎🏊‍♂️🚻

The High Rim Trail has received a lot of attention recently, thanks to a new brochure and trail clearing over the last few years. This moderate backpacking trip can be done as a day or multi night trip. The 55 km (34 mi) trail follows the mountain ridge along the east side of Okanagan Lake and has many viewpoints of the valley. To hike the whole route will take two or three days. Access points such as Oyama, Beaver or Postill Lake Roads east of Lake Country provide shorter stretches. The terminus access points are Cosens Bay in Kalamalka Lake Park in the north and Philpot Road on Highway 33 in the south.

Okanagan Highlands Trail (Map 10/A3–E1) 🏕️🚶‍♂️🏊‍♂️🚻

This trail has seen a lot of work over recent years and now extends from Highway 33 near Mission Creek all the way to Chute Lake over a distance of 68 km (42 mi). Recent improvements include the building of new single track trails, upgrading existing trail surfaces, removing hazardous trees and clearing overgrowth. Along the way hikers will find many viewpoints, campsites, shelters, lakes, creeks and streams. This trail can be broken up into sections for those not looking for a long distance hike. From the Okanagan High Rim trailhead on Highway 33 to McCulloch Lake and the Nordic cabin, it is about 18 km. The next 37 km section follows the trail down to Little White Mountain s in good shape. The trail then tracks west to Big Meadow Lake before connecting with Chute Lake.

Okanagan Mountain Park (Map 9/F3) 🏕️🚶‍♂️🚴‍♂️🐎🏊‍♂️🚻

This wilderness park was devastated by fire in 2003 and is only now beginning to recover. Access is by the Lakeshore Road from the north, Chute Lake Road from the south or by boat to the west. Within the park, there are miles of interconnecting trails with the highlights including canyons, four mountain lakes, sandy beaches, and six marine camping areas. Mountain biking is allowed on all trails, but the terrain is challenging and not intended for beginners. Be sure to bring along plenty of water and your bug repellent.

The main route into the heart of the park from the north is the Divide Lake North Trail. This is the only trail open to horseback riders. It is an 8 km (5 mi) one-way trek following the old microwave road to Divide Lake that can be very scenic in late May to early June because of the wildflowers near the lake. The Wild Horse Canyon Trail is perhaps the most popular trail in the park and starts from the north parking lot. It extends 22 km (13.5 mi) into a spectacular canyon and past a few offshoot trails leading down to the lakeside camping areas. The trail initially dips into the creek draw before climbing the hillside with granite rock bluffs offering impressive vantage points of Okanagan Lake. The Boulder Loop Trail also leads from the north parking lot and covers 5 km along Dead Horse Creek. It is possible to extend the trail along Goode's Basin Trail. From the south the Mountain Goat Trail climbs steadily to Divide Lake. The 10 km (6 mi) return trail is not maintained and the surface in places requires the sure footedness of a mountain goat. Linking Baker Lake with the Wildhorse Canyon Trail, the Frederick Creek Trail is a popular 4 km (2.4 mi) trail.

Boulder Loop Trail

This is an easy 5 km (3 mi) loop that starts at the north parking lot and follows the Boulder Trail to Dead Horse Creek and Golden Mile Road. Panoramic views of Okanagan Lake and downtown Kelowna reward hikers along this trail, which gains 300 m (985 ft) in elevation.

Divide Lake North Trail

This 8 km (5 mi) one-way trail runs from the Rimrock Gate to Divide Lake. This is the only trail in the park that is open to horseback riders and serves as the main route into the heart of the park. This trail is particularly scenic in late May and early June when there are plenty of blooming wildflowers. Expect an overall elevation gain of 980 m (3,215 ft).

Frederick Creek Trail

Accessed from the south parking lot, a moderate 4 km (2.5 mi) one-way trail climbs 560 m (1,840 ft) to Baker Lake from the Wild Horse Canyon Trail. Adding in the Wild Horse section, the trail runs 10 km (6 mi) to the lake. The trail can be hard to track, but is the preferred route into the heart of the park from the south since the Divide Lake South Trail is permanently closed.

Goode's Basin Trail

Stretching between Dead Horse Creek and the Pinnacles, this is a moderate 2.5 km (1.6 mi) one-way trail is accessed from the junction of the Boulder Loop and the Wild Horse Canyon Trail. It climbs 280 m (920 ft) to the Pinnacles.

Mountain Goat Trail

From the south parking lot a steep, difficult 5 km (3 mi) one-way trail leads to Divide Lake. As the name would suggest, sure footing is necessary along this route, which gains 540 m (1,180 ft).

Wild Horse Canyon Trail

This is perhaps the most popular trail in the park and starts from the north parking lot. It extends 22 km (13.5 mi) into a spectacular canyon and past a few offshoot trails leading down to the lakeside camping areas (Buchan Bay, Commando Bay and Goode's Creek). The trail initially dips into the creek draw before climbing the hillside with granite rock bluffs offering impressive vantage points of Okanagan Lake, including from a short 1 km branch called the Rim Trail. Expect an overall elevation gain of 560 m (1,840 ft).

Orchard Lake Trails (Map 28/E4) 🚶‍♂️🐎🚻

The Orchard Lake area features open forests and meadows that are popular with horseback riders. There are fifteen trails in the area, all between 5 km and 7 km (3–4 mi) long. Some of the trail names and destinations include Loon Lake, Range Gate, Chalaforchie Lake Loop and Coyote Lake.

Oyama Lookout Trail (Map 17/D3) 🚶‍♂️🚻

From the junction at Oyama Lake Road, this easy 9 km (5.6 mi) roundtrip walk takes you along a deteriorating road beyond Damer Lake before the trail branches left to the transmitter and lookout. From the lookout, there is an impressive view of the north Okanagan Valley. Overall the elevation gain is 150 m (490 ft). Allow four hours to complete.

OKANAGAN MOUNTAIN PARK TRAILS

	MAP	DIFFICULTY	LENGTH	ELEVATION GAIN	BIKE	CAMP	FISH	HIKE	HORSE	SNOWSHOE	VIEW
Baker Lake Trail	Map 9/G3	Easy	2 km (1.2 mi)	240 m (785 ft)	•	•	•	•	•	•	•
Boulder Loop Trail	Map 9/G2	Easy	5 km (3 mi)	300 m (985 ft)	•	•		•		•	•
Buchan Bay Trail	Map 9/E3	Moderate	1.5 km (0.9 mi)	140 m (460 ft)		•		•		•	
Commando Bay Trail	Map 9/E3	Moderate	2 km (1.2 mi)	140 m (460 ft)		•		•		•	
Divide Lake North Trail	Map 9/G2	Moderate	8 km (5 mi)	980 m (3,215 ft)	•			•	•	•	
Frederick Creek Trail	Map 9/G3	Moderate	4 km (2.5 mi)	560 m (1,840 ft)				•		•	•
Gemmill Lake Trail	Map 9/G3	Easy	2 km (1.2 mi)	160 m (525 ft)		•		•		•	
Goode's Basin Trail	Map 9/F2	Moderate	2.5 km (1.6 mi)	280 m (920 ft)		•		•		•	•
Goode's Creek Trail	Map 9/E3	Difficult	3 km (1.9 mi)	180 m (590 ft)		•		•		•	
Lookout Trail	Map 9/G3	Easy	0.5 km (0.3 mi)	40 m (130 ft)		•		•		•	•
Mountain Goat Trail	Map 9/G3	Difficult	5 km (3 mi)	540 m (1,770 ft)				•		•	•
Old CN Trail	Map 9/G2	Easy	3 km (1.9 mi)	360 m (1,180 ft)	•			•		•	
Wild Horse Canyon Trail	Map 9/F2	Difficult	22 km (13.5 mi)	560 m (1,840 ft)	•	•		•		•	•

Packsaddle Creek Loop (Map 47/B3)
The Packsaddle Creek loop is 6 km (3.6 mi) out and back, gaining 150 m (500 ft) of elevation. This is a pleasant hike at most times, but especially in spring, when the creek is in full run-off. The trail is found about 5 km down the Canoe Forest Service Road. From the parking lot you can hike 200 metres along the main road to the far side of Packsaddle Creek or along an old logging road that leaves from the back of the parking area.

Paradise Trail (Map 49/B1)
This trail can be found off the north side of Mountainview Road north of McBride. Look for a small parking area that marks the trailhead to this moderate 14 km (8.7 mi) route. The trail provides great views of the Rocky Mountain Trench as it ascends 1,480 m (4,855 ft) up Mount Monroe.

Parbury Falls Trail (Map 43/B6)
From the Mud Lake Recreation Site, the Parbury Falls Trail is wet and over-grown, but people can still traverse east along the north shore of the lake to the sight of Parbury Falls. The trail is about 2.5 km (1.6 mi) in length.

Park Hill Area Trails (Map 30/C7)
Found just north of Salmon Arm near the community of Canoe, the relatively new trail system on Park Hill offers hikers, bikers and snowshoers up to 5 km (3 mi) of trails. These trails can take you from the shores of Shuswap Lake at Canoe Beach up to the western and eastern slopes of Park Hill. The trails are of various lengths and difficulty; so there is something for everyone here.

Peachland Lookout Ridge Trail (Map 9/D2)
Part of the Peachland trail system, this trail starts 8.7 km up Princeton Avenue. Offering a panorama view of Ok Lake, it is an ideal half day trek for hikers, snowshoers, cyclists and horseback riders. For those not interested in the entire loop, keep right at the first fork for the 2 km climb to the lookout.

Pennask Lake Trails (Map 15/G5)
Linking a variety of lakes in and around the Pennask Plateau, these short trails are frequented by anglers in the summer and snowmobilers in the winter. Access is from Mellin Forest Service Road to the north or Pennask Lake to the south.

Peter Lake Trail (Map 6/E2)
This difficult 5.4 km (3.3 mi) trail starts at the railway crossing 2 km north of Farron outside Gladstone Provincial Park's east boundary. From here, the trail climbs along a small creek. Actually, climb is not the right word, as you go up and down repeatedly over a series of hummocks. After a while, the trail begins climbing steadily to Other Pass before descending to Peter Lake. Watch out for devils club closer to the lake. It is possible to camp at the lake.

Phoenix Forest Trails (Map 5/G5)
This series of trails and old roads dissect the Phoenix Interpretive Forest between Greenwood and Grand Forks. The longest trail–the Outside Loop–is about 31 km (19 mi) long. These trails hook up with the Boundary Trail to the north and the Marshall Lake Ski Trails. Be careful when exploring the old mine works and please stay out of private property in the area. Another popular trail is the Phoenix Wagon Road Trail. Look for the trailhead to this old wagon road at the sharp bend near the first bridge over Twin Creek on the Greenwood side of the Phoenix Road. At the time of this writing, only 1.5 km (0.9 mi) of this historic route had been cleared, although there is an alternate trail that climbs steeply to the right where a fence currently blocks the route. Heading left to parallel the creek will bring you to an old forestry road, which in turn will bring you back to Phoenix Road.

Pincushion Mountain Trail (Map 9/E2)
From the end of Ponderosa Drive in Peachland, this scenic trail leads 3.5 km (2.2 mi) return to the summit. In all you climb over 390 m (1,280 ft). Many continue north along the ridge north of the summit for an additional 3.5 km, 200 m (655 ft) venture.

Pinnacle Lake Trail (Map 19/C2)
The Pinnacles are a popular destination with those in the know; towering spires with lots of options for scrambling. The trail to beautiful Pinnacles Lake is one of the main access routes into the area and is about 4.5 km one-way from the trailhead, gaining 450 m (1,465 ft) to the lake.

Placer Lake Trail (Map 2/B6)
The trailhead is found at Placer Lake, which is a challenge to access in its own right, and makes its way to the Trapper Lake Trail. At only 2.3 km (1.4 mi) one-way this trail is not overly long but it is a hard hike. Most of the hike up from the lake is at a grade of 25%-35% climbing 390 m (1,280 ft) until you reach the alpine meadows surrounded by snowcapped mountains. Camping can be found at Placer Lake and along the Trapper Lake Trail.

Polecutter Trail (Map 2/F3)
This network of trails passes through historic logging and mining sites. While you will cover about 4 km (2.4 mi) to do a basic loop, there are many old logging roads and trails to explore. The area has open rangeland mixed with stands of aspen, fir and pine.

Postill Mountain Bike Trails (Map 17/C5)
Once the domain of hardcore mountain bikers, this area is being overrun with ATVers and four-wheel drive enthusiasts. However, hidden amongst the endless off-road trails is one of the most amazing manmade mountain bike berms ever created. It has fallen into disuse, but riders can still sample some of the stunts and the small network of difficult trails in the area. Unless you're comfortable with hardcore riding, give this one a pass.

Postill-Swalwell Lake Trails (Map 17/E5)
A 65 km (40 mi) network of trails extends around Postill Lake and Swalwell/Beaver Lake with one trail (Postill Lake Trail) connecting the two trail networks. The trails range in length from 5 km to 11 km and are accessed by the Postill Lake or Beaver Lake Roads.

Potts Farm Trail (Map 32/E3)
This easy 14 km (8.6 mi) round trip is located at the west end of Lac des Roches and leads past a large fir tree to a series of ponds and Grizzly Lake. The trailhead can be found on the north side of Highway 24, east of Gerald Crescent. The overall elevation gain is 75 m (245 ft). Visitors can enjoy hiking, or snowshoeing and cross-country skiing in winter. Be wary of thin ice in winter.

Predator Ridge Trails (Map 17/B2)
The famed golf course and resort area offers trail enthusiasts endless trails to explore. Around the new Sparkling Hills Resort area, the cross-country ski trails offer year round enjoyment. The 7.8 km (4.8 mi) system loops around the golf course. Further afield, trails start in Ellison Park and lead up to the ridge creating scenic loops in all directions. The long term plan is to link Lake Country in the south with Vernon in the north along this ridge system.

Pukeashun Trail (Map 30/B1–35/B7)
From the Kwikoit Creek Forest Service Road, this 13 km (7.9 mi) moderate hike takes you to the open meadows of a seemingly endless alpine. The area is popular with horseback riders, guide outfitters and, in winter, snowmobilers.

Queest Mountain Trail (Map 30/G4–31/A4)
This trail runs through sub-alpine meadows that have many wildflowers in July as well as excellent views. The trailhead is found just past the 14 km marker on the Queest Mountain Forest Service Road. It leads 12 km (7.5 mi) to a snowmobile chalet and onto the lookout tower on Queest Mountain. It is possible to camp or stay in the chalet and explore the alpine area.

R.W. Starratt Wildlife Sanctuary Trail (Map 47/A3)
The sanctuary lies just south of the town of Valemount off the east side of Highway 5. The sanctuary helps protect an important tract of wetland habitat, vital for waterfowl. From the parking area, the trail traverses 7 km (4.3 mi) providing information plaques along the route to help educate visitors on the wetland and its wildlife. The trail passes through a mix of forest and at times along the dyke system where open views of the wetland can be seen. There are also two lookout towers along the trail.

Raft Peak Trail (Map 38/A6)
Follow the Raft Creek Forest Service Road as far as possible (no motor vehicles allowed past km 14) and continue on foot along the road, which shortly turns into a foot trail through a bit of forest before emerging into the alpine. The route up is straightforward but steep, making for a roughly 5 km (3 mi) return hike climbing 565 m (1,855 ft). From the rocky summit you can enjoy 360° views of the surrounding area.

Rainbow Falls Trail (Map 25/G4)
The old trailhead leading into Monashee Provincial Park is being restored beyond the current trail that leads to the scenic falls. Some scrambling might be involved to make the 12 km (7.2 mi) one-way trek to Spectrum Lake. Once you reach the park, many backcountry fishing and camping opportunities await you.

Rainbow Trail System (Map 14/B5) 🏕🥾🚵🐎🚻

The Rainbow Trail system is a challenging trail system developed by the Endurance Riders Association of BC. There are over 160 km (100 mi) of trails in the area, with up to 2,700 m (8,860 ft) of vertical gain. Along the way, you will ride logging roads, cow paths and game trails. There are eight trails, each marked with its own colour (thus the name of the system). The longest trail is the 53 km (33 mi) Orange Trail, while the shortest trail is the 8 km (5 mi) Short White Trail.

Ravine Edge Trail (Map 17/D2) 🥾🚻

Offering views of Kalamalka Park and the Camels Hump, this 7.5 km (4.7 mi) loop trail starts from King Edward Forest Service Road outside of Vernon. The trail actually drops over 165 m (540 ft) in elevation.

Rea Lake Circuit (Map 28/B3) 🏕🥾🛶

This 12 km (7.3 mi) moderate wilderness circuit leads past several remote wilderness lakes. The trail is generally well marked but can be tough to follow in places. The circuit also links up with the Tsintsunko Lake and Master Subalpine Trails to extend your journey. The trailhead is found at the end of Bob Lake Road or Rea Lake Road.

Reinecker Creek Trails (Map 30/D7) 🥾🚵🚶🚻

There are several different trail options along Reinecker Creek, which drains into Shuswap Lake at Herald Park. The most popular is the short Margaret Falls Trail that leads to an impressive canyon. Also starting from the park is the 3.4 km (2.1 mi) return Upper Canyon Trail. It is recommended to start this moderate trail on the steeper east side of the creek, where several vantage points offer nice views over Shuswap Lake and the park. Continuing north, the Reinecker Creek East Trail allows for a 13 km (8.1 mi) loop that climbs about 350 m (1,150 ft) before following an old road down the west side of the creek. This old road is called the Reinecker Creek West Trail and is a multi-use trail that is popular with mountain bikers and ATVers. It is possible to continue past the north end of the trail system on an unmarked route that connects to the forest service road into the White Lake Valley. Mountain bikers can avoid the steep lower sections by accessing the trail from the Bastion Mountain Forest Service Road. Follow the signs to the trailhead.

Riddle Road [Three Blind Mice] Trails (Map 9/G5–10/A5) 🚵🚻

A series of mountain bike trails are found at the end of the steep Riddle Road, which in turn is found north of Penticton on the Naramata Road. From the gate at the end of the road, a great single track trail is yours to explore. It is possible to pick your way north to Naramata while you enjoy the terrific views of Okanagan Lake and the spring wildflowers. Due to the maze of trails in the area, the nickname Three Blind Mice is appropriate.

Proper footwear, such as quality hiking boots, can be the difference between a great hike and a painful struggle.

Rim Rocks Trail (Map 17/E2) 🥾🚵🚻

The Rim Rocks Trail follows the edge of a unique rock pit where you will find spires of volcanic rock towering over an almost alien landscape. The hike in is only 2 km (1.2 mi) along an old road off the King Edward Forest Service Road, but there is some moderate scrambling around the rocky landscape, including a trail through the "Eye of the Needle." It is also possible to do a 6 km (3.7 mi) loop over to Baldy Mountain. This loop climbs about 170 m (560 ft).

Ripley Lake Trail (Map 3/G3) 🥾

This 5 km (3 mi) trail follows the Ripley Lake shoreline, but there are also many old roads in the area to explore. It is possible (though difficult) to make your way south to Madden Lake.

Rock Ovens/Adra Tunnel (Map 9/G4) 🥾🚵🐎🚻

If you want to explore the history of the Kettle Valley Railway, this 20 km (12 mi) section of abandoned track is a good choice. Many hikers/bikers begin where Smethurst Road meets the railgrade and work their way up past Adra and Little Tunnels to the Rock Ovens. Despite the gentle grade, you actually climb almost 900 m (2,955 ft) with excellent views of Okanagan Lake along the way. Unfortunately, the 484 metre (1,590 ft) long Adra Tunnel is sealed off because it is partly collapsed. Cyclists often continue past Chute Lake to the trestle bridges of the spectacular Myra Canyon.

Roderick Haig-Brown Park (Map 29/E5) 🥾🚵🚤🚶🚻

Within the provincial park are 26 km (16 mi) of well-developed trails, mostly along both sides of Adams River from Adams Lake to the Shuswap Lake. The trails are generally flat and easy to follow. The area is famous for its Sockeye Salmon spawning beginning in October with the peak years being every 4 years (2018, 2022, etc.) and there is a wheelchair accessible trail to the viewing platform. Unfortunately, the popular Bear Creek Flume Trail is currently closed due to several bridges being washed out or in a state of disrepair.

Roscoe Lake Trails (Map 21/B7) 🥾🚵🚻

The trail around Roscoe Lake is well-marked (with yellow triangles), has little elevation gain and is well maintained. It is a 4 km (2.4 mi) easy walk through an immature pine stand that circles the lake. Near the south end of the lake, a 2.5 km trail climbs the bluff for a nice view.

Rose Valley Trails (Map 16/G7) 🥾🚵🚻

The popular Rose Valley Reservoir can be reached via several trailheads, including at Rose Valley Elementary, on West Lake Road just north of Peak Point Road, and from the very end of West Kelowna Road. Some popular trails in this system are the Rose Valley Lake Loop (15 km/9 mi long), Rose Valley Regional Park Trail (13 km/8 mi long), and the Rose Valley Trail (7 km/4.5 mi long). For mountain bikers, these trails are considered moderate in difficulty – there are no stunts but there are some steep climbs and drop-offs. Hikers can enjoy the panoramic views and check out caves formed by ancient volcanic activity.

Round Lake Trail (Map 27/F2) 🏕🥾🛶

From the 8 km mark on the Deadman Creek Road, this 3 km (1.8 mi) one-way hike leads through a second growth Lodgepole pine stand with little elevation gain. While it is not a long trail, it is seldom used and can be quite difficult to follow the old blaze marks.

Rubberhead Mountain Bike Trails (Map 30/D7) 🥾🚵🚶🚻

Mainly used by mountain bikers, this trail system includes almost 20 trails including a variety of downhill options for advance riders. From steep and rooty to open trails, this system has something for everyone. The 110 Forest Service Road snakes through the entire system, offering access to most of the trails over a 9 km (5.5 mi) distance. Supermans Trail is one of the longest in this trail group, zig zagging in a steady down or uphill for 5 km (3 mi).

Saddle Mountain Trail (Map 43/B7) 🥾🚻

Found just east of the town of Blue River, the Smoke Creek Forest Service Road leads to a rough branch road leading up the mountain. Depending how far you can drive, the trail is about 6.5 km (4 mi) one-way climbing 980 m (3,215 ft). Most of the elevation gain occurs within the first 2 km, with the majority of this trail being a ridge walk to an alpine lake.

Sandner Creek Trail (Map 6/D3) 🏕🥾🚵🐎🛶🚻

Give yourself the better part of a day (or two) to explore the old homestead and unique geological formations that are accessed by this trail that follows Sandner Creek. It begins at the north end of Christina Lake and extends some 18 km (11 mi) return along the valley bottom. Please respect private property at the north end of the lake.

Scotch Creek Lookout Trail & Hlina Loop (Map 30/A4) 🥾🚵🐎🚶🚻

Part of the Shuswap Trails network, this trail starts off Scotch Creek Hlina Forest Service Road, which leads north from Leopold Road. Currently the 4 km (2.5 mi) trail loops through a mixed forest to a fantastic viewpoint over the lake. Those wanting to hike more of a route rather than a trail can explore the Hlina Loop. This 5.5 km (3.4 mi) loop is for experienced hikers with good route finding skills. This loop can be found at the northwest corner of the Scotch Creek Lookout Trail.

Selwyn Traverse Trail (Map 47/B3) 🥾🚻

This 11 km (6.7 mi) trail climbs 150 m (500 ft) if hiked from north to south and about three times that if hiked the opposite direction. The trail walks along the toes of the Rockies just east of Valemount. For the more hardcore hiker, it is possible to make your way up to McKirdy Meadow along the trail described earlier.

Seven Sisters Trail (Map 28/E1–33/D7) 🥾🐎🚻

The Seven Sisters Trail is a 19 km (12 mi) trail over Mount McGregor between the Westsyde Road and Bonaparte Road. You gain about 280 m (920 ft) to the high point. Hikers usually turn around at the viewpoint at the summit. There is also an extensive series of horseback trails in the area.

Seymour Lookout Trail (Map 35/G4) 🥾🚻

To reach this former forestry lookout requires a steep, difficult 3.8 km (2.3 mi) one-way grunt up a poorly maintained trail through the sub-alpine. The trailhead is found at the 66 km marker on the Ratchford Creek Forest Service Road.

Shannon Beach Park Trail (Map 30/D4)

Accessed off Eagles Bay Road, two short loop trails climb uphill from this popular beach area for a total hiking distance of 2 km. The easy-to-access trails are popular with hikers, mountain bikers, snowshoers and wildlife viewers.

Shannon Lake Trail (Map 9/F1–16/F7)

Do not be confused by the name, this grueling hike actually leads from Shannon Heights Place up to a vantage point high above the lake. The trail climbs close to 600 m (1,970 ft) over 3 km (1.9 mi) one-way. Enjoy the view before looping back down along Drinkwater Creek.

Sheridan Lake Trails (Map 32/A3)

At the west end of Sheridan Lake is a nest of old roads and multi-use trails. Access to these trails is off the Boulanger Road, which in turn is off West Sheridan Lake Road. These trails are used by snowmobilers in winter and by most everyone else in summer. There are over 200 km (130 mi) of trails here (in truth, mostly old roads), not all of which are worthwhile for hikers unless looking for exercise.

Shorts Creek Canyon Trail (Map 16/F3)

From the parking lot on a spur road of the Whiteman Creek Road, this is a 10.5 km (6.5 mi) return trail. The moderate hike gains 240 m (785 ft) and follows a well-developed trail along the edge of the Short Creek Canyon. After viewing the canyon, you can continue down the creek to the Westside Road near Fintry for an additional 8 km (4.9 mi) one-way.

Silver Daisy Mountain Trail (Map 1/B5)

It is possible to do this 20 km (12 mi) trail up to the summit of Silver Daisy Mountain in about 9 hours. The trail starts at the Sumallo Grove Picnic Area off Highway 3, crosses the Skagit River and switchbacks its way up a steep hill to a saddle, which offers great views of the Skagit Valley. From here, the trail continues through a meadow to the 2,040 metre (6,690 ft) summit, gaining 1,435 m (4,700 ft) along the way. Part of the trail follows an old mining tram. The trail is best left for late summer/early fall.

Silver Star Mountain (Map 24/F6)

Silver Star Mountain provides excellent hiking opportunities in July through September from the top of the ski lift (which can be ridden in the summer months for a fee). The trails, which are found along the ski runs and access roads, provide a chance to walk through beautiful wildflowers in the sub-alpine. In summer, portions of the mountain are converted into a lift-accessed mountain bike park. There are also extensive cross-country ski trails that make fine biking and snowshoeing options as well. One popular area is around the Knoll, which links the village with the Silver Queen Lift.

Skaha Bluff Trails (Map 9/G7–10/A7)

This area has long been a top mountain climbing destination, and with the addition of the parking area and easier access, it is now a hot spot for hiking and mountain biking. Access the parking lot by turning onto Smythe Road off of Lakeside Road and following it to the end. For mountain bikers, there are a lot of challenging black-diamond trails, including the 3.5 km (2 mi) long Whips and Chains and the 3 km long DZL. Rock Oven connects the system to an exit at the Eastside Road Boat Launch over a distance of 6 km (4 mi) and a 1,055 m (3,460 ft) descent.

Skihist Provincial Park Trails (Map 13/B2)

From the top of the campground, access can be found to approximately 8 km of trails that provide excellent views of the canyon and the surrounding mountains. A popular section of trail leads to Gladwin Lookout where mountain goats can often be seen navigating the steep hillside opposite the lookout (allow one and a half hours round trip). Another section loops along the Cariboo Wagon Road and takes two to three hours to complete.

Skmana Lake Trails (Map 29/D6)

At Skmana Lake off the Loakin-Bear Creek Road, there are 10 km (6 mi) of groomed cross-country ski trails. During the off-season, the trails offer a stroll or mountain bike ride around the marshy lake that provides the ideal setting for wildlife viewing.

Skoatl Point Trail (Map 28/A2)

Most people start this trek to the dramatic volcanic cone in Bonaparte Provincial Park from the Windy Lake Recreation Site. From here it is about 12 km (7.3 mi) return. The actual trailhead is found northwest of the lake cutting the trail distance to 9 km return. The trail skirts by Adler Lake halfway to the cone.

Skull Mountain Trail System (Map 28/E2)

Found on the northwest side of the Thompson River between Barrière and McLure, there are 34 km (21 mi) of trails in this area. The trails are mostly easy, but there are a few stiff climbs for non-motorized recreation only. The area was burned out in the 2003 wildfire and the burned trees have been removed, meaning that the views from here are terrific. In the heart of summer, though, the area can be extremely hot and offers little cover from the heat.

Skyline II Trail (Map 1/B7–D7)

The western trailhead to the Skyline II Trail is accessed off the Silver Skagit Road at the parking lot right north of Ross Lake. The trail leads 26 km (16 mi) from the valley bottom to an alpine ridge at Camp Mowich in Manning Provincial Park. Along the way, the trail climbs steeply, gaining 1,310 m (4,300 ft) to the ridge. The hike initially begins in a forest and then crosses several creeks before proceeding into some sub-alpine meadows and then along the ridge. Part of the historic Centennial Trail, it is possible to continue on to Lightning Lake via the Skyline I Trail.

Small River Trail (Map 50/E5)

Northwest of Tête Jaune Cache, this trail follows an old logging road north into the Small River Valley. Logging practices are visible along the way, but overall, this moderate 40+ km (25+ mi) route offers some nice scenery. Near the upper reaches of the route, some great views of Mount Langstaff and the surrounding glaciers can be seen. The stream may difficult to cross, as several of the bridges have been washed out. Most turn around at the 18 km mark where the bridge is out.

Smith Creek Trails (Map 9/F1–16/F7)

Located in Westbank off the Old Okanagan Highway, the Smith Creek area offers some great intermediate cross-country riding. The main loop is one of the few in the area that climbs up along a single track trail instead of an old road, weaving its way up the mountain. The last uphill section is quite steep and may need to be walked, while the downhill can be quite fast, with sections of loose gravel that can be dangerous if you don't control your speed. Other trails include Gruel-Dump, Santa's Revenge and the 2.5 km long Holy Pail (a 430 m/1,410 ft climb).

Snehumption Creek Trail (Map 3/D7–E7)

This trail follows Snehumption Creek deep into the heart of the Snowy Protected area just inside the Canada/US border. The trail is not well maintained and is difficult to follow at points as it climbs into the open sub-alpine on the south slopes of Snowy Mountain. It would be possible to come in on this trail and out on the Snowy Mountain Trail, though there would be a fairly long road walk to end the hike. The trailhead is found off the Chopaka Road, about 3 km (1.8 mi) before the US border.

Snowy Mountain Loop (Map 3/A5–E6)

This route is popular with experienced backcountry horse riders. Most people on foot hit the alpine around Snowy Mountain from the east. This route follows the Ewart Creek Trail to the Centennial Trail, then along animal paths and roughly defined trails south, then east, to Snowy Mountain, looping past Newby Lake on the way. There are plenty of cow paths in the area and getting off the right route is easy. Riders can do the loop in three days, but to really enjoy the scenery six days is recommended.

Snowy Mountain Trail (Map 3/D7)

This 12 km (7.3 mi) hike begins along a well-maintained trail, but ends with a scramble to the top of the mountain through alpine meadows. From the top, you will be rewarded with an excellent view of pristine wilderness between the mountain and the US border. It is possible to extend the hike along the routes described above.

South Canoe Trails (Map 24/D2)

This network of trails is accessed by 10th Avenue, southeast of Salmon Arm. One of the most popular trail networks in the area, there are close to 40 trails to choose from and new ones being added regularly. From this trail system, it is possible to link up with the 40 km (25 mi) long Larch Hills Traverse.

South Okanagan Grasslands (Map 3/F5–4/A7)

There are no developed trails in this park, but there is a series of old routes, roads and trails that are heavily used. Probably the most popular trail in this park is the Mount Kobau-Testalinden Trail; a 5 km (3 mi) trail (actually an access road for the fire lookout) that circles the mountain then climbs to a fire lookout, where there are 360 degree views of the surrounding area. There are other trails, including a 6 km (3.6 mi) trail which follows old mining roads through the park, past an old mine (which has been covered up). There are also old roads over Black Mountain and four-wheel drive trails leading up Kruger Mountain.

Spaist Mountain Trail (Map 20/G7)

This 2.6 km (1.6 mi) one-way trail is found at the western end of Pimainus Lake and heads up Spaist Mountain for an elevation gain of 320 m (1,050 ft). The trail is extremely steep in sections; fixed ropes are in place for assistance.

Spanish Lake Trail (Map 37/B1)

From the end of the Spanish Creek Forest Service Road, it is necessary to cross the creek and follow an overgrown road to the actual trailhead. From here, the easy trail leads about 5 km (3 mi) to the site of ancient lava beds and the extinct Flourmills Volcano.

Spion Kopje Mountain Trails (Map 17/B4)

Pronounced Spine-cop, a new trail system has been marked by the local hiking club providing a variety of trails leading up and around this popular mountain in the heart of Lake Country. To cut down on the elevation gain, the system is best accessed from the new hiking trailheads at the end of Alex Drive in the Lakes Subdivision off Oceola Road or off Moberly to Ravenridge Road on the road to Carrs Landing. The trails follow old roads and single track trails that climb to the summit for a great view of the four lakes that make up Lake Country. Hikers should allow a couple hours to reach the summit.

Spooner Creek Trails (Map 6/D5)

There are several mountain bike trails around Spooner Creek that can be accessed off the Stewart Creek Road at the southwest end of Christina Lake. The Spooner Creek Trail is a difficult 4.3 km biking or moderate hiking trail that follows the creek down to West Lake Drive and offers some nice views over Christina Lake. The trail is accessed from a trailhead near the 9 km mark of Stewart Creek Road and loses about 580 m (1,900 ft) in elevation. Across the road is the short, 600 metre There's Willis Trail, while to the south the Boris and Upper Boris Trail offer about 3.4 km of trail to explore. The TNT Trail connects with Highland Road and covers about 4.5 km of fairly steep terrain. Linking TNT with Boris is the 1.2 km Wheel Chair Trail.

Stake Lake Ski Trails (Map 22/A5)

One of the more popular mountain biking destinations near Kamloops, there are a total of 45 km (28 mi) of trails to explore. The roller coaster trail network offers good riding for all abilities.

State Lake Trail (Map 11/C5)

This is an easy 1.5 km trail from the trailhead at the 9.5 km mark on the Sandrift/Barth Creek Forest Service Roads. The trail leads to a small tenting site with a toilet at the north end of the lake.

Stinky Lake Trail (Map 3/G5)

Winding its way up the backside of Oliver Mountain, this trail follows old mining roads across mostly open grasslands over a distance of 5 km (3 mi), with a 260 m (850 ft) elevation gain. There are some great views over Oliver and it is possible to descend to town near the water tower.

Strawberry Creek Trail (Map 4/B7)

Accessed from the west end of Osoyoos, this trail starts out along a sidewalk before joining an old gravel road that winds its way up a hillside, eventually narrowing to become an honest-to-goodness trail. The route passes an abandoned mine, then back into town over its 6 km (4 mi) distance, gaining 120 m (395 ft) in elevation along the way.

Sugar Mountain Trail (Map 25/G5)

An old four-wheel drive road heads up to an abandoned fire lookout on Sugar Mountain. From the junction with the Kate Creek Forest Service Road this is a steep 10.5 km (6.5 mi) one-way route that is more often explored by ATVers. The spectacular views from the top help compensate for the tough 1,230 m (4,035 ft) elevation gain. Beware of bears.

Sugarloaf Mountain Trail (Map 16/G2)

Access is off of Sugarloaf Forest Service Road, which branches north from Westside Road. To reach the summit of Sugarloaf requires a 350 m (1,500 ft) climb from the trailhead. The 4.6 km (2.9 mi) round trip follows an old skid road and well-marked trail to a deteriorating lookout platform overlooking Okanagan Lake.

Sun Peaks Trails (Map 29/B5)

While this area is best known for its downhill skiing, in summer, a series of lift accessed downhill mountain bike trails can be accessed off the Sunburst Express. Some people think the lift is cheating, but most riders can bomb down the trails and back up a couple of times before the die-hards have finished grunting their way to the top. In all there are over 40 km (25 mi) of single track trails that access 610 m (2,000 ft) of vertical along with stunts and obstacles to enjoy. And if that is not enough, there are ten hiking trails, including the difficult Tod Peak Trail and four trails that are open to horseback riding, including the easy village loop and the difficult Top of the World Trail.

Sunset Properties Trail (Map 17/B2)

Named after the subdivision in the area, these popular local trails are well marked and not difficult to follow. Depending on what route you take, it is possible to string together over 6 km (3.7 mi) of trails to explore (longer if you link with the trails along Predator Ridge). The views of Okanagan Lake are fantastic.

Swakum Mountain Trails (Map 14/E1)

The slopes below Swakum Mountain are home to 78 km (48 mi) of interconnecting trails and logging roads for the snowmobilers in the winter. In the summer, Helmer Road is closed to vehicle travel but the area does offer a hike-in campsite and opportunities to fish and explore. Helmer Road is accessed from Exit 315 on the Coquihalla Connector.

Swift Alpine Trails (Map 47/A2)

The most popular route is the road that climbs up to the former site of the Valemount Lookout Tower. Past the viewpoint are picturesque alpine meadows that are accessed on the McKirdy Meadows Trail. The Swift Alpine Trail can range from 5 km (3.1 mi) to 15 km (9.3 mi) in length, depending on where you begin and how far you wish to travel.

Syphon Falls Trail (Map 24/B1)

This 3 km (1.9 mi) return trip gains 140 m (460 ft) as you make your way to the scenic falls and up Gayle Creek. This trail is found northwest of Salmon Arm off of 40th Avenue or 60th Street.

Tahaetkun Mountain Trail (Map 16/D2)

In the mountains west of Okanagan Lake, this is another of a series of peaks that area hikers explore. Depending on how far you can drive up the side road leading off the Whiteman Creek Forest Service Road system, the trail is close to 4.5 km (2.8 mi) return. You climb about 290 m (950 ft) in elevation.

Tappen Bluffs Trail (Map 30/A7)

Found about 2.5 km down the Skimikin Lake Road, this trail follows a forestry road to the nice vantage point over Tappen Valley and Salmon Arm. The trail is 4 km (2.5 mi) one-way and all but the last short section can be ridden on a bike or ATV. Those looking for a longer ride can hook up with the Skimikin Lake Trails.

Teepee Lakes Trail (Map 8/D2)

Found north of Bankier, the trio of lakes that make up the Teepee Lakes are accessible by a looping 12 km (7.5 mi) trail with minimal elevation gain. Ostensibly for anglers to access the lakes, the trail is also used by hikers.

Terrace Mountain Trail (Map 16/F4)

The highest peak in the area, the lookout road is quickly deteriorating and is best walked or biked. From the summit, you get a great view of Okanagan Lake. A major forest fire in 2009 has affected the area and created a lot of burned trees to be wary of; exercise extreme caution, especially on windy days.

Terry Fox Trail (Map 46/G2–47/A1)

This moderate 12 km (7.5 mi) trail ascends Mount Terry Fox eventually reaching the scenic alpine area below the peak. Look for the access road off the east side of Highway 5, south of Tête Jaune Cache. The trail and provincial park were established in 1982 as a permanent natural monument to the Canadian hero, Terry Fox.

Texas Creek Trail (Map 6/E5)

From the Texas Creek boat launch on Christina Lake, this 2 km trail heads north to a footbridge over Texas Point. The trail joins the Deer Point/Troy Creek Trail for a much longer extension. Bikers will find some sections a little tricky, but hikers will have no problems.

The Harpolds Trails (Map 6/C6)

Baby Harpold and Papa Harpold are home to some of the best mountain biking in Grand Forks and there is a maze of difficult mountain bike trails around and over these hills. Expect to take at least an hour to ride any of these routes, or just spend the day exploring. The trailhead is found off Highway 3 at Sand Creek Road (near the Welcome to Grand Forks Sign). Depending on your route, it could be a 12 km return ride gaining 465 m (1,525 ft).

Thimble Mountain Trails (Map 6/A5)

This trail system begins at about the 3 km mark on the Knob Hill Forest Service Road, which is found to the south of Wilgress Lake on Highway 3. The hiking trail up Thimble is an 8 km (5 mi) one-way trail which ascends

510 m (1,675 ft) as it makes its way up to and around the base of Thimble Mountain. This trail is popular both with hikers and mountain bikers and offers great views of the Granby River Valley from a lookout a little way past Thimble Mountain.

Thomas Hayes Ecological Trail (Map 24/C6) 🚶

There are over 4 km (2.5 mi) of trails in the ecological reserve found south of Otter Lake. The easy trail system has little elevation gain making it a nice shoulder season hike.

Trapper Lake Trail (Map 2/B6) 🏕🚶🐴🎣🚵

This difficult 20 km (12 mi) trail extends from a branch road of the Pasayten River Forest Service Road into some remote wilderness area to the west of Cathedral Provincial Park, gaining 1,220 m (4,000 ft) along the way. The historic pack trail once led from Similkameen Falls, but logging activity has made it easier to drive further up the valley. At Trapper Lake, the trail connects with the Centennial and Border Lake Trails (see above), while further south Flat Top Mountain and Placer Lake are accessible. Many hikers use Trapper Lake as a base camp for further excursions around the area. This area is popular with off-road vehicles and runs through the Placer Mountain to Border Lake Motorized Recreation Regulated Area, though this trail is not motorized.

Trinity-Ricardo Trails (Map 24/F6–G4) 🏕🚶🐴🎿🚵🚵

For adventurous hikers and bikers, a fantastic 40 km (25 mi) one-way adventure will take you from Silver Star Park north to the Shuswap River east of Enderby. From the Sovereign Lake Cross-Country Area climb 10 km (6 mi) to the park boundary along Repeater Road and Ganzeveld Trail. From the boundary, continue along the main (Ganzeveld) trail as it descends toward the Shuswap River. Along the way, you will pass the snowmobile chalet and several side trails.

Trout Creek Trail (Map 9/E5) 🚵🚵

This 4 km (2.5 mi) loop gains and loses 275 m (900 ft) of elevation. The trailhead is found next to the Summerland Golf and Country Club at the end of Mountain Avenue.

Trudeau Trail [Skihill Mountain Trail] (Map 46/F3) 🚵🚵

This trail is only 2 km (1.2 mi) long. Which does not sound too bad until you realize that the distance you climb is 450 m (1,500 ft), or almost one vertical metre gained for each four hiked. That is a pretty stiff climb up to the alpine. Fortunately, once you are at the first lake, you can wander around in the alpine.

Tsintsunko Lake Trails (Map 27/G3–28/A3) 🚵🚣🚤🐴🚵

From the 14 km mark on the Shelley Lake/Beaverhut Road, this 4 km (2.5 mi) easy walk follows a well-marked trail through second growth timber to the Tsintsunko Lake. At the north end of the lake, it is possible to join up with a few other trails in the area, including a rustic 3 km one-way route to Caribou Lake.

Tsuius Mountain Trails (Map 25/G2–31/G6) 🏕🚵🚵

To access Tsuius Mountain, you can take any one of four trails. The most popular trail is the shortest; a 6 km (3.7 mi) one-way trip from a logging spur off the North Shuswap Forest Service Road past Mirror Lake gaining 900 m (2,955 ft). The longest trail is a 16 km (9.8 mi) hike from Tsuius Creek Road along Paintbrush Ridge. This scenic route should take the better part of a day. When you reach the mountaintop, you will be rewarded with spectacular scenery and views of distant snowfields. Many hikers use Mirror Lake as a base camp for wilderness hikes north to Joss Mountain and Joss Pass.

Twenty Mile Creek Trail (Map 3/B1–2/G1) 🏕🚵🚣🚵

This difficult trail leads 22 km (13.5 mi) one-way from Apex Mountain to Hedley, with an overall loss of elevation of 1,400 m (4,595 ft) as you pass by remnants of old gold mines to the valley below. The rugged route follows old roads and crosses several unbridged creeks and it is necessary to bring ropes (for the creek crossings), a topographic map and a compass. The trail begins from the Nickel Plate Cross-Country Ski Area.

Twin Lakes Trail (Map 19/C1) 🏕🚵🚤🚵

Twin Lakes are located at the north end of the Pinnacles and accessed about 14 km down the North Fork Forest Service Road. A four-wheel drive vehicle is recommended to reach the trailhead. It should take about 5 hours for hikers to cover the 7.6 km (4.7 mi) to the lakes climbing about 420 m (1,380 ft). The first part of the popular trail is very steep, but the view of emerald blue Twin Lakes below is worth the effort. It is possible to continue south on the Mark Berger Traverse to the beautiful Monashee Lake.

Tuktakamin Mountain Trail (Map 23/F5) 🚵🚤🚵

South of Falkland, this imposing mountain makes a scenic hike or backcountry ski destination. This difficult loop trail is about a 12 km (7.5 mi) in length and leads people up and through forest slopes and into the exposed alpine ridge where there are fantastic views and wildflowers (when in season), gaining 360 m (1,180 ft) along the way. The return section drops back into the forested western slope and accesses the road where a short hike takes you back to your car. Although easy to follow for the most part, expect a bit of scrambling along the ridgeline.

Valley View Loop (Map 4/A2) 🚵🚵

The trailhead for this 9.5 km (5.9 mi) loop is found on Oliver Ranch Road, north of Oliver. The trail features a climb and descent of 314 m (1,030 ft) as it passes through the Vaseux Protected Area just above Vaseux Lake.

Valleyview–Barnhartvale Area (Map 22/E2) 🚵🚤🚵

From the Valleyview Arena on Todd Road to the east of Kamloops, an easy 4.5 km (2.7 mi) one-way hike leads along an old road through the hills. The main route accesses a plateau above Valleyview for a view of Kamloops and the Thompson River. Mountain bikers often explore a number of additional trails that are found in the area.

Vancouver, Victoria and Eastern Railway (Maps 3, 4, 5) 🚵🚤🐴🚵

This old railway used to run 220 km (134 mi) from Midway to Princeton. Unfortunately, most of the old railbed has disappeared. The best section is from Bridesville to Myncaster, although some sections are overgrown. This 34 km (21 mi) section descends 250 m (820 ft) through the dry ranch country.

Vernon Hill Trails (Map 17/E1) 🚵🚤🚵🐴🚵

To the east of Vernon along the Becker Lake Road, the Interpretive Forest showcases 1,850 hectares (4,570 ac) of good forest practices in the Okanagan. A number of trails allow you to explore different forest ecosystems and enjoy the wildlife of the area. The Vernon Hill Interpretive Forest Trail is a 7.4 km (4.6 mi) hike that drops about 165 m (540 ft) and offers nice views over the Coldstream Valley. The Easthill Trail is the only trail with a steep climb, but you will be rewarded with a good view of the pond and the Coldstream Valley when you reach the top. The Vernon Hill trail is a moderate 12 km (7.3 mi) hike that gains 600 m (1,970 ft) to the summit. It follows an old road from the John Park Road and is also used by ATVers.

Short breaks taken at regular intervals will optimize your overall performance and keep your hiking rhythm steady. You will have an easier time maintaining a consistent speed if you take a two minute break every 25 to 30 minutes.

Vidler Ridge Trail (Map 25/G6) 🚵🚵

Vidler Ridge is a ridge southeast of Sugar Lake. Getting to the trailhead can be a bit tricky, but once you have found it, the route is fairly easy to follow, though quite steep. The trail is 14 km (8.7 mi) long and will take a good six hours to hike.

Vista Pass Trail (Map 19/C2) 🚵🐴🚵

The steep, difficult 9.5 km (5.9 mi) return trail to Vista Pass climbs 715 m (2,345 ft) to the divide between the Okanagan and Arrow Lakes with spectacular views of the Pinnacle Peaks. The trailhead is found about 21.5 km up the South Fork Forest Service Road, near the end of the four-wheel drive road that runs up Railroad Creek. The trail hooks up with the Barnes Creek Trail, creating a 14 km (8.5 mi) hike through the beautiful pass.

Volcanic Trail (Map 6/B4) 🚵🚤

The Volcanic Creek Forest Service Road branches east from the North Fork Road, providing access to a mountain bike loop trail. Most ride up the road to the trailhead at either 2.5 km or 4.5 km. The upper trail has more challenging climbs, while the lower trail access leads to the fast flowing downhill section of the trail. The trail itself is 5.4 km (3.4 mi) one-way and leads back to the forestry road. A complete loop would be about 10 km.

Wells Gray Park Trails (Maps 37, 38, 41, 42, 45, 46)

This large park features an extensive trail system, leading to some of the most spectacular scenery to be found. Despite the popularity of frontcountry destinations, many of the backcountry trails are only lightly used. Trails range from easy, short distance jaunts such as the Bailey's Chute Trail, which leads hikers to ancient lava flow, to difficult treks such as the Central Mountain Trail, which leads to breathtaking panoramic views of the alpine above Murtle Lake. Battle Mountain/Alpine Meadows and Trophy Mountain Trails are other challenging routes that lead through beautiful alpine meadows to a seemingly endless backcountry adventure. One of the most popular trails in the park is the easy Helmcken Falls Rim Trail which leads to a viewpoint over Canada's fourth tallest falls – a must-see for all visitors to the park. Those interested in doing the hut to hut trail between Battle Creek and Trophy Mountain need to make reservations by calling (250) 587-6444.

Bailey's Chute Trail (Map 37/D1)

The trailhead for Bailey's Chute can be found at km 59 along the Clearwater Valley Road. An easy 2.5 km round trip takes you to a viewing platform that offers an up-close look at some massive salmon runs during spawning season.

Battle Mountain/Philip Lake Area Trails (Map 37/G4–38/A3)

The access road to this remote alpine trail area can be found about 6 km south of the park gate. The rough four-wheel drive road travels into the mountain area ending at the trailhead along Battle Creek. This area is known for its wildflowers and spectacular views, with sprawling alpine meadows and several backcountry campsites available. It also connects with the hut system linking Trophy Mountain with the Fight Meadow Chalet. Be cautious of bears in the area – this is grizzly country.

Chain Meadow/Easter Bluffs Loop (Map 41/D6)

Accessed across from the Clearwater Lake Campground, this 16 km (10 mi) loop leads past Sticto Falls on Falls Creek to Chain Lake and the Easter Bluffs. At the Easter Bluffs, hikers can take in a great view of Clearwater Lake before returning along the shore of the big lake.

Green Mountain Canyonlands Trails (Map 37/E3–F4)

This is the only trail system in Wells Gray that is open to horse use. The most common access points are at the Flat Iron and Whitehorse Bluffs trailheads. There is some wilderness camping available along the Clearwater River and trail maps are posted at all trailheads and junctions.

Helmcken Falls Rim Trail (Map 37/D3)

This trail is one of the highlights in Wells Gray Park. It is an easy 4 km (2.5 mi) one-way trip to view the amazing 141 metre (465 ft) high waterfall on Murtle River. If the fourth highest falls in Canada is not impressive enough, there are some other, much smaller falls downstream. The trailhead is located beside Dawson Falls Campground.

Murtle Lagoon Trail (Map 38/E1)

This 5.4 km (3.4 mi) trail is mostly used as a portage for accessing Murtle Lake and its many campsites and features little elevation gain. The trail is also popular with highway travellers stopping in on the park for a day trip.

Trophy Mountain Trails (Map 37/G6–38/A5)

Located in the southern portion of Wells Gray Park, Trophy Mountain offers hikers one of the easiest-to access alpine meadow areas in BC, while the north side of the mountain features steep glacial terrain. The alpine meadows are particularly impressive when wildflowers bloom in late June and early July and it is possible to camp at Sheila Lake. In winter this area becomes popular with snowshoers and backcountry skiers since it is possible to link the Trophy Mountain Chalet with the Battle Creek/Phillip Lake trailhead. This multi-day route passes Discovery Cabin (11 km/ 6 hours one-way) and the Fight Meadow Chalet (a further 16 km/10 mi). Cabin reservations are required. Follow Roads 80, 10, and 201 from the Clearwater Valley Road to find the parking lot and trailhead.

Westlake Trail (Map 6/E6)

While this trail can be walked (and there are some great views over Christina Lake that may draw hikers), it is best known as a hardcore mountain biking trail, complete with white knuckle descents and an offshoot trail with stunts and bridges. This 4.5 km (3 mi) trail is accessed from Highland Road and requires a climb of 525 m (1,725 ft).

Westridge Hut Trail (Map 46/F4)

There are a bunch of steep trails around Valemount and this is one of the steepest, climbing 750 m (2,460 ft) in 3 km (1.8 mi) to the YORA hut. From there, the open alpine provides a perfect backdrop for endless days of exploring. The area is used by Canadian Mountain Holidays for guided heli-hiking, which is a good option if you do not want the uphill grunt. You can reserve the hut by calling 250-566-4225.

Whatcom Trail (Map 1/B4–D1)

Starting along the Dewdney Trail from the Cascade Recreation Area parking lot off of Highway 3, this 13 km (8 mi) one-way trail climbs 1,080 m (3,545 ft). Wilderness camping is available at Snass View, while Punchbowl Lake offers a relaxing spot for a break or a cool swim following the steep climb. The trail continues down into the Paradise Valley and the Tulameen River near Wells Lake where a variety of trails continue on. The hike is best done in late summer or early fall.

White Lake Trail (Map 3/G3)

There is a parking area and information shelter for this trail located off of Fairview-White Lake Road. The first section of this trail stretches for 3 km (1.9 mi) towards Mahoney Lake, through the dry, rugged terrain of the White Lake Grasslands past a chain of alkali lakes. From Mahoney Lake another 7.5 km (4.5 mi) of trail leads back to White Lake and the parking area.

White Lake Trails (Map 30/C5)

In and around White Lake are a series of trails to explore. At the east end of the lake, a trail starts at the Settle Road turnaround and leads 5 km (3 mi) one-way along the southern shore of the lake. The trail bisects a cedar and hemlock forest as well as an old burn before reaching the 5 km mark on the Bastion-White Lake Forest Service Road. The trail can be quite swampy and wet, especially during the spring. You can also access the series of ski trails at the east end of the lake. From Pari Road, a 3 km (1.8 mi) easy hike leads up the cliffs at the north end of White Lake. The area has an abundance of wildflowers and wildlife as well as a good view of the Tappen Valley from the cliffs.

Another option is found at a gravel pullout off Fairveiw-White Lake Road. The trail heads southeast into the White Lake Grasslands Protected Area, past alkali ponds, rock bluffs and ridges to Mahoney Lake. From Mahoney Lake, the trail links up with Green Lake Road and continues to the top of Mount Keogan. This trail runs approximately 6.5 km (4 mi) round trip with an elevation gain of 450 m (1,472 ft).

Wolfcub Road (Map 4/C5)

Found east of Oliver, this series of old logging roads leads to a popular wildlife watching area overlooking a lake. You can continue along the lake to connect with the Camp McKinney Road, which will bring you back to your vehicle.

Wright Lake Trail (Map 30/F1)

This boat access trail is found on the east side of the Seymour Arm of Shuswap Lake. The easy 2.5 km one-way trail has minimal elevation gain and begins on the south side of Wright Creek before crossing to the north side en route to the remote fishing lake. A sign should mark the trailhead.

Wrinkly Face Cliffs (Map 17/C5)

From the signed High Rim trailhead about 11 km up the Beaver Lake Road, this moderate hiking or snowshoe trail climbs 175 m (575 ft) to a nice view-point from Wrinkly Face Provincial Park. Allow at least a couple hours to enjoy the 3.3 km (2 mi) one-way trail that is well marked and easy to follow. It is possible to continue the journey on the High Rim Trail north past Oyama Lake Road.

Xenia–Christina Lake Trail (Map 6/C3)

This trail links the Granby River drainage with Christina Lake. You will need a boat to access the Christina Lake end, while most two-wheel drive vehicles can access the trailhead at the end of the Miller Creek Forest Service Road. It is a fairly steep and difficult 6 km (3.7 mi) one-way hike that should take less than three hours. Xenia Lake is a good fishing hole complete with a rustic camping area. Please note that recent reports are saying that this trail is becoming overgrown; this might increase the amount of time it takes to hike the trail.

Yeoward Mountain Trail (Map 19/A2)

Found along Yeoward Mountain Road, which in turn is found off the South Fork Road east of Lumby, this 6 km (3.6 mi) hike climbs 700 m (2,295 ft) onto this prominent Monashee Peak. The views are very rewarding.

WELLS GRAY PARK TRAILS

Trail	Map	Difficulty	Length	Elevation Gain	Bike	Cabin	Camp	Fish	Hike	Horse	Ski	Snowshoe	View
Anderson Lake Trail	42/B6	Easy	4 km (2.5 mi)	Minimal				•	•				•
Bailey's Chute Trail	37/D1	Easy	2.5 km (1.5 mi)	Minimal					•				•
Horseshoe Trail	37/D1	Easy	6 km (3.7 mi)	Minimal					•				•
Battle Mountain/Alpine Meadows Route	37/G4-38/A3	Difficult	32 km (20 mi)	1,670 m (5,480 ft)	•	•			•		•		•
Canim/Mahood Falls Trail	19/D1 (CCBC)	Easy	1 km (0.6 mi)	Minimal					•				•
Canim River Trail	19/D1 (CCBC)	Easy	2 km (1.2 mi)	Minimal				•	•				•
Caribou Meadows Trail	38/A3	Difficult	7.5 km (4.7 mi)	1,070 m (3,510 ft)	•	•			•		•		•
Central Mountain Trail	42/B7	Difficult	7.5 km (4.7 mi)	1,000 m (3,280 ft)					•				•
Chain Meadow/Easter Bluffs Loop	41/D6	Moderate	16 km (10 mi)	280 m (920 ft)					•				•
C W Shook/Dragon's Tongue Trail	41/D6	Easy	1.5 km (0.9 mi)	60 m (195 ft)					•				•
Dawson Falls Trails	37/E3	Moderate	2.5 km (1.5 mi)	Minimal					•				•
Deception Falls Trail	19/E1 (CCBC)	Easy	0.8 km (0.5 mi)	140 m (460 ft)					•				•
Diver's Bluff Route	41/C6	Moderate	1.5 km (0.9 mi)	n/a				•					
Flat Iron Trail	37/F4	Moderate	4.5 km (2.8 mi)	220 m (720 ft)					•				•
Fight Lake Trail	38/A3	Difficult	4.5 km (2.8 mi)	1,000 m (3,280 ft)	•	•		•	•				•
Flourmills Trail	37/B1	Difficult	12.5 km (7.8 mi)	n/a				•					•
Foot Lake Trail	37/E3	Easy	1 km (0.6 mi)	Minimal					•				•
Gattling Gorge Trail	37/D3	Easy	4 km (2.5 mi)	Minimal					•				•
Helmcken Falls Rim Trail	37/D3	Easy	4 km (2.5 mi)	80 m (260 ft)					•				•
Henrietta Lake Trail	38/D1	Easy	0.5 km (0.3 mi)	40 m (130 ft)				•	•				•
Hobson Lake Trail	41/B3	Moderate	13 km (8 mi)	300 m (985 ft)				•	•				•
Huntley Column Trail	41/C3	Difficult	4 km (2.5 mi)	1,300 m (4,265 ft)					•				•
Long Hill Trail	38/A5	Difficult	3.5 km (2.2 mi)	640 m (2,100 ft)					•				•
Mahood Lake Trail	37/C3	Moderate	12 km (7.5 mi)	260 m (850 ft)					•				•
Mahood River Trail	37/D4	Easy	4.7 km (3 mi)	100 m (330 ft)				•	•				•
Marcus-Myanth Falls Trail	37/D1	Easy	3.5 km (2.2 mi)	Minimal					•				•
Majerus Farm/Loopet Trails	37/F2	Varies	26 km (16 mi)	Varies	•	•			•				•
McDougall Falls Trail	42/A7	Moderate	5 km (3.1 mi)	100 m (330 ft)					•				•
Moul Falls Trail	37/F5	Easy	2.7 km (1.7 mi)	35 m (115 ft)					•				•
Mount Philip Trail	37/G4-38/A4	Difficult	9 km (5.6 mi)	1,060 m (3,480 ft)	•	•			•		•		•
Murtle Lagoon Trail	38/E1	Easy	5.4 km (3.4 mi)	40 m (130 ft)				•	•				•
Murtle River Trail	37/E2-F1	Moderate	14 km (8.7 mi)	140 m (460 ft)					•				•
Philip Lake Trail	38/A4	Moderate	2.5 km (1.5 mi)	780 m (2,560 ft)					•				•
Placid Lake Trail	37/E3-E4	Easy	2.5 km (1.5 mi)	200 m (655 ft)					•		•		•
Pyramid Mountain Trail	37/D1	Moderate	5.5 km (3.4 mi)	240 m (790 ft)					•				•
Rainbow Falls Trail	41/F3	Easy	0.5 km (0.3 mi)	Minimal					•				•
Ray Farm Mineral Spring Trail	37/D1	Easy	4.5 km (2.8 mi)	Minimal					•				•
Shadden Lookout Trail	37/F6	Easy	1 km (0.6 mi)	Minimal					•				•
Sheila Lake Trail	38/A5	Moderate	5 km (3.1 mi)	380 m (1,250 ft)				•	•				•
Silvertip Falls Trail	38/A6	Easy	2 km (1.2 mi)	100 m (330 ft)					•				•
Smith Lake Loop	37/F3	Easy	5 km (3.1 mi)	80 m (260 ft)	•				•				•
Spahats Falls Trail	37/F6	Easy	3 km (1.9 mi)	Minimal					•				•
Spahats Forest Loop	37/F6	Easy	700 m (0.4 mi)	Minimal					•				•
Stevens Lake Route	38/C2	Difficult	10 km (6.2 mi)	120 m (390 ft)			•	•	•				•
Stillwater Route	37/G1-38/A1	Difficult	12 km (7.5 mi)	300 m (985 ft)			•	•	•				•
Strait Lake Trail	42/E6	Moderate	5 km (3.1 mi)	120 m (390 ft)				•	•				•
Summit Lake Trail	45/C6	Difficult	6.9 km (4.3 mi)	160 m (525 ft)					•				•
Sylvia and Goodwin Falls Trail	37/D4	Easy	7 km (4.3 mi)	n/a					•				•
Trophy Flower Meadows/Shepherd's Hut Trail	38/A5	Moderate	3.5 km (2.2 mi)	840 m (2,755 ft)	•	•			•		•		•
Trophy Skyline Trail	38/A5	Difficult	5 km (3.1 mi)	n/a					•				•
Ursus Trail	37/G4–38/B4	Difficult	11.5 km (7.1 mi)	700 m (2,295 ft)			•		•				•
Wavy Crest Trail	42/E6	Difficult	7 km (4.3 mi)	1,240 m (4,070 ft)					•				•
West Lake Loop	37/D1	Easy	3 km (1.9 mi)	40 m (130 ft)				•	•				•
West Rim Tote Trail	37/E4	Easy	8 km (5 mi)	520 m (1,710 ft)					•				•
Whale Lake Trail	19/D1 (CCBC)	Moderate	5 km (3.1 mi)	300 m (984 ft)				•	•				•
Whitehorse Bluffs and Rock Roses Trail	37/E3	Moderate	6.5 km (4 mi)	200 m (655 ft)				•	•				•
Zodiak Peak Route	41/D4	Difficult	9 km (5.6 mi)	1,600 m (5,250 ft)					•				•

ATV [OHV] ADVENTURES

The warm weather and relatively sparse population of British Columbia makes the centrally located Thompson Okanagan one of the best off-road riding areas in the country. The dirt and gravel roads in the region date back to the 1800s and were mostly created by the mining and forestry industries.

Today, these roads combine with countless trails and old railroad beds that lead to ghost towns and old mine sites, as well as communities that cater to this growing sport.

The trails in this region vary with some routes designated for motorized off-road use, while other routes are designated for horseback riders, hikers and mountain bikers. Make sure you plan ahead before heading out; motorized riders are always under heavy scrutiny, so tread lightly. ATVers have received a bad reputation in some areas due to irresponsible riding by a notable minority. The Okanagan's dry climate has caused many new rules and closures to be established, so spark arrestors are required at many of these riding areas, as is liability insurance.

In order to truly explore this beautiful part of the Canadian backcountry you will need a four-wheel drive or all-terrain vehicle. There are thousands of kilometres of old logging trails that criss-cross the backwoods of the scenic Thompson Okanagan region. Adding to this are off-road trail systems that provide a host of sights and sounds to experience. From scenic mountain rides to exploring the maze of trails and roads around the many lakes in the area, there is no shortage of places to ride.

Surprisingly, most people that visit BC seldom venture out into the backroads and experience the wilderness that the province is famous for. This is where tour operators can help. Tour companies offer full-day, half-day and weekend excursions that include scenic mountain tours designed for all skill levels.

For locals, we recommend one of the many riding clubs in the area. The list is long, so it is best to start by visiting www.atvbc.ca to find out about local clubs and the latest rules and regulations.

When off-roading in the region it is always wise to have a well prepared trip plan and good equipment. The weather has been known to change quickly on people while exploring the BC wilderness, in the past floods have washed out bridges, active logging has altered road patterns and fallen trees from wind storms have blocked roads in and out. So plan ahead and bring all the necessary gear, make sure you respect all closed areas, and above all, have fun and explore!

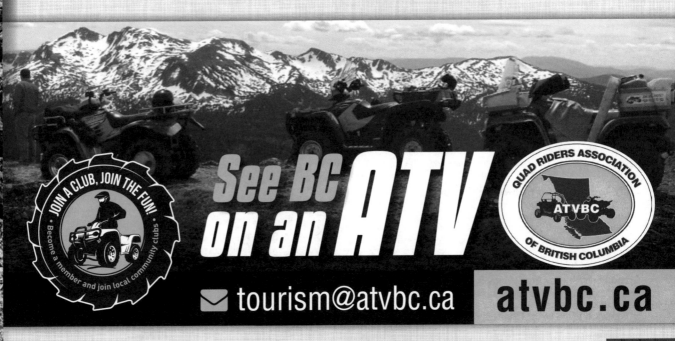

Apex Motorized Trails (Map 3/C3–9/D7)

Situated around the popular Apex Mountain ski resort, there are some 175 km (110 mi) of rideable motorized trails in the area. The trails can be accessed from the west at two points along Highway 3A. Van Wallegham Road in Olalla provides access, as does a point further north on Highway 3A near Cedar Creek. The Hedley-Nickelplate Road also intersects the trails from the east side, while Green Mountain and Apex Mountain Roads provide better road access in the north and west respectively.

Batchelor Heights Area (Map 22/B1)

This designated riding area is found just north of Kamloops, outside the Lac Du Bois Provincial Park boundaries. There are areas for all skill levels with lots of dirt and rutted trails. For an interesting ride follow the trails through the trees that cross creek beds and offer a different experience than the dry, dusty hill climbs Bachelor Heights is known for. This area is subject to seasonal closures and riding is somewhat limited, but it is close to Kamloops. There is also a four-wheel track further west off Tranquille Road up to Wheeler Mountain.

Bear Creek Motorized Recreation Area (Map 16/D4–G5)

The largest recreation site in BC, this site covers 35,000 hectares (21,735 ac). Trails are managed, marked and designated for motorcycles, ATVs and UTVs less than 1.3 metres (50 in) wide. There are one-way trails, loop trails and hundreds of logging roads to explore. Environmentally friendly riding is the key here, and with over 130 km (80 mi) of double track trails (not including roads), rules are strictly enforced. There are two staging areas, the Aspen Trailhead is located at the 8 km mark off the Bear Main Road and the Upper Pits is located at the 11 km mark. Trail fees are in effect from April through October.

Campbell Range/Scuitto Lake Area (Map 22/F4)

The entire Campbell Range area has extensive year-round riding opportunities suitable for all experience levels. This is a large area perfect for weekend trips, with a maze of ATV and snowmobile trails and forestry roads branching from the Scuitto Creek Forest Service Road. Please obey posted signs and keep off the grasslands. Access is off Robbins Range Road, which leads to the Campbell Range Road and eventually the Scuitto Creek FSR.

Chuwels Mountain Trails (Map 21/G4–22/A5)

There are 47 km (29 mi) of single track motorcycle trails in the area, as well as wider snowmobile trails and spur roads. The southern loop is part of the Dragon Spray Race Course and another route leads up to a microwave tower for a nice view of the surrounding area. In addition, trails connect to the Greenstone Mountain and Inks Lake area for days of riding. Access is off the Lac Le Jeune Road where the Chuwels Mountain Road leads west under the Coquihalla Highway.

Clearwater Area Trails (Maps 33, 34)

Situated south and east of Clearwater, this 320 km (200 mi) network of trails can be accessed right from town or from several points along the Birch Island – Lost Creek Road. These trails run along the eastern border of the Dunn Peak Protected Area and connect with North Barrière Lake to the south. Also popular with snowmobilers in winter, parts of the trail network follow the Harper Snowmobile Trails.

Crowfoot Mountain Trails (Map 30/B3–C2)

To get to the popular Crowfoot Mountain multi-use area, head north on Garland Road, where there is a parking lot found shortly down the forest service road. Follow the road to the Sheep Trail sign where a steep, well-defined route follows the old road about 8 km (5 mi) to the top and the beautiful alpine meadow area overlooking Shuswap Lake. Most continue to the lookout on Crowfoot Mountain, but it is possible to access Mobley Mountain or drop down to Scotch Creek and back up to Grizzly Lake. The large trail network is also accessible via the Ross Creek Road near Magna Bay.

Duffy–Greenstone Off Highway Vehicle Area (Map 21/E3–22/A4)

Part of the newly established Duffy – Greenstone Off Highway Vehicle Area, the trail systems boasts over 75 campsites and 130 km (80 mi) of signed, designated trails. There is a wide variety of trails for all levels, with an estimated 80% being rated easy to moderate. On top of the Greenstone Trails there are connecting routes to the Chuwels and Inks Lake riding areas. Bring extra gas and try the 80 km (50 mi) loop. Riding is allowed only on the designated trails.

Grand Forks/Granby Area (Maps 5, 6, 11, 12)

This is a very large riding area comprising close to 1,500 km (930 mi) of trails, stretching between Grand Forks and Greenwood in the south all the way to Edgewood in the north. There are many ghost towns and old mining sites

to explore in the Eholt and Greenwood/Phoenix area, while the further north you travel, the more scenic and remote your surroundings become. There are many remotes lakes to access in this area for some excellent fishing, including Xenia Lake, while some gorgeous isolated campsites can be found along Lower Arrow Lake. There are plenty of mountains to climb in the area – Bluejoint is one of the more prominent peaks and offers a good challenge for riders. The opportunities for exploring here are endless, but be aware that this is grizzly bear territory and ATVs are not allowed on trails in Gladstone Provincial Park.

Hunters Range Trails (Map 24/F3–31/C6)

Better known as a winter destination, this area offers endless meadows and alpine vistas. Trails and roads extend north to the Mara Mountain or Owlhead Trail systems, which lead all around the Sicamous area.

Inks Lake Area (Map 22/A3)

This area is found off the Coquihalla Highway (Hwy 5), just 13 km south of Kamloops. Take the Inks Lake U-turn exit then go under the culvert and park by the salt/sand shed. The trails begin just across the cattleguard; there is potential for camping across the cattleguard too. This large network has hundreds of kilometres of trails ranging from challenging motorcycle and mountain bike trails to ATV trails suitable for beginners and advanced riders. Be wary that many of the trails area very steep and the trails built by mountain bikers are not for ATV use. It is also easy to get lost in the maze of routes that crisscross each other. The network links with Timber Lake Road in the south.

Beware of trucks and equipment transporting logs. Always pull over and let them pass in order to protect yourself from flying stones and dust clouds.

Kettle River Area Trails (Maps 18, 19)

Also known as the Kettle Lightning Trails, this 55 km (34 mi) network of trails is located just north of Granby Provincial Park. Access can be found via the Kettle River Forest Service Road off of Highway 6.

Lake Country Area (Map 17)

There are countless roads and trails that explore the series of lakes that rest on the plateau that runs east of Okanagan Valley. Access is readily found off any of the main roads, including James Lake or Bata Lake in the south, Postill Lake, Beaver Lake or Oyama Lake near Lake Country or King Edward Lake in the north. Recreation sites provide camping and most people bring along their fishing rods. For great views of the area, head up to the Oyama Lake Lookout via the steep hill climb.

Larson Hill (Map 7/C2)

Larson Hill is a popular destination used frequently as a staging area for club gatherings. Take the Larson Hill exit off the Coquihalla Highway (Hwy 5) and head east towards Brookmere. In addition to following the Kettle Valley Railway/Trans Canada Trail, there are also old roads and a network of trails leading north to Shovelnose Mountain and south to Thynne Mountains.

Mabel Lake (Map 25/D2–31/E7)

This large north-south running lake offers trails from the south end near Mabel Lake Provincial Park to the north end near Wap Creek Provincial Park. From the north, explore the area off Mable-Iron and Derry Creek Roads up to Two Moon Lake at 1,882 metres (6,175 ft). Halfway down Mabel Lake, the Cottonwood Beach Recreation Site is a good starting point to access the Tsuius Creek Road and the route up to Mount Mabel. From the south near Mabel Lake Provincial Park, follow Chambers Road east to the Sugar Lake Riding Area. There are riding opportunities along the old roads on the west side of the lake as well.

McBride Area (Map 49/B1–D1)

Off highway riding is limited in the North Thompson area due to ranchland and concerns over Caribou, however the McBride area does have a few areas to sample. These include the Homes / Beaver River area, Bell and Lucille Mountain and the Renshaw Area. ATVs are not allowed in the alpine, but there are a number of roads that can be ridden. Close to town, try the route to McBride Peak. There is an ATV trail to an abandoned fire lookout along with an offshoot to Mount Teare, providing great views of the area.

Merritt Area (Maps 7, 14)

The entire Merritt region is a hotbed for off highway vehicles. A good option is to pick a campsite in the area between Highway 5 and Highway 5A and start exploring. This area includes a large portion of the Kettle Valley Railway/Trans Canada Trail where you can ride right into Tulameen and even all the way to Castlegar. There are also multi-use trails that will take you up to high elevations around Thynne Mountain, Lodestone, Sugarloaf Mountain and more. You can ride for days without crossing the same path.

Munro Lake Trails (Map 9/B3)

There are many kilometres of trails heading west from Peachland that create a maze around the Darke Lake and Eneas Lake Provincial Parks. These trails are a mix of decommissioned forestry roads, active logging roads and many side trails. Access is found off the four-wheel drive/ATV Eneas Lakes Road from the north, or the better Munro Lake Forest Service Road from the south.

Penticton Area Trails (Map 10)

A great OHV ride heads northeast from Penticton around the back of Mount Campbell. Here riders will find an easy network of trails great for beginners. Further south the Steward Creek Forest Service Road is a good option with a route that extends into Beaverdell and Carmi area. To the north, the Greyback Forest Service Road leads riders to a lake and scenic waterfall. Some of the side roads in the area can be quite technical and muddy so it is best to explore with at least two quads.

Okanagan Falls Riding Area (Map 4/B2)

Just east of the small town of Okanagan Falls is a great riding area offering over 40 km (25 mi) of trails. There are some beginner level trails, but most are for advanced riders. Offering a mixture of single track trail and old roads, the riding is on dusty and loose dirt surface with some rocky sections. The network accesses some nice viewpoints and wetter sections as well. To get here, head 3 km east from McLean Creek Road on Allendale Lake Road and look for the parking area just past the landfill.

Placer Mountain Area (Map 2/A5–D7)

This area is popular with four wheelers and horseback riders, with the best access found east of the Manning Park East Gate. Turn at the first culvert after the gas station and head through the campground towards Placer Lake Recreation Site. Trails in this area are marked and provide nice loops over Placer Mountain all the way north to Copper Mountain. The east side of Placer Mountain has a steep, switch-backed road made of nothing but red rock pulled from mining sites.

Sicamous Trails (Map 30/G5–31/D2)

In the area north of Sicamous there are countless logging roads and trails to ride. From the Queest Mountain area you can ride west to the shores of Shuswap Lake and north to Anstey-Hunakwa Provincial Park. The snowmobile route becomes a multi-use trail that leads past the snowmobile club cabin to loop around and down the Wilson Branch Forest Service Road. Another popular ride is the route up to Eagle Pass. South of the highway, trails lead past the 'Last Spike' in Craigellachie.

Stemwinder Motorized Trails (Map 2/G1–9/A6)

Accessed from Stemwinder Mountain Forest Service Road off of Highway 3 west of Hedley, 45 km (28 mi) of trails extend north into the mountains, eventually linking up with the Isintok Trails. These trails also access Barton Lake and Little Willy Lake, both popular fishing spots.

Sugar Lake Riding Area (Map 25/F5)

This beautiful area, found east of Mabel Lake, offers some excellent riding over a large area. It is said you can ride for days without ever covering the same trails twice. A popular ride is the 11 km (7 mi) trail that leads to the summit and an old fire lookout atop Sugar Mountain. You will climb over 1,230 metres (4,000 ft) to the 2,130 metre (6,990 ft) summit with very rewarding views.

Summerland Trails (Map 9/E4)

Closest to town, the Upper Summerland Trails follow loose sandy surfaces and often leads to dead ends. Three kilometres from town is the Race Course Loop. This is a moderate 6 km (3.7 mi) trail that makes its way back to the Summerland Road. It is also possible to ride up Giants Head Mountain and enjoy the great view overlooking Penticton to the south. To get to a much larger group of trails follow the Princeton-Summerland Road west of town. Here you can follow the Kettle Valley Railway/Trans Canada Trail west past Osprey Lake into Tulameen or branch off to the Crump Trails and connect with the Isintok Trails that go south to the Stemwinder Provincial Park, off Highway 3.

Tranquille Plateau (Maps 27, 28)

Located northeast of Kamloops, this large riding area offers some 535 km (332 mi) of trails that can be accessed from multiple points, including via Lac Du Bois Road from Kamloops and O'Conner Lake Road off of Westsyde Road. The expansive trail system cuts through Porcupine Meadows Provincial Park as well as the southern portion of Bonaparte Provincial Park. There are many spots to explore for fishing and camping in this scenic area. These trails become very popular with snowmobilers once the snow falls.

Tulameen Area (Map 7)

The discovery of gold in 1885 helped develop this area around Granite City near present-day Coalmont. Today, the Granite Creek Recreation Site acts as a popular base to explore the Lodestone Mountain area. Here countless roads and trails make for some exciting riding leading into the mountains. Across the river and Coalmont Road, riders can also explore a mix of roads and trails that lead into the ATV friendly town of Tulameen. From here, routes continue west and north up into the Coquihalla Lakes and Mount Henning area. The area offers something for everyone with routes like the Kettle Valley Railway/Trans Canada Trail that are relatively smooth and flat to challenging offshoots that climb up mountains into advanced terrain.

> *Liability insurance is now required in order to ride on any forest service road in BC. For more information and to purchase trail passes with insurance visit bcorma.ca.*

Tunkwa–Duffy Off Highway Vehicle Area (Maps 21, 22)

The Tunkwa-Duffy ORV Area was established to protect the sensitive grasslands and provide opportunities of ATV and motorcycle riders. Closures in this area include Tunkwa Provincial Park and the area immediately east, Six Mile, Cherry Creek and Logan Lake Ski Trails. However, there are designated ATV trails around Forge Mountain (85 km/50 mi), Logan Lake Face-Paska (65 km/40 mi) and Logan Lake South (30 km/20 mi) as well as designated motorcycle trails in the Duffy- Greenstone area (130 km/80 mi). Each riding area has designated staging areas and there are more than 20 campsites in the area.

Valemount Area (Maps 46, 47)

Some 185 km (115 mi) of trails can be found close to the small town of Valemount. These trails climb high into the mountains offering stunning views of the Rocky Mountains. Family friendly riding can be found on the West Ridge Family Loop, a low elevation 22 km (14 mi) long trail that offers fantastic views and a warming hut to take a break at. One of the most popular areas for Valemount sledders, and usually the first to open each year, is Allen Creek, where you can find lakes, meadows, bowls and steep climbs suitable for the most advanced riders. Overnight trail riders can check out Yellowjacket and Horse Creek Campgrounds on Kinbasket Lake for some great spots to spend the night. For panoramic views of the entire area, riders can climb the Sea to Sky Trail to the viewpoint at the top of Canoe Mountain.

Vernon Hill Trails (Map 17/E1–24/F7)

In the area just east of Vernon there are well over 150 km (90 mi) of trails to ride. Trail maintenance has been going on for more than 20 years, with many trails utilizing the area's old logging roads. There are two main sections. The trails near Becker Lake range from beginner to moderate with a combination of forestry roads, powerline trails and single track side trails. Further east, the Bardolph Lake area is often used as a gateway for a longer ride that courses north to the boundary of the Silver Star Provincial Park. Keep an eye out for two warming shelters in the area – the Silver Star Chalet and the Armstrong Chalet, both maintained by the Vernon Snowmobile Association. There are also 200 km (120 mi) of motocross trails that can challenge even the best of riders.

Whipsaw Creek Riding Area (Map 1/E3–2/A2)

This 185 km (115 mi) trail system is found south of Princeton and can be accessed by the Whipsaw Forest Service Road off Highway 3. It is possible to loop past the Garrison Lakes Rec Site and link up with Highway 3 further south via the Sunday Summit Forest Service Road. Alternatively, trails lead north to join the Lodestone Trails out of Tulameen. Popular with four-wheel drive vehicles as well, parts of these trails also follow the Old Dewdney Trail.

SNOWMOBILE ADVENTURES

British Columbia offers some of the best snowmobiling terrain in Canada. Sledders will find a mix of groomed trails, massive glaciers, hill climbs and thousands of kilometres of logging roads to explore. This holds true in the Thompson Okanagan area, which boasts beautiful regional hot spots like Kamloops, Kelowna, Merritt, the Shuswap, Sicamous and Valemount.

Families and novice riders often enjoy the ability to travel along established routes, exploring the forests and meadows in areas with warming sheds and established parking lots. Advanced sledders will love the remote alpine riding areas and the thousands of kilometres of unmarked logging roads that extend throughout the region. Snowfall is generous in this part of BC and there is always a lot of powder during the riding season which extends until spring in the high alpine areas.

In the Thompson Okanagan almost every community has an extensive network of snowmobile trails and logging roads nearby. In most cases there are multiple riding destinations near each town that result from the combination of vast countryside and prime snowmobiling weather. In fact, in some communities snowmobiles are the preferred mode of transport as the gravel roads, ATV trails and some hiking trails all become snowmobile routes in the winter. Larger communities like Kamloops offer a lot of amenities with lots of routes surrounding the city; however, the smaller towns are full of friendly residents and passionate sledders that will often have tips and new trails to tell you about.

If you are new to snowmobiling, or just want to rent a sled, there are tour companies in most communities that will take you out for a day or a couple hours. These adventure companies provide tours and lessons; some companies even offer multi-day trips with accommodations and meals. There are also more than 70 snowmobile clubs in British Columbia, each one maintaining extensive trail networks and riding areas. These associations create the snowmobile routes and maintain sections of the mountain assigned for snowmobile use only.

If you plan on heading out for a snowmobile trip then contacting a club is a good way to start planning. Generally, permits are needed to access the club maintained areas – these permits help to offset the maintenance cost. If you are more adventurous, the ungroomed trails will still take you through picturesque terrain where moose sightings are not uncommon. Check out the BC Snowmobile Federation at *bcsf.org* or *abcsnow.ca* for more information.

© Gillene Gauthier

Adams Lake Snowmobile Trails (Map 29/C1–F4)

This unorganized riding area is found north of Chase, between Adams Lake and Scotch Creek. You can ride to the top of the 1,893 metre (6,210 ft) Pisima Mountain and along the Adams Plateau. There is a shelter in the meadows at the head of Nikwikwaia Creek and a mining cabin at the edge of the meadows near Nikwikwaia Lake. The area is quite large, with trails found on the east and west side of the lake. It is best left to experienced riders looking for a quieter place to ride.

Adams Lake West Snowmobile Trails (Map 29/C1–34/C7)

Located between Adams Lake and the Barrière Lakes, this area has over 200 km (125 mi) of informal trails to explore. Access can be found off South Barrière Lake or Johnson Lake Forest Service Road.

Allan Creek Snowmobile Trail (Map 47/B7)

The Allan Creek area is usually the first region to open for the sledding season. Accessed off the Allan Creek Forest Service Road, which begins off the west side of Highway 5 about 35 km south of Valemount, and follow a groomed but steep 10 km (6 mi) trail to the cabin. You can climb upwards of 1,000 m (3,300 ft) to access big powder and steep hills around the hidden lakes, bowls and meadows in the area. Family friendly riding can be found around the cabin and lakes as soon as you enter the alpine. A trail pass is required to ride here.

Allen Creek Snowmobile Trails (Map 26/A4)

Located 13 km south of Clinton or 26 km north of Cache Creek, access is just off Highway 97 near the Carquile Rest Area. Experienced snowmobilers can ride the popular route into a vast alpine area which opens up to large bowls and untouched areas. Riders must use caution and be fully prepared for emergency situations.

Barnett Perimeter Trail (Maps 32, 33)

Most of this 400 km (240 mi) long trail runs north of this book in the south Cariboo. The section in this book runs east from the Green Lake Trail system to Bonaparte Lake. The trail then climbs up to the Akehurst Lake region crossing under Highway 24 near Phinetta Lake. Veer west and north to the Wavey Lake Road, then down the rough creek trail to head up Windy Mountain and around the first bench to come down to the Mahood Lake Road. The trail is marked with black arrows on a yellow sign.

Barrière Snowmobile Trails (Map 33/E6–34/A5)

Located between the Dunn Lake Road and North Barrière Lake, this riding area has a series of snowmobile trails with some moderately difficult alpine riding. Going around Dunn Peak Protected Area there are plenty of easy routes to keep the family happy. Routes extend east from North Barrière Lake to link with the Harp Mountain Trails.

Bear Creek Motorized Recreation Area (Map 16/D4–G6)

The Bear Creek riding area found north of West Kelowna provides access to hundreds of unploughed logging roads and clearcuts. Considered more of a summer hotspot for ATVers, the local snowmobile club does maintain a shelter at Esperon Lake. Trails climb up to 2,195 metre (7,200 ft) in elevation. Note the area is active with logging so roads may be plowed.

Blue River Trails (Map 42/G7–43/C6)

There are close to 185 km (115 mi) of trails found around Blue River. To access the Parberry and North Blue River riding areas, parking can be found at the Red Sands parking lot just north of Blue River. The Parberry Trails are best left to advanced snowmobilers as the high alpine terrain can be quite challenging.

Bonaparte Provincial Park (Map 27/G1–28/A3)

Bonaparte Provincial Park is one of the few provincial parks that allows motorized use. The rolling, forested hills offer opportunities for a variety of trails, which are maintained by the Kamloops Snowmobile Association. The well-established system runs through the southern portion of the park and includes public winter cabins. Currently, there is no park use permit or letter of permission required. Please note that snowmobiling is permissible in the Natural Environment Zone but not in the Wilderness Recreation Zone of the park. There are also trails northeast of the park that link to the Barnett Perimeter Trail.

Boulder Mountain Snowmobile Area (Map 31/G3)

Just a section of this popular snowmobiling area near Revelstoke is found in the Thompson Okanagan region of BC. The trail system is accessed from the parking lot at Highway 1 or 4–6 km along the Jordan Forest Road (if it is ploughed). The terrain is suitable for all levels of snowmobilers and the Revelstoke Snowmobile Club has developed the area by signing and grooming

50 km (30 mi) of trails. The chalet at the top of the mountain at 2,100 m (6,890 feet) is a popular rendezvous for snowmobilers who can access the over 80 km² of terrain. It is found at the end of Bezanson, Kirkup and Veideman Trails.

Blue Lake Snowmobile Trails (31/C5)

Recent trail work and the Blue Lake Cabin have helped this area become very popular. There are some big, high alpine areas and the trails are groomed. The trails begin at the Yard Creek Provincial Park turn off, south of Malakwa or about 17 km east of Sicamous.

Brown Creek Snowmobile Trail (Map 32/F6)

The Brown Creek Trail refers to the portion of the Barnett Perimeter Trail north of Bonaparte Lake to where it joins the Windy Mountain Trail. The Brown Creek portion is 17 km (10.5 mi) long and starts at the Bonaparte Lake Recreation Site; there are no guarantees that access to the recreation site or the trail will be groomed.

Cabin Lake Area (Map 13/F6)

The easiest access to this area is south of Highway 8 along the Prospect Creek Forest Service Road. The main route involves following a 7 km (4 mi) rough four-wheel drive road that gains about 215 metres (700 ft) to the lake. Other options include the old road to the Stoyama summit, a 4 km (2.5 mi) trail to the 1974 plane crash site found south of Cabin Lake, and the steep and challenging Heather Basin Trail. Another option is to head to Lightning Lake, which involves a steep 5 km (3 mi) excursion along an old road.

Caribou Basin (Map 40/D7–36/E2)

About 108 km north of Revelstoke off Highway 23 there is an area with some great tree riding opening up to two massive bowls. It is quite a distance from Revelstoke, but well worth the trip. Be aware of seasonal closures (January 1st to April 15th) and avalanche hazards. You can find access off the Brewster Forest Service Road.

Chappell Creek Snowmobile Trails (Map 43/B2)

The trailhead to this system is located north of Blue River off the west side of Highway 5, about 58 km south of Valemount. The parking area has maps and picnic tables. From here, the route follows 20 km (12 mi) of logging roads and about 26 km (16 mi) of groomed and marked trail leading into the alpine. Expect to climb about 600 metres (2,000 ft) as the trails wind around Mount Chappell. Please respect all closures as the system travels within winter range for the mountain caribou. A trail pass is required to ride here.

Check the weather forecast and trail conditions before you go out to assess whether there is danger of an avalanche.

Christina Lake Snowmobile Trails (Map 6/F6)

Most of the riding in this region is at the Paulson Summit and the Walker Creek area, however, closer to town the Fife and Santa Rosa Road are easily accessible areas suitable for everyone. The riding is mainly done over logging roads and into cleared logging areas. Some years when the lake freezes over, riders can travel the length of the lake for an exciting snowmobile experience. There are also many smaller mountain lakes to sled to for a day of ice fishing.

Chuwels Mountain Trails (Map 21/G4–22/A5)

At the base of Chuwels Mountain, there are about 50 km (30 mi) of snowmobile trails along the vast network of forestry roads and old side roads to explore. Snow is present from late fall to early spring. The trail system is best accessed off the Chuwels Mountain Road, which branches west from the Lac Le Jeune Road and under the Coquihalla Highway (Hwy 5), adjacent to Stake Lake Recreation Area.

Clemina Creek Snowmobile Trails (Map 47/C6–E7)

This area can be found about 30 km south of Valemount off the east side of Highway 5. From the Clemina–Dixon Albreda and Keyhole Riding Staging Area you can head south to the Clemina Creek Forest Service Road via a regularly groomed 17 km (10 mi) long trail that takes you to the Clemina Cabin. Access trails break off at the 15 km and 19 km mark for the Morning Glory Trail and the Wind Tunnel Trail. At the 21 km mark, the Valley Trail takes you into the Goat Ridge Bowl. North from the staging area is the smaller Keyhole Riding Area, which offers more technical riding with rolls, pits and halfpipe-like areas.

Coquihalla Summit Snowmobile Area (Map 7/B4–E6)

The Coquihalla Summit Snowmobile Club offers a large riding area between Hope and Merritt off the Coquihalla Highway (Hwy 5) at Exit 228 leading to the Britton Creek Rest Area. Park at the lot 200 metres down the Tulameen Forest Service Road. The club grooms over 60 km (37 mi) of trails to make for easy access to the alpine. The Henning alpine is 6 km (3.7 mi) from the parking lot and the 10-K alpine is 15 km (9 mi) in. For less experienced riders there are some groomed trails through the alpine. Trails also follow unplowed forest service roads southeast from the lakes and can be easily ridden all the way to Tulameen and beyond. The Coquihalla Lake Lodge is found right next to the trailhead, while the club also has two cabins in the alpine stocked with firewood. The parking lot has lots of room for any size rig, as well as a loading dock and a heated changing room. There is a fee to ride here.

Crowfoot Mountain Trails (Map 30/B4–D2)

The Crowfoot Snowmobile Club maintains this established trail network that offers about 28 km (17 mi) of groomed trails and three day-use chalets in a 20 km2 (12.5 mi2) area. Access is found 30 km east of Highway 1 to the north of Celista. Follow the signs to Garland Road and continue to the main parking lot a kilometre up the logging road. From here follow the tracks up to the open alpine area where there are plenty of areas to play on, including groomed trails and deep, untouched powder. From the main chalet, most ride up to the old forestry lookout on Crowfoot. From here it is possible to ride over to Mount Mobley or drop down into the Scotch Creek drainage to link up with the Lichen Mountain Trails. A trail pass is required to ride here.

Eagle Pass Mountain Trail (Map 31/C3–E2)

This area is found 29 km northeast of Sicamous off Highway 1, at the start of the East Perry Forest Service Road. The access road is groomed close to the alpine, a distance of about 25 km (15 mi). There are no marked trails past the end of the grooming and the terrain is rugged and remote. Be wary of avalanche conditions when riding here.

Fawn Lake Trail (Map 32/B3)

Found off Highway 24, about 25 km east of Highway 97, Fawn Lake offers a resort and access to some snowmobiling areas. The route is about 26 km (16 mi) long and goes from Fawn Lake Road, in the west, to the Windy Mountain Snowmobile Trails in the east. The Fawn Lake Trail is a level, easy graded route but opens up as you head east.

Fly Hills Snowmobile Trails (Map 23/G2–30/A7)

Just 10 minutes west of Salmon Arm, the Fly Hills offer about 200 km (124 mi) of snowmobile trails forming three loops in a 50 km2 (30 mi2) area. There is a chalet and some warm-up huts available and an excellent variety of trails. The routes are well mapped and signed for family friendly riding. Access to the area from Salmon Arm is via the Fly Hill or the Charcoal Creek Forest Service Roads. The trails rest around 1,372 metres (4,500 ft) in elevation so the conditions are good from mid-November to March. Maintained by the Salmon Arm Snow Blazers, a trail pass is required to ride here.

Graystokes Snowmobile Area (Map 17/F7–18/C4)

There are four warming chalets and 350 km (215 mi) of groomed trails found in this huge area 41 km east of Kelowna. The vast majority of the trail network centres on the Graystokes Plateau, but there are also connectors to the Big White and McCulloch Lakes areas and even Lumby in the north. The Graystokes Provincial Park section offers 150 km (93 mi) of marked looped trails with routes leading to lakes, mountain peaks and various cabins. This is a very popular place to ride.

Greenstone Mountain Trails (Map 21/E3–22/A4)

Located southwest of Kamloops, the Greenstone Mountain riding area features ungroomed riding along unploughed forestry and ranching roads. There is access to the extensive trails to the south and west towards Logan Lake area. The Greenstone Mountain Provincial Park allows snowmobiles and there is a lookout and emergency shelter located at the top of the mountain.

Griffin Riding Area (Map 31/F4)

This is another popular area found just 22 km west of Revelstoke off Highway 1 at the Wap Lake Forest Service Road. The ungroomed trails in this area follow the road to the upper cutblocks before leading through some treed trails and into the alpine.

Grizzly Lakes/Clearwater Area (Map 38)

There are over 90 km (55 mi) of trails in this area found northwest of Clearwater. Access is found off several roads including Camp 2 Road, while a well-maintained cabin can be found at Grizzly Lakes.

Groundhog Snowmobile Trails (Map 39/A3–B4)

Travelling south from Blue River, turn left off of Highway 5 onto Finn Creek Forest Service Road to access this riding area leading to Groundhog Mountain. This area is suitable for beginner riders, while the Salmon Lakes and Foam Creek areas, also accessible from Finn Creek Road, are best left to expert riders. Be careful of mountain caribou in the higher elevations.

Harper Creek/Harp Mountain Area (Map 34/A2–B5)

Located 50 minutes north of Kamloops, this remote riding area offers tons of unofficial trails and loops. West of Harper Creek there is an unmaintained trail leading to Granite Mountain, while Foghorn Mountain has a club maintained shelter in the meadows as well as a linking trail to Clearwater. In addition, there is a maintained shelter on Harp Mountain as well as a historic ranger cabin along one of the southern access routes. Access is from the unploughed Harper Creek Forest Service Road at North Barrière Lake or from Vavenby off Highway 5. Due to the remoteness and the maze of side trails this area is best left to intermediate or advanced riders.

Headwater Lakes Area (Map 9/C2–15/G7)

Endless logging roads, powerlines and clearcuts take riders as far west as Nicola Lake. Access is off Brenda Mine Road, just west of Peachland and West Kelowna, or by following the route to Pennask Creek Provincial Park just south of the Coquihalla Connector (Hwy 97C). The trails can also be picked up at the resort on Headwaters Lake. From here head up to the top of Mount Pennask for some great views.

Helmer Lake/Swakum Mountain Snowmobile Trails (Map 14/E2–21/D7)

From the Helmer Exit off the Coquihalla Highway (Hwy 5), about 80 km (50 mi) of snowmobile trails offer fine views along with plenty of variety. The trails to the south lead along a series of logging roads at the base of Swakum Mountain. To the north, the route from Helmer to Mamit Lake is a popular riding area. Helmer Lake is part of a group of lakes connected by the network of gravel roads in the Swakum Mountain range. Most people start at Helmer Lake because it is the only campground in the region with direct access to the trails.

Holmes River Snowmobile Trails (Maps 49, 50)

Accessed off Highway 16 southeast of McBride, 60 km (39 mi) of trails extend north and east along the Holmes River. This route follows the Holmes River Forest Service Road, eventually branching north towards the Alberta border.

Hunters Range Snowmobile Trails (Map 24/F3–31/C6)

Located east of Enderby, there are two trailheads found off the Mable Lake Road. The Ashton Brash trailhead is 7 km up, then left on Watershed Road, while the LaForge trailhead is 30 km from Enderby on the Three Valley Gap Forest Service Road. Each trailhead offers membership and day passes to access the over 240 km (150 mi) of trails, including about 90 km (55 mi) of groomed trail. There are warming cabins along with challenging hills and deep bowls in the alpine. This system links to trails from the north and east that wind their way up Mount Mara and into the extensive alpine meadows in that area.

Idabel Lake/McCullough Snowmobile Trails (Map 10/C2–F6)

This is a family friendly diverse riding zone around the Little White Mountain area combined with groomed trails along the Kettle Valley Railway. To access this area head 6 km past the Big White turn-off on Highway 33, then turn onto McCulloch Road and head towards the Idabel Lake community. A groomer stationed at Idabel Lake maintains an extensive network of about 200 km (125 mi) of trails around eight lakes in the region. Lodging can be found at Idabel Lake and McCulloch Lake with good access off the Okanagan Falls Forest Service Road (Rd 201) as well.

Interlakes Snowmobile Area (Map 32/A1–C3)

The Sheridan Lake area has over 200 km (120 mi) of signed and mapped trails maintained by the South Cariboo Quad Squad, Friends of Sheridan Lake and the Interlakes Snowmobile Club. A map can be found at the Sheridan Lake Resort. The system follows mostly old logging roads, skid trails and animal trails and can be accessed from the parking area on Boulanger Road.

Inks Lake Snowmobile Trails (Map 22/A3)

Linking with the Chuwels Mountain Trails and the Greenstone Mountain Trails, these trails are a maze of old roads and ATV tracks west of the Coquihalla Highway (Hwy 5). There are some marked trails in the area and some single track motorcycle only trails. The system is best suited for intermediate riders and can be quite popular.

Jamieson Creek Snowmobile Area (Map 28/C5)

Located just 30 minutes north of Kamloops, this area is loaded with unorganized trails. The Kamloops Snowmobile Association maintains some trails in the region and these, combined with the forestry roads, allow riders to gain access to numerous meadows and lakes to ride. The area is quite popular and links to a much larger network of trails such as the Tranquille/Sawmill system.

Joss Snowmobile Area (Map 31/F6)

Joss is another area best left for a sunny day due to avalanche risk. There are two routes in, both off Three Valley-Wap Lake Forest Service Road, which is found south off Highway 1, about 24 km west of Revelstoke. The longer route is around 50 km (30 mi) off Iron Road, whereas the shorter route takes you through some extreme and expert terrain. Whichever route you decide once you get into the alpine you will enjoy wide open riding and you can explore the route back through Two Moon Lake.

Lac Le Jeune Snowmobile Trails (Map 21/G6–22/C4)

Located 20 minutes south of Kamloops, the Kamloops Snowmobile Association maintains trails that stretch south and east from Lac Le Jeune. This unorganized trail system runs through rolling hillsides, meadows and lakes on unplowed forestry and ranch roads. The area around the lake is quite busy, but as you make your way south, there are fewer users. This area is also accessed through Edith Lake to the northeast and Ross More Lake to the east.

New regulations by the BC Government have made it legal for snowmobiles to cross a plowed forest service road. The only requirement is that you have liability insurance and a valid driver's licence.

Lake Country Area (Map 17)

This system follows the endless road and trail system along the plateau that runs east of the Okanagan Valley. Access is readily found off any of the main roads, including James Lake or Bata Lake in the south, Postill Lake, Beaver Lake or Oyama Lake near Lake Country or King Edward Lake in the north. Recreation sites provide places to camp or picnic, while ice fishing is possible on the lakes. The Oyama Lake Lookout is a popular destination with a fun hill climb and nice view.

Lichen Mountain Snowmobile Trails (Map 29/G3–30/B2)

These trails are groomed and some head up to the alpine. There is a small chalet available and a series of trails around the base of Little Lichen Mountain as well. Trails also link with the Crowfoot Mountain system and there are lots of unofficial areas between Lichen and Grizzly (Fowler) Mountains offering terrain for intermediate and expert riders. You can climb over 1,000 metres (3,300 ft) and find deep, untracked snow along with some amazing views here.

Lodestone Snowmobile Trails (Map 7/F6–1/D1)

The Lodestone Snowmobile Trails are accessed just west of Coalmont along the Lodestone Lake and Arrastra Creek Forest Service Roads. There are about 100 km (60 mi) of informal trails in the area that head up to Mount Jackson and Lodestone Mountain. A well-used side trail leads to Wells Lake near the northern boundary of Manning Park. It is also possible to follow trails to Tulameen where the Coquihalla Summit Trails lead over to the Mount Henning and Thynne Mountain areas.

Logan Lake Area (Map 21/C7–F4)

Logan Lake has over 100 km (60 mi) of routes to explore, offering mostly wide open terrain and easy trails. The Bose Lake/Forge Mountain area has three peaks over 1,600 metres (5,300 ft), with little avalanche danger. To the southwest there is the Tupper Lake area with mostly unploughed logging roads, while Dominic Lake to the northeast is another popular destination.

McBride Area (Map 49/A2–D1)

Amid the beauty and splendour of the Rocky Mountains, the McBride area offers some of the best backcountry snowmobiling in the province, with an average snowfall of over 3 metres (10 ft) combined with riding elevations between 1,065 and 2,745 metres (3,500-9,000 ft). There are three designated sledding areas (Belle Mountain, Lucille Mountain and the Renshaw Trails) with groomed trails from the parking lots to the riding areas. Trail passes are sold at the trailheads. Homes River also offers some informal riding.

Belle Mountain Trails (Map 49/A2)

This family oriented riding area has around 15 km (9 mi) of groomed trails. A parking lot at the 5 km (3 mi) mark of the Bell Mountain Forest Service Road is shared with the Yellowhead Ski Club, while a cabin sits at the end of the groomed trail.

Lucille Mountain Trails (Map 49/B3)

This trail system features every type of riding experience, from groomed trails to extreme hill climbs. There is parking about 500 metres up the Lucille Mountain Forest Service Road, where there is a loading ramp and toilets. There is also a cabin at the end of the 15 km (9 mi) groomed trail.

Holmes River Trails (Maps 49, 50)

Accessed off Highway 16 southeast of McBride, 60 km (39 mi) of trails extend north and east along the Holmes River. This route follows the Holmes River Forest Service Road, eventually branching north towards the Alberta border.

Renshaw Trails (Map 49/B1–D1)

Possibly the largest mapped riding area in BC, these trails are found just 15 minutes from McBride; follow Mountainview Road to the McKale River Forest Service Road. From here, there is a groomed trail that is 30 km (19 mi) long and leads to the remote riding areas. It is recommended that you carry beacons, shovels and extra gas when riding in this area.

Monashee Motorized Trails (Map 19)

Found north and west of Highway 6, there are over 275 km (170 mi) of trails to explore in this area. The Pinnacles area offers more advanced alpine riding, while the areas around Holmes Lake follow mostly old and active logging roads. The Lumby/Mabel Lake Snowmobile Club grooms some of the trails and also has a trail map of the area. Visit *lmla-bcsf.silkstart.com* to request maps for this area.

Mount Henning Area (Map 7/C5)

Access to the Coquihalla Summit Snowmobile Club Trails, including Mount Henning, is off the Coquihalla Highway (Hwy 5) at the Britton Creek Rest Area. There are fees to ride the Coquihalla Summit Snowmobile Trails, whereas the Timberline Cruisers Snowmobile Club Trails out of Tulameen have no fees. The Timberline Trails link to the Coquihalla system via the Riddell Creek Rabbit Mountain and Lawless Creek Forest Service Roads. There are no less than 50 km (30 mi) of trails around Mount Henning plus a 7.5 km (4.6 mi) trail that links this system with the 55 km (34 mi) of trails around Thynne Mountain.

Nehalliston Snowmobile Trails (Map 33/B3–37/B7)

North of Highway 24, between Bridge Lake and Taweel Lake is the Nehalliston Plateau. This high elevation area is riddled with small fishing lakes and old roads that make up a series of fine snowmobile trails. The Windy Mountain Connector links this system with the trails around Bowers and Needa Lake. The Barrett Perimeter Trails also run through this area.

Olalla to Apex Mountain (Map 3/D3–B1)

This unmaintained 20 km (12 mi) trail needs a lot of snow on the ground before there is enough clearance to get over the blowdowns and stumps. This route should be left to experienced riders as it crosses over high mountainous areas where weather conditions can change rapidly. Follow Olalla Creek Forest Service Road to the trailhead.

Osprey-Paradise Snowmobile Trails (Maps 8, 15)

This informal riding area is found north and south of Highway 97C, about halfway between Aspen Grove and Kelowna. Access can be found off the Sunset or Elkhart Exits. There are close to 190 km (120 mi) of trails to explore in this high plateau area.

Owlhead/Mara Mountain Snowmobile Trails (Map 30/G6–31/B6)

Logging roads wind their way up Mara Mountain and into extensive alpine meadows where the high elevation (over 2,000 metres/6,500 ft) ensures good riding until late spring. The local snowmobile club groom the road and maintain a warming chalet about 21 km (13 mi) up the trail. The Super Bowl is a popular destination for those wanting to do some hill climbing. There is parking at the start of the Owlhead Forest Service Road off the MacLean/MacPherson Road.

Park Range Snowmobile Trails (Map 25/D5–F3)

North of Lumby, near Mabel Lake Provincial Park, is a sprawling area comprised of trails and unploughed logging roads, offering a mix of terrain, including a series of alpine sections and cut blocks. Accessed off either Squaw Valley or Traylor Creek Roads, the Lumby/Mabel Lake Snowmobile Club grooms the trails and maintains a chalet near Ireland Creek.

Paulson Summit (Map 6/F3–G2)

This sprawling area is found 26 km northeast of Christina Lake or 9 km west of Nancy Greene Provincial Park at the 24 Mile Staging Area. Riders can head up to the Walker Creek Cabin or up to the Mount Shields area via the Bulldog Forest Service Road. There are more than 200 km (120 mi) of trails in the area, with at least 30 km (18 mi) of them groomed by the West Kootenay Snowmobile Association. Beyond the groomed trails, the riding is more challenging, with some old cutblocks to play in and some interesting areas around Mount Shields. You need to be a club member to ride here and you can usually purchase a pass at the trailhead.

Porcupine Meadows Snowmobile Trails (Map 27/F5–28/A4)

Part of the Tranquille/Sawmill Trails north of Kamloops, Porcupine Meadows Provincial Park is open to snowmobiles from December 15th to April 15th and offers ungroomed trails to explore. Access is from the chalet at the 31.5 km mark on the Sawmill Main Forest Service Road where there are plenty of groomed trails and unplowed roads to ride.

Prospect/Honeymoon Snowmobile Area (Map 13/E6–14/A5)

Near Merritt, Stoyoma Mountain receives early snowfall and the Merritt Snowmobile Club maintains more than 85 km (50 mi) of trails in the area. The system leads into high mountain country and avalanche territory including trails around Cabin Lake and Stoyoma Mountain as well as the Honeymoon area further west. From Highway 8 turn onto the Spius Creek Road and look for snowmobile signs, at the 7.5 km mark there is a gravel parking lot and a kiosk with a trail map. If the road is plowed continue to the 24 km mark.

Queest Mountain Trails (Map 30/G5–31/A3)

Queest Mountain lies just north of Sicamous and offers about 35 km² (22 mi²) of riding with deep powder and exciting hill climbs. There is a warming chalet 26 km (16 mi) up, where there is a great view of Shuswap Lake. Take the Queest Mountain or 1800 Forest Service Road to the base, where the grooming typically starts. If the road is ploughed then continue to the parking area just after the 14 km mark.

Raft Mountain Snowmobile Trails (Map 37/G7–38/A6)

Northeast of Clearwater riders can explore over 50 km (30 mi) of logging roads and 26 km (16 mi) of trails around Raft Mountain. The area offers everything from easy, low elevation routes to high elevation alpine trails. The Clearwater Sno-Drifters club maintains the trails and the two cabins found near the treeline. Access and parking is off Clearwater Valley Road.

Sawmill Snowmobile Connector (Map 27/D3)

Located northwest of Kamloops, snowmobile riders will find the 29 km (18 mi) Sawmill Snowmobile Connector off of Deadman Vidette Road. This snowmobile route connects the Deadman Valley to the Tranquille Plateau as well as to the trails around Bonaparte Park.

Spa Hills (Map 23/F4–24/A3)

North of Falkland, there are multiple access points to this riding area. There are about 80 km (50 mi) of marked trails in the Bolean, Arthur and Spa Lakes area along with warm up shelters at Bolean Lake and near Spa Lake. Riding is along roads, through clear cuts, meadows and burned off areas, but road access is subject to logging activity. Connecting trails link to the Fly Hills system out of Salmon Arm for days of riding.

Silver Star Trails/Vernon Snowmobile Area (Map 24/F6–G4)

There are 50 km (30 mi) of trails within Silver Star Provincial Park and another 150 km (90 mi) of trails outside the park. The area also features two chalets; the Silver Star Chalet and the Armstrong Chalet. A popular route is the Trinity-Ricardo Trail, which links the Silver Star area with the Trinity Valley to the north. This network of 60 km (37 mi) of groomed trails starts by following the Ganzeveld Trail over the summit.

Summit Seekers Snowmobile Trails (Maps 1, 2)

Accessed by Whipsaw Creek Forest Service Road, there are about 50 km (30 mi) of trails running just north of Manning Provincial Park. The trails are groomed on occasion and lead to an emergency shelter at Frog Hollow. They also connect to the Lodestone Trail network out of Tulameen. Across the highway, the Placer Mountain area is also maintained by the same club. There is an emergency shelter on Placer Mountain as well.

Thuya Lakes Snowmobile Trails (Map 33/B5)

West of the town of Little Fort, you can find the trailhead to this system off the Thuya Lake Road south of Eakin Creek Road. This collection of trails and roads connects a number of small lakes in the area and is usually well marked. Although the area is subject to logging and some connector roads may be plowed, when conditions are good, riders can easily cover 100 km (60 mi) in a day.

Thynne Mountain Trails (Map 7/B5–D2)

Part of the Merritt Snowmobile Club, the staging area for the Thynne Mountain Trails is found near Brookmere, where the Thynne Mountain Forest Service Road starts. There are 55 km (34 mi) of trails to explore here, and the majority of them are groomed and signed. The club also maintains two shelters known as the Tin Shed and Andy's Lake Emergency Shelter. Andy's Lake Shelter is on the north shore of Andy's Lake, while it is possible to link with the Mount Henning area to the south. All fees go directly to the maintenance of these shelters and trails.

Tod Mountain Snowmobile Area (Map 28/G5–29/C7)

Found behind Sun Peaks Ski Village, the Tod Mountain system is managed by the Kamloops Snowmobile Association. Follow signs from Sun Peaks to the public snowmobile parking area. The snowmobile trails snake up the backside of Tod Mountain and riders must stay on defined trails as this is a skiing area as well. The trails follow mostly unplowed forestry roads, but some are groomed by Sun Peaks Adventure Tours. There is a club shelter on the western side of Cahilty Mountain.

Tranquille/Sawmill Snowmobile Trails (Maps 27, 28)

This large riding area is accessed from the Kamloops Clubhouse at km 31.5 on the Sawmill Main Forest Service Road. There are plenty of groomed trails and unploughed roads to ride northeast of Tranquille Lake. Riders will find two shelters in the area, one just outside the Porcupine Meadows Park, as well as an old forest lookout at the height of land. Further north, riders can enjoy the trails around Bonaparte Provincial Park, while the Jamieson Creek Area is also known for its excellent snowmobile trails through beautiful meadows and lakes. Adding to the mix are a series of roads and trails leading further west to explore the plateau and connect up with the Deadman River. The main route leads past Gisborne Lake, over Criss Creek and past a series of lakes en route to Uren Lake. Continuing north from the Deadman River area trails lead past Hammer and Bonaparte Lake to eventually link with the Barnett Perimeter Trail.

Snowmobiles should have brightly coloured antenna flags mounted on rods that are 1.2 to 2.4 metres (4-8 ft) long located on the back of the snowmobile. This is especially important if you're driving in a hilly area so that others can see you.

Tunkwa Lake Loop (Map 21/C3)

Located in and around the Tunkwa Provincial Park this loop provides a scenic, flat ride through trees and meadows. This is family friendly riding with no major hills or cliffs. You can ride the loop along some nice tree lined trails for about 50 km (30 mi) worth of riding. There is a staging area bordering the North Leighton Campground.

West Ridge Snowmobile Trail (Map 46/G3)

Just west of Valemount this area is an ideal place for family friendly riding. A 22 km (14 mi) circuit starting from the west side of Highway 5 leads you along the sporadically groomed trails that provide access to alpine powder. There is a warming cabin at the far end of the area. For more adventure there are numerous cutblocks and detours to explore. The West Ridge Loop connects to the larger West Ridge riding area and offers more technical riding and large open bowls for the advanced riders. Note the ridge and alpine areas above the trail are closed to snowmobiling.

WILDLIFE ADVENTURES

One of the greatest things about being in the wilderness is spotting the residents in their natural environments. British Columbia has an international reputation as being an excellent place to see wildlife. Despite the development and hot, dry climate, the Southern Interior offers an abundance of species to view. In addition to birds and animals common to the rest of BC, this region is one of the best areas of the province to see mountain goats and California bighorn sheep.

The hot, arid climate of the south Okanagan is home to species that are not generally found elsewhere in the province.

Some wildlife is easy to spot. Salmon viewing, for instance, is a matter of getting down to the right stream at the right time. On the other hand, many birds and animals tend to flee when they hear, see or smell humans. In order to improve your chances of spotting these more elusive creatures, wear natural colours and unscented lotions. Bring along binoculars or scopes so you can observe from a distance and move slowly but steadily. Keep pets on a leash, or better yet, leave them at home, as they will only decrease your chances to spot wildlife. Early mornings and late evenings are usually the best time to see most birds and animals.

Never approach an animal directly and for heaven's sake, do not try and bring animals to you by offering them food. Animals can become conditioned to handouts, which may put both of you in harm's way. Rather, figure out what natural foods they prefer, and situate yourself near where these animals will feed.

This list is certainly far from a complete list of everywhere you can see a bird or beast. For instance, it is nearly impossible to peddle certain sections of the Kettle Valley Railway in late summer without coming across a black bear feeding on berries or a deer on foliage. This is, however, a very good start.

Most wildlife watching is seasonal. Migratory birds are seen in spring and fall, while reptiles are rarely seen outside of summer. As you discover the joys of watching wildlife, you will learn the rhythms of the seasons.

Remember, not all wildlife watching sites are created equal. Some of the sites below cater mostly to birders, while other sites feature large mammals like deer and bighorn sheep. Still other sites focus on fish. All of them are worth checking out. For more information on wildlife watching, contact an area club, like the Kamloops Naturalist Club or the South Okanagan Naturalist Club.

DID YOU KNOW?

WE HAVE A THRIVING INSTAGRAM COMMUNITY

@backroadmapbooks
Follow us and discover Canada from a whole new perspective. Our gallery features some of the most stunning photos of Canada's backcountry.

#brmb
Tag us in your photos: join one of Canada's fastest growing outdoor communities for a chance to get featured in our feed.

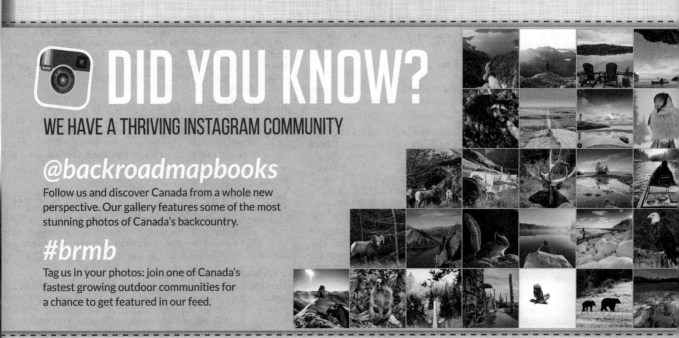

WILDLIFE ADVENTURES

Anstey Hunakwa Provincial Park (Map 30/G1–31/A1; 35/G7–36/A7)
The habitats of grizzly, black bear, moose, mule deer, pine marten, Townsend's big-eared bat and fisher are found within the park. This is also spawning ground for Coho and sockeye salmon, kokanee, lake trout and rainbow trout.

Blue Earth Lake Provincial Park (Map 20/B4)
Located about 30 km southwest of Cache Creek, Blue Earth Lake Provincial Park is accessed from the gravel Venables Road off the Trans-Canada Highway north of Spences Bridge. Within this 705 hectare (1,740 ac) park you will find numerous lakes, wetlands and riparian areas supporting various species of songbird and migrating waterfowl.

Blue River Provincial Parks (Map 43/A7–A6)
The deep oxbows and meandering sections of this northern part of the Thompson River are important spawning grounds for rainbow and bull trout, as well as Chinook and Coho salmon. Large stands of rare black spruce provide nesting grounds for great blue heron, who feed on the fish along with a large black bear population. Moose and mule deer also frequent the area.

Bonaparte Provincial Park (Map 27/G1–28/A2)
This is a wild, undeveloped watershed containing sub-alpine spruce forest, lakes and sedge meadows which host a diverse array of species, including cranes, rainbow trout, deer, black bear, beaver, timber wolf, moose, great horned owl and many others.

Boothman Oxbows (Map 6/C6)
This site just east of Grand Forks contains a large wetland. Bird lovers will find a variety of species ranging from songbird to woodpeckers and waterfowl. April to September is the best time to visit.

Botanie Creek Valley (Map 13/A2–20/A6)
The Botanie Creek Valley has a high diversity of wildlife, from rattlesnake to spotted bat to bald eagle. But the big viewing opportunity is for bighorn sheep. The sheep are often found along the road or on the cliffs across the creek. There are a number of fire roads leading up into the sub-alpine, which is famous for its proliferation of wildflowers.

Buse Lake Protected Area (Map 22/G3)
Approximately 20 km southeast of Kamloops, Buse Lake is a prime spot for bird watchers as its rich alkaline shoreline brings waterfowl and shorebirds of all shapes and sizes. Rare species such as the American avocet can be spotted on occasion. Buse Hill also offers expansive views of the surrounding Thompson Basin and those with binoculars may spy a bear or two rummaging for berries.

Darke Lake Provincial Park (Map 9/C3)
This off-the-beaten-path location sits amongst the fir and pine clad hills of the Okanagan, northwest of Summerland off Highway 97. White-tailed deer are common in this area as they pick their way through the forest on silent hooves. Darke Lake also provides habitat for blue and red listed bird species and shorebirds, notably the barn and flammulated owl and Northern goshawk.

Douglas Lake–Monte Creek Corridor (Map 15/E3–23/B5)
Between Douglas Lake and Monte Lake you will frequently see birds (hawks, grouse, pelicans and waterfowl) and mammals such as mule deer and coyote along the side of the road.

E.C. Manning Provincial Park (Map 1/A5–G7)
Backcountry enthusiasts that frequent this year-round recreation area will be treated to a variety of species to view. There have been 206 separate species of birds and 63 species of mammals recorded here. Some of the species are quite common, such as the common pika and Columbian ground squirrel, while less common inhabitants include the Cascade golden-mantled squirrel, mountain beaver and wolverine. The threatened grizzly bear also calls the park and the associated Cascade Recreation home. Another at risk species found here is the spotted owl.

Elephant Hill Provincial Park (Map 20/E1)
At 995 hectares (2,460 ac), this natural protected area includes parcels of ungrazed and lightly grazed grasslands in some of the driest conditions in the province. There are often rattlesnakes and gopher snakes huddled in the underbrush, while mule deer, coyote and various species of birds like the common merganser, chukar, belted kingfisher, rosy finch and sharp-tailed grouse can be seen here.

Emar Lakes Provincial Park (Map 33/B3)
A chain of small lakes and wetlands in this 1,604 hectare (3,965 ac) park provides habitat for the black tern, common loon, great horned owl, ruffed grouse and moose.

Goldpan Provincial Park (Map 20/C7)
Established in 1956, this park preserves the historical nature of the area, while California bighorn sheep can be viewed on the surrounding hills by Spences Bridge. Also look for osprey flying overhead and salmon, trout and steelhead in the Thompson River.

Graystokes Provincial Park (Map 18/B4–C7)
The extensive complex of swamps, streams and wetland meadows mixed with forest within this park make it unique to the Southern Interior. Forest types range from mid-elevation to alpine and include extensive old growth Engelmann spruce and Douglas fir. The park provides habitats for a number of large mammals like moose, mule and white-tailed deer, mountain caribou and bear. Lynx, wolverines, ptarmigan and grouse also call this area home.

Haynes Point Provincial Park (Map 4/B7)
Haynes Point sits on a pencil of land jutting into Osoyoos Lake. Families of California quail are common in summer, while from April through September watch for marsh wrens, eastern kingbirds, gray catbirds, cedar waxwings, yellow-headed blackbirds and orioles. The best viewing times are when there are fewer visitors in the park.

Hedley–Keremeos Cliffs (Map 3/B4)
More than 150 mountain goats call the south-facing cliffs along Highway 3 between Hedley and Keremeos home. Viewing is best done with binoculars from the highway since the goats are usually high up on the hillside. Although present year round, the goats are best seen from April to October.

Juniper Beach Provincial Park (Map 20/G1–26/G7)
This park is located in between Cache Creek and Kamloops and is home to the western rattlesnake as well as a few deer. The main attraction here is the bird watching for species such as mountain blue bird, northern oriole and the western tanager.

> *When observing wildlife from a vehicle, slow down to ensure the animal's safety, but do not come to a complete stop. This is recommended to avoid the habituation of wildlife to high-traffic areas.*

Kalamalka Lake Provincial Park & Protected Area (Map 17/D2)
This park has a little something for everyone with a variety of mammals, birds and reptiles residing in this mosaic of grassland communities. Larger herbivores like the white-tailed and mule deer mix with predators such as cougar, black bear, coyote, red fox and bobcat. A great spot for birdwatchers, the park provides habitat for the Canada goose, canyon wren, white-throated swift and western screech and flammulated owl. The variety of reptiles here is also vast, including pacific rubber boa, western rattlesnake, western yellow-bellied racer, gopher snake, western painted turtle, Great Basin spadefoot toad and northern alligator lizard.

Kingfisher Interpretive Centre & Hatchery (Map 25/B3)
This hatchery rears Chinook and Coho salmon and rainbow trout and has an interpretive trail. It is located along Cooke Creek about 21 km east of Enderby on the Mabel Lake Road. Closer to town, the Shuswap River is a good place to view osprey and their nests on the hydro towers. Chinook, Coho and sockeye salmon as well as kokanee can also be seen spawning in the river from mid-September to mid-October.

Lac du Bois Grasslands Provincial Park (Maps 21, 22, 27, 28)
Rising above the hot, dry Thompson Valley, this area helps protect three grassland communities surrounded by forested hills. California bighorn sheep, mule deer, moose and waterfowl are common residents and visitors to the park, while the western rattlesnake, sharp-tailed grouse and flammulated owl live more secretive lives within its boundaries.

Loon Creek Hatchery (Map 26/C4)
The Loon Creek Hatchery is one of five such hatcheries run by the province. This one produces kokanee and rainbow trout. Combined, these hatcheries populate about 1,200 lakes with between 10 and 12 million fish each year. The hatchery is located 20 km north of Cache Creek on the paved Loon Lake Road.

Momich Lakes Provincial Park (Map 34/G5–35/B5)

Momich Lakes Park encompasses frontage on Adams Lake and three smaller lakes as well as their associated wetlands. The Momich River and its flood plain are also a part of the habitat for beaver, black bear, moose, mule deer and muskrat. There are also sockeye salmon and native stocks of trout and other fish species in the river.

Mud Lake Delta Provincial Park (Map 43/C7)

For the true nature enthusiast, this secluded 500 hectare (1,235 ac) park provides habitats of rich floodplain wetlands, back channels, beaver ponds and oxbow lakes. The steep slopes surrounding this area are a mixture of old growth cedar, hemlock and spruce. Within this area you may witness bull trout and Coho salmon spawning, moose and other larger herbivores roaming through the wet valley and various species of songbirds. Be careful and aware of your surroundings as this area can be a spring grizzly bear range as well, due to the abundance of spawning fish.

Okanagan Mountain Provincial Park (Map 9/F3)

Above Okanagan Lake, this large park covers over 10,000 hectares (24,700 ac) of rugged landscape with mountain lakes, grasslands as well as spruce and fir forests. The park is only accessible by boat, on foot, horseback or bicycle and is a good bird watching area. A variety of large and small mammals can also be seen on occasion.

Osoyoos Oxbows Wildlife Reserve (Map 4/A6)

The Okanagan River north of Osoyoos is a great spot for birders, and an amazing list of species may be observed here. There is dyke and road access along the river as well as many trails for visitors to get close to the various habitats.

Paul Lake Provincial Park (Map 22/F1)

This park can be extremely busy during the summer. Birdwatchers may find it more difficult to see the bald eagles, falcons, osprey, swallows, and white-throated swifts common to the area. The park also protects habitat for coyote and mule deer.

Pritchard Provincial Park (Map 23/C2)

This park protects one of the few spots along the Thompson River between Chase and Kamloops that is not under private ownership. Visitors can spot trumpeter swan and a variety of other waterfowl and shorebirds, as well as beaver, muskrat, otter and passerines.

Raft River (Map 33/G1–38/D3)

In fall, the Raft River is home to returning sockeye and Chinook salmon. Raptors such as bald eagles and turkey vultures can also be seen here: turkey vultures are common in summer, while eagles are seen frequently in winter.

Roderick Haig-Brown Provincial Park (Map 29/F5)

This section of the Adams River is world famous for its sockeye salmon run. This amazing display of nature occurs every fall, but it is the dominant runs, where millions of fish jam the stream that attracts all of the attention. The dominant runs occur every four years – 2010, 2014, 2018, etc. At other times of the year, birds and small mammals can be seen along the well-developed trail system in the park.

Salmon Arm Nature Park (Map 24/C1)

The Salmon Arm Nature Bay Enhancement Society operates an information centre at Marine Park in the north end of town. In addition to bird blinds, every May there is a Grebe Festival in honour of the western grebes that make this area home.

Shuswap River Hatchery (Map 18/D1)

Chinook salmon are raised at this small hatchery on a scenic section of the Shuswap River. The hatchery is open to the public, and is found about 32 km east of Vernon.

Skihist Provincial Park (Map 13/B2)

This hot, dry area is home to a variety of birds, which frequent the campsite and the nature trail taking you to the scenic bench above the river. There is also a herd of elk that have been introduced in the area along with California big horn sheep and bear.

South Okanagan Grasslands Protected Area (Map 3/F5–4/A7)

This protected area encompasses 9,364 hectares (23,130 ac) comprising of four sites: Mount Kobau, Kilpoola, Chopaka East and Chopaka West. Habitats for an astonishing number of rare and endangered birds, mammals, reptiles and amphibians can be found within this large area. Mount Kobau is home to a bighorn sheep and mule deer range with the feature bird being the Brewer's sparrow. In Chopaka East and West and the Kilpoola site birders will find the sage thrasher and grasshopper sparrow. In fact, Chopaka West is the only place in the province that these birds regularly breed. Of course, many other bird species can be seen flying around or resting in the trees.

Spences Bridge (Map 20/D6)

Large herds of bighorn sheep are visible in and around the community of Spences Bridge throughout the year. Although the site of the sheep excites visitors, they do cause the local residents grief by often eating laundry that is hanging to dry. A patient observer may also see elk, deer, coyote, black bears, cougar, bobcat, lynx, bald eagles, ospreys and many other wildlife species.

Spius Creek Hatchery (Map 14/A4)

Approximately 15 km west of Merritt on Sunshine Valley Road, this hatchery features self-guided tours, and is open every day except Christmas, Boxing Day and New Years. The hatchery raises Chinook salmon, which return in September, and Coho salmon, which return in November. Juveniles can be seen all year.

Summerland Trout Hatchery (Map 9/F5)

This provincial hatchery is popular with visitors looking to learn more about rainbow trout and brook trout. Facilities include a fisheries interpretative centre and spawning channels. The hatchery is located 14 km north of Penticton on Highway 97. Turn right on Lakeside Drive and continue for a kilometre.

Swan Lake (Map 24/D7)

Swan Lake is a birding hotspot in the North Okanagan area. During the spring and fall migration, Sharp-tailed sandpiper and lesser golden-plover are spotted on occasion, while American avocet, black-necked stilt and black-crowned night-heron are seen less frequently. Common waterfowl species includes green-winged, blue-winged and cinnamon teals, ruddy duck, barrows and common goldeneyes, bufflehead, Canada geese and American coot.

Taweel Provincial Park (Map 33/B1–37/A7)

Access into this 4,558 hectare (11,260 ac) park is limited since the access road to the southeast shore of Taweel Lake is privately owned and controlled by the resorts on the lake. This helps maintain the habitat in this park for the wild native rainbow trout, marten, moose, timber wolf and birds such as the barrow's goldeneye, common loon and the three-toed woodpecker.

Tranquille Marsh (Map 22/A1)

Located 10 km west of North Kamloops on Tranquille Road, the marsh is often completely flooded in late spring. Access is difficult at this time but improves from May to mid-June. Fall is also a good time to visit. Tranquille Marsh is known for migratory waterfowl, especially swans.

Tunkwa Provincial Park (Map 21/C3)

Located between Savona and Logan Lake, this park is a mosaic of grasslands and interior Douglas-fir forests with several lakes and wetlands providing ideal habitat for spawning trout in May. The park is also home to moose, mule and white-tailed deer and birds such as the Canada goose, common snipe, mallard, mountain bluebird and vesper sparrow.

Upper Adams River Provincial Park (Map 34/G4–39/D3)

River otter, elk, moose and black bear are inhabitants of this park located between Adams and Tumtum Lakes.

Vaseux Lake Wildlife Area (Map 4/A3–B3)

The best time to visit this trail-accessed area is in spring and fall, especially during bird migrations. The National Waterfowl Sanctuary is host to a wide variety of bird species. In winter watch for California bighorn sheep in the hillsides east of the parking area.

Ward's Lake (Map 6/A6)

This small lake contains good habitat for birds and migratory waterfowl. In recent years the water level has been a problem. When water levels are up, watch for yellowlegs and sandpipers, while many songbirds, including bluebirds, blackbirds, kingbirds, flycatchers, sparrows and warblers, can be seen from April to September.

Wells Gray Park (Maps 37, 38, 41, 42)

Wells Gray is a big park, and has an extensive variety of ecosystems. There are many types of wildlife here, from predators like wolf, cougar, lynx, bobcat, wolverine, and grizzly and black bear to large ungulates such as moose, deer, goat and caribou. There have been 219 species of birds seen in the park.

White Lake Provincial Park (Map 30/C5)

White Lake is home to an intermountain-Rocky Mountain population of the western painted turtle which is the only native pond turtle left in British Columbia.

WINTER ADVENTURES

People living in the Southern Interior have long known that winter is a sacred time. Although the days are shorter, there is a certain beauty and stillness that only winter brings. Even better, many of the trail systems are often abandoned during the week allowing for a more peaceful adventure.

This is a moderate climate and the winters, while not as warm as on the coast, are still quite pleasant. In fact, there are areas in the Okanagan Valley and Boundary Region where snow rarely falls and lakes do not freeze over. However, a slight rise in elevation changes all of that. Cross-country skiers can often be out on the trails by mid to late November through March.

This slightly cooler climate is a boon for winter enthusiasts. While the so-called wet-coast concrete is falling at Whistler, places like Sun Peaks, Silver Star and Big White are being blanketed in light, fluffy snow that the locals call champagne powder. Also nicknamed hero's powder, this snow can make moderately talented skiers look (and feel) like experts.

Big White is second only to Whistler in sheer size, but all the interior resorts have been adding new runs and expanding. Yes, there is more to skiing BC than just Whistler/Blackcomb. Fortunately, most of the ski hills retain the charm and friendly attitude that made them such a popular getaway for Vancouver skiers in the know just a decade ago and, more recently, for Australians.

Cross-country skiing remains a very popular activity in the interior. Some of the province's best trails are located in this area, from the extremely popular trails at Nickel Plate to the sprawling interconnected trail system at Silver Star Mountain/Sovereign Lake. And if groomed trails do not do it for you, there are plenty of places for the adventurous backcountry skier to explore.

Snowshoeing is a sport that has been rapidly gaining popularity for snowbound hikers. Part of its newfound appeal can be attributed to the radical design innovations that have taken place over the last few years. Snowshoes have gone from unwieldy racquets attached to the feet to devices that are only slightly larger than a pair of boots and are just as easy to walk in.

It is important to remember that backcountry travel comes with a degree of risk that, while manageable, is never non-existent. Be sure to stick to established trails or known backcountry routes. If possible, travel with someone who has more experience or take a lesson on avalanche safety. And, always, always carry an avalanche transceiver.

Apex Mountain Ski Area (Map 3/C2)

Apex Mountain Resort is the smallest of the big resorts in the Okanagan, with 73 downhill runs, the longest one being 5 km, all accessed by four lifts. There are also ungroomed backcountry ski trails at the resort. A 6 km return trail leads from the bunny hill near the lodge around the far side of the ski hill to Mount Riordan. The same trail accesses a route to Beaconsfield Mountain, which is about 10 km return, gaining 350 m (1,140 ft) along the way. From Apex Mountain, a 6 km cross-country trail links to the Nickel Plate Lake Ski Trails. Terrain parks, a Tube Park (open day and night) and a 1 km night lit skating loop also add to the resort's appeal. Visit the resort website at *apexresort.com* for additional details.

Barrière Forks Cross-Country Ski Trails (Map 34/A7)

Maintained by the Barrière Outdoor Club, this small cross-country ski area has 6 km (3.7 mi) of groomed trails that are open to the public without fees. There is a warming hut on site.

Belle Mountain Ski Trails (Map 49/B2)

Offering over 20 km (12.5 mi) of easy to difficult trails, groomed for classic and skate skiing, this system traverses through a mix of wooded and open areas, with occasional viewpoints of the valley below. The trailhead, located 8 km east of McBride, is also home to a warm up cabin and outhouses. Nearby Dore Valley also offers some ungroomed trails for snowshoeing and backcountry skiers. The trails are maintained by the Yellowhead Ski Club and there is now a 10 person cabin on the Pine Lake Loop available for booking. Contact Terri at 250-569-3362 for booking and to check trail conditions or visit their Facebook page.

Big Bar/Clinton Cross-Country Trails (Map 26/A2)

Found just north of Clinton, there are over 50 km (30 mi) of trails in the area, with about half of them groomed for cross-country skiing at any given time. Several trails head to viewpoints over the Marble Range. The trails are easily accessed of Big Bar Road and snowshoeing is an option.

Big White Ski Area (Map 11/B2)

With 3,052 hectares of skiable terrain and 118 designated trails accessed by 16 lifts, Big White is the second largest downhill ski area in the entire province. The mountain has a great mix of terrain, but the area is best known for open bowls full of champagne powder. Cross-country skiers will find about 25 km (16 mi) of groomed trails, while snowshoers can access 15 km (9 mi) of mapped trails at the base of the resort. The resort also offers a Terrain Park and a Tube Park. Visit *bigwhite.com* for more information.

Blue River Trails (Map 38/G1–43/A7)

The Blue River Trails are located in the east part of town near Eleanor Lake and the Thompson River. There are about 5 km (3.2 mi) of easy, scenic trails. Further to the northeast is the River Loop Trail, while those seeking a bit more challenge can explore the Murtle Lake Ski Trails west of town. The 10 km (6.25 mi) system is found off the south side of the Murtle Lake Forest Service Road.

Camp Creek Ski Trails (Map 47/B3)

The Camp Creek trail system is found off the Camp Creek Road south of Valemount. The 10 km (6.25 mi) trail system is regularly groomed and offers loops ranging from easy to difficult. There is plenty of parking available at the trailhead, along with picnic tables and a cooking shelter for visitors to enjoy. Additional trails can be found at Jackman Flats, or you can get out in the fresh powder and carve your own path at Tete Jaune.

Candle Creek Trails (Map 37/G7)

North of the town of Clearwater, you can find the Candle Creek Trails off the west side of Clearwater Valley Road. There is a parking area available complete with a warming cabin and outhouses for visitors. The trail system is maintained throughout the winter and offers 28 km (17.5 mi) of easy to difficult interconnecting loops. The longest is the 13.9 km Outside Loop.

Carmi Ski Trails (Map 10/B6)

Located in the Ellis Creek Demonstration Forest are 17 km (10.6 mi) of well-marked trails. The trails are not groomed in the winter, but are easy to follow and are usually well broken. The main trail is quite challenging with steep hills (up to 17 degrees). There is also a popular toboggan hill next to the parking lot.

China Ridge Ski Trails (Map 7/G6–8/A7)

Located west of Princeton at the recently closed Snowpatch Ski Hill, there is a 40 km (25 mi) network of snowshoe and ski trails, with 20 km (12.5 mi) of the trails groomed. The trails follow old roads through open timber, cutblocks and across natural grassy slopes, with 20 km groomed for cross-country skiing. The trails offer a view of the Tulameen River Valley as well as shelters and

warm-up huts. Additionally, there are specific trails for skiing with your dog and another 5 km (3.1 mi) of snowshoe trails. Maps and additional details can be found on the ski club website at *chinaridgetrails.com*.

Crystal Mountain Ski Hill (Map 16/E7)

Crystal Mountain is a small ski hill located near Westbank on the outskirts of Kelowna. There are 30 runs of various degrees of difficulty serviced by three lifts as well as a terrain park. There are also 12 km (7.5 mi) of snowshoe trails in the area. Visit *crystalresort.com* for more information.

Harper Mountain Ski Hill (Map 22/F1)

Found east of Kamloops on the Paul Lake Road, this small community ski hill has 16 runs accessed by three lifts. The hill also has an 8 km (5 mi) cross-country trail system that is not patrolled and is track set occasionally, as well as a tube park and a terrain park to enjoy. Visit *harpermountain.com* for more information.

Jackman Flats Trails (Map 46/F1)

There are a number of groomed ski trails just off Highway 5 near Valemount ranging in length from 1.4 km to 6.2 km (3.9 mi). The trails traverse through both wetlands and sand dunes that make for interesting sites in winter. Additional trails can be found at Camp Creek.

Jewel Lake Ski Trails (Map 5/F4)

From the Jewel Lake Lodge at the south end of the lake, three short loop trails (up to 5.8 km/3.6 mi long) lead through the pine forest. These trails are well marked and groomed and provide an enjoyable outing for all levels of skiers. Also in the area is the more challenging Calypso Trail, which leads up Mount Roderick Dhu. This route is a popular snowmobile destination.

Johnson Lake Ski Trails (Map 29/C1)

Over 58 km (36 mi) of cross-country and snowshoe trails can be found here with the longest trail being the Johnson Lake Loop Trail at 22.4 km (14 mi). Access to the trails can be found at the Johnson Lake Recreational Site or at the Johnson Lake Resort. However, the resort closes around mid-December each year for the winter. Snowmobile clubs use the area in the winter as well.

Kane Valley Cross-Country Trails (Map 14/F6)

The beautiful Kane Valley is home to a well-established 50 km (30 mi) trail system. Designed for beginner to intermediate skiers, the trails follow old roads and trails through open timber and across sloping meadows. The ski season runs from December to March and there is a good map found on the ski club website, *nicolanordic.ca*, to help pick your route, with six different trailheads to choose from. Generally speaking, there is easier terrain found around the second trailhead, while the perimeter trail offers a more challenging route.

Be sure to dress in layers, in order to enable you to peel off or add clothing as needed to adjust your comfort level.

Lac Le Jeune Ski Trails (Map 22/A5)

This network of trails and old roads circle the popular recreational lake south of Kamloops. The moderate to difficult trail system is not groomed and features some long, steep climbs. Including the trails around Stake and McConnell Lakes, there are 73 km (45 mi) of trails, including snowshoe and dog friendly trails, passing through a variety of terrain, from open meadows and hillsides to narrow forested trails. Snowmobilers also access the trails.

Larch Hills Ski Trails (Map 24/D1–30/D7)

Located on Edgar Road east of Salmon Arm, Larch Hills has over 150 km (94 mi) of ski trails to explore (43 km of the trails are groomed and 98 km are ungroomed). There are several chalets and shelters to help take the edge off those cool days. The trail system follows a network of old and new logging roads, which criss-cross their way throughout the area. In addition, there are marked snowshoe trails and a dog friendly multi-use trail. Donations are encouraged to help with trail maintenance. Trail maps and more can be found on the Larch Hills Nordic Society webpage, *skilarchhills.ca*.

Logan Lake Cross-Country Trails (Map 21/D5)

At Logan Lake, there are 36 km (22 mi) of groomed ski trails, ranging from 1 km to 6 km, suitable for all abilities. The trails are tracked set for both skating and classic skiing and include 2 km of lit trails for night skiing. In addition, there are 7.5 km of shared trails and an additional 5 km of dedicated trails for snowshoeing. Trail maps and more can be found at *highlandvalleyoutdoorassociation.com*.

Manning Park (Map 1)

Manning Park is a great winter destination offering a resort and everything from backcountry skiing to downhill skiing. The main cross-country area has two warming huts and over 30 km (19 mi) of groomed trails, including 17 km (10.5 mi) of skate skiing trails, which weave around the rolling forested hills near Lightning Lake. There are also over 160 km of backcountry routes leading to the end of Lightning Lake, around Cambie Creek and even up the ridge of the Three Brothers. Snowshoers can travel the backcountry as well, or enjoy the 13 km (8 mi) of trails at Manning Park Resort. Gibson Pass Ski Area is a nice family downhill area with over 30 runs and four lifts. Visit *manningpark.com* for more information.

Marshall Lake Ski Trails (Map 5/G5)

Easily accessed on the Phoenix Mountain Road west of Grand Forks, Marshall Lake is a popular cross-country ski area with 17.5 km (11 mi) of trails that are also used by snowshoers and even snowmobilers (please stay off the set ski tracks). The cross-country ski trails link to the nearby Phoenix Alpine Ski Area, which is a community run hill.

McCulloch Cross-Country Trails (Map 10/E2)

The Kelowna Nordic Ski Club has been quite active in this area. Currently, there are about 75 km (47 mi) of cross-country trails and 75 km (47 mi) of snowshoe trails in the McCulloch/Hydraulic Lake area. Included are 21 km (13 mi) of dog friendly trails, one of only a few such options in the province. Dogs are also welcome on all the snowshoe trails. There is a heated cabin at the trailhead and three others along the system. To get here, take Highway 33 from Kelowna and look for the turn-off just over 6 km past the Big White Road. The large parking lot is found opposite the resort. Visit *kelownanordic.com* for additional details, trail maps and more.

McKinney Nordic Ski Club (Map 4/E5)

Located to the east of Oliver on the south side of McKinney Road at kilometre 26.4, there are 14 km (8.7 mi) of groomed trails that are formed into a series of loops. The shortest possible loop is just over 3 km and the longest is 8.7 km. A day shelter can be found at about half way around the outside loop. Visit *mckinneynordicskiclub.com* for more information.

Mount Baldy Ski Area (Map 4/E5)

Mount Baldy is a small community ski hill, serving the towns of Oliver and Osoyoos. Currently closed, the hill did offer 35 runs accessed by a T-bar, magic carpet and two quad chairs. There is also a terrain park. Visitors can also find 20 km (12.5 mi) of previously groomed cross-country ski trails, as well as 20 km of marked, but ungroomed ski/snowshoe trails.

Mount Morrissey Ski Trails (Map 29/B6)

Found just east of the Sun Peaks Ski Area, there are 20 km (12.5 mi) of both track set ski trails and ungroomed trails. A day-use cabin is found at Morrissey Lake.

Nickel Plate Nordic Centre (Map 3/B1)

Nickel Plate Nordic Centre is home to 85 km (53 mi) of ski trails for all levels of ability. In total, there are 65 km of groomed trails that are track set for skating and classic skiing, while the other 20 km offer more challenging ski-touring opportunities. In particular, the Okanagan Vista Trail offers a nice 8 km (5 mi) loop and the Burn Perimeter Trail provides a 12 km (7.5 mi) loop. There are also 24 km (15 mi) of marked snowshoe trails to explore. A large log cabin at the trailhead offers a stop over after a long day of skiing. The ski season lasts from November until April. Visit *nickelplatenordic.org* for trail maps and additional information.

Phoenix Mountain Ski Area (Map 5/G5)

Located west of Grand Forks, Phoenix Mountain is a community run ski hill with 16 runs. Serviced by a T-bar and rope tow, the longest run is 1.6 km long and the terrain is often steep with a lot of interesting features. This charming ski hill also features a terrain park and weekly night skiing. Visit *skiphoenix.com* for more information.

Postill/Swalwell [Beaver] Lake Ski Trails (Map 17/D5)

A 40 km (25 mi) network of trails extends around Postill Lake and Beaver Lake northeast of Kelowna. The Postill Lake Trail connects the two networks. The trails range in length from 5 km to 11 km and are fairly level, with a maximum elevation gain of 150 m (490 ft). There are also snowshoe and snowmobile trails to explore in both areas.

Silver Star Ski Area (Map 24/F6)

One of the bigger ski hills in the interior of BC, there are 131 marked runs on 1,328 hectares of skiable terrain found east of Vernon. The front side attracts the family with blue cruisers, while the backside is the domain of powder hounds and double blacks. At the base of the mountain are 52 km (32.5 mi) of groomed cross-country trails, which connect up with the Sovereign Lake Ski Trails to offer over 100 km (60 mi) of trails with at least 70 km of these trails being groomed daily. Adding to the mix is a 4 km (2.5 mi) track set trail lit for night skiing, while snowshoers can find 16 km (10 mi) of signed single-track trails as well. Visit *skisilverstar.com* for more information.

Skmana Lake Ski Trails (Map 29/D6)

There are 18 km (11 mi) of groomed and track set trails for beginners to advanced skiers here. One of the easiest and most popular of these is a 4.5 km (2.8 mi) trail around Skmana Lake itself, while the rest of the trails wind through the surrounding hills along old logging roads. There is a small warming hut near the lake about 500 metres from the parking area. There are also numerous designated snowshoe trails, all maintained by the Skmana Ski Club. Donations are gratefully accepted.

Sovereign Lake Ski Area (Map 24/E6)

The Sovereign Lake trail system is one of the premier ski areas in Canada. It offers 50 km (31.25 mi) of groomed cross-country ski trails together with a day lodge and three warm-up huts. The series of short loop trails (up to 5.5 km long) dissect the beautiful sub-alpine meadows of the area. It is also possible to link up with the Silver Star and Trinity-Ricardo Trail networks or explore the 14 km (8.75 mi) of snowshoe trails available in the area. Visit *sovereignlake.com* for more information.

Stake Lake Ski Trails (Map 22/A5)

These trails are located to the south of Stake Lake and offer over 45 km (28 mi) of track set cross-country trails for all abilities. Included here are 3.7 km of trails lit for night skiing, 5 km of trails groomed for dogs and snowshoe trails. The roller coaster trail network offers a warm-up hut at the Stake Lake parking lot. Full details, maps and more can be found on the ski club website, *overlanderskiclub.com*.

Sun Peaks Ski Area (Map 29/B5)

Sun Peaks has 121 named trails across three mountains, including extensive glade areas. There are 12 lifts servicing the sprawling downhill area. It is best known for big, open blue cruisers, but has a good mix of terrain. There are also over 40 km (25 mi) of groomed and track set cross-country trails as well as 18 km (11.25 mi) of ungroomed backcountry ski trails and 12 km (7.5 mi) of trails set aside for snowshoeing. Specific trails can also be skied with dogs. Visit *sunpeaksresort.com* for more information.

Telemark Cross-Country Trails (Map 9/E1–16/E7)

Near the Crystal Mountain Ski Hill on the Glenrosa Road, there are over 50 km (30 mi) of cross-country trails that are groomed for classic and freestyle skiing. The trails run anywhere from 1.5 km to 10 km long and include a 4.3 km lit track for night skiing. Visitors will also find 62 km (39 mi) of snowshoe trails here. Visit *telemarknordic.com* for more information.

Wells Gray Park (Map 37/E2–38/B6)

Located near the main gate to Wells Gray Park are 50 km (30 mi) of well-maintained trails for all levels of classic style skiers maintained by Helmken Falls Lodge. Another 80 km (50 mi) of groomed trails, also in the park, are maintained by two local clubs. In addition, the park offers fantastic backcountry skiing, with a well-established series of backcountry huts between Battle Creek and Trophy Mountain. This area is a skier's paradise offering scenic sub-alpine meadows and high alpine areas with open bowls. Most begin their traverse north from the Trophy Mountain Chalet, a twelve-person hut. It is about 11 km (6.9 mi) or six hours to the rustic Discovery Cabin and a further 16 km (10 mi) or seven hours past Table Mountain to the Fight Meadow Chalet, another twelve person hut with amenities. Reservations for hut space must be made beforehand arrival by calling (250) 587-6444.

White Lake Area Trails (Map 30/C5)

At the east end of White Lake there is a 30 km (19 mi) network of trails for you to explore in the summer or winter. Other possibilities are to head south on the second road east of the 5 km marker on the Bastion-White Lake Forest Road, which takes you along Reinnecker Creek to the Bastion Mountain Road.

THE OKANAGAN
BRITISH COLUMBIA

Summerland - Tim Buss

Osoyoos - Angelica Perez Anzures

Bertram Beach, Kelowna - Stuart Madden

The Okanagan Valley lies in the southern interior of British Columbia and is well known as one of the warmest areas in Canada. With sparkling lakes, draping vineyards and epic trails, it is no wonder the valley is a key destination for adventurers of all kinds. Made up of the cities of Kelowna, Penticton, Vernon, Osoyoos, and many other small communities, there is endless opportunity for adventure in the Valley. Over 60 Provincial parks are found among the inland desert landscape of the Okanagan, with plenty of choices from rustic backcountry trails to luxurious ski resorts.

Filled with rich Indigenous and settler history, each township and city in the Okanagan Valley boasts ample historic sites and monuments. From the bustling city of Kelowna to the quaint village of Lumby, communities in the valley are welcoming and friendly to visitors eager to enjoy their many incredible tourist attractions. From wine tours to guided historic trail walks, there is plenty of opportunity to live and breathe everything Okanagan.

The warm dry heat and the clear blue summer skies make the Okanagan Valley a popular destination for a blissful summer retreat. Explore the wide open backcountry with two wheels or two feet, with no bushwhacking required, or kick back in the sand in any of the sprawling lakeside beaches – you can find

your own personal paradise in the Okanagan. World renowned golf courses line the valley while classic wineries border the blooming vineyards, all within mere kilometers of dazzling Okanagan Lake.

SUPER, NATURAL BRITISH COLUMBIA ☘ CANADA

Offering year round adventure, the Okanagan Valley is home to world-class mountain resorts such as Silver Star and Big White. Carve the powdery slopes by day and relax fireside in the evening with some exquisite valley wine – your getaway will be packed with as much adventure as you decide to fit in.

The Okanagan's diverse climate creates abundant habitat for a variety of wildlife, and even the famed cryptid of Okanagan Lake, affectionately referred to as Ogopogo. Said to be approximately 40-50 feet long, sightings of the slithering sea serpent have been reported from Rattlesnake Island all the way to Peachland. While you might not get a glimpse of the secretive snake, you will certainly see plenty of other animals – deer, caribou, moose, cougars, rattlesnakes and many others call this region home.

Relaxation and adventure await you year round in the Okanagan – say yes to a little bit of paradise.

EXPLORE THE OKANAGAN
Hwy 97 runs north-south through the Okanagan, connecting with Hwy 1 and 3 on either end.

WELCOME TO Armstrong

THE ROAD LESS TRAVELLED

The charming town of Armstrong, located just north of Vernon along Highway 97A, is the perfect countryside escape in the Okanagan. Blooming pastures and stunning blue skies create a picturesque setting for a city with an authentic western twang, where you might just feel like you have taken a step back in time. Rustic, but not primitive, Armstrong Spallumcheen has ample amenities to make your stay comfortable while you chase excitement in the great outdoors.

With heritage buildings lining the downtown streets of Armstrong, history and culture are literally all around you. A rich history of agriculture maintains strong roots in the community, with farming still serving as the backbone of the local economy. Dutch immigrants played a large role in this heritage and contributed to Armstrong Spallumcheen's widely renowned reputation as a producer of top-quality cheeses. Load up on some local dairy delicacies to take to one of the beautiful picnic spots you can find in any direction from town.

It is not all farmland in Spallumcheen though! There is plenty to see and do and there are huge adventures waiting to be had all around this small town. Hiking enthusiasts of all levels will enjoy the incredible trails leading to breathtaking views of the valley. Bird watchers can take a stroll around Otter Lake with their binoculars, while cyclists can take to the 200 km of picturesque country roads that surround the town.

Diverse Okanagan terrain and cool winter months make Armstrong Spallumcheen a winter wonderland as well. Nearby Silverstar Mountain offers world-class downhill skiing and snowboarding, with over 120 runs and 760 m (2,500 ft) of vertical. Snowshoers can take to any of the trails around Armstrong Spallumcheen, and the Caravan Farm Theatre's winter show, complete with horse-drawn wagons, is a local favourite.

Of course, Armstrong Spallumcheen's culture is more than just country – the city is alive with events and festivals all year round. An 11 day run of celebrations lead up to Canada Day, and the annual Harvest Pumpkin Festival features attractions such as the Great Pumpkin Catapult. In the fall, excite your taste buds at the Cheese… It's a Natural tasting, seminar and demonstration event.

Cultivate your love for the outdoors and experience small town culture with a unique twist in Armstrong Spallumcheen!

> **The secret is out! Our residents are quite friendly and love to share their favorite spots with visitors. Just ask – and take the roads less travelled – it's worth it**

TO LEARN MORE, CONTACT

Armstrong Spallumcheen Visitor Centre
3550 Bridge St, Armstrong, BC V03 1B0
Ph: 250-546-8155
www.aschamber.com

From top to bottom: Rose Swanson (Mount Rose Lookout) - Kam Phung; Otter Lake - Kimberly Vezeau; Railway Divider - City of Armstrong; Rose Swanson (Mount Rose Lookout) - Kam Phung.

WELCOME TO Vernon

ACTIVATE YOUR ADVENTURE

Vernon's sloping mountains, three gorgeous lakes and panoramic views will have you seeing the beauty that surrounds this charming city. Despite a quaint population, Vernon is bustling with adventure opportunities. Located in the central part of the North Okanagan, Vernon can be your base for exploration with sandy beaches, refreshing lakes, world famous ski resorts, pristine golf courses and endless scenic trails. Events are lively, and the community is eager to share their experiences and local tips for adventure in and around Vernon.

As the oldest community in the Okanagan, Vernon has strong ties to its agricultural heritage. The moderate climate, enriched soils, and flourishing valley has sustained the community for thousands of years. Originally populated by the Salish natives, European settlement of the area began in the early 1900s, making Vernon into the bustling fruit growing economy it is today. Proud of its mature history, the downtown buildings of Vernon feature 27 murals depicting the detailed past of the town.

Vernon may be old in age, but it beckons fresh journeys for all ages to discover. Annually, Vernon hosts the perfect weather for every season's best activities and events to celebrate them as well. Whether you dive into the summer and immerse yourself in any of the glimmering lakes, or scurry to the mountain to test your tricks on the slopes or trails, Vernon is home to every adventure you may be looking for!

❝ Your Vernon adventures are only as limited as the number of hours in a day. ❞

Rise with the radiant sun in the warmth of the Okanagan summer and start your day with a stroll on any of the dozens of panoramic trails Vernon has to offer. Amp up your adrenaline bounding down the path of "Honest Ed," an epic 32km mountain bike loop, or take the whole family out for a leisurely ride around BX Creek at Silver Star. The cool forest covering along the rugged valley terrain makes for a refreshing summer stroll as well. Crisp air will fill your lungs as you breathe in the colourful lake views and mountain backdrops. Whether you walk, bike, snowshoe, or cross-country ski along any of the countless trails in Vernon, you're guaranteed to see stunning viewpoints and experience true Okanagan nature at its best.

A hot days hike through the trails of Vernon, calls for a refreshing dip of course! Cool off in the evening as you waterski, kayak, paddle board, fish or swim the invigorating waters in any of the pristine local lakes. Calm currents and sheltered coves easily make Vernon one of the top destinations for stand up paddle board enthusiasts. All summer long every local lake is scattered with paddle boarders, and the sport is celebrated in Vernon annually at the Kalamalka Classic Stand Up Paddleboard Festival, Canada's largest SUP festival. For a sweet cruise around Sugar Lake, rent a kayak and experience

true tranquility as you float along the crystal waters or grab your tackle box and catch some fun fishing in Swan Lake. With 100 lakes within an hour's drive of Vernon, you will be able to find some cool water adventures.

Vernon's summers create the ideal conditions for sun seekers to explore, however the winter months make the valley the perfect winter getaway. The most popular winter sports in Vernon are skiing and snowboarding, but it's no surprise with the ample freshly powdered mountains in the area. Silver Star Mountain Resort draws in adrenaline junkies with 132 runs of champagne powder, forming the perfect slopes to ski, board, fat bike, tube or sled down, and even features a "Rockstar Park" with courageous jumps and rails to show off your skills at. Sovereign Lake Nordic Centre and SilverStar Mountain Resort share 105 km of daily groom cross country trails for those seeking a more relaxed way to explore the mountains.

You don't have to wait for spring to bike around Vernon, fat biking provides a whole new snow experience. February celebrates the innovative winter sport, and you can join in the fun renting one of the fat tired bikes at Silver Star Mountain. The Sovereign Lake Nordic Centre features 14km of snowshoe trails and 50km of cross-country trails to take you through the clearly marked and serene pathways. Even head out with some four legged friends to dog sled across the frozen wonderland on a two-day, one-night adventure.

If you're looking for even more ways to cram more into your days visiting Vernon, they've got you covered morning to night. Experience their live theatre, car races, festivals and events any time of the year to see why the community is so proud to call Vernon home. Bask in the entertainment of the theatre under the stars or give a standing ovation as you cheer on the performers from around the world at the Okanagan Military Tattoo shows. Ring in the coming of fall with a round of the roots 'n' brews festival celebrating harvest and of course, beer, and heat up your winter at the Vernon Winter Carnival. Chill night life and comforting community spirit will captivate you and make you fall in love with Greater Vernon.

Head to the oldest community in the Okanagan Valley to have the chance to experience the freshest, most exhilarating adventures in the fascinating terrain that surrounds Vernon. Come see for yourself why this place is so great!

TO LEARN MORE, CONTACT

Vernon Visitor Centre
3004 39th Ave, Vernon, BC , V1T 3C3
Ph: 250-542-1415 TF: 1-800-665-0795
www.tourismvernon.com

MAP 17

 From top to bottom: Kalamalka Lake - Thomas Bullock; Historic O'Keefe Ranch; Kalamalka Lake Provincial Park - Robb Thompson; Silver Star Mountain - Silver Star Mountain Resort.

WELCOME TO
Kelowna
LAKESIDE URBAN OASIS

Kelowna is the largest city in the Okanagan Valley, maintaining a bustling urban atmosphere next to a limitless outdoor recreation playground where you will have no trouble getting away from it all, whether you are testing your limits on the trails or just soaking in the amazing views. Surrounded by impressive mountains, crystal lakes, rich forests and bountiful orchards and vineyards, Kelowna will take your breath away before you have even started your adventure.

The name Kelowna comes from an indigenous term for grizzly bear, and Sylix and Okanagan First Nations continue to prominently contribute to Kelowna's cultural landscape to this day. The abundant fishing and hunting in the area have sustained a local population for over 6,000 years, while large scale European settlement and farming began shortly after the turn of the 20th century. These days, the name Kelowna is associated more with bountiful fruit harvests, wineries, golf courses and outdoor adventure than with grizzly bears.

During the hot summer months, Kelowna's lakes become oases for locals and visitors alike looking to cool down and relax. With over 30 beaches to choose from around Kelowna, Okanagan Lake is a swimmer's and beachgoer's paradise. Many beaches offer amenities like playgrounds, concessions and bathrooms and are a great place to take the family and keep the kids occupied. For a more serene experience you can find isolated beaches where the water's soft lapping and occasional chirp of a songbird set the soundtrack to a tranquil escape from the rushing pace of modern life just a short drive away.

> ❝ An exciting hybrid of amazing food and wine, vibrant culture, and beach-based vacations on the shores of Okanagan Lake. ❞

Watersport enthusiasts can kick it up a notch with some of the best wakeboarding and waterskiing in Canada, catching some air or laying into a hard carve across the sparkling blue water, or take to the cable park and get technical on a wide range of jibs and jumps. Okanagan Lake has no shortage of high speed white-knuckle action. Alternately, many lake-goers prefer a motor-less adventure exploring the lake with a stand up paddleboard (SUP), kayak or canoe, often bringing along a snorkel to explore that hidden cove or bay a little more closely. Keep your eye out for Ogopogo – Okanagan Lake's resident cryptid, a massive snake-like water dweller who makes an appearance every so often to pose for a grainy photograph.

With over 200 freshwater lakes to choose from within easy driving distance, anglers will find no shortage of spots to drop a line around Kelowna. Wood Lake is a hidden gem, with large populations of land-locked kokanee salmon that are easily trolled for – if you see a boat making erratic looping turns, that is probably a sign of a skilled fisherman, and not someone who has overindulged in one of Kelowna's award-winning wines. Nearby

 From top to bottom: Kelowna Waterfront - Shawn Talbot Photography; Myra Canyon Trail - Tourism Kelowna; Okanagan Lake - Rodney's Reel Outdoors; Don-o-Ray Vegetables - Shawn Talbot Photography.

183

HOT SUMMER DAYS + REFRESHING WATER = ENDLESS FUN!

BIRTHPLACE OF BC WINE

MYRA CANYON KETTLE VALLEY TRAIL
18 TRESTLES & 2 TUNNELS

FARM TO TABLE
WHERE FRESH IS FROM

KNOX MTN.
RIGHT DOWNTOWN!

Kalamalka Lake offers the chance to reel in some monster lake trout and rainbows, with the calcite-rich waters turning the lake mesmerizing shades of cyan and indigo – make sure to bring your camera.

Hikers, bikers and horseback riders can all explore the area around Kelowna via an extensive network of trails that are easily accessed – trailheads can often be found right in town. One spectacular highlight in the area is the Myra Canyon, which runs along a portion of the Kettle River Railway and features two tunnels and 18 trestle bridges. The breathtaking views from these trestles include sweeping vistas of deep ravines and distant mountain peaks.

Located just north of downtown, the 310 hectare Knox Mountain Park is a hub for local hikers and mountain bikers. Panoramic views and a diverse landscape of riparian, wetland, grassland and forest habitat will win over any nature lover, and a well-maintained multi-use trail system makes this one of Kelowna's most popular outdoor destinations. This park is just one of many excellent mountain bike areas around Kelowna – hundreds of kilometers of trails stretch into the surrounding mountains in every direction. Whether you are looking for a leisurely pleasure cruise or a limit-pushing technical descent, there is something for everyone here. Come find out why Kelowna is one of BC's top mountain bike destinations!

No visit to Kelowna would be complete without checking some of the 32+ wineries that are within a 20 minute drive of the city. Kelowna's warm climate is conducive to a rich and bold grape harvest, with local wines consistently winning national and international awards. Take some time to sip, savour and celebrate with a different wine for every day of the year – your taste buds will thank you. If you prefer your drinks cold and carbonated, Kelowna has a booming craft beer culture – check out Freddy's Brew Pub, Tree Brewing or BNA Brewing Co and sample the skills of the local brewmasters. After you have quenched your thirst, why not take in some free live music at Kelowna's annual Parks Alive! concert series, an outdoor family friendly celebration of the arts, featuring local and internationally renowned performers throughout the months of July and August, or check out the year-round indie music scene thoughout the city.

In the heart of the Okanagan, you will fall in love with Kelowna's sights, sounds and limitless bucket list adventures.

MAP 17

TO LEARN MORE, CONTACT

Kelowna Visitor Centre
544 Harvey Ave, Kelowna, BC V1Y 6C9
Ph: 250-861-1515 TF: 1-800-663-4345
www.tourismkelowna.com

WELCOME TO Oliver

WINE CAPITAL OF CANADA

Cradled in the South end of the Okanagan Valley, the town of Oliver lies within the only desert area of Canada, featuring inviting summer temperatures and welcoming tourist attractions. Soak in the most of the beaming desert sun hiking the backcountry, visiting the plethora of fishing holes or touring any of the incredible wineries. The diverse landscape of monumental mountains, sage grasslands, glistening lakes and flowing rivers make Oliver a diverse backcountry playground. Easy to reach via plane, bus, or car, Oliver is a small town with a big personality.

Back in 1918, "Honest" John Oliver, 19th premier of British Columbia, set out to irrigate the land in Oliver and create a place to work and live for WWI veterans feeling the sting of a declining economy. The warm climate and fertile soil allowed his project to flourish, and the roots of the South Okanagan fruit growing industry took hold. Today, Oliver is still known for its abundant, delicious fruit and vegetable harvest – growing top quality produce is ingrained deeply in Oliver's heritage. No visit to Oliver will be complete without sinking your teeth into a juicy tree-ripened peach or a handful of ruby-red cherries.

❝ Desert-like conditions mean Oliver is home to a variety of unique flora and fauna, and new trails to explore evolve every few years. ❞

While the abundant sunshine makes for a productive growing season, it creates an attractive playground for outdoor recreationists of all kinds, as well. Explore the unique inland desert landscape around Oliver through a variety of trails that surround the city, on two feet or two wheels. The Hike and Bike trail is a local favourite, easily accessed with a flat grade and mostly paved surface. Spring and summer bring colour to the many oxbows and ponds around Oliver, with bright pink flowering lilies, while fall paints the landscape a full spectrum of oranges, reds and yellows creating scenery you will not be able to stop yourself from photographing.

Birders and naturalists are advised to bring their binoculars when visiting Oliver, as the surrounding wetlands are oases for herons, eagles, painted turtles and many other fascinating creatures looking for a place to cool down and soak up some moisture. For a chance to see a bluebird or two, hike the Golden Mile Trail, part of the National Bluebird Trail. Or, climb into the surrounding mountains and you may stumble across a herd of Bighorn Sheep grazing amid the ancient antelope brush and wild grey sage. Be patient and keep a close eye on your surroundings – there is no telling who you might run into in this unique ecosystem.

On a hot summer's day, the only thing better than a chilled glass of one of Oliver's award winning white wines is a dip into a local swimming hole.

From top to bottom: Road 13 Winery - Darren Robinson; Cycling - Lionel Trudel; Fly Fishing - Mike Turner; Ice Sailing - Gord Wylie.

PICTURESQUE **MCINTYRE BLUFFS**

WINE CAPITAL OF CANADA

OLIVER
HIKE & BIKE TRAIL
18.8 KM

AUTUMN
SALMON RUN

MCKINNEY
NORDIC
SKI TRAIL

Tuc-el-nuit Lake has large beaches and a playground and is the perfect spot to bring the family for a picnic. The Okanagan River runs right through Oliver and offers a ton of options for cooling down, having a soak and splashing around. Or, slap on some sunscreen and blow up a tube or air mattress for a relaxing ride down the river's gentle currents – it does not get much more relaxing than this.

If you are looking to cook a dinner of fresh fish to pair with the local produce, take a trip to Vaseux Lake. With the dramatic McIntyre bluffs in the background, this lake hosts a diverse array of fish and is teeming with large bass, carp, trout, perch, kokanee and others. You will have no problem bagging your limit as blue-winged teals swoop overhead and trumpeter swans glide past you along the lake's calm waters.

In winter, the nearby McKinney Nordic Ski Club maintains around 14 km of ski and snowshoe trails for exploring the snow covered forest. Take a break at the Eagle Lookout ski shelter with a thermos full of hot coffee or tea as you look over the majestic winter landscape, breathing in the silence and fresh mountain air – a ski through the woods is the perfect way to get that moment of serene, peaceful reflection. Downhill skiers and boarders flock to the nearby Mount Baldy Ski Area, located just east of town. Mount Baldy offers 22 runs for every level of rider, with a generous annual snowpack and a relaxed small-mountain atmosphere. With no shortage of terrain to explore and plenty of hidden powder stashes to find, this hill is a hidden gem of the southern interior.

A small town with a lot of passion for culture and community, Oliver hosts a variety of festivals and events each year. Learn about endangered ecosystems at the Meadowlark Festival in May, test your strength with the Half Ironman Triathlon in June, make your July sparkle with the Sunshine Festival and Parade or ring in the fall at the Festival of the Grape in October. With many outdoor concerts and colourful culture events, Oliver is always a lively place – no matter the season.

The desirable year-round climate, breathtaking natural panoramic views and endless recreational options will draw you to Oliver – but it will be the memories you make that will keep you coming back.

MAP

TO LEARN MORE, CONTACT
Oliver Visitor Centre
6431 Station St, Oliver, BC V0H 1T0
Ph: 778-439-2363 TF: 1-844-896-3300
www.winecapitalofcanada.com

 From top to bottom: McIntyre Bluffs - Luke Friesen; Okanagan River - Darren Robinson; Oliver Mountain - Lionel Trudel; Mt. Baldy - Oliver Recreation.

WELCOME TO

Osoyoos

CANADA'S WARMEST WELCOME

Situated right at the gateway of the Okanagan Valley along the US border, Osoyoos is the passage to incredible adventures. Drink in the inviting climate of Canada's only living desert and sip on award winning wine, while devouring juicy Okanagan fruit and filling up on inspiring history. Not only home to warm temperatures and hot adventures, Osoyoos also features the warmest freshwater lake in Canada, ideal for any water sport your heart desires. With plenty to see, do, and learn about, the small town of 5,115 residents will leave a big impact on you.

Osoyoos is as rich in history as it is in warm weather and wine culture. The name Osoyoos is derived from the Syilx word soo-yoos, and refers to the narrows that are formed by two spits crossing the lake. While Sylix people have been living in the valley for thousands of years, the first Europeans to arrive were scouts for the Pacific Fur Company who used the Okanagan River to access Osoyoos Lake and the land further north. The Okanagan Valley took off as a major trade route for supplies to inland forts with the arrival of the Hudson's Bay Company, and before long became a stopping point for miners and prospectors caught up in the great gold rush of the 1860s. The frontier spirit lives on in Osoyoos, as does a strong and proud Sylix culture.

" A diverse, natural place of great beauty on a widespread system of trails "

The unique terrain of Osoyoos makes it one of North America's most delicate ecosystems. Every inhabitant of the Osoyoos area, both plant and animal, rely on the others for coexistence. You can learn about this incredible environment at the Osoyoos Desert Center, or get a firsthand look by taking an educational walk at the Nk'Mip Desert Cultural Centre. A guided tour with Great Horned Owl Eco-Tours will get you up close and personal with some of the area's most interesting avian residents. These wise, wide-eyed birds share the skies with many unique species, including mountain bluebirds and red tailed hawks. Make sure to bring your binoculars when visiting Osoyoos! Do not forgot to look underfoot, either, as you might catch a glimpse of a scurrying salamander or a rubber boa snaking its way through the sand. The Osoyoos area is even home to the northern scorpion, but do not worry, as these critters are not known to sting humans. With such a diverse collection of local wildlife, Osoyoos is a naturalist's dream.

The warm, temperate summers have made agriculture and tourism economic staples for Osoyoos for generations. The first commercial orchard was established in Osoyoos in 1907, while grapes began to be cultivated in the 1960s. Today, you can enjoy a tour around any of the impressive

From top to bottom: Vineyard - Destination Osoyoos; Nk'Mip Cellars - Destination Osoyoos; Osoyoos Lake - Destination Osoyoos; Path to Spirit Ridge - Destination Osoyoos.

187

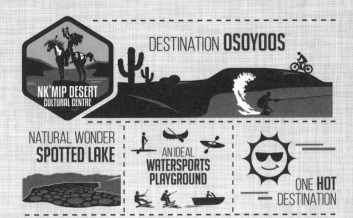

DESTINATION **OSOYOOS**

NK'MIP DESERT CULTURAL CENTRE

NATURAL WONDER **SPOTTED LAKE**

AN IDEAL **WATERSPORTS PLAYGROUND**

ONE **HOT** DESTINATION

wineries in Osoyoos, boasting a variety of wines such as Merlot, Pinot Noir, Pinot Gris, Chardonnay and many more. Or check out some of the bustling farms and farmer's markets to pick up a flat of juicy ripe Okanagan peaches.

You will not want to let your sunny days slip away while you are in Osoyoos. With clear blue skies overhead and plenty of sunshine, Osoyoos Lake is a real summertime dream. Take your pick of swimming, kayaking, canoeing, stand up paddling, tubing, water skiing, wakeboarding or just lounging on the beach to experience the incredible beach culture of Osoyoos.

Anglers can take to the lake for a chance to reel in one of 43 species of fish that swim the warm waters. Rainbow trout and salmon are plentiful in the spring and fall, while bass are a favourite catch during the summer. For your best chances of catching that trophy bass, however, take a trip to Vaseux Lake, where 4 kg (9 lb) bass are frequently reeled in. Enjoy a barbecue under the open summer sky with your fresh catch – remember that trout is best enjoyed with rosè or dry Riesling, while bass pairs well with most whites. Savour the distinct local flavours and the satisfaction of your catch while you watch the sun set over rolling hills and vineyards – what could be better than that?

Those looking to explore the area on foot can take to one of many trails in and around Osoyoos – trails wind around Osoyoos Lake, into the overlooking hills and along estuaries. Wheelchair accessible trails pass by glorious gardens right in town, while interpretive trails run through the oxbows at the north end of the lake, providing a fascinating look into the area's only wetland. In Osoyoos, adventure is found right outside your doorstep.

A small town with a big heart, Osoyoos is known for its incredible hospitality to all who visit. July long weekend hosts the Osoyoos Annual Cherry Fiesta, while street dances can be enjoyed in both July and August. Other events such as the Meadowlark Nature Festival in May and the Festival of the Grape in October make Osoyoos a place for all-season celebration.

Heat up your next adventure and come see Osoyoos for yourself!

TO LEARN MORE, CONTACT

Destination Osoyoos
8701 Main St, Osoyoos, BC V0H 1V0
Ph: 250-495-5070
www.destinationosoyoos.com

MAP4

 From top to bottom: Spotted Lake - Destination Osoyoos; Mountain Biking - Destination Osoyoos; Osoyoos Lake - Destination Osoyoos; Osoyoos Lake - Destination Osoyoos.

WELCOME TO Summerland
TAKE YOUR TIME

Conveniently located on Highway 97 between Penticton and Kelowna, Summerland is a charming lakeside town where you can escape the bustle of the city, take a deep breath and relax.

Sitting in the heart of the Okanagan Valley, famous for its vineyards and orchards, Summerland explodes in a kaleidoscope of colours when fresh vegetables and fruit blanket the countryside. Sprawling grasslands, scattered ponderosa pine and fragrant sagebrush make up the landscape of this inland desert region, with the iconic Giant's Head extinct volcano setting the backdrop for this friendly community.

Summerland's diverse terrain offers endless opportunity for adventure for every kind of explorer. Hot summer days will have you eager to journey to Rotary Beach for a kayak or paddle board excursion. The warm August evenings are ideal for a hike or bike around the many trails and parks or a horseback tour through the valley. Summerland lives up to its name with stunning blue skies and endless adventures.

The mild winter months and surrounding mountains allow Summerland to boast ample adventures throughout the entire year. Hike up snow-capped Giant's Head to enjoy the views, or bike or snowshoe along one of the town's many trails.

From bursting orchards in summer to glistening winter nights, there is always something to celebrate in Summerland. The season kicks off with the Chain of Events bike festival in May. Then join the fun at Action Fest in June with three days of sports, music and food. Music in the vineyards or on the water, local markets and a variety of sporting events for every skill level take you into fall. Don't miss the Okanagan's premier winter party - the Summerland Festival of Lights and Light up the Vines at the end of November.

The stunning landscape and welcoming community of Summerland is just waiting for you to discover and explore!

> **" Summerland's diverse terrain offers endless opportunity for adventure for every kind of explorer. "**

TO LEARN MORE, CONTACT
Summerland Visitor Centre
15600 Hwy 97, Summerland, BC V0H 1Z0
Ph: 250-494-2686
www.tourismsummerland.com

189

From top to bottom: Giant's Head Mountain - Kelly Funk/TOTA/SCC; Okanagan Lake near Rotary Beach - Eric Simard/TOTA/SCC; Mount Conkle - Eric Simard/TOTA/SCC; Cartwright Mountain - Sophia Jackson.

THE SHUSWAP
BRITISH COLUMBIA

Little Shuswap Lake - Village of Chase

Sicamous Creek Falls - Darren Robinson Photography

Eagle River - Darren Robinson Photography

Scattered around the inviting waters of Shuswap Lake and surrounded by the majestic peaks and highlands of the Monashee Mountains, the Shuswap is home to seven quaint areas – Chase, South Shuswap, North Shuswap, Salmon Arm, Sicamous and Eagle Valley, Falkland and Enderby – creating an outdoor adventurer's paradise. The area is just a short drive along Highway 97 from the Okanagan region to the south, and offers a more laid-back and relaxed atmosphere. Country roads branch off of Highway 97 in all directions, leading to hidden gems just waiting to be discovered by curious backroads explorers.

The pristine natural beauty of Shuswap Lake paints an idyllic background mural for life in the Shuswap region. The refreshing, revitalizing waters are sure to please all the senses, whether you are jumping in off a roof of a houseboat on a hot summer's day or peacefully enjoying the sunset's amber reflection from a white sandy beach. Boaters, kayakers and canoers all enjoy exploring the brilliant waters of Shuswap Lake and the 1,000 km of shoreline that offers countless beaches, campsites and hiking trails. With marine parks scattered across all corners of this expansive lake, there is no shortage of secluded campsites to post up at and enjoy a little slice of serenity. While taking in the silent calm of your private paradise, listen and watch for

one of 250 species of birds that either call the lake home or, like you, are just stopping by to enjoy the view and have a splash in the water (and maybe munch on a few bugs).

In winter, the Shuswap area is coated with generous helpings of fluffy interior powder, creating an enchanted landscape that is fully navigable

SUPER, NATURAL BRITISH COLUMBIA ♦ CANADA

by an extensive network of cross-country ski, snowshoe and snowmobile trails. The lake, when frozen, becomes a hub for Canada's greatest pastime, outdoor hockey, while those with a little bit of patience can drill through the ice and try their luck at pulling out some of the lake's delicious,

juicy rainbow trout. Rather than hindering outdoor adventure, Old Man Winter simply provides more options for the Shuswap region.

For a taste of local culture, take a tour of one (or all) of six local wineries – the region's hot days and cool nights create a distinctive flavour – or sample some homegrown goodness at a farmer's market. After your taste buds have been tantalized, feast your ears on the vibrant Shuswap music scene, the crown jewel of which is the annual Salmon Arm Roots and Blues Festival.

Stimulate your body and your senses, or just relax and soak it all in in the beautiful Shuswap!

EXPLORE THE SHUSWAP
Midway between Vancouver and Calgary, the Shuswap is easily accessed by Hwy 1 or by Hwy 97 from the south.

Craigellachie · Malakwa · Seymour Arm · St. Ives · Anglemont · Magna Bay · Celista · Scotch Creek · Lee Creek · Chase · Sorrento · Notch Hill Balmoral · Blind Bay · Eagle Bay · Wild Rose Bay · White Lake · Sunnybrae · Tappen · Salmon Arm · Canoe · Sicamous · Mara · Grindrod Kingfisher · Ashton · Enderby · Gardom Lake · Deep Creek · Ranchero · Silver Creek · Salmon Valley

WELCOME TO
Sicamous
GATEWAY TO THE SHUSWAP

Sicamous is an understated community perched on the narrows between Shuswap and Mara Lakes, and sees a lot of lively activity on the beautiful sparkling blue waters that surround it. With the Eagle River snaking its way out of the mountains past the north end of town, Sicamous is defined by water, but offers so much more for the adventurous outdoor explorer.

Dubbed the "houseboat capital of Canada," hundreds of these watercraft are available for rental right in town (three houseboat rental companies to chose from), and contribute to a large boom in population from May to October. During the season the lake will be peppered with leisure crafts, with the nearby Cinnemousun Narrows Provincial Park offering a spectacular destination for kayakers and canoers as well. This park is found at the convergence of the four arms of Shuswap Lake and is one of the most popular spots to swim and waterski in the BC Interior. Several walk-in forested campsites are available for those looking to soak in the beauty of the area overnight – the reflection of distant stars sparkling on the tranquil lake, with silhouettes of thickly forested mountains looming overhead, creates a surreal and unforgettable scene.

Anglers can cast a line for one of 19 species of fish that swim the Shuswap, while the Eagle River has prime fishing for trout and char. The mountains that dominate the surrounding landscape can be scaled along a web of well-maintained hiking trails, offering spectacular views of Sicamous and the brilliant lakes below. In winter, the Sicamous area turns into a snowmobiler's playground, with deep deposits of dry interior powder accumulating each year. Many trails are groomed, and local snowmobile clubs maintain some cozy huts in the surrounding mountains, where you can warm up next to a roaring wood stove after a day of sledding in fluffy champagne powder. Cross country skiers can take the serene but strenuous Larch Hills Traverse, which leads all the way to Salmon Arm with awe-inspiring vistas to enjoy along the way.

From lakes to mountains to rivers, Sicamous is just waiting to be explored and enjoyed!

" Sicamous is a recreation destination for all seasons. Sicamous, a place to come to play, and decide to stay. "

MAP30

TO LEARN MORE, CONTACT
Sicamous Visitor Centre
3-446 Main St, Sicamous, BC V0E 2V0
Ph: 250-836-3313 TF: 1-866-250-4055
www.sicamouschamber.bc.ca

From top to bottom: Hangliding Ramp at Sicamous Lookout - Darren Robinson Photography; Shuswap - Waterway Houseboats; Sicamous Creek Falls - Darren Robinson Photography; Eagle Pass - Patrick Garbutt.

WELCOME TO Chase

A SHUSWAP EXPERIENCE

Chase is an idyllic, peaceful village located on the shores of Shuswap Lake. Characteristic of the region, Chase is surrounded by lofty, thickly forested mountains whose reflections shine on the sparkling blue canvas of the lake, creating a remarkable contrast against the lush lowlands that the town rests upon.

The most popular place to enjoy the outdoors in Chase is at the centrally located public beach, where boaters, kayakers and canoers can set off to explore the immaculate lake, while others choose to just laze on the golden sand and take the occasional dive off the wharf to cool off. Visitors will find a friendly, welcoming atmosphere at the beach, with children's laughter and the amicable buzz of a laid-back rural community creating a relaxing setting for an afternoon in the sun.

For those looking to explore the wilderness around Chase, there are many moderate hiking trails located close to town. Niskonlith Lake is a particularly scenic destination, featuring kaleidoscopic displays of wildflowers in late spring and early summer. Chase Creek Falls are another must-see, with crystal-clear mountain water cascading down a three-tiered drop. To the north of town, Roderick-Haig Brown Provincial Park features an extensive trail system along and around the Adams River, which is world famous for its massive sockeye salmon run. The returning salmon paint the river a bright red, while majestic eagles glide through the sky above in search of an easy meal. The salmon run is truly a sight to behold.

Adrenaline junkies can soar through the air across the Chase Canyon at Treetop Flyers Zipline, or head out for an exciting day of snowmobiling once winter arrives and the snow begins to fall. Nearby Crowfoot and Grizzly mountains offer excellent snowmobile terrain and a consistently deep snowpack that will challenge all levels of sledders.

For a taste of Chase's small town culture, check out the burgeoning live music scene. The Music on the Lake series runs every Tuesday in July and August in Memorial Park, right on the shores of Shuswap Lake. Or, check out the Art in the Park exhibits and the local Farmer's Market for even more local talent. Chase's "Shop Local/Dine Local" campaign makes it easy indulge in the unique flavours of this vibrant community. Come for a visit and let yourself be charmed by Chase's Shuswap experience!

> **Chase attracts visitors with its interesting history, hot climate and abundance of outdoor adventures.**

MAP 29

TO LEARN MORE, CONTACT

Chase Visitor Centre
400 Shuswap Ave, Chase, BC V0E 1M0
Ph: 250-679-8432
www.chasechamber.com

From top to bottom: Chase; Little Shuswap River and South Thompson River viewed from the North - Village of Chase; Pulling Together Canoe Journey from Memorial Park - Village of Chase; ATV fun near Niskonlith Lake - Village of Chase; Ziplining with Treetop Flyers Zipline - Village of Chase.

WELCOME TO Salmon Arm

HEART OF THE SHUSWAP

Salmon Arm sits in a rolling, fertile valley at the southern end of Shuswap Lake, with impressive, thickly forested mountains rising in all directions, creating a splendorous natural setting for a city that retains a rich small-town charm despite being the Shuswap's largest urban centre. From a colourful history of First Nations culture and gold rush fever to a modern heritage of outdoor recreation and arts and culture, Salmon Arm offers diverse experiences and endless possibilities set amidst a dramatic and gorgeous landscape.

Salmon Arm is found on the identically named Salmon Arm of Shuswap Lake, one of four sections that make up this unique H-shaped water body. The lake not only gives the city its name, but also serves as its focal point for outdoor recreation. The lake's sparkling waters beckon to swimmers, boaters, paddlers and anglers, creating an irresistible draw to the area for visitors from all over. Located just across the Arm, nearby Herald Provincial Park is a favourite place for locals and visitors alike to enjoy Shuswap Lake's pristine waters. The park sports an attractive beach, while hikers can venture inland up an enchanting canyon to Margaret Falls. The canyon's unique microclimate is home to many species of rare flowers, trees and shrubs while the falls themselves tumble down a sheer rock face, creating a natural shower to dip under after a hot day of hiking. These falls are just one example of the many gems that Mother Nature has hidden around Salmon Arm.

"Whether you are looking for fun in the sun or winter wonderland adventures, Salmon Arm is the place to be, whatever the time of year."

Anglers will delight in casting a line into Shuswap Lake either from shore or from a boat, with many more surrounding lakes and rivers creating limitless opportunities for reeling in one of 20 resident fish species. Shuswap Lake is particularly famous for its large rainbow trout – with a bit of luck, skilled anglers can pull in rainbows up to 10 kg (22 lb) in size, while 2 kg (4 lb) fish are caught regularly. With a total surface area of 310 km² and around 1,000 km of shoreline, your biggest challenge will be choosing a spot to fish.

After getting to know the lake up close, why not get a different perspective by taking one of many local hiking trails to a panoramic viewpoint? The Shuswap Trail Alliance maintains an elaborate trail network that extends deep into the surrounding mountains, offering a unique challenge for every

 From top to bottom: Bastion Mountain Lookout - Darren Robinson Photography; Chase Creek - Darren Robinson Photography; Shuswap River - Darren Robinson Photography; Adams River - Darren Robinson Photography.

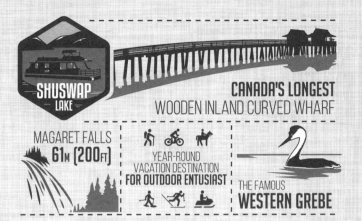

SHUSWAP LAKE

CANADA'S LONGEST
WOODEN INLAND CURVED WHARF

MAGARET FALLS
61M (200FT)

YEAR-ROUND
VACATION DESTINATION
FOR OUTDOOR ENTUSIAST

THE FAMOUS
WESTERN GREBE

skill level. While you stroll along towering corridors of cedar, spruce and Douglas fir, listen and watch for one of the 250 species of birds that live or pass through the area. Absorb the serenity of the forest and get a feel for being part of something bigger than yourself in these traditional lands of the Southern Secwepemc First Nations, whose history and spirit permeate the breathtaking landscape around Salmon Arm.

To get a closer look at the many birds of the Salmon Arm area, take a walk along Salmon Arm Bay, breeding ground for the famous and fascinating Western Grebe, among countless other species. If you are lucky you can catch the elegant courting display of the Grebes, during which a couple will rise out of the water onto their feet and run across its surface in a perfectly choreographed ballet-like motion – it is nothing short of impressive. The Grebes stick around to build floating nests and hatch their young before returning south to warmer climates. These birds are truly a sight to behold, whether you are an avid birder or not.

Although it is true that the Salmon Arm area is spectacular during summertime, when the snow falls in winter a whole new range of outdoor recreation opportunities opens up. Trails around Salmon Arm turn into premier snowshoeing and cross-country skiing destinations, and the beauty of the surrounding forests and mountains is only amplified by the generous dumps of white, feathery snow that make the area famous for winter recreation. While gliding along these trails in winter, the absolute stillness of your surroundings transmits a powerful, lasting calmness. For those looking for more of an adrenaline-charged outing, there is no shortage of snowmobiling terrain around Salmon Arm, while backcountry skiers and snowboarders can tackle steep and deep runs at several points along the Larch Hills traverse.

Additionally, there are plenty of opportunities to kick back and take it easy and enjoy a unique experience without leaving town. Take a relaxing walk along North America's longest curved inland wharf, or tune in to some world-class music at the annual Salmon Arm Roots and Blues Festival. Load up on locally grown organic produce at the farmer's market, or stimulate your palette with a local wine. For taste, culture, nature and adventure, you just can't beat Salmon Arm!

MAP 24

TO LEARN MORE, CONTACT
Salmon Arm Visitor Centre
Suite 101, 20 Hudson Ave NE, Salmon Arm, BC V1E 4P2
Ph: 250-832-2230 TF: 1-877-725-6667
www.sachamber.bc.ca

 From top to bottom: Salmon Arm Wharf - Darren Robinson Photography; South Canoe Trails - Randi & Jason Photography; Margaret Falls - Darren Robinson Photography; Raven Trail - Darren Robinson Photography.

194

WELCOME TO Enderby

WHERE THE SHUSWAP MEETS THE OKANAGAN

Enderby is a charming little city nestled against the crystal clear Shuswap River, with the iconic Enderby Cliffs rising in the near distance, creating a majestic background for this charismatic town. The quiet but character rich streets of Enderby harken back to an earlier time, and the surrounding landscape enchants the senses and stimulates the soul. Hot, sun-filled summers and plenty of snow in the winter make this area a real outdoor adventurer's playground.

The Shuswap River cuts a meandering path around Enderby and is the most popular place to spend a sunny day for locals and visitors alike. Countless sandy beaches, long and lazy curves and a variety of shallow and deep sections make this river a hotspot for swimming, tubing or just lazing on the beach. But, be warned, dip your toes in on a hot summer day and you will not be able to resist gong for the full plunge. Tubing has long been a go-to summer activity for the locals, and now the secret is out. Bring along some snacks, drinks and your best buddies and you will not want to get off the river. Just be sure to wear sunscreen!

While enjoying the pristine waters of the Shuswap, keep an eye out for one of the many species of birds that live and hunt on the river's banks. Eagles, great blue herons and belted kingfishers are just some of the species you can see performing aerial acrobatics in the pursuit of a tasty sushi lunch. Anglers can take part in the hunt as well, with an abundant trout population year-round and four species of salmon swimming the river starting in late summer. If you are looking for a more secluded and quiet day on the water, there are many surrounding lakes in the Enderby area that are perfect for a peaceful paddle or a solitary cast.

When the snow falls, a wealth of winter recreation opportunities arises in the Enderby area. Sprawling networks of cross-country ski, snowshoe and snowmobile trails surround the town, with plenty of the interior's famous champagne powder piling up each year to keep the steep terrain deep, while many trails are track-set or groomed. Tons of ice-fishing hotspots and several nearby downhill ski areas add to make winter a truly magical time to visit Enderby.

On the water, in the mountains and in between, Enderby has something special to offer no matter the season!

> **A great destination for small-town spirit and big city excitement, natural beauty and rich cultural experiences.**

MAP 24

TO LEARN MORE, CONTACT

Enderby Visitor Centre
700 Railway St, Enderby, BC V0E 1V0
Ph: 250-838-6727
www.exploringenderby.com

From top to bottom: Enderby Cliffs – Darren Robinson Photography; Shuswap River – Darren Robinson Photography; Shuswap River – Darren Robinson Photography; Larch Hills – Darren Robinson Photography.

THOMPSON VALLEY

BRITISH COLUMBIA

Clearwater, Wells Gray - Hinterland Adventure

South Thompson Hoodos - Allen Jones

Paul Lake Campground - Allen Jones

Divided into the North and South Thompson along the two arms of the Thompson River, this region is made up of bustling cities, sleepy towns, sprawling wildlands and some of Canada's most stunning provincial parks. The Thompson is a land of contrast, where dry desert-like terrain meets lush forests and rushing rivers, and lowland valleys jut against towering mountains. In the Thompson, urban amenities come with a dose of small-town charm, making this an outdoor explorer's paradise.

With a vast amount of land, and even more extensive geological variation, the options for adventure in the Thompson are endless, no matter the season. Explore the mountains and waterfalls of Wells Gray Provincial Park, or canoe the glistening blue waters of Murtle Lake to your own private beachfront campsite. The many rivers in the region create a playground for kayakers, rafters and canoers, while alpinists can elevate their adventure and scale one of the many mountain summits. When the snow falls, skiers and boarders flock to Sun Peaks, Canada's second largest ski resort, for 126 marked runs and plenty of surrounding backcountry. Nordic skiers have trails galore to choose from as well, and snowshoers can roam through white-blanketed forests and along sprawling mountain ridges. Whether you are travelling downhill or uphill, by

land, water or snow, the Thompson is the perfect place to get your fix of outdoor excitement.

Humble and quaint, the towns that make up the Thompson are often small, with big history and even bigger heart. The region's natural abundance has

SUPER, NATURAL BRITISH COLUMBIA ❦ CANADA

supported a thriving Salish First Nations culture for countless generations, and a rich European settler heritage has sown deep roots here. A strong sense of community and diversity can be felt as you wander the peaceful city streets of the Thompson.

From broad valleys to craggy mountain peaks, the dramatic geography of the Thompson makes for a flourishing wildlife habitat. Fishers, hunters and wildlife viewers all enjoy this diverse ecosystem, home to bears, moose, eagles, deer, salmon and countless other species that have been calling this region home since time immemorial. Whether under a shining bluebird sky or a sparkling star-filled moonscape, the Thompson is teeming with critters large and small, reminding us that we are not alone.

From the moment the first snowflake falls in winter to the first bud blooming in summer and beyond, the Thompson is a pristine example of the true Canadian outdoors. Look for your next adventure in the heart of British Columbia and fall in love with the Thompson's limitless beauty.

EXPLORE THE THOMPSON VALLEY
Hwy 5 provides north-south access, while Hwy 1 travels east-west through this region.

NORTH THOMPSON: *Mount Robson · Tete Jaune Cache · Valemount · Blue River · Blackpool · Avola · Vavenby · Birch Island · Clearwater / Wells Gray Little Fort · Darfield · Louis Creek · Barriere · McLure · Sun Peaks · Heffley Creek*
SOUTH THOMPSON: *Pinantan Lake · Tranquille · Tobiano Lac Le Jeune · Kamloops · Knutsford · Pritchard · Monte Lake · Westwold · Falkland*

WELCOME
TO
Valemount
LET THE MOUNTAINS MOVE YOU

Planning a Rocky Mountains vacation? Valemount is the ideal place to start. Nestled between three majestic mountain ranges—the Cariboo, the Monashee and the Rocky Mountains—the Village of Valemount has earned its reputation as a year-round playground for travelers to British Columbia.

This friendly spot on Yellowhead Highway 5 offers all the services and amenities you need, with several gas stations, charming diners and restaurants, outdoor guides and attractions, and a 9-hole golf course! Our Visitor Information Centre is located on Yellowhead Hwy 5. Be sure to drop in for all your travel information needs.

Comfort and charm combine to make Valemount the perfect stop for visitors to BC or those on their way to Vancouver or Jasper National Park. Enjoy quality lodging with more than 30 friendly hotels, motels, inns and bed and breakfast options, as well as several campgrounds and RV parks.

" Blue skies and gorgeous snow-capped peaks form the backdrop for your epic and unforgettable vacation in Valemount. "

Have a hunger of a different sort? From fine dining in relaxed atmospheres to homemade sandwiches at our coffee shops, you will find a surprising number and variety of restaurants and eateries in Valemount to satisfy any appetite.

Make sure you have your camera ready because Valemount has some of the most spectacular scenery in British Columbia. We are proud to be the home of Mount Robson, the highest peak in the Canadian Rockies, and a short drive from Jasper National Park. Valemount is close to many Regional and Provincial parks, including Cedarside Regional Park, the perfect stop for a picnic and a swim; Rearguard Falls Provincial Park where you may witness salmon leaping up the falls towards their final spawning grounds; George Hicks Regional Park, located on Swift Creek next to the Valemount Visitor Information Centre; Jackman Flats Provincial Park an ecological wonder of shifting sand dunes and rare plant life; Mount Terry Fox Provincial Park, dedicated to Terry Fox for his remarkable achievements; and Mount Robson Provincial Park, famous for its many lakes, trails and wildlife — all within a 20-minute drive from the village.

Valemount is well known for its winter activities. Feel the adrenaline rush as you explore hundreds of kilometers of snowmobile trails. Or create your own tracks through fresh powder by accessing the backcountry on your alpine tour skis, on a sled on Crystal Ridge Sled-Assisted Ski Hill, or by a comfortable snowcat . Other activities include dogsledding, cross-country skiing, snowshoeing and skating.

 From top to bottom: Mount Robson-Berg Lake - Kelly Funk; Valemount Guided Trail Rides - Kelly Funk; Valemount Mountain Bike Park - Dan Roberts; Kinbasket Lake - Megan Pawliuk.

OVERLANDER FALLS

MT. ROBSON 3954 m

BERG LAKE ADVENTURES

LET THE MOUNTAINS MOVE YOU

ALPINE ADVENTURES

There are many summer activities including heli-sightseeing, whitewater rafting, golfing, hiking, canoeing, mountain biking, geocaching and fishing. Explore the backcountry on horseback or on a guided ATV tour.

A great addition to Valemount is the Mountain Bike Park. For the experienced and more adventurous mountain biker, the Valemount Mountain Bike Park offers a variety of trails from old school single track downhill, to new school machine built cross country and downhill trails. Located minutes from the town core, the Valemount Bike Park will be sure to please every mountain biker with its variety of offerings. For more info contact VARDA at *info@ridevalemount.com* or check out *www.ridevalemount.com*.

Located amidst amazing scenery, the Valemount (Canoe Reach) Marina offers a boat launch, moorage facilities, small campground and warming hut, as well as a playground for the kids. Kinbasket Lake is a large hydroelectric reservoir stretching from Valemount all the way down to the Golden area, with water elevation levels that vary dramatically, depending on the time of year. Water levels recede during the winter and generally advance to accessible levels in late spring reaching its highest levels in late summer. Enjoy boating, camping and fishing on beautiful Kinbasket Lake.

The Starratt Wildlife Sanctuary, locally known as Cranberry Marsh, offers a scenic 6-km loop with two viewing towers along the way. The main dike, which is only a couple hundred metres from the Best Western, has spectacular bird watching opportunities particularly in May and June. Another great bird viewing opportunity can be had from the north side of the marsh on the newly constructed section of boardwalk and trail. This new section is approximately 0.9 km long; one can continue around the trail from there or, if time is limited, just a quick walk in and back is still a nice option.

While you are here, check out one of the many events Valemount has to offer including the Mount Robson Marathon, Robson Valley Music Festival or Canoe Mountain Rodeo. These are just a few of events Valemount has to offer, check out the website for more listings.

Get inspired. Get out of your comfort zone. Get to Valemount and let the mountains move you.

MAP 47

TO LEARN MORE, CONTACT
Valemount Visitor Centre
785 Cranberry Lake Rd, Valemount, BC V0E 2Z0
Ph: 250-566-9893
www.visitvalemount.ca

From top to bottom: Mount Robson-Berg Lake - Kelly Funk; Fraser River - Kelly Funk; Jackman Flats - Kelly Funk; Keyhole - VARDA.

WELCOME TO
Clearwater
THE CANADA YOU IMAGINED

Nestled along the Yellowhead Highway, approximately 126 km north of Kamloops, Clearwater is loaded with spectacular landscapes and raw, incredible adventures. With a relaxing lifestyle enveloped by breathtaking mountain, rivers, and luscious meadow views, it is easy to see why more and more people are visiting and staying in Clearwater.

Clearwater is the gateway to Wells Gray Provincial Park and offers all the services necessary for outfitting the many adventures available into and out of the spectacular park. Wells Gray Provincial Park, accessed through the north end of Clearwater via Clearwater Valley Road, is the fourth largest park in Canada and is brimming with outstanding backcountry adventures. With 5,250 square kilometres of true Canadian wilderness, crowds are never an issue, even in the busiest of seasons. The rugged terrain, made up of ancient volcanic fields, azure glacier fed lakes, lush wildflower meadows, towering mountain peaks and crashing waterfalls, creates spectacular views and extraordinary experiences.

A haven for any hiker, Wells Gray Park has ample trails to take a casual peruse along, or trek to the top of a summit. Take a walk through history in the remains of the Ray Family Farm and Majerus Homestead where empty

> **Known as a world-class destination for canoeing, rafting, kayaking, fly-fishing, hiking, camping and horseback riding, it is a must stop on any tour of British Columbia.**

pioneer shacks have slowly been reclaimed by the forest. A well-beaten path cuts a corridor through thick brush to these relics of a bygone era, offering a window into early pioneer life. With a kaleidoscope of bursting meadows and dense forests, Trophy Mountain is easily one of the most popular hikes in the park, and can be hiked in just 45 minutes. Or, kick your adventure up another notch on a multi-day hut to hut hiking excursion. Wells Gray Adventures offers three, five and seven day outings as you scramble to the top of peaks and cool down with a dive into a chilly alpine lake, dreaming the nights away in cozy wilderness cabins.

Propel yourself into a paddle around Murtle Lake, the largest non-motorized paddle-only lake in the North America, and pull up shore side to your very own lakefront campsite. The smaller lakes dotted throughout the park and around Clearwater offer ample opportunity to catch some new adventures. The two hundred lakes in the area are teeming with diverse varieties of fish and, as one of the last great wilderness preserves, Wells Gray Park and Clearwater are ultimate destinations for anglers.

 From top to bottom: Wells Gray Provincial Park - Tourism Wells Gray; Dutch Lake - Tourism Wells Gray; Clearwater Lake - Wells Gray Adventures; Trophy Mountain - Wells Gray Adventures.

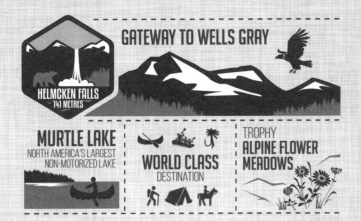

GATEWAY TO WELLS GRAY

HELMCKEN FALLS 141 METRES

MURTLE LAKE NORTH AMERICA'S LARGEST NON-MOTORIZED LAKE

WORLD CLASS DESTINATION

TROPHY **ALPINE FLOWER MEADOWS**

With six months of winter, Wells Gray and Clearwater's abundant winter adventures will have you wishing the snow stuck around for even longer. Warm up in the cool winter air in the expansive backcountry as the 100 kilometers worth of snowshoeing trails keep your winter adventures blazing, and the groomed trails create perfect track for cross-country skiing. Dash down the thrilling runs of Clearwater Ski Hill and ski above the treeline on the famous Trophy Mountains. A stunning and popular viewpoint in the spring and summer, Helmcken Falls is unbelievably more wondrous in the winter. A glistening ice cone builds up around the raging falls as it plunges into the deep bowl of the canyon.

You will be enveloped in 360 degree views of mind bending nature as soon as you enter Wells Gray and Clearwater. The diverse ecosystem and terrain is home to a variety of wildlife. Guided or on your own, let the adventure take you on a journey to view black bears, grizzlies, moose, mountain goats, caribou, deer, wolves, beavers, along with over 250 species of birds in their natural habitat.

With short or long excursions, you can chase any of the 39 named waterfalls throughout the park, including the iconic Helmcken Falls. The 141 m tumbling waterfall is Canada's fourth largest falls and one of the most impressive. Just steps from the road leads you right to the well-maintained viewing platform with scenic views of the blue waters cascading down into the canyon below. A hike along Rim Trail will get you an even more astonishing bird's eye view of the falls. Located in the heart of British Columbia, a visit to Clearwater and Wells Gray Provincial Park will have you falling in love with the adventurous wilderness and charm of the welcoming town.

MAP 33
MAP 37

TO LEARN MORE, CONTACT

Clearwater/ Wells Gray Park Visitor Centre
416 Eden Rd, Clearwater, BC V0E 1N1
Ph: 250-674-3334
www.wellsgraypark.info
www.wellsgray.ca

From top to bottom: Helmcken Falls - Tourism Wells Gray; Murtle Lake - Tourism Wells Gray; Clearwater River - Riverside Adventures; Battle Mountain - Wells Gray Adventures.

WELCOME TO Barriere

GATEWAY TO THE NORTH THOMPSON

Located 66 kilometers north of Kamloops, in the centre of the North Thompson Valley, Barriere is a rustic and alluring destination for a truly authentic backcountry experience. With a population of less than 7,000, the people who live here are tight knit, easygoing, friendly and love to celebrate the wild badlands of Barriere with those who visit. Set along the shores of the North Thompson River, the meadows are lavish, the lakes are bountiful and the ranch lands are right out of your favourite Western movie. The kind-hearted community and breathtaking backcountry will make you see why Barriere is not only a gateway to the North Thompson Valley, but a passage to your next incredible adventure.

Located just off of Highway 5, the panoramic views of Barriere will captivate you simply from the seat of your car, but dive into the fascinating landscapes of this rustic backcountry and you will find yourself steeped in history, community and adventure.

With over 100 lakes and ample roaring rivers, you will want to dip right in to the summer adventures Barriere has to offer. As one of the largest lakes in the area, Adam's Lake has no limits on motor size or adventure capacity. Whatever sport floats your boat, you can enjoy it on Adam's Lake. The strong winds make it ideal for windsurfing, or try something new and explore some underwater caves at one of several top-notch diving sites. Bring your adrenaline to new heights with an intense white water raft down Adam's River, exploring every twist and turn it has to offer.

> ❝ Adventure awaits you in Barriere. Badlands, forests, ranchlands, hiking trails, lakes and rivers are yours to explore. ❞

Barriere is the perfect place to get caught up in fishing, with 100 lakes populated with Rainbow trout, Kokanee and Coho salmon, Kamloops trout, whitefish, white sturgeon and steelhead. Coast along any of the major lakes waiting for your next catch, or take your fishing experience to the most serene level and head to a more remote location. Accessible only by boat or float plane, Caverhill Fly Fishing Lodge boasts more than 15 nearby lakes teeming with rainbow trout and a peaceful atmosphere. With so many lakes to check out around Barriere, you will be submerged in adventure as soon as your arrive.

Well known for its lavish ranch lands, Barriere has hundreds of trails for you to explore any time of year. Saddle up and feel the crisp valley wind in your hair as you travel through the thick bush and blooming meadows on horseback along the limitless backcountry trails, on your own or

 From top to bottom: North Thompson Valley - Allen Jones; Bonaparte Lake - Allen Jones; Trails Galore - Allen Jones; Sun Peak Ski Resort - Allen Jones.

100+ LAKES TO CHOOSE FROM

NORTH THOMPSON
FALL FAIR & PRO RODEO

KAMLOOPA POW WOW

TRAILS GALORE

SOCKEYE SALMON RUN

with a guide. The Seven Sisters Trail System offers hundreds of trails for every level of hiking fanatic, and the Johnson Lake Loop takes you above Adam's Lake for amazing views of its crystal clear waters. For maximum adventure, cruise down the slopes of Sun Peaks in the summer, freeriding the alpine trails on your mountain bike. Lavish meadows, pristine lakes and mesmerizing views await you around every corner of every trail, through every season.

When the snow falls, Barriere and its surrounding area turns into a real winter wonderland. Local skiers and snowboarders flock to Sun Peaks Resort, which boasts a generous annual snowpack and 880 m (2,890 ft) of vertical, with 11 lifts servicing eager downhillers. Explore the alpine, dip into the trees for a hidden stash of powder or cut a clean carve across a corduroy groomer – Sun Peaks offers one of the best downhill experiences in BC. For sled-heads, the Barriere Snowmobile Club maintains many trails and hosts a variety of events in the area, with Green and Harp Mountains being popular destinations. Snowshoers, cross-country skiers and dogsledders can skip the motors and do some exploring of their own – take along a fishing road and auger and try your luck at pulling a trout out of a frozen lake for an unforgettable winter experience. No matter your activity of choice, winter is a blessed time to be in Barriere.

You can find even more adventure in Barriere by hunting down any of the several geocaches in the area. Start off with the more easily accessible caches along the popular hiking trails, or take your scavenger hunt to the next level digging into the backcountry to reach the more difficult hidden treasures.

Barrière thrives not only on spectacular natural features, but a stunning sense of community. Check out the Wildfire Dragon Monument in nearby Louis Creek for a dramatic example of this region's community pride. Ambitious and passionate, the people of Barriere love to celebrate, especially with those who visit. The North Thompson Fall Fair and Rodeo is an annual favourite for locals and visitors alike, drawing large crowds for three days of family-friendly fun.

From the breathtaking views to the kind-hearted community, visit Barriere to celebrate the beauty of life and adventure in the best ways possible!

TO LEARN MORE, CONTACT
Barriere Tourist/Visitor Info Booth
#3 – 4353 Conner Rd, Barriere, BC V0E 1E0
Ph: 250-672-9221
www.visitbarriere.com
www.norththompson.ca

MAP 28

WELCOME
TO
Kamloops
PLAYTIME. REDEFINED.

Kamloops is a bustling city located amid a rugged and breathtaking landscape of ancient rock formations and sun-drenched grasslands. The semi-arid landscape is intersected by rushing rivers and bordered by lush forests of lodgepole pine and trembling aspen, creating a unique playground for outdoor enthusiasts in an environment that is sure to stimulate the soul.

Hikers can explore a far-reaching network of trails that extends from Kamloops deep into the surrounding mountains. Breathe in the fragrant sagebrush as you marvel at the glacially carved hoodoos, then turn in the other direction and witness the sun casting crimson shadows on a placid mountain lake – the scenery around Kamloops is straight out of a painting and may just awaken your inner artist.

Mountain bikers can get their adrenaline fix at the Kamloops Bike Ranch, the most technically advanced municipal bike park in Canada, or take to the hills and explore an expansive trail system accommodating every skill level. Kamloops is considered the birthplace of freeriding and mountain biking has deep roots in the city. Whether you are looking to drop down a sheer cliff face or just enjoy the views from a well maintained pleasure trail, you can find exactly what you are looking for.

Anglers have plenty to get excited about with over 100 fishing lakes found within a one hour drive of Kamloops. Many are home to the famous Kamloops Rainbow Trout – these fish are fast, agile, and grow big and strong, presenting a worthy challenge for even the most seasoned fishers. Reeling in one of these freshwater monsters is sure to be an unforgettable experience.

When the snow falls the area around Kamloops opens up to a wealth of outdoor adventure opportunities. Nearby Sun Peaks Resort is the second largest ski hill in BC, offering world class skiing and boarding on over 3,600 acres of terrain. For a more low-key family oriented day on the slopes, check out the smaller Harper Mountain, located just northeast of town. Or, head out on a pair of snowshoes or cross country skis to explore the endless backcountry. Snowmobilers have no shortage of terrain to chart their own path on, either.

Regardless of the season, the terrain or your choice of activity, Kamloops is nature's playground to discover!

> **Sandstone canyons, grasslands and evergreen timberlands play host to incredible hiking, mountain biking and camping.**

MAP 22

TO LEARN MORE, CONTACT
Kamloops Visitor Centre
1290 West Trans Canada Hwy, Kamloops, BC V2C 6R3
Ph: 250-374-3377
www.tourismkamloops.com

From top to bottom: Harper Mountain - Tourism Kamloops, Campbell Lake - Tourism Kamloops, Stake Lake Trails - Tourism Kamloops, Kenna Cartwright Park - Tourism Kamloops.

GOLD COUNTRY
BRITISH COLUMBIA

Crater Lake - Douglas Lake Ranch

Sundance Guest Ranch - Brett Beadle

Logan Lake - Tyler Meade Photography

Situated in the heart of BC's interior, Gold Country is a land rich in history and nature. Encompassing golden, arid hillsides, lush green forests, meandering mountain creeks and so much more, Gold Country's diverse landscape is a unique puzzle with independently breathtaking pieces. Though gold fever no longer grips the hearts of visitors like it used to, outdoor explorers can find a different type of treasure in the stunning scenery and adventure opportunities that abound in Gold Country.

For those who like to spend their time on the water, Gold Country offers a huge selection of rivers and lakes to choose from. Anglers can try for a variety of fish, including numerous species of trout and salmon that populate the region's waters in abundance. Nicola Lake alone reportedly holds twenty six species of fish – with options like this, it would be safe to call Gold Country an angler's paradise. You might even hear the local phrase "a lake a day as long as you stay" while visiting Gold Country – try put this to the test and you might never leave!

Take a step back in time and embark on a family-friendly gold panning adventure. The Fraser and Thompson rivers are both popular gold-panning destinations, as are numerous local creeks. Dip your pan into the cool, clear water of Gold Country

and see what you can find! Even if you do not strike it rich, the beautiful scenery and abundant wildlife is sure to leave a lasting impression. Keep your eye out for one of the many species of birds that populate this region – stellar's jays or bald eagles

might be circling overhead. Wildlife viewers can also spot some of the large mammals that call this region home – from deer to moose to bighorn sheep and many others, Gold Country is teeming with wildlife.

Those looking for high elevation adventure can tackle one of Gold Country's many hiking trails to access striking panoramic views of this beautiful region, or pedal to the top and test your skills with a thrilling descent down a top-notch mountain bike trail. Horseback riders can enjoy fragrant sagebrush and multicolored wildflowers as they traverse the area in a time-honoured fashion. If you prefer the comfort of your vehicle, take the Gold Country Circle Tour and explore the local wineries, farms, artisan studios and golf courses, all conveniently located next to major roads. No matter what your preferred method of transportation is, Gold Country has plenty for you to explore. Stake a claim for adventure and come see Gold Country for yourself!

SUPER, NATURAL BRITISH COLUMBIA CANADA

EXPLORE THE GOLD COUNTRY
Highways 5 and 1, as well as several smaller connectors, provide access to Gold Country's many communities.

Bookmere · Aspen Grove · Douglas Lake · Quilchena · Merritt · Lower Nicola · Coyle · Canford · Logan Lake · Thunwa Lake · Savona · Walhachin
Cache Creek · Ashcroft · Spences Bridge · Keefers · Lytton · Lillooet · Hat Creek Ranch · Cooper Creek · Deadman Valley · Loon Lake · Clinton
Jesmond · 70 Mile House · Green Lake

204

WELCOME TO Ashcroft
WELLNESS AWAITS YOU

Ashcroft rests along the banks of the Thompson River amid a unique inland desert landscape, with golden hills rolling and rising away from the town to form the Highland Valley Plateau. Aromatic sagebrush covers the lower reaches of these hills, while dry pine proliferates on the surrounding heights, forming a picturesque setting reminiscent of the Old West.

Although Ashcroft is situated in a dry climate, the Thompson River, as well as numerous lakes and streams, provide ample water-based recreation opportunities. Barnes Lake is favourite among locals for fishing, paddling or just enjoying the cool lake breeze from shore. Nearby Oregon Jack Provincial Park offers visitors a chance to check out some spectacular waterfalls that cut their way through a limestone canyon, while the wetlands above are home to a variety of wildlife, including moose and plenty of waterfowl. This area has a rich history of First Nations use – rock petroglyphs denote its spiritual significance, while culturally modified trees provide insight into traditional methods of sustenance and environmental stewardship. This area is a must see, both for its history and its scenery.

Scenic camping along the Thompson River can be found right in Ashcroft at the Legacy Campground, a community built site that offers family-friendly riverside accommodations and a frontier-era historic atmosphere. For those looking for a more adventurous camping experience, Blue Earth Lake Provincial Park has rustic camping in a lush wetland setting, where the splashing of trout and chirping of songbirds will set the mood for a relaxing getaway. Nearby Cornwall Hills Provincial Park is famous for its massive wildflower bloom in July and August, while Elephant Hill Provincial Park is home to the rare western rattlesnake. While snake lovers keep their eyes on the ground, birders can gaze upwards for a chance to spot belted kingfishers and rosy finches.

A variety of trails and four-wheel drive roads weave their way through the mountains and hills surrounding Ashcroft, allowing hikers, mountain bikers, dirt bikers and ATVers a chance to access stunning viewpoints for some of the best sunsets in BC. A whole spectrum of gold, amber and ochre colours are sure to dazzle and inspire.

For clean air, fresh water, a warm climate and stunning scenery, look no further than the charming and friendly village of Ashcroft.

> **A small town nestled along the banks of the Thompson River with clean air, fresh water, ample hiking and walking opportunities.**

TO LEARN MORE, CONTACT
Ashcroft Museum
402 Brink St, Ashcroft, BC V0K 1A0
Ph: 250-453-9161
www.ashcroftbc.ca

From top to bottom: Sundance Guest Ranch - Laetitia Algrim; Black Canyon - Barbara Roden; Thompson River - Cole Evans; Cornwall Hills Provincial Park - Alicia Leech.

WELCOME TO Logan Lake
DISCOVER OUR NATURE

Logan Lake is a progressive, family-oriented community nestled in the mountains of British Columbia's interior, surrounded by vibrant forests and pristine lakes and streams. Gorgeous scenery, expansive backcountry and a laid-back small town feel make Logan Lake a must-visit spot for any outdoor adventurer.

For anglers, the town's namesake lake offers abundant opportunity. Two aerators, a spawning channel and a consistent stocking program ensure that you can get your fishing fix without having to leave town. For those looking for a little more adventure with their cast, there are more than a dozen fishable lakes within a half hour drive of Logan Lake. These lakes vary from vehicle accessible to hiking-only, and many have campsites to turn your fishing trip into a pleasant overnight getaway.

ATVers and dirtbikers can explore the hundreds of kilometers of maintained trails that extend from Logan Lake deep into the surrounding mountains. The Logan Lake ATV club is very active in trail building and upkeep and hosts events throughout the year. Extensive mining and logging operations in the area have created a sweeping network of backroads, as well, and these are popular travel routes for hunters who comb the forest for deer, moose and grouse. The sheer size of the remote backcountry that surrounds Logan Lake creates low hunting pressure, and chances are good for bagging that prize buck.

Birders and wildlife viewers can check out the duck pond and any of the surrounding lakes to catch a glimpse of the area's colourful local and migratory bird population. Yellow-Headed Blackbirds, Pileated Woodpeckers and Barn Swallow Cajays are just a few of the species you can see fluttering around town.

When the snow falls, the area around Logan Lake opens up to cross-country skiers, snowshoers and snowmobilers – the untamed wilderness that surrounds the town is only made more spectacular by a thick blanket of fluffy interior powder.

For an all season, all ages and all natural adventure getaway, come and explore Logan Lake!

> **Logan Lake has matured from an exclusively mining-based town to a multi-activity outdoor adventure locale.**

TO LEARN MORE, CONTACT

Logan Lake Visitor Centre
31 Chartrand Ave, Logan Lake, BC V0K 1W0
Ph: 250-523-6322 TF: 1-800-331-6495
www.loganlake.ca

MAP

 From top to bottom: Logan Lake - Tyler Meade Photography; Logan Lake Campground - Tyler Meade Photography; Logan Lake Ranchland - Tyler Meade Photography; Savona Mountain - District of Logan Lake.

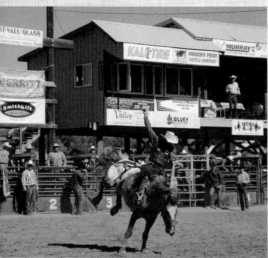

WELCOME TO
Merritt

COUNTRY MUSIC CAPITAL OF CANADA

Situated in the heart of the Nicola Valley, Merritt is a bustling city with a laid-back country approach. Rich in history and culture, with no shortage of exciting attractions, Merritt combines small-town charm with big-city comforts surrounded by a stunning landscape of rolling meadows and rugged mountains

Country music fans rejoice – you have come to the right place! From the Canadian Country Music Hall of Fame to the Walk of Stars, Merritt is proud to call itself the "Country Music Capital of Canada". Larger than life murals adorn Merritt's city streets with some of country's most celebrated personalities, and the twang of that classic country sound resonates deep within the city's soul.

For over 50 years Merritt has celebrated its cowboy and ranching roots at the annual Nicola Valley Pro Rodeo, where roaring crowds cheer on the wild bucking action. The Ty Pozzobon Invitational PBR features Canada's best bullriders testing their limits and showing off their skills. For a boot-stompin' hand-clappin' good time check out the Rockin' River Music Fest, which brings some of country's hottest stars to Merritt each year. Or, for a

> **Rolling meadows meet the ridge of the Coastal Mountain range, rising over our sun-drenched valley, creating a natural backdrop for outdoor adventures.**

change of pace, check out the annual Bass Coast Electronic Music Festival, which features an eclectic mix of music, visuals and art – Merritt is more than just cowboys and country music.

For a look into the city's past, take the Heritage Walking Tour around some of Merritt's oldest buildings and the tales of intrigue, mystery and romance that surround them. Learn about Merritt's pre-European history at the Nicola Valley Museum and Archives and celebrate the vibrant Salish First Nations culture at the annual Aboriginal Day Celebration, a community gathering filled with song and dance.

Conveniently located on the Coquihalla Highway, Merritt is a great place to stop for a break during your travels. But, be warned, with so much to see and do, you may find yourself staying longer than you planned!

 From top to bottom: By Lions Memorial Park - Darren Robinson Photography; Nicola Valley Pro Rodeo - Darren Robinson Photography; Fly Fishing in the Nicola Valley - Kelly Funk Photography; Nicola Lake from Monck Provincial Park - Kelly Funk Photography.

EXPLORE NICOLA VALLEY

COWBOY COUNTRY

Welcome to **NICOLA LAKE** MONCK PROV. PARK

HISTORICAL **BAILLIE HOUSE** SINCE 1908

COUNTRY UNBRIDLED

COUNTRY MUSIC CAPITAL OF CANADA

Merritt enjoys hot summers, plenty of winter snowfall and vibrant springs and autumns. The pronounced seasons and a vast backcountry of lush forests, towering mountains and pristine waterways create endless opportunities for outdoor recreation.

Anglers can find an almost overwhelming abundance of places to drop a line around Merritt. A lake a day as long as you stay, with over 200 fish bearing lakes and streams in the area, freshwater fishing for rainbow trout and kokanee is second to none. Nicola Lake is the most popular place to try your luck, with up to 26 species of fish calling this lake home – the quality of the fishing is rivaled only by the breathtaking scenery. Swimmers, stand up paddle boarders, kayakers, waterskiers and wakeboarders all flock here as well, while the strong winds that pick up along the 22 km long lake have created a thriving windsurfing scene.

For trail explorers, plenty of options abound in every direction. Those looking to get into the alpine and ascend some serious elevation can climb Stoyoma Mountain with its snow-capped peaks and sprawling rocky vistas. Nature lovers can explore the area around Harmon Lake, which features interpretive signs and an abundant bird population. Be sure to bring your binoculars for a chance to see trumpeter swans, red necked grebes and yellow-headed blackbirds, among many others – this area is a bird watcher's paradise.

For a more high-speed trail adventure, check out one of the Merritt area's many mountain bike, horseback riding, hiking and ATVing trails. The riding season here is one of the longest in BC, stretching from March until November. Whether you are a first-timer or a seasoned vet looking to push your limits, Merritt has a trail just for you. If you prefer your trail riding experience with a little more torque, link up with the Nicola Valley Dirt Riders Association for some high-octane options in the area. In winter, Nordic skiers glide along the Kane Valley Trails, comprising 50 km of terrain, with scenery straight out of a Christmas card.

The possibilities for fun and adventure in Merritt are endless – come and make some memories!

MAP 14

TO LEARN MORE, CONTACT

Merritt Tourist/Visitor Info Booth
2202 Voght St, Merritt, BC V1K 1B8
Ph: 250-378-0349
www.bailliehouse.com

Tourism Nicola Valley
www.tourismmerritt.com

From top to bottom: A-P Guest Ranch - Kelly Funk Photography; Near Marquart Lake - Darren Robinson Photography; Overlooking Nicola Lake - Darren Robinson Photography; Treasure Mountain towards Kane Valley (southeast of Merritt) - Kelly Funk Photography.

SIMILKAMEEN VALLEY
BRITISH COLUMBIA

Horses up Jura - Darren Robinson Photography

Similkameen River - Darren Robinson Photography

Cathedral Lakes Park - Darren Robinson Photography

The Similkameen Valley is carved out of the majestic Cascade Mountains, situated between the Okanagan and Lower Mainland regions of BC, running for 200 km along the meandering Similkameen River. The river and abundant sunshine fuel the fertile lowlands that extend out to the base of the skyscraping, craggy peaks lining the valley in either direction. While the scenery is breathtaking, those who take the time to explore the area will be rewarded with an abundance of outdoor recreation opportunities.

Beachgoers flock to the Similkameen River in the summer for its crystal clear water and soft, sandy beaches. Take a dip in the deep pools at Bromley Rock and feel the adrenaline as some climb to the top to take the leap of their life. Or, spread out your trusty beach blanket and let your worries drift away with the current as you soak up the rays and lose yourself in your daydreams. Or, unwind on the move as you float down the river on a tube or air mattress with your best friends, some cold drinks and not a care in the world.

Work up a sweat and find the ultimate viewpoint on one of the valley's many hiking trails. The rugged and secluded Cathedral Provincial Park attracts hikers from far and wide, offering unrivaled vistas of vertigo-inducing jagged peaks, shining sapphire lakes and sprawling emerald forests. Watch nature's greatest mountaineers, bighorn sheep and mountain goats, nimbly maneuver the steep terrain and marvel at the adaptability of these agile ungulates. Spend your evening around a campfire reveling in the epic sights beneath the open star-strewn sky.

When the snow falls in winter, Nordic skiers and snowmobilers take to the surrounding mountains to reap the generous deposits of fluffy champagne powder. Manning Park is a winter wonderland for

SUPER, NATURAL BRITISH COLUMBIA
♦ CANADA

adults and children alike. You can snowboard, ski, cross country ski, snowshoe, toboggan, skate, or tube the Polar Coaster! China Ridge in Princeton has over 45 km of expertly maintained cross-country trails – bring a picnic lunch and warm up in the China Ridge Hut after a peaceful day of gliding through the snow-dipped forest. Sledders

can search for the ultimate powder anywhere between Princeton and Manning Park, where trails extend deep into the surrounding mountains.

For an authentic Similkameen experience, you might not even have to leave the highway. Stop at one of a dozen fruit stands that line the roadside for a full spectrum of locally grown organic fruits and veggies – the Similkameen's bountiful harvest will have your mouth watering. For the thirsty traveler, endless summer sunshine and steady winds create a unique grape-growing climate, and the Similkameen's wineries offer a range of flavours sure to delight even the most discerning palate.

With all this and more, come and see for yourself why the Similkameen, one of BC's best kept secrets, is no longer a secret.

EXPLORE THE SIMILKAMEEN VALLEY
Hwy 3 runs straight through the Similkameen Valley, stretching for 180 km from east to west.

WELCOME
TO
Princeton

PEACEFUL, PLEASANT, PROGRESSIVE AND PROUD

Located just east of the Cascade Mountains, Princeton is a quiet town tucked into the forks of the Similkameen and Tulameen Rivers. Visitors to Princeton will find a charming, welcoming community that prides itself on its open spaces, trails, rivers and lakes, conveniently accessed by the Crowsnest Highway.

Princeton enjoys dry, hot summers thanks to the rain shadow of the Cascade Mountains. Thankfully, two of the cleanest and warmest rivers in BC flow right through town, and there are some 50 lakes found within a 30 minute drive from Princeton. On a hot July day there is no better place to be than in the water! Grab some refreshments, slap on some sunscreen and float a tube down the Similkameen to the Bromley Rock Provincial Park – it is a good idea to arrange for a shuttle back to town after your float down the river's relaxing currents. Or, grab a rod and reel and catch yourself a fresh trout dinner at one of the area's many fishing hotspots – Allison and Chain Lakes are a couple of local favourites. Kayakers and canoers will have no shortage of routes to explore, either – however you prefer to spend your time on the water, the Princeton area has an activity just for you.

Hikers can take to the hills and explore some of the open pine and old growth forests that surround Princeton along the China Ridge trail system, offering spectacular views of the Tulameen Valley. Recent trail builds have made this area popular with mountain bikers, and in the winter China Ridge is a hub for Nordic skiers and snowshoers. Bikers can traverse the Kettle Valley Rail Trail – Princeton sits right in the middle of a 100 km maintained trail system that is sure to excite any trail rider. For a more high-powered experience, ATVers and snowmobilers can explore deep into the surrounding mountains. Birders can grab a pair of binoculars and head to Swan Lake, a 57 hectare wildlife sanctuary that has recorded sightings of 128 different bird species including the red-breasted sapsucker and the northern saw-whet owl.

Rich with adventure and full of small-town charm, Princeton is just waiting for you to come and explore!

" Time slows down here in Princeton and you can get away on uncrowded lakes, rivers, trails and beaches. "

TO LEARN MORE, CONTACT
Princeton Visitor Centre
169 Bridge St, Princeton, BC V0X 1W0
Ph: 250-295-0235
www.princeton.ca

MAP

From top to bottom: Palmers Pond - Sharon Anderson; China Ridge Trails - Darren Robinson Photography; Fishing one of our 50 Lakes - Darren Robinson Photography; Tulameen backcountry - Nadine McEwen.

BOUNDARY COUNTRY
BRITISH COLUMBIA

Christina Lake - Samuel Numsen

Jewel Lake - Ciel Sanders

Phoenix Mountain - Ciel Sanders

Located along the US border between the Okanagan and Kootenay regions, this little-known paradise is characterized by sunshine, fresh water, sprawling mountains and friendly, outgoing locals. From Rock Creek in the west to Christina Lake in the east, there is a limitless amount of swimming holes, hiking trails, campsites, fishing spots and much, much more to explore in the Boundary.

In the summer, life in the Boundary revolves around its rivers and lakes, which are some of the cleanest and warmest in BC. For a relaxing day on the water, tube the Kettle River, lazily floating along its meandering course. Fish dart underneath and deer forage on the river bank as you take your pick between numerous sandy beaches to stop at. Laid back but wild, this is the definitive Boundary experience. For whitewater thrills and a more remote adventure, kayakers take to the Granby River. With sparkling crystal clear water surrounded by lush wetland and towering mountains, the excitement of the rushing rapids will be rivaled only by the spectacular scenery.

Anglers love dropping a line in the Kettle and the Granby, and maybe even more so in the many stocked lakes that dot the landscape, where aggressive trout reside in abundance, just waiting to chomp down on a tasty worm. If bass is your target, try Christina Lake, where trophy fish are pulled regularly out of the unusually warm waters. Be warned, you might not be able to resist taking a dip yourself after a day of fishing.

Hikers can challenge themselves in Gladstone Provincial Park, where trails loop around the north end of Christina Lake and over to the Granby River valley, through old growth cedar and hemlock forests that provide important habitat for a wide range of wild critters. You will surely be inspired by this untouched wilderness. Explore some Boundary history by hiking around one of the area's many ghost towns. The old Phoenix town site provides a fascinating look into the boom-and-bust pattern that saw cities appear and disappear virtually overnight. The lingering resonance of fortunes won and lost can still be felt here.

In winter, take to the slopes at Phoenix Mountain, the best little mountain in BC. Do not let the mountain's small size fool you – there are plenty of steep and deep turns to be had, with a full-sized terrain park to practice tweaking your methods. Sledders flock to the alpine bowls of the Paulson Summit, while cross-country skiers can explore the trails around Marshall Lake for a peaceful jaunt through the enchanting forest. No matter the season, the Boundary has something exciting to offer with a distinctly local flavour.

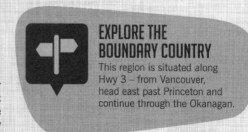

SUPER, NATURAL BRITISH COLUMBIA ❦ CANADA

EXPLORE THE BOUNDARY COUNTRY
This region is situated along Hwy 3 – from Vancouver, head east past Princeton and continue through the Okanagan.

Christina Lake · Grand Forks · Carson · Greenwood · Kettle Valley Midway · Carmi · Beaverdell · Westbridge · Rock Creek · Bridesville

WELCOME TO Christina Lake
COME HOME TO THE LAKE

Located in the heart of BC's southern interior, Christina Lake is a small, unique community that welcomes visitors with open arms – there is just too much natural beauty not to share. The lake itself is fed by dozens of crystal-clear creeks which cascade down the surrounding mountains, with hidden waterfalls nestled amid stands of old-growth forest. First Nations pictographs attest to the area's long-standing allure. The pristine waters remain a draw to this day, turning the town into a hub of activity during the summer.

Stretching for 18.5 km (11.5 mi) from north to south, Christina Lake, offers numerous irresistible beaches all along its length. From the family-friendly Provincial Park Beach at the lake's south end, where aspiring architects can build sand castles and wade in the shallow water, to the boat-access beaches at the lake's north end, there is a beach for everyone on Canada's warmest tree-lined lake. Nearby, Christina Creek and Kettle River offer yet another option for those looking for a cooler dip.

Also famous for fishing, Christina Lake offers rainbow trout, kokanee salmon and both small and largemouth bass. Water sports enthusiasts flock to the lake to enjoy the calm waters by boat, kayak and paddle boards. The local marina and adventure sports stores can help you out with all your rental and equipment needs.

For those looking to work up a sweat before hitting the water, or take a leisurely walk or bike ride check out the Trans Canada Trail once the Kettle Valley Railway. Among an elaborate web of hiking trails around the lake, offering stunning viewpoints and adventure for all skill levels. Mountain bikers can test their mettle on a state-of-the-art downhill trail network. The Christina Lake Golf Courses offer world- class golfing beneath a stunning backdrop of the Monashee and Selkirk Mountains. No need to travel far, with auto and rv services, to groceries and pharmacy, to wellness options, all the amenities and services you need for your stay are at the lake. Visit the Welcome Centre and local Gallery and check out the unique shops and sights along the way. Stop by the local bakeries for your favourite home baked treats, and visit the array of local flavours at our cafés and restaurants.

Christina Lake is more than just a summer paradise. Although the town quiets down in the off season, it provides the perfect fall, winter or spring getaway, where you can explore the outdoors and enjoy the peacefulness of this time of year while having all the comforts of home in the variety of accommodations available to suit your needs. Discover the trails on snowshoes, cross country skis or Fat bikes, and be captured by the natural beauty here at all times of the year.

With all of this to offer and much, much more, your first visit to Christina Lake will not be your last.

" ... there is just too much natural beauty not to share. "

TO LEARN MORE, CONTACT
1675 Hwy 3, Christina Lake,
British Columbia V0H 1E2
Ph: 250-447-6161
www.christinalake.ca

From top to bottom: Friends Hiking-Break time - Christina Gateway CDA, Tubing - Trudy Hallam, Pictographs by Kayak Connie Riesterer, Biking in spring on Trans Canada Trail - Connie Riesterer

WELCOME TO
Greenwood
CANADA'S SMALLEST CITY

Discover a window into the past in Greenwood, where a mining boom town history sets the backdrop for a modern outdoor recreation hotspot. Situated right along Highway 3, the boundary between this quaint city and the surrounding forest is pleasantly undefined – fragrant evergreens reach up to and around Greenwood's many immaculate heritage buildings. This blending of natural beauty and manmade resilience gives Greenwood a unique charm that beckons to be experienced up close.

For outdoor recreationists, there is plenty to do in and around Greenwood. Bikers and hikers can trek the Trans Canada Trail, the world's longest recreational trail system that passes right through Greenwood. To the east, the trail heads towards Eholt, a former railway boom town that was once home to several raucous saloons, now completely overtaken by grassland and forest. To the west the trail leads towards Midway and several irresistible swimming holes along the Kettle River – the sparkling, temperate water is the perfect refresher after a walk in the summer sun.

Anglers and paddlers can take to the water at Jewel Lake, a pristine lake that offers guaranteed quiet and some excellent trout fishing and swimming. Relax and breathe in the fresh mountain air as you wait (never too long) for the strike of a juicy rainbow. Spend the night at Jewel Lake Resort and watch the sun set behind the pine covered mountaintops, turning the lake into a vivid canvas of oranges and reds.

Spend the day in town and take a walk along the self-guided heritage tour, featuring some of the best preserved turn-of-the-century buildings in BC. You will feel like you have truly taken a step backwards in time. Bike or drive through the Phoenix Interpretive Forest in the mountains above town, where the scant remains of the Mile High City offer glimpses of a bygone era. Pause and listen for the echoes of miner's picks and grinding railcars, which some say can still be heard today.

With a rich history in an even richer natural setting, there is a whole world to explore in Canada's smallest city.

> **Camping, hiking and fishing are king during summertime in the Monashee Mountains surrounding Greenwood.**

MAP

TO LEARN MORE, CONTACT

Greenwood Visitor Centre
214 S Copper Ave, Greenwood, BC V0H 1J0
Ph: 250-445-6355
www.greenwoodmuseum.com

From top to bottom: Mountain Trail overlooking - Ciel Sanders; Road cycling Boundary Creek - Ciel Sanders; Jewel Lake - D. Mackle; Boundary Falls - Ciel Sanders.

INDEX

The **Map Index** listings consist of: listing name, page number/coordinates. In the example found on the left, Duncan is found on page 11/E6.

For the **Adventure Index**, the listing also consists of the Reference Page number, where the description of the listing is found. In the example below, the Stuart Channel listing description is found on page 89.

Stuart Channel...........11/B1-G4,**89** → Reference Page

Name   Map Page/Coordinate

R.S. = Recreation Site   P.P. = Provincial Park

The grid lines found in the example are used for illustration purposes only. The blue grid lines found on the maps refer to UTM coordinates.

ADVENTURE INDEX

SALMON RUN IN THE ADAMS RIVER, KAMLOOPS, BC

© Daniel Mackle

FISHING ON JEWEL LAKE, BC

© Kevin Chow

HIKING TO MURTLE LAKE IN WELLS GRAY PROVINCIAL PARK

HUNTING ADVENTURES

PADDLING ADVENTURES

VASEUX LAKE IN THE OKANAGAN VALLEY

STROLLING ALONG THE TRAILS OF KALAMOIR REGIONAL PARK, KELOWNA

© Laura Johnson

© Samuel Numsen

FORDING THE KETTLE RIVER

ACTIVITY CHART

Cathedral Park Trails

PAGE.....................141
TOTAL TRAILS.........16

TRAIL ADVENTURES

BIKING ON THE KETTLE VALLEY RAILWAY, OKANAGAN, BC

ATV (OHV) ADVENTURES

DAWSON FALLS, WELLS GRAY PROVINCIAL PARK

SNOWMOBILE ADVENTURES

WILDLIFE ADVENTURES

WINTER ADVENTURES

© Jesse Olund

ICE HOCKEY ON LOGAN LAKE

MAP INDEX
(Name, Page/Coordinates)

© Alyssia Leong

TRAIL RIDING, ASHCROFT, BC

COLDWATER RIVER, MERRITT, BC

DUTCH LAKE, CLEARWATER, BC

KALAMALKA LAKE, BC

KINNEY LAKE, VALEMOUNT, BC

ATV TRAILS SHUSWAP LAKE, BC

PADDLING THE SHUSWAP RIVER © Kat Tancock

SPOTTED LAKE, OSOYOOS, BC

© Hoodoo Adventures

PADDLING VASEAUX LAKE LAGOONS